'Digby Tantam has worked with people with autism s[...] over 30 years. This experience has made him aware of th[...] in the clinical pictures to be found in people in the spe[...] just one aspect, they can vary from those with severe or profound learning disability right up to those of remarkably high ability, even genius level, in specific areas. However, the author emphasizes that they all share a major problem affecting non-verbal communication. This type of communication he considers essential for the "unconscious link between people". Is this the basis of the social instinct?

The author discusses in detail, but with great clarity, what is known of the physical, neurological and genetic findings in people with autism spectrum conditions, and the developmental, social and emotional factors, including changes with age, that have an equally important effect upon the clinical picture. He also discusses the prevalence and methods of treatment.

This fascinating, and intriguing analysis of the remarkably diverse picture to be found in autism spectrum conditions makes this book especially unusual in the published literature of the field, and essential reading for both professionals and parents.'

– Dr Lorna Wing, Consultant to the NAS Lorna Wing Centre for Autism

'This is a unique and timely contribution to the literature on autism. The National Autistic Society of the UK will be 50 years old in 2012. Many of the children who attended its first school are now approaching old age.

In this astonishingly comprehensive and well researched book on autism through the life span, Digby Tantam's long and eminent career as a leading academic, researcher and clinician is evident throughout. His thorough examination of the science and the various theories of autism is matched by an engaging and straightforward style that makes even the most complex aspects accessible. His use of case examples also reveals a deep understanding of the true nature of autism – empathy for "autistic thinking" and recognition of the "strengths" of autism juxtaposed with recognition of the very real difficulties that may be present. Respect for difference and diversity is noticeably informed by research and a solid first hand clinical background and experience. It is consequently unsentimental, wise and practical.

Due to the breadth and depth of this book I would recommend it as an investment that will be invaluable not just for academics, clinicians and researchers but a much wider readership that will include the autistic community and those who support them.'

– Richard Mills, Director of Research, The National Autistic Society
UK and Research Director, Research Autism, London

'This authoritative, comprehensive textbook by Professor Tantam, an internationally recognized expert, provides an overview of Autistic Disorder ranging from an historical perspective to our current knowledge of its clinical presentation, life course, underlying pathology, etiology, and treatment. It fills a void in the literature, and I predict it will become "the standard reference" for students, clinicians, and researchers working with Autistic Disorder.'

– Edward R. Ritvo, MD, Professor Emeritus, UCLA School of Medicine, USA

'This is probably the most comprehensive and wide ranging book on ASD I have ever read. It is an extraordinarily rich mine of information from neurobiology to treatment, and from infancy to adulthood. "No stone is left unturned." An original and perhaps controversial feature is the highlighting of links between ASD and ADHD.'

– Professor Margot Prior, AO, FASSA, FAPS, Department of Psychology, University of Melbourne, Australia

AUTISM
SPECTRUM
DISORDERS
THROUGH THE
LIFE SPAN

by the same author

Can the World Afford Autistic Spectrum Disorder?
Nonverbal Communication, Asperger Syndrome and the Interbrain
Digby Tantam
ISBN 978 1 84310 694 4
eISBN 978 1 84642 936 1

of related interest

An A-Z of Genetic Factors in Autism
A Handbook for Professionals
Kenneth J. Aitken
ISBN 978 1 84310 976 1
eISBN 978 0 85700 490 1

The Complete Guide to Asperger's Syndrome
Tony Attwood
ISBN 978 1 84310 495 7 (hardback)
ISBN 978 1 84310 669 2 (paperback)
eISBN 978 1 84642 559 2

The Imprinted Brain
How Genes Set the Balance Between Autism and Psychosis
Christopher Badcock
ISBN 978 1 84905 023 4
eISBN 978 1 84642 950 7

DIGBY TANTAM

AUTISM SPECTRUM DISORDERS THROUGH THE LIFE SPAN

Jessica Kingsley *Publishers*
London and Philadelphia

First published in 2012
This edition published in 2013
by Jessica Kingsley Publishers
116 Pentonville Road
London N1 9JB, UK
and
400 Market Street, Suite 400
Philadelphia, PA 19106, USA

www.jkp.com

Library of Congress Cataloging in Publication Data
A CIP catalog record for this book is available from the Library of Congress

British Library Cataloguing in Publication Data
A CIP catalogue record for this book is available from the British Library

ISBN 978 1 84905 344 0
eISBN 978 0 85700 511 3

Printed and bound in Great Britain

To my dearest wife Emmy, as always,
and to our four children, Sasha, Ben, Grace, and Robert

CONTENTS

4   DEVELOPMENTAL, SOCIAL AND EMOTIONAL CONSIDERATIONS   89

5   SOCIAL ORIENTATION, COMMUNICATION AND LANGUAGE   110

PART 2 CLINICAL ASPECTS OF ASD

ACKNOWLEDGEMENTS

Many colleagues over the years have encouraged me in my education and training in psychiatry and psychology, and have provided me with the space in which I could pursue my own interests, especially my interest in Asperger syndrome. Although listing individual names inevitably risks inadvertent omissions, I want to express my gratitude explicitly to the late Douglas Bennett, for his inspiring demonstration of person-centred psychiatry; to Jon Borus for providing me with the opportunity for post-residency training at Massachusetts General Hospital and the Harvard School of Public Health; to the late Gerry Klerman, for believing in me enough to select me for this programme and act as my research supervisor; to Lorna and the late John Wing who introduced me to Asperger syndrome; and, especially, to Uta Frith who took me as an untested PhD student and stimulated me over and over again to question 'clinical judgement' and buttress it with evidence and analysis as she guided me through my first, formative research into Asperger syndrome and to the completion of my doctoral thesis. Uta also arranged seminars for other PhD students at the then MRC cognitive psychology unit, which included Simon Baron-Cohen, Tony Attwood, and Peter Hobson, who have all made distinguished contributions to autism and Asperger syndrome subsequently.

In more recent years, I have been supported by the NHS Trust and its officers in which I have been working since the late 1990s and which has enabled the development of the Sheffield Asperger Syndrome Service, and the possibility of working with multidisciplinary colleagues, as well as a consultant colleague, Sobhi Girgis. I am particularly grateful to Richard Bulmer, Andy Bragg and my line managers, Tim and Katie Kendall for their support for these developments.

Ron Akehurst, the Dean of the School of Health and Related Research at the University of Sheffield, enabled me to take a year's study leave, and I was able to re-establish contact with Simon Baron-Cohen and work part-time in the developmental psychiatry section of the Department of Psychiatry at Cambridge University. I am very grateful to Tony Holland, who made this possible, and to other colleagues in Cambridge who have provided me with support and assistance, including Adrian Grounds, who sponsored my associate fellowship at Darwin College, Peter Jones, who approved my honorary appointment, and Ian Goodyer, who supported it. I am especially grateful to Simon Baron-Cohen for valuable discussions with him and with some of his doctoral students, not least Michael Lombardo. For someone so eminent in his field, Simon has been remarkable for his openness and modesty, and I have greatly benefited from this.

I am grateful to my publisher, Jessica Kingsley, who, when my previous publisher got cold feet about the length and duration of gestation of this book and rescinded my contract with them, was willing to take on the project and to allow me to develop it as I thought necessary. Her own contribution to the field of autism spectrum disorders (ASD) through her energy, her support for anyone with something of value to say about ASD, and her willingness to publish them, has been remarkable.

Finally, I am grateful to the many patients and parents over the years who have educated me about ASD, and in the process have shown me a great deal about the worth of family life.

As always, I am indebted to the pillar of my own family life, Emmy van Deurzen, without whose love, encouragement and intellectual companionship, this book would not have been written.

COPYRIGHT ACKNOWLEDGEMENTS

Every effort has been made to trace copyright holders and to obtain their permission for the use of copyright material. The authors and the publisher apologize for any omissions and would be grateful if notified of any acknowledgements that should be incorporated in future reprints or editions of this book.

Figure I.1 on p.16 reprinted from *Neuroscience* **164**(1), Bilder, R., F. W. Sabb, *et al.* (2009). Phenomics: The systematic study of phenotypes on a genome-wide scale, 30–42, with permission from Elsevier.

Figure 3.1 on p.77 reprinted from *Neuron* **67**(1), van de Lagemaat, L. N. and S. G. N. Grant (2010). Genome variation and complexity in the autism spectrum, 8–10, with permission from Elsevier.

Table 3.1 on p.81 reprinted from *NeuroImage* **29**(4), Burgel, U., K. Amunts, *et al.* (2006). White matter fiber tracts of the human brain: Three-dimensional mapping at microscopic resolution, typography and intersubject variability, 1092–1105, with permission from Elsevier.

Figure 3.2 on p.82 reprinted from *The Lancet Neurology* **7**(8), Ciccarelli, O., M. Catani, *et al.* (2008). Diffusion-based tractography in neurological disorders: Concepts, applications, and future developments, 715–727, with permission from *The Lancet*.

Figure 3.3 on p.86 reprinted from *Annals of the New York Academy of Sciences* **1124**, Buckner, R. L., J. R. Andrews-Hanna, *et al.* (2008). The brain's default network: Anatomy, function, and relevance to disease, 1–38, with permission from John Wiley and Sons.

Figure 6.1 on p.143 reprinted from Frith, U. (2003). *Explaining the Enigma* (2nd edition). Oxford: Blackwell, with permission from the illustrator, Axel Scheffer.

Figure 8.1 on p.179 reprinted from National Autistic Society (2011). Asperger syndrome: the triad of impairments, with permission from the National Autistic Society, www.autism.org.uk.

Table 9.1 on p.212 reprinted from *Research in Autism Spectrum Disorders* **3**(3), Myers, B. J., V. H. Mackintosh, *et al.* (2007). My greatest joy and my greatest heartache: Parents' own words on how having a child on the autism spectrum has affected their lives and their families, 670–407, with permission from Elsevier.

Table 10.5 on p.238 reprinted from *Research in Developmental Disabilities* **29**(5), Peters-Scheffer, N., R. Didden, *et al.* (2008). The behavior flexibility rating scale-revised (BFRS-R): Factor analysis, internal consistency, inter-rater and intra-rater reliability, and convergent validity, 398–407, with permission from Elsevier.

Table 10.7 on p.246 reprinted from *Archives of Internal Medicine* **166**, Spitzer, R. L., K. Kroenke, et al. (2006). A Brief Measure for Assessing Generalized Anxiety Disorder: The GAD-7, 1092–1097, with permission from PHQ Screeners.

Table 10.8 on p.247 reprinted from *Journal of General Internal Medicine* **16**(9), Kroenke, K., R. L. Spitzer, *et al.* (2001). The PHQ-9: Validity of a Brief Depression Severity Measure, 606–613, with permission from PHQ Screeners.

Box 12.4 on p.324 is reprinted from New York State Department of Health (1999). Clinical Practice Guideline, Report of the Recommendations, Autism/Pervasive Developmental Disorders, Assessment and Intervention for Young Children (Age 0–3 Years), with permission from the New York State Department of Health.

Crown copyright material is reproduced with the permission of the controller of the HMSO and the Queen's Printer for Scotland.

PREFACE

'Writing a preface is like sharpening a scythe, like tuning a guitar, like talking to a child, like spitting out of the window…like ringing someone's door bell to trick him.'

Kierkegaard, in *Prefaces, Light Reading for People in Various Estates According to Time and Opportunity* by Nicolaus Notabende.[1]

I first heard of Asperger syndrome in 1977. I had spent several months in the Widener library at Harvard University reading about nonverbal communication, because this had seemed to me to be an important, but neglected, subject in psychiatry. Now I had returned to the UK, hoping to get a job at the Maudsley Hospital. I went to see John Wing, then the Professor of Social Psychiatry at the Institute of Psychiatry in London, and told him I was interested in nonverbal communication. He said that his wife, Lorna, was very interested in this subject, too, particularly in a group of people with a disorder like autism, who seemed to have a particular deficit in nonverbal communication. That whetted an interest that in 1980 led to an MRC fellowship and a full-time research project on Asperger syndrome, supervised by Uta Frith, and then to clinical work with people with Asperger syndrome, which has never subsequently abated.

This book is the result of those 30 years of clinical work and of that interest. I have kept detailed records of many of the patients with autism spectrum disorders that I have seen over this time – some 1500 people of all ages and of all levels of ability – and have drawn on this information as well as on the substantial amount of research information that has been accumulated.

WHY THIS BOOK

People with an autism spectrum disorder (ASD) may seek help for the first time in adulthood, or they may be referred to specialist services at the age of one or two years. They may lack language, or be able to use words with ease and precision. They may have intellectual disability or intelligence way above the average. Some may be looking for help into employment, others may be university professors and even doctors. Some may be in good health, others may have disabling conditions that are associated with their ASD and affect their mobility, their self-care, or their independence. Some may be impulsive and have attention deficit hyperactivity disorder (ADHD), others may be careful and conscientious, with many rituals or routines that prevent them from a quick response to change. Some may have brothers and sisters with an autism spectrum disorder, possibly with a known genetic disorder, others may seem to have developed their autism spectrum disorder with no explanation. Some may develop serious psychiatric disorders. A few may commit murder or other serious crimes. Most want to belong, although almost everyone with an autism spectrum disorder will have experienced bullying, and nearly half will develop an anxiety disorder in their teens or twenties.

Autism spectrum disorder may affect people very differently at different ages, and in all of these different situations. It is therefore difficult for any particular doctor to get a comprehensive picture of autism spectrum disorders, particularly as most of the study of them has been by paediatricians, child psychologists and child psychiatrists, and mostly of affected children, yet childhood accounts for only a quarter of most people's lives, including people with Asperger syndrome. I have been fortunate to have been asked to assess and advise about people suspected with autism spectrum disorder for over 30 years, and during that time I have worked with people in all settings, including special hospitals, prisons, mental health units, schools, special schools, community settings and, mainly, families. First and foremost a clinician – a general adult psychiatrist, psychologist and psychotherapist – I have drawn on this experience to provide the first completely comprehensive coverage of autism spectrum disorder.

I have been helped by John Wing's comment from 1977. For I have found that he and Lorna were right, the fundamental feature of the autism spectrum disorders is, so far as I am concerned, a disorder of nonverbal communication or, to be more specific, a disorder of the unconscious linkage between people, mediated by nonverbal communication, that I have called the 'interbrain'.[2] Having a way to formulate what an autism spectrum disorder is has been a great help in explaining to people with one, their families, or others concerned with them what the problem is. It also helps to be able to separate out what is due to their developmental disorder, and what is attributable to other factors, not least the emotional factors that affect outcome.

Having a clear defining characteristic of the autism spectrum disorders is also helpful when training others in assessing people with these conditions and advising about treatment. But training has increasingly involved introducing doctors, psychologists and others to the rapidly developing cognitive neurosciences. The difficulties of many people with autism spectrum disorders do not stop with their partial disconnection from the interbrain, but extend to language, movement, learning, empathizing, and many other 'higher functions'. Research into these areas is rapidly expanding, partly propelled by a substantial increase in funding for research into autism in recent years.

PLAN OF THE BOOK

Those sciences that are basic to an understanding of the autism spectrum disorders are considered in Part 1 of the book, which draws on an exhaustive review of the current literature, tempered by my own clinical experience of which research findings are likely to be of particular clinical relevance. Most of the studies cited in Part 1 have been published since 2005.

Part 2 is a detailed clinical overview of autism spectrum disorder. The account will draw on my own clinical experience, on psychiatric research, on research by developmental psychologists, and on work by educationalists and therapists. Part 2 includes case descriptions, based on the amalgamation of several cases of ASD personally known to me, illustrating not only the direct consequences of having a disorder of psychological development but also the different, often creative and original, ways that a person can accommodate to it.

In fact, my experience has shown that the way that a person, and their carers, reacts to a developmental disorder determines much more of the outcome of the disorder than is commonly assumed. This should not have come as a surprise. A cerebrovascular accident, a stroke, is an unequivocally neurological disorder. Yet, the outcome of rehabilitation is more influenced by psychological factors than by the volume of brain that has been infarcted.

STIGMA

Autism spectrum disorders can be mysterious to people who are unfamiliar with them. This justifies some people treating people with an autism spectrum disorder with a lack of understanding, and a few people reacting with unkindness or even hostility. People with an autism spectrum disorder and their families often feel isolated and sometimes embattled. Understanding the problem and trying to get help for it may be the only way out of this isolation.

How a parent understands the disorder is usually more practical, and almost always more empathic, than how a scientist understands it. Practitioners have to try to combine both perspectives. This is particularly difficult when one perspective is of a neurodevelopmental disorder, with demonstrable abnormality in the brains of a substantial minority, and the other perspective is of vulnerable people who are unable to succeed in a society that values the person who can charm, deceive, or seduce most effectively. These are two of the perspectives that have been taken by observers of autism spectrum disorders. Neither of them is completely accurate. For one thing, there is considerable variation in brain structure in the general population. And, for another, people with autism spectrum disorders are not just victims. They can be aggressors, too.

BIOLOGICAL VERSUS EXPERIENTIAL

However, any practitioner does have to find a way of synthesizing a biological and an experiential perspective if he or she is to be able to relate fully with either patients or carers. I think that each practitioner has to do this for him- or herself. The challenge is so similar to the existential challenge for all of us of coming to terms with our own limitations that it has to be according to the same values and beliefs. I did not have a child or close relative with an autism spectrum disorder, unlike many of the first generation of researchers. Despite this, I had no difficulty in understanding the experience of having an autism spectrum disorder – my friends were kind enough to tell me that they had always found me different from other people – but it took me rather longer to begin to piece together a biological understanding of the disorder. This was even though John Wing's observation that autism spectrum disorder was a disorder of nonverbal communication seemed to fit my own observations from the beginning.

LIMITS

It seems to me that autism and Asperger syndrome could be understood only by combining the psychological and the neurological perspectives. This required more of me than the middle way pursued by many general psychiatrists who sidestep the issue by concentrating on what works in practice, mixing psychological and biological interventions as necessary. For one thing, many parents wanted to know how far their son or daughter could go in the way of adaptation, to quote from the title of one of Kanner's later papers.[3] It seemed to me that the only way to be able to predict this was to separate out the underlying neurological impairment from the functional disability that it caused, since the functional effect of the impairment was clearly affected by a person's psychology and by the social resources available to them, their limits or, to use a term of Dorothy Stock Whitaker, their 'frontier'.[4]

The realization of my own limits came to me rather late. It comes much earlier to people with an autism spectrum disorder or, if not to them, to their carers. These limits seem particularly cruel because they are not limits of character. Character, like our faces, is the product of our own actions and reactions once we reach middle age. Limitations that arise because of geography, ethnicity, the social position of our parents or biology are all harder to accept. They seem like limits that are assigned to us in some unfair kind of lottery. Other people may not see ascribed limits as limits at all, but as deficits or failings, but if we are born with them it is clearly inappropriate to blame someone for being limited, and yet we all are.

The courage with which many people with autism spectrum disorders tackle their limits has often encouraged me to face up more honestly to mine; as a result, I have gained as well as given from my companionship with my patients.

At the time that I write this, the doctor's bedside manner is a facet of medical life that has receded almost as far into the past as the wing collar or the surgeon's bow tie. Talking about the bedside manner conjures up a vivid memory of a hard night that I spent as a newly qualified doctor. I had tried without success to insert a central venous line by the then-preferred subclavian route, and was a bit desperate. The surgical registrar on-call drifted by and, contrary to my expectations of the indifference of a relatively senior surgical colleague to the discomfiture of a mere houseman, offered to help, and succeeded easily where I had failed. Later I went to thank him, and found him by the bedside of a patient in the intensive care unit. I watched him for a while. He didn't seem to be doing anything. So I asked him what he was doing. 'Watching my patient get better,' he said. Being by the patient's bedside is a form of companionship that is, in my experience, restricted to those who witness together at one of life's moments of emotional intensity. This intensity can sometimes be present when a person realizes that all their struggles in life may have to do with a particular disability that it is their lot to bear, and not because of their, or their family's, failings. Sharing in the relief and renewed determination that often accompanies this realization has been, and continues to be, one of my most rewarding experiences as a doctor and therapist.

I hope that this book informs and educates but most, I hope that it helps other doctors to witness with patients and carers the frustrations, originality, sadness and wonders of having an autism spectrum disorder.

INTRODUCTION

The term 'autism' has undergone many vicissitudes since it was briefly employed by Eugen Bleuler in one edition of his influential textbook on schizophrenia. Both Hans Asperger and Leo Kanner, paediatricians working in Vienna and Chicago respectively but both trained in central Europe, annexed it to apply to children with unusual social difficulties, terming them respectively children with 'autistische Psychopathen' (autistic personality disorder),[1] and children with 'autistic disturbance of affective contact'.[2] The disorder that Kanner described has since then been known as infantile autism, early childhood autism, childhood autism, childhood schizophrenia and, most recently, autistic disorder. The 'autistic personality disorders' that Asperger described were rediscovered by English-speaking psychiatrists in the late 1970s and early 1980s, mainly as a result of the work of Lorna Wing,[3] and her proposal to call them people with 'Asperger's syndrome' or 'Asperger syndrome' has been widely adopted since then.

Asperger's interest was in the social abilities of the children he described; Kanner's interest was in their emotions. 'A lack of emotional or social reciprocity' remains one of the criteria in the *Diagnostic and Statistical Manual* of the American Psychiatric Association at least up to its fourth, text revised edition (DSM-IV-TR),[4] for a diagnosis of either autistic disorder or Asperger syndrome. Neither Asperger nor Kanner knew of each other's work until some time after the end of the war that had divided the Anglophone and German-speaking scientific worlds. They differed over whether these disorders were related: Kanner thought not, Asperger thought that they were.[5] Nowadays this issue has been resolved by considering that there is an 'autism spectrum' which includes both conditions, as well as some other 'autism spectrum disorders'.

Nor did either Asperger or Kanner appear to know of previous descriptions of similar disorders, such as the 'dementia infantilis' described by De Sanctis[6] and Heller.[7] Their cases had a more organic flavour and might be likely to be diagnosed today as having another related disorder, disintegrative disorder. De Sanctis and Heller both considered that these conditions were related to the dementia praecox that had been described by Kraepelin, hence their term 'dementia infantilis'. Dementia praecox was the basis for Bleuler's description of the group of schizophrenias. Case reports similar to those of De Sanctis and Heller continued to be published after Bleuler's terminology was widely accepted, but now under the name of 'childhood schizophrenia'. There may have been an even earlier report of a person with autism. In 1898, Barr described a 22-year-old man with learning difficulty, echolalic speech and a remarkable memory.[8]

Autistic disorders are unlikely to have emerged in the late nineteenth century, any more than schizophrenia did, even though there are no medical descriptions of it before this time. There are biographical descriptions that seem to meet ASD criteria dating back to the

Reformation. Fitzgerald has provided many possible instances of these.[9] Other examples include Francis Potter and the Warwickshire calendrical calculator. Potter, a friend of John Aubrey whose biography appears in Aubrey's *Brief Lives*, was fascinated by the number 666, thought that disease might be cured by blood transfusions, and was a lifelong bachelor of 'a very tender constitution'. He was denounced to a Puritan committee of inquiry but rather than being interrogated, was given a pint of wine, and sent home. The Warwickshire prodigy (from the Warwickshire records kept in Solihull public library) could walk around a field and calculate its area in his head, could do other calculations so amazing that he appeared before the House of Lords as a wonder, and announced on the day of his death exactly how many pints of beer he had drunk his whole life through.

In the glossary, the framers of DSM-IV explain that lack of social and emotional reciprocity is apparent when someone treats another person like an object.[4] Psychoanalytic theorists of autism have taken this to be the defining feature of autism,[10] as indeed did Kanner. Both Kanner and Asperger were trained in the German psychiatric tradition and both knew of Bleuler's attempt to define the fundamental characteristics of the 'group of schizophrenias'. In one edition of his textbook Bleuler gave a lack of affective contact as one of these, and termed it 'autism', derived from the Greek for self, meaning a person living in their own world and not the world of others. Bleuler replaced 'autism' in later editions with a term that he had taken from Ronald Fairbairn, via Melanie Klein – 'schizoid' or, as we might say, 'cut off', but it was the characteristic of being lost in their own world that struck both Kanner and Asperger in the children that they were perplexed by and so they both described them, independently, as autistic.

The category of 'Pervasive Developmental Disorders' (PDD) was first introduced in the third edition of the *Diagnostic and Statistical Manual* of the American Psychiatric Association (DSM-III).[11] It included 'Infantile autism', 'Atypical ASD' and 'Childhood Onset ASD'. PDD was also adopted as a category in the tenth edition (ICD-10) of the other main official diagnostic system, the *International Classification of Diseases*.[12] Asperger syndrome was first recognized as an independent syndrome in the tenth edition of the *International Classification of Diseases*.[12] It is likely that in DSM-V and ICD-11, PDD will be replaced by 'Autism Spectrum Disorder', because the notion of pervasive developmental disorder has been criticized for its confusion of impact, which is certainly pervasive, with aetiology, which seems increasingly specific rather than 'pervasive'. In anticipation of this, this book has been entitled *Autism Spectrum Disorders* rather than 'pervasive developmental disorders' as they were originally intended to be called.

Asperger syndrome was also included in ICD-10 along with 'Childhood autism', Rett syndrome, 'Other childhood disintegrative disorder', 'Overactive disorder associated with intellectual disability and stereotyped movements' and a number of other, atypical, and not otherwise specified residual categories. DSM-IV has also included Rett syndrome (but calling it Rett's disorder) and childhood disintegrative disorder, but not 'Overactive disorder associated with intellectual disability'.

The term 'pervasive' was chosen to stress the wide range of situations that are affected by the triad. Autism spectrum disorders are not a manifestation of intellectual disability and yet, as Rimland pointed out many years ago,[13] intellectual disability is truly a pervasive developmental disorder, affecting almost every aspect of psychological and social life. Wing herself has proposed an alternative term, the autism spectrum,[13] and as matters currently stand pervasive developmental disorder and autism spectrum disorder are interchangeable terms.

FUTURE ENLARGEMENT OF THE ASDs

ICD-10 already includes one disorder within the PDDs, 'overactive disorder associated with intellectual disability and stereotyped movements', that is closer to hyperkinetic disorder (or attention deficit hyperactivity disorder) than to an autism spectrum disorder. Tic disorders and hyperkinetic disorders in children without intellectual disability are classified in ICD-10 as behavioural and emotional disorders. Clearly this inconsistency will press for resolution in future editions. One simple way that this might be done is to include hyperkinetic disorder (or attention deficit/hyperactivity disorders as they are termed in DSM-IV) in a larger category of neurodevelopmental disorders alongside the ASDs.

If that happens, there are likely to be several other candidates for new pervasive developmental disorders. Intellectual disability may itself be one if, as seems possible, common forms of intellectual disability are no longer attributed to an inefficiency of all cognitive processes but to a specific, if pervasive, cognitive impairment.[14] 'Dysexecutive syndrome' is another candidate. This disabling condition is not currently represented anywhere in either of the major diagnostic classifications. Its symptoms are described in 'Organic personality disorder' in ICD-10 and are recognizable in the DSM-IV description of 'grossly disorganized behaviour' in the definition of schizophrenia. Some symptoms also appear in the characteristics of inattention in the DSM-IV definition of attention deficit hyperactivity disorder. None of these definitions is applicable to the person who has what used to be known as a frontal lobe syndrome, but who has no frontal lobe lesion and no psychosis. But such cases do exist – one is described in Chapter 16.

Psychiatrists often have to take account of changing diagnostic categories. The inexorable rise of post-traumatic stress disorder since the Vietnam war is one example. The reported prevalence of many of the ASDs has also climbed steadily and progressively since 2001. Autistic disorder was estimated, in 2000, to affect 4 children in every 10,000.[15] Even this was an increase on previous estimates. The rate reflects the narrowness of the criteria that were accepted then. Wing and Gould, using the triad of social impairments that are the basis of current criteria, had found in 1979 that 22 children in every 10,000 in Camberwell had an autism spectrum disorder,[16] and that 20 of them had an IQ of 70 or below.[17] But even these rates are low compared to the rates of 1 in 250 for autistic disorder and 1 in 150 for autism spectrum disorders that were reported in 2001 from New Jersey in the United States.[18] They are not an isolated finding. Comparable rates have been reported in Cambridgeshire in the UK of 1 affected child in 175 (this issue is discussed in detail in Chapter 7).

The prevalence of the autism spectrum disorders is small compared to that of ADHD. Recent estimates put the community prevalence of this disorder at between 4 and 12 per cent of children aged between 6 and 12.[20] This is even higher than the lifetime prevalence of PTSD in the community.[21]

THE CHALLENGE OF THE ASDs FOR ALL MENTAL HEALTH PROFESSIONALS

The official recognition of the ASDs means that all psychiatrists and clinical psychologists, and not just those who work with children, have to take account of development. This has an immediate practical implication. Since a detailed developmental history is usually necessary for a confident diagnosis of an ASD, psychiatrists and psychologists working with adults who rarely think it appropriate to interview parents will have to find some acceptable way not only of doing so, but also of taking a detailed history from them. Lest this seems too ambitious, it has also been suggested that the clinicians dealing with developmental disorders also require an expert knowledge of neuroscience,[22] and in recognition of this, Part 1 of this book contains reviews of current neuroscience, neurogenetics and neuropsychology as well as that other hand-maiden of psychiatry, social science.

There is already a slow but inexorable intrusion of developmental disorders like the autism spectrum disorders and ADHD into the concerns of clinicians dealing with adults. Understanding people with these disorders demands a developmental perspective that is likely to change the clinicians' perception of their other patients, too. The developmental perspective emphasizes change as well as stability. Developmental thinking challenges clinicians to consider the factors that determine long-term as well as short-term outcome. Often these are unrelated to symptom severity or behavioural disturbance, although these may be the factors that determine short-term management. Developmental thinking is not just applicable to the ASDs. Long-term studies of schizophrenia and of personality disorder have demonstrated that these apparently intractable conditions change with time, although often over longer spans of time than the duration of episodes of psychiatric care. One consequence of coming to terms with ASDs may therefore be that clinicians working with adults will pay more attention to developmental factors in other conditions that affect their patients.

Few services for adults are geared up to follow people throughout their lives. Unless people are acutely ill, they run the risk of getting lost to medical services, even people with schizophrenia who would benefit from more active community treatment.[23] ASDs are very often lifelong conditions, but the disabilities that they cause may change as a person gets older, or as their social situation changes. The disability may be similar to that caused by other psychiatric conditions and there is often a danger of misdiagnosis. The disability may be no disability at all during some periods of a person's life, and at those times the person concerned may rather be considered normal than suffering from an ASD. Many people with an ASD recognize that they are different but yet wonder, some would say justifiably, whether it is they who need to change, or the society that cannot find a place for them.[24]

ASDs cause enormous distress as well as disability. The services for people with ASDs are still developing, at best, and rudimentary at worst. Many of the services are located within the services for people with learning disability and are not appropriate for the majority of people with an ASD who do not have general learning difficulties, even if they have specific ones. Special schooling and educational programmes are being developed in many places, but there is much less follow-on provision. Adults with ASDs may often become socially excluded, relying completely on elderly parents or, even worse, becoming homeless.

Hard facts complement these clinical impressions. It has been estimated, for example, that the health care costs of children with ADHD are over twice those of normally developing children.[25] Even more strikingly, it has been estimated that the total direct cost to the UK of autism is £1 billion,[26] with elevated costs for medical care in childhood,[27] and as a result of a lack of suitable employment in adults.[28] For comparison, the direct costs of schizophrenia are estimated by the same group to be £1.3 billion.[29] Admittedly, the figures for schizophrenia are for England and those for ASD are for the UK as a whole. However, the prevalence figures for autism assumed by Jarbrink and Knapp were 5 per 10,000,[27] and, as already noted, that may be one-tenth of the actual prevalence figure. The actual costs of ASDs to the health and social services are therefore likely to be substantially higher – and perhaps more than those of schizophrenia.

CHALLENGE AND OPPORTUNITY

People with ASDs may be distraught, or mute, or utterly at odds with others. But they are rarely mad. They and their carers expect to be partners in the management of their difficulties. Very often they or their carers know more about the condition than the doctor or psychologist treating them. So it is very much to the clinician's advantage to make them a partner. Because people with ASDs have often been ignored by statutory services, they have had to develop support groups and to innovate, for example by using the internet. Treating them can be a challenge, but it offers new opportunities to the clinician.

Perhaps one of the largest opportunities is one of the most difficult to describe. People with ASD, and their carers, think about things that most of us take for granted. They think about how long a minute is, as in 'just a minute'. Or they wonder why street furniture is numbered, and what happened to the missing number. Or why there are so many different types of electricity pylon. These are, of course, some of the more obviously weird questions. But some questions that people with an ASD ask go deeply to the heart of many philosophical questions. 'Why', for example, 'would someone want to be my friend?' or 'What does a girl want in a man?' Clinicians who try to grapple with the questions that a person with ASD puts to them, if they are able to empathize with the emotional intensity that lies behind these questions, will find themselves having to question their own values and life equally carefully.

This is particularly so if the clinician is asked the question that people with an autism spectrum disorder often ask, 'What is a friend?' Many people with an ASD count acquaintances as friends, and I often follow the question, 'Who are your friends?' with further questions about whether or not the friend visits or is visited at home, or whether it is someone who the patient goes out with on social occasions. My daughter recently pointed out that many of her friends were virtual friends: people who she met occasionally but with whom she had more frequent contact by email. Email, chatrooms, discussion lists, social networking services and other opportunities of social contact using the internet are increasingly used by people with ASD. So the question remains, 'What is a friend?' Clearly one sort of answer is that a friend is a person with whom you have a relationship. Two differences between a relationship and a social contact are that the relationship persists even when the person is absent because one thinks about the other person, and that a relationship entails more than a social contact.[30] Relationships involve connecting up what the people involved would consider their selves, and not their public personae. Allowing people, to use Goffman's phrase, behind the scenes.[31] Making friends is therefore a matter of making and maintaining connections. It involves effort, thoughtfulness and empathy.

The challenge of replying to the question, 'What is a friend?' is to discuss the tasks of making and keeping friends without calling on the intuition or common sense of the person with an ASD, since it is precisely this lack of intuition that led to their question in the first place. The opportunity for clinicians is to reflect on themselves. It is easy for professionals, too, to become disconnected from other people. Not, admittedly, because they have an ASD – although a few do – but because of the nature of work and its demands. Talking about friendship to someone with ASD means getting back to basics for the clinician, too. It provides an opportunity for self-reflection on how disconnected the clinician has become, or might become, in their own life. Maybe it is good for each of us to ask, from time to time, 'How many of my so-called friends are really acquaintances and how many of my acquaintances would I like to be my friends?'

COVERAGE OF THE BOOK

ADHD, dysexecutive syndrome and the autism spectrum disorders occur more frequently together than would be expected by chance (see Chapter 9 for a review). This may be because each of them is a disorder of the frontostriatal brain system. Bradshaw and Sheppard define this to include the dorsolateral prefrontal cortex, lateral orbitofrontal cortex, anterior cingulate, supplementary motor area and associated basal ganglia structures,[32] to which I would add superior temporal sulcus, fusiform cortex, amygdala, insula, inferior parietal cortex and cerebellum. ADHD and dysexecutive syndrome may affect the outcome of an ASD, especially during adolescence, as much as the autistic syndrome itself. A full consideration of ASD must therefore include discussion of these other conditions, and I have chosen to include them, inasmuch as they co-occur with ASD, in this book. An advantage of doing this is that it facilitates taking a lifelong perspective on these disorders, which has been neglected in the past. A further advantage is that it seems likely that the ASD category will become expanded to include these, and perhaps other, as yet undescribed, neurodevelopmental disorders, in the future.

Therefore, while this book is mainly about the autism spectrum – about autistic disorder, Asperger syndrome or disorder, and 'pervasive disorder not otherwise specified' – I shall also consider syndromes like Rett syndrome, disintegrative psychosis, dysexecutive syndrome and attention deficit hyperactivity disorder as they overlap with or lie along the boundary of ASD. I shall give more attention to ADHD as there is growing evidence of overlap with Asperger syndrome and, my clinical experience suggests, with a particular 'atypical' subtype, which is sometimes called ASD 'not otherwise specified' (ASD-NOS), atypical autism or, my own preferred nomenclature, atypical Asperger syndrome. This condition is described fully in the chapter on adolescent presentations of ASD (Chapter 16).

I shall refer generically to all of the autism spectrum disorders as ASDs, and to attention deficit hyperactivity disorder as ADHD (for the sake of brevity I shall consider that ADHD is a unitary condition). I shall use AS to mean Asperger syndrome or high functioning autism, that is having an ASD but in the absence of intellectual disability and with normal or near normal speech and language. To refer specifically to the combination of ASD, intellectual disability and speech and language impairment, I shall use either 'Kanner syndrome' or autistic disorder.

The brain and developmental disorders
ASD

Autistic disorder was once considered to be psychological in origin, the result of the failure of a parent to provide love to the child over and above physical nurturance.[33, 2] But Kanner revised this opinion early on,[34, 35] attributing autism to both innate and experiential factors. In the 50 years since Kanner came to this conclusion, the evidence for the importance of innate factors has become overwhelming. Physical illnesses, neurological conditions and genetic disorders have all been identified that are associated with an increased risk of autism (for details, see Chapter 11). Even when no known genetic disorders have been identified, the risk of developing an autism spectrum disorder is increased by having an affected family member,[36] and ASD is considered to be the most heritable childhood psychiatric disorder.[37]

In clinical practice, many people with ASD have no family history of the disorder and no significant illness or overt disorder, other than the ASD itself, that might provide a cause. However, careful investigation may still show milder abnormalities. Parents, for example, are more likely to show some of the behaviours that are characteristic of ASD, for example unusual face scanning strategies.[38] Siblings, too, have been shown to look less at faces, like their sibs with ASD but unlike neurotypicals, and to show less fusiform gyrus activation.[39] More minor physical abnormalities can be found on detailed physical examination;[40] and most strikingly, because it directly reflects unusual brain development, volumetric studies of the brain show reduced cerebellar volumes and increased ventricular/brain ratios in people with an ASD versus controls.[41]

One complication of the latter finding is that the brain, like most other bodily organs, shows disease atrophy. Brain volume drops, largely as a result of the reduction of dendrites and association fibres, if the brain is inactive. So reduced brain volume may simply reflect a lack of use, such as might occur as a consequence of the social exclusion that many people with an ASD experience, and therefore be a consequence not a cause of ASD. However, there is another line of evidence for assuming that unusual brain development precedes the development of an ASD. This relies on the stretchability of the child's skull, which is not yet completely ossified but has fibrous connections between suture lines. Head circumference in children can therefore be used as an indication of how much the brain has pressed outwards against the skull as the brain grows, and therefore how big the brain and its associated structures (meninges and ventricles) are. Head circumference in infants who will later be diagnosed with an ASD is the same in the second trimester of pregnancy,[42] the same or smaller from birth to two weeks of age, but then becomes larger by a year,[43] and remains this way for several years. The magnitude of the size difference is correlated with the amount of social impairment found on later assessment months.[44] One possible reason for the increase of head circumferences may be that there is early myelination of the association fibres in white matter,[45] and this may be a consequence of accelerated development of all parts of the body mass.[45]

ADHD

There have been many studies of brain volume in people with ADHD, too, and widespread changes have been reported,[47] although the greatest changes are either confined to the grey matter of the cerebral cortex,[47] or to specific areas within the brain.[48, 49, 50, 51] Young people with ADHD and ASD were found, in one study, to have reduced grey matter volumes in the left temporal lobe and increased grey matter volume in the left parietal lobe, compared to controls. They differed in that the young people with the ASD also had increased grey matter in the right supramarginal gyrus, also known as the temporoparietal junction, since it is the area of the brain that is at the caudal end of the temporal lobe adjacent to the parietal lobe.[52]

These studies indicate that ADHD is associated with having an atypical development of the brain, just like ASD. Indeed the Brieber *et al.* study suggests that there is an overlap between the atypical development of the brain in ADHD and in ASD. The abnormal brain development is unlikely to be secondary to ADHD because some of them can be found in neurotypical siblings. In one study, boys with ADHD and their neurotypical siblings both showed reductions in right prefrontal grey matter and left occipital grey and white matter compared to controls: the boys with ADHD had additional reductions in right cerebellar volume that seemed to tip them into overt ADHD.[53]

The reader will note that the same points are being made for ADHD – that there is an association with a generalized alteration in brain size, and that some of the differences in the brain can also be found in apparently neurotypical family members – as were made for ASD. This is one of the many reasons that I suspect that ADHD and ASD will be classified together in the future.

The similarities between them are even greater when their genetics are considered. Both may be a feature of rare genetic syndromes, but even when none of these conditions are present, ADHD like ASD has a high heritability,[54] and, like the disposition for ASD,[55] is continuously distributed throughout the general population.[56] It may even be the same genes that contribute to the risk for both although the extent of the genetic overlap is disputed.[57]

Swedenborg's hypothesis

The philosopher and theologian Emmanual Swedenborg was the first to suggest that the cerebral cortex was organized functionally, with particular areas of it having specific functions. This doctrine was neglected at first but has become generally accepted.

The surface of the cerebral cortex is wrinkled with a pattern of ridges ('gyri') and grooves ('sulci'). These are variable and it is not easy to differentiate any but the largest areas. However, they may have functional significance as it has been suggested that blocks of brain tissue that have efferent fibres going to the same area of the brain tend to stick together, and that adjacent areas of brain that are connected to different brain areas tend to pull apart, forming sulci.[58] Korbinian Brodmann, centuries after Swedenborg, painstakingly examined sections of the cerebral cortex and described variations in the topography of the pyramidal neurons in the six layered (four layered in some older parts of the forebrain, or palaeopallium) 'grey matter' which overlies the thickly bundled, myelinated axons of fibres ('white matter') that provide afferent and efferent connections to it. He classified 52 different 'cytoarchitectures' each belonging to a different area. Although Brodmann's areas have been criticized – there are advocates for the later classification of von Economa and Koskinas, for example – Brodmann's areas continue to be widely used.

The only definitive way of finding out what the Brodmann area of a particular part of a particular brain belongs to is to examine it histopathologically. This is clearly not feasible when the brain is a living one being examined in a scanner. Jean Tailarach, a neurosurgeon, used the axis of a line drawn between the anterior and posterior commissures to a particular brain to create a three-dimensional coordinate system that, although developed for this particular brain, can be used as a standard by transforming the dimensions of other brains so that the line between their anterior and posterior commissures is in the same plane and has the same length.

A hypothesis that is the basis for much current neuroimaging is that the arrangement of cells in each of Brodmann's areas, their 'cytoarchitectonics', differed because each area had a different function. On the assumptions that the topography of Brodmann areas is the same from brain to brain, and that a Brodmann area corresponds to a particular function, Tailarach coordinates can be used as markers for functional units of the brain. But these assumptions are only approximate, and may sometimes lead to erroneous conclusions.

Modern neuroimaging methods (for example, positron emission tomography and functional magnetic resonance imaging) make it possible to measure the uptake of oxygen and sometimes other ligands by brain cells and neuroglia. This provides an indication of blood flow and therefore neural activity. So these and other methods provide a map of those areas of the brain that are active during the performance of tasks chosen by the investigators. Mapping brain function has provided considerable information about areas of the brain whose apparent function could not be deduced from lesion or animal studies. Many of these functions have been particularly relevant to ASD and, in turn, the study of people with ASD has provided information about neurotypical function. These exciting developments are summarized in Chapters 1, 2 and 3.

COULD SOME KINDS OF ASD BE PURELY PSYCHOGENIC?

Despite the massive preponderance of neurobiological evidence supporting the importance of the innate factors that Kanner himself came to consider to be essential, there are still some people who argue that ASD is psychogenic, and many people who argue this for ADHD. One reason for this is that children who experience extreme social and emotional isolation are known to develop ASD-like symptoms. Parents have probably known this from time immemorial, but little account was made of it until the work of Bowlby and his co-workers became widely known.[59] Children were routinely separated from their parents in hospitals or institutions throughout most of the twentieth century.

Bowlby was originally commissioned by the World Health Organization to look at the mental health of children displaced by the Second World War. His findings were consistent with those in primates who were experimentally deprived of parenting,[60] and in other animals, including dogs.[61] Bowlby adopted the terminology of ethology, and attributed this syndrome to the accumulation of anxiety due to everyday threats which were not buffered by 'attachment'.[62]

Attachment theory might explain some of the symptoms experienced by many children with ASD,[63] but Tinbergen, a Nobel laureate in ethology, and his wife suggested that extreme insecurity, or anxiety, in children might be enough to cause ASD.

The Tinbergens' hypothesis is probably the most plausible psychogenic hypothesis, not least because it is consistent with the high levels of anxiety that do seem to be inextricably bound up with ASD. It is also consistent with Kanner's own view, that children were particularly at risk of ASD if their parents were overseas graduate students who were both socially isolated and highly intellectual 'refrigerator' parents. One feature of ASD that cannot be explained by the attachment hypothesis is that studies of parents of children with ASD do not show that they are emotionally depriving parents. Nor does ASD obviously remit if children are placed with adoptive parents., although it could be argued that this is because the effects of emotional deprivation are greatest during a critical period and before the adoption has taken place.

There is another reason why the psychogenic hypothesis of ASD is attractive. Individuals with ASD should not, or so it may seem to lay people, 'get away' with blaming their difficult behaviour on some kind of brain abnormality, but should take responsibility for their own actions or, if they are still young, their parents should do so for not providing them with the correct upbringing.

An independent, although related, argument is that to attribute ASD to innate factors is too pessimistic because that would suggest that only a physical intervention could help, and despite many claims to the contrary, no physical intervention has ever been proven.

Both groups – those who oppose medical exemption from responsibility and those who oppose medical nihilism – assume that if ASD were psychogenic then a person with ASD could be expected to change themselves and so both fault-finding and an expectation of recovery would be justified.

It would clearly be unjustified to conduct an experiment to whether extreme emotional or social deprivation can cause permanent ASD, but there is evidence available from pseudo-experiments, in which children who have experienced extreme social deprivation can be studied *post hoc*. There are a few single case studies of feral children who have either been brought up by a delusional parent, who has locked them up and kept them isolated, or children who have been abandoned but survived, sometimes reputedly being nourished by wild animals (wolf children, ape children, and so on).[64, 65, 66, 67] Many of these studies have focused as did Cambyses, the ancient Persian king described by Herodotus, on language acquisition. They have provided surprisingly little information about the role of early socialization, or its absence, in the development of autism spectrum disorder.

Economic conditions in Eastern Europe led, in the recent past, to many parents handing over their children to the state for maintenance, and to the consequent development by the state of large 'orphanages', particularly in Romania, Moldova and Russia. Children in these orphanages were given the basics of physical care but sometimes no emotional care and no organized opportunity for socialization. Children in these circumstances become withdrawn, as attachment theory indicates, stop communicating with those around them, and pay reduced attention to their environment. They may develop restlessness, rituals and stereotypies. Their behaviour may, in other words, become similar in some respects to ASD.

When the consequences of state adoption of children became widely known, schemes, including some illicit ones, were introduced to provide adoptive parents for these children in the West. Some infants may have been confined to their cots for long periods of time with extremely restricted opportunities for social interaction. Some of these children had no parents, but others were placed there by their parents, in some cases because they were presenting developmental challenges but mainly, apparently, because the parents could not afford to keep them.

Romanian ex-orphanage children, adopted in the UK, and comparison groups of Romanian children and of UK children who were not institutionalized but who were also adopted in the UK, have now been followed up into their early teens. There were higher rates of inattention and overactivity at both 6 and 11 years of age in the boys who had spent six months or more in an orphanage, but no higher rates in girls who had spent six months or more in an orphanage or any of the other subgroups.[68] Inattention and overactivity was sufficiently similar in these boys to consider it a manifestation of ADHD, and it was associated with conduct disorder, relationship problems, and executive impairment, just as is ADHD of whatever aetiology.

That only boys, but not girls, were at increased risk of ADHD indicates that even in these extreme psychological circumstances, innate factors are still important. But the study also points to the importance of experience in turning a disposition into a disorder.

ASD was also found in a small (6%) subgroup of the Romanian ex-orphanage children at the age of four, but in none of the adopted children born in the UK. However, their ASD was more likely to improve at the age of six than would be the case for ASD in other children, they did not have greater than normal head circumferences, and the boy/girl ratio was equal.[69] Comparable results have been found in an independent cohort of ex-orphanage children adopted in the Netherlands.[70]

Impaired executive function and reduced theory of mind accounted for most of the ASD symptoms,[71] and were associated with inattention and overactivity and 'disinhibited attachment'. This symptom profile is characteristic of atypical AS.

These studies do seem to suggest that a small proportion of children, under conditions of extreme neglect, may develop an atypical ASD, but even in them innate factors may still contribute. Children showing early signs of ASD may be more likely to be given up for adoption, and parents with an ASD may be more likely to give up their children for adoption as well as passing on a hereditary disposition to ASD to their children.

What can definitely be concluded from these studies is that experiential factors do play a part in the aetiology of the ASDs. But they are against psychogenesis alone being a cause for all, but rare if any cases of ASD.

Emotional isolation caused by ASD

Several of the theories suggested to be fundamental impairment in ASD might act as barriers to social and emotional relatedness with others, and therefore produce a lack of attachment from within. Examples include my own theory of a lack of interbrain connection, Hobson's theory that autism is an innate failure of intersubjectivity,[72] and a recent hypothesis that ASD results from a failure to 'bond' because the infant does not elicit the normal peptide surge in the mother that triggers maternal behaviour in mammals.[73, 74] None of these theories can explain many of the features of ASD unless some additional factor supervenes. Study of the Romanian orphans suggest that some aspects of ASD which are often taken to be neurological and therefore the consequence of an innate impairment, like theory of mind or executive function, are actually the result of impaired early social interaction and that, even in neurotypicals, normal development of these cognitive functions requires socialization.

Can experience sculpt the brain? Epigenesis and learning

If deprivation can cause executive dysfunction and an impairment in theory of mind judgements (see Chapter 6 for a definition and discussion of these impairments), might it also cause the functional changes in the areas of the brain that have been shown to be associated with these impairments in ASD? In other words, does the presence of altered neurological function provide proof of innateness? There is good reason to think not.

Some areas of the brain become smaller when they are not exercised, and larger when they are 'exercised'. London cab drivers have larger posterior hippocampal grey matter volume (although at the expense of anterior grey matter) as a result of having to learn a detailed mental map of London.[75] Many people with ASD avoid situations in which their lack of skill can be shown up. So it is possible that a reduction in brain activity may reflect a kind of disuse atrophy rather than being the cause of the lack of skill.

Epigenesis is another way in which experience can influence neurology, and not the other way around. Epigenesis refers to the environmental effect on genes, which, it is becoming apparent, is substantial. Genes can be turned off or on by adding or removing methyl groups, or by being covered or uncovered by their protein coating of histones.[76, 77] These epigenetic effects are themselves enabled or disabled by genes, such as the genes that code for an enzyme, histone deacetylase, which esterifies histone side chains causing the protein to fold more tightly around its DNA core, and so blocking access by mRNA. HDAC inhibitors, which include butyrate, reverse this process.[78]

Epigenetic effects explain the changes in the relative sizes of the brain with development, and the timing of myelinization of the axons of brain cells and therefore the speed of transmission of neural networks. Epigenetic factors probably account, too, for the increase in receptor sites and increased arborization or dendritic branching that occurs at junctions between nerve cells that receive more traffic than usual, and the reversal of this process, and in embryo the apoptosis or cell death that accompanies a lack of transmission. The brain's development is also influenced by emotion, again probably through epigenesis. There is an excitotoxic theory of trauma that argues that trauma exposes the developing brain to high levels of corticosteroids which lead to reduced brain volume,[79] and possibly other more selective effects. There is also evidence, from mammalian studies,[80] that the early relationship between mother and offspring in social prairie voles releases genes in the amygdala that increase oxytocin release in adult life and that increased levels of oxytocin release in response to pairing leads to stronger pair bonding. Epigenetic factors are probably important in ASD, and may influence the functional development of the brain.[81]

The plastic effects of experience on the brain, through learning, through interaction with the environment,[82] or through epigenesis, constitute a new field.[81] The implications for ASD are likely to be considerable but they lie in the future and will have to be covered in future editions of this, or similar books, rather than in this one.

One likely contribution of this new field will be to model more effectively the extent to which innate and experiential factors contribute to the severity of ASD in any particular case, or subtype of these disorders. This is likely to lead, in turn, to better methods of predicting outcome and of targeting interventions. It might go some way, too, towards answering the recurring question of whether or not families and others contribute to, reduce, or simply respond to the challenges of a person with ASD. This issue often comes up most acutely when the state becomes involved in parenting, and it will be considered further in Chapter 10 in connection with providing medical reports to family courts and child care panels.

THE LIMITS OF NEUROIMAGING

The resolution of fMRI has improved, and is now about a millimetre or slightly larger than a cortical column.[83] fMRI localization proceeds by averaging and abstraction: images obtained on repeated trials are overlaid and only the ones that appear in all of the trials are retained. The results from groups of participants are similarly averaged, and this may introduce a substantial loss of resolution if, as seems likely, the functional map of different brains varies slightly.

There are some other difficulties about inferring anything clinically useful about ASD from studies of brains, even though it may be alterations in the brain that are the cause of ASD.

The first is that the rule that generates a behaviour may be very different from the apparent function of the behaviour. An example of this is the way that birds behave in a flock. It seems wondrously complex – complex enough in fact for us to watch a large flock just to see what will happen. Its function is more obvious. Birds flock so that they can follow a leader to food or to shelter. At the same time, they seem to be socializing. Birds seem to break away and then realize their mistake, flying more quickly to catch up and rejoin the flock. If we were to design the flocking 'mechanism' in a bird's brain, we would probably want to include some perception like 'leader', 'flock' and 'wanting to be with other flock members'. Convincing computer simulations of flocks of birds can be generated much more simply, by the application of simple rules, requiring only that an individual bird maintains the same topographical distance between itself and the birds in its immediate vicinity. These rules also predict the behaviour of actual flocks.[84] We interpret the behaviour of flocking birds functionally, in terms of leadership and socialization. But the generation of this behaviour, its cause, has nothing to do with these abstractions but with a much simpler rule.

Brains follow rules, not functional descriptions. So when we ascribe a function to an area of the brain, we may be in error. The superior temporal gyrus is, for example, apparently specialized in breaking up sequences into components, or assembling sequences into components. In the left hemisphere the superior temporal gyrus is required for speech production, but it would be wrong to call it the location of speech production since this is a description of the consequence of what the superior temporal gyrus does, which is to break up utterances into phonemes or morphemes, or to assemble phonemes into utterances. This is essential for speech production, but is not itself the production of speech.

In the first chapters of this book, I review the considerable information that is now available about the activation of different brain areas and the light that this information casts on the impairments of people with ASD. But it will be important to remember that there is a considerable gap between what the brain does and what happens as a result. One example is a study of the prefrontal cortex. In a summary of their findings, the authors of one study write: 'We propose two hypotheses about the neurobiology of self-control: (i) Goal-directed decisions have their basis in a common value signal encoded in ventromedial prefrontal cortex (vmPFC), and (ii) exercising self-control involves the modulation of this value signal by dorsolateral prefrontal cortex (DLPFC).'[85] The dorsolateral prefrontal cortex is sometimes known as the 'frontal eye field', and its functions are discussed in Chapter 1. The authors' evidence that activation of this area is associated with what is recognizably self-control is convincing. But what if the process of 'self-control' is actually a process of scrutinizing oneself from another person's perspective, and that to imagine this requires drawing on the frontal eye fields to create the inner sense of being looked at by another person? Self-control would not be exercised by the DLPFC at all, but be the consequence of a mental process which used the DLPFC to simulate being looked at, just as a program may draw heavily on information stored in RAM or on the hard disk.

Information about brain activity is often given disproportionate weight by scientists and the general public, but the inference of mental processes from observations of brain activity is a kind of 'reverse inference', which is logically flawed.[86] It is a backwards kind of logic or 'affirmation of the consequent'. A more obvious example of this would be: 'if I finish writing this book, I will have finished writing all of the chapters in it, too. I have finished this chapter. So I have finished the book.'

How clinically useful is a study of the brain?

Functional neuroimaging is creating new challenges for determining when activation of a brain area should be considered significant and when it is spurious, and also for developing new tests that will disclose relevant brain activation. The goal is to map particular brain areas onto particular psychological functions, but that may be a chimaera. Dual aspect monists would not find it so.[87] They consider that when we use mental terms we mean no more, or no less, than if we could describe a sequence of events in the brain. Of course, our knowledge of the brain is much less developed than our knowledge of the mind. But the rapid developments in neuroscience applied to the brain (when I refer to neuroscience in the remainder of this book, I shall be referring to brain neuroscience unless otherwise specified) are rapidly increasing our knowledge.

Many neuroscientists in fact use descriptions of brain process and mental processes interchangeably. For example, in a paper on the neurobiology of narrative, the author writes, 'Posterior regions of the cingulate may be responsible for the retrieval of elaborative information such as personal experience, in order to enrich comprehension or add realism to a produced story.'[88] Mar's mixing of psychological terms like 'responsible', 'in order to' or 'add realism' and neurological ones like 'posterior regions of the cingulate' and 'retrieval of… information' is common in papers, like this one, which are based on neuroimaging data. Like many other authors, Mar assumes that spatial organization of the brain ('posterior region') corresponds to function ('responsible for retrieval…'): an assumption that may be premature (but see below). Mar also mixed together functions that are easily instantiated by automatic systems, such as information retrieval, with those that we would normally consider acts, requiring planning or intention. Story telling would probably be considered by many to be a particularly demanding example of an act of human creativity (one, incidentally, that is particularly difficult for many people with an ASD). But Mar suggests that the posterior cingulate participates directly in this creative act.

But there is one obvious and one less obvious problem with mixing up psychological and neurological descriptions indiscriminately. The obvious problem is that posed to Gall, the founder of phrenology, who argued that the size of areas of the brain is linked to the development of the capacities that might be linked to those areas. Albert Einstein is a case in point. His achievements in physics are considered to be superlative by many people, but his brain, far from being correspondingly enormous, was rather smaller than the average. Detailed analysis showed only that Einstein had a larger parietal lobe than the average,[89] and more glial cells, the latter possibly explicable if Einstein had Asperger syndrome[90] as some have argued.[91] The parietal lobe is not the part of the brain normally associated with abstract thought, or even with mental imagery. So it seems unlikely that there is a direct correspondence between hypertrophy of this area in Einstein, and his physical and mathematical creativity.

NETWORKS

There is growing evidence that parts of the brain interact through networks, some of which run from the very front of the brain, originating in the prefrontal cortex to the very back, the cerebellum. It seems increasingly likely, too, that dysfunction in these networks is more closely related to the symptoms of ASDs than dysfunction in any particular place in the brain that is a way station on the network. I have also hypothesized that brains are not only internally networked but also typically wirelessly networked with other brains.[92] Studying specific areas of the brain may provide only indirect evidence about the network and therefore indirect evidence about the neurological substrate of ASD.

Evidence about networks is slowly beginning to accumulate and I shall consider some of it in Chapter 3.

Emergent properties

Some kinds of psychological phenomena are algorithmic, or rule bound, as I previously proposed that neurobiological processes were. One can easily conceive of computerizing them, or of imagining them carried out by neurobiological processes, for example the storage and retrieval of information. Other phenomena, like intuition or aesthetic judgements, do not appear to be rule bound at all, even allowing for the kinds of fuzzy, trainable systems that neural nets allow. Social intuition is one of these phenomena that looks like it can be accounted for only by processes that are new to psychology, and are not found in neurobiology, but 'emergent' from it.[93] The concept of emergence had little scientific credence during the height of monism, when mind and body seemed to be no more than descriptions of the same thing. But the human genome project has undermined that simplicity: the range of possible variation in the human genome, while astronomically large overall, does not seem enough to explain the difference between, say, a chimpanzee and a person. Bilder *et al.* put it this way:

> The human genome, with only 3 billion bases, selected from a pool of only four nucleic acids, organized in a neat one-dimensional sequence, pales in comparison to the human phenome, which contains an unknown number of elements, many of which are characterized by enormous inter-individual variation that is at best only partially understood, and for which the dimensionality remains unknown. Phenomics – operationally defined as the systematic study of phenotypes on a genome-wide scale – is critically important to provide traction for biomedical advances in the post-genomic era.[94]

They provide a graphic to demonstrate the points at which new phenomena may emerge (Figure I.1).

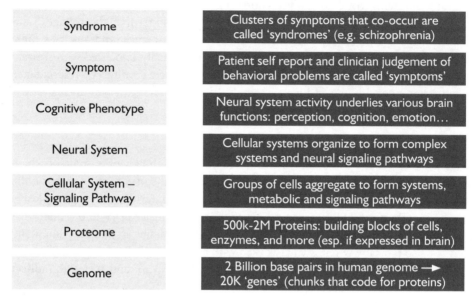

Syndrome	Clusters of symptoms that co-occur are called 'syndromes' (e.g. schizophrenia)
Symptom	Patient self report and clinician judgement of behavioral problems are called 'symptoms'
Cognitive Phenotype	Neural system activity underlies various brain functions: perception, cognition, emotion…
Neural System	Cellular systems organize to form complex systems and neural signaling pathways
Cellular System – Signaling Pathway	Groups of cells aggregate to form systems, metabolic and signaling pathways
Proteome	500k-2M Proteins: building blocks of cells, enzymes, and more (esp. if expressed in brain)
Genome	2 Billion base pairs in human genome → 20K 'genes' (chunks that code for proteins)

Figure I.1 Levels of description of pathology
Source: Reproduced from Bilder, Saab, *et al.*, 2009 with permission from Elsevier.

Mixing up neurological and psychological explanations overlooks these emergent properties, and prematurely oversimplifies the aetiology of the ASDs. Many geneticists are, for now, concentrating on finding more direct manifestations of genotypes, what Bilder *et al.* call 'cognitive phenotypes' but are more generally called 'endophenotypes'.[95] The gulf between neurology and psychology may take a long time to fill, not least because psychological explanations, or reasons, are often applied *post hoc* and, while they may cause future actions, are rarely the cause of the action for which they supply a reason.[95] I have therefore devoted a separate chapter (Chapter 7) to psychological functions, linking them where possible to neurobiology but recognizing that these links may prove misleading ultimately. Epilepsy is included among these 'psychological' functions because it has some of the same emergent properties.

One possible explanation for emergence is that parts of the brain interact together, producing a system that has functions that cannot be inferred from the functions of its parts. Another is that language acts as a kind of instruction set that alters the function of individual parts of the brain. An analogy to the latter that is often used is to computer function. Computers run programs, instantiated as memorized instructions, and a computer process cannot be understood without reference to this software. The brain also uses software, including the inner language described by Vygotsky,[96] but also more elusive, nonverbal algorithms deriving from experience. I have a personal computer that uses the Microsoft Windows operating system. Much of my computer is taken up by cooling fans, controllers and input-output devices, like my hard disk or memory arrays. The Windows operating system requires all of these to be functioning for it to work, but I can run my version on a different computer that might have a larger hard disk, less memory, different cooling systems and so on. Clearly, the functions that Windows enables, the 'functionality' of Windows as IT people call it, does not reside in any particular part of the computer, or even particular part of the hard disk. The functions of the software 'emerge' from the functions of the hardware, but do not correspond to them. Those dualist philosophers who argue that the same applies to the brain argue that mind and brain cannot therefore be two aspects of one thing, but two quite different things.

NEURODIVERSITY

Genes interact with experience, and experience also shapes the developing brain. How people put their brain to use adds a further element of emergence. It is premature in these circumstances to assume that there is an ideal brain, or even an average brain, and that deviations from this confer disadvantage let alone disability. People with AS have long argued that this is a neurotypical perspective, with neurotypicals being those people who not only share a common neurotype but also assume that this neurotype is in some way superior to all others.

Human evolution has involved substantial changes in the brain which are often presented as progressive, with *Homo sapiens* being the ultimate goal of evolution. Evolution occurs as organisms change their phenotype and in so doing survive more successfully in a new ecological niche. Human culture tends to minimize adaptation pressure, but this may change. Biologists have come to the conclusion that biodiversity is the best preparation for adaptation. The same argument applies to neurodiversity as a preparation against future new adaptation pressures on the brain. One obvious candidate is the increasing symbiosis with machines as a means of communication, memory and information processing. People with AS have already distinguished themselves in communicating with computers. People with ADHD may have had greater selection advantage in the past when in warfare or hunting, reckless but rapid decision-making was at a higher premium. We cannot at this stage assume that neurotypicality will always be the most adapted human neurobiology.

OTHER SOCIAL CONSIDERATIONS

The theoretical argument for neurodiversity is gainsaid by the practical reality that people who do not fit in are likely to be pressured to change to try to force them to conform. The most direct expression of this is bullying. These pressures to conform when neurodiversity affects socialization, neurotypicals are predisposed to try to bend.

One of the reasons that ASD is so complex is that life experience and temperament make a considerable difference to the level and type of disability that the same core impairment produces in different people.[97] The impact of bullying for people with an ASD is only now becoming apparent, for example. Some of these factors are considered in Chapter 6.

SCOPE AND PLAN OF THE BOOK

Each chapter of the book contains a brief summary of relevant neurotypical function and, where appropriate, structure, before considering how people with an autism spectrum disorder, and where it might be relevant, people with other kinds of neurodevelopmental disorder, might differ.

Part 1 covers the relevant theory and Part 2 relevant practice. The first two chapters are on the brain, arbitrarily divided into superficial areas (Chapter 1) and mainly comprising the phylogenetically recent parts of the brain and deep structures (Chapter 2).

Selected brain areas are considered in each chapter, each with an account of normal anatomy and presumed function, and then sections on animal studies (if sufficient have been carried out), the functional effect of lesions in adulthood and childhood, and structural and functional changes reported in the ASDs and where appropriate in other neurodevelopmental disorders.

Chapter 3 covers neurogenetics, the interaction of genes in networks, and the interaction of neurons in networks.

Chapter 4 covers the experiential, familial, personal and other 'psychosocial' factors that influence the development of a person with an ASD. This is particularly important because having the kind of different brain described in Chapters 1 to 3 results in being different but not necessarily impaired. An autism spectrum 'condition' may or may not have adverse consequences. Whether it does or not depends on whether or not it is disabling, and that may depend on how far society is prepared to go to enable the person.

Chapter 5 covers communication and linguistic theories that are of foundational important to an understanding of ASD. The neurology of speech and language are considered, followed by a brief introduction to psycholinguistics in neurotypicals and in people with an ASD.

Chapter 6 focuses on nonverbal communication and its links to the fundamental impairments in ASD, including empathy and reduced theory of mind.

Chapter 7 covers other aspects of neuropsychology that are relevant to disorders that are co-morbid with ASD. Like Chapters 1 and 2, this is divided into topic areas, although this time functional rather than anatomic ones. Within each function area, there is a consideration of neurotypical function, testing and the significance for ASD.

Part 2 begins with a discussion of the autistic syndrome in Chapter 8, opening with a consideration of whether or not there are specific autism spectrum disorders or whether, as Lorna Wing suggested, there is an autism spectrum. The evidence points strongly to there being a spectrum of disorder or rather a complex amalgamation of several continua, at least one of which corresponds to the fundamental lack of social contact that justified the term 'autism' in the first place. Reviewing current diagnostic practice suggests that the description of 'autistic disorder' in the current edition of the *Diagnostic and Statistical Manual* of the American Psychiatric Association (DSM-IV-TR)[4] provides a reliable basis for diagnosing the presence or absence of the autistic (or the ASD) spectrum but that it is best considered to be the characterization of a syndrome and not of a disorder.

Chapter 9 covers what is known about the course and aetiology of the autistic syndrome itself. This chapter therefore provides information that is common to all of the ASDs, including best practice for diagnosis, investigation and treatment. Chapters 10 and 11 cover clinical assessment and aetiology, respectively.

The remaining chapters of the book, from Chapters 12 to 17, provide a detailed clinical account of the ASDs organized by their characteristic presentations at particular developmental stages: Chapter 12 on presentation in infancy, Chapters 13 and 14 in middle childhood, Chapters 15 and 16 in adolescence and Chapter 17 in adulthood. There are two chapters for middle childhood since it is at this stage of development that high and low functioning ASD diverge. Chapter 13 is on high functioning ASD or Asperger syndrome, and Chapter 14 on Kanner syndrome. In adolescence there is a further divergence between typical (Chapter 15) and atypical AS (Chapter 16). Since atypical AS is associated with ADHD, there is a consideration of this condition in Chapter 16 too.

This principle of organization has been chosen because people affected by an ASD often first seek help, or have help sought for them by their carers, at times of transition between developmental stages. Each of these transitions calls for new skills or new forms of adaptation. Many people with ASD cope with their condition without any specific help until they find themselves in a situation that makes too many demands on them. Often these new demands correspond to a transition. The first demands of peer relationships in infancy, or the long-term demands of relationships at work or in family life for adults in middle adulthood, are two examples. I begin each of these chapters with a brief account of what these transitional demands might be for the particular age group considered in the chapter.

Transitions may create difficulties for many people with diagnosed ASD. They also bring out the existence of an ASD in a new group of sufferers who were previously unrecognized. And a few people with an ASD may find less difficulty in the new stage of life, and may cease to need professional help. So at each transition a new group of children, adolescents or adults present with hitherto unsuspected problems and their mode of presentation, and the nature of their underlying problems, is characteristic of the transition.

Clinicians will find it convenient to use age at first presentation as an easy source of reference when researching a new patient or client whom they suspect of having an ASD. Researchers, experts and people particularly interested in ASD, including some dedicated parents and some people with ASD themselves will want to read the book more systematically. In this way, the book will appeal to two readerships. There will be clinicians who take a special interest in the ASDs, perhaps acting as the lead clinicians in their organization for these disorders. I would hope that these specialists will read the book in its entirety. There will also be a much larger group of psychiatrists, psychologists, counsellors, specialist nurses and others who may have the responsibility of caring for occasional patients or clients with Asperger syndrome. These clinicians will, I expect, want only to study those sections of the book that concern a particular subtype of ASD. Naturally, I hope that some of them will be sufficiently intrigued to want to read the remainder of the book, too.

It is not currently clear whether these additional factors occur more frequently with ASD because they are genetically related, because they are functional consequences of brain areas that are shared with those that lead to the 'autistic factor', or because there is an underlying genetic, biochemical or intra-uterine condition that is common to each of them.

Every person with an ASD is different. That seems simplistic until as a clinician meeting a succession of people with an ASD, one has to try to discern what they have in common that justifies each of them having the same diagnosis. A useful approach to this is to think of each person with an ASD as having a functional profile with high or low function on relevant dimensions. However, functional descriptions are unwieldy and cannot be translated into the categorical diagnoses that are required administratively and socially. So experienced clinicians often return to using diagnostic categories, like Asperger syndrome or Kanner syndrome (the term that is used in this book to apply to what is otherwise sometimes called low functioning autism or typical autism), recognizing that these paradigms are useful labels even if they are not labels of separate disorders.

In the remainder of Part 2, the clinical chapters from Chapter 12 onwards are based on these useful labels. They all begin with a summary of the developmental tasks that correspond to that stage of life. This is important because, as the authors of DSM-IV-TR put it, 'the qualitative impairments that define these conditions are distinctly deviant relative to the individual's developmental level and age'.[4a] Developmental tasks are determined by social arrangements interacting with developmental processes intrinsic to neurotypical development,[99] or 'developmental levels'. Clinicians wishing to know therefore whether a person's impairments are distinctly deviant must first know what is appropriate to the developmental level. Each chapter is further divided into sections according to the type of ASD most likely to present at that age.

The practitioner confronted with, say, a 12-year-old who is unexpectedly failing at school and developing behavioural problems can therefore easily turn to Chapter 15 on presentation in later childhood for help with diagnosis. There they will find accounts of the ASDs that are most likely to become salient during later childhood and adolescence. These include Asperger syndrome, atypical Asperger syndrome and dysexecutive syndrome. This is not to say that these disorders may not present either earlier or later. Indeed, Chapter 17 on adulthood also considers Asperger syndrome becoming salient for the first time. However, the type of expression of Asperger syndrome at age 12, and perhaps the severity or pattern of the core impairment, is different from that in adulthood.

This last remark should not be taken too far. There are often substantial differences between 12-year-olds with Asperger syndrome, just as there are between people of Asperger syndrome at every age. So much so that I once concluded, in a kind of desperation, that the characteristic feature of Asperger syndrome was that everyone with it was more individual than was normal. At that stage in my getting to know people with this condition, each of them seemed so different from each other that I despaired of finding any common factor. One reason for this is that emotional and social factors, like age, have a substantial impact on the functional disability that ASDs cause.

Another reason is that people with an autism spectrum disorder are born – as I have noted previously – disconnected from other people.[93] This is not something they choose. Nor is it an emotional reaction to an unkind world, as psychoanalysts used to think. To use a computer analogy, it is rather that their brains cannot handshake with the wide area social network. This network is mediated by the constant nonverbal communication that passes between people. The network is both directive and permissive. Lacking its direction, some people with an ASD develop in strikingly original ways. Others simply become defeated, and inert. Lacking its permissiveness, some people with ASD develop their own world of gratification and reward. Others become depressed, or uneasily linked to others through more tenuous means of communication. Whatever the consequence, the person with an ASD, especially if they have an autism spectrum disorder, has to explore the world anew since the maps and landmarks that society places in it are invisible to them. As a result, each person with an ASD has something of the quality of the explorer about them: self-sufficient, methodical in preparation, eccentric and awkward because they spend so much time alone, uneasy in the company of their peers, and courageous. I hope that in this book I can manage to convey some of these positive attributes as well as any of the impairments of people with these disabling conditions.

Part I

SCIENCES BASIC TO ASD

Chapter I

NEUROLOGY OF THE SUPERFICIAL STRUCTURES OF THE BRAIN

This chapter and Chapters 2 and 3 deal with the neurology of areas of the brain that have been particularly implicated in the ASDs. It is a highly selective review of recent studies of the brain with a particular emphasis on neuroimaging studies. Some areas of the brain that may turn out to be important, such as the basal ganglia, the hippocampus (which has been reported to be abnormal in ASD or ADHD)[1] and the hypothalamus, have been excluded for reasons of brevity.

Each of the chosen areas, in contrast, receives quite detailed coverage, although I have included only those findings that have a clear relevance to clinical features of ASD. The rapid accumulation of findings in the field has outpaced the development of synthesis. Some sections may read more as lists of findings even though in these sections I have often limited cited studies to those published within a year or so of publication of the completion of this text and I have included only those studies that offer promising new leads about ASD. Where possible I have included one of the increasing number of systematic reviews.

I have used headings to try to order the material although it has not always been possible to apply them. Function, for example, is so often tied in with structure that separating some findings about structure from those about function would reduce comprehensibility and not increase it.

RIGHT HEMISPHERE
Anatomy
The right hemisphere is that half of the cerebral cortex that is on a person's right side. The dominant hemisphere is the one that contains the speech centre. In all but a tiny proportion of right-handers and half of left-handers, the left hemisphere is dominant, i.e. in about 97 per cent of the population. Throughout this book the use of 'right hemisphere' should be taken to imply non-dominant hemisphere unless otherwise specified. The cerebral cortex is the phylogenetically most recent part of the brain. Its particularly large, pyramidal, neurons are well ordered with a zone of cells and terminals ('grey matter') arranged in six layers (in the neocortex or neopallium; four in the older small brain, or archipallium) separated from a zone of axonal fibres ('white matter'). Layers I–III are mainly composed of interneurons connecting to the neurons in layers IV–VI and possibly act as local processors. Layers IV–VI subserve thalamic input, output to effectors, and thalamic output respectively.

The two hemispheres connect indirectly via their projections to lower centres but are also directly connected with each other through a bridge of nerve fibres, the corpus callosum.

The surface of the cerebral cortex is folded into prominences (gyri) and grooves (sulci). Areas of the cortex were previously described on the basis of the appearance of the surface and the divisions apparently created by the sulci. Areas are now defined by the appearance of the cellular architecture under the microscope, and the most influential of these cytoarchitectonic schemes is based on a map of 52 cytoarchitectonically distinguishable areas developed by Korbinian Brodmann.

Normal function

Barr noted some time ago that there was less than full understanding of the functions of the right cerebral hemisphere,[2] and this remains true. It is clear that the cerebral hemisphere is particularly involved with visuospatial perception, and that its ability to produce language is limited although not completely absent.[3] The right hemisphere uses a different visual search strategy to the left, and is more attuned to expressions of negative affect. There is evidence that the right temporal hemisphere responds to the emotional connotation of words before the words are lexically decoded.[4]

Some of the functions that are normally restricted to the right hemisphere, such as gaze following and holistic or gestalt face processing are particularly affected by ASD.[5]

Functional effect of lesions in adulthood

Cerebral lesions acquired in adulthood may mimic some aspects of ASDs. Infarction in the right cerebral hemisphere may produce an inability to recognize familiar faces and facial expressions of emotion (prosopagnosia), a lack of expression in spontaneous speech (aprosodia),[6] and reduced performance in 'theory of mind' tasks.[7] Interpretation of facial expressions of emotion and the interpretation and expression of emotional prosody are impaired in people who have had right hemisphere, but not left hemisphere, strokes.[8] Tests of pragmatic communication in autism show impairment relative to controls similar to that demonstrated in people who have had right hemisphere strokes.[9]

Functional effect of lesions in childhood

Case studies suggest that right hemisphere lesions in childhood result in key functions, such as social processing, being transferred to the left hemisphere.[10] This may be so effective that agenesis of the right hemisphere may remain undetected.

Structural and functional changes in the ASDs

Although focal lesions of the right hemisphere have been demonstrated in the brains of many people with autism or Asperger syndrome, they are not universal and, when lesions are found on CT or MRI scans, they are no more likely in the right hemisphere than elsewhere.[11, 12] Some older studies have shown a preponderance of left hemisphere lesions in people with autism, possibly because older diagnostic criteria for autism favoured children and adults with narrower, Kanner-type autism who had substantial language as well as social impairment. Right hemisphere lesions in infancy do result in impairments in nonverbal communication,[13] but right hemisphere functions can be switched to the left hemisphere if lesions occur in early childhood,[14] and it cannot therefore be assumed that a focal lesion in the right hemisphere in infancy will have the same effect in later life as a focal lesion occurring after the loss of this plasticity.

In a study of children with intractable epilepsy referred for possible surgery, 4 of the 11 children with Kanner syndrome and 6 out of 8 children with Asperger syndrome had an abnormality in the right hemisphere.[15] Similar results were obtained in a series of children referred to the Maudsley Hospital.[15] Since Kanner syndrome involves both language and nonverbal impairment, but AS involves mainly nonverbal impairment, the preponderance of right side abnormalities in the AS group suggests that the source of the nonverbal impairment in ASD might be linked to right hemisphere damage or dysfunction.

A thinner right hemisphere cortex has been found in ADHD,[16] but this affects the angular and supramarginal gyri, that is, the areas lying between temporal, parietal and occipital lobes that are connected via fibre tracts to the cingulate and to the dorsolateral prefrontal cortex. The authors suggest that their findings represent an abnormality of the whole attention network, in which these structures are involved, rather than localized right hemisphere pathology.

PARIETAL CORTEX

The parietal lobe is behind the frontal lobe, from which it is separated by the central sulcus, and so is in the caudal (rear) half of the cerebral hemispheres. It is above the temporal lobe, and separated from it by the lateral sulcus or Sylvian fissure. Behind it is the much smaller occipital lobe, the boundary between them being marked by another sulcus, the parieto-occipital fissure. There is no guarantee that these sulci are true functional boundaries, although they seem so to the human eye. However, sulci or grooves may be created by bundles of association neurons pulling brain tissue in different directions and this may well mean that at the broadest level the parietal lobe does have a common input and output, and therefore some degree of functional unity. The parietal lobe is the final common pathway for the general senses, such as touch or joint movement, and outputs to striated muscle and muscular control systems in the brain.

Inferior parietal lobule
Normal function
The inferior parietal lobule, at least in monkeys, has neurons that respond to actions rather than behaviours. For example, some might fire when a monkey grasps something to eat, but not when the monkey grasps something to move. Some neurons in this lobule fire equally when an action is taken and when it is perceived. These are known as 'mirror neurons'. It has been argued that when one monkey watches another monkey performing an action and when the observing monkey does the action itself, there is one common feature, the idea of what that action achieves – the intention behind that action. Mirror neurons are therefore sometimes

said to be activated by intentions rather than actions,[17] although the assumptions behind the hypothesis are no longer considered as persuasive as when hypothesis was first put forward.[18] fMRI studies of people undertaking economic games show that the inferior parietal lobule and the superior temporal sulcus also light up when the most difficult determinations of the other player's intentions are taking place.[19]

The evidence for a mirror neuron system in people is still equivocal. Areas of the brain around the inferior parietal lobule are activated when people watch facial expressions or hand gestures: if they are asked to imitate these, then the left hemisphere is active along with the right; if they are just asked to watch, the right hemisphere is active.[20] It is claimed that one component of the electroencephalogram, the mu rhythm, is attributable to the coordinated firing of sensorimotor neurons that include mirror neurons and that suppression of the mu rhythm is an indication that these neurons are not in their resting state but responding to 'intentions'. Desynchronization of the mu rhythm, it is suggested, can therefore be used as a marker of mirror neuron activation.[21]

Some circumstantial support for this is that mu suppression is greatest when women (assumed to be the more empathic sex) watch hand gestures, that it is correlated with the personal distress subscale of an empathy questionnaire, the Interpersonal Reactivity Index, and that it is negatively correlated with the tendency to classify or 'systemize' [sic], thought to be a male propensity.[21]

The inferior parietal lobule, along with the frontal operculum and the superior temporal sulcus, are the most likely candidates to be the mirror neuron system in people (if there is such a system). These areas are activated when looking at faces, and more activated when looking at emotional, rather than neutral, faces.[22] It has been suggested the frontal operculum is more activated in imitating facial expression and the inferior parietal lobule in imitating social gestures.[23] The inferior parietal lobule shares in the activation of the adjacent superior temporal sulcus to gaze direction and to the intentions of the person gazing in adults,[24] and in children.[25]

Inferior parietal lobule has been considered to be one element in a network activated when shapes are perceived as animated. Gobbini et al. also include the frontal operculum, the fusiform cortex, and the superior temporal sulcus, particularly its posterior part, in this intention-attributing network and distinguish it from the network activated during false belief stories, which includes both the anterior and the posterior cingulate cortex, and the temporoparietal junction.[26] The participation of the inferior parietal lobule in attributing intentions may account for its activation during 'gloating'.[27]

Decety and Lamm, after reviewing over 70 studies, conclude that the temporoparietal junction has a more specific role in false belief tasks, being particularly active when agency is being considered.[28]

Structural and functional changes in the ASDs

In a three-way comparison between young people with ASD (ASD and ADHD), young people with ADHD only, and matched neurotypicals, both of the ASD groups showed reductions in grey matter in the left medial temporal lobe, and an increase in the inferior parietal lobule, but only the ASD group had increased grey matter at the right temporoparietal junction (right supramarginal gyrus).[29] This led the authors to suggest that the autistic syndrome of impairments in social communication and interaction that were shown by the young people with ASD and ADHD, but not the comparison group of young people with ADHD, were associated with this right supramarginal gyrus abnormality.

In another study of young people with ADHD there was reduced activation of the inferior parietal lobule when they were required to rotate a shape in their minds, however the index group performed as well.[30]

A defect in mirror neurons has been proposed to be the fundamental disorder in ASD,[31] but the evidence for this is not strong.[32]

TEMPORAL CORTEX

Anatomy

The temporal cortices are partly separated from the remainder of the hemispheres by a deep vertical cleft, the Sylvian fissure. Each hemisphere has three prominent gyri on its surface. They, the superior, middle and inferior gyri, are arranged in parallel and almost horizontally. The inferior gyri wrap round the bottom of the temporal lobe on to its medial surface where they abut one of the structures considered in Chapter 2, the fusiform gyrus. The medial surface of the temporal lobe is also closely connected to other structures considered in Chapter 2, such as the amygdala, the cingulate and the cortex. Adjacent structures, including the insula and its overlying opercula and the medial prefrontal cortex, are also relevant to ASD and will also be considered in detail in Chapter 2. Several of these structures are palaeocortex. Their grey matter is agranular and not composed from six layers as is the grey matter of all of the neocortical structures considered in this chapter, but of four.

The superior gyrus of the dominant temporal lobe is often included with the gyrus (the pars orbicularis or Brodmann's area 44), and areas of orbitofrontal and parietal cortex, in the operculum. This structure also includes the posterior part of the left inferior frontal gyrus (Broca's area) rostrally (Brodmann areas 44 and 45). Broca's area is essential for speech production. Wernicke's area (Brodmann area 22) is in the posterior part of the left superior temporal gyrus and is at the caudal end of the operculum and adjacent to both the parietal and the occipital lobes. Its position is likely to reflect the close links that there are between shape perception and recognition of written words, the auditory association cortex which lies anterior to it, and input from the mouth, lip and tongue movements that accompany speaking, reading and listening.

Wernicke's area is required for semantic processing and therefore for speech comprehension, and the operculum as a whole is often thought of as the speech system of the brain. The inner part of Wernicke's area, the planum temporale, is larger in the dominant hemisphere than in the non-dominant hemisphere and this size differential is apparent from the thirty-first week of gestation indicating that it precedes the use of the language that it ultimately comes to support.

Normal function

The temporal cortex is mainly involved with memory, its storage, and its use in interpreting incoming input. The inferior temporal gyrus seems to be specialized for visual input, and the superior temporal gyrus for auditory input. The left temporal cortex is dedicated to symbolic recognition, particularly the recognition of words. The right temporal cortex is concerned with other patterns. As well as recognized words or patterns, the temporal lobes probably play a part in assimilating them into 'concepts'. It is in the right temporal lobe that adjustments are made for size, orientation and other accidentals enabling shapes to be recognized and, correspondingly, the left temporal lobe links words with their associations activating what psychologists call 'schemata'.

The superior temporal gyrus (Brodmann area 22) functions as an associative auditory cortex and is therefore particularly concerned with the patterns in sound: in the non-dominant hemisphere this includes reactions to music, and in the dominant hemisphere to vocal communication. Wernicke's area is located posteriorly in the left superior temporal gyrus, adjacent to both the parietal and the occipital lobes. Its position may be important in the synthesis of visual input from the written word, sensory input from mouthing words, and from the auditory association cortex which lies anterior to it, both structures that have often been implicated in the ASDs.

The anterior part of the superior temporal gyrus plays a part in emotional discrimination. There is some overlap between the temporal gyri and the superior temporal sulcus, and ablation of the gyri bilaterally in monkeys destroys previous learnt gaze discrimination.[33]

The superior temporal sulcus (the grey matter at the base of the sulcus) is especially concerned with following a directional cue. It is active when another's gaze direction is being determined and, in primates, in following the direction of another person's gaze with the eyes or looking in the direction of a pointing finger.[34] Gaze following involves prioritizing looking at the eyes of a conspecific (or in the case of primates an individual in a related species, since chimpanzees follow the gaze of humans, and vice versa) and then turning the head, the eyes, or the focus of attention, or all three, to the object at which the other's eyes appear to be looking. Gaze following develops between the ages of 3 and 18 months in normally developing infant humans, but it is much later (probably age 5) that infants can infer from what they see when they follow another person's gaze to the knowledge that this is what the other person is seeing too, and therefore what the other person might be thinking about.[35]

The superior temporal sulcus is also activated in seeing another's facial expression (see inferior parietal lobule above) and is also activated, although in a slightly different part, when gaze is returned rather than averted.[36]

The inferior frontal gyrus on the right has overlapping functions with superior temporal cortex on the right and with the inferior parietal lobule. Although these structures are not so anatomically differentiated as they are in the dominant hemisphere, where they constitute the operculum or speech centre, they are sometimes also referred to as constituting an operculum in the right hemisphere and it is feasible to consider that these structures also make up a centre in the non-dominant hemisphere, but subserving social gaze rather than language.

The temporal lobes can be also functionally divided into anterior, middle and posterior regions. The superior temporal gyrus anteriorly is specialized in social concepts or schemata. Both the right and the left anterior and superior temporal lobe is activated when subjects judge whether or not social concepts (like honour or bravery) apply to stimuli, but not when they are judging whether or not non-social concepts apply (like nutritious or useful).[37]

The anterior part of the temporal cortex plays a part in emotional discrimination. The middle part of the temporal lobe is thought to be involved in declarative memory,[38] that is memory that can be retrieved using some kind of index, whether that is a thought or 'conscious effort', a sensation like a smell, or an emotion. There may possibly be some lateral specialization in that the left temporal lobe may be particularly concerned with the registration and recall of verbally linked, declarative memories,[39] and the right temporal lobe with emotionally linked memories.[40] The more superior and anterior the temporal lobe, the more its function seems to involve judgement and 'abstract conceptual representations'.[37]

Middle and posterior left temporal areas surrounding Wernicke's area are activated during speech and language processing, and may be particularly concerned with processing of irregular word forms which require the retrieval of explicitly remembered lexical items. The middle temporal lobe is activated in tasks requiring the naming of famous faces,[41] and when names are being associated to faces.[42] Face concepts seem to be handled particularly by the right middle temporal lobe.

The middle part of the temporal lobe includes some of the most ancient areas of the brain involved originally in smell perception. These are the entorhinal and perirhinal cortices, the perihippocampal cortex, the hippocampus and the amygdala. Animals use smell to cue emotional responses through direct signals (pheromones) and more non-specifically by providing information in the form of scent marks. Smell therefore provides information about the attitude that an animal should take to an object, but unlike vision, smell provides much less information about the physical properties of an object. A significant part of the smell brain, the perirhinal cortex, is therefore given over to the problem of inferring object identity from smell, and in combination with visual and other sensory input.[43] The perirhinal cortex is also involved in the incidental recognition of facial identity in a facial perception task.[41]

The posterior temporal lobe is particularly involved in detecting incongruity.[44]

Functional effect of lesions in animals

Bachevalier et al. observed the dyadic social interactions of macaques at three and six months of age.[45] Monkeys with lesions in the medial temporal lobe or the inferior temporal visual area showed impairments in emotional expression and in social behaviour in comparison to unlesioned controls. The authors thought that these were similar to the behaviours shown by children with autism.

Functional effect of lesions in adulthood

Temporal lobectomy in adults results in impairments in matching facial identities and expressions of emotion that are similar to those of frontally lobectomized patients, and are not specific to either the right or the left hemisphere. Many of the errors in the patients with frontal lobectomies and an equal number of those who have lobectomies of the temporal lobe are perseverative: that is, they result in the repetition of a response from a previous test to the new one.[46]

The posterior temporal sulcus is contiguous to the parietal operculum, and overlaps in function with it. A lesion in this area in a reported case was associated with an inability to infer the preferences indicated by gaze direction depicted in a cartoon face (see Chapter 5 for more details about the 'What does Charlie want?' test).[47]

Functional effect of lesions in childhood

Published series of children with temporal lobe foci being considered for surgical treatment of intractable epilepsy have high rates of disruptive behaviour not otherwise specified, ADHD, and autism spectrum disorder.

Structural and functional changes in ADHD and the ASDs

One MRI survey of the brains of children with autism and of a neurotypical control group have demonstrated white matter volume reductions in temporal lobe and cerebellum and grey matter volume reductions in only one area of the brain, the superior temporal lobe,[48, 49] although a more recent study, using an arguably more sensitive method (PET scanning), found widespread grey and white matter abnormalities in many brain areas and not just temporal lobe.[50] Grey matter is also reduced in people with non-specific learning disability, and the DeVito *et al.* findings may have been confounded by the association of learning disability with autism in their participants.[51] Other studies have however shown volume *increases* in temporal lobe,[52] which were confined to middle temporal areas in one study,[53] although not in another.[54]

Another study, of high functioning young people with autism, who had normal PET or SPECT scans, showed a relative hypoperfusion in the left temporal lobe compared to the right temporal lobe.[55] SPECT studies of 5-HT2A receptor binding have shown dysfunction in the superior temporal area in people with Asperger syndrome, and in the cingulate, left parietal lobe and frontal lobe.[56] Another study showed a correlation between the extent of underperfusion of the superior temporal lobe and the number and severity of symptoms of autism.[57]

Pathological examination also supports temporal lobe abnormality in autism with small tightly packed neurons being reported in the entorhinal cortex.[58, 59] Abnormal minicolumns (see Chapter 3) with reduced neuropil have also been reported in frontal and temporal lobes in ASD.[60] On balance there seems support for the view that the superior temporal lobe is specifically impaired in ASD.[61]

Autism and the language areas

In people with autism, frontal and temporal language areas are smaller on the left than the corresponding structures on the right, and are smaller than in normal controls.[62] The pattern of activation of the language centres is also different in high functioning people with autism compared to controls during a sentence comprehension task.[63]

Face processing and the fusiform gyrus

It is well attested that face processing recruits more brain areas outside the fusiform gyrus in people with autism than in neurotypicals.[64] Functional MRI studies of face processing demonstrate a reduced activation of fusiform gyrus, amygdala and, for dynamic faces, in superior temporal sulcus in people with autism compared to neurotypical controls.[65]

ADHD

Generalized grey and white matter reductions have been reported in the brains of young people with ADHD,[66, 67] with white matter being more reduced in never medicated participants than medicated ones; the only particular region that is disproportionately affected is the cerebellum.[68] One comparison of people with ADHD and AS demonstrated little difference in the pattern of grey matter reduction. However, the participants with AS in this study had as many symptoms of ADHD as the ADHD only participants. There was, however, an increase in grey matter at the right temporoparietal junction in the AS group,[69] which the authors took to be an indication of abnormality in the AS group.

Temporoparietal junction and parietal operculum

Accumulating evidence from cognitive neuroscience indicates that the right inferior parietal cortex, at the junction with the posterior temporal cortex, plays a critical role in various aspects of social cognition such as theory of mind and empathy. With a quantitative meta-analysis of 70 functional neuroimaging studies, the authors demonstrate that this area is also engaged in lower level (bottom-up) computational processes associated with the sense of agency and reorienting attention to salient stimuli. It is argued that this domain-general computational mechanism is crucial for higher level social cognitive processing.[70]

FRONTAL CORTEX

Anatomy

The frontal lobes in human beings begin about halfway along the top surface of the brain and extend to the front (rostrum) and back down the underside of the brain, between the temporal lobes on each side, but only as far back as the central sulcus. This amounts to almost half of the cerebral cortex. The frontal lobes are one of the areas of the brain that are most developed in apes compared to other primates, and in humans compared to other apes. The frontal lobes are slightly larger in children with an ASD compared to neurotypical children, and there is a proportionate reduction in many caudal cerebral areas and in cerebellar vermis (see Chapter 2) with abnormal patterns of connectivity being the most likely cause of these volumetric changes.[71] The frontal lobes tend to be slightly smaller than those of neurotypical children in people with ADHD with particular reductions in dorsolateral prefrontal cortex and supplementary motor cortex.[72]

The brain adheres to Beer's Law in that its ontogeny recapitulates its phylogeny.[73] The more rostral the frontal lobe area is, the more it is developed in human beings and the longer it takes to mature. So the prefrontal cortex is the most recent area of the brain, pylogenetically, and the dorsolateral area is more recent than the ventromedial area.[74] Orbitofrontal cortex (area 10) is not completely myelinated until the end of adolescence at 18 or 19 years, and cell numbers decrease while dendritic branching increases throughout this period of maturation.[75] MECP2, the gene whose expression is abnormal in Rett syndrome, is particularly richly expressed in the prefrontal cortex.[76] Layers I–III, the most recently evolved, outermost, layers are particularly thick in prefrontal cortex, and their pyramidal neuron have more dendrites than other cortical neurons.[74]

Normal function

Caudal areas of the frontal cortex have specialized integrative function, for example the frontal eye fields occupy area 8, just rostral to the supplementary motor cortex, and are responsible for coordinating the eye movements into the intentional action of 'gaze'. The inferior frontal lobe is also involved in gaze control, but is also active during imitation, particularly of facial expression.[23] It is suggested that it contains mirror neurons. The inferior frontal lobe is adjacent to the anterior insula, and in one study, it was activated by unpleasant tastes – as the insula is – and also by looking at photographs of disgusted faces. The degree of activation was correlated with scores on an empathy test (the Interpersonal Reactivity Index).[77] Inferior frontal lobe is also activated during embarrassment,[78] the right inferior frontal lobe is involved in response inhibition,[79] and the left inferior frontal gyrus activates when there is conflict between emotional valence of words and emotional prosody.

Embarrassment is a self-conscious emotion, and was in this case stimulated by extracting unflattering stills from video recordings and asking participants to rate how photogenic such stills of themselves or of others looked. The area that showed the greatest differential activation of self over other ratings was the right precentral gyrus, and the authors concluded that this area made an important contribution to self-recognition in this study.[79] This differentiation then fed forward into the inferior frontal lobe where it was combined with emotional appraisal in response to the experimental task of making an embarrassing self-assessment. This is an example of the hierarchical way that the more recently developed layers of prefrontal cortex may take processing from lower layers, and process it further by combining it with other information streams.

PREFRONTAL CORTEX
Anatomy

Neuroimaging has demonstrated that the frontal lobes consist of functionally distinct, although overlapping, areas, with the most rostral areas in the prefrontal cortex having the richest connections with the remainder of the brain.

Cytoarchitectonic differences (differences in the orientation of the neurons within the layers of the neocortex) can be used to distinguish areas that correspond approximately to functionally distinct areas. The mapping of 52 areas developed by Brodmann is the most widely used.[80] Brodmann's map of prefrontal brain areas is shown in Figures 1.1 (lateral view) and 1.2 (medial view of separated hemisphere) with the functional areas and the numbers of the Brodmann areas both shown.

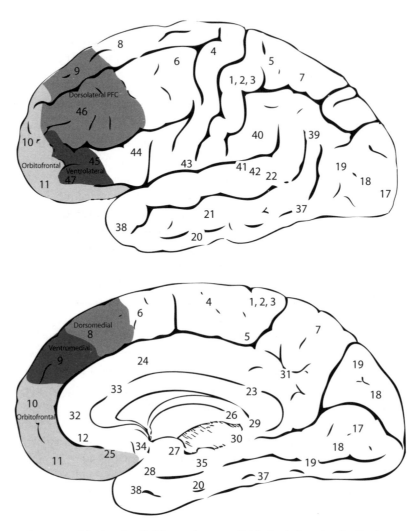

Figures 1.1 and 1.2 Lateral (top) and medial (bottom) aspects of right hemisphere showing Brodmann areas with the areas of prefrontal cortex shaded in

Normal function

The prefrontal cortex (PFC) is often thought of as having executive or control functions over the remainder of the brain, often by inhibiting or suppressing a repeated action. Damage to some prefrontal areas may have surprisingly little effect on the performance of everyday tasks but can cause substantial social impairment through what carers may call a change of personality or, even more loosely, may summarize in the comment that, 'he's become a different person'.

If Freud had located the super-ego anywhere, he would likely have located it in the frontal lobes. Their function is often to suppress a tendency of the brain to act automatically in response to an environmental affordance ('utilization behaviour') or by continuing with a previous sequence of actions ('perseveration') that are no longer appropriate. One commonly used test of frontal lobe function, the Towers of Hanoi test, requires that an expert player apparently make their situation worse before getting better. In this test, a player has to arrange disks of varying circumference into piles according to the diameter of each disk. The disks are threaded on to three, five or any number of poles, depending on the complexity of the task. The only allowable move is to take the topmost disk from one pole and thread it onto another. The rule 'only place a smaller disk on a larger one' will, if repeatedly applied, reach the finish. Children, and people with a frontal lobe lesion, cannot suppress this rule but adults who can do so solve the problem more quickly.

The Towers of Hanoi task may test another, more subtle, function of the frontal lobe which is to inhibit behaviour which some particular aspect of the environment evokes or, to use Gibson's term, 'affords'.[81] At its most basic, this may mean inhibiting primitive reflexes like the grasp reflex, in which touching the palm of the hand provokes a grasp. At the next level, it means inhibiting more complex automatic behaviour associated with an object. Lhermitte described this as 'utilization behaviour': an example would be seeing one's glasses and picking them up and putting them on.[82] One would only do this if one were not normally wearing glasses, but people with frontal lobes may continue to put on glasses so that they are wearing three or four pairs if glasses continue to be presented to them. Problems similar to utilisation behaviour may be a substantial problem in people with ADHD or atypical Asperger syndrome, as in the example below.

Case example

> A young man was visiting his father and his stepmother, who he thought had alienated his father's affections. He had not wanted to go, and had been drinking heavily. After he arrived, he was made welcome but he did not want to sit down, and so stood with his back leaning against the draining board (his father lived in a bedsit). As his hand was feeling behind his back to check that there was nothing there that he might dislodge, it felt a knife which he picked up and put down several times, all behind his back and outside his vision. He picked it up one more time, and then lunged at his stepmother, whom he had no thought of harming until that moment. He stabbed her so forcefully with the knife that she died on the spot.

Another way of considering utilization behaviour is that it is not planful. To solve the Towers of Hanoi task, it may be necessary to imagine the completed task and then consider the penultimate step, the antepenultimate step, and so on, reasoning back to the current situation. Being about to formulate a plan by manipulating a model or image of the final goal may be another aspect of frontal lobe functioning involving as it does inner speech and working memory (for a more detailed consideration of these, see Chapter 7).

The right prefrontal cortex may have a particular role in suppressing risky behaviour.[83] Lesions in the left medial frontal lobe may cause echolalia and hyperlexia, both symptoms of ASD.[84, 85]

There is considerable evidence for differences in the PFC of neurotypicals and people with ASD. Using levels of N-acetylaspartate (NAA), creatine and phosphocreatine (Cr + PCr) and choline (Cho) as indicators of neuronal density and mitochondrial metabolism, phosphate metabolism and membrane turnover, Murphy *et al.* concluded that 'subjects with AS have abnormalities in neuronal integrity of the prefrontal lobe [but not the parietal lobe], which is related to severity of clinical symptoms'.[86] However, this and other studies have not taken account of the possible secondary effects on the PFC of primary impairments elsewhere. Nor have they allowed for the possible confounding effects of ADHD. It is now apparent that at least 70 per cent of people with ASD also meet ADHD diagnostic criteria. So findings that were thought to be specific to ASD may turn out to be associated with ADHD and not specific to ASD.

ASDs and related conditions

A review of ten published cases of mixed PFC pathology beginning in childhood led Eslinger *et al.* to suggest that there were three distinct developmental trajectories resulting from dorsolateral, medial and orbitofrontal lesions.[87] Dorsolateral lesions resulted in visuospatial (they had data only on right-sided lesions) and attentional impairment with little other effects; medial and ventral lesions and white matter disconnection led to a loss of initiative and motivation 'as well as inattention and emotional dependency' and orbitofrontal lesions led to 'intractable deficits in self-regulation, emotion, and executive functions'.[87]

Neuropsychological and imaging studies have shown that attention deficit hyperactivity disorder is associated with alterations in prefrontal cortex, particularly dorsolateral PFC, and its connections to striatum and cerebellum. Research in animals, in combination with observations of patients with cortical lesions, has shown that the PFC is critical for the regulation of behaviour, attention and affect using representational knowledge. The PFC is important for sustaining attention over a delay, inhibiting distraction, and dividing attention, while more posterior cortical areas are essential for perception and the allocation of attentional resources. The PFC in the right hemisphere is especially important for behavioural inhibition. Lesions to the PFC produce a profile of distractibility, forgetfulness, impulsivity, poor planning and locomotor hyperactivity. The PFC is very sensitive to its neurochemical environment, and optimal levels of norepinephrine and dopamine are needed for proper PFC control of behaviour and attention. Electrophysiologic studies in animals suggest that norepinephrine enhances 'signals' through postsynaptic alpha2A-adrenoceptors in PFC, while dopamine decreases 'noise' through modest levels of D1-receptor stimulation. Blockade of alpha2-receptors in the monkey PFC recreates the symptoms of ADHD, resulting in impaired working memory, increased impulsivity and locomotor hyperactivity. Genetic alterations in catecholamine pathways may contribute to dysregulation of PFC circuits in this disorder. Stimulant medications may have some of their therapeutic effects by increasing endogenous stimulation of alpha2A-adrenoceptors and dopamine D1-receptors in the PFC, optimizing PFC regulation of behaviour and attention.[88]

In a review in 2003, Wood and Grafman divide the prefrontal cortex into two areas: a ventromedial and a dorsolateral.[74] They suggest that the former has particular links with emotional processing and the amygdala, with memory and the hippocampus, and with higher order sensory processing and the temporal visual association areas. The ventromedial PFC can be further subdivided into the orbitofrontal PFC (Brodmann areas 10 and 11), dorsomedial PFC (area 8) and the ventromedial PFC proper (area 9). The ventromedial area abuts the inferior frontal lobe, with the operculum containing the speech centre on the left, and an important nonverbal communication node on the right. A small part of the orbitofrontal PFC wraps around the frontal pole of the brain, and is visible on the surface. The dorsolateral area can be subdivided in the dorsolateral area proper (areas 9 and 46) and the ventrolateral (area 47). These areas abut the frontal eye fields. Other adjacent areas to dorsolateral PFC are area 6, which is thought on the basis of animal models to contain mirror neurons responding to goal directed movements and to neurons controlling switches of gaze in response to non-social environmental stimuli. The ventromedial PFC lies between the orbitofrontal cortex and the dorsomedial PFC and has, like them, a common boundary with the cingulate. The orbitofrontal cortex is adjacent to the paracingulate, a continuation forwards of the cingulate gyrus on its inferior surface, and of the insula on its anterior surface. It also has particularly strong network connections to the amygdala and the hippocampus.

DORSOMEDIAL PFC

Anatomy

The dorsomedial PFC abuts, and may form a functional unit with, adjacent dorsal anterior cingulate (Brodmann area 32).

Normal function

The dorsomedial PFC is one of the areas of the brain, along with medial parietal cortex, that shows more activity when participants in fMRI studies are not engaged in tasks and are supposedly resting. They are sometimes said to be active in the 'default state' of the brain.[89] One possible explanation for this is that these areas are active in going over something that has happened previously. Phan et al., for example, showed participants arousing or aversive pictures, and then asked them to think about them or to try to switch off their feelings.[90] Increased negative affect was associated with amygdala activation, as expected, and successful reduction of negative affect and of amygdala activity was associated with dorsomedial PFC activity.

Dorsomedial PFC is involved in using gaze direction as a means of obtaining social information, linking shift in gaze direction to shifts in intentional perspective.[91] There is dorsomedial PFC activation when watching a film of two people interacting,[92] and considering questions like 'Are you sociable?', 'Is Caroline [a close friend] sociable?', 'Does Caroline consider that you are sociable?'[93] The authors of the last study consider that dorsomedial PFC is involved in self-referential processing and perspective taking.[94] Mundy reaches a similar conclusion after reviewing relevant studies,[94] considering that dorsomedial PFC and anterior cingulate are necessary for social orienting, and as such provide a foundation for the development of joint attention in infants, later on for the development of intersubjectivity and of a theory of mind.

Dorsomedial PFC and anterior cingulate are activated by social oddball tasks, which is consistent with Mundy's hypothesis about its action.[95] Reductions in grey matter in the medial PFC in people with schizophrenia correlate with reduced performance on emotional attribution to others.[96]

Functional effect of lesions in animals

Stimulation of the area in monkeys which is thought to be equivalent to the dorsomedial PFC resulted in large gaze shifts sometimes associated with movements of the eye and the whole head.[97] These findings must be interpreted with caution as the homologues of monkey and human brain are not fully known, and the authors may have stimulated what in humans is the frontal eye field.

Functional changes in the ASDs

Dorsal anterior cingulate, and possibly dorsomedial PFC, is more active in people with ASD than in neurotypicals in an oddball task whether social or non-social stimuli are used, although the activation is greater for social stimuli. This overactivation correlated in this study with social impairment and, the authors suggest, may indicate a deficit in social orientation.[95]

VENTROMEDIAL PFC

Normal function

The ventromedial PFC modulates peripheral responses to emotionally arousing stimuli, with the left ventromedial mainly influencing the vagus, and the parasympathetic system, and the right ventromedial PFC linking to amygdala and the sympathetic nervous system. Hänsel and von Känel suggest that it plays a particular role in appraising threat levels, and therefore in maintaining or extinguishing conditioned responses.[98]

The ventromedial cortex is activated in a range of socially relevant tasks, such as joint attention,[99] processing social rather than mechanical stimuli, imitating facial expressions of anger and fear,[100] judging self-relevance,[101] and making emotional discriminations.[102] Processing social cues involves mutual activation with the right amygdala, presumably providing emotional input, and with temporoparietal junction, where low-level processing relevant to agency takes place (and see also section on inferior parietal lobule above).[103]

Only one of these studies has reported ventromedial PFC activation in a joint emotion task,[104] and it is possible that there was some overlap in this study between ventral and dorsomedial areas.

Two studies have shown increased activation in ventromedial PFC when subjects are asked to link pictures of emotional faces and words: one showed an increase in activity when the word was the right label for the emotion compared to when it was the wrong one,[105] and one showed increased activation when there was a discrepancy between emotional expression and the story being told by an actor adopting that expression.[106]

Activation during high level emotional processing is the most replicated finding in fMRI studies of ventromedial PFC, particularly when the emotion involves comparison with others. Schadenfreude, for example, is associated with ventromedial PFC activation.[107] This in turn has been linked to two general functions of the ventromedial PFC: gut feelings and empathy.

Ventromedial PFC is particularly connected to the amygdala and other areas of the brain linked to autonomic function. Damasio has suggested that emotional arousal is linked to situations and stored in the ventromedial PFC as a 'somatic marker' that can be re-evoked by comparable situations in the future, even if no contemporaneous arousal is taking place.[108]

Damasio *et al.* have proposed that risky situations evoke gut feelings of alarm, based on these somatic markers or memories, and these inhibit the likelihood of risky actions being undertaken.[109] The idea has proved a highly persuasive one, although the evidence for it has been disputed.[110] An alternative formulation is that ventromedial PFC coordinates a network subserving 'affective evaluation' and that it is responsible for 'emotionally flavouring' memories (see page 63).[111]

Ventromedial PFC is not only linked to other areas of the brain, but also linked to other brains. When two people playing charades are simultaneously scanned, the activity of their two ventromedial PFCs is synchronized.[112] This may be linked to its role in empathizing, but another possibility is that ventromedial PFC stores the emotional component of other people's responses from which an internal simulation of the other person can be constructed.[113]

Functional effect of lesions in adulthood

Lesion studies confirm the involvement of ventromedial PFC in the anticipation of social and emotional response, and consequent modulation of behaviour. The single most influential of these is the case study of the railwayman, Phineas Gage, whose frontal lobe was transected by a crowbar. Pathological reconstructions show that this passed through his dorsolateral PFC and then his ventromedial PFC before exiting his skull.[114]

In one study, survivors of strokes selectively affecting the ventromedial PFC were unimpaired when making purely rational – utilitarian – moral judgements, but were impaired when empathy also had to be taken into account, for example being more willing to sacrifice one person for the sake of others than controls with intact prefrontal cortices (the authors of this paper summarize the data by suggesting that this represents a shift from deontological ethics to utilitarian ones).[115]

A single case study of a 57-year-old man (MW) with frontal variant frontotemporal dementia (fv-FTD) with particular involvement of the ventromedial PFC is relevant to the ASDs in that although standard tests of frontal executive function were largely unremarkable, MW had impaired theory of mind.[116] He challenged others by his aggressive and disruptive behaviour, and also tended to wander off, and checked obsessively, for example rocking his car before driving away to make sure that the suspension was intact.

People who have suffered closed head injury seem particularly at risk of orbitofrontal and ventromedial PFC damage, and studies show that they are less likely to respond autonomically to negative emotional expressions, or to be able to identify them. Probably as a consequence, they have particular impairments in social adaptation coupled with a lack of insight. Anosmia may be a useful clinical sign of this kind of damage.[117] In another case series of people who had suffered brain injuries, the most profound empathy impairments were shown in people with ventromedial PFC involvement.[118]

Structural and functional changes in the ASDs

A review of fMIR studies of tasks requiring social cognition in people with an ASD concluded that there was a pattern of reduced activation in ventromedial prefrontal cortex, temporo-parietal junction, amygdala and periamygdaloid cortex, along with aberrantly increased activation in primary sensory cortices.[119]

Irony, a particularly challenging social concept for people with an ASD, requires the ability to contrast real and expressed communicative intent. It therefore relies on knowing what people might really be thinking. In one study, 18 boys aged 7–17 with an ASD were impaired in their ability to attend to nonverbal cues, such as facial expression and tone of voice, in an irony task when compared to neurotypical controls. This impaired performance was associated with reduced activation of medial PFC and superior temporal gyrus and the reduction in activation was correlated with symptom scores.[120]

Reduced right ventromedial volume has been reported in boys who are impulsive in comparison with boys who are not.[121]

Functional changes in other disorders

Ventromedial PFC is also implicated in post-traumatic stress disorder (PTSD), a condition in which highly emotionally charged memories are repeatedly triggered by everyday happenings that, in some way, put the person in mind of the event or events that they are remembering in this way. The event(s) are typically unpleasant and often frightening (hence 'traumatic') and their re-evocation is associated with an unpleasantly high degree of autonomic arousal (hence 'stress'). PTSD is considered a disorder because there is a failure to process the original trauma, possibly because the person concerned cuts off, or dissociates from, the emotions associated with the trauma.

Animals that are repeatedly frightened show reduced benzodiazepine binding in their frontal lobes, probably as a result of a reduction in GABAergic interneurons which act as inhibitors to the pathway from frontal lobe to amygdala which acts to down-regulate amygdalar responsiveness. Vietnam veterans with combat-related PTSD also have reduced benzodiazepine binding relative to controls on single photon emission computed tomography (SPECT) imaging following administration of a benzodiazepine ligand (iomazenil) doped with a radio-isotope. The reduction is particularly marked in the ventromedial PFC.[122] In a meta-analysis of fMRI and PET scan studies carried out in anxiety-related disorders, there was greater activation of amygdala and insula whenever anxiety was increased relative to control subjects, and activation of ventromedial PFC in participants with PFC, but only in them, not in the participants with other anxiety disorders.

These studies suggest that the ventromedial PFC is involved not only in linking, storing and recalling emotions and situations, but also in somehow working through emotional experience so that it can be safely put away. Some evidence is provided by a functional connectivity analysis, with reference to the right anterior cingulate (Brodmann area 92), of fMRI scans conducted while subjects were visualizing traumatic memories. There were several differences in the connectivity maps of participants with PTSD and those without, but one of them was that subjects without PTSD had greater correlations between activation intensity in the reference area 9 and activation in left ventromedial PFC than did the subjects with PTSD.[123]

Other studies mentioned previously suggested that ventromedial PFC is involved in empathizing. It is not clear how these two might be linked, unless coming to terms with a trauma involves being able to empathize with the person (or the agency) responsible. This is supported by studies of PTSD following road traffic accidents, and the place of forgiveness in predicting good outcome.[124] Giving people stories to read about transgressors, and the instruction to forgive them, results in activation of various brain areas, including the left ventromedial PFC.[125]

One possible reason that people may not be willing to forgive is that there is a moral repugnance against unfair dealing, and sometimes it seems that forgiving someone is to reward their unfairness. Transcranial magnetic stimulation (TMS) over the right temple temporally inactivates the right dorsolateral PFC which lies below this part of the skull, and predisposes gamblers to accept risky bids that they would normally reject.[126] It also reduces the vicarious perception of pain, and perhaps also feelings of pain.[127] Courses of TMS to this area in people with PTSD assuage their PTSD symptoms, perhaps because they are not inhibited by a fairness requirement in letting go, and forgiving.[128]

How this links with structural evidence of impaired ventromedial PFC in people with an ASD is not clear. Perhaps it is linked to the lack of empathy often shown by people with an ASD (considered in Chapter 3), perhaps with the lack of emotional processing that is often a clinical problem in people with Asperger syndrome (see Chapter 15), or perhaps it is linked with the high degree of stress that many people with an ASD experience from a very early age, i.e. that it is caused by stress rather than a cause of ASD-related stress.

VENTROLATERAL PFC

Normal function

Little is known about the ventrolateral PFC: its neighbouring area, the dorsolateral PFC has been studied much more extensively. Human neuroimaging confirms ablation data in animals that the ventrolateral PFC is a kind of pre-processor for visual working memory and dorsolateral PFC activation.[129] The ventrolateral PFC receives its input directly from sensory cortex and outputting to the dorsolateral PFC. For example, simply rehearsing a phone number activates ventrolateral PFC function while saying the same number backwards activates dorsolateral PFC function.

This account almost certainly underestimates the important of ventrolateral PFC. Ramnani and Owen reviewed studies of PFC function.[130] They concluded that the ventrolateral PFC may be involved in:

> the selection, comparison and judgement of stimuli held in short-term and long-term memory, holding non-spatial information 'online', task switching, reversal learning, stimulus selection, the specification of retrieval cues and the 'elaboration encoding' of information into episodic memory.[130a]

Raposo *et al.* provide evidence that left ventrolateral PFC generates the semantic tags by which memories can be retrieved,[131] an important aspect of working memory. Right ventrolateral PFC has been linked to spatial working memory in another study.[132]

Ventrolateral PFC are more strongly influenced by reward than dorsolateral PFC.[133] Beating a computer at the rock-paper-scissors game results in ventrolateral PFC activation, along with activation of adjacent areas and activation of the globus pallidum.[134] The ventrolateral PFC may also play a part in the evaluation of risk, and therefore in decision-making in conditions of risk. In one study, adolescents showed less ventrolateral PFC activation (and also activation of their dorsal anterior cingulate) than adults when engaged in a monetary decision-making task[135] and in another monetary reward on a working memory task increased ventrolateral PFC activation.[136]

Deception motivated by the avoidance of unpleasantness, a cognitively and affectively complex activity, may be associated by a peak of activation in the ventrolateral PFC (although others locate this in dorsolateral PFC).[137]

Single neuron recording studies in monkeys in the brain area corresponding to ventrolateral PFC have found neurons that respond to faces and to primate vocalizations, suggesting the the ventrolateral PFC synthesizes visual and vocal communications.[138]

Structural and functional changes in the ASDs
ASD
In normally developing human adolescents, there is ventrolateral PFC activation when viewing pictures of faces with gaze directly forwards compared to faces with gaze averted: there is no activation in matched participants with ASD.[139]

ADHD
Sowell *et al.* found hypotrophy not only in ventrolateral PFC but also in anterior temporal lobes.[140] In another PET study, people with ADHD who were given a decision-making task in which short-term rewards had to be weighed against long-term losses showed activation of both ventrolateral and dorsolateral PFC, but this was not associated with as much activation of insula, hippocampus and anterior cingulate as it was in controls, leading the authors to suggest that the PFC was cut off from information from emotional and memory processes in people with ADHD in comparison with controls.[141] More recent studies have confirmed reduced network connectivity involving these areas.[142]

DORSOLATERAL PFC
Anatomy
The dorsolateral PFC has links to the dorsal action control system of parietal lobe, superior temporal lobe and cerebellum, but only in sighted individuals.[143]

Normal function
Ramnani and Owen conclude in a review that dorsolateral cortex:

> has been implicated in many cognitive functions, including holding spatial information 'on-line', monitoring and manipulation within working memory, response selection, the implementation of strategies to facilitate memory, the organization of material before encoding and the verification and evaluation of representations that have been retrieved from long-term memory.[130a]

Dorsolateral PFC is implicated in self-aware decision-making, for example in making choices[144] (the ventromedial PFC is involved in affective evaluations) and in self-regulation.[145] The dorsolateral PFC, especially the principal sulcus, is required for the memory or application of rules, but the orbitofrontal cortex is used for selecting which rules are important, in conjunction with ACC (anterior cingulate cortex).[146]

Working memory

A common factor in all of these operations is the ability to hold data in a form that can enable it to be operated on in real time, much as computers call data into RAM or volatile memory so that every byte can be accessed directly by the central processor. The human equivalent of this is termed 'working memory' (see also Chapter 7). Dorsolateral PFC is the brain area that is most often associated with working memory, either because working memory is instantiated there or because it is the brain's principle access into working memory.[147] The former is suggested by a transcranial magnetic stimulation study in which the dorsolateral PFC was temporarily disrupted by a double TMS pulse just after participants had read sentences from the reading span test, a test of verbal working memory. The TMS pulse impaired performance on the test suggesting that it had disrupted the committal of the sentences to working memory and that this occurred in the dorsolateral PFC.[148]

Procedural learning

Working memory is required for serial tasks, and therefore for procedural learning. The dorsofrontal cortex and cerebellar vermis seem to act cooperatively in procedural learning, with procedures being established first in the dorsolateral cortex and then becoming more durably established as procedural memories in the cerebellum. A single case study suggests that these relationships are more complex than this simple statement suggests. Right dorsolateral PFC and left cerebellar vermis subserve procedures learnt with the left hand, left dorsolateral PFC and right cerebellar vermis subserve procedures learnt with the right hand, and the two pairs acting as antagonists.[149]

Deliberate self-control

Dorsolateral PFC is also activated during many deliberate mental actions, including the inhibition of prepotent responses (in other words, deliberately not doing something that has become habitual, and either doing nothing or doing something new).[150]

Failed inhibition of prepotent responses accounts for 'perseveration', a well-known clinical sign of frontal lobe dysfunction.

Inhibiting prepotent learnt responses is only one facet of dorsolateral PFC activation when deliberate control is being exerted over an action tendency, presumably one linked with activation in some other brain area. Dorsolateral PFC is activated, along with cingulate cortex, when involuntary emotional responses are being controlled,[151] although dominant dorsolateral PFC is activated only during amygdala down-regulation: up-regulation seems to require wider PFC involvement.[152]

The emotional selectivity of dorsolateral PFC control may reflect a bias towards greater activation associated with positive emotions. There is also a bias in dorsolateral PFC, as there is in the cerebral cortex as a whole, for the dominant area to be more active in association with positive emotions, and the non-dominant area more active in association with negative emotions. So the left dorsolateral PFC is most biased towards positive emotions, and the right ventromedial PFC towards negative ones.[153] It is likely that dorsolateral PFC is active during voluntary or social smiling.

Conscious deception is also associated with dorsolateral PFC activation (although there are some reservations about the involvement of the ventrolateral PFC).[154] This, too, can be thought of as being a control task if, as seems the case, to tell the truth is the prepotent response.

Another, but much more complex, prepotent response is for game players to go against their own interests in the interests of fairness. Games, such as the ultimatum game, have been devised to demonstrate this. Players of the ultimatum game typically refuse offers that are in their interests if they have observed the player making the offer acting unfairly previously.[155] But players who receive repeated transcranial magnetic stimulation of their right dorsolateral PFC, which temporarily disrupts its function, continue to recognize when another player is being unfair, but are willing to accept unfair offers, when they would have resisted them previously.[156]

Dorsolateral PFC is also implicated in the control of distraction by visual stimuli.[157]

Dorsolateral PFC has a special links with language, and in conversations activation in dorsolateral PFC is temporally coupled with activations in speech production areas of the speaker – although, perhaps surprisingly with activation of the listener's dorsolateral PFC anticipating the activation of the speaker's speech production area.[158]

Greater tonic activation of the right dorsolateral PFC is associated with trait behavioural inhibition.[159]

Mental effort, volition or willpower

However, dorsolateral PFC may also be activated simply by effortful deliberation not involving conflict, for example recalling something from memory,[160] deliberate imitation,[161] deployment of attention, meditation[162] and reading facial expressions.[163] A further link between willed action and the dorsolateral PFC is that, at least in one small study, activation is associated with organizing facts into a narrative.[164] Dorsolateral PFC is also activated when participants who have been made to feel ill by being given a typhoid inoculation are asked to perform cognitively demanding tasks. Participants who have not received the vaccine do not activate their dorsolateral PFC, but those who have (whose insula is also strongly active, in parallel to their feelings of malaise) do.[165] Finally, dorsolateral PFC is activated during a taste test.[166]

Stress reduces the capacity for mental effort, and in a comparison of women shown extremely violent film clips and women shown less violent ones, the stressed women performed a working memory task requiring mental effort less efficiently and also showed less dorsolateral PFC activation than the women shown nonviolent film clips.[167]

Perspective taking

Perspective taking is another self-control task, in that seeing someone else's point of view often means suppressing one's own. Not surprisingly, perspective-taking, but not other aspects of empathy, is linked to dorsolateral PFC function, as estimated in one study by glutamate concentration.[168]

Functional effect of lesions in adulthood

Dorsolateral PFC is affected early on in the course of frontotemporal dementia, although generally no more than other PFC areas. Some neurologists do distinguish predominantly dorsolateral involvement, where the symptoms are perseveration, automatic behaviour, and a lack of account of goal or environmental constraints; and predominantly orbitotemporal involvement, where the main symptoms are apathy, loss of personal hygiene, stereotypia, disinhibition, loss of concern for consequences of acts, lack of attention to social rules or to danger, and lack of empathy.[169] Lesions of dorsolateral PFC may reduce social perception, although possibly by impairing deliberate strategies for reading nonverbal cues. Dorsolateral PFC lesions are particularly associated with a lack of awareness of impaired social perception.[170] A single case study of a 15-year-old boy who had extensive right dorsolateral PFC damage following rupture and repair of an arteriovenous malformation at the age of 7 years suggests a particular link of dorsolateral PFC and ADHD. This boy recovered from the acute effects of the stroke, but then his attention gradually deteriorated, and he became more impulsive, developing what amounted to an acquired ADHD.[171]

Chronic ketamine misuse leads to dopaminergic up-regulation, which affects dorsolateral PFC and dorsolateral striatum particularly. It is associated with a reduction in working memory, impaired executive function and increased dissociability.[172]

Patients with schizophrenia, who perform poorly on the interpretation of eye expressions, also have a reduced volume of prefrontal grey matter, but it is only the reduction in grey matter in their dorsolateral PFC that is correlated with scores on a test of eye expression, suggesting that dorsolateral PFC may be particularly involved in this.[173]

Structural and functional changes in the ASDs and related conditions
ASD

The dorsolateral PFC may be particularly affected in people with an ASD combined with a language disorder (typical autism, or low functioning autism) with one study showing reduced grey matter in the dorsolateral PFC only in this subgroup. Abnormal P3a responses and reduced amplitude P3b waves were also found in this group, but not in the high functioning group, possibly suggesting more general neurological differences.[174] However, even in more able people with ASD there is reduced activation in dorsolateral PFC during a spatial memory task than in controls.[175] No abnormality was found in visually guided saccades in this study, but in a more recent one, *increased* activation of the dorsolateral PFC was found in a visually guided saccade task, which the authors take to be the consequence of the PFC compensating for a lower level impairment in eye movement control.[176]

That there may be an abnormality in dorsolateral PFC in ASD is suggested by several studies of molecular biology. One showed that a particular gene (SLC25A12, found on the long arm of chromosome 2 in the region 2q31-q33) is over-expressed in autism. SLC25A12 begins to be expressed at mid-term, when the brain starts to develop its surface architecture of gyri and sulci. The gene is more highly expressed in developing mice in lateral prefrontal and ventral temporal cortex from which dorsolateral prefrontal cortex, the inferior frontal operculum, and the fusiform gyrus develop. SLC25A12 concentrations influence the mobility of dendrite mitochondria and dendrite length in mouse embryonic cortical neurons. They also modify dendrite length and the mobility of dendritic mitochondria. So an increase in activity of this gene would have an impact on several of the structures considered to be relevant to autism.[177] Grey matter (i.e. cells) are increased in both medial and dorsolateral PFC but along with reduced white matter, suggesting lower connectivity,[178] which could be the consequence of altered intra-uterine development. It seems unlikely that any one gene is solely involved in autism, however, but there is one reported case of a narrowly defined deletion on chromosome 2, just outside the region considered above, this time at 2q34 on the paternal chromosome, leading to autism.[179] One of the genes on 2q34 is MAP2, a gene also involved in Rett syndrome. This gene was under-expressed in the dorsolateral PFC, although this was a study of only two people. Ill-defined cortical layers and reduced dendrite numbers in dorsolateral PFC were also found in this study.[180]

Performance on a test of inferring emotions from the eye regions (the Reading the Mind in the Eyes test) has been shown to be best in neurotypical women and worst in parents of both sexes of children with ASD. Neurotypical men are intermediate in scores. The performance on this test was correlated with activation of the left dorsolateral PFC and left medial temporal gyrus as demonstrated on fMRI conducted while the test was being done.[163] An independent study of judging emotions from the eyes using dense-array event-related potential recording also found activation in medial temporal lobe and prefrontal cortex, although this time on the right side.[181]

There is one test that is performed better by people with an ASD than by neurotypicals: the embedded figures test. In this test, subjects are given a complex line drawing whose outline depicts a recognizable object, but which contains internal lines, seemingly at random, but one of which depicts a smaller, 'embedded' object. Lee et al. scanned children between the ages of 7 and 12 with ASD and a group of age and IQ matched controls while they were performing the embedded figures test.[182] Neurotypical children had active left dorsolateral PFC, premotor frontal cortex and extensive temporal activation while doing the test. The children with an ASD had much more limited activity, in one area of premotor cortex, with no activation of either temporal lobe or PFC.[182] One interpretation of this finding is that the neurotypical children were seeing something that the children with an ASD were not, and this was actually distracting them from the task. One tempting conclusion is that they were seeing the wood (the larger figure) and not the trees (the smaller areas demarcated by the internal lines, which included the embedded figure). A comparable task, in which the wrong answer interferes with finding the right answer, is the matchstick task, in which matchsticks can either figure as units which can be handled digitally or as the boundaries of shapes, which are to be handled as analogues. Adults with lesions in their dorsolateral PFC are more successful than neurotypical controls on the matchstick task, presumably because the digital use of the matches as normally apprehended by a process involving dorsolateral cortex does not occur and therefore does not inhibit performance of the required analogue task.[183]

ADHD

Several studies suggest that ADHD is associated with abnormalities in dorsolateral PFC, although most stress that this is only one component of an abnormality in an attentional network. Sowell *et al.* found hypotrophy not only in ventrolateral PFC but also in anterior temporal lobes.[140] A SPECT study showed hypoperfusion in temporal cortex, although not always in the same areas, in children with ADHD, along with hypoperfusion in the thalamus and the caudate (in a minority) and in PFC.[184] In another SPECT study, the hypoperfusion was particularly apparent in left dorsolateral PFC and the extent of the hypoperfusion relative to the perfusion of the right dorsolateral PFC was correlated with symptom scores and neuropsychological test results.[185] In a further study, this time using the N-acetylaspartate marker of neuronal health, reduced N-acetylaspartate concentrations were found in left dorsolateral PFC but only for people with hyperactivity and not for those people who met criteria for attention deficit disorder (ADD) and not ADHD.[186] This result was partly confirmed in another study, using the particular sensitive method of proton magnetic resonance spectroscopy (H-MRS), in which girls with ADHD had lower N-acetylaspartate concentrations in dorsolateral PFC. In this study, right but not left dorsolateral PFC volumes were reduced in all participants with ADHD, irrespective of gender, and there was a correlation between a test of ADHD (Continuous Performance Test), volume and the creatine-phosphocreatine peak signal on H-MRS.[187]

The attentional impairment is not necessarily linked to control, that is inhibition of prepotent responses. In one study, 6–10-year-olds with ADHD relied *more* on dorsolateral PFC to make no go responses after a series of go responses.[188]

Cortical thinning of dorsolateral PFC has been described in ADHD, but in association with thinning in other brain areas thought to be nodes in an attentional network. These include inferior parietal lobule and anterior cingulate. These are areas also implicated in ASD, and it is possible that the participants in this study had elements of ASD, too.[189] Event-related potential studies in people with ADHD suggest quite widespread abnormalities.[190] Berger *et al.* conclude, in their review of self-regulation as it applies to ADHD, that 'Overall, the neuroimaging and genetic evidence support the involvement in ADHD of all the brain areas included in the executive attention network, that is, the basal ganglia, PFC and the cerebellum.'[191]

ORBITOFRONTAL PFC

Anatomy

The orbitofrontal cortex is larger, in proportion to the total brain volume, in humans than it is in any other vertebrate, including the other primates. Some of its neurons, spindle or von Economo neurons, are of a type only found here and in adjacent structures (insula, anterior cingulate, dorsolateral PFC) and are more vulnerable than other neurons to the particular kind of degeneration seen in frontotemporal dementia.[192]

Phylogenetically, the orbitofrontal PFC is an outgrowth from the olfactory cortex, each lobe of which has a thin projection into the ipsilateral nostril where it interfaces with olfactory epithelium.[193] This core is composed of piriform cortex around which is layered, most thickly posteriorly transitional cortex, and the whole is covered by 6 layer isocortex, the most recent cortex phylogenetically. Each of these different cortices follows a different developmental trajectory.[194]

The orbitofrontal PFC not only is connected to all of the other PFC areas, but also shares a border with the insula, across which there are many connections, and with the paracingulate cortex, an extension of the cingulate. It has two main connections with the amygdala, one direct and one indirect, via mediodorsal thalamus.[195] There are also connections between orbitofrontal PFC and amygdala, and orbitofrontal PFC and cingulate cortex. Through these projections the orbitofrontal PFC may influence the cholinergic and monoaminergic innervation of widespread cortical and subcortical regions of the forebrain. The orbitofrontal PFC also has links with the lateral and posterior hypothalamus, and may therefore modulate autonomic arousal. Prefrontal fibres even extend to the spinal cord.

The orbitofrontal cortex is larger than normal in older male children with an ASD, but this is mainly accounted for by a hypertrophy in non-neural tissue.[196]

Normal function

The large size of the orbitofrontal PFC, its development in humans relative to other animals and the effects of lesions have suggested to many neuroscientists that the orbitofrontal PFC has a kind of chief executive role. It has been suggested that it prioritizes resources at the highest level by switching attention, for example from environmental stimuli to internal representations,[197] or by guiding attention to objects of importance, for example fearful faces,[198] and it is invoked by error messages from 'lower' centres. Ramnani and Owen term the orbitofrontal PFC 'Summa inter pares'; and suggest that there is 'a specific role for this region in integrating the outcomes of two or more separate cognitive operations in the pursuit of a higher behavioural goal'.[130b] They also suggest that the orbitofrontal PFC achieves this by combining emotional and cognitive information, so as to provide motivation. Adolphs arrives at a similar synthesis, although adding communication to the kinds of function that the orbitofrontal PFC integrates.[199]

The orbitofrontal PFC connections are widespread but many of them are with areas like other PFC areas or anterior cingulate that are themselves integrative. It is implicated in the amygdalar up- and down-regulation, thus influencing overall responsiveness to threat.[200] So these suggestions about the functions of the orbitofrontal PFC are consistent with its anatomy, and also fit in with contemporary conceptions of leadership, and of what Isaiah Berlin called the 'hare' version of change and motivation. They are also consistent with the hierarchical thinking that is implicit in much discussion about the central nervous system, for example in terming some areas, 'higher' centres and some 'lower'.[201]

These claims for the orbitofrontal PFC are somewhat reminiscent of post-Cartesian claims for the homunculus: that within the brain there is a command centre that performs the brain's most mysterious operations, but in a compass much smaller than the brain itself.

The orbitofrontal PFC may be important in emotional attachment. Primiparous mothers shown pictures of their own babies had greater bilateral activation of orbitofrontal PFC and of visual cortex than when shown pictures of other people's babies. The activation of orbitofrontal PFC, but not visual cortex, was in proportion to the positive feelings that the mothers had in viewing their babies.[202] However, familiarity may have been a confounding factor, because greater familiarity with a face increases orbitofrontal PFC activation.[203]

The orbitofrontal PFC is the main processing area for taste and olfaction,[204] and is activated during judgements about the familiarity of smells.[205] In macaques, the firing of single neurons in the orbitofrontal cortex is modulated when they are given food or food is withheld.[206] Lateral orbitofrontal PFC is activated by eating unpleasant foods, and medial orbitofrontal PFC by eating pleasant foods; its response is altered by hunger and satiety.[207]

An alternative hypothesis is that the orbitofrontal PFC acts as a 'cache' for a history of recent experiences which can be accessed when there is no direct access to social experience.[208] There is some supportive evidence for this, in that orbitofrontal PFC, amygdala, and hippocampus are all activated in an emotion recognition task in which there is a delay in the presentation of the matching stimulus, although this delay was only ten seconds in this particular experiment.[209] Further evidence is that orbitofrontal cortex is activated in a game playing situation in which the person being scanned bases their moves on their opponent's previous reciprocity, or lack of it.[210]

If this 'cache' theory is correct, the orbitofrontal PFC activation observed during direct gaze,[211] which is augmented by interpersonal valence,[212] may not be a consequence of the orbitofrontal PFC having control over the response to the direct gaze, but that its cache is being upgraded. The orbitofrontal PFC's access to taste and smell experiences may provide a means of accessing these prior experiences, by means of the emotional 'flavour' that they leave behind.[213] Activation of the orbitofrontal PFC may indicate interrogation of this cache,[214] especially when the experimental task requires the participant to have a theory about how other people might react,[215] or when there has been much recent visual attention – that is gazing at – another person.

Emery in an influential review concluded that there is a gaze-following system hardwired into the brain that is subserved by a circuit linking superior temporal sulcus, amygdala and orbitofrontal PFC.[216] The implication is that orbitofrontal PFC executes gaze following, but an alternative explanation is that gaze following activates the 'caching' function of orbitofrontal PFC, which then stores this new perspective.

Functional effect of lesions in adulthood

Frontotemporal degeneration selectively targets von Economo neurons, and therefore orbitofrontal PFC, although there may be different clinical courses, with different areas that are primarily affected. Indirect evidence about the orbitofrontal PFC may therefore be provided by the deficits seen in people in the early stages of frontotemporal dementia. Early effects include impaired social interaction,[217] with impaired self-management and self-presentation,[218] and reduced empathy.[219] In a study of people who had parts of their PFC removed surgically, some patients with lesions to their orbitofrontal cortex (and also some patients who had lesions to ventromedial PFC) had deficits in interpreting emotional expressions, particularly vocal ones,[220] and these impairments were more likely in people with bilateral lesions, some of whom also had a change in their emotional responses ('affective lability') and in social interaction. However, people who had lesions in the anterior cingulate cortex showed the same types of impairment, but with even greater severity.

Structural and functional changes in the ASDs

Two people with neuroaxonal dystrophy involving orbitofrontal PFC are reported to have behavioural symptoms characteristic of autism but the dystrophy was widespread in other areas of the brain, too.[221] In another study, people with Asperger syndrome did not show as much activation in orbitofrontal PFC in response to fearful faces as did controls.[222] Increased grey matter density has been reported in orbitofrontal PFC in people with an ASD, affecting the particular area that is activated in a joint attention task.[223] However, another study found decreased grey matter in right lateral orbitofrontal PFC and that, although there was evidence of social deficits in the children with autism who were being studied, this correlated with white matter, but not grey matter.[224] In another study, people with Asperger syndrome did not show as much activation in orbitofrontal PFC in response to fearful faces as did controls.[225]

One particular test of executive function, but not others, has been associated with different activation in orbitofrontal PFC in people with an ASD as compared to controls.[226] The performance on orbitofrontal-amygdala tasks in people with autism is disproportionately impaired,[227] compared to neurotypicals, in those with *higher* verbal IQs.

Chapter 2

THE CEREBELLUM AND DEEP STRUCTURES IN THE FOREBRAIN

Although the ASDs affect what are often called the higher functions of the brain, and these functions are associated with the phylogenetically most recent areas of the human brain, research suggests that older areas of the brain may change their function as newer areas develop,[1] and so become drawn into higher functions, too. The cerebellum is a case in point. The lateral lobes of the cerebellum are larger, as a ratio of total brain volume, in humans compared to other primates.[2] Their development has been linked to the development of the grasping hand and of speech, rather than to social organization. However, the contribution of the cerebellum and of other brain areas involved in motor control, like the caudate, may extend from the control of movement to the control of thinking, and therefore of cognition.[3]

This would not be such a big step if thinking does, as Vygotsky suggests,[4] involve inner speech and sub-vocal movements of the speech apparatus since a thought could be interrupted by stopping the imperceptible movements of the lip and tongue that accompany speech. Thinking may also involve imagery, and may be accompanied by supportive movement, including looking in a particular direction,[5] or even, when imagining something involving steering a passage between two risks, extruding the tip of the tongue between the lips. An image may be interruptible by changing the direction of gaze or retracting the tongue. This may be the basis for the therapeutically disrupting effects of eye-movement desensitization therapy on recurrent, anxiety-ridden images or 'flashbacks'.

Counter-intuitively, the cerebellum's absence, like the absence of the corpus callosum or one of the cerebral hemispheres, may have almost no functional effect so long as it had never developed. The impact of its loss, once developed, is substantial.[6]

CEREBELLUM

Anatomy

The cerebellum receives input from sensory fibres in the spinal cord via the inferior olive in the medulla, and from the neocortex via the pons. Each olivary neuron, or 'climbing fibre', invests and has multiple synapses with the dendrites of one of the large and characteristic Purkinje cells in the cerebellar cortex. The second major afferents are pontine neurons, or 'mossy fibres', which synapse with granular cells whose branching axons form a kind of cable of parallel fibres running through the dendritic trees of the Purkinje cells. Each parallel fibre synapses with hundreds of thousands of different Purkinje cells. The output from Purkinje cells is the resultant of the intense activation that it receives from one spinal afferent, counteracted by a haze of interactions with afferents from cerebral cortex via the pons. The output goes to one of the three nuclei deep in the cerebellum, where it inhibits their tonic activity.

It is currently thought that each of the nuclei is specialized in their function to some degree: the dentate nucleus projects to motor cortex, and may be involved with the control and coordination of purposeful movements like reaching or grasping; the interpositus nucleus sends signals to motor cortex and spinal cord, and may smooth out movement to avoid tremor or marked changes of muscle tone; and the fastigial nucleus receives signals from vestibular systems and is probably linked to balance, truncal posture and eye movements, particularly the maintenance of a stable visual axis despite movements of the head and body.

Although most of the cerebellar projections via the thalamus are to frontal or parietal cortex, some from the dentate nucleus are to prefrontal cortex terminating in glutaminergic endings there. This circuit also involves basal ganglia, notably caudate nucleus and putamen. These may be particularly relevant to the autism spectrum disorders.

Normal function

The cerebellum plays an important role in coordinating movement, and the cerebellar vermis is the area involved in the control of eye movement.[7, 8, 9] As well as smoothing out movement, the cerebellum plays an important role in timing movement, and therefore in learning and reproducing sequences.

The cerebellum is also involved in the control of attention,[10, 11] and in working memory, the mental equivalent of the computer's random access memory. Switching thoughts or imagery by suppressing competing thoughts or images in favour of a single, desired thought or image, cognitive control, is central to the deployment of attention,[12] and its involvement in attention may be an extension of this. Similarly, the contribution of the cerebellum to memory may also be an extension of motor control if 'keeping something in mind' involves sub-vocalizing.

Having a working model of how someone else thinks and feels – having a theory of mind – is important in social interactions. One hypothesis about theory of mind is that we know about other people by mimicking their actions, a hypothesis that has received a strong impetus from the finding of mirror neurons, discussed in the later section of this chapter on the supplementary motor cortex.

In one study of this simulation theory of mind hypothesis, subjects in an MRI scanner watched videos of themselves lifting a box, and videos of other people lifting a box. The subjects were asked whether the other people anticipated that the box was heavy or light. When the subjects watched either video, there was increased blood flow, as shown by fMRI activation, in their supplementary motor cortex, where mirror neurons are located. When the subjects thought that the other person lifting the box had falsely anticipated its weight, there was also activation in areas associated in other studies with theory of mind tasks (superior temporal sulcus, orbitofrontal, paracingulate cortex) and also cerebellum.[13] This network, including the cerebellum, amounts to an action observation network.[14]

The cerebellum has a much wider role than even the previous findings suggest, since it is also involved in affective responses. There is increased cerebellar activity during separation from loved ones,[15] and activation during the experience of a painful stimulus and also when watching a loved one experiencing a painful stimulus.[16] In the latter situation, it appears not to be sympathetic pain, but distress at the pain experienced by the other person which activates the anterior insula bilaterally (often activated during conditions of disgust), the anterior cingulate cortex, shown to be active in many empathy studies, brainstem and cerebellum.

Schmahmann has suggested that the lateral lobes of the cerebellum are involved in modulating thought, language and planning, perhaps through their involvement, which could be accounted for by their involvement in the intention movements that might accompany these activities.[3] He has also suggested that the cerebellar vermis contributes to a cognitive affective system by performing the same role in affective circuits as in motor circuits, by smoothing out the signal or 'modulating behaviour automatically around a homeostatic baseline'.[3a]

Courchesne proposed that the:

> cerebellum is not a motor device, a sensory device, or a cognitive device, but rather a general purpose device (e.g. sensory, motor, autonomic, memory, attention, affect, language) which may be needed in upcoming moments…for instance, previous work from our laboratory has shown that cerebellar pathology does not eliminate the ability to shift attention, but instead makes attention shifts slow and inaccurate.[17]

Functional effect of lesions in animals

Colchicine-induced lesions in the dentate nucleus of infant Sprague-Dawley rats impair sequential learning,[18] but have no effect on social interaction. Midline cerebellar lesions of ten-day-old rats of a different laboratory strain (DN/HAN) produced a different picture: more motor activity, more perseveration, and less response to environmental cues, including threat and social cues.[19]

The development of cerebellar Purkinje neurons in rats is impaired both by social and movement restriction during neonatal development,[20, 21] which may be partly reversible if the restriction is later lifted.

Neonatal Borna disease virus infection in rats has been suggested as an animal model of autism,[22] as has hypothyroidism. Bornavirus targets pyramidal cells in the cerebral cortex, Purkinje cells in the cerebellum, and granule cells in the dentate nucleus.[23] Infected rats spend less time in social interaction and more time passively following a partner. They are also less likely than controls to show aggression to an intruder.[22] Hypothyroidism in neonatal rats results in not only a reduction of granule cells in the cerebellum, but also changes in the cerebral cortex similar to those in Rett syndrome in humans.[24]

Hypothyroidism may regulate genes that are important in embryogenesis. One such gene, although not one that is regulated by thyroid hormone, is the Engrailed-2 gene. This is a homeobox gene governing midline development in the mid and hind brain but not expressed in the forebrain. It governs the development of the cerbellar vermis. Mice lacking the gene have abnormalities of the vermis, and also of the placement of the amygdala. They show behaviours that are suggestive of autism.[25] Engrailed has been considered by some workers a candidate gene for autism.[26]

Mice who are exposed to viral infection during the mid-trimester of pregnancy have offspring with cerebellar abnormality that 'is strikingly similar to that observed in autism', possibly because the infection triggers an auto-immune attack on embryonic Purkinje cells.[27]

Functional effect of lesions in adulthood

Excessive repeated alcohol use is the commonest cause of cerebellar dysfunction in adulthood, but alcohol also affects other areas of brain including pons and cerebral cortex. However, loss of volume in the anterior vermis but not in cerebral cortex is correlated with deterioration in balance confirming the well-known clinical association of cerebellar lesions and ataxia. Perhaps, more surprisingly, reduction in volume of the vermis (and associated thalamus) predicted scores on the Wisconsin card sort test, but these scores were not correlated with loss of prefrontal cortex volume. Visuospatial test performance was correlated with a loss of cerebellar white matter, but not the loss of volume of parietal cortex.[28]

Ischaemic damage to the cerebellum reduces the intensity of pleasurable emotions subsequently. The response to frightening stimuli is subjectivity unchanged, but H_2O^{15} PET scans show reduced activity in response to frightening stimuli in the cerebellum, and also in right ventral lateral and left dorsolateral prefrontal cortex, amygdala, thalamus and retrosplenial cingulate gyrus; they show increased activity in the ventral medial prefrontal, anterior cingulate, pulvinar and insular cortex. The authors of this study suggest that this reflects the activation of an alternative circuit for responding to frightening stimuli.[29]

Functional effect of lesions in childhood

The outcome of cerebellar dysgenesis varies according to the areas and layers involved.[30] Dysgenesis of the cerebellar vermis occurs rarely, and usually in association with more or less widespread dysgenesis of other midline structures in the brain, including the corpus callosum and the pons, and often renal and hepatic abnormalities. A study of one of these named syndromes (Joubert syndrome) suggests that the vermian dysgenesis may account for episodic hyperpnoea and apnoea (Cheyne-Stokes breathing), hypotonia, developmental delay, truncal ataxia and ophthalmological abnormalities resulting from nystagmus and disruption of pursuit movements, saccades and other rapid eye movements. In a study of 15 people with Joubert syndrome, 11 were given a battery of neuropsychological tests and found to be impaired both in attentional and social skills out of proportion to their language abilities,[31] although comparisons of these children with children with autism indicate that there are differences.[32]

Congenital non-progressive cerebellar ataxia is associated with learning difficulties, but typically involves greater impairment of nonverbal than verbal scores on intelligence testing.[33] Spinocerebellar ataxia, a hereditary ataxia caused by the synthesis of a key protein containing a supernumerary glutamine group, affects language, memory and executive function, that is those functions which are associated with network between cerebellar cortex and dorsolateral PFC. In a study of 15 patients with spinocerebellar ataxia, theory of mind was also impaired, but visuospatial processing, calculation, and the social and emotional functions associated with ASD were unaffected.[34]

Older children who have received partial cerebellar resections because of tumours are left with disabilities that are predictable from the functions of the cerebellar areas that they have lost. Resection of the right (dominant) cerebellum impairs auditory sequential memory and language processing, and resection of the left lateral lobe impairs spatial and visual sequential memory. Resection of vermian tumours (usually medulloblastomas) typically leads either to an autistic-like syndrome or to dysarthria preventing intelligible speech. Speech partially recovers, but remains 'telegraphic' with normal content, but a persistent loss of voice prosody similar to that of people with left-sided (non-dominant) frontal lobe lesions. Children whose vermis has been resected also show a persistent lack of syntactic comprehension and a lack of spontaneous speech. All of these abnormalities may be linked to the impaired auditory sequential memory, which is a further consequence of the surgery.

Children with resection of only the lower part of the vermis also develop monotonous speech, but not dysarthria. Some of them go through a period of mutism, although their language understanding seems unaffected. In the short term, these children also avoid reciprocal gaze, withdraw from social and physical contact with others, and do not use language for communication. Many of these symptoms are similar to those of a frontal lobe syndrome. One child who was particularly severely affected demonstrated confabulation, thought disorder, and increased verbal fluency. Her scores on an autism checklist were in the autistic range. Although many of these symptoms settled down, she showed persistent lack of empathy. All of the children with vermian resection had persistent slowness in task performance.[35]

Infarction of the lateral cerebellar lobes leads to an impairment of procedural learning.[36] Complete cerebellar resection leads to a posterior fossa syndrome that includes the symptoms of vermal ablation plus a loss of procedural memory. Interestingly, there is some recovery, blood flow is altered in the areas of cerebral cortex that are associated with the cerebellum and this, along with the persistence of cognitive and affective impairments, suggests that normal function requires the existence of the whole frontocerebellar network and not just intact frontal lobes.[37]

Foetal alcohol syndrome results from the exposure of the foetus to high blood levels of alcohol as a result of the mother's drinking. The consequence may be characteristic facial anomalies, microcephaly or generalized cortical atrophy, callosal agenesis, or cerebellar hypoplasia.[38] Widespread brain damage is the most common consequence.[39] Attentional and dysexecutive impairment are characteristic of the syndrome, and are similar to those seen in ADHD.[40] The cerebellum is typically involved, especially the dentate nucleus, as are parietal and frontal cortices, frontal white matter, corpus callosum and thalamus. Magnetic resonance scanning suggests that glia are more involved than neurons.[41]

Structural and functional changes in the ASDs and related conditions
ASD

It was a considerable surprise that Courchesne *et al.* found that there was an association between abnormalities of the cerebellar vermis and autism,[42] as the cerebellum had not seemed to be a participant in what was then being called the social brain. However, subsequent research has confirmed that dysplasia of the cerebellar vermis is a common, and replicable, finding in young people with autism spectrum disorder. The relationship is so established that it is claimed a clinical diagnosis of autism at the age of five years can be correctly classified on the basis of MRI brain measures in 95.3 per cent of children with an ASD and 92.3 per cent of children without.[43]

Cerebral and cerebellar white matter, and anterior vermis volume were all greater in this study in the ASD group than in the controls. Not all studies have reported an increased volume in the posterior vermis: some have indeed reported hypoplasia. One possible explanation has been provided by an MRI study that included children with autism in the absence of other disorder, children with a fragile X chromosome, and children with trisomy 21. The children who had only autism had smaller volumes in lobule VI and VII of their (posterior) vermis, but the children with fragile X disease who also had autism had hyperplasia of these lobules.[44]

The relative size of these structures reverses with age in comparison to controls, and their larger size in very young children with autism gives way to a significant reduction in volume relative to controls in older children and adults.[45] Cerebellar volume in girls with autism is at least as reduced, compared to controls, as that of boys.[46] Volume loss may reflect, at least in part, reduced cell size of the Purkinje cells.[47]

There is a significant association between tuberous sclerosis (TS) and the occurrence of autism. In one study of TS, the total number of brain tubers correlated with intellectual impairment but not with autistic symptoms, unless only the number of cerebellar tubers is counted, when an increased number is associated with greater autistic symptoms.[48, 49] In an independent replication of this study using magnetic resonance imaging and positron emission tomography, the TS group with cerebellar lesions had more autistic symptoms, and those with tubers in the right cerebellum (the dominant cerebellum) were more socially isolated and had greater communicative and developmental disturbance.[50]

The particular significance of the right cerebellum is also suggested by a study of a monozygotic twin pair in which the lower functioning twin had a smaller right cerebellum (and a larger left frontal lobe volume to total brain volume).[51]

It is unclear what the significance of cerebellar hyperplasia is in younger children, but the evidence suggests that it is associated with a loss of function relative to neurotypical children just as the relatively lower volume indicates reduced function in older children. Evidence for this comes from clinical studies showing cerebellar type gait disturbance in children with newly diagnosed autism (average age 5 years 10 months) compared to neurotypical children.[52] Further evidence is that cerebellar Purkinje cells and their inhibitory interneurons have reduced levels of the glutamate decarboxylase enzyme (in both its isoforms GAD65 and the commoner, GAD67) required to turn glutamate into a second, and distinct transmitter, gamma-aminobutyric acid (GABA). This is likely to lead to disruptions in the activity of the dentate nucleus in people with an ASD compared to neurotypicals.[53, 54, 55]

Proton magnetic resonance studies of the cerebellum in autism are just beginning, but one showed a trend towards reduced N-acetylaspartate and a reduction of glutamate and its precursor glutamine (the latter consistent with the studies by Yip *et al.*, mentioned in the paragraph above) which the authors take as an indication of reduced activity of neuronal bodies and therefore of grey matter.[56] Intriguingly, given the apparent association between autism and bipolar disorder (see Chapter 10), proton magnetic resonance scans of children with mood disorders plus at least one parent with bipolar disorder also show reduced N-acetylaspartate levels in cerebellar vermis, and these are linked to abnormally high myo-inositol levels in frontal cortex.[57]

Diffusion tensor magnetic resonance tractography has been used in studies of cerebellum. One such study, of people with AS and controls, suggested abnormalities in intracerebellar networks of white matter, and in the white matter of the superior cerebellar peduncle which carries efferents to the pons and thence to the parietal cortex. The authors of this study conclude that this is evidence of 'cerbellar disconnection' in ASD.[58]

There is a suggestion that mutations in the long arm of chromosome 7 are associated with ASD. One study appears to have localized this effect to one of the homeobox transcription factors Engrailed-2 (EN2) that is involved in neural organization in the segment giving rise to the cerebellum. In this large study, haplotypes of EN2 differing by single nucleotide polymorphisms were found to protect against (one haplotype) or increase the risk of (the other haplotype) ASD and the authors suggest that the gene may have this effect via the gene's influence on the development of cerebellum or cerebellar connectivity.[59]

One study has found that 21 per cent of people with an ASD have antibodies to a cerebellar protein with an apparent molecular weight of approximately 52 kDa, but only 2 per cent of the typically developing controls – a highly significant difference – had the same antibody. The antibody appears to target the Golgi cell.[60]

ADHD

MRI scans of the cerebellum in attention deficit hyperactivity disorder have not always been consistent in finding reduced cerebellar volume compared to controls, but a meta-analysis confirms that ADHD is associated with volume reduction,[61] particularly marked in the posterior inferior vermis, in contrast to ASD, where it is the anterior vermis that is implicated.[62]

One study considered in Valera *et al.*'s meta-analysis included non-affected brothers as a second control group.[63] The total intracranial volume of the boys with ADHD was reduced compared to the non-related controls suggesting the involvement of many brain areas, but the volume reduction was restricted to the cerebellum (and especially the right, or dominant, cerebellum in this study) if comparison was made with unaffected brothers. One possible explanation for this is the hypothesis put forward by Halperin and Schulz,[64] that in at least some cases of ADHD, the primary disorder lies in cerebellar dysgenesis, and that other areas of brain are only secondarily affected, as a result of their neuronal linkage with the cerebellum. According to this theory, recovery occurs only when these secondarily affected areas, notably the prefrontal cortex, are able to compensate for the primary cerebellar disorder.

Several studies have found reductions in grey matter, but tensor imaging also shows that white matter is affected, with particular losses in the left cerebellum, in contrast to the study of Durston *et al.* cited above.[65]

The relatively small volume of the vermis is non-progressive but persists irrespective of outcome. Children whose symptoms worsen tend in addition to have relatively smaller lateral cerebellar volumes as they get older, suggesting that this may be linked to having a poor outcome.[66]

Williams syndrome

The cerebellar vermis in Williams syndrome is proportionately larger than controls, and the forebrain proportionately smaller.[67] This is the inverse of the situation in autism spectrum disorder, and has been suggested to be a possible explanation for the symptom profile of Williams syndrome, which is also the inverse of that in ASD in that communication, both linguistic and nonverbal, is disproportionately good in people with Williams syndrome, relative to their impaired reasoning, spatial ability, motor coordination, arithmetical ability and problem solving.

AMYGDALAE

Anatomy

The amygdalae are paired structures that abut the third ventricle. Each amygdala ('almond') is composed of a group of nuclei lying within each temporal lobe, close to the medial surface. The lateral, basal and accessory nuclei lie more deeply within the cortex and receive input from the smell brain, the association areas of other sensory cortices, and from the frontal lobes. The medial and central nuclei output to the hypothalamus (which controls many endocrine hormones); to the brainstem autonomic centres, controlling the vagus nerve and therefore influencing the activity of the heart, the bronchi and the smooth muscle of the gut; and to the sympathetic nervous system, which partly opposes the cholinergic parasympathetic system. The amygdala also influences the output of the adrenal medulla and therefore the levels of circulating epinephrine (adrenaline) and norepinephrine through the sympathetic system.

The central nucleus of the amygdala in rats projects to the periaqueductal grey matter, the freeze system, and to the cerebellum, which mediates fear-induced startle. The lateral nucleus disinhibits the neurons of the central nucleus by GABAergic neurons (which are the site of the sedative action of the benzodiazepines). The high level of dendritic plasticity of the neurons in both nuclear groups enables fear conditioning to take place, and having an intact amygdala is essential for fear conditioning.

Normal function

The right and left amygdalae have different functions, with the left being more responsive to specific emotions and the right to the level of arousal irrespective of emotion,[68] but there is also considerable overlap. A review concludes that the amygdalae are inconsistently, weakly activated by positive stimuli but are consistently, strongly activated by aversive stimuli, irrespective of sensory modality.[69] Their response is stronger when arousal level is already high, when the stimulus is more aversive, and when the stimulus acts as a motivation for action. Amygdalar response rapidly habituates, and occurs to stimuli that are subliminal. There is an independent and parallel process leading to the conscious appraisal of the hedonic tone of a stimulus. Amygdalar activations increase motor readiness, alter autonomic activity, and change the direction of attention and the storage and retrieval of memories. Emotional arousal enhances memorization via activation of the amygdala.[70] Whether a stimulus affects the right or the left amygdala depends on gender, personality and mood. Although deliberate reflection cannot trigger the amygdalar response, it can prolong it,[71] evidence that negative thinking may influence emotional disposition.

The amygdalae were once primarily thought to be a fear and anxiety system. Gray and McNaughton,[72] in this connection, define fear as defensive avoidance and anxiety as defensive approach. Defensive approach includes defensive attack as well as guarded approach. They argue that the amygdala mediate defensive avoidance and defensive attack with the medial hypothalamus organizing fleeing, the periaqueductal grey freezing (panic in humans), and the septo-hippocampal system, defensive approach.[72]

Brothers proposed that the amygdalae, the superior temporal sulcus, and the orbitofrontal cortex form a 'social brain' (see also later section on social intelligence).[73] This idea has proved influential in the study of social disorders, such as the hypothetical disorder 'psychopathy' as well as ASD,[74] and it has led to this small structure being credited with extraordinary, and probably disproportionate, importance.

One possible explanation is that fear conditioning has much more widespread ramifications than is usually considered. For example, the central nucleus of the amygdala is connected to the medial preoptic area, part of the limbic system involved in maternal behaviour. But the amygdala's contribution to maternal care may simply be that nulliparous rat females avoid newborn rat pups through a conditioned aversive response mediated by the amygdala. This conditioning is reversed,[75] by the normal release of the vasoactive peptides oxytocin and vasopressin at birth.[76]

The amygdalae are adjacent to the superior temporal sulcus and have strong interconnections with perisulcal neurons.[77] The superior temporal sulcus is involved in the interpretation of eye direction, and the superior temporal gyrus in making other socially relevant judgements about faces, for example familiarity. Superior temporal sulcus is activated in a task in which subjects are asked to detect when the face cue with which they are presented appears to be looking directly at them, and additional amygdalar activation occurred when there was no such face in one series of trials.[78] In a study of gaze direction co-varied with facial expression, the BOLD signal of the left (an indication of the deoxygenation of haemoglobin and therefore of blood flow and neural activity), but not the right, amygdala, was greater in response to an angry face appearing to gaze directly at the viewer and for a frightened face appearing to look away than for a looking away angry face or a directly looking frightened face. Simply looking at a face produces some amygdalar activation, but this is less if the face is familiar, perhaps, as one study has suggested, because there is less need for a 'guarded attitude'.[79]

The amygdalae respond to any stimulus which is conditioned by fear avoidance, so any threatening stimulus is likely to evoke an amygdalar response.[80] This will include stimuli that are not normally associated with threat, such as faces and other social stimuli, and may be the explanation of the regular activation of the amygdalae in social tasks. Greater amygdalar activation occurs even when threat is low level as, for example, when furniture with sharp, as opposed to rounded, corners is viewed.[81] Threat recognition does not require conscious processing, and the amygdalae will respond to stimuli which are masked from conscious awareness.[82] Amygdalar activation occurs when emotional processing is occurring both implicitly and explicitly, although there is greater activation during explicit processing.[83]

A finding that amygdalar volume is proportional to the size of social networks is consistent with the idea that the amygdala monitors social interaction for threat.[84]

Functional effect of lesions in animals

Lesions of the amygdalae in immature (day 7) rat pups lead to locomotor stereotypies that worsen after puberty. Lesions of the amygdalae in nearly mature rats (day 21) result in many fewer behavioural changes. This strongly suggests that amygdalar abnormality during development may have different consequences to those of lesions acquired in adulthood. Rats bred for amygdalar excitability ('fast kindling') are worse at learning the correct path in a Morris water-maze test, and show attentional deficits analogous to some people with ADHD.[85]

Amygdalar lesions in primates impair social interaction in a fashion that has been thought to be similar to autism although this has been challenged.[86] Ablation of the amygdalae in rhesus monkeys blocks acute, unconditioned fear but not trait-like fear responses, which are associated with increased EEG activation in right frontal lobe.[87] Ibotenic acid ablation of the amygdalae in one study of two-week-old macaques results in alterations in emotional and social behaviour, which are not shown if the amygdalae of adults are ablated. The latter interact normally with conspecifics. The neonates with amygdalar lesions have normal facial expressions, grooming and play behaviour and the authors of this particular study concluded,[88] like Prather et al.,[86] that amygdalectomized macaques were not autistic, but that their symptoms were the consequence of being unable to make appropriate threat assessments in social interactions.

Functional effect of lesions in adulthood

Urbach-Wiethe disease, a rare lipid storage disease most common in the Afrikaans, often has its origins in infancy. It causes lipid deposits in epithelial tissues and bilateral amygdalar damage, leading to epilepsy and rage attacks. Siebert et al. conducted a series of psychological tests in ten adults with Urbach-Wiethe disease in whom there was brain imaging evidence of bilateral amygdalar damage (and also some adjacent damage to the posterior temporal lobe).[89] The participants' ability to recognize photographs of facial expressions was less impaired than previous studies had suggested, and the ability to recognize basic emotions was within age norms. There was a tendency for negative emotions to be ignored in favour of positive emotions when the expressions were of blended emotions. However, emotionally driven memorization was markedly impaired. Participants often did not recognize facial expressions which they had seen previously (particular if they were of smiling faces), and their ability to learn paired associations between smells and figures was also markedly impaired.[89]

Functional effect of lesions in childhood

Dysembryoblastic neuroepithelioma tumours are among the rare conditions that selectively affect the amygdalae in childhood. Adults with amygdalar lesions have been reported to have theory of mind deficits,[90] but in another study, although this was true of adults who had undergone amygdalotomy as a result of seizures attributable to DNET (dysembryoplastic neuroepithilial tumor) – and therefore having amygdalar lesions dating from childhood – adults whose amygdalae were surgically removed because of amygdalar lesions acquired in adulthood did not have theory of mind deficit.[91] This supports Frith and Frith's suggestion that the amygdalae play a role in acquiring a theory of mind, but not in mediating it.[92]

Structure and function in the ASDs
Structural changes in the ASDs

There is no consistent structural abnormality in the amygdalae in unselected groups of people with autism.[93, 94] Amygdalar enlargement has been reported in children with autism spectrum disorder,[95] and high functioning autism,[96] but a reduction has been reported by others.[97] Later studies have replicated the finding of an increased volume, especially on the right, with the volume correlated with communicative impairment.[98] In a second study, the hypertrophy of the amygdalae in children with ASD relative to neurotypicals had been completed by the age of two years, with further proportional increase in size at the age of four years being no more in children with ASD with controls. In this study, amygdalar volume was correlated with joint attention in the four-year-olds with ASD.[99] People with Asperger syndrome have larger left amygdalar volumes than people with autism,[100] but this may be a consequence of the anxiety that is more often associated with Asperger syndrome, as children with generalized anxiety disorders also have larger than normal amygdalae.[101]

Reported cytoarchitectonic abnormalities in autism include smaller and more tightly packed cell bodies than normal in the medial nuclei of the amygdalae.[102]

There is a suggestion in one study of surface area reductions, but not volumetric reductions, in the amygdalae of young people with ADHD but this may be secondary to reduced connectivity with the prefrontal cortex as the authors suggest.[103]

Functional changes in the ASDs

Baron-Cohen *et al.* have demonstrated reduced activation in the left amygdala on a theory of mind task, both in people with autism and people with Asperger syndrome.[104] Proton MRS studies have shown reduced resting N-acetyl-aspartate levels in the right amygdalar/hippocampal,[105] and in the left amygdalar regions,[106] in children and adolescents with autism compared with controls, which may be an indication of reduced activity as N-methyl-D-glutamate (NMDA) is an important amygdala transmitter that is crucial for second-order conditioning.[107]

Amygdalar activation normally occurs when fearful faces are being viewed, with the degree and side (left versus right amygdala) of response reflecting the strength of depicted expression. This graded response was not shown by a group of people with Asperger syndrome in one study,[108] although this may reflect other changes in face processing,[109] evinced in this study in the greater superior temporal sulcus and anterior cingulate activation in the AS group and a reduced activation of their orbitofrontal cortex.

High anxiety proneness is typical of people with autism and it is unclear whether these amygdalar changes are a consequence of this, and therefore a non-specific consequence of having an autism spectrum disorder, or whether they play a primary role.

ADHD

There are small changes in amygdalar volume in people with ADHD, but possibly more substantial changes in the connectivity of prefrontal cortex and the amygdala that, the authors suggest, could be responsible for the increased risk of mood disorder.[103]

CINGULATE

Anatomy

The cingulum (Latin for 'belt') runs in each cerebral hemisphere around the fibrous bundle connecting the two hemispheres, the corpus callosum. Its medial surface abuts grey matter in the cingulate gyrus, the cingulate cortex, and its superior surface abuts grey matter in the cingulate sulcus. These structures cannot be distinguished on scans, and the whole complex is often referred to as the cingulate. The anterior part of the cingulate cortex is part of the palaeocortex, the penultimate area of the cerebral cortex to develop phylogenetically, before the neocortex. The posterior is composed of phylogenetically later isocortex. Palaeocortex does have a six layered structure like the neocortex and because of this, palaeocortex and neocortex are sometimes termed 'isocortex' in contrast to the three layered 'allocortex' of which the hippocampus and insula are examples. But palaeocortical neurons are agranular, unlike those of the isocortex that comprises most of the cerebral cortex as well as the posterior cingulate cortex.

The anterior insula, like the anterior cingulate, contains a high proportion of spindle neurons (or von Economo neurons). These have been found elsewhere in the brain only in the dorsolateral prefrontal cortex, where they are present in fewer numbers,[110] and the orbitofrontal cortex. Spindle neurons have been found only in the great apes, elephants and toothed whales, leading to speculation that they are involved with the 'theory of mind' judgements,[111] which are apparently demonstrable only in these animals, or at least with social communication.[112] It has been suggested that a loss of spindle neurons may be the cause of autism, but a first count of their numbers has not shown them to be reduced compared to controls.[113]

The anterior cingulate receives input from the midline thalamus and related nuclei, the posterior cingulate from the superficial nucleus of the thalamus and from the hippocampus.

The cingulate sulcus contains motor neurons providing input to the motor cortex, and directly to motor neurons in the spinal cord.[114] The posterior cingulate and the precuneus may form a functional unit.

Normal function

Broca included the cingulate gyrus in his 'grand lobe limbique', considering it a part of the emotional brain along with the amygdala, hippocampus, orbitofrontal cortex and other structures. The limbic system, as Maclean reinterpreted it,[115] was supposedly a primitive core of 'old mammalian brain', which constituted an emotional brain inside the 'higher mammalian' cognitive brain. However, there is little evidence that these two traditional categories correspond to how the brain handles processing, or indeed that palaeocortical functions are necessarily more 'ancient' than neocortical ones.[116] Papez described the cingulate as the 'seat of emotional consciousness',[117] and le Doux suggested that there is a link between the involvement of the anterior cingulate in working memory and this involvement in consciousness.[118] Cingular activation is increased by tasks that involve the recognition of the human body.[119]

The anatomy of the anterior and posterior cingulate indicates, as noted above, that they have a different phylogeny, and they also have distinct functions with the posterior cingulate being linked to conscious self-awareness and a part of the default network, and the anterior cingulate, and the insula, linked to reflexive emotional experience.[120] Thinking about duties and obligations increases posterior cingulate cortex activity, and thinking about hopes and aspirations increases the activity of anterior cingulate cortex.[121] A review of 120 fMRI studies of semantic memory led the reviewers to suggest that the anterior cingulate plays a role in self-directed memory retrieval, and the posterior cingulate in preparing episodes for storing semantically.[122]

Anterior cingulate
Mood
Psychotic disorders are associated with cingulate abnormalities, with a particular association between bipolar disorder (more common in people with ASD, and their families) and anterior cingulate abnormality. There is also less activation in anterior cingulate when people with fragile X view photographs of emotional expressions than when neurotypicals do.[123] Fragile X is associated with ASD, and also with an increased risk of depression and anxiety, especially in the minority of women who are affected by the condition.

Rostral anterior cingulate is activated when distracting stimuli are present, and dorsal anterior cingulate along with dorsolateral prefrontal cortex when attention is strengthened so that it can be maintained without being distracted by them.[124] The anterior cingulate is active during cravings when attention focuses on a particular goal or desire.

Emotional flavour
I have argued that most of what we experience has a valence of 'palatability' or emotional flavour that is the result of the simultaneous awareness of the experience and our emotional reaction to it. I suggested in that paper that the anterior cingulate may play a special role in adding emotional flavour.[125] There is some evidence for this in studies of the empathic reactions to pain.[126, 127, 128] The anterior part of the anterior cingulate, along with the posterior cingulate, is more reactive to positive emotional flavours, and to the possibility of gain in decision-making tasks; the middle and posterior part of the anterior cingulate is more active in response to negative emotions and the possibility of losing.[129] The anterior cingulate is also activated during judgements of social status,[130] and trust or distrust.

Posterior cingulate
The posterior cingulate and precuneus are linked with the medial prefrontal cortex and the inferior parietal cortex in a 'default network'[131] (see Chapter 3). The default network, and the posterior cingulate, is active during social reflection – the kind of imagination that is lacking in people with ASD. This kind of imagination involves narrative, and it is therefore notable that posterior cingulate activity is linked to language, and its volume is smaller in children with autistic disorder and language impairment.[132] Thinking about social situations involving highly familiar people, such as family or friends, is associated with posterior cingulate activation,[133] as is forming impressions of someone new.[134]

The posterior cingulate is also active during false belief tasks,[135] during narratives involving an alteration of spatial perspective,[136] and in the Stroop effect, when there is a conflict between the meaning of a word and its presentation, as for example when the word 'red' is shown in the colour green.[137]

Functional effect of lesions in adulthood

As might be expected from the wide range of roles apparently performed by the anterior cingulate cortex, lesions result in a similarly wide range of effects, although all involve emotion in some way. An infarction in the left anterior cingulate cortex of a man with a pre-existing haemangioma has been reported to result in a transient hyperfamiliarity with the faces of others.[138] Surgical cingulotomies are, rarely, performed for obsessive compulsive disorder (OCD), and result in reduced anxiety. In rats, anterior cingulate lesions reduce escape/ avoidance behaviour in response to painful stimuli.[139] This may be because anterior cingulate is, in association with the 'reward centre', the nucleus accumbens, required to evaluate the effort to put into a task in comparison to the likely reward.[140] Posterior cingulate is affected by senile dementia of Alzheimer type early on during the course of the illness, and this may account for the early onset of misidentifications of familiar others.

Structural and functional changes in the ASDs and related conditions

Anterior cingulate dysfunction has been increasingly implicated in ASD and ADHD. In a review of 24 studies, ASD participants given social tasks that they typically perform less well than neurotypicals, for example theory of mind or face-processing tasks, had reduced blood flow, relative to controls, in their perigenual anterior cingulate (and also in their insula). In 15 studies ASD participants given *non*-social tasks that they and people with ADHD often perform less well, for example tests of attention control and working memory, had a reduced flow in dorsal anterior cingulate (and an increased flow in rostral anterior cingulate).[141] Reduced connectivity between the anterior cingulate and the insula was correlated with autistic traits in another study from the same laboratory,[142] although it is possible that this is a secondary consequence of reduced social learning as a result of ASD. The anterior cingulate has a role in switching attention in response to emotional stimuli,[143] and it has been speculated that it may therefore be involved in selective attention to facial stimuli and the social orientation that is a fundamental deficit in ASD.[144] A clinical consequence of reduced face-reading ability in people with ASD is that they are over-trusting. One study has shown a reduced activation of anterior cingulate during a trust game.[145]

The creation of an emotional flavour may be how the anterior cingulate is linked to repetitive behaviour. One comprehensive fMRI study has provided evidence of abnormal connectivity of the anterior cingulate in people with ASD, and linked this to the abnormal activations of anterior cingulate following successful task performance. The authors suggest that successful completion of tasks in people with ASD may not be experienced as successful because the emotional flavour is that of failure, due to this abnormal anterior cingulate, and so the task is repeated, leading to cycles of repetition.[146] An increased N-acetylaspartate/ creatinine ratio, with a correlation between the ratio and the total Yale-Brown obsessional scale score, has been reported in two studies of the prefrontal cortex and the anterior cingulate of untreated people with ASD.[147, 148]

The inverse problem may occur in ADHD: hypoactivation of the anterior cingulate following errors may reduce error detection and lead to an overestimation of success.[149] There are increased choline levels in anterior cingulate in ADHD, rather than reduced ones.[150] Reduced error detection extends to undiagnosed siblings, and may be an endophenotype for ADHD.[151]

Posterior cingulate connectivity with amygdala is reduced in people with ASD during face processing.[152]

INSULA
Anatomy
The insula is, like the orbitofrontal prefrontal cortex, a development of olfactory cortex, which, to accommodate this hypertrophy, invaginates at this point. So the insula appears to be an island (hence its name) lying in a trough covered over by gyri jutting caudally back from the frontal lobe (frontal operculum, or pars orbicularis), forward or rostrally from the parietal lobe (parietal operculum) and from below, from the temporal lobe (temporal operculum). Like the cingulate, it has a posterior granulate portion, similar to other neocortex, and an anterior agranular, or palaeocortical, portion. The anterior part of the insula contains a high density of D1 dopaminergic neurons, and these are depleted, with a reduction of grey matter volume, in people with schizophrenia or people who are chronic cocaine users. It receives visceral sensation from the gut, airways and cardiovascular system, via the thalamus. It outputs directly to these structures, too. The posterior part receives input from the thalamus, and so from peripheral sensory nerve endings, particularly the slowly conducting nerves specialized for information pain, itch and pleasurable touch.[153]

Normal function
The insula may be particular concerned with internal sensation, 'introception'.[154] By extension, the insula is activated by unpleasant internal sensations that reach consciousness such as suffocation, nausea and, by disgust,[155] an emotion that is tied to what we find 'nauseating'. It may be particularly involved in self-conscious feelings, and therefore subjective awareness,[156] possibly in collaboration with other palaeocortical areas containing spindle neurons such as the anterior cingulate, and ventromedial parts of the prefrontal cortex.

The anterior part of the monkey insula contains many single neurons that respond to reward,[157] and the insula, along with orbitofrontal and dorsolateral prefrontal cortex and the anterior cingulate, is activated by cue-induced craving in people with addictions.[153]

Functional effect of lesions in adulthood
Infarcts in the right insula, following strokes, are associated with an increased risk of death from cardiac arrhythmias in the subsequent three months,[158] presumably because of the disruption of the insula's normal control over the milieu interne.

Structural and functional changes in the ASDs

Surface morphometry indicates a folding abnormality of the left frontal operculum in less able people with an ASD.[159] This area involves Broca's language centre, but it overlies the insula and the shape difference may reflect an abnormality in either Broca's area or the insula underneath it, or both. Broca's area is a more likely candidate, given the known language problems in people with autistic disorder. The abnormality was more marked in children compared to adolescents, which would be consistent with some children recovering language function.

fMRI studies have shown that the perception of facial disgust expressions specifically activates the insula. The present fMRI study investigated whether this structure is also involved in the processing of visual stimuli depicting non-mimic disgust elicitors compared to fear-inducing and neutral scenes. Twelve female subjects were scanned while viewing alternating blocks of 40 disgust inducing, 40 fear inducing and 40 affectively neutral pictures, shown for 1.5 seconds each. Afterwards, affective ratings were assessed. The disgust pictures, rated as highly repulsive, induced activation in the insula, the amygdala, the orbitofrontal and occipito-temporal cortex. Since during the fear condition the insula was also involved, our findings do not fit with the idea of the insula as a specific disgust processor.[160]

Insula, like anterior cingulate cortex, is less active in people with an ASD during the performance of a social task, compared to neurotypicals.[158, 161] It is also less active in people with ASD compared to neurotypicals, again as is the anterior cingulate cortex, in tasks in which an incongruent flanking stimulus has to be ignored in order to attend to a central stimulus.[158, 162] Attention to a stimulus is intensified in neurotypicals if it is preceded by a highly arousing stimulus. This is associated with insula activation. Neither occurs in autism.[163]

Both of these findings may be part of a more general impairment in inhibitory circuitry in ASD, and a reflection of underconnectivity between brain areas.[164] The insula and the anterior cingulate cortex may therefore contribute to the difficulty of people with an ASD to see 'the wood for the trees' and is also activated by a high arousing stimulus.

ADHD

Insula and anterior cingulate are less highly active in boys with ADHD during an interference task than during other tasks, and less than in neurotypicals engaged in the same task.[165]

FUSIFORM GYRUS

Anatomy

The fusiform gyrus occupies much of the inferior surface of the temporal lobe, and has strong connections to occipital cortex, and so to the visual pathways leading back from the eyes through the lateral geniculate ganglion lying just above the medial surface of the inferior temporal gyrus and therefore medial to the middle temporal gyrus.

Normal function

The fusiform gyrus is activated during the perception of familiar objects or properties, such as colours, words, numbers and, in the fusiform face area, faces. Radiologists show more right fusiform gyrus activation and, less activation of their left occipital cortex, than novices when viewing chest radiographs.[166] It is likely that the fusiform area supports learning through repeated practice, or 'over-learning'. An example of this is the ability of experienced radiologists to interpret radiographs. They use patterns or gestalts, and it is likely that is these that are stored in, or accessed via, the fusiform gyrus.[167]

Fusiform cortex probably passes processing on to the middle and posterior temporal gyrus where semantic categorization occurs.[167]

'Reading' faces is an over-learnt skill that is normally acquired passively as a result of the innate tendency to focus on faces. There is strong evidence that faces are scanned by a rapid but simplified route, in which there is a particular focus on the eye region, with some tracking upwards and downwards towards the nasolabial folds. It is possible that the fusiform gyrus stores this strategy, and that the integrity of the fusiform cortex is essential to it being invoked when faces are viewed.

Functional effect of lesions in adulthood

Lesions of the right fusiform gyrus result in impairments of the ability to perceive facial configurations and hence to prosopagnosia,[168] and left-sided lesions to anomia and to synaesthesiae.

Structural and functional changes in the ASDs

There is substantial evidence that people with an ASD make more errors in face interpretation than neurotypicals, that they scan faces in a different way,[169] showing less preference for scanning the eye region,[170] and that the fusiform gyrus is less likely to be activated during face processing. Presumably all of these findings are interlinked. One possible explanation is that people with an ASD do not look sufficiently at faces to learn privileged methods of discrimination, and therefore to embed face-processing strategies in their fusiform gyrus. Some evidence comes from fMRI in children with an ASD, who show normal fusiform gyrus activation when viewing faces of their mothers or a familiar child, but not when viewing an unfamiliar face.[171] There may be differences between people with AS and people with autism.[172]

Fusiform gyrus neurons have been reported to be fewer and smaller in people with autism compared to controls.[173] It is possible that fusiform gyrus is primarily affected in ASD, but this would be gainsaid by the precise discriminations that people with an ASD regularly make in the pursuit of their special interests. It therefore seems more likely that the lack of activation of a fusiform face area is connected with the lack of over-learning of faces.

Frank prosopagnosia is reported to be rare in AS.[174]

Chapter 3

INTERACTIONS IN GENES
AND NEURONS

The increasingly strong evidence for a neurological basis for the ASDs has been summarized in Chapters 1 and 2. There is equally strong evidence that these neurological changes are genetically determined.[1]

A variety of brain areas implicated in ASD were considered in Chapters 1 and 2, but no focus in the brain emerged as commonly causing ASD. There is no autism producing lesion. The lesion approach to communication disorders had already been challenged by Geschwind[2] who resurrected the connectionist approaches of the nineteenth century. He argued that symptoms occurred not because of an area of brain damage, but because brain areas were disconnected. A connectionist, or network, approach to ASD is now widely accepted, as is the brain's interaction with the environment. This new network model, and the evidence for it, is considered in the second part of this chapter.

The genetics of ASD are covered in the first part. It is consistent with the network approach to ASD that candidate genes for ASD include many that code for synaptic proteins since the synapses are to networks what connectors are to cables. What may be more unexpected is that a focal genetics has, like lesion-based neurology, given way to a genomic understanding of ASD that increasingly includes interactions between genes and between genes and the environment.

This homology between the new interactive genomics and the new connectionist neurology is the justification for considering both genetics and networks in this chapter. But it can only be coincidence that a disorder of social interaction is attributed to an impairment of the interaction of parts of the brain which is attributed to a dysfunctional interaction between parts of the genome.

The chapter begins with a general introduction to genomics as it relates to ASD.

INTRODUCTION TO GENOMICS AND TO GENETIC INTERACTIONS

There are specific mutations that are associated with a risk, sometimes a very high risk, of the development of ASD (these are considered in Chapter 12) but these are rare, as are focal lesions in the brain causing ASD.

This has until recently been attributed to the cumulative or polygenic effect of genes that each contribute a structural or functional abnormality, not substantial enough in itself to cause disorder, but in combination with the subclinical contribution of other genes, disorder results.

This model of ASD has dictated much of the genetic research until recently, searching for candidate genes that would be frequently associated with ASD.[3] However, attention has now switched to the interaction between genes themselves via the proteins that are transcribed from them, either through an interaction between these protein products or because one gene product can control the activity of another gene.

Genes, chromosomes and DNA

The genetic material of people and other higher organisms, or eukaryotes, is contained in long threads or chromatids contained within a cell nucleus. The chromatid has a core of deoxyribonucleic acid. DNA is made up of two chains, or polymers, of a five-ringed sugar or pentose (deoxyribose in DNA) linked by a phosphate group. Each pentose is linked to one of four 'nucleobases': adenine (A), thymine (T), guanine (G) and cytosine (C). In ribonucleic acid, RNA, the sugar is ribose, and T is replaced by uracil (U), but the structure is otherwise the same. The phosphate, sugar, nucleobase complex is called a nucleotide. Single stranded DNA is highly chemically active, and A shows a strong affinity for T (or U) and C for G. Two complementary DNA strands are paired together in the chromatid, with the sugars in one strand running from a phosphate molecule (the 5' end) and in the other strand from a sugar molecule (the 3' end), with each A linked to a T, and each C to a G in a 'base pair'. Because of the forces between them, the double stranded DNA coils into a helix, and then coils again into a double helix. The 3' ends of each strand are non-overlapping but wrap back onto themselves to form the 'telomere': a structure that may be related to ageing.

There is also a small amount of genetic material in a separate organelle within the cell, the mitochondrion (green plants also have DNA in chloroplasts). This material is thought to have originated in a bacterium that colonized the cells of a primitive organism, and made such a useful energetic contribution that evolution has favoured its conservation in all subsequent organisms, by ensuring the each egg of these organisms contains some of the mother's mitochondria that are thereby passed on to any progeny, either male or female, that develop from that egg.

Unless the cell is preparing to divide or actually dividing, the chromatids are involved in protein synthesis, and are much longer than the diameter of the nucleus. They are not normally visible under a light microscope even with special stains (with the exception of X chromatids, which are visible as 'Barr bodies'). When the cell is preparing to divide, the DNA double helix is successively straightened out, unstitched, copied, the copied fragments joined into two new strands, and each new strand linked to an old strand to form two double strands. These are normally identical by virtue of the affinity of C for G, A for T, and vice versa.

This results in the creation of a duplicate, sister chromatid, joined to the original at a specially adapted DNA segment, the centromere. As cell division proceeds, the histone coat of the chromatids contracts and twists resulting in a condensed structure, the chromosome, which is visible, on staining, under the light microscope. All but one of the human chromosomes looks roughly like an X, with the centromere at the centre of the X, two short or p arms and two long or q arms corresponding to the condensed sister chromatids. The chromatids are pulled apart when the cell divides during normal growth (mitosis), and once a cell wall and a nucleus have re-established themselves, each daughter cell has one identical chromatid each.

Cytogenetic testing until quite recently has relied on the appearance of the chromosomes to determine genetic abnormalities, sometimes supplemented by combining or hybridizing with fragments of DNA that are known to bind to specific areas of interest and that can themselves be bound to a fluorescent compound that can be seen in a light microscope (the fluorescent in situ hybridization or FISH test). Chromosome maps were produced based on the bands that could be seen when the chromosome was stained by particular rearrangements. The position or locus of the phenylketonuria gene, for example, is 12q22-q24.1. This means (reading from left to right) that it is on chromosome 12, on the long arm (q), beyond the twenty-second band counting out from the centromere to the telomere, but short of the twenty-fourth band, or rather short of the first sub-band (24.1) after the twenty-fourth band.

It was once thought that histone carried the genetic information, but it is now known that it is DNA that does, with sections of DNA along the long strand of DNA in each cell being a 'gene', and each gene normally carrying the information for assembling a protein from individual amino acids.

In diploid organisms like people, there are normally two approximate copies or homologues of each chromosome in each cell, with the exception of the sex chromosomes that determine the sex of the cell. One of the sex chromosomes looks similar to the other non-sex or 'autosomal' chromosomes, and so because of this appearance is conventionally called the 'X' chromosome. The other seems to have a bit chopped off and so is called the 'Y' chromosome. In people, there are normally 46 chromosomes in all. Other great apes have more, 48, because they have two chromosomes corresponding to the human chromosome 2. So the human complement is usually represented as 46, XY for most men, and 46, XX for most women. The 44 autosomes are paired: one coming from the father and one from the mother. These copies are normally identical in all of the respects that make the cells viable. Their difference constitutes 'normal variation', such as eye or hair colour.

Ova and sperm are haploid: they contain only one copy of each autosome, plus an X chromosome in the ovum, and either an X or a Y chromosome in the sperm. A special cell division process leads to the formation of ova or sperm in which homologous chromosomes pair up so closely that they can exchange genetic material in a crossover. As a result the chromosomes are recombined, each having some new, exchanged genes. Recombination is required to preserve genetic diversity: large areas of the Y chromosome that are protected from recombination are effectively junk, as already noted. Misalignment of the homologous chromosomes may result in an unequal exchange of genetic material, so that one chromosome may lose some genes – deletions – and the other chromosome may gain some – duplications. Crossover may also break one or both chromatids in one of the chromosomes involved in the crossover. DNA polymerase will stitch these breaks back together, but may do so with the DNA fragment reversed – an inversion. Deletions, duplications, and inversions are known as copy number variations.

Meiosis is completed by a further cell division that pulls the homologous chromosomes apart first from each other, and then in a further cell division into their separate chromatids. The daughter cells have only one of the two homologous chromatids that belonged to the parent. Fertilization of one of these haploid ova with a haploid spermatozoon means that the nucleus of the fertilized egg now has the full diploid complement of chromosomes again.

A gene on one chromosome and its variant on another are called 'alleles'. Having two copies of each chromosome may mean that more protein is transcribed, that is an increase in the genetic dose. So farmed wheat, which is polyploid, is larger in all respects than wild wheat, which is mostly diploid and the highest gluten yield is found in the hexaploid, cultivated durum wheat. In people, muscle tissue is also polyploid, one effect of which is to increase the genetic dose of the DNA for transcribing the contractile protein, beta-myosin.[4]

Genes and the genome

The definition of a gene was derived from work with a fly that is readily available in California, the fruit-fly Drosophila. Distinctive morphological or functional features are easily detected in mutants of wild type Drosophila. A gene was a length of chromosome that corresponded to one of these features, as demonstrated by the fact that a change in the DNA, a mutation, at any point in this length would cause a change in the feature for which the gene was named. Mutations were more or less closely linked depending on how often they would be conserved together in subsequent generations, and a map of the genes could be drawn up for simple organisms.

Originally, it was expected that DNA would turn out to be a string of genes, but it is now estimated that only about 1 per cent of DNA is expressed, that is transcribed into messenger RNA (mRNA) that is then being translated into a polypeptide. A further complication is that some mRNA molecules are cut and spliced into new molecules, from each of which a polypeptide is transcribed. So the one gene/one protein hypothesis that followed on from the Drosphila work no longer holds. It is therefore more usual now to use the term 'genome' (originally coined in the 1930s) to refer to the totality of the nuclear DNA, and not 'genes' that refer only to 'exons': DNA whose code is ultimately translated into a specific polypeptide.

Expression, inactivation and imprinting

There may be no occasion in which all of the genes on a particular DNA strand are active at the same time. The investment of DNA by histone prevents access by the RNA polymerase complex required to synthesize the RNA molecule complementary to the gene. Making a gene active requires that the histone unwinds and is lifted away (and that a number of other actions take place in the polymerization process). Controlling the histone/histone and histone/DNA bonds over a gene is therefore one way of allowing mRNA synthesis to take place, in which case the gene is active, or 'expressed'. Proteins called chromatic remodelling complexes do this, possibly by acetylating or esterifying the amino acids of the histone, thus reducing the bond with the bases constituting DNA and opening a gap for the polymerase to get access, or by acetylation that restores the histone's acidity and closes gaps. mRNA transcription may also be controlled, sometimes by the pre-existing level of the protein that is being transcribed.

As stem cells differentiate, they become less competent and more specialized, which means that some of their genes, and the corresponding functions, have to be turned off and some turned on.[5]

While gene expression may be turned on and off during the lifetime of an animal, some genes are silenced for ever, or inactivated, soon after fertilization. Women do not have twice as many functional X chromosomes as men, but almost the same number, since one of their X chromosomes is partly inactivated and becomes permanently coiled up and therefore visible even between cell divisions (the Barr body already mentioned). However, even this chromosome may not be completely inactive as XO women with Turner syndrome lack some necessary genes compared to XX women.

Genes or chromosome segments may also be inactivated selectively, and previously inactivated genes may be activated again, during and immediately after fertilization. If this process is determined by which parent provided the gene, this is called 'imprinting'. Methylation of histone that results in a tighter coil of the chromatid blocking DNA transcription is one of the common mechanisms of inactivation. Demethylation leads to re-activation.

Angelman and Prader-Willi syndrome are due to deletions or duplications of nucleotide sequences (or copy number variations, as described below) CNVs in an area in the long, q, arm of chromosome, 15, 15q11-15q13. Normally the SNRP gene in this area is maternally imprinted, and the UBE3A, a ubiquitin gene, is paternally imprinted. If a child inherits a defective SNRP gene from the mother, the father's gene, which may be normal, cannot compensate as it is normally imprinted and so is not available for transcription, and Angelman syndrome results (see Chapter 12). If a child inherits a defective UBE3A gene from the father, and as it is the mother's gene is imprinted and so unavailable, Prader-Willi syndrome results.

Expression, inactivation, and imprinting and inactivation are means to reduce genetic dose, to prevent competition between alleles, and to alter the structure and function of organs or parts of organs. Expression is also the reason that one allele is dominant over another. If a gene has two alleles, D and r, and a diploid individual has both DD alleles, they are said to be homozygous for DD. If another, heterozygous individual that has D on one chromatic and r on the other (written as having Dr) and they have the same phenotypic features as a DD individual, D is said to be the dominant allele, because the gene product of the r allele has not been expressed. In this example, enough of the product of the D allele is produced by just one D being active that it is 'haplosufficient': there is no shortfall of the gene product compared to the DD homoozygote.

Imprinting has been proposed as a factor in the genesis of the ASDs.[6]

Epigenesis
Non-genomic factors can influence the expression of genes. Evidence from one study suggests that adverse life events may alter the expression in the brain of serotonin receptors[7] and in prairie voles maternal care influences expression of the oxytocin receptor gene in the pup's brain. There is a single case where it has been suggested that the failure to express a normal oxytocin gene in humans has led on to autism, although this is in a family where other family members have a polymorphism in this gene.[8]

Penetrance
Epigenetic factors influence the extent to which a gene's protein product is present in or affects an individual bearing the gene. The form and function of mature individuals in a species are thought to be variants of a paradigm member of that species whose form and function is called the phenotype (from the Greek for 'showing' or 'appearance' and the usual English usage of 'type'). Phenotype might also be loosely used for the actual form and function of a

particular individual. So the previous statement about epigenesis could be modified to read: epigenetic factors influence the alterations in phenotype produced by a variant gene.

The general term for factors that interpose between a gene and a phenotype is 'penetrance'. Gene variants whose impact can be ameliorated by non-genetic factors have reduced penetrance, others that almost always affect phenotype (such as the polymorphism that causes ASD and Rett syndrome) are highly penetrant. Penetrance is one possible explanation for simplex families with one member with an ASD: that in fact there are other family members with the gene variant that has led to overt ASD in the affected family member, but the variant is of low penetrance and so has not altered the phenotype of these other 'carriers', the common term for people with genetic variant that has not affected them but when transmitted to the next generation will cause pathological change.

Copy number variation, discussed in a later section, is now thought to provide a more common explanation both for simplex families where the affected family member has a genetically caused ASD. Carrier status may also be explained by CNVs as in fragile X, also discussed in the later section, but also by sex-linked factors as in Rett syndrome (discussed in detail in Chapter 12) and by the gene in question being recessive (see previous section), in which case it is only expressed when a child has inherited two copies of the recessive gene, one from each parent.

Phenylketonuria (PKU) is an example of a recessive disorder. Untreated PKU leads to intellectual disability and, possibly, ASD[9] although more often ADHD. It is caused by a lack of phenylalanine hydroxylase that converts phenylalanine into tyrosine. Phenylalanine cannot be degraded in the absence of this enzyme in the liver, and so accumulates leading to toxicity that is especially damaging to the developing brain. There are at least 400 known polymorphisms in the PKU gene, which lies in the region 12q22-q24.1 on chromosome 12. Since both genes are normally expressed, and one allele is haplosufficient, that is codes enough enzyme to degrade phenylalanine sufficiently, a child can only develop PKU if he or she receives a defective copy of the gene from the mother and the other from the father.

Mapping the human genome

The human genome contains 3.2 gigabases: or 3,2000,000,000 nucleotides. The Human Genome Project successfully worked out the sequence of 90 per cent of these (highly repetitive, or heterochromatic, regions were not all sequenced) in an unknown number of people who had donated samples – but some sequences may be derived from a much smaller number of people, possibly only one.[10] The human genome project used a complex combination of methods to work out sequences, but since then there has been an increasing availability of microarrays, or chips, onto which fragments of denatured or single-stranded DNA of known sequence have been deposited. Each deposit can be of any length, from a few nucleotides up to the length of a bacterial chromosome (200,000 bases), and modern commercially available chips may have as many as a million different deposits. The sample DNA is denatured, labelled with a fluorescent dye, and applied to the chip. Once unbound DNA is eluted, the level of fluorescence at each deposit on the chip is an indication of whether or not sample DNA was bound there, and therefore whether or not the DNA sequence of the target DNA was found in the sample DNA.

With these semi-automated methods of aCMH (array-based comparative genomic hybridization) it has become much cheaper and quicker to sequence a genome, and it is possible for individual genomes to be sequenced. James Watson, who with Crick identified the double helix, was the first named person, but it is expected that there will be many others: in fact, it is possible that this may become a regular part of a medical work-up in the future. There are a number of websites of record that publish genome sequence, and some additional groups are allowing individuals to publish their own personal sequences, as they are performed.

Fewer genes were found than expected in the human genome (25–30,000) although the number varies somewhat depending on how a gene is defined. This is about the same number as is found in rice or mustard grass. The project confirmed that only a small portion of DNA was within an exon or region that might be transcribed into mRNA. Other DNA was highly repetitive (the heterochromatic material already mentioned) or part of a start or stop region, or an intron (material that is translated into RNA, but then cleaved off before polypeptide transcription).

When individuals have been compared, about 99 per cent of their DNA is identical, but about 95 per cent of human DNA is identical with the chimpanzee, and there are a substantial number of genes that are conserved between very different species. An example is one cluster of genes that has evolved rapidly and is possibly associated with human brain development, but it contains regions conserved in chickens as well as chimpanzees.[11]

This situation is not dissimilar to the present understanding of the brain. There are large areas of cerebral cortex whose function is unknown. In fact, even in my career as a doctor, I have known surgeons to remove some of these areas as being a cause of mental illness with the expectation that this would not cause harm because these areas were simply 'association' areas. Many of these regions are also to be found in other vertebrates, but are much more substantial in people.

Single nucleotide polymorphisms (SNPs, 'snips')

The most common cause of variation is recombination at meiosis. It was at one time thought that the most common cause of damaging variation – or mutation – was when one nucleotide was knocked out by radiation, or mistranscribed during cell division. These often used to be called point mutations, but are now termed single nucleotide polymorphisms since the mutation comes about through the substitution of one base pair for another. Changes – variations or polymorphisms – in a single nucleotide may have no effect, may change a codon leading to a changed amino acid in the encoded polypeptide, may change a codon but not lead to a changed amino acid (as the genetic code is redundant), or may change one of the control regions (start or 'promoter' regions, or stop regions) causing a more substantial effect. Changes with no effect in one tissue may have an effect in another if the gene is only expressed in that other tissue. SNPs that cause changes are known as replacement SNPs, or if they change a control region, expression SNPs: those that do not cause changes are synonymous SNPs.

Databases of SNPs are now available, and DNA chips can be produced to reveal them. Linkage studies can be conducted with SNPs probes on families where there are affected and unaffected members. SNPs that are found more frequently in the affected members should include those that might be a gene for ASD. However, the results have been disappointing in that many loci on many chromosomes have been identified in different kindreds, but there have been few overlaps. Candidate gene association studies, in which the frequency of occurrence of SNPs in people with an ASD is compared with the frequency of the SNPs in the general population, have improved specificity, but not by much.[12] One reason may be that SNPs are frequent, possibly occurring every thousandth base pair.

The genes for synaptic receptors and enzymes active in the synaptic cleft have an unusually high frequency of SNPs. The dopamine 4 receptor and the enzyme catechol O-methyl transferase (COMT) affect the time course of dopamine in the synaptic cleft, therefore its action in prefrontal areas, and so influence reward and, possibly, proneness to ADHD. They exist in different versions corresponding to variants, or alleles, in the underlying gene. COMT Catechol-O-methyltransferase enzyme activity is modified by a valine to methonine substitution resulting from A-G (adenosine–guanine base pair) being substituted for G-G (guanine–guanine) at codon 158, resulting in a substitution of valine (Val) to methionine (Met).[13] MetCOMT has been thought to be associated with ADHD and does appear to be linked to aggressivity in children.[14] Other SNPs in COMT have been linked to intellectual disability in Han Chinese.[15]

There are many single gene diseases that increase the risk of ASD (see Chapter 11), and a few that cause ASD in almost all affected members, but these are very rare disorders and cannot account for most of the heritability of ASD. Other, and more complex, genetic models are required.

Expression maps
Only those SNPs that are expressed in relevant tissues in the brain are likely to be relevant to ASD. It is now possible to detect genes that are expressed *in situ*, by hybridizing them with DNA arrays, and it has been suggested that this may lead to a narrower, and therefore more useful, list of candidate genes.[16]

Copy number variants
SNPs are hereditary. So if a person with an SNP has children, the SNP will be transmitted according to Mendelian principles, that is if there is one allele only affected, half of the children are likely to get this, and the other half the unaffected allele.

Mutations may occur during meiosis, when gametes are being created and stored. Unlike SNPs, these mutations are not inherited from parents, although they may be passed on to offspring. Meiosis involves tearing chromosomes apart and inevitably some repair is required. The power of enzymes to repair DNA has only recently been realized. They are able to fix broken strands, but in the process may invert them, duplicate them, or delete loops that fail to adhere to the main chain. This results in sequences of nucleotides being lost, being repeated, or being patched back in but in reverse order (inverted). These mutations are collectively known as Copy Number Variations or CNVs. CNVs provide one possible explanation for genetic factors playing a part in the aetiology of ASD even in simplex families, with only one affected member.

CNVs, like SNPs, may be of no apparent significance, fatal, or somewhere in between. Approximately 0.4 per cent of a human genome may be composed of CNVs, and even identical twins may differ genetically because of different CNVs. CNVs like SNPs can be identified using commercially available nucleotide arrays 'chips' each with over a million probes and using these probes to find any CNVs in any part of the genome, a method known as genome-wide association study.

CNVs involving large (over 1000 bases or 1 kilobase in length)[17] are particularly important causes of polymorphism. CNVs may result in an inactive gene or, in the case of duplications, in an increased dose of the gene product.

CNVs may confer advantage and be passed on into the next generation.[18] One variant of the dopamine 1 transporter (DAT1) gene has nine tandem repeats in a normally repetitive region, while the most common gene has ten repeats. The nine repeat gene may produce less DAT and therefore less dopamine release at synapses, although the evidence is mixed, but it does confer better ability to learn implicit regularities in sequences when compared to the typical gene.[19]

There is increasing evidence of CNVs being implicated in ASD, as well as in schizophrenia and intellectual disability.[20] In one large multicentre study,[21] large CNVs affecting several genes and mainly occurring de novo were more common in the ASD group than in their siblings (the odds of having autism and having one of these CNVs was 5.6 times more than the odds of not having autism and having a large CNV). The CNVs occurred in many different loci (the authors estimate between 130 and 234) although many of them were adjacent. Chromosomal areas where loci of large CNVs were particularly likely to be found were 7q11.23, 15q11.2-13.1, 16p11.2, and Neurexin 1 (the possible functions of these areas are discussed in Chapter 11). Similar findings in another study[22] led the authors to conclude that: (1) CNVs are commoner in children with ASD in simplex families and (2) in these families more common in the children with ASD than in their siblings; (3) CNVs involving duplications are more likely to be transmitted but (4) deletions are more common than duplications in children with ASD; (5) the CNVs are unusual ones ('ultrarare') and (6) are more common, and larger, in women with ASD in simplex families (my numbering). A third study has reached similar conclusions.

In this study, the genomes of nearly a thousand people with ASD and their parents were investigated using DNA microarrays. A significantly increased rate of copy number variants, that is deletions or duplications of nucleotide sequences in the people with an ASD (the rate was actually 1.19 times higher than in their parents) were not restricted to a few sites known or suspected to be associated with an increased risk of ASD, but affected genes on many different chromosomes whose function, where it was known, was linked to receptor formation, cytoskeleton or G protein synthesis (guanosine triphosphatase (GTPase).[23] The final common pathway of these genes is not known, but a plausible speculation is that it is linked to the interaction between neurons, and the creation of networks. Van de Lagemaat and Grant provide a model of how some of the genes identified in the Pinto *et al.* study might interact, and how they may link to the neural disconnections that are increasingly linked to the ASDs.[24] In Figure 3.1, which is taken from their paper, they show how linked genes might code for proteins that constitute steps in the construction of synapse.

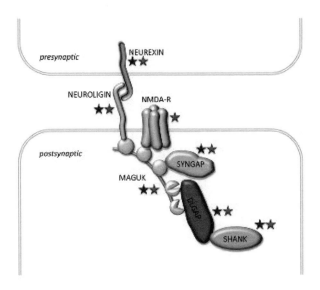

Figure 3.1 Proteins involved in the construction of synapses, many of them being products of candidate genes in ASD
Source: Reproduced from van de Lagemaat and Grant, 2010 with permission from Elsevier.

Linked proteins have also been mapped by a method developed by Zoghbi *et al.* They term these linked proteins an 'interactome', and they have applied this method to ASD, suggesting some novel reasons why genes implicated in ASD may interact indirectly through the partnership between their gene products.[25] They identify, like van de Lagemaat and Grant,[25] genes coding for proteins involved in connections between neurons, although in the post-synaptic space rather than in the construction of the synapse itself.

Tandem repeats

A special kind of CNV is the tandem repeat, a sequence of non-coding base pairs that, under some circumstances, can grow in length (a process that leads to a reducing efficiency of any related genes over successive generations, termed 'anticipation'). The FRAX gene is on the long arm of the X chromosome. Termination of the transcription of the gene is signalled by a tandem repeat of about 40 in a CGG triplet to a repeat of over more than 200 times over several generations. At the length of 40 the repeat acts as a signal for mRNA to disengage; at 200 mRNA gets tangled and its production, and therefore the production of the protein, FMR1, that it codes for, drops leading to fragile X syndrome, a syndrome associated with learning disability and ASD in males (see Chapter 11).

The middle (centromere) and ends (telomeres) of chromosomes are highly repetitive, with the lengths of the repetitions of telomeres decreasing with biological age. This has been suggested to be a cause of ageing changes in non-genetic tissue.

Repeats of a CAG trinucleotide occur normally in the Huntingtin gene leading to a chain of glutamines in the Huntingtin protein that it codes for. However, in Huntington's disease the number of repeats increases beyond 40 leading to lengthening of the protein by the insertion of this number of glutamines into its normal chain, and the manifestation of the disease. Huntingtin regulates the expression of the gene for brain-derived neurotrophic factor, but it is not clear whether this is linked to the aetiology of Huntington's disease.

Epistasis

The Huntingtin gene is an example of a gene that influences the expression of another gene via its gene product, a phenomenon termed 'epistasis'. Epistasis may be one way in which the apparent similarity between the chimpanzee and the human genome may turn out to be misleading: that genes act in concert with each other and not simply as isolated controls, each with a single functional product. Again, there are striking similarities with the brain, where networks between archaic structures may produce new, emergent properties that could not be predicted from the function of each of the structures alone.

Many of the latest genomic studies in ASD have focused on these epigenetic effects. Voineagu *et al.* used post-mortem brain slices from 19 people with an ASD and 17 controls. They used chips to probe for RNA (as an indication that a gene has been expressed) and focused on areas that they assumed were particularly associated with ASD: cerebellar vermis, superior temporal gyrus, and prefrontal cortex. Using statistical methods, they calculated which genes were more likely to be active together ('co-expressed') in these tissues, arguing that these genes might constitute a superordinate category of interacting genes or 'transcriptome'. Two statistical clusters looked like good candidates for an ASD transcriptome, both found in PFC and STG, but not so markedly in cerebellar vermis. One was under-expressed in ASD, and contained FOX1, an mRNA splicing factor gene, already suspected of being implicated in ASD. The other transcriptome of interest was over-expressed in ASD, and was linked to glial activity: possibly representing an inflammatory response.[26]

NETWORKS IN THE BRAIN

Local area networks: minicolumns

Anatomy

Cortical neurons seem to be organized in local networks of neurons in vertical columns that are 40–50 microns in diameter in people, and contain between 80 and 100 neurons (with the exception of minicolumns in occipital cortex, which are probably twice as large). Each minicolumn contains interneurons (mainly but not solely GABAergic and inhibitory), glutaminergic pyramidal cells which project freely up and down the minicolumn as well as projecting myelinated axons out of the minicolumn and so are the efferent cells, and a small number of cells interfacing with afferent axons. It has been speculated that there are about as many minicolumns as there are fibres in the corpus callosum, suggesting that each minicolumn may also be in contact with minicolumn from the other hemisphere.[27] It has also been suggested that astrocytes, normally considered as part of the connective, glial tissue in the brain, are elements in the minicolumn too, although linked magnetically and not electrically, and play a part in memory and other cognitive processes.[28]

Normal function

An obvious analogy exists between minicolumns and microprocessors, but there are many contradictory findings and some researchers doubt that there are functional units corresponding to minicolumns at all.

Functional effect of lesions

Ageing female rhesus monkeys that have failing memory and reduced ability to learn, comparable to Alzheimer syndrome in humans, also have disorganization of the minicolumns in area 46 (corresponding to dorsolateral prefrontal cortex in humans), although no reduction in total neuronal numbers. Minicolumnopathy has also been reported in schizophrenia.

Structural and functional changes in the ASDs

Casanova has been an energetic advocate of minicolumnopathy as a cause of Rett syndrome and other ASDs.[29] Neuropathological examinations of post-mortem brains have shown a variety of abnormalities, including an increased number of smaller pyramidal cells in cerebral cortex that would be consistent with minicolumnopathy.[30]

The cortical excitability hypothesis

Transcranial magnetic stimulation (TMS) is a technique by which a coil is placed close to the skull and a transient but powerful magnetic field is generated by the passage of a pulse of current in the coil. The field temporarily inhibits the firing of pyramidal cells in areas close to the coil, possibly by an effect on the minicolumns. TMS has been used to provide information about minicolumnar function, and chronic TMS is now being promoted by some researchers as a means of overcoming 'minicolumnar pathology' in which, it is supposed, minicolumns have a reduction in inhibitory interneuron activity, and are consequently not sufficiently isolated from each other. This leads to a greater spread of cortical excitation in response to afferent stimulation than there should be. Chronic TMS, it is supposed, can counteract this and it has been used in a surprisingly wide range of disorders, including schizophrenia,[31] depression, obsessive compulsive disorder, Tourette syndrome and ASD.[32] All of these are disorders known to be markedly influenced by placebo effects, at least in the short term, and these early findings cannot be taken as evidence of the cortical over-excitability hypothesis.

Conclusion

Since minicolumns are not universally accepted as units of cerebral organization and they cannot be observed directly in vivo, their significance for the ASDs is currently uncertain.[33]

Working memory networks

Minicolumnar organization, if it turns out to be a valid concept, will reflect the secular organization of cortex: susceptible to change, but over a long period. Some brain tasks require more rapid, but more transient networks, notably the scratch pad of working memory (see Chapter 7). This memory, like that of random access memory in a computer, has to be easily retrieved by a variety of routes but can be volatile. In a computer, it is lost as soon as the machine is turned off. Functional networks corresponding to RAM and subserving spatial working memory have been identified in rhesus monkeys. The network functions by electrical resonance linking pyramidal cells that are mutually excited in a microcircuit whose constituent neurons are a representational map of the physical environment being remembered. Neurons are included or excluded by means of cyclic AMP receptors on dendritic spines that can turn on or turn off channels that either enable or disable the neurons response to excitation by other neurons with terminals on the spine. These hyperpolarization-activated cyclic-nucleotide-gated (HCN) channels are controlled by alpha2A adrenoreceptors.[34] It has been suggested that one of the actions of clonidine is to stimulate this receptor, and that this may account for its beneficial effect in ADHD. Guanfacine, another drug developed for the treatment of hypertension, is a more specific alpha2 agonist, and is currently being trialled as a possible ADHD treatment, although the effect size appears to be low.[35]

Functional networks and fibre tracts

Networks linking brain areas have become established as the likely basis for at least some of the impairment in a number of 'frontostriatal' disorders including schizophrenia and autism.[36] Study of some of these disorders has led, in turn, to a clearer delineation of distinct networks subserving identifiable, or nearly identifiable, functions. Post-hoc 'connectivity' analysis of fMRI provides evidence of functional connectedness, although the findings may be affected by age, which reduces the functional connectivity of frontal networks at least in the resting state.[37] Connectedness may be estimated by time correlations, coherence, or other methods.[38] Connectedness between areas that are active even when the brain is at 'rest' can be detected by very low frequency oscillations in the electrical activity of the brain, and are detectable by scalp electrodes,[39] and also by using spontaneous low frequency fluctuations in oxygen uptake (BOLD signals).[40] If the same rhythm of activation and inactivation is found in two sites, they are considered to be time coupled and to have a functional connection between them. By taking one area or node as the 'seed', the areas that are time coupled to it constitute further nodes on a functional network that includes the starting node. Statistical analysis of the signals from many brain areas is another 'model-free' way of detecting correlations between signals that can be used to generate maps of functional connections.[41] Functional networks that have consistently been found in many laboratories involve the following structures: sensorimotor cortex, occipital cortex and extra-striate visual areas, bilateral temporal/insular and anterior cingulate cortex, left and right lateralized networks consisting of superior parietal and superior frontal regions, and the so-called default mode network consisting of precuneus, medial frontal, inferior parietal cortical regions and medial temporal lobe.

Many of these connections were known from previous fMRI studies that demonstrated that anatomically distinct brain areas were often activated by the same stimuli suggesting that they shared some common function. Several correspond to known structural connections (and perhaps all of the functional connections will eventually be found to have a structural basis) mediated by known, automatically defined nerve fibre tracts. These can be detected in vivo by repeated fMRI scans that allow estimates of water diffusion (diffusion tensor imaging), and may also be detectable in post-mortem dissections of macroscopic fibre tracts. It has been suggested the fibre tract development is wholly or partly under genetic control.[42]

Anatomy

Large fibre tracts have been recognized from post-mortem dissections of brains for centuries, with three main structures being macroscopically discriminable and therefore named: the corpus callosum between the hemisphere, the internal capsule between the basal ganglia and the ventricles, and the external capsule between the ventricles and the grey matter of the cortex. The internal capsule includes corticospinal tracts, and blends caudally into the optic radiation, and into the auditory radiation (see Table 3.1). Tensor diffusion imaging and microdissection suggests that the external capsule actually consists of three distinct networks too:[43] the superior and inferior occipitofrontal tracts and the uncinate tract.[44] These methods have also delineated three other major fibre tracts (see Table 3.1).

Table 3.1 Characterization of fibre tracts

Fasciculus (fibre tract)	Connecting	With
Corticospinal	Primary motor cortex (area 4)	Spinal cord/motor neurons
Optic radiation	Lateral geniculate body	Primary visual cortex (area 17)
Acoustic radiation	Medial geniculate body	Primary acoustic cortex (area 41/42)
Fornix	Hippocampus	Mammillary body
Cingulum	Anterior thalamus	Hippocampus
Corpus callosum	Connecting right and left hemispheres	
Superior longitudinal	Frontal lobe (e.g., Broca's region)	Occipital (visual cortex), parietal and temporal (Wernicke's region) cortices (this part also called arcuate fasciculus)
Inferior longitudinal	Temporal pole	Occipital pole
Superior occipito-frontal	Prefrontal cortex	Limbic/paralimbic areas
Inferior occipito-frontal	Frontobasal cortex	Parietal cortex
Uncinate	Orbital cortices	Cortex/hippocampal formation

Source: Reproduced from Burgel, Amunts, *et al.*, 2006 with permission from Elsevier.

Future studies are likely to alter some of the details shown in Table 3.1 and are also likely to link the functional imaging of tract anatomy with connectivity studies (see next section).

Mantini *et al.* analysed EEGs and found local rhythms that could be linked to simultaneous fMRI images,[45] providing in vivo evidence for some of the networks in Table 3.1. One connected inferior parietal lobule, posterior cingulate, with prefrontal areas. Mantini *et al.* also describe a dorsal attention network connecting dorsolateral PFC to rostral cortical areas; a visual processing, occipitotemporal network; an auditory processing, superior temporal cortical network; a frontoparietal network; and a medial PFC, anterior cingulate, hypothalamus and cerebellar network (see Figure 3.2).[45]

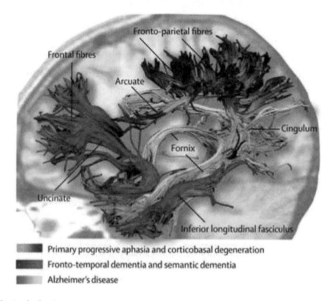

Figure 3.2 Networks in the brain
Source: Reproduced from Ciccarelli, Catani, *et al.*, 2008 with permission from *The Lancet.*

Hagmann *et al.*, for example, have used diffusion tensor imaging to map a 'structural core within posterior medial and parietal cerebral cortex' which corresponds to the default network disclosed by connectivity analyses.[46]

One of the most recent studies of networks has compared changes with age from 8 years to 30 years. Longer networks replace shorter ones, as might be expected, but it is more surprising that local networks diminish, particularly those crossing from one side of the brain to another,[47] perhaps correlated with the increasing specialization of the left hemisphere for language. The largest centre for network development is anteriorly in the right prefrontal area. This is followed by the precuneus. These are both in what the authors call the cingulo-opercular network. Other networks that they describe are frontoparietal, sensory motor, default, occipital and cerebellum (see Figure 3.3).[47]

Corpus callosum

More is known about the corpus callosum than the other fibre tracts, partly because it is such a large structure that is relatively easy to visualize. It is a thick fibre bundle of between 2 and 3 per cent of all fibres in the brain and connecting the right and left hemispheres. The width of the corpus callosum continues to increase until middle age, and is correlated inversely with the volume of orbitofrontal and dorsolateral PFC.

The corpus callosum allows sensory information presented to one hemisphere to be available to the other, connects the two motor cortices, and links association areas. It includes a range of fibre sizes with different degrees of myelination; the smaller the fibre, the slower its connection, and the more likely that it will link association areas. The spatial relationship of the cortical areas is topographically represented in the corpus callosum.[48]

Developmental anatomy

Diffusion tensor imaging has begun to be used as a means of tracking developmental changes in fibre bundles. In one study of 100 neurotypical children between the ages of 5 and 18, fractional anisotropy (a marker for white matter organization) was used to follow the development of white matter in the left frontal lobe, in frontoparietal connections, and in the arcuate fasciculus. There was a positive correlation between the development of the arcuate fasciculus and intelligence in girls, but a negative association in boys.[49] This and other results are consistent with the heterogeneity of brain substrates that underlie 'g' or the common factor of intelligence (discussed further in Chapter 7). They also point to differences in the organization of male and female that may be related to the increased incidence of some frontostriatal disorders, such as ASD, ADHD and early onset 'process' schizophrenia in boys and men compared to girls and women. Corpus callosum thickness is proportional to brain volume and although the corpus callosum is thicker in women than in men, this difference disappears if brain volume is controlled.[50]

Normal function

Wider networks are more active in the older than the younger brain.[51]

The superior and inferior longitudinal tracts are both implicated in attention. The uncinate tract links up the anterior temporal pole with orbitofrontal PFC and adjacent areas. It is therefore an important constituent of a temporal pole system, which has particular significance for the introduction of emotion into conscious processing, especially on the right side. Much less is known about these tracts than about the corpus callosum, and what is known about all of them is mainly inferred from lesion studies, although diffusion tensor imaging is now providing *in vivo* information.[52]

Functional effect of lesions in childhood

Absence or dysgenesis of the corpus callosum is the most common hereditary abnormality of the brain, and is associated with a large number of chromosome abnormalities. Its most common clinical features are loss of muscle tone, speech delay and learning difficulty, in that order.[53] Sleep problems in very young children, and attentional and social impairments, similar to those of ASD, have been reported in some children.[54]

Some aminoacidurias, such as L–2-hydroxyglutaric aciduria (L–2-HGA),[55] and maple syrup disease,[56] cause leucodystrophies which may particularly affect intracerebral tracts. Their symptoms include not only ASD, but also impaired speech development, and learning difficulty, and are non-specific.

Infants born pre-term have a reduced volume of white matter, including corpus callosum volume, and this persists in boys up to at least six months, but not in girls.[57]

Functional effect of lesions in adulthood

Adults may have few or no symptoms of corpus callosum deficits in everyday life, but acute injury may lead to an inability of the language centres in the left hemisphere to access sensation and movement being processed in the right hemisphere, leading to anomia for objects held in the left hand, an inability to make the left arm act (left arm ideomotor apraxia) and an inability to write or read in the left visual field (left visual field dyslexia and dysnomia).[58] A now famous series of studies on patients with callosotomies performed for intractable epilepsy have shown that in many ways the self is divided following the operation, with the right and left hemispheres behaving independently and sometimes competing for the control of the limbs to perform actions. Some interhemispheric transfer does persist, for example between superior colliculi, and in the anterior and posterior commissures, that may attenuate the impairment.[59]

It is hypothesized that lesions affecting other white matter tracts cause specific disconnection syndromes but the number of reported cases is too small to generalize about the functions of specific tracts.

Structural and functional changes in the ASDs
ASD

It has been reported that the thickness of the corpus callosum is reduced in ASD,[60] especially in the caudal part.[61] In one study, the size of the reduction was correlated with performance IQ, and was confined to a subgroup who had particularly low performance IQ.[62] The reduced thickness has been reported to be associated with under-connectivity between cortical areas.[63] Keary et al. found a reduction in corpus callosum volume in people with ASD compared to controls, and found a correlation between volume and performance on a frontal lobe test (the Towers of Hanoi test) although there was a slight, and non-significant, reduction of performance IQ in the subjects.[64] The reduction in white matter may also be apparent in the internal capsule, and persists well into adulthood.[65] One study exclusively of people with AS did not find the expected reduction of corpus callosal volume, suggesting that any changes in volume are a secondary feature of ASD.[50]

Case example

> Andrew was first diagnosed as having AS when he was 13. His verbal IQ was estimated to be 130 when he was aged 8, but his sequencing, number and spelling abilities were all at a much lower level. He mastered the piano to grade 5, but could not progress beyond this (expert musicians use both right and left hemispheres, but less expert musicians use only the right hemisphere). He had difficulty with other skills requiring the coordination of both of his hands, including swimming, catching a ball and using cutlery.

Just et al. found a reduction in the cross-sectional area of the corpus callosum in people with AS, compared to neurotypicals, and also found a reduction in frontoparietal synchronization suggesting reduced connectivity between these areas. Corpus callosum thickness and frontoparietal synchronization were correlated in the ASD group, but not the neurotypicals.[66]

ADHD

The size of the splenium of the corpus callosum is reduced in girls with ADHD, but not in boys. Boys, though, have a smaller rostral part compared to girls and to neurotypicals.[67] Overall, the corpus callosum is thinner.[68] The superior occipito-frontal tract is reduced in size in ADHD.[69]

Functional aggregates, modules or systems

It is likely that the study of networks will make a greater contribution to understanding ASD in the future than it does now, as there is a widespread view that the ASDs will turn out to be disorders of connectivity.

Although direct studies of connecting pathways are in their infancy, patterns are already emerging that suggest that particular brain areas regularly interact with others and act as a kind of aggregate, module or system. Some candidates for those systems that are relevant to the ASDs, and their possible constituents, are shown in Table 3.1.

All but the first two of these systems I have labelled by function, and further details about these functions will be considered in later chapters, and are not therefore considered further here.

Table 3.2 Suggested brain systems relevant to the ASDs, and their possible components

Function	Possible nodes within the responsible network
Emotional contagion	Dorsal anterior cingulate/mid cingulate/supplementary motor area/ventromedial prefrontal cortex, orbitofrontal cortex
Cognitive empathy	Anterior cingulate, insula, dorsolateral prefrontal cortex, orbitofrontal cortex
Social orienting and shared social attention ('the interbrain')	Anterior cingulate, superior temporal sulcus, inferior parietal lobule, ventral prefrontal cortex, orbitofrontal cortex
Repetitiveness	Anterior cingulate, basal ganglia, corpus callosum

The default network

Several of the systems listed in Table 3.2 are active when participants are waiting to undertake a task in the scanner but are not actively involved in one. Because this is a kind of default condition, the areas that are more active during it are said to constitute a default network (Figure 3.3).

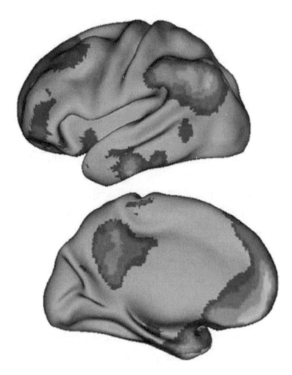

Figure 3.3 Nodes of the default network
Source: Reproduced from Buckner, Andrews-Harra, *et al.*, 2008 with permission from John Wiley and Sons.

Normal anatomy

The default network is variously typified, but there seems to be agreement that it includes three subsystems based on the posterior cingulate, medial prefrontal cortex and bilateral inferior parietal cortex.[70] Buckner *et al.* add the hippocampus, and differentiate between dorsomedial PFC (linked with the posterior cingulate) and ventromedial PFC linked in the medial prefrontal cortex of Bluhm *et al.* with anterior cingulate.[71] Other studies suggest that the mid, pregenual area, of the cingulate is a critical node, and that the insula may also be involved.

Normal function

The default network is active not only during wool-gathering or daydreaming, but also in more focused forms of introspection such as autobiographical memory, thinking about the future, undertaking theory of mind tasks, estimating the best strategy to follow in a game, and making moral judgements.[71]

Another network, opposed or 'anti-correlated' to the default network, is active when a task is being focussed on. The two opposing attentional networks, the default network evoked during introspection and the external attention network evoked when carrying out a task, correspond to two styles of cognition that Baron-Cohen has termed 'empathizing' and 'systemizing'.[72]

Functional impairment in default network in ASD and ADHD

ASD

Reduced connectivity has been reported between the frontal and temporoparietal components of the default network in people with autism compared to neurotypical controls.[73] Differences have also been reported in other studies, affecting both white and grey matter, with both reductions and increases of volume relative to neurotypicals consistent with an imbalance due to reduced connectivity.[74, 75] Giving participants a variety of true or false judgement tasks normally increases default network activation, but does so less for participants with ASD than for neurotypicals. There was a tendency for the reduction to be particularly marked when the task being given required a psychological rather than a physical judgement.[76] Di Martino *et al.* have found a correlation between a measure of 'autistic traits' (the social responsiveness scale: see Chapter 11) and activity in two areas implicated in the default network, pregenual cingulate and insula.[77]

A difficulty in interpreting these findings is that introspection is gossiping or chatting carried on with oneself, in the absence of anyone else to chat to. Chatting is the social task, par excellence, that is disrupted by the 'low bandwidth interbrain connection' (see Chapter 5) of people with ASD. Reduced activity in the default network may therefore be a consequence of ASD.

ADHD

There is reduced connectivity in the default network in people with ADHD,[78, 79] and it has been argued that the characteristic symptoms of ADHD may be attributable to this.[80]

The anti-correlated, task focused network

The task-focussed network involves activation of the dorsolateral PFC, inferior parietal cortex and supplementary motor area. Activation of the task-focussed network switches off the default network, and when the task focus is 'switched off' the default network activates.[80] It has been suggested that anterior cingulate cortex may participate in this switching, that these are fundamental states which exist even in infancy, and that one brain state is linked to introspection and the other is linked to exterior perception and activity in the world.[81]

Attention disorders and the anti-correlated networks

One of the prevailing theories of attention deficit is that effort is required to resist distraction and that a lack of effort, or effort being taken up by some other task, leads to the attention deficit. A more recent theory revives the teachers' conventional wisdom that it is daydreaming that prevents children concentrating – that is, that reduced activity of the task processing network, and therefore reduced task attention, is brought about by interference by the activation of its anti-correlated, default network. There are some aspects of attention that are heightened by default network activation, too, for example response times to unpredictable stimuli, suggesting that there is a link between mind-wandering, mindfulness and alertness.

Functional disorders of anti-correlated networks and the ASDs

Senile dementia of Alzheimer type involves an early uncoupling of the default network from the hippocampus, leading to a loss of autobiographical memory. Schizophrenia is reported to show greater connectivity within each of the anti-correlated networks, attributed to a lack of inhibition or an excess excitation. This leads to increased switching from one to the other.

In contrast to schizophrenia, adolescents and adults with ASD show reduced connectivity in the default network, especially apparent in weak connections with the medial PFC.[82] People with ADHD also have reduced connectivity, but this time it is particularly between the posterior cingulate cortex and precuneus, and anterior components of the default network.

Chapter 4

DEVELOPMENTAL, SOCIAL AND EMOTIONAL CONSIDERATIONS

What is striking about the group of 'frontostriatal' disorders is that they are all influenced by culture as well as biology. The preoccupations of people with obsessive compulsive psychosis are those of their culture, but exaggerated. The coprolalia of Gilles de la Tourette syndrome is defined culturally: the repeated vocalizations are not just sounds, or common words, they are expletives, defined as taboo words in the culture from which the sufferer comes. There are writers who have argued that attention deficit hyperactivity disorder is not a disorder of the person, but of the culture, and similarly for schizophrenia. It has been suggested that children with autism may have greater survival ability than non-autistic children if isolated: the maladaptiveness of autism is in relation to living with other people.

These social and cultural factors that influence the autism spectrum disorders will be considered in this chapter. Some may influence the manifestation of ASD, while others, its impact.

SOCIAL FACTORS
Social factors in determining whether or not there is a disorder
The social construction of the ASDs
Autism spectrum disorders rarely, if ever, are the consequence of purely psychosocial factors (see Introduction). Though, like other neurological conditions, they may manifest more severely as a result of psychological factors. Severe and long-standing (more than six months) social deprivation in early childhood may produce a disorder in adolescence that has many ADHD-like features.[1] In a study of children who spent their first years in Russian orphanages (average four years) before being adopted, 82 per cent had a recognized educational need at follow-up between the ages of 9 and 13. Around 62 per cent had a disorder of language communication, and 42 per cent had ADHD. Girls and children with low birth weights were particularly affected. This study, like other adoption studies, did not take into account children who had developmental disorders before entering the orphanage.[2]

Another potential source of social disadvantage is to be brought up by a parent or parents who are addicted to heroin. Children of heroin addicts who are brought up by their birth parents have a lower IQ, on average, than those children of heroin-addicted parents who are adopted. Lower socioeconomic status and education contribute to the disadvantage. However, the risk of developing ADHD, which is raised, is not reduced by adoption, suggesting that ADHD is genetically rather than socially determined.[3]

It is now generally accepted that there is a spectrum of ASD running from the most severely disabled through to people who have no 'traits' of ASD; those people who have traits, or have what they consider to be a non-pathological autistic spectrum condition, lie somewhere in between. Services are based on dichotomous or categorical judgements: either a person has, or they do not have, a disorder. Fudging this, for example by saying that someone has 'autistic traits', is rarely satisfactory in a clinical setting as it carries with it a kind of stigma without a person having a legitimate reason, a diagnosis, for obtaining services. Yet, as sociologists legitimately argue, diagnosis does not easily take account of the plasticity of development, such that a person may have a disability, in relation to the psychological or social demands placed on them at one time point, but no longer have a disability at another.[4] Using group norms, for example averaged developmental milestones in children, may seem objective, but conceals the social process that problematized the child's 'normality' in the first place.[5] Attributing the disability to an impairment in the child may shift the focus of intervention from the family or society that fails to enable the child.[6]

It has been argued that the politics of diagnosis have been hijacked by those wishing to normalize all children irrespective of whether or not that is in the child's interest. It has sometimes been suggested, too, that 'normalization' or 'mainstreaming' not only has been driven by 'political correctness', but also has had a more cynical background in that withholding a diagnosis can justify withholding expensive resources, too. But a contrary argument has also been made: that parents who have the articulacy to do so, have used a diagnosis of an ASD as a means to obtain more resources for their child than they should. 'Mainstreaming' for example is more likely if parents are of higher social class.[7]

Similar issues have arisen in the debate about ADHD, but with the added political dimension of ethnicity. More African Americans are diagnosed with ADHD than white Americans,[8] and African Americans in the US, and other minority groups elsewhere, have sometimes suspected that their children are being medicated by a predominant majority who fear the behaviour and folk ways of minority children.[9] In one study of inner city African American parents, nearly a quarter thought that too many children were being medicated for ADHD, and only two-thirds would recommend stimulant treatment for the child of a friend or family member.[10]

Tipping the balance

It is well recognized that situational stress may aggravate the symptoms of an ASD, possibly mediated by anxiety or depressed mood.[11] So another consequence of the autism spectrum concept is that persistent and severe anxiety or depression might so worsen the symptoms of ASD that they push a person across the tipping point where clinical ratings move from non-impaired traits to impairment and therefore 'disorder'.

One consequence of this is that social factors may appear to 'create' ASD when they simply disclose it. A further implication is that ASD may be an episodic disorder if symptom severity is close to the threshold at which impairment is caused.

Social situations which are stressful are likely to be those in which there is substantial social interaction required, with groups and not just individuals, where expectations are implicit and not explicit, and where tasks and performance criteria may suddenly and unexpectedly change.

A two factor model

There is accumulating evidence that at least some (3–25%) young children with an ASD 'recover', mostly in response to intensive behavioural training.[12] Recovery was defined by Helt *et al.* as 'entering the normal range of cognitive, adaptive, and social skills', although it did not exclude 'residual vulnerabilities in higher-order communication and attention'.[12a]

ASD develops typically in infancy. It impacts on all social interactions – in Chapter 5, it is argued that its fundamental symptoms are the consequences of an impairment in nonverbal communication and therefore the glue of social interaction – and therefore on social development and its cognitive consequences. If intensive behavioural intervention can push even a small minority of children with an ASD back on to a normal path of social development, this suggests that the usual consequences of ASD involve not only the primary impairment but also the accumulated consequences of pursuing an uncorrected, idiosyncratic social developmental path.

It is generally assumed that ADHD remits after childhood, but ASD does not. The facts are against this. In one large study, the likelihood of future social recovery with the disappearance of the typical phenotype was greater in 12-year-old children with an ASD than for those with ADHD.[13]

Advantages to society in ASD and ADHD
ASD

It is clear from the foregoing that the ASDs are not simply a social construction. There is overwhelming evidence that there is an unusual brain organization linked to them that differs from the neurotypical brain. People with this brain organization often experience social disadvantage, although this may be variable, and is influenced by environmental factors.

Could it be that under some environmental circumstances, the ASDs are actually advantageous to humankind? If they were, it would go some way to explaining the persistence of the genome or genomes that dispose to them.

Autism spectrum disorder is not an uncommon condition, affecting perhaps as many as 1 per cent of the population. ASD is highly hereditary, and yet many people with an ASD remain childless throughout their lives. What is it that maintains the genetic disposition in the population? There may be several explanations for this, including the effect of increased paternal age in increasing mutations in spermatozoa, but 'balanced selection' is another possibility. 'Balanced selection' means that the genetic advantage of heterozygosity leads to a selection pressure to conserve the genes or the liability to copy number variation that lead to ASD, which is opposed by the reproductive disadvantage of a person who is homozygous for these genes. If heterozygotes are more frequent than homozygotes, there will be a level of conservation of the genes at which the two selection pressures are balanced.[14]

Heterozygotes are likely to have some features or 'traits' of ASD without having the full syndrome. ASD 'traits' are much more common than cases of ASD, and it has been suggested that they do confer some reproductive advantage that ensures the survival of the genes predisposing to the full condition, although traits are also associated with an increased risk of depression, anxiety and interpersonal difficulties.[11] Possible advantages might be a superior ability at mathematics, physics, or related subjects requiring 'systemizing',[15] or an ability to develop circumscribed skills to a superior level ('savant' skills). 'Savant' abilities might be particularly linked to a disposition to restricted and repetitive behaviours,[16] which people with an ASD often have, along with children at risk of obsessive compulsive disorder or anorexia nervosa. An alternative explanation is that savants are able to dispense with higher level processing, and thus find quicker and less effortful methods of performing the mental operations connected with savant skills like 'calendrical calculation' (see also Chapter 7).[17]

People with ASD are superior at visual searching than neurotypicals.[18] In addition, I have speculated that AS, and possibly ASD traits, may confer a particular ability to interface with control systems, and therefore with electronic devices like computers.[19] This fits in with a speculation by some people with AS that they are the next evolutionary stage of humankind.

ADHD

Many people with ADHD have a polymorphism of the dopamine transporter gene (DAT1) that reduces dopaminergic transmission in nucleus accumbens,[20] and is associated with more reward hunger and greater reward seeking behaviour, including frequent sexual intercourse.[21] This in itself might have ensured the reproductive preservation of this gene, but it may also confer evolutionary advantage in other ways. It has been argued that people with ADHD have faster response times, which would have ensured better defence against predators, better hunting performance, more effective territorial defence and a greater capacity for mobility and settling.[22]

However, the disposition to risk-taking, also associated with ADHD, leads to an increase in accidents that may limit survival into adult life, and may have reduced the selection advantage of ADHD in more settled social groups although not in groups moving into new environments. Williams *et al.* imagined a hunter-gatherer group, and the benefits of having members who are unusually, and riskily, inquisitive – another behavioural trait of ADHD.[23] They concluded that there would be an ideal proportion of such risk takers, who would have a higher mortality, and other less curious, and more conservative, members of society. Risk takers would be more able to find novel sources of food, especially during migration when old food sources would no longer be accessible. Their speculation was limited by a lack of information about the reproductive success of people with ADHD but speculated that the ADHD genes may be conserved at the present levels (a prevalence of between 5 and 10 per cent of the population meet diagnostic criteria for ADHD, they argue – but see Chapter 9) by a selection balance between the benefits and the costs of risk-taking.[24]

Socioeconomic factors and ASD

There is a correlation between psychiatric disorder, ASD and socioeconomic disadvantage,[25] but this is attributable to the increase in psychiatric disorder attributable to socioeconomic disadvantage: ASD prevalence is not affected by familial socioeconomic status.[26] However, ascertainment is. The age at which ASD is diagnosed in Taiwan,[27] and in the US,[23] is later in more rural areas, and in families who are more socially deprived.

Ethnic factors and ASD

Ethnicity, like socioeconomic status, is not related to the prevalence of ASD but ascertainment is, with lower rates of ascertainment in ethnic minority groups, although these rates can be increased to that in the ethnic majority by the use of structured instruments.[28] Evidence reviewed in Chapter 9 suggests that the children of parents from the Caribbean who emigrate to the UK have an increased risk of ASD.

Social factors affecting the symptom profile of ASD

The expression of disorder is influenced by the presence or absence of co-morbidity, by personal factors, by social circumstances, and by culture.

All of the ASDs are associated with an increased risk of co-morbid conditions. Epilepsy, learning difficulties, other neurological disorders, other conditions associated with the factors causing the ASD – for example, other conditions associated with placental insufficiency if that is implicated in a particular person – and the degree of overlap between one ASD and another, may all affect presentation and course. These issues are addressed in the later clinical chapters (Chapters 12 to 17) as the effects of co-morbidity vary according to age group.

Pathoplastic effects of temperament

Personal factors include coping styles, life experience and character. Only character has been much studied. However, character itself is a composite that may include some developmental characteristics, and many of these studies cannot be applied directly to the clinical situation. Moreover, temperament is influenced by life experience, and that of people with both ASD and ADHD may be negative, either because of bullying (considered below) or simply because of difficulties in fitting in because of the disorder itself.[29, 30]

Schwartz *et al.* used a self-report measure of temperament, measuring extroversion, negative emotionality, effortful control, and agreeableness/adaptability (from the revised Early Adolescent Temperament Questionnaire of Ellis and Rothbart), measures of autistic symptoms, and a measure that parents completed to rate their child's social and emotional functioning.[31] They compared 44 young people (aged 8 to 16) with AS with 38 typically developing young people, and found that surgency and effortful control were correlated with better social and behavioural scores, from which they concluded that self-control made a contribution, independent of the autistic syndrome, to outcome.[31] However, they recognized that there may have been potential confounds in co-morbid anxiety disorder or ADHD.

Clinical experience confirms that personal factors do affect outcome, and two of the most important are friendliness and the absence of hostility.

Schizoid personality disorder and ASD

The overlap between schizoid personality disorder and AS has led to suggestions that the two conditions are one and the same,[32] an argument that was more persuasive when there was thought to be a link between schizophrenia and autism (which for a period was re-termed 'early childhood schizophrenia') on the one hand, and between schizoid personality and schizophrenia on the other. The schizoid personality of Kretschmer and other German psychiatrists, whose definition was used by Wolff and her collaborators,[33] has been replaced in ICD-10 and DSM-IV by two diagnostic categories: schizoid and schizotypal. Schizoid personality disorder as now defined is close to Fairbairn's original description,[34] and is a disorder associated with shame- and anxiety-proneness leading to the avoidance of situations that may provoke social comparisons, social withdrawal, and difficulty in making emotional commitments. Schizoid personality traits may overlap with the premorbid symptoms of schizophrenia, provoking further diagnostic confusion. Schizoid traits were common in one sample of people with AS,[35] possibly because they are more at risk of failures in early relationships with carers, and therefore of 'avoidant' ('dismissive') attachment.[36] But schizoid personality disorder is a description of emotional style, and could therefore be applied to anyone, irrespective of his or her communicative impairment or lack of it. It is therefore unlikely that there is a causal link between ASD and schizoid personality, only a contingent one.

Schizotypal personality disorder presents a rather different problem. Its characteristics potentially include communicative impairment ('inappropriate or constricted affect' is one criterion, 'appearance that is odd, eccentric, or peculiar' is part of another) as well as odd beliefs that might be difficult to distinguish from the idiosyncratic, though rational, beliefs that people with ASD might have, and odd thinking and speech that could easily be the label placed on the pragmatically impaired speech of many people with AS. In fact, the other criteria – lack of close friends, social anxiety, suspiciousness of other people, and even ideas of reference (which encompasses the sensitive ideas of many adolescents with social phobia) might all occur in people with an ASD who have secondary anxiety. ASD is an excluded diagnosis for schizotypal personality disorder. That is, if ASD is diagnosed, schizotypal personality disorder should not be. But mild expressions of ASD may go unrecognized, particularly if they present in adulthood. Esterberg used the Autism Diagnostic Interview (ADI) to probe the parents of adolescents with a diagnosis of schizotypal personality disorder for symptoms of ASD in these adolescents childhood, and found that many did have such symptoms.[37] The most parsimonious explanation is that Wolff was partly right, and some adolescents diagnosed as having schizotypal personality disorder, but not those diagnosed as having schizoid personality disorder, have ASD that has been misdiagnosed.

Social and familial influences on the expression of ASD

Clinical experience is that although friendly families sometimes have friendly children, the negative experiences that people with an ASD have with their peers may easily break this transmission. Values may be more robust, and families that emphasize prosocial behaviour do influence the attitudes and beliefs of their children. This may not hold true for those children who feel particularly powerless in adolescence, and blame others for their social exclusion (see the discussion of atypical AS in Chapter 16). Parental attributions of the causes of asocial behaviour in children with ADHD may also influence how disruptive that behaviour is.[38] Caucasian parents may be more likely to consider biological or medical explanations.[39] Fathers are more likely to make moral judgements, and mothers to seek neutral ways to manage the behaviour.[40]

Peer influences on the expression of AS or ADHD

Many parents have experienced a young adolescent with an ASD adopting behaviour or bad habits from other young people, often choosing those behaviours or habits that are particularly upsetting to others.

The imitation may apparently be because the young person sees the effectiveness – or at least the outrage – that the imitated behaviour causes, and wants to be able to reproduce it. Or it may be because a social group, usually itself a marginalized one, offers a place to the young person but expects some extreme or antisocial behaviour to justify the place.

People with AS or ADHD may also buy themselves into social groups, either by paying for drink, sweets or other goods, or by doing favours, including sexual favours, or by playing the fall guy in criminal or other antisocial activities.

This situation may easily open the young person to exploitation in which others make use of this willingness to victimize themselves, augmenting it by pretending a friendliness or trustworthiness that their intended victim cannot see through.

Social dominance, power and authority

Interpersonal relations are determined by competition, as well as by affiliation.[41] An adequate degree of dominance, as well as an adequate amount of affiliation, is necessary for satisfactory relationships. Sometimes called self-efficacy,[42] or social influencing power,[43] it is a consequence of social status as well as the possession of social skills, including persuasion, conflict management and negotiation. Self-efficacy is linked to mutual trust in friendships and self-confidence, but is inversely correlated with autistic traits.[44] Young people with ADHD, similarly, lack social status and have more negative than positive influence over others.[45]

Anger, aggression and violence

Anger is a universal emotion, triggered by conflict (sometimes called aggressive anger) or threat (sometimes called defensive anger). It is associated with a characteristic arousal pattern largely mediated by the sympathetic nervous system and including both noradrenergic and cholinergic (for example, in piloerection) effectors. This arousal is not specific to anger but is a more general reflex preparatory to action, being active, for example, in predators during feeding attacks. However, predation is not triggered by threat but by hunger and, possibly, other desires as evinced, some suppose, by foxes who will kill all the hens in a hen house even though they may carry only one off to eat.

Whether the arousal is the defining characteristic of anger or whether it is the action tendency to which it is linked is the basis for the disagreement about emotions between James and Lange on the one hand, and Cannon on the other.[46] In fact, they are so closely linked that the distinction has little value. The action tendency to which action leads is attack and is common to both anger and predation in predators.

Sympathetic arousal is associated with an increase in blood pressure and increased skin blood flow, leading to one of the inadvertent signs of anger, going red. The distribution of the erythema is the same as that of embarrassment with flushing of the face and upper chest. However, the characteristic action tendencies are different. In anger the tendency is to go forward into someone's territory or space, and the red, jutting face of the colonel whose face is bristling because of piloerection is the human expression of the angry dominant primate. As well as jutting the face forwards and staring, sometimes with the eyes actually bulging, an opponent's space is invaded by reducing interpersonal distance. Raising the volume of the voice enables auditory intrusion, and an outpouring of strong-smelling sebaceous sweat is an intrusion into the olfactory domain. Angry feelings include the perception of these bodily changes: people feel hopping mad, or red with rage, 'in your face' or even they just 'see red', but these feelings may get caught up with desires or fantasies like wanting to smash someone's face, feeling an urge to pick something up and throw it, and so on. Other signals of anger include intention movements such as balling the fist, in animals that hit with their fists, or baring the teeth, in animals that bite.

Anger may also be expressed by characteristic displays, including the brow lowering, the jaw clenching, and the corners of the mouth dropping, a characteristic vocalization like a snarl, and a variety of conventional displays, for example giving someone the finger or swearing at them.

Anger and status

Anger is a social emotion, and is therefore closely linked to social factors, such as status. Social status or standing is rooted in who one chooses to stand with. At the level of relationship, this is influenced by liking or affiliation. At the level of acquaintanceship, this is linked to power or influence. One wants to stand with the person who can offer the most protection or give the best guidance. Where physical proximity is limited, for example in a classroom, high status children get looked at more than low status children. They get more attention. Low status individuals are sometimes considered to envy this and be motivated by 'attention-seeking', although this assumes that angry attention is equivalent to admiring attention, which seems unlikely.

High status animals guard groups, including groups of females; the larger the group that is guarded, for example the larger the harem, the more status the individual needs to have and demonstrably does have. However, as well as guarding against outside threats, high status animals guard against internal threats. In apes, dominant or alpha males chase away those greedy individuals who want more of the common resource of food than is their due, although subdominant males may gang up and displace dominant males who become oppressive.[47]

Dominant males may get their pick of food and access to females, but the pay-off for the group may be that intra-group fighting or conflict is minimized. Thomas Hobbes speculated that this is why human groups are so ready to make themselves subservient to kings and other tyrants.[48]

The behaviour of many animal species is constrained by dominance hierarchies. People, including people with an ASD, are more alert to facial expressions of anger than to other emotions,[49] possibly because these signals bid for dominance or at least challenges that could lead to changes in dominance.

Assertion and anger

A distinction is sometimes made between being assertive and being angry. In assertiveness training, people are shown how to be assertive without having to be angry. Assertiveness is potential anger that is locked into having a higher status or rank than someone else. Pulling rank on someone else works only while that someone else is recognizing the legitimacy of the rank, that is the person shares the social assumptions on which the rank is based. If this is repudiated, assertiveness can lead only to backing down, or getting angry. Assertiveness training may therefore be based on the false assumption that people have status, but fail to use it. Although this may be the case, most unassertive people's claim to status is rejected by others, and they have to become angry to make their impact, or they are afraid that if they do get into a fight, they will be defeated and so they back down.

How is anger switched off?

Some emotions, like happiness, are typically fleeting. Others, like anger, may persist for as long as the conflict or the threat lasts. Persistent anger, or hostility, increases coronary artery disease in people if it is associated with defeat.[50] Once anger leads to overt fighting there are further costs, including mortality in fights such as wars, bar brawls, domestic altercations and suicide. Evolutionary psychologists have argued that the mortality in young males attributable to fighting may have little social disadvantage, as only a small number of males are required to inseminate the population of females. Some mammals even take advantage of this, living in small groups of several females with one dominant male who drives out successive generations of sons, who may become loners or band together in loose peer groups unless they can displace a dominant male in another group. This arrangement is possible only in widely dispersed social groups, such as the 'wild west'. It is not appropriate for towns and cities, that is for civilization. People with anger problems including people with an ASD may be drawn to wilderness living, but many people with an ASD rely on other people in other ways and have to find ways of switching aggression off.

If, as the previous paragraphs suggest, winning, although it works for the victor, does not work for the vanquished in large and interdependent societies, what alternatives are there?

Anger and fear, dominance and submission

Fights can be averted by appeasement. In many animals, this involves signalling a loss of status relative to the aggressor. Submission is a common method of averting aggression in primates, including people. Human submission displays include lowering the gaze and the head, even falling to one's knees (all of these gestures have been incorporated into courtly protocol by many monarchs), conciliatory touching, and apologizing while lauding the strength or wisdom of the opponent. In chimpanzees the absence of counter-aggressive intent includes movements that increase vulnerability to attack, such as baring the throat.

If anger is the emotion associated with offence, then fear is the emotion associated with submission. Submission may be generalized, when an individual submits to a whole group. The particular kind of anxiety associated with this is 'shame'.

When submission fails in dealing with someone with an ASD

Overpowering is a common method for fathers to deal with threats from other males, including their sons. This may seem surprisingly successful when the child is young and physically vulnerable, and may be one reason that fathers often experience their sons with an ASD or ADHD as being more neurotypical than do their mothers. However, as the child with ASD gets older and falls behind in the acquisition of the rituals of submission, fathers may find their absence increasingly threatening. He never apologizes, he just carries on grinning, or he just doesn't know where to draw the line or when I'm getting to the end of my tether, are all things that fathers say. Later on, the father's physical dominance may no longer be enough to face their child down, and it is the father, not the child, who might submit. Fathers who model this kind of conflict management strategy are more likely to have sons who use it, too, and physical aggression during the teenage years may as a result be more frequent. Repeated submission, particularly if it is shaming, can lead to a disposition to experience shame, or low self-esteem, that may be countered by being more than usually quick to take offence, and more than usually ready to escalate conflict into violence.

Submitting to people with an ASD as a policy is no more successful than always submitting to anyone else, however unreasonable. It places the person with ASD in a position of perpetual dominance and this predisposes to tyranny. Even though few people with ASD are tyrannical over other people's respect, love or agreement, there is a significant risk of people with an ASD being tyrannical about rituals, routines or prohibitions.

Case examples

Frank was easily upset by disorder, but he got comfort from routines. His parents ran a restaurant, and for a few weeks they were pleased that he would go into the room in which they stored the cutlery for the tables, and arrange it. However, one day, he was not finished when the staff came to lay the tables and he got worked up when his parents asked him to stop. So they told the staff to get on with other jobs. Over the next weeks, Frank's ordering became more complex and the staff was more and more delayed in being able to get the cutlery. Came the day, when Frank forbade them to, as it would mess up his order. There was an aggressive confrontation during which Frank stabbed himself with a knife, although not seriously. His parents went out and bought a duplicate set of cutlery for the restaurant, and told the staff to lay the tables using the new set that they stored in the kitchen. It was inconvenient, but anything to avoid a further confrontation. But then, Frank found out about the new stock and insisted that he should check that, too.

Arthur may have found blond hair sexy; he certainly liked to stroke it. One day, a staff member objected to him doing so, and Arthur bit her. He began to bite any blond staff member, and the management decided to order that only non-blond staff should have any personal contact with him. But then Arthur began to stroke the hair of young female staff who were brunette, too.

When submission fails in dealing with neurotypicals

Agonistic conflict resolution proceeds by moves, or displays. Many of these are acquired socially. When to call someone out, what words to use, what epithets are strong enough and which too strong, how to make use of allies – all of these are as applicable to the playground, at least for boys, as they are for chimps. More often than not people with an ASD will not have a secure enough grasp of these rules to know how to call an offender to account, and how to split them from their allies so that they can be dominated, and made to submit. More often than not people with an ASD will experience anger when they have been offended against, but will not display aggression or try to make the offender submit. The anger will therefore persist, and will be discharged as attack and not in an agonistic display. This may mean that someone else, in some other time and place, may suddenly be hit or punched.

Placation

Chimpanzees are omnivores, who use tools, make war and peace, and live in organized societies. Their genome is closer to the human one than it is to any other organism, bar one (but see below). Not surprisingly, they have been used as models of humanity. The concept of a 'theory of mind' was, for example, first adumbrated in relation to chimpanzees. More recently, mirror neurons found in primates have provided a new model of ASD.[51] Theories about dominance, about violence and about depression have all been based on studies of chimpanzees and some primatological terms have been passed into common parlance about people – 'alpha male' is an example. Chimpanzees, according to one philosopher, have minds in Brentano's sense of being able to deal with intentionality, although they do so gesturally rather than conceptually,[52] leading this philosopher to a similar position to that of myself, that the fundamental deficit in the ASDs is a disorder of social orienting.

Chimpanzees are dangerous animals to human handlers, and models of violence based on chimpanzee evidence have tended to stress the potential for violence, and the need for its constant suppression, often by individuals of superior status. 'Pygmy chimpanzees' or bonobos provide a rather different perspective on our primate heritage. Violence is less common in bonobo groups than in chimpanzees.[53] Bonobos, Pan paniscus, although closely related to chimpanzees (Pan troglodytes), are smaller and live in a circumscribed area south of the Congo River. Bonobo females may be dominant over males, and bonobos live in groups that are, unusually, composed of related males and unrelated females: it is the young females and not the males who leave the family group to join an unrelated group at puberty.[54] Bonobo social development takes longer than chimpanzees,[55] and bonobos play in a more human-like way than chimpanzees with human children.[56] One bonobo, Kanzi, can use 200 words, having acquired these by watching his mother being taught, without success, to use a keyboard.

Bonobos manage conflict peacefully more often than chimpanzees. This is because bonobos are more ready to switch from fight/flight or approach/avoidance social dimensions to affiliation or 'tend and befriend' dimensions,[57] the latter being what in humans would be called 'placation'. The switch may be mediated by oxytocin and vasopressin (see Chapter 11). Placation in bonobos involves some kind of pleasuring, which may be sexual (adult bonobos may have homosexual and heterosexual intercourse many times a day), but may also be offering food, grooming, or even tickling. Bonobos manage conflict by anticipating status threats and providing affiliative compensation – 'placation' – before the threat becomes actual, thus preventing anger reaching a level where it becomes self-sustaining. Doing this, however, requires a higher level of interaction and a greater use of affective and cognitive empathy.

When placation fails in dealing with someone with an ASD

Placation may fail because it is dismissed as a strategy ('You are just indulging him', a person might say), because it is applied too late, often because the earliest signs of anger have not been shown in a way or in a context in which they might be recognized and so the opportunity for placation was missed, or because it is not followed by dialogue. Anger revives if the cause of the anger persists, or if the person has not been able to voice the complaint that provoked the anger in the first place.

When placation fails in dealing with neurotypicals

Placation is a particularly difficult challenge for low status boys, as it is easily misperceived as submission. It requires a high level of empathy, and is therefore difficult for many people with an ASD. Submission reduces status further, whereas placation may increase it. Submitting in one situation makes it more likely that submission will be required in another. Many children with ASD try to use placation as a means of averting conflict, for example by buying sweets for peers, 'playing the fool', or doing dares. However, these often lead to further loss of status and an increase rather than a decrease in aggression towards them.

Placation presents the further challenge that it requires setting aside the placator's feelings – which are often angry ones – to focus on those of the person being placated. Self-control of this kind presupposes the development of cognitive empathy and of its substrate in the frontal lobes.[58] Children with ADHD may therefore find placation particularly difficult.

Dialogue

Even if anger is turned aside in some way, it will recur unless the underlying conflict is resolved. Resolution may happen spontaneously. Anger at a sudden change of plan may melt away with time. But more often anger is revived if the underlying issue is not resolved. Dialogue about the cause of the anger is therefore normally required to prevent this recrudescence. Having difficulty in formulating a grievance might be expected to increase the risk of aggression, and generalized learning disability or language disorder are, with ADHD, the three greatest risk factors for aggression in children.

Anticipation

Anticipation of anger and the early application of restitution or propitiation, if occurring early enough, can turn anger off, well before it leads to aggression or violence, assuming that others are willing and able to propitiate. Individuals may also suppress anger if they anticipate that other people may react in a negative way to it. Both kinds of anticipation draw on cognitive empathy, and adolescent, neurotypical frontal lobe function.[58]

Violence inhibition

Once a violent attack has been launched, it is desirable that it is terminated as quickly as possible. The submission/fear response typically does that,[59] amounting to a 'violence inhibitory inhibitory mechanism'.[60] Recent evidence supports this. Children considered to have callous-unemotional traits are worse than peers at detecting fearful facial expressions, whereas antisocial behaviour was associated with impaired anger detection, although undiminished (in fact heightened) fear detection. Abused children are better at identifying fear and sadness.[61] The amygdalae play a key role in coordinating responses to fear, including others' expressions of fear. One study summarizes the current thinking on violence inhibition, and suggests the existence of two pathways. In summary, it is proposed that rapid detection of negative expression causes the activation of the left amygdala, leading to an aggressive response. But slower processing, involving the fusiform cortex, inhibits right amygdala activation and this inhibits anger.[62] This is consistent with the increased aggression associated with blunted fear responses either as a result of experience (the most likely explanation in the sample of Leist and Dadds,[63] or in ASD, where it may result from a primary disorder of emotional contagion.[64]

Social factors affecting the quality of life of people with ASD
Marginalization

Quality of life is impaired, compared to neurotypical peers, in people with AS.[65] Although the symptoms of autistic disorder are more severe than those of AS, the quality of life of people with Asperger syndrome may be worse than it is for people with autistic disorder.[66] A likely reason for this is that people with AS compare themselves unfavourably to others.[67]

Many young people with AS are observers, rather than participants, from an early age. Young people with ADHD tend to participate, but sometimes in a way that others see as rough, or one-sided. Marginalization of both people with AS or ADHD often begins from the age of eight, although it may be later. It usually intensifies from the age of 11 on, possibly because that coincides with the change from primary to secondary school, although the onset of puberty, the development of same sex peer groups, and an increasing emphasis on popularity and social competency may all play a part. Once established, loneliness often persists throughout life, along with feeling disconnected from other people.[68] In people with ASD, the quality of relationship with a best friend is the strongest corollary of loneliness,[69] but in ADHD, loneliness at home and paternal warmth are both factors that strongly influence the quality of peer relationships.[70]

Loneliness, further social withdrawal and anxiety – often social anxiety – are interrelated. In one study of 'experimentally induced' ostracism, adolescents with ASD experienced an increase in anxiety, an increase in shame, and a reduction in mastery, belonging, and in the sense that life has meaning.[71] This triad contributes to the social disability produced by the AS,[72] possibly accounting for almost as much as the AS itself in adolescence. Even if a young person with ASD does not experience loneliness, they may often be marginalized.[73]

Marginalization in neurotypicals reduces altruism.[74] Loneliness also normally increases a focus on others' distress, and reduces the rewards of social interaction.[75] So some of the asocial behaviours of people with an ASD may be consequences of their treatment by others, and not of the condition itself.

Loneliness

Weiss made an important distinction between emotional and social loneliness.[76] Emotional loneliness refers to the feeling of a lack of attachment, of not mattering to another person as an individual; social loneliness to the feeling of being out of the social circle, having no social role, place or influence. Emotional loneliness is the consequence of a lack of affiliates, social loneliness of a lack of social efficacy. People with an ASD may experience both forms of loneliness. Although the two are usually linked in practice, it can be helpful to keep the distinction in mind when providing advice, counselling or treatment. One of the reasons that bullying can have such devastating consequences is that it is an attack both on emotional attachments to others, and on social influence.

Friendship

Friendships counteract emotional isolation, and are a context in which social influence can be honed. They influence attitudes, beliefs and habits, and provide models on which a person can pattern themselves. Friends, by definition, share, and are therefore open to social influence by each other. Friendships are shaped by how much influence one or other of the friends can exert.

At one time, it was thought that people with an ASD were unable to make friends. This was attributed to coldness and aloofness in people with ASD, and to belligerence in people with ADHD. It is true that sociability does determine the interest in making friends, and sociability may be reduced in people with ASD (see the discussion of schizoidia in Chapter 8), but sociability is by no means always reduced in a person with ASD. People with an ASD have difficulty in making friends, but may be able to overcome it. Making friends is anyway easier in early childhood when social expectations are much less. So having had friends is not inconsistent with a diagnosis of an ASD. Loneliness increases as people get older, when the social demands of one friend by another increase, and when social conformity becomes a factor in the choice of friend.

In an informal analysis of cases seen in my practice, social adjustment was correlated with exposure to peer relationships more than to symptom severity. It may be that there is no direct relationship between the two, but that both reflect some underlying trait of sociability. However, clinical experience is that interacting with neurotypicals, so long as it is not abusive or exploitative, does provides people with an ASD with a stimulus towards developing a wider and more representative range of social skills. Bauminger et al. found that a child with an ASD who was friends with a neurotypical showed greater responsiveness, stronger receptive language skills, more prosocial orientation, and more complex coordinated play than a child with an ASD who was friends with another child with a disability.[77] The authors conclude that 'Exposure to typical peers appears to have significant effects on friendship behaviours,'[77a] although it is possible that the reverse is truly the causal relationship, and that children with more effective friendship behaviours are more likely to have neurotypical friends.

Friendships are not always positive because friends cannot always be relied upon to be caring. In one study of adolescents, best friends of the group with AS were of poorer quality than those of the neurotypical comparison group. The adolescents with AS were, not surprisingly, less motivated to seek friendships. Their levels of loneliness and of depressive symptoms correlated inversely with the quality of their best friendships and positively with the levels of conflict and betrayal that were often high in the conduct of the best friends of people with AS.[78] The study supports what people with AS often say in the clinic, that it was only in retrospect that they realized how the people who they thought were friends were actually laughing at them or exploiting them.

Bullying

In one community survey of adolescents and adults, 90 per cent of respondents said that they considered that they had been bullied at some time, and over 30 per cent that they were still being bullied.[79] Similar figures, of 94 per cent being bullied, have been reported in surveys of mothers about their child or adolescent offspring.[80] Having ASD symptoms seems to act as a particular incitement to bullying.[81] In a large study of all children in England and Wales, children with special needs and autism were 7.1 times more likely to be bullied than children without special needs bullying.[82] Almost all young people with ASD are bullied at school, and this is a factor in their avoiding, or being excluded from, areas in school in which many children congregate,[83] and as adults, choose cinemas and libraries at their main community resources.[84]

Bullying in younger children can cause somatic symptoms, anxiety and depression.[85] In adolescence it is a cause of school avoidance, suicidal thoughts and study problems. Later in life it can cause long-term loss of self-esteem, with sensitivity to slights that can lead to problems at home in accepting limit-setting, or with authority in later life. Bullying can also lead to an increase of anxiety, and to school refusal. An alternative response to bullying is to try to pay the bullies back. People with AS are rarely effective at this. The planned retaliation may cause even greater humiliation if it is directed at the bullies themselves. Sometimes people with AS may take out their frustration with bullying on younger children or other more vulnerable targets. This is one factor that can cause problems of aggression in AS (to be discussed below).

Bullying has hit the headlines, but it may seem like yesterday's news, with more emphasis now on youth violence, the low standing of the UK in international tables for quality of life for children, and the risks and consequences of the religious radicalization of young people. However, the reasons that bullying has hit the headlines – its devastating effects on young people and their families, for example – have not gone away. And there may be links between bullying and some of the youth problems that seem more salient at the moment. Bullying may be linked to a culture of violence, and to a lack of resistance to the processes of marginalization. Social disidentification with the majority, something commonly experienced by people with Asperger syndrome who have been bullied, increases the risk of terrorism,[86] and reduces wellbeing. Bullies and bully victims may be more likely to become violent youth.[87] Bullying by teachers, something often reported by young people with Asperger syndrome, is associated with an increased school suspension rate,[88] and suspension may become permanent exclusion, leading to a failed education with all its implications for adult employment and social integration.

The stigma of people with mental health problems begins early, at infant school. This would seem to be a good time to implement preventative measures, but a systematic review of 40 studies of intervention concluded that there were, so far, few conclusions that could be drawn about what works, except that familiarity often reduces stigma, particularly if children act as buddies to someone with a mental health problem. How much teaching about empathy and inclusiveness adds to this is less clear.[89]

CULTURAL FACTORS

ASD symptoms can be recognized in children in every culture, but the threshold at which the signs are considered to be indicative of a disorder varies from one culture to another,[90] as does the expression of associated symptoms.[91] One way of looking at this is that an ASD is an identity to which a child may or may not be assimilated. Adopting the identity leads to societal reactions to that identity, and also changes to the perceived identity of the individual self: to being an 'Aspie', for example.

Cultural factors influence psychological capacities including attention,[92] and empathy. So culture may contribute to the manifestation of ASD. However, in this section, I shall concentrate on cultural influences on identity, a much older and therefore more studied area.

The construction of deviant identities

Sociologists have often been troubled by the possibility that psychological disorders are largely cultural artefacts: that, in other words, the so-called mental illnesses are not illnesses at all, but merely labels into which people who deviate from social norms are shoehorned.[93] The concept of illness is strongest when it approximates to the Virchovian concept of disease:[94] is a reliably reproducible bodily response, or pathology, to specified disease agents, such as toxins or pathological organisms. Although psychiatrists regularly speak of 'psychopathology' and refer to specific causes of psychopathology such as trauma, these are not physical states that any observer can see under the microscope or measure in the blood. Nor are traumata the psychic equivalent to toxins. Nietszche's dictum, 'what does not kill you, makes you strong',[95] might apply to adversity, but not to tuberculosis. ASD does seem disease-like in that many symptoms are qualitatively different from everyday behaviour, and because of its regular association with demonstrable genetic and brain abnormalities, but it too has been criticized as an unhelpful label,[96] and the medical model of ASD has come increasingly under attack. Currently there are many who would like to replace the term 'Autism spectrum disorder' with 'Autism spectrum condition'. ADHD is less obviously disease like, and some have argued that it is a means of pathologizing ethnic or class differences in behaviour.

An alternative approach to deviancy theory is Mechanic's theory of 'illness behaviour'.[97] Mechanic argued that a sickness role was a legitimate social role for anyone who was displaying illness behaviour, so long as this was combined with accepting the authority of socially appointed carers. The sick role therefore carried with it an expectation that a person was relieved of some duties and social obligations in exchange for carrying out the duties and obligations that went with their treatment.[97] There was a corollary expectation that if they did this, they would be more able to take up their obligations later.

It could be argued that both of these models are applicable to ASD. If there are duties that a person can shoulder that will lead to greater social involvement, and reduced illness behaviour, then the Mechanic model applies. For these temporary occupants of the social role, the label or diagnosis of disorder may enable a reduction of social deviance.

In other circumstances, there is no remedial behaviour and no authority to legitimate the illness behaviour. Adopting the sick role reduces social obligation, and therefore social involvement, with no subsequent reversal and recovery. Diagnosis or treatment may be much less appropriate for this group, and for them, the term 'autism spectrum condition' may be more appropriate.

Cultural explanations of the causes of ASD

Explanations of what causes ASD tend to reflect the models of deviancy in the culture. Thus in Nigeria, only 58 per cent of healthcare workers thought that ASD had a natural explanation, and 27 per cent thought that it was supernaturally caused. The assumed aetiology influences beliefs about treatment.[98] In this same study, 55 per cent of health care workers thought that ASD was treatable, and 32 per cent that it was preventable. Direct knowledge of working with a child with ASD altered expectations of treatability and experience of more than five years in this work changed beliefs about prevention.[98]

Normalization

Some of the force of this argument has powered the 'normalization' movement. Normalization is unexceptionable when it claims for people with disabilities that they should have as 'normal' a life as possible. The resulting de-institutionalization has probably increased the quality of life of many people with psychiatric disorders and learning disability, although its impact on people with ASD has not been separately evaluated.

Other aspects of normalization include the use of adoption or fostering as an alternative to children's homes, adult fostering schemes to provide some family life for adults with learning difficulties, buddy and befriending schemes, and 'mainstreaming' young people into 'mainstream' schools and colleges. The potential advantages of this kind of normalization are obvious, but little attention has been paid to any negative consequences although, to the practising clinician, these can be striking.

Normalization as an empirically based practice is one thing, but adherents of normalization have sometimes seen it as a proof that autism can be cured, or even that autism does not exist except in the minds of the people who falsely label others with spurious diagnoses. Normalization can, therefore, arouse considerable passions. On one side are those who want to rescue ordinary people from the perils of being imprisoned in a diagnosis. On the other are the diagnosticians themselves – carers as well as professionals – who feel betrayed by not having their struggles with a 'real' problem validated by a label.

Deviancy theory

There is little evidence that the use of ASD diagnoses does lead to the 'self-fulfilling prophecy',[99] or the secondary deviance that deviancy theory posits as the consequence of labelling, although some evidence that expectancy bias does affect neurotypicals' social interactions.[100] However, most clinicians will be aware of the impact of individual carers' and teachers' expectations on the apparent communicative competence and learning ability of the people with ASD with whom they interact. Some of the variance may be due to skill, some to the communicative ability of the carer or teacher, some to the emotional demands generated by the carer or teacher, but some to their expectations.

Adopting a pathological identity

Deviancy theory predicts not only that societal reaction will push a person towards more deviant action, but also that a person adopts more deviant behaviour in response to the 'anomic' consequences of being disempowered by the label. There is little direct evidence for this, but more evidence of differential association having the consequence of amplifying deviance. Differential association results from individuals who are considered marginal, for example by virtue of having a stigmatized label, associating with other marginalized individuals. There is some evidence of this occurring in adolescence,[101] although it is not clear to what extent the diagnosis contributes to this, and to what extent it is simply due to marginalization occurring spontaneously.

It has been suggested that antisocial behaviour in ADHD before early adolescence occurs solely or mainly in response to stress or provocation, but that after adolescence people with ADHD may initiate antisocial behaviour ('proactive' rather than 'reactive' antisocial behaviour) as a consequence of an identity that includes such antisocial behaviour as a characteristic.[102]

There is often debate between educational psychologists on the one hand, and doctors such as community paediatricians on the other, about whether diagnosis is a good or a bad thing. It is bad if it increases stigma and so increases the marginalization of a young person, and therefore increases the risk of differential socialization. It is good if it helps to explain reactive antisocial behaviour, increases others' ability to deal with it, and reduces rejection and marginalization. It is an empirical question that could readily be tested, but the test has not been done.

Acquiring an identity

Identity is acquired through identification, that is taking on the values and culture of the referent social group in order that people can identify you as being a member of that group. Identity is also used to mean a unique identifier, in recognition perhaps that it is composed of several identifications – for example, I am a father and an insurance salesman. Identifications may be passive, as they are when we put on a uniform, but they are then skin deep. Or they may be enacted with our whole being, so that little gap remains between the enactment (or social role, or social performance, to use different but overlapping metaphors developed by different sociologists) and our being.

People with an ASD seem to have a strong identity to others because of their idiosyncrasies, but they may be unsure themselves who they are, even to the extent of having difficulty acquiring or expressing personal preferences. This is particularly so for people with an ASD. Young people with AS are less likely than a comparison group to remember words that relate to themselves as opposed to words that relate to others.[103] In this study, self-referenced memory performance increased with age in both groups, and was not correlated with theory of mind performance. It was correlated, however, with social problems. Young people with AS had fewer social problems if they had better self-referenced memory.[103]

One reason for a reduced sense of self, that is of identity, may be that people with an ASD may lack a referent group with whom to identify. Identity therefore needs to be created without the benefit of prefabricated models. Referent groups are usually selected from among an acquaintanceship. People with an ASD who may have limited or no face-to-face interactions with groups who might have the potential to be referents, may choose a group that exists as an idea, a virtual group. Sometimes this is a group of marginalized people, with whom the person with AS can identify. Murderers, criminals, the Nazi party or World Wide Wrestlers may all provide groups with which people with an AS want to identify, sometimes because they are powerful as well as being marginalized.

Sexual identity
The lack of identity may also affect gender identity and sexuality. People with an ASD often feel that they are different from others, and this feeling of not belonging in society may not be dissimilar to that of people with a gender identity disorder, who believe that if they were of the opposite gender they would feel at home, but in the gender that is determined by their biological sexuality, they feel alien. A significant minority of people with ASD may develop gender dysphoria,[104] and may seek gender reassignment surgery, hormone treatment or cosmetic treatment of facial hair.[105] Several of those people with AS and gender identity disorder that I have personally assessed have adopted their gender role of choice, and one of them had formed a stable partnership in that gender.

Identity shapes not only gender roles, but also the expression of sexuality. These issues are discussed more in Chapter 15.

Off the peg identity
What constitutes a gender identity is not acquired simply through common sense or through modelling, both processes that may be opaque to people with an ASD, but are explicitly defined in innumerable internet and magazine discussions about what girls do or what boys do. An inability to feel at home in such discussions may be a reason that people with AS are drawn to gender dysphoria as an exploration of their ill-defined sense of being different from others.

There are other identities which are explicitly defined that may be attractive to people with an ASD, and that can also account for the sense of difference. Some are deviant identities, others are persecuted identities; others are out of place, or out of time. People with AS may feel at home within strong but marginalized religious movements or cults, model themselves on people from another culture or from countries they have never visited, or identify with their parents' generation, listening to the pop songs or dressing as if they belong to that generation and not their own.

These explicit identities are 'off the peg' in that they do not need to be constructed, but can simply be adopted. In recent years, as more people have recognized that they have AS, new 'off the peg' identities have developed, which are more AS friendly. These include being a 'nerd' or a 'geek', or even being an 'Aspie'. These identities have often been created, at least in part, on the internet. There are Aspie bulletin boards, websites and discussion forums, and an Aspie island in the virtual world, 'Second life'. Sociologists dealing with ethnic minorities term the adoption of an appropriate minority culture as 'enculturation' and contrast it with 'acculturation', in which minority groups are compelled to adopt the identity of the majority culture. In a study of one such ethnic minority, acculturation led to more substance misuse, less happiness and more psychosocial stress than enculturation.[106] If this also applies to people with AS, then Aspie-dom and other enculturating influences for people with AS are likely to provide mental health benefits.

The internet also offers the possibility of virtual identities in which a person can claim an identity that is discrepant from one that they might realistically claim in reality.

Family interaction

Many people with an ASD avoid social interaction, including family interaction, particularly at times when conversational load is highest, for example at meal times. In one study, 20 families with one child with autism and 10 families with neurotypical children were videotaped at meal times. The children with autism acted as conversation stoppers, making fewer bids for interactions, commenting less often, dropping conversational turns more often, and responding less to bids for interaction. Many young people with an ASD spend most of their time in their bedroom, sometimes venturing downstairs only to watch television, when social interaction is a minimum. Many young people with an ASD have tense relationships with one parent, often fathers, and this can lead to conflict between parents. If father has an ASD himself, the reverse may occur, and there may be a bond between child and father, although this may, so far as mother is concerned, lead to an excessive permissiveness and a reduction in the expectations of normal socialization.

Female members of the family may be more understanding but paradoxically this may lead to more aggression towards them, possibly as a way of reducing social demand. Mothers are often the target of displaced aggression. Many people with ASD are aware of the potential for others to retaliate and this may be one reason that mothers, and not fathers, become targets. Younger siblings or sisters of any age may also be targets. Sometimes the aggression is triggered, although remotely by frustration at some other agonistic encounter. At other times, it may be continual. In these cases, ADHD is more likely to be the main or co-morbid diagnosis.

Some people with ASD are more than usually gentle, either some of the time – when this state can be interspersed by periods of 'losing it' or 'getting wound up' – or all of the time. A close relationship may grow up with one or both parents in this situation, and this may last longer into adult life than would normally be the case with neurotypical grown-up children.

Family members may feel guilt, often inappropriately, that they have been unable to save the person with ASD either from their condition, or from the bullying or marginalization of other people. This may be compounded by criticism, either perceived or actual, from other people that they have failed as parents, or accusations that they were exaggerating their child's difficulties. The accusations of exaggerated or inappropriate help-seeking often precede diagnosis and are one reason that parents are often so keen to obtain a diagnosis. In this situation of the family against a hostile world (or sometimes, one parent and the children against the other parent and the hostile world), 'enmeshment' may occur. Enmeshment means that the parent believes that they know their child's needs without the child needing to articulate them; that other people who believe they also know the child's needs are a potential threat; and that the parent's life has to be put on hold until their child has got these needs met. This is a particularly difficult situation when the child is thought to need services that are unavailable, or care that goes beyond the professional.

Siblings may be neglected as a result of having a child with an ASD in the family, but can make an important contribution to the development of their affected sibling. In one study, adolescents with an ASD experienced greater social support, and gained more emotion-focused and fewer problem-focused coping strategies from a sibling than from a parent. This was most true of a girl with an ASD and a sister, and least true of a boy with ASD and a sister. However, the amount of time together and the amount of positive feeling in the relationship was in inverse proportion to the number of behavioural problems shown by the adolescent with the ASD.[107]

Chapter 5

SOCIAL ORIENTATION, COMMUNICATION AND LANGUAGE

SOCIAL ORIENTATION

Looking preferentially at human faces, or picking human voices out of ambient sound for particular attention, are requirements if infants are to communicate with their parents. Both are probably innate and reflexive responses, which become shaped by experience. Infants show a preference for looking at other children, rather than geometric shapes (although this preference is reversed in children with an ASD).[1] The orientation is not under conscious control, and indeed most of the time people are unaware of it happening. However, occasionally the orientation recruits prefrontal conscious attention areas to enable further processing, such as when one catches someone saying one's name in a hubbub, or when someone is staring at oneself from a crowd.[2]

Eye orientation

Interest in the eyes is common to many vertebrates, many of whom interpret direct gaze from another animal, to be threatening, whether or not a conspecific. Gaze has evolved to have an additional directional function in primates,[3] crows and parrots, in that conspecifics preferentially look in the direction of each other's gaze. Orientation to and by the eyes of other people has become particularly important in humans,[4] and by four months infants are able to scan right-way-up pictures of faces much faster than inverted faces, and to respond to their apparent direction of gaze.[5] As children get older, parents can direct or elicit the gaze of their own children independently of other children, even in groups of children playing together,[6] using pointing or verbalization, but based on gaze.[6]

Mutual gaze is threatening in non-human primates, and results in either a fight or a submission display. Humans may be unique in being able to learn, within the first few months of life, to find mutual gaze rewarding under particular circumstances,[7] thus enabling mutual gaze to be used in a signalling role.[8] Averted gaze and mutual gaze both result in right superior temporal sulcus activation, but in slightly different areas. Looking at pictures of eyes also results in activation of inferior occipital gyri, fusiform gyri and inferior frontal gyrus.[9] Direct gaze evokes a stronger orienting response (as shown by a negative wave at around 170 milliseconds, or N170) on EEG, and spreads to areas of the brain that are activated during 'theory of mind' tasks (see Chapter 6).[10] Being looked at increases the tendency to imitate the person doing the looking in neurotypicals, but not in children with ASD.[11]

I have argued elsewhere that impairment of gaze orientation may be fundamental to the ASDs,[12] an argument that has also been made by others much more recently,[13] and there is evidence that gaze produces a reduced orientation response, as estimated by a positive wave at 400 milliseconds (P400) in the evoked potential, in people with an ASD and even in their siblings,[14] suggesting that there may be a hereditary basis to this. Neurotypical children are better at detecting direct gaze than averted gaze, but this is not true of children with an ASD.[15] People with ASD, unlike neurotypicals, do not give preferential attention to faces when working out depictions of complex social situations.[16]

Gaze following

Following in the direction of averted gaze provides important information about what others are looking at. This may identify a potential food source, or a potential threat, but in people it may also provide information about another person's thoughts.[17] Neurotypical children and adults, as well as people with an ASD, reflexively or 'covertly' follow the direction of gaze of others' eyes,[18, 19] but the accuracy of doing this is reduced in people with ASD, possibly because they spend less time looking at the other person's eyes before tracking away in the apparent gaze direction.[20] Children who reflexively orientate to other people's gaze learn to use other cues to orientation, including head posture and the point, most often made with a finger or an arm, but possibly with any part of the body that has a defined axis.

Having learnt to follow points, children learn to attract other people's gaze or attention by showing; for example, in a face-to-face encounter with a parent who is spooning food into the child, the child may lift up a spoon or a cup. By the age of 12 months, children are beginning to use the point themselves to direct other's attention by that means.[21] This kind of point – proto-declarative pointing – is distinct from pointing that is an extension of the reach, and used to show what one wants ('proto-imperative' pointing). If anything it is a kind of imitation of gaze, and not surprisingly involves activation of the frontal lobes,[22] where gaze control is situated.

Inference from gaze or movement direction
Gaze direction

Crows and parrots, along with great apes and humans, can deduce not only the direction of a conspecific's gaze, but also that the gaze can be impeded by an object that is not in the line of sight of the observing bird but is in the line of sight of the bird being observed. Crows and parrots can therefore know when something is hidden from a conspecific that is visible to them. Bonobos are the most like humans in following gaze, and will repeatedly turn their gaze on to an apparent barrier in the view of a person with whom they are interacting and who appears to be trying to look through the barrier.[23]

This may, or may not, be related to 'perspective taking', the situation when people say that 'they can see her point of view', or 'she changed her perspective after he had explained how he saw things'. Perspective taking is required in situations other than when empathizing with others, as the case history demonstrates.

Case history: Roger

Roger could not fit in, and his mother thought she knew why after seeing a television programme about Asperger syndrome. Her subsequent reading further heightened her suspicions that Roger had this disorder and she sought out a specialist who could make the diagnosis one way or another. Roger had many typical features in his childhood, but his mother said some of them were gradually improving. In particular, his nonverbal expression, which had been almost lacking when he was a child, was beginning to normalize. He still had that undefinable air of being lost in his own world where he could be constantly intrigued and fascinated by details that would be unimportant to anyone else. At the time he was seen, his particular interest was in aerodynamics and Roger was getting considerable satisfaction from designing, making and testing fairings for his bicycle that would reduce drag and make it go faster. Despite being bullied, he seemed to be content, perhaps because he was oblivious to much of the sarcasm that he received from the bullies.

The specialist confirmed the diagnosis, but 18 months later was asked to see Roger again. Roger had lost his former air of guilelessness and contentment. He was angry and miserable. He had spoken to his parents about suicide. He laughed bitterly when he was asked about his former interest in aerodynamics. One day, he said, he had seen, really seen, the look on someone's face as he rode past them and realized what he, and his bike, looked like to them. 'Bonkers,' he said. 'They must have thought I was bonkers.' Since then, he had become self-conscious about everything, and more and more discontent with himself and his life. He wished he could be more like other people, and picked up every hint of criticism or condemnation in what other people said about him.

Roger's Asperger syndrome was spontaneously remitting, as seems to happen in a proportion of the most able teenagers. Along with that, his awareness of himself was growing to the point that he suddenly grasped how he seemed to others, a profoundly disturbing realization for him which led to him becoming dysthymic.

Orientation and ASD

Many of the actions described in the original description of 'joint attention' and its reduction in ASD are orientation behaviours, which are reduced in the participants with ASD.[24] Young children with an ASD orientate less to faces than normally developing children, whereas a matched group of children with Williams syndrome spend more time looking at faces than normally developing children.[20] Children with autism are also less accurate than normally developing children in inferring what another person is looking at.[25] Children with ASD were also more likely to look at the pointing finger, and less likely to look in the direction that the finger was pointing than normally developing children in one study.[26] Children with ASD were also less likely to look at a parent and engage the parent's interest than the normally developing group.[27] Children with an ASD are less likely to use pointing to direct interest (proto-declarative pointing) than normally developing children, but this is not because of an inability to form the point gesture, as they are as likely to use pointing to show what they want (proto-imperative pointing).[28] Measures of social orientation impairment show promises for the reliable, early detection of ASD.[29]

Gazing at an object may be a signal of moving towards or otherwise engaging with the object, and may therefore be a biological basis for 'intention' and agency.[30] This may be one of the characteristics that distinguishes biological from physical movement. Two-year-old normally developing children orientate particularly to biological movement, but two-year-old children with an ASD do not.[31]

Orientation is also important for the later phases of language development, presumably because ostensive learning requires that children and adults both share the same object of attention when being taught a new word. Children's responsiveness to adults' orientation and adults' responsiveness to children's orientation during play are both predictors of language development in children with ASD.[32]

Finally, the fathers of children with autism also show slower gaze orientation in response to others' gaze compared to arrow symbols, unlike the fathers of neurotypical children.[33]

IMITATION

Mutual gaze is an instance of imitation, in which one person copies what another person does. In macaques, there are populations of neurons that fire when the gaze is turned in a particular direction, and some of these neurons also fire when another monkey is observed to be gazing that direction,[34] indicating that this imitation is at a neural level, at least in one of our primate cousins. Imitation plays a special role in child development. Adults repeatedly imitate their children and, as the child gets older, vary the imitation so that it is closer to the normative than the child's utterance or performance. Neonates imitate adults too,[35] as do day-old rhesus macaque infants,[36] although in the particular experimental set-up used, the adult had a still face, moved directly into an expression and then returned to a still face so that neither infant had to recognize a facial expression in a dynamic face. Sounds or movements that are imitated in later life often occur within a continuous stream of sound or movement, and part of imitation is to know when the relevant sound or action begins and ends within this stream (see the discussion of chunking on page 115).

The word 'imitation', like the word 'copying', is used to mean both conscious or deliberate mimicry (the latter confusingly also used for a phenomenal similarity created by an evolutionary pressure to disguise a harmless animal as a dangerous one, or vice versa) and unconscious or reflexive imitation, such as when someone puts out a hand and, without thinking, one puts out one's hand in response.[37, 38] I shall use imitation in this latter sense. Imitation in the former sense may also be impaired in ASD,[39, 37] but probably as a consequence of dyspraxia rather than an inability to recognize what needed to be copied.[40] People with an ASD may be very good at consciously imitating, or mimicking, another person.

Facial expressions in response to another person's facial expression may take up to a second,[41] but micro-responses indicating imitation of emotional expressions can be detected by electromyography at between 17 and 40 milliseconds. These responses are always congruent: that is, they are always the same as the expressions that they are responses to, but they may be inhibited before they become manifest on the face.[42] There may be a later, incongruent response, which is influenced by emotional priming, for example seeing an angry face may lead to adopting a fearful expression, especially if having previously viewed a fear-inducing photograph.[42] It seems likely that the fast response represents an immediate or contagious spread of emotional expression that is normally not manifested but inhibited, probably by a frontal/basal ganglion network acting directly on motor cortex,[43] and that the delayed response results from further processing, most likely also involving the amygdala, and fusiform cortex where the effect of priming is likely to be exerted.[44] Even though the first, reflexive response is covert, it can be expected that if the later reflective response is incongruent there will be less of a delay in producing it than if it is discongruent. Lee et al. tested this using a control task (the Simon task),[45] and electromyography to ensure accurate recording of response latency, and fMRI. Both an immediate, reflexive response and a later, overt response can be detected electromyographically, even if the immediate response is inhibited and does not result in visible facial expression. As expected the incongruent response was delayed and producing it required more activation of ventrolateral prefrontal cortex (Brodmann area 47), supplementary motor area, posterior superior temporal sulcus and right anterior insula. The non-emotional interference task used as a control was associated with activation in another frontostriatal network. Questionnaire scores on ratings of empathy and emotion control style correlated with activation of ventrolateral prefrontal cortex and the superior temporal sulcus.[45]

Single cell recordings in the F5 area of macaque cortex (thought to correspond to human premotor cortex) demonstrated the existence of cells that responded both when a movement was initiated and when it was observed ('mirror neurons') and when an action was required ('canonical neurons'), for example 'grasping' irrespective of the movement that might be required to accomplish it (grasping someone's hand is very different in movement from grasping a pin or a ball).[46]

There is controversy about the importance of mirror and canonical neurons in people,[47, 48] partly because single cell recordings are only ethically possible in limited situations, for example in people having neurosurgery. However, there is a general view that, first, they are important in understanding ASDs; second, that if understanding what someone is doing is understood by neurologically rehearsing doing it oneself, then imitation must be a more fundamental operation in processing than was previously thought; and third, aims or targets are anterior to movements, so what processing deals with may be intentions which later get translated into actions.[48]

Imitation and ASD

Clifford et al. studied 45 home videos of infants, 15 of whom were later diagnosed as having autistic disorder, 15 of whom later showed developmental or language delay, and 15 of whom developed normally.[49] The infants with an autistic disorder differed from the other two groups in showing less 'peer interest', more 'gaze aversion', fewer 'anticipatory postures', and less 'proto-declarative showing'. Imitation deficits and impaired joint attention each, independently, contribute to delayed social development.[50]

People with autism spend less time looking at the eyes of others in evaluating complex scenes,[51] although not when evaluating simple emotions.[52] That, it is suggested, leads to greater social impairment, for example in being able to differentiate posed and genuine smiles,[53] and to a reduction in the acuity with which others' gaze direction can be judged.[25] Children as young as two with an ASD do not orientate to an approaching adult's eyes as neurotypical two-year-olds do.[54] Merin et al. used the still face condition (an alarming experience, even for an observer, when a carer interacting with a baby suddenly shuts off all expression) as a complex social stimulus for six-month-olds, and measured the direction of the infant's gaze.[55] A cluster analysis of the ratio of fixation times to the eyes and to the mouth, averaged over three still face episodes, disclosed a cluster of 11 six-month-olds with a significantly lower eye to mouth fixation time. Of these 11 children, 10 had an autistic sibling, whereas 21 of the remaining 44 children did.[55]

When children with an ASD are instructed to look more at the eyes, they show an increase in contagious facial and bodily expression to neurotypical levels.[56]

Children with autistic disorder who have not developed usable language make less use of orientation and imitation than other children with an ASD,[57] suggesting that language development in ASD requires the prior development of some degree of orientation and imitation. Some of the impairment of imitation in children with ASD may be accounted for by not attending to the socially salient cues that call out for imitation,[58] and in consequence, children with ASD can be taught to improve their imitation skills.[59]

There is evidence to support the clinical observation that many children with an ASD cannot learn by imitation, only by doing. Children with an ASD learning to use a new tool make more use of proprioceptive feedback from the tool than normally developing children,[60] pointing possibly to a greater than normal skill in dealing with the physical universe. However, this reliance on proprioception was, in this study, in inverse proportion to the children's social and imitative ability.

It has been speculated that the imitation impairment is partly, if not wholly, the immediate contagious or mirroring kind of imitation, and that this indicates that there is a relative paucity of mirror neurons in the frontoparietal area in people with ASD than there is in neurotypicals.[61, 62, 63, 64] In one study, children with an ASD used fewer hand gestures spontaneously, and, as shown on home videos, used fewer hand gestures during early development than neurotypicals, but their ability to deliberately copy hand gestures was also reduced.[65]

In the latter study, the use of gesture was negatively correlated with speech fluency.[65] Other studies also suggest that imitation may be a precursor of language development. Gesture use was strongly correlated with both receptive and language skill in infants in one study.[66] Responding to joint attention initiatives is strongly correlated with receptive language in this study,[75] and also predicted a diagnosis of autistic disorder and a failure to develop language before the age of five years in a mixed group of children with ASDs.[67]

CHUNKING

Social events, unlike merely physical ones, are composed of recognizable elements that are distinguished from each other and from their background context by some boundary: pauses or pitch changes in speech are examples. Understanding social stimuli requires that these recognizable elements are identified and separately processed,[68] or 'chunked'. De Saussure first proposed that these elements are 'syntagmatically' strung together to form larger groups, and each element is one instance or paradigm of a class of interchangeable elements.[69] Speech is composed of phonemes that are distinct from each other, and from any ambient sound, and perceived as such. Movement can be segmented into actions, including communicative actions, such as gestures. Communication requires that a continuous signal is 'digitized', that is broken down into its chunks. One strong piece of evidence for this is that we rarely hear near words. Irrespective of whether it is a warbling infant or a growling old man, a person with a thick BBC accent or a colourless rural manner of speaking, a person speaking in a wind or a person speaking in a tomb, we hear them say words. This first step in recognizing certain stimuli as social, and in parsing them into their signicative elements, is reliant on activity of centres in and around the superior temporal sulcus.[70] Digitizing language and parsing nonverbal communication may involve the same centres,[71] and is the most likely explanation for the bilateral activation of centres in right and left hemisphere that occurs when speech is heard.[72]

Once sounds have been segmented into phonemes, their processing as linguistic elements takes place mainly in the dominant hemisphere, although there is some residual verbal recognition in the non-dominant hemisphere too. Communicative actions, such as gestures and facial expressions, draw on the processing resources of the fusiform cortex,[73, 74] especially on the right fusiform cortex where overlearnt, reflexive or 'gestalt' processing takes place. Gestalt processing, unlike featural processing, is sensitive to the effects of inversion: although inverted faces can be processed, it takes longer suggesting that there are two face reading processes;[75] one is rapid, and may be particularly affected in ASD, and the other is a slower, more deliberate one that may be unimpaired in ASD.

Gaze plays a part in chunking. The start of a gesture may be signalled by a brief gaze at the eyes of the person to whom the gesture is directed, this gaze both serving the instrumental function of making sure that the other person is looking so that the gesture is not overlooked, and the communicative function of indicating that an expression is on the way. In speech there is a momentary pause between phonemes, and this can be detected visually, by a cessation of movement in the lips of the speaker. However, it is unlikely that purely perceptual processes can account for chunking, but inner motor matching, such as is supposed to be provided by mirror neurons, is also required. Observation of action scenes by normally developing children is associated with desynchronization of the EEG over temporal and frontal cortex as well as over motor cortex, not present when the children were viewing still scenes, which would be consistent with the activation of the mirror neuron system.[76] Motor matching, or embodiment, also provides an explanation for the normal overestimation of the duration of facial expressions.[77]

Chunking and ASD

In a small study, children with autism who interacted with robots used more orientation and imitated unfamiliar actions more than children interacting with adults.[78] One possible explanation is that robotic actions are more clearly delineated, or chunked, because they occur in the context of inaction rather than the continuous distractions of non-communicative human movement.[79] Some further evidence for this is that slowing down the presentation of facial expressions and associated sounds enhances recognition and correct imitation of the sounds in people with ASD.[80, 81]

Chunking may involve two systems, a purely perceptual one – visual in the case of chunking movements into gestures – and a motor matching one, possibly involving mirror neurons. Children with an ASD who were viewing action scenes did not show activity over the presumed mirror neuron areas, unlike normally developing children who did, suggesting that the motor matching process was offline in the autistic children, who had to rely purely on perception to break the sensory input up into meaningful chunks.[82]

Children with autistic disorder and specific language impairment, but not matched children with Asperger syndrome and normal language development, have delayed right temporal lobe responses on magnetoencephalogy, which would be consistent with a disorder of speech chunking that is phonemic segmentation of speech.[83]

COMMUNICATION

'Marked impairment in the use of multiple nonverbal behaviours such as eye-to-eye gaze, facial expression, body postures, and gestures to regulate social interaction' is the first diagnostic criterion of Asperger disorder listed in DSM-IV.[84] Factor analytic approaches to the ASDs indicate that there are either two or three factors, of which the one with the greatest loading and greatest construct validity is 'social and communication' (see Chapter 8), the topic of this chapter.

The use of the word 'behaviour' rather than 'communication' in the DSM-IV definition was in keeping with the behavioural approach to communication developed by Skinner and George Miller.[85] This behavioural approach is now considered outmoded, not least because it fails to capture the notion that communication is an exchange.

Classical approaches to communication

The earliest Indian Brahmanic and later Buddhist scholars studied phonology, the combinatorial rules of syllables, syntax, or the combinatorial rules or words into sentences, as well as semantics, or the meaning of words. Their main aim was to develop mnemonic methods to ensure the accurate transgenerational transmission of the Vedas and the Tripitaka.

Once there was a method of recording utterances, then less attention was given to accuracy. Poets who read their work out would include different elements according to the audience, or would add contemporary interest or local colour. The social rather than the archival function of stories was more important. The Greeks added logic to the Brahmanic study of grammar, originally as a codification of one important social use of speech, in discourse or argument. Another principal study was rhetoric, or the power of communication to move others emotionally, and so to persuade them to some desired end. Rhetoric was closely related to performance not only in the theatre, but also in the law courts. Cicero and other Roman lawyers considered rhetoric to be just one element in a performance designed to win over the jury, a performance that also included the behaviour, dress and demeanour of the plaintiff. Rhetoric used the sound associations of works (onomatopoeia), and their connotations as means of increasing their persuasiveness. Rhetoric, singing and dancing were understood by the Greeks to be varieties of performance art.

Aristotle proposed in his Rhetoric that effective persuasion required a credible speaker, a good argument, and the right emotional state in the audience. The enthymeme was the rhetorical equivalent of the syllogism in logic: a kind of deduction, but based not on the meaning of the words themselves but on an accepted association between signs and events. So, to say that 'the days are much longer than the nights, so it must be summer' is a syllogism, but to say that 'swallows have arrived, so it must be summer' is an enthymeme.

Semiotics, or the study of signs (also known as semiology), originates with the work of the logician Charles Peirce.[86] He formalized Aristotle's theory of signs in various ways, but his lasting contribution was to expose the inner relation of the enthymeme: how signs signify. Swallows signify summer because there is a regular, empirical association between the two: when the swallows come the days are warm and long. This, Peirce said, makes swallows an index of the summer, and this sign is an indexical sign. If we wanted to indicate summer in a stage set, we might have lots of swallows flying around or we might fly the picture of a large sun above the centre of the stage. The sun picture would resemble the sun seen in the sky on a summer's day, and so would stand for/represent/signify (many different words are used for the inner relation of the enthymeme) summer 'iconically' in Peirce's terms (in language indexes are sometimes called metonyms, and icons, metaphors). Draping a banner by the side of the stage saying 'Summer' would be a symbolic sign, or symbol tout court in Peirce's terms – more often nowadays referred to as an arbitrary or conventional sign.

Linguistics

Ferdinand de Saussure, a diplomat and teacher of Indo-European languages, further developed Peirce's sign theory into a general theory of the structure of language that became the basis for linguistics and for structuralism in psychology.[69] He recognized that the symbol had properties that the other signs did not, properties which enable symbols to be part of a system or language, and therefore to be independent both of what they represented and of the way that the brain processed the system. Language is a system because any unit can form a unit of language so long as it can be represented in the appropriate modality (gesture, speech or writing typically, but other sounds or visual symbols may also form a language) and it was clearly discriminable from every other. This 'principle of difference' applied (memorably guyed by Derrida in his neologism 'différance')[87] both to what was represented (the signified) and what represented it (the signifier). Green and blue things look clearly different and so there are two signifieds, 'green' and 'blue', each requiring a different signifier. These are arbitrarily connected: so in English they could be words 'green' or 'blue' or the sounds these words make when we read them aloud, and in French they could be 'vert' and 'bleu'. But linguistic practice would quickly suppress the use of 'broun' and 'rett' as the two signifiers for green and blue, because there is not enough difference between 'brown' and 'broun' or 'rett' and 'red' to allow for unambiguous communication. Nor does the word 'grue' get much use because there is no use in differentiating between blue and greenish blue and between green and blueish green, so there is no demand for a colour word, 'grue', for it.[88]

De Saussure supposed that sentences were composed of strings of linguistic signs with each place on the string having a defined – or syntagmatic – relation to the next place. So the simplest sentence string has two places: noun and verb phrase. The linguistic signs that may fill each of these two places come from classes – nouns, verbs, pronouns, and so on – that are paradigmatically related: only one paradigm or example of that class may be chosen.

Modern syntactic theory, and therefore theories about the development of speech, have been heavily influenced by de Saussure's syntagmatic concept.[69] Chomsky proposed that phrases when they are first thought have a simpler, 'deep' structure that is independent of the grammatical rules of the language being used: indeed, it may even be universal.[89] Language specific grammatical forms, or surface structures, can then be generated by a process of transformation of the deep structures. The details of this are no longer exactly as Chomsky proposed them, but most if not all psycholinguists now adhere to some sort of 'generative' or 'transformational' grammar.

The principle of difference has also been influential. It is generally accepted that each language has a set of distinguishable sounds (phonemes) or written signs (graphemes) that underlie utterances which are then realized phonetically or graphically. Languages are also now analysed in terms of units of meaning, or morphemes, which are combined into spoken or written words. So 'words' is the combination of two English morphemes: 'word' and '-s'. The affix 's' inflecting the meaning of 'word' to mean 'more than one word'.

De Saussure distinguished between an utterance and a sentence string.[69] An utterance – what someone says, writes or sings – is the performance of a sentence string. There is a process from the generation of the sentence mentally to its utterance in which errors might be introduced. Errors in producing the sentence string are errors in competence. Errors in translating it into an utterance are errors in performance. The difference roughly corresponds with the neurological distinction between receptive and expressive. Receptive dysphasia is a disorder of competence, leading to a failure of language comprehension. Expressive dysphasia is a disorder of performance leading to a failure of speech production, although in practice these two types may not be so clearly differentiable.

Digital communication

Information theory focused on communication as a kind of code,[90] similar to that used so frequently in the Second World War. Possibly the most famous code was that of the Wehrmacht, encoded using an Enigma machine first developed some 30 years before. The Enigma machine used rotors and other mechanical devices to convert letters, entered using a keyboard by the operator, into a particular lamp display which could be read off as another encoded letter. The process was based on an arbitrary string that was fed in each day by the operator. The code could be decoded by using another Enigma machine that performed the same operation, but inversely, so long as the initial seed string was known. By using redundancy in the message, security leaks and other information, Allied code-breakers, based at Bletchley Park, were able to create their own Enigma machine and break German Naval messages, enabling the position of hunter-killer submarines that were based in the Atlantic to intercept Allied convoys, to be located and destroyed by depth charges.

Shannon's contribution was to indicate how important redundancy was in digital messages, introducing the notion of error checking to counteract the errors or entropy that regularly affect messages, and also introducing the notion of 'channels'.[90] If a message is transmitted by several changes such as encrypted Morse code and encrypted text, it is possible to check the two signals between channels, identify errors, and remove them.

Shannon thought of information as the signal, and that the error or 'noise' in it was formally equivalent to entropy in thermodynamic theory. Information was therefore 'negentropy'. Messages can be digitized, and the quantity of information measured on the basis of the number of non-redundant bits, with redundant bits being those that can be removed without loss of information. Redundant bits do, however, serve a function, for error checking. It has been estimated that most spoken utterances contain about 50 per cent redundancy.

Shannon proposed that errors could be reduced not only by internal checking using redundant, duplicated information, but also by using different channels to convey the same message, so that errors can be reduced by checking between channels.[90] Channels of communication include written and spoken communication, as well as facial expression, gaze, voice prosody, gesture, postural shift and proxemic information (spacing of the body from other people).

Design features of a language

The sharp distinction that thinking clearly tries to make between categories probably belies the blurring of the boundaries within communication in reality. Language is not as code-like as Shannon suggested, nor as free from communicative context as linguistics might want.[91] However, languages do have distinct design features. It is possible to say 'no' or 'not' in a language; it is possible to speak about things that do not exist, or have not happened (Brentano's criterion of 'intentionality' and of mind),[92] and language can be self-reflective referring back to itself or its production. 'Inner' speech or psychological processes can therefore be described by inner speech, itself a product of inner processing.

The medium and the message

Communication media are channels that can all carry messages, or intentional communications in Shannon's terms.[90] The same report can be printed in the newspapers, transmitted over the radio or television, promulgated in a podcast, or provided in conversation by the person next door. It has been argued, for example, by McLuhan (the medium is the message), that the nature of the message carried by these and other media is changed by the medium itself.[93] But that is to alter Shannon's definition of the term. By confining 'message' to intentional communications, Shannon meant that they were the result of a reflective process. Although messages can be conveyed iconically, for example by mime, these methods are unreliable compared to messages using arbitrary linguistic units, or, in Peirce's terms, symbols. Arguments, or logic, can be conveyed only as a result of reflective processing.[94] Messages are therefore almost always encoded in a language.

When McLuhan wrote that the medium is the message, he was drawing attention to the other function of communication in the Aristotelian scheme, rhetoric.[93] Television for example, with its combination of sound and imagery may have a rhetorical punch lacking to the next door neighbour to accompany many of its messages, although a few may be more persuasive if coming from talking to the next door neighbour in the flesh.

Combinatorial approaches to communication

A document produced by a committee may seem like a single text, and indeed somebody on the committee will have had the task of ensuring that it is internally consistent and that it 'flows'. However, a reader may find within it a political bias, or several biases if the members of the committee have opposing views; a hesitancy or a whole hearted assertion of its conclusions; and the work of this hand or that in particular passages. Communications, even constrained ones like committee papers, are multistranded.

One view of any communication is that it is the end result of a collaboration between different functional brain areas, and so very much like a document produced by a committee.

Any particular communication may be deconstructed, like the committee's communiqué, into distinct messages. Here is an example from a detective story by Carlo Lucarelli. The protagonist, Commissario De Luca, has a balding boss who repeatedly smooths down what brilliantined hair he has left over his pate. He does so with a jerk of his hand upwards, and then a backward swipe of his hand over his scalp, so fast that it is 'almost like a tic'. In their first interview, 'the chief's hand shot up, and De Luca was suckered in. He extended his own hand, at the precise moment that the chief bent his arm at the elbow, and he was left with his hand suspended in midair. He concealed his faux pas by pretending to bat away a fly.'[95]

De Luca involuntarily imitates his boss, then realizes that this has another level of meaning and could be seen as ridiculing him. So he adds an extra movement – batting away a fly – which, when combined with the earlier movement, obscures the former's communicative significance. Interpenetration of the medium and the message is another example of combination as in this, fictionalized, account of a flood:

> **Flooding in Kansas**
> A flash flood today threatened to engulf parts of Kansas City. The fire service were deluged with calls. The fire chief paid tribute to staff taking the calls. 'They were like an island in a sea of chaos. They deserve gallons of thanks,' he said.

Combination of several expressions or channels of communication may allow emotional expressions to be blended, tinged with irony or sincerity, or appearing to be superficially or deeply felt.

The combination of nonverbal and verbal communication allows even more complexity, including the possibility of communicating conflicting ideas. This style of communication was famously seen as being used by parents to control their children: the 'double bind' described by the ethologists and psychiatrists working in the Stanford Center for Communication.[96]

Many people with an ASD find blends of emotions or other combinations of different subtexts of communication particularly difficult. They prefer their language concrete, and their emotions black or white.

Two fundamental types of communication

One model of the interaction of brain and communication is to consider the brain as a kind of Enigma machine, decoding incoming signal traffic such as speech or writing, turning it into digitizable brain code that can be processed and then re-emitted following a second application of the cipher machine, as speech or writing. Digitizability is a key criterion of human language.[97]

The Enigma machine, like the human brain, or a speech recognition program running on a computer, turns speech into information which can be digitized, processed, and then recompiled. All of these communications are 'symbolic'.[86] This model is one version of how human language and the language processor works, and was the dominant model in psycholinguistics,[98] until transformational grammar models focused attention on the structure of language itself, effectively creating a new science of linguistics out of psychology.[99]

The digital theory of communication fits best with communication using symbols with an arbitrary or 'conventional' meaning.[100] For this reason, it is usual to distinguish language-based or verbal communication, which is uniquely human and digital, from that kind of nonverbal communication, which is used by other vertebrates and is analogic (although there are some non-verbal symbols, too, such as American Sign Language, these are based on language).

Nonverbal communication is best understood as signal traffic coupling one brain with another,[101] an interconnectedness that has parallels with the internet which couples one computer with another by virtue of a wireless network. I have suggested the term 'interbrain' for this coupling.[102] There are no modems in the human brain, or radio signals connecting one brain to another, but I argue that nonverbal signals function like the wireless network, and the centres that encode and decode them correspond to modems. Examples of this coupling between brains are contagious yawning,[103] and smiling,[104] in which one brain encodes a yawn or a smile, an expressive action which, when perceived by others reflexively causes them to be more likely to yawn or smile, too. People with an ASD are less likely than neurotypicals to contagiously yawn or smile.[105]

Contagious smiling is subliminal, and emotional contagion can therefore be contrasted with the mimicry that people with an ASD are often very good at. In fact, 'echolalia' or repeating back what a person says without changing the words is more common in people with an ASD than in neurotypicals. People with an ASD may also be very good at reproducing what another person has said, retaining the quality of the voice as well as the words so they may sound exactly like that other person. Although nonverbal expression is not impaired in ADHD, there is evidence that nonverbal interpretation may be.

The interpretation and expression of speech are handled by centres which are separated by the length of the temporal lobe. The interpretation or decoding of language occurs in Wernicke's area at the caudal end of the temporal lobe, and lesions here lead to receptive dysphasia. The encoding of thought into language occurs in Broca's area, at the rostral end of the temporal lobe where it joins the prefrontal cortex, and lesions of this area are associated with expressive dysphasia. Nonverbal expression and interpretation are not functionally and therefore not anatomically distinct.

Another difference between the two types of communication is that most nonverbal communication cannot be understood as the transfer of packets of information, or messages, but as a continuous bias or influence, more like analogue than digital communication. A final difference is that speaking and writing are intentional processes, and we can reflect on them. Indeed one strong theory of consciousness is that it is mediated by internal language,[106] and it has been suggested that this is the reason that we can typically be aware of left hemisphere processing, but not of right hemisphere processing even though these may be just as 'intelligent'.[107] This use of inner language may be impaired in people with an ASD,[108] although possibly not in those with AS and no language disorder. Right hemisphere processes are 'reflexive' rather than a 'reflective' process,[109] or, to use an overlapping dichotomy, automatic rather than intentional.

From the foregoing, it is apparent that there are two poles of communication: at one end is digital, intentional, symbolic, reflective communication mainly using words, and is the kind of communication that can be called a language. At the other end is analogue, automatic, iconic or indexical, reflexive communication, which is usually termed 'nonverbal communication', although word use, for example involuntary swearing, may also be close to this pole. Nonverbal communication, for example that developed by and for deaf people, may on the other hand be at the language pole. Usage dictates that one pole is called 'verbal communication' and the other 'nonverbal communication' and I shall accede to this, but just because words are used does not mean that communication meets these 'verbal' criteria; similarly, just because words are not used does not mean that the communication meets the nonverbal criteria.

In practice, communication in real life is almost always blended. Although, as will become apparent below, impairments affecting language are distinguishable from those affecting nonverbal communication, utterances are processed simultaneously digitally and analogically. Encoding an utterance about emotions or emotive situations is coupled with feeling and may lead to the display of the appropriate emotion, even if the task is simply to read a sentence displayed on a computer, with no relevance to one's actual situation – or so a study of people receiving facial botulinum toxin injections for cosmetic reasons indicates.[110] The 38 female participants were receiving injections into the corrugator supercilii muscle to remove frown lines on their foreheads. The corrugator supercilii contracts during anger and during fear, and its paralysis by the botulinum toxin injection delayed the reading times of angry and fearful sentences but not of happy sentences.[110]

Anatomical approaches to communication

Some body areas are specialized for communication. The vocal apparatus in humans is capable of a wide range of sounds, and the ear of discerning them. The hand is dexterous enough to make a range of gestures, and the eyes to see them. The placement of the eyes, the contrast of the pigmented iris with the white sclera, the outlining of the eye with hair makes eye expressions particularly easy to see and, in combination with the contrast between the hairless face and hairy scalp, means that direction of gaze can be interpreted from a distance. Both hands and faces are not normally clothed or covered in many cultures, enabling their expressions to be seen easily. The human face has evolved as an expressive organ, with at least six distinct patterns of muscular contraction and relaxation that are recognized universally as the fundamental expressions of emotion.[111] These expressions appear on the faces of congenitally blind people as well as sighted individuals in appropriate emotional contexts.[112]

Channels of communication are more or less highly adapted for communication. Foot posture can be reflectively used as a medium of expression, for example in ballet, but is generally neglected when communicative effort is being made, and so reflexive expressions may more readily leak out through the feet.[113] However, the paucity of foot postures, and the requirements of the feet to adjust their posture to locomotion, means that they are much less expressive than the hands. The hands are capable of communicating whole languages, such as British or American Sign Language, but are more often used for reflexive communication in gesture.

The vocal apparatus may be used reflexively for involuntary communication by sound, or reflectively (i.e. deliberately) for speech or for mimicking other sounds, like animal noises, but it is less effective at communicating over a distance than are the hands.

Although anatomy and physiology of individual channels does constrain communication using them, Shannon's postulate – that messages can be duplicated across channels – means that many channels are capable of carrying the same messages.[90] Indeed the channel may switch mid-message. If we are speaking to someone, we may interrupt our speaking to write something down or spell it out, and then revert seamlessly to speech. Or if we are gesturing to someone who is moving away our gesture may expand from a simple hand gesture to an arm gesture.

McLuhan's aphorism that the medium is the message may apply to reflexive as well as to reflective communication:[93] a clenched fist plus a frown is, for example, a stronger message than just a frown.

LANGUAGE, SPEECH AND WRITING

A language is a system of communication which relies on symbols that can be expressed acoustically or graphically. Knowing a language requires exposure to the language, principally through participating in a community of users of that language. Hearing deficits may delay acquisition of language, and motor deficits delay the use of language to communicate. Both are more common in people with an ASD. Particular kinds of motor deficit may affect the ability to use writing (dysgraphia) or speech (expressive dysphasia), but not necessarily to use language, although a language disorder may be a cause of dysgraphia or dysphasia. A failure to understand language (receptive dysphasia) is more likely to be an indication of an impairment in language use. A failure to understand writing may also be an instance of impairment in language, but may also reflect a specific problem in translating letters into sounds and vice versa – dyslexia, or a specific impairment of writing and reading.

Language use is rarely if ever divorced from communication more generally, and the choice of words or expressions, or the tones of voice or stress patterns with which words are uttered, are influenced by nonverbal communicative demands as well as purely linguistic ones. One consequence of this is that the boundaries of what is specifically linguistic about communication difficulties has often changed and at the present time there are no generally accepted criteria for what constitutes a specific language impairment. Professionals trained in dealing with communication are called 'speech and language' therapists in recognition of the wider influences on verbal communication.

Anatomy

Left-sided strokes may result in dysphasia in right handers and about half of left handers, whereas right-sided strokes very rarely affect speech except in the half of left handers with dominant right hemispheres, although they may affect other aspects of communication, such as the expression of emotion. It can be assumed from this that the left hemisphere contains the language centre or centres in 95 per cent of the population, and this is reflected in an anatomical difference between the right and left hemisphere which is visible to the naked eye.

Neuroanatomy and language

Neuroimaging studies reinforce psycholinguists' distinction between syntax and semantics in that grammar and semantics are processed by functionally separate areas,[114] with grammar processing requiring phonological short-term memory.[115] Grammar and language-specific word forms are generated in Broca's area, which is the area of inferior frontal cortex immediately adjacent to the temporal cortex. Speech generation is under the control of the more rostral Wernicke's area, which is at the other end of the temporal cortex where it abuts the inferior parietal cortex. It is presumed that activation of Broca's area leads to the activation of Wernicke's area via a series of grey matter based activations during which words are inserted into the grammatical frame and then phonological and paralinguistic information is added, the latter probably provided by right hemisphere processing transferred via the corpus callosum.[116]

The output of Wernicke's area can be interpreted by other parts of the brain outputting as the vocal cord contractions and chest movements that produce speech, or into the hand movements that produce writing. Wernicke's area, like other areas of the temporal lobe, receives input from the ear and the eye. So the output of Wernicke's area is probably subject to constant monitoring and modified so that the actual output is recognizable, despite changing environmental conditions which might alter it (think, for example, of writing in a moving car, and the efforts to make the words legible). Translating the output of Wernicke's area into meaningful speech or writing therefore requires adequate functioning of the productive apparatus down to and including the muscles and muscle spindles of the hand, thorax and chest, and also the sensory projections back to the temporal cortex.

Dysphasia may result from dysfunction in the connections between Wernicke's area, the effectors of speech or writing, and the sensors that monitor the status of the effectors and feedback to Wernicke's area. Geschwind revived the concept of disconnection disorders to describe these dysphasias,[117] and wide area networks are now thought to be more involved in language production than was once thought. Dyslexia is, for example, now suggested to be a disorder of phonology based in the dysfunction of a network of brain areas.[118] Grammar generation also involves the frontotemporal network subserving working memory.[119] Network explanations of speech and language impairment have received further support from speculations that the sensors and effectors of the speech and writing apparatus are one and the same, that is that a mirror neuron system is linked to the production and interpretation of language.

There are macroscopic differences between right and left hemispheres which correspond to the language centres being on the left, as they are in 95 per cent of people, including all right handers and about half of left handers. Although fMRI studies show considerable activation in both hemispheres when speech is being processed,[72] irrespective of handedness, the 'message' or linguistic element of speech is regularly associated with left superior temporal sulcus activation. This has been elegantly demonstrated by comparisons of the processing of sound tones in the speakers of languages like Mandarin, in which tonal variants carry meaning, and the speakers of non-tonal languages. Mandarin speakers showed activation of their left superior temporal sulcus and their right inferior frontal gyrus when listening to lexically meaningful tonal contrasts, whereas English speakers (a non-tonal language) showed only the right inferior frontal gyrus activation.[120] In another comparable study of female Chinese musicians, listening to Mandarin in which there was a lexically incorrect pitch variation was associated with a left front late positive component in an evoked potential (ERP) study, whereas listening to music where a note was either flat or sharp led to a right-sided late positive potential in the frontal leads.[121] In other words, an error in speech intonation is picked up in the dominant, left hemisphere, but an out-of-tune note is picked up in the right hemisphere of the brain. In another study, this time of the processing of deviant vowels with paralinguistic sounds, only the variant vowels activated left superior temporal sulcus.[122]

There is a close anatomical relationship between the auditory cortex and the temporal areas dealing with language, suggesting that language processing has its evolutionary basis in analysing complex sounds. Severely deaf children, whose primary language is based on signing and not speech, show greater activation of their posterior superior temporal sulcus and gyrus in response to signs than do hearing vocalizers. This suggests that language processing is not modality specific.[123]

Development

Language exists independently of the language user. Language users may contribute to it, but are mainly constrained by it in that they must use the same morphology, phonology and semantics of a particular language in order to communicate with other users of that language. Acquisition of the ability to use a language during development is not fully understood. Particular points of controversy are the part played by an innate 'language acquisition device' (to use Chomsky's terms),[124] and the importance of nonverbal communication as a basis for language development, notably the relationship of language to the protolinguistic use of gestures like waving or pointing. Language acquisition is accelerated by exposure to speech in that language and, since writing was invented only in the historical period, speech must be considered to be the basic form of language. It is not clear whether there is a critical period after which language can no longer be acquired, although there is strong evidence that it takes longer and is more effortful to acquire language in later childhood. The chance of acquiring useful language drops off particularly after the age of five years. Learning a second language involves a different process, more akin to the rote teaching and learning of multiplication tables than the acquisition of a first language. The children of severely deaf, non-speaking but signing parents may learn sign language before speech.[125]

The first utterances of a child are single words, although it seems like these words contain both a noun and a predicate, that they are, in fact, phrases or 'holophrases'. Further development of speech requires the development of vocabulary and also the ability to deal with grammar. There is a transitional stage in grammar acquisition in which children apply grammatical rules even to irregular words, such as saying 'wented' instead of the English past participle of 'go', which is 'went'.

Normal function

Speech has a social or phatic function,[126] cementing social relationships or changing others' emotions or motivations. Dunbar has estimated that two-thirds of the time that people are simply in conversations that are not focused on a task or goal (i.e. 'chatting') is taken up with this kind of gossip.[127] He has also suggested that the larger the primary social group, the more processing demand that chatting makes, and that this may have been the driver for the increase in cerebral cortex volume in the primates.[127]

Speech which is not just chatting but directed at some end or goal may be used for description, negotiation or persuasion, or instruction, among many other purposes. Benjamin Whorf, an insurance claims assessor and amateur anthropologist, noted that the words with which people described things altered their appraisal of them.[128] For example, barrels of petrol that were described as full were treated with care, and rarely caused fire, but barrels that were thought of as empty, after the liquid petrol had been removed, were empty of petrol but full of petrol vapour. People smoked near empty barrels, thinking of them as empty and therefore safe, and fires were much more likely to be started by an explosion in an empty barrel than a full one. Preventing this kind of fire meant changing people's linguistic habits from thinking to themselves, 'It's OK. It's empty' to thinking to themselves, 'It's dangerous because it's still full of fumes.' This kind of redescription, or 'cognitive change', is the basis for many kinds of psychological treatment, notably 'cognitive therapy'.

Speech may also instruct. Vygotsky argued that much of what is called 'thinking' is a process of inner speech in which one talks to oneself (sometimes slight jaw movements indicate that the speech apparatus is actually being used).[106] Talking to oneself creates an impression that one may be both speaker and the person spoken to: that there is an 'I' and a 'me'. Accordingly, one may give oneself instructions that can assist skilled motor performance ('remember, play more slowly') or one can describe a problem to oneself and then self-consciously plan how to solve it. The mix of description and instruction is often considered to be part of the narrative function of speech, and self-awareness is often considered to be closely linked to the capacity for 'self-narration' or the body of conversations that one has had with oneself about oneself.

Impairment: speech and language disorder

Speech and language disorders range from simple sound substitutions to the inability to understand or use language or use the oral-motor mechanism for functional speech and feeding. Some causes of speech and language disorders include hearing loss, neurological disorders, brain injury, intellectual disability, drug abuse, physical impairments such as cleft lip or palate, and vocal abuse or misuse. Frequently, however, the cause is unknown.

Over a million students in special education in US public (i.e. state-funded) schools in the 2000–2001 school year were categorized as having a speech or language impairment, and it is estimated that communication disorders (including speech, language and hearing disorders) affect one in every ten people in the United States.

Adult onset speech and language disorder

Adults with lesions affecting Broca's area or Wernicke's area have distinctive speech and language impairments, or 'dysphasias'.

Anterior dysphasia

Anterior or receptive dysphasia results from lesions in Broca's area. Any speech that is preserved following a lesion is fluent but shows syntactical errors (agrammatism) and randomly selected words or words that are made up (neologisms). Anterior dysphasia is associated with a lack of understanding of other people's utterances, and an inability to deliberately mime actions ('ideomotor apraxia').

Posterior dysphasia

Posterior dysphasia, the consequence of lesions to Wernicke's area or adjacent cortex, is associated with hesitancy as if creating sentences requires unusual effort and speaking is, in consequence, dysfluent. Semantic impairment is apparent in the difficulty in finding words – nominal dysphasia – but sufficient language processing remains intact so that if substitute words are produced, they are not neologisms but synonyms or periphrases, for instance 'the glass thing that people put liquids in', instead of 'bottle'. So neologisms do not occur. Posterior dysphasia does not lead to syntactical errors either, but it is associated with impaired understanding of conventional signs, although with no impairment in mimicking them, and impaired writing.

Both types of dysphasia are associated with impaired reading, but anterior dysphasia particularly affects a person's ability to read regular word forms (for example 'affected' as the past form of 'affect'), and posterior dysphasia particularly affects the reading of irregular word forms (for example, 'read' as the past form of 'read'). The difference may result from regular word forms being understood by the application of a grammatical rule, and irregular forms being understood by retrieval from lexical memory. People with anterior dysphasia show greater impairment when being asked to read out loud, or when writing to dictation.[129]

Developmental speech and language disorder

The plasticity of brain development means that clear-cut differences between anterior or posterior dysphasia do not occur in children, although it is often possible to determine whether a particular child's speech and language problems are predominantly expressive or involve both the expression and the understanding of speech.

Predominantly expressive disorders ('speech sound disorders')

Disorders of language expression may occur despite a normal understanding of language, although this may be rarer than once thought.

Expressive disorders may be the result of impaired encoding of language ('phonological disorders'), in which case 'inner speech' or language-based thinking is also affected, or of translating language into appropriate movements ('articulation disorders'), in which case inner speech may be intact. Writing impairment may be due to specific dyspraxia of writing or 'dysgraphia', often associated with poorly formed and slowly produced letters, or to errors in the formation of letters and words (dyslexia).

Articulation disorders

The commonest articulation disorder is a speech dysfluency, such as stuttering. Stuttering is not associated with any of the ASDs, and does not lead to delay in speaking. Speech disorder resulting from impaired formation of speech sounds, for example saying 'see' instead of 'ski', may be associated with delay in speaking.

Speech and language therapists may classify an impairment in the pitch, volume or quality of the voice as an articulation disorder, but this kind of impairment is more properly classified as a disorder of nonverbal expression and a child who has this kind of speech impairment should be screened for an ASD.

Speech dyspraxia ('phonological disorder')

Speech dyspraxia was first described by Rapin.[130] Speech dyspraxia is an acoustic version of dyslexia. It is associated with impaired production of all phonemes leading to speech that it is difficult to understand. Like other dyspraxias it is a disorder of movement planning and so is distinct from the speech problems ('dysarthria') that may occur as a result of weakness of the tongue, lips or other voluntary speech organs. Speech dyspraxia leads to speech being produced on inspiration as well as expiration, unusual accentation, and other more incapacitating impairments in the programming of the vocal apparatus that can make speech indecipherable.

Speech dyspraxia may result in an absence of cooing or babbling as an infant, delayed use of speech, problems coordinating sounds with delays between sounds and a lack of variation of sounds leading to fewer consonants and vowels being used, and an avoidance of difficult to produce sounds. Infants with speech dyspraxia may have other oropharyngeal dyspraxias, and have problems feeding as a baby and later eating from a spoon or sucking from a cup.

Older children may make sound errors, appear to be struggling to produce sounds, have difficulty in copying speech, in pronouncing longer words, and be hard to understand for an unfamiliar listener. Anxiety makes the problem worse.

Speech dyspraxia may be associated with paralinguistic impairment. Speech may be monotonous, that is lacking in variation in tone, unusually stressed or lacking variation in pitch, or lacking a normal rhythm (the latter having clinical similarity to the 'scanning speech' seen in some cerebellar lesions). If these paralinguistic problems are associated with nonverbal expressive impairment in other modalities, then an ASD should be suspected.

Phonological disorders

Phonological disorders may also affect the production of particular phonemes leading to systematic phonemic errors, for example substituting dental sounds, normally made in the front of the mouth ('t' and 'd' sounds) with glottal sounds, normally made in the back of the mouth ('k' and 'g' sounds): saying 'tup' for 'cup' for example, or 'das' for 'gas'. Some phonic variations are appropriate to particular dialects of English, for example, 'dis' for 'this' or the obsolete upper class dialect in which 'w' was substituted for 'r'. Another common phonological error is to omit the second consonant in words that begin with two consonants: 'boken' instead of 'broken', for example.

Phonological errors commonly occur during speech development, and only their age-inappropriate persistence should be taken as an indication of a phonological disorder.

Specific reading and writing impairment (dyslexia)

Dyslexia is a common cause of educational disadvantage. It has only recently been generally accepted to be a disorder in its own right in children, and is still contested outside professional circles in adults. There is a strong link between ADHD and dyslexia (see Chapter 13). Dyslexia is most often one consequence of a wider phonological impairment with both reflecting difficulties in chunking input into phonemes or morphemes.[131] However, dyslexia may also occur in the absence of phonological disorder, when the reduced ability to chunk into morphemes applies only to visual stimuli.[132] Reversing letters and numbers when writing, common symptoms of dyslexia, may be a sign of this difficulty in visual processing.

As well as its effect on reading and spelling, dyslexia may impair the ability to handle mathematical symbols, for example in algebra, to remember multiplication tables or to handle changes. All of these disorders, like phonological disorder itself, may be associated with working memory impairment.

Dyscalculia, more narrowly defined, or 'number blindness' results from lesions or dysgenesis in the intraparietal sulcus.[133]

Dyslexia may be the first diagnosis in a child who will eventually be diagnosed as having an ASD.

Relation to ASD

Many people with Asperger syndrome, who by definition have no language impairment, may have some degree of speech apraxia, possibly as one manifestation of a more general dyspraxia.

A proportion of people with an ASD may also have more specific phonological disorders, which may or may not be associated with specific language impairment.[134]

Receptive language disorders ('specific language impairment')

Children with delayed use of speech may also have a delayed understanding, too, and this may indicate that language processing is selectively impaired, compared to other cognitive abilities. Specific language impairment, as this is currently termed, occurs as often as autistic disorder in the general population and may persist into adulthood although when it does, it is rarely recognized. Specific language impairment is particularly associated with syntactical errors but semantic errors also occur, leading to malapropisms and neologisms. Characteristic errors include omitting tense markers (e.g. 'he talk' instead of 'he talked' or 'he talks'), having difficulty in repeating a sentence immediately after someone says it, and or in repeating a grammatically well-formed non-word (e.g. saying 'redbusting', and then asking the child to repeat it).

Pragmatic impairments are the consequence of both nonverbal and linguistic impairment,[135] and although typical of ASD and ADHD,[136] may also occur in association with specific language impairment.

Syntactic errors

Syntactic errors are errors of grammar. They may be apparent in unusual word order, in a lack of appropriate tense, in the use of regular forms in the place of grammatically correct irregular ones ('he wented'), in a lack of agreement between tense or case, or a lack of grammar ('Sorry me cry you' instead of 'I'm sorry I made you cry').

Semantic errors

Semantic errors are errors of word meaning. Gross errors may lead to a person not being able to say what they mean. Mild errors may lead to the use of made-up words (neologisms) or almost correct words (malapropisms). Neologisms are not always indicative of semantic error, however. Some people with Asperger syndrome want to name things for which there is no word, for example, a particular sort of electricity pylon that has three arms and eight insulators.

Pragmatic errors

Pragmatic errors arise because context is not provided, or is not used appropriately, to disambiguate speech. 'Anaphors' are words that refer back to some previous word in an utterance, and it is this previous word that provides the anaphor's meaning. Anaphors are a common cause of pragmatic errors. Almost all of the pronouns are anaphors. The pronouns that provide the greatest difficulty, however, are those in which the context is provided by the social circumstance of the utterance, and not to be found in the utterance at all. Examples are the personal pronouns 'I' and 'you', and place markers like 'here' or 'there'. These are words that have only a situated meaning: where I mean by 'here' will depend on where I am physically located. If I ring someone on my mobile and say, 'I'm here,' the person on the other end would rightly say, 'But where is that?' Although mixing up 'I' and 'you' is the most often pronominal reversal associated with ASD, getting other, anaphorical, pronouns wrong occurs as often in my own clinical experience. Pronominal reversal is not, of itself, an indication of a specific language impairment.

Speech may take account of context in other ways, for example the needs of my auditor have to be taken into account. If he or she is a baby, I will adjust my vocabulary and even the pitch of my voice accordingly. If it is a person demanding respect, my speech will become less personal and more formal. (A young man of my acquaintance who had successfully negotiated an entrance interview with the headmaster of a new school was asked if he had any questions, and said, 'Yes. How old are you?') This aspect of pragmatics shades into sociolinguistics or the way that speech conventions propagate power and gender relations.

Speech prosody may also play a pragmatic role as well as communicating information about the relationship of speaker and auditor. For example, in speech the only way of differentiating the two meanings of a recent book title,[137] which could be about a gunslinger or a herbivore but is actually about punctuation and grammar: 'Eats, shoots, and leaves' and 'Eats shoots and leaves', is for the commas to be indicated in speech by pauses.

Pragmatic impairment may be difficult to pick up on standard tests,[138] but automatic methods exist for assessing voice prosody,[139] at least one of which can be used in very young children in the babble or pre-linguistic phase.[140] Oller *et al.* used whole-day samples of children who were presumed to be neurotypical, to have Kanner syndrome, or to have language delay.[140] They were able to discriminate between the neurotypical children and the other two groups with a high degree of accuracy, based solely on the computerized vocal analysis, but it is not clear how much of the prosodic impairment was meta-linguistic and how much para-linguistic. The first principal component differentiating the groups (802 recordings were analysed), and accounting for 40 per cent of the variance, had three main factors: first, normal formant transitions (shifts in tone or pitch) marking syllables;

second, giving more voice energy to the syllable in a word that is normally stressed (often the first syllable in English, but the last syllable in French); and third, normal variations in pitch and tone during utterances.

Semantic-pragmatic disorder

Semantic-pragmatic disorder was developed by Rapin in her attempt to provide a systematic classification of childhood speech and language disorders.[130] It is sometimes applied to children whose speech is normal syntactically and phonologically, but who have speech and communication difficulties. For some time it has been differentiated from ASD as a specific disorder with a different outcome, and there are certainly some children with mild specific language impairment who present mainly with neologisms or word finding difficulties, and make pragmatic errors (examples of these are given below). But it is now thought that, except for these rare instances when it is a presentation of specific language impairment, it is always associated with impaired nonverbal expression and is therefore a presentation of ASD.

Selective mutism

Selective mutism (previously termed, 'elective mutism') is the descriptive term for a condition in which a person – normally a child – can speak, and does so in one behaviour setting such as home, but does not speak ('mutism') in other settings or with other people. The mutism is persistent (lasting for longer than a month is sometimes specified) and complete, in that setting. Some young children will, for example, speak only to a sibling, whose language demands are less rigorous than a parent, and who can therefore make adjustments for the child's speech errors. The occurrence of selective mutism peaks at about the age of five, coinciding with the child's first school, and it is most often school that is the setting in which children are mute. There may be many possible reasons for selective mutism,[141] but in at least some cases, the child has a mild specific language impairment associated with reduced verbal working memory,[142] which is not sufficient to prevent speaking in low anxiety settings, but enough to inhibit language processing in settings where the child is anxious. There is an association between selective mutism and anxiety disorders like shyness in children.

Is the language impairment in ASD a specific language impairment?

A parsimonious, and therefore attractive, hypothesis about ASD is that AS is the consequence of a nonverbal communicative impairment, and autistic disorder the consequence of this plus a super-added specific language impairment.[143] Young children with autistic disorder and those with specific language impairment do have similar language difficulties, but these diverge as children get older. Children with autistic disorder are more likely use echolalia than children with specific language impairment. With increasing age it is more apparent that the linguistic errors made by children with autistic disorder and children with specific language impairment are not quite the same.[144, 145, 146] Both groups of children make syntactical errors but children with an autistic disorder are less likely to make semantic errors,[147] and less likely to have articulation disorders. The molecular biology, neuroimaging and genetics of specific language disorder do not show the overlap with ASD that they would be expected to if the autistic disorder was AS plus specific language impairment.[145] Grammatical ability is inversely correlated with speech delay and the number of symptoms of autism,[148] and in another study was inversely correlated with self-injury, temper tantrums and more restricted or repetitive behaviours,[149] suggesting that syntactical impairment in autistic disorder is more a measure of severity than of an independent syndrome.

In comparisons of spontaneous narratives produced by children with autism and children with a specific language impairment, both groups make syntactic errors, but children with autism also make more pragmatic errors, for example using more ambiguous referents (e.g. 'here'),[150] or in shifting perspective to different protagonists.[151] Children with ASD may also make errors in repeating sentences that are suggestive of working memory impairments,[152] but make fewer syntactic errors than children with specific language impairment when demands are made on working memory.[153] Groehn *et al.* conclude, in a review of the literature, that the language disorder in ASD is best understood as a kind of disconnection aphasia,[144] like conduction aphasia but involving more widespread disconnection than that within the arcuate fascicle that is implicated in acquired conduction dysphasia following a stroke or other localized lesion.[154]

It is unlikely that the overlap between specific language impairment and autistic disorder will be resolved by psychological or linguistic research unless the relative contributions of culture and neurobiology to the development of language – a debate originating in the controversy between Piaget and Chomsky about the origins of language – can be decided. This is more likely to happen through the development of neurobiological markers,[155] or genetic markers for language,[156] than through research into language use.[157]

Despite the uncertainty about the aetiology of language impairment in autism, it is useful clinically to think of the functional impairment of ASD as being due to a nonverbal communicative disorder and an additional but varying degree of impairment in producing grammatically well-formed utterances,[158, 159] with people with AS having relatively little or no specific language impairment and people with an autistic disorder having a significant degree of it. Research indicates that language understanding may also be impaired in people with ADHD.[136]

Patterns of speech and language impairment in the ASDs

Echolalia (repeating word for word what someone has just said) palilalia (repeating over and over what one is saying),[160] and jargon speech (the out of context repetition of catch phrases) are commonly associated with the speech of people with an autistic disorder. The use of this kind of speech is now thought to be an attempt to interact, but in the face of inadequate language.[161]

Even where language is normally developed, the social use of language is impaired, leading to pragmatic and sociolinguistic errors. This may be one facet of the fundamental disorder of nonverbal communication in the ASDs. One study has found that everyone in a sample of people with AS had an idiosyncratic voice prosody in comparison with a neurotypical sample.[162]

Prevalence of types of speech and language disorders

A study of children with language delay found on screening unselected two-year-olds that 61 per cent had a phonological or articulation disorder alone, 17 per cent had some degree of specific language impairment in addition but no other developmental problem, and 22 per cent had a language and nonverbal impairment. The authors judged that the nonverbal impairment was significant in 10 per cent, of whom 4 per cent met criteria for an autistic disorder.[163]

Management of speech and language disorders

Although it is beyond the scope of this book to discuss this in any depth, it is worth mentioning here that there are many possible causes of speech delay or selective mutism other than an ASD or a speech and language disorder. Routine assessment should include an assessment of hearing, where suggested by the history, an assessment of non-speech mouth and tongue actions to check for motor control of the speech apparatus, for example by asking the child to mime licking a lollipop and then to actually lick one, and checking cerebellar function, for example by asking the child to repeat strings of alternating sounds such as puh-tuh-kuh as quickly as possible.

Prosody should be assessed by listening to the child speaking and noting the distribution of stress, variations in pitch, and variations in tone. Prosody is used to mark phrases within sentences, and to differentiate statements from questions. The child's ability to do this should be assessed.

Unclear pronunciation of vowels, consonants and whole words or phrases may indicate a speech sound disorder.

Care should be taken that the child is being assessed in their first language, that is, the one that they normally speak at home.

Chapter 6

NONVERBAL COMMUNICATION, EMPATHY AND THEORY OF MIND

NONVERBAL COMMUNICATION

Many of the current psychological theories of the fundamental impairment in ASD implicate nonverbal communication. Nonverbal expression rated at two years of age was a better predictor of outcome in ASD at the age of seven than any other measure in one study,[1] and ratings of nonverbal communication were proposed as a screening tool in another.[2] Much of nonverbal communication happens without conscious awareness, unlike language. If I am in a meeting with three people and I think that I am getting a disproportionate amount of attention from a speaker, I will look over at the third, silent person and within seconds the speaker will start to direct remarks to him or her. Nonverbal communication is an effective means of influencing others, but its effects are usually not attended to. This lack of conscious awareness distinguishes language-like nonverbal symbols, for example metaphorical gestures that activate left as well as right hemisphere,[3] from the reflexive to and fro of socially embedded nonverbal communication.

Right hand gestures in most people are more likely to be associated with utterances that have a positive emotional valence, and left hand gestures with speech that has a negative valence. In a very small sample of individuals (although a large sample of utterances), this was reversed in two left handers,[4] suggesting that speech and possibly voluntary control are more readily exercised over positive messages than over negative ones, which are more likely to be involuntary and therefore 'true'.

Are all nonverbal communication channels affected in ASD?

Studies of nonverbal communication have often focused on the anatomical area used for expression. Body parts vary in the extent to which they are normally consciously monitored (the face is monitored more than the feet) and faces express both conscious or deliberate expressions, and involuntary ones. Movements of the feet when a person is sitting are much more likely to be involuntary and have been used to give clues to emotional states that a person might be trying to conceal.[5] Interpretation of nonverbal communication by television pundits or political observers purports to use this 'leakage' to discover other people's 'real' feelings.[6]

People with an ASD may not be impaired in their conscious – or reflective, to use the term used in Chapter 5 – ability to use nonverbal communication, or to consciously use leakage. They use nonverbal expressions, although idiosyncratically, as if they are alone.[7] Nor is their imitation of goal-directed actions impaired.[8] However, people with an ASD are impaired in their involuntary, 'reflexive', use of nonverbal communication: that is, they are impaired in the immediate unthinking recognition of and response to gestures, facial expressions, gaze direction, tone of voice and other kinds of nonverbal communition.

Both nonverbal expression and the interpretation of others' nonverbal expressions are implicated. In fact, the mirror neuron theory of ASD suggests that it is only by responding in imitation that we are able to interpret another person's nonverbal cue. This kind of nonverbal communication is the basis of continuous interpersonal interchange that I term the interbrain connection, and which creates the experience of 'intersubjectivity'.[9, 10, 11]

Nonverbal communication is redundant, and has often been considered to be divisible into channels,[12] as discussed in Chapter 5. People who have had radical surgery for laryngeal tumours may sometimes relearn oesophageal speech, but are unable to modulate this well enough to regain voice prosody. However, they continue to be effective nonverbal communicators in other channels: knocking out one channel of communication does not knock out others.

In ASD, all channels of nonverbal communication are impaired including voice prosody,[13, 14, 15, 16] hand gestures,[17] posture,[18] and gaze.[19, 20, 21] This suggests that there is a common basis for nonverbal communication, irrespective of channel or modality, just as the language areas are involved in the production of words, whether they are written, sung or spoken. Some evidence for this comes from a study of multiplex families with more than one sibling having an ASD. Linkage analysis of the genotypies of the families who had the most severe impairment of nonverbal communication demonstrated that genes on 8q22-23 and 16p12-13 had the highest lod scores;[22] 8q22 is the site of a hydroxylase gene implication in congenital adrenal hyperplasia, and 16p the site of a gene whose deletion leads to tuberous sclerosis.

Nonverbal expression is also reduced in people with intellectual disability compared to neurotypicals,[23] but not to the same degree.

ORIENTING ATTENTION, SALIENCE AND INTERPERSONAL COMMUNICATION

Selecting elements of the environment to attend to is crucial for the survival of any animal. Humans are no exception. To some degree acoustic and tactile attention can be made selective by priming, but in humans and other primates the main modality for attention is visual. Eye movements, and where necessary associated head movements, are under the control of the frontal eye fields, and initiating an eye movement probably requires activation of the dorsomedial area of prefrontal cortex.[24] In one study, participants were shown either an arrow or a photograph of a person looking sideways in a particular direction as a priming stimulus, and then shown an object in their peripheral visual field that was either in the direction pointed at by the arrow or the gaze in the photo that they had seen, or was not. An additional non-priming condition, in which participants saw a photo of a face apparently looking directly at them or a simple non-directional line segment, were also used. Priming reduced reaction time, as expected, but the arrow cue elicited much greater activation than did the gaze cue, with additional activation of the left parietal area and both temporal areas, and in the frontal eye fields.[25] The authors suggest that arrows require intentional, or reflective, visual attention,[25] which would be consistent with the arrow being a symbol, that is a directional cue that has had to be learnt and therefore requires reflective access to its learnt significance, and corresponding action.

Gaze while listening to speech is normally under the control of the left hemisphere and directed more to the mouth, which provides disambiguating information about phonemes, than to the eyes. However, when voice prosody becomes negative, gaze switches in neurotypicals, but not in people with an ASD, to right hemisphere control and is more often directed to the eyes, which provide better information about emotions.[26]

People with an ASD attend to their physical environment, and to changes in it, with greater effectiveness than neurotypicals,[27] although possibly doing this by a different processing route.[28] Some aspects of reflexive attention are therefore unimpaired in people with an ASD. What seems to be impaired is reflexive attention to social stimuli across the board, including a reduced attention to the linguistic rather than the perceptual quality of speech.[29]

This difference in stimulus salience is likely to be present from birth in many people with an ASD. It cannot therefore be attributed to being able to make complex judgements about what is social, but must be due to some much more basic characteristic of stimuli. Two likely candidates are attention to eyes,[30, 31] and attention to movement that has a biological or purposive character,[32] which, like attention to the eyes, has perceptual privilege in neurotypicals but not people with an ASD.[33] Movements of a biological and purposive kind are likely to be movements that an infant might themselves make, for example movements that evoke the same mirror neuron activation as do the baby's own movements. Both of these types of stimuli result in activation in visual cortex, the frontal eye fields, right temporal cortex and adjacent parietal cortex.[34] The temporoparietal junction is implicated in orienting to biological movement,[35, 36] and connectivity between this area and other areas implicated in attention is reduced in people with an ASD.[36]

Orienting attention is not impaired in ADHD, but maintaining it in the face of distractors, a function of the rostral anterior cingulate, is.[37] ADHD, like other ASDs, is also associated with impairment of right hemisphere attentional networks.[38]

Recognition of emotional expression

There has been a considerable literature on whether or not people with an ASD can recognize facial expressions as efficiently as neurotypicals. The original studies used photographs of facial expressions, which were not always standardized. Even when standardized photographs were used,[39] there were problems about choosing matched populations, whether or not people with an ASD might use idiosyncratic categorization rather than a simple failure of recognition, and ceiling effects. How much photographs emulate everyday face reading was also moot. Repeated studies have supported most of the original findings, however: that facial expression recognition is impaired in ASD,[40] and also in ADHD, that facial identity and facial expression is usually determined by a kind of privileged or gestalt processing which is not used for facial gender,[40] and that the way that faces are scanned in people with an ASD probably accounts for the local processing rather than gestalt processing effect.[40]

Faces, arguably, do not receive the same degree of attention from people with an ASD as they do from neurotypicals. Although there is consistent evidence that the fusiform face area is implicated in face processing,[41] and is underdeveloped in people with an ASD,[42,43] it may be that this is because it is not recruited by repeated task performance, as it is in neurotypicals,[44] than that there is a primary impairment in the fusiform area.

Face recognition ability varies even within the neurotypical population, and is genetically determined.[45]

EMPATHY

The term empathy was coined by the Englishman Edward Titchener, who, before emigrating to the United States, studied in Europe, where he was influenced by the aesthetics of Friedrich Vischer. Vischer had coined the term *Einfühlung* to describe the general human ability to feel at one with nature. He ascribed this to the human ability to mimic movement: so when a tree sways, a human observer has the sensation of swaying too, and in experiencing the feelings that go with swaying, attributes them to the tree. Theodore Lipps, under whom Titchener studied, had applied this to psychology, and to the problem of knowing other people's feelings.[46] In the US, Titchener founded the psychology laboratory at Cornell, and continued to work on the human applications of *Einfühlung*, which he translated for the benefit of English speaking colleagues as 'empathy'. The word has no relation to the modern Greek ἐμπάθεια, which means something more like 'prejudice'.

Unexpected emotional responses to others are a common source of burden to the carers of people with an ASD,[47] especially when there is a lack of response to distress. Lack of empathy is considered to be a defining characteristic of an ASD, and it has been proposed that the ASDs should be included in a larger class of 'empathy disorders'.[48] Empathy is currently considered to be a combination of two dissociable processes: affective empathy, based on emotional contagion, and cognitive empathy, based on a 'theory of mind'.[49] It is further suggested that these are neurologically, phylogenetically and probably developmentally distinct components, with contagious emotion being linked to face perception and activation of the most rostral part of superior temporal cortex (Brodmann area 44) and adjacent prefrontal cortex, and theory of mind being linked to imagination, and the orbitofrontal cortex (Brodmann areas 10, 11).[50, 51, 52] Other studies support the importance of these two areas, along with presumed mirror neuron areas.[53]

AFFECTIVE EMPATHY

Emotional contagion

It is still agreed that empathy's roots are, as Lipps surmised,[46] in the contagion of emotional expression, leading to the carry over of the emotion associated with that expression,[54] a phenomenon sometimes termed 'emotional contagion'.[55] On top of this base are layered levels of processing that involve, at the least, capacities for imagination or theory of mind (considered below), focus on or indifference to the emotional stimulus, and a general attitude of concern or 'compassion'.[56]

Emotional contagion may be a momentary response that can be inhibited within milliseconds but where top-down processing is inhibited, for example in crowds, it may spread and swell leading to a persisting emotional tone, or mood, that infects almost everyone in a crowd. It has even been suggested that emotional contagion may spread through social networks within a population with a time course of years. Hill *et al.* have used data collected for the Framingham Heart Study to model this and suggest that a person has their probability of contentment increased by 0.02 per year for each person in their network who is content, and to have their contentment decreased by 0.04 for each person who is discontented.[57] It is interesting to note that, if these estimates are correct, low mood is twice as contagious as good mood.

Emotional contagion and ASD

Neurotypical adults seeing a video of another person receiving apparently painful stimulation to a part of their body reflexively inhibit the corticospinal activation of their own musculature for that part as well as showing autonomic arousal proportional to the imagined pain. Adults with AS also experience autonomic arousal but not in proportion to the imagined pain, and they do not inhibit corticospinal activation.[58]

Imitation by another person facilitates social interaction in neurotypicals and in people with ASD,[59] but people with an ASD are less likely to imitate others (see Chapter 5 for details). There is strong evidence that emotional contagion, based both on facial and other bodily expressions, is reduced in ASD.[60, 61] There is an interaction between autistic traits and gender, presumably because women are more responsive than men to facial expression. In one study, being a woman and having low autistic trait scores were independent predictors of spontaneous facial mimicry (electromyographic activity of corrugator supercilii muscle) but not correlation with social smiling (electromyography of zygomaticus major).[62]

The impairment in motor imitation may be due to an impairment in the neurological substrate of copying a movement,[63] but it is also affected by the gaze of the person being imitated in the case of neurotypicals, but not children with an ASD.[64] Children with an ASD who do not show emotional contagion do so if they are instructed to look at the other person's eyes,[65] suggesting that gaze and orientation plays a part even in emotional contagion. A similar finding has been made in a woman with bilateral amygdala lesions, who did not spontaneously look at the eye region and whose acuity at detecting facial expressions increased when she was instructed to do so, although she soon forgot the instruction and reverted back to her previous eye avoidant face scanning.[66]

People with diagnoses of antisocial personality, who are low on empathy, also spend less time looking at another person's eyes but this may be a learnt response, of suppressing eye orientation, rather than a primary failure of eye orientation as is most likely in ASD.

Emotional contagion and affective empathy

Contagion of emotions is potentially dangerous to individuals[67] and a means of blocking it, without blocking endogenous feelings, develops to protect against it, presumably during infancy. Psychoanalytic theory has speculated for over a century that infants achieve this, and make their first steps towards self-awareness, by being able to distinguish feelings that originate in themselves from feelings that originate in others. The ability to do this is also essential for the development of empathy.[68]

The way that emotional contagion is blocked probably involves being able to make general distinctions between self- and other-generated processes. This ability is subverted by disinhibition. So in crowd situations, or when intoxicated, people might still act as if contagious feelings are really their own, leading to groups of people behaving almost like single organisms with only one mind. It can also be subverted by an effort of imagination: neurotypicals watching painful operations on another person's orbits experienced more tensing of their own orbicularis oculi muscle around the eye if they were told to imagine that it was themselves having the operation, than if they were told to remember it was someone else.[69]

Some evidence points to an association between a reduced ability to distinguish self from other and a reduced ability to describe one's own feelings, sometimes called alexithymia, and a consequent reduction in cognitive coping with emotions.[70]

Attributing consequences to one's own versus another's actions is associated with a self-recognition system, possibly centred on the temporoparietal junction and inferior parietal lobule[71] and activations of anterior cingulate cortex.[72] The anterior cingulate is also more active, along with orbitofrontal cortex, when observing one's face as compared to that of others.[73]

Self-recognition

The ability to distinguish self from other is often tested using the mirror recognition test, in which an infant has a spot of rouge put on her or his cheek and is then sat in front of a mirror. Infants who recognize the spot as a blemish, and try to wipe it away, are assumed to have recognized themselves in the mirror and therefore to have a concept of self. Other animals that show this kind of self-awareness include chimpanzees,[74, 75] bottlenose dolphins,[76] Indian elephants,[77] and parrots and members of the crow family.[78] Parrots also show cage stereotypies that have features similar to those in autism.[79] Animal species that pass self-recognition tests have certain similarities. They are species that are tameable or trainable, can learn human language and have complex calls of their own, and they can make lasting relationships with humans; their cognitive capacity increases if they are brought up by humans.

In humans, self-recognition often seems to involve inferior prefrontal cortex, suggesting the involvement of inner speech in some but not all tasks.[80, 81]

Self-recognition is unimpaired in people with a ASD.[82, 83]

Self- and other-judgements in ASD

People with ASD make fewer distinctions between themselves and others,[84] do not show increased activation on EEG when viewing their own versus others' faces, as neurotypicals do;[85] they do not show activation of the inferior parietal lobule when viewing faces that are the product of morphing their own face with that of another person, and do not show enhanced cingulate cortex activation in association with their own moves in an iterative trust game, as neurotypicals do.[86] They are reported to be more alexithymic, and this is associated with a reduced distinction between self and others, and reduced empathy,[87] although the authors of this article, unlike Chiu *et al.*, conclude that it is insula rather than the anatomically proximate anterior cingulate that is the area in the brain linked with this judgement.

Envy and gloating are both emotions that are linked to Schadenfreude, the satisfaction of other people's misfortunes. Schadenfreude is satisfying only if other people's feelings are sharply distinguished from one's own. It is therefore reliant on the self–other distinction, and might therefore be expected to be reduced in people with an ASD, which one study suggests that it is.[88]

Modulating affective empathy
Modulating affective empathy by orientation

Schadenfreude is an example of the ability of neurotypicals to shut off, or at least diminish empathic responding. One way that this might be achieved is to be aware of another's pain, and to rejoice in it. Another, simpler way is to inhibit attention to someone else's pain, or to another's facial expressions, and the simplest way of doing this is to reduce attention to the person's eyes.[89] Although the net result may be the same as someone with an ASD who is not drawn to another person's eyes, this strategy is a learnt and reflective one, rather than the reflexive impairment of someone with an ASD.

Modulating affective empathy by emotional sensitivity

Attending to facial expressions in others is just the first step in affective empathy. The next step is facial imitation (see Chapter 5), and then the evocation of endogenous emotion by the mimicked facial expression. The imitation and affective response networks are separable, and separably modulated or impaired.

Empathy is correlated with sensitivity to feelings and, since the emotional brain is derived from the rhinencaphalon, sensitivity to smell, too. Ratings on an affective empathy rating scale are correlated with the ability to differentiate smells to the right nostril (olfaction is ipsilateral, and so the right nostril is linked to the right hemisphere).[90] When deducing the intentions of cartoon characters and naming their feelings are compared, the feeling condition results in additional activation in cingulate, paracingulate and amygdala, suggesting that these areas may be implicated in emotional sensitivity.[91] Other studies also implicate insula and prefrontal cortex.

Emotional sensitivity and ASD

Emotional sensitivity during face processing may be reduced in ASD.[92]

COGNITIVE EMPATHY

Affective empathy involves, as discussed in detail above, the direct communication of emotion using nonverbal means. Imagine two one-year-olds playing together. One is clearly enjoying shaking a rattle until an adult takes it away from her. Her face scrunches up and she is ready to burst into tears, and we might observe the other one-year-old's face also scrunch up, even though it was not his rattle that was taken away. The girl's distress communicated itself directly to the boy through emotional contagion, principally mediated by mirroring of facial expression. From about 18 months, the second child may not only empathize but also respond with solicitous gestures: this is the beginnings of what is often referred to as prosocial competence. However, from this age, a new kind of empathy is apparent, too. In our thought experiment, even if the first child does not react expressively to the toy being taken away, the second child may still show solicitude.[93] Somehow, even though there is no facial expression to be mirrored and therefore no emotional contagion, the boy seems to empathize with the girl. He knows what it would be like to have a pleasurable toy taken away, he sees this happening to the girl, and so he deduces that she, too, is feeling as he would in a similar situation. This application of imagination, of putting oneself in someone else's shoes, is often termed cognitive empathy. It requires the same kind of ability to take another person's perspective that is required in many theory of mind tasks.

Theory of mind

The current period of very active research can be dated back to 1978, to an article entitled 'Does the chimpanzee have a theory of mind?' by Premack and Woodruff. It was based on experiments with one of the chimps, Sarah, who lived in the chimpanzee colony established by the Premacks.[94] Premack and Woodruff wrote in this article that 'An individual has a theory of mind if he imputes mental states to others' and defined mental states to include 'purpose or intention, as well as knowledge, belief, thinking, doubt, guessing, pretending, liking and so forth.'[94a] Theory of mind and cognitive empathy are often used interchangeably, with theory of mind being the currently favoured term despite it being infelicitous. It seems very unlikely that we can learn much about other people by theorizing about them, or their minds. As Wittgenstein wrote, 'My attitude towards him is an attitude towards the soul. I am not of the opinion that he has a soul.'[95]

A number of distinct experimental paradigms have been used to test theory of mind. The original Premack and Woodruff study required Sarah to choose between photographs in response to having seen a video in which her favourite keeper, Keith, was trying to achieve something but lacked what he needed to do it. One of the photographs, which Sarah normally chose, was of what Keith was missing, the other or others were not. In a third experiment, the test was repeated but using a video made by Bill, a person that Sarah reportedly disliked. This time Sarah chose a photograph that showed Bill in even greater difficulty, for example putting his foot through the box rather than standing on it to get the bananas.

Testing theory of mind

One interpretation of these findings is that Sarah chose a photograph of what she would have wanted for the human she saw in the video. She wanted some help for Keith, and had the knowledge to know what that was, but she wanted something bad for Bill. Perhaps because it is not directly a test of the ability to impute a mental state to another, a different false belief task has been widely adopted in human studies. This is based on a paradigm of Wimmer and Perner,[96] and are tests of the ability to judge what another person knows, but not what another person doubts, guesses, pretends, to name some of the other mental states that Premack and Woodruff thought constituted having a theory of mind.[94] Another type of theory of mind test, the Strange Stories test developed by Happé, tests the imputation of some of these mental states.[97] Nonverbal tests of theory of mind include replications of false belief tasks in which the testee indicates her or his expectations by means of gaze direction,[98] the Reading the Mind in the Eyes test, and tests requiring participants to arrange cartoon pictures in an appropriate sequence.[91, 99] Tests of self-recognition (see above) and of inference from gaze direction or biological movement have also been used as tests of theory of mind.

False belief and other narrative tests

The original task used to assess theory of mind in children with ASD was Wimmer and Perner's 'Sally-Anne' task,[100] in which an experimenter enacts a scene with two dolls, Sally and Anne.[101] Sally is shown placing a ball in her basket, putting the lid on, and then exiting the scene. Anne then moves the ball to her own box, and puts the lid on. Sally then comes back, and the question for the observing child – the 'testee' – is where will Sally look for her ball: where it really is, or where Sally, but not the testee, last saw it. In other words, does Sally know less than the testee, who has seen Anne move the ball, and so knows that it is in Anne's box (see Figure 6.1).

Figure 6.1 The Sally-Anne test of theory of mind
Source: Reproduced from Frith, 2003 with permission from the illustrator, Axel Scheffer.

If the testee says that Sally will look for the ball in her own basket, he or she is said to have a theory of mind ability. Neurotypical children acquire the ability to pass this test from about three years onwards, and most neurotypical children have acquired the ability to pass the test by four years. Neurotypical children pass a slightly more difficult second order theory of mind test between the ages of six and eight.[102] Children or adults with ASD and a verbal age of over 12 are likely also to pass the test.[103] Children with congenital deafness, but no ASD, are delayed,[104] and even in adulthood may not pass the test if they have not been brought up to sign, although children with sign language can pass the test.[105] This suggests that the performance on false belief tasks is strongly influenced by language ability (using language widely as in Chapter 5 to encompass sign as well as word languages), or perhaps more generally, of 'inner speech' or narrative ability. 'Nonverbal' versions of false belief tasks, using gaze direction (see below) to indicate what the testee thinks that Sally would do, have been used to overcome this narrative difficulty, but do not remove the likelihood that the testee is using propositional thinking or inner narrative to arrive at their conclusion about Sally's behaviour, even if they do not articulate their conclusion but signal it. However, looking at what other people will look at might be a normal developmental step from looking at what they are looking at, and may be a precursor to a theory of mind.[106]

Spontaneous narrative and theory of mind

Mothers talk to their children about the personalities, mental states and motives of other people from when their children are 18 months old. Deaf children and children with ASD who cannot participate in these dialogues may not be stimulated to develop narratives about other children which can provide for false belief judgements. In a mixed group of children with language delay followed up until they were seven or eight, all had impaired oral narrative skills, irrespective of whether or not they had an additional ASD diagnosis.[107] In another study, the conversation of children with an ASD was compared to that of neurotypical children and of children with specific language impairment. The children with an ASD named more things, and made more statements about what they wanted, but provided fewer explanations, references to other people's state of mind, or references to their own thoughts or beliefs.[108] A lack of oral narrative is a possible explanation for a lack of theory of mind in some institutionalized children who have been deprived of conversation with carers. These children are more likely to grow up showing the symptoms of 'quasi-autism'.[109]

Congenitally blind neurotypicals are able to make normal ratings of the emotional valence of stories about people, and the same brain areas are active when they do so as in non-blind neurotypicals,[110] suggesting an independence of this component of theory of mind from components that are based on perspective-taking.

The same brain areas that are active in theory of mind tasks are also active during self-appraisal,[111] suggesting that we know about our own minds by the same means that we know about other people's minds.[112] Success on false belief tasks probably correlates with narrative ability more generally,[113] and this may be linked to the extent to which individuals discuss and reorder autobiographical memory. People with an ASD spend considerable time in going over remembered events, but do not think of them as having denouements, suggesting that the social context of the remembered events is not recalled.[114]

Self-conscious activities like thinking about memories, and presumably false belief tasks too, involve inner language,[115] and, consequently, activation of Broca's area (left inferior frontal gyrus).

Social intelligence and theory of mind

Children with ASD are delayed or may never acquire the ability to pass Sally-Anne type false belief tests, but children with AS appear to do so at the same age as neurotypical children. To see if a more subtle test could disclose theory of mind, narrative methods of testing have been developed including the Strange Stories test.[116] Other comparable narrative methods include the Stories from Everyday Life test.[117] There is a correlation between the results of these tests in people with AS, and a correlation with verbal IQ, which is much higher than it is in neurotypicals and has been interpreted to mean that people with AS are using language to solve the puzzle.[118] Nonverbal tests, such as cartoon tests or the Reading the Mind in the Eyes test, may be less amenable to these alternative strategies.

Cartoon tests of theory of mind

Putting cartoon drawings into a correct social sequence has been used to test theory of mind in schizophrenia,[119] but used less in autism although the attribution of intentions to animated drawings of shapes has been studied. On this test, children with an ASD show less use of mental state descriptions than neurotypical children.[120, 121]

Cartoon tasks have been used to invoke theory of mind processing in MRI scanners,[91, 122] and these have been interpreted to be supportive of the distinction between affective and cognitive empathy in that it has been suggested that each is served by a different but overlapping network. Vollm *et al.* conclude that the overlap includes the medial prefrontal cortex, temporoparietal junction and temporal poles; affective empathy is associated with enhanced activations of paracingulate, anterior and posterior cingulate and amygdala; and theory of mind tasks are associated with activation of lateral orbitofrontal cortex, middle frontal gyrus, cuneus and superior temporal gyrus.[91]

Simulation theory or theory theory?

Theory of mind is sometimes presented as an alternative strategy to empathy in knowing what someone else is thinking or feeling – perhaps even a strategy that able people with an ASD, such as people with AS, may be able to use since it involves language.

Theory of mind tests demonstrate that people with AS have more difficulty than neurotypicals in narrative tests, although they do also suggest that the strategy that people with AS use to interpret the stories may be more language based,[123] and so might represent a kind of compensatory effort.

There are many aspects of language use, of narrative, that are influenced by the emotional state, attention, or other personal characteristics of the listener – many, but not all, of these can be considered to be pragmatic features. One example, which has sometimes been considered to be a test of the theory of mind, is the 'faux pas' test in which people with an ASD are compared to neurotypicals on their ability to detect embarrassing or socially inappropriate utterances – 'faux pas' – in written narratives. Faux pas typically cause a characteristic feeling, embarrassment or 'cringing', specific facial signals (rubbing or touching the nose as one would if there was a bad smell), and activation of the rhinencephalon, specifically the insula. People with an ASD perform less well than neurotypicals on the faux pas test, tending to make too many judgements that faux pas are occurring.[124] Clinically, some people with AS and also with atypical AS will report that they tell themselves not to make a faux pas, for example telling themselves that they must not comment on a new acquaintance's weight and then, without thinking, they say 'Why are you so fat?'

These considerations have led to the suggestion that cognitive and affective empathy must be conjoined, and that cognitive empathy, far from being a cool, rational 'theory', is more like a kind of working model of someone else, a model with thoughts and feelings, something like the 'internal object' first described by Freud.[125] This 'simulation' theory of mind has been applied to ASD.[126, 127]

Taking a person's perspective is assisted by being there, with the person. It is possible to empathize with their feelings, and gauge from their gaze what they are thinking. Being able to recruit gaze may add considerable processing ability too. When someone is not there, it is necessary to imagine how they might have responded. One likely explanation of this is that we can 'simulate' the responses of people that we have met, or somehow know about. As a person becomes more familiar, so these simulations become more detailed and we are willing to make more predictions. Predicting how another person behaves also requires that one's own responses are suppressed.[128] The results of one study suggest that simulations involve activation of orbitofrontal cortex and that suppression of one's own perspective is associated with activation of left dorsomedial prefrontal cortex.[129] Self-reflection and making mental state inferences about someone perceived to be like oneself were both associated with activation of ventromedial prefrontal cortex in another study, whereas attributing mental states to a person seen as dissimilar involved activation of more dorsal areas.[130]

In a magnetic spectrum tomographic study of an adjacent brain area, dorsolateral prefrontal cortex, glutamate levels were correlated with perspective-taking, but not other dimensions of empathy, rated by questionnaire. ADHD is associated with increased glutamate in prefrontal cortex,[131] and the ability to consider another person's perspective in the abstract in social problem solving is reduced in ADHD.[132]

Perspective-taking and theory of mind

In a classic experiment, Baron-Cohen *et al.* demonstrated that neurotypical children, but not children with an ASD, could make a judgement about what a cartoon character ('Charlie') wanted by looking at his direction of gaze.[133] I had put forward a similar proposal, based largely on clinical observations, independently and at the same time.[134] Replication studies have shown that the impaired use of cue to detect desire is not due to the child's own desires being prepotent, but does extend to other signs of direction, such as arrows,[135] and therefore, presumably, pointing. However, children with an ASD do not respond more strongly to gaze direction over arrows, although neurotypical children do.[136]

Inferences about intention and agency from biological motion

Knowing what someone wants from their gaze direction is closely related to knowing what someone wants from their movement towards an object, or knowing what someone fears or dislikes from their movement away. Motion potential provides even more information, in that it might give clues to the intentions behind the movement. In fact, a particular class of movements, often called 'biological' or active as opposed to 'physical' or passive ones, are experienced as if they are motivated by intentions and the entities that are moving are experienced as agents. Even if the movements are sketchy movements of simple geographical shapes, neurotypicals will interpret them, if the movements are self-correcting, as being goal directed, and therefore the shapes as having intentions and being agents.[137] Some, but not all, studies have suggested that people with an ASD are less able to follow biological motion,[138] but there is stronger evidence that people with ASD are less likely to interpret motion as biological. Judgements involving agency involve caudal areas of superior temporal sulcus and adjacent parietal cortex, an area often termed the temporoparietal junction. Repeated studies have indicated that right temporoparietal junction is involved in perceiving movement as biological.[139] A patient with a lesion in posterior temporal sulcus was unable to perform a related task, of inferring preferences from observations of another person's actions.[140]

The left temporoparietal junction may be implicated in perceiving another person as being a 'narrative agent'.[141] The temporoparietal junction is less active during motor inhibition tasks in people with ADHD,[142] and is less well connected to prefrontal cortex in people with ASD.[143] People with an ASD are less likely to perceive motion as biological,[33] and have reduced temporoparietal activation compared to neurotypicals and are less likely to attribute agency to cartoon movements.[144]

The Reading the Mind in the Eyes test

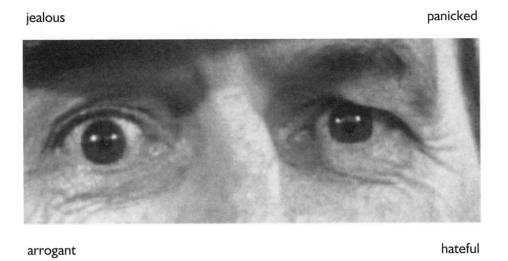

Figure 6.2 One task from the Reading the Mind in the Eyes test
Source: Picture supplied courtesy of Simon Baron-Cohen.

The Reading the Mind in the Eyes test requires the participant to look at a photograph of the region of the face that runs in a strip from just below one ear to just below the other, and that contains the eyes. Using only the information in this strip, the testee has to determine what the mental state was of the person who was photographed (see Figure 6.2). The test requires almost all of the steps considered in this section on empathy (see Figure 6.3). It requires the eyes to be the focus of attention (although there is a good deal less distracting redundancy than in photographs of the whole face), the normal threat response that involves amygdala activation to be inhibited, and for the emotion engendered by the expression to be felt. That emotion needs to be put into a narrative context, since the terms that the participant is asked to choose are not emotion words, but moral judgements – 'hateful', 'arrogant', 'jealous' and 'panicked' in Figure 6.2. The normal response to the picture in Figure 6.2 is 'panicked'.

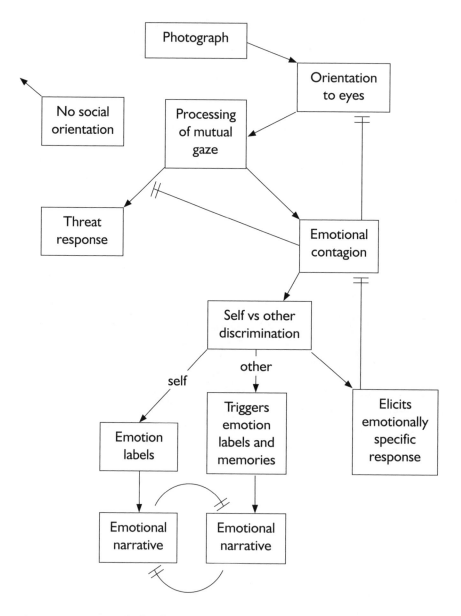

Figure 6.3 Putative steps leading from emotional contagion and internal narrative to empathy and a theory of mind

Key

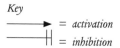 = *activation*

= *inhibition*

Accurate responses on the eyes test require that all of these steps, involving both affective and cognitive empathy, are completed successfully. People with an ASD consistently perform less well on the eyes test than neurotypicals, but it remains open at which step or steps they fail. Acquiring a theory of mind requires all of the steps needed to perform theory of mind tests. So it also remains open at what developmental level (as each of these steps is mastered at a different age, and to some degree builds on the previous step) theory of mind errors actually arise. Although performance on the Reading the Mind in the Eyes test is impaired in people with ASD, it is not impaired in people with ADHD. Nor is a more naturalistic empathic task, although self- and other-informant reports of people with ADHD were significantly lower than normally developing adolescents in this study.[146]

WHEN THEORY OF MIND AND EMPATHY CONFLICT

Conflicts between what a person says, and what they mean, or imply, or signal nonverbally have been the subject of considerable interest since the Mental Research Institute in Palo Alto proposed that 'double-bind' communications of this sort led to schizophrenia.[145] One fMRI study suggests that comparable conflicts might arise between theory of mind and empathy, and when they occurred the anterior cingulate and ventrolateral PFC were activated, arguably in order to resolve the conflict. When emotional contagion cues were prioritized, network analysis suggested a connection between ACC and right premotor cortex. When theory of mind judgement predominated, the favoured connections were with language and memory areas: bilateral temporal poles and rostral medial PFC.[147]

EMPATHY HAS TO BE MERITED

An empathic response is the product of a cascade of neural responses from the initial one of emotional contagion, accompanied by the partly independent perspective-taking and self-conscious perception of another person's feelings and thoughts. However many, if not all, of these responses are down- or up-regulated by reflection and learning.[148] The extent of the empathic response may be influenced by autonomic responsivity,[149] independently of the accuracy of the empathic response.

The affective and the cognitive empathy centres may each influence the functioning of the other. For example, pain perception is greater when viewing others from one's own ethnic group, than when viewing out-group faces expressing an equal intensity of pain expression.[150] The most likely explanation is that Caucasians and East Asians (the faces used in the study) scan faces differently: Caucasians scan a triangle between eyes and mouth, East Asians scan around the nose, presumably because this provides more useful, affective information in East Asian faces.[151] Empathy with pain in children is also influenced by knowledge about emotions, and also about the emotional style of their mothers.[152]

There is a common sense idea that adults learn to empathize more as they can identify with a wider range of people, and to see that, as people often say, 'we are none of us black or white but shades of grey'. Observation suggests otherwise: that when one infant cries all other infants within hearing distance cry, that is, infants empathize with other infants without making exceptions. Young children may empathize with other young mammals to an extent that they have to be protected against distress from normal human actions like slaughtering and eating young mammals and birds. Explicit learning about empathy often involves empathy suppression, for example for those who are 'not worth consideration' or people who have 'brought it upon themselves' or even, just people who are not like us, 'they don't feel normal emotions. They just pretend they do, to get your sympathy'.

Empathy modulation
Tribalism
Adults normally have the capacity to turn empathy off in response to an evaluation of whether or not the other 'deserves' empathy.[153] It has been argued that this capacity underlies the otherwise inexplicable but reliable observation that men who are considered kind, stable and loving at home can commit rape and murder in a theatre of war.[154]

This kind of judgement may be made by people with an ASD too, who consider that all neurotypicals form a class, none of whose members deserve empathy. One neurotypical's bullying or aggression can therefore be paid back on another neurotypical because 'all neurotypicals are the same'.

Affective reactivity
It is well known that empathy diminishes in populations who are numbed or shocked into apathy. Conversely, increased emotional sensitivity is associated with an increase in empathy, especially in boys.[155, 156]

Fear
The developmental studies mentioned above provide evidence that self-regulation is also correlated with empathy.[157, 158] One reason for this may be that compassion, even in the presence of intact self–other differentiation, raises some degree of the shared emotion in the observer that needs to be processed. This is particularly so when the pain of another person is being observed, when brain areas that are normally activated by threat in the immediate environment are also activated.[159] The response to another person's pain may be more or less empathic depending on the extent to which the observer fears the other's pain, and wants to avoid it.

Rules trump empathy
Many people with an ASD are idealistic and believe strongly in the importance of care and affection in the world. They may be easily moved to tears by stories of children or animals being ill-treated, and yet may, without seeing the inconsistency, strike the family pet because it was 'naughty', or lock a younger sibling in the bedroom because they are a 'nuisance'.

People with an ASD are very like neurotypicals in this respect. One has to be 'cruel to be kind'. One must avoid making 'special exceptions', however pitiable they seem. One must 'harden one's heart' in life. One difference though is that people with an ASD can be even more rigid in the application of rules, and the rules are often of a specific rather than a general kind.

Case example

> Ronald was looking after his young nephew and niece when his niece came to him in tears saying that her brother had pushed her. Ronald grabbed his nephew and took him into the garden where he repeatedly punched him to teach him that boys should never be aggressive to girls.

Read my lips

In 1988, US Vice-President George H. W. Bush used the phrase 'Read my lips' as a synonym for 'Believe me'. It was not clear why he said this, but it was perhaps prescient as subsequent research indicates that there is often a discrepancy between the positive message that politicians convey in debates in their words – and which they may emphasize with the gestures of their dominant arm – and negative gestures in the non-dominant limb. Observers are aware of the positive messages, but may be unaware of the negative message, although they may be empathically influenced by it. In people who are right brain dominant, the involuntary gestures are made by the right hand. Careful observers who look to the left hand for the 'real truth' may be fooled by the left-handed politician, although it would be far-fetched to attribute the success of contemporary left handers (Tony Blair and Barack Obama are examples) to this.[160] Such channel discrepancies were first described by the Palo Alto communications laboratory[161, 162] and may represent a particular challenge for empathizing for someone, such as a person with an ASD, whose empathy is impaired.

Implications for ASD

Reduced empathy reduces the quality of intimate relationships, and so increases the burden for carers. It may also contribute to later difficulty in making or maintaining sexual relationships, and in child-rearing.

It is often thought that reduced empathy makes a substantial contribution to violence or antisocial behaviour, although there is little evidence for this.[163] However, blunted responses to other people's pain or fear may increase the risk of violence becoming prolonged or going 'too far'.

The main impact of reduced empathy may be on social problem solving, particular conflict resolution, and negotiation.[164] Both of these 'prosocial competencies' become increasingly important as children grow older, and both are linked to children's popularity.[165]

The lack of empathy of people with an ASD may be paid for by themselves in the long run, in the pain of social exclusion and unpopularity, which further reduce prosocial responding,[166] and so create a vicious circle of social marginalization.

Chapter 7

NEUROPSYCHOLOGY OF ASD

INTRODUCTION

Particular brain structures are repeatedly implicated in studies of ASD. The short-list of the areas considered in Chapters 1 and 2 has included cerebellum, basal ganglia and prefrontal cortex in ADHD; right superior temporal lobe, cingulum, inferior parietal lobule and fusiform gyrus, amygdala, frontal operculum and medial prefrontal cortex in ASD, and, in addition, in autistic disorder with language impairment, dorsolateral prefrontal cortex and left superior temporal lobe. But there is no evidence that a focal lesion in any of these structures will be enough to cause an ASD. And other conditions that are causes of ASD, like Rett syndrome or velocardiofacial syndrome, or are associated with ASD, like epilepsy, dyslexia or Tourette syndrome, are even less localized.

Usually, the ASDs are the consequence of instability or impairment in networks linking brain centres, an approach to neurological impairment first made in the nineteenth century by Hughlings Jackson and others, but revived in the twentieth century by Norman Geschwind,[1] and popularized by Antony Damasio.[2]

Network dysfunction does not necessarily result from abnormal neurons, or grey matter, but might happen if insufficient interconnections have not developed, as suggested in the underconnectivity hypothesis of Just et al.,[3] or it may be the consequence of a biochemical lesion affecting one particular transmitter, the dopamine explanation of ADHD. It has also been suggested that glial dysfunction may cause network instability, too.[4] At the moment, the techniques for examining network function are in their infancy.

Dysfunction in a neurological network leads to new ways of looking at psychological impairment, too. Networks may fail only under load, for example, and so psychological impairments may be demonstrable only under load, too. Load in this context includes anxiety, fatigue and interpersonal demand, as well as concurrent cognitive processing.[5] The psychological consequences of network impairment are therefore influenced by what an older generation might have considered to be 'functional' factors.

Psychological impairments in consequence of network instability are also more ecologically sensitive. The neurologist, Victor Adams, liked to use as an illustration of frontal lobe dysfunction a patient of his who could have a conversation with him over the telephone when he called her from outside her hospital room, but as soon as he walked in she became mute and was apparently unable to speak to him at all.[6] One can suppose that her dorsolateral PFC and temporal lobe language centre function was prejudiced by her need to use frontal operculum to process nonverbal communications, too, and that the consequence was a failure of network function when Dr Adams was present in the flesh. In the past, this kind of variability has too often been written off as purely psychological, and appropriate tests of it have not been developed.

INTELLIGENCE

Age and IQ are numbers, and the dimensions on which they lie are linear. However, neither age nor IQ is like this in real life. A person is likely to change much more between birth and the age of 5, than between 20 and 25. Intelligence, too, is not a linear dimension. A drop of IQ from 80 to 60 is much more disabling than a drop of IQ from 140 to 120, for example. Unlike IQ, intelligence is not simple. IQ is a general factor of intelligence, extracted originally by Spearman from a range of sub-tests of intelligence. This general factor does not account for all the variance of even the standard intelligence tests. Reanalyses of intelligence test datasets, using modern measures of goodness of fit of factor solutions, indicate that three factors, rather than one, fit the data better.[7] Cattell termed these three factors *fluid intelligence*, the ability to develop new solutions for problems; *crystallized intelligence*, the ability to recognize that a new problem is a variant of an old one and apply the solution of the old one to the new one; and *visual-spatial reasoning*, the ability to represent a problem visually, and use visual imagery to solve it.[7, 8] Fluid intelligence is closely correlated to working memory (discussed below).[9]

Intelligence is not a measure of total brain function, but of a function, called 'problem-solving' in the previous paragraph, which comes into many other cognitive processes. However, the relation between intelligence and these other processes depends on whether intelligence is limiting. A computer analogy may be appropriate. The intelligence of a computer is a reflection of its central processing unit (CPU). If this is slow, and can handle only short strings at a time, the whole computer will be slow and limited. However, if the CPU is fast, but the graphics chip is slow or there is a shortage of random access memory, the computer will still be slow, particularly at tasks that draw particularly on graphics processing or RAM. Haier and others have argued for a frontoparietal connection as being a reliable basis for spatial intelligence (often described as being well developed in people with ASD),[10] but when people with comparable IQs on testing are compared, there are considerable differences in activation patterns in their brains, suggesting that there are different neurological routes to the same 'g'.[11] However, a more recent study of 241 patients with focal lesions seems to confirm the importance to IQ of a frontoparietal network linking 'regions that integrate verbal, visuospatial, working memory, and executive processes'.[12]

Some of the difficulty in interpreting the neuroimaging findings may result from the contribution of processing efficiency to IQ, since processing efficiency reduces rather than increases brain activity.[13, 14] As IQ scores fall, there is greater correlation between sub-test scores, meaning that the impact of a single, general factor of intelligence becomes greater. This may be because connectivity is a general neurological factor that is a necessary but not sufficient criterion for intelligence.[15] Conditions that affect white matter, such as tuberous sclerosis, may be particularly associated with reduced intelligence for this reason.[16]

The computer analogy is misleading in one way. There is no single locus for intelligence that corresponds to the CPU. But nor is intelligence a general property of the whole brain. Intelligence is best understood as an expression of the function of a network of centres. Similarly, the autistic impairment can also be understood as an expression of the function of another network, involving other centres.[17] In one study of people with autism, for example, intelligence was linked with electrophysiological activity in centro-parietal areas, and the autistic impairment with temporal electrical activity,[18] an area known to be associated with face processing in people with autism.[19]

It has been argued that some cognitive skills are not correlated with intelligence. Musicality and mathematical ability are examples. More contentiously, it has been argued that there exists a separate intelligence, 'emotional intelligence', which is correlated with interpersonal skill, although this has not been accepted by many experts.[20]

Intelligence is often expressed as the percentage of the score obtained to that of the general population of the same age as the testee: the intelligence quotient, or IQ. It is generally accepted that intelligence tests based on language or symbolic skills may give a different IQ score, often known as the verbal IQ, to that of nonverbal measures, the performance IQ. In the general population verbal IQ equals performance IQ and is approximately 103 (the average IQ of the whole tested population has slightly increased since norms were developed). Although there are many factors that influence verbal and performance scores, including speed (which particularly influenced performance IQ) and education (which influences verbal IQ), reduced verbal versus performance IQ may be an indicator of a speech and language disorder and reduced performance versus verbal IQ may be an indication of dyspraxia.[21] Although left hemisphere lesions in adults (in those whose left hemisphere is dominant) particularly affect language, and right hemisphere lesions in adults particularly affect motor performance, right-sided lesions in children may or may not produce a verbal performance discrepancy.[22] Left-sided lesions in children are associated with impaired speech and language and with verbal performance discrepancies but, surprisingly, verbal IQ may exceed performance IQ as often as verbal IQ is inferior to performance IQ.[23]

Authorities often urge that IQ is not used to make the diagnosis of intellectual disability, which should be based on a full clinical assessment. But although it may not be sufficient to make a diagnosis of intellectual disability, it is necessary. The omission of an IQ test when learning disability is suspected, or indeed in many cases when a cognitive impairment is suspected, is negligent. The World Health Organization recommends the bands shown in Table 7.1.

Table 7.1 Bands of mental retardation and intellectual disability recognized by WHO

Term	IQ
Profound mental retardation/intellectual disability	Below 21
Severe mental retardation/intellectual disability	20–34
Moderate mental retardation/intellectual disability	35–49
Mild mental retardation/intellectual disability	50–69
Borderline intellectual functioning	70–80

Note: Adaptive functioning should be considered as well as IQ
Source: World Health Organization, 1992.

Testing

Intelligence testing dates back to the early years of the twentieth century, when the French psychologist Alfred Binet developed a test to measure the educability of children. The most generally accepted test is currently the Wechsler Adult Intelligence Scale (WAIS); the childhood version is the Wechsler Intelligence Scale for Children (WISC). These tests have been criticized for being culture bound, and culture-free tests also exist. The WISC and the WAIS have up to the most recent edition divided the individual test items, or subscales, into verbal and performance groups, and IQ scores have been given as verbal, performance and full-scale IQs. Verbal IQ is affected by language development. Reading age in cultures where there is univeral literacy is often a usable, temporary proxy for the verbal IQ.

The differentiation between verbal and performance IQ has become so established that I will continue to use it in the remainder of this section. However, the fourth editions of the WAIS and the WISC have four, not two, subscales: perceptual reasoning, verbal comprehension indices, working memory and processing speed.[23, 24]

Intelligence testing in people with an ASD shows considerable variation from test to test, both in full scale score, and in the magnitude of the verbal-performance discrepancy (the difference between verbal and performance IQ scores). Motivation, concurrent medication, the patience and skill of the tester, even the expectations of the tester, all may cause this unreliability. Another factor may be that the most widely used tests, such as the WISC, may underestimate performance IQ in comparison to tests that require minimal language such as Raven's progressive matrices (up to a 30 point difference in one study).[25] The progressive matrices are normally administered using printed patterns, but a puzzle version may be more convenient and more reliable for people with a significant learning disability.[26]

Network dysfunction

IQ is reduced following head injury, particular when the frontal lobes are involved. The reduction may not affect all types of intelligence equally. In particular, there might be a dysjunction between verbal and performance IQ. This has led to a particular theory about the discrepancy of verbal performance IQ scores: that it is due to a reduction of white matter in the right hemisphere (supposed to be the hemisphere responsible for nonverbal intelligence). There is no evidence for this, but there remains an intriguing subgroup of people who have markedly higher verbal than performance intelligence. It has been speculated that this group may include people with Asperger syndrome, although this seems unlikely as visuomotor intelligence may be a strength of people with Asperger syndrome,[27] verbal superiority over performance in IQ scores is true of a majority of people with AS but not all, and in any case the verbal performance discrepancy often disappears later in childhood. [27]

Nonverbal learning difficulty

Rourke originally formulated nonverbal learning difficulty as:

> bilateral tactile-perceptual deficits, worse on the left side of the body; impaired visuo-spatial organizational abilities; impaired coordination of willed activity, especially on the left side of the body (habitual motor skills, or motor activities

that have become habitual, like writing, may be unaffected; poor or inappropriate responses to novel stimuli; speech dyspraxia with reduced speech prosody, verbosity, phonological paraphasias, impaired pragmatics, and reliance upon language as a principal means for social relating; impaired reading comprehension in the presence of normal decoding of single words and the ability to read and spell; dyscalculia; impaired problem solving and concept formation; and impaired social perception, social judgement and social interaction.[28]

Rourke has suggested that this syndrome is the consequence of dysfunction of the non-dominant cerebral hemisphere produced not by a loss of grey matter, but lesions in white matter.[29] The long axons that make up white matter are formed into bundles running from side to side of the brain (commissural fibres), from front to back (association fibres), and between lower and higher brain centres (projection fibres). Rourke argues that intact association fibres are necessary for the development but not maintenance of dominant hemisphere functions, so that any major interruption of white matter tracts interferes disproportionately with the function of the non-dominant hemisphere. Acquired white matter lesions are therefore likely to result in a disproportionate impairment of non-dominant hemisphere function for which there can be no compensation.[29]

The neuropsychological profile of nonverbal learning disability (NLD) does fit some but not all individuals with known lesions of white matter, including dysgenesis of the corpus callosum,[29, 30] agenesis of the corpus callosum associated with prosodic impairments,[31] disorders of the midline such as velocardiofacial syndrome,[32] and demyelinating disorders such as metachromatic leucodystrophy.[33]

However, ASD does not necessarily involve a superiority of verbal over nonverbal IQ, even if only AS is considered. Nor are the learning disabilities that Rourke considers to be characteristic of NLD always present in AS.[29] NLD is not therefore another name for AS.

Relation to ASD

Intelligence is one of the current differentiata in international diagnostic criteria for the diagnosis of autistic disorder rather than Asperger syndrome. The other differentiata are delay in language and delay in other developmental milestones. Each of these differentiata is correlated, suggesting that reduced IQ may be linked with delayed language. There is a strong association between autistic disorder and IQ, but in one study,[34] the IQ of people with Asperger syndrome was normally distributed, suggesting that there is no particular association between AS and IQ, although there may be a less strong common factor of g in what intelligence tests measure in AS.[35]

Lower verbal IQ than performance IQ is often found, as might be expected because of their language impairment, in people with an autistic disorder, but not always. There does not seem to be any regularity in the verbal–performance ratio in Asperger syndrome. The expected pattern of much higher verbal IQ to performance IQ may occur, but the opposite ratio also occurs, and it is difficult to predict which way it will be clinically.

Using the fourth edition of the WISC, Mayes and Calhoun found that children with AS had above average scores on the perceptual reasoning and verbal comprehension indices, and below average scores on working memory, and processing speed.[36] Writing speech was also reduced. Similar results were found from WISC-IV testing of children with ADHD.[37] Mayes and Calhoun thought the WISC-IV was better for children with ASD, not least because it captured their visual reasoning and verbal comprehension strengths.[36] However, the WISC is influenced by language ability, and may underestimate intelligence in people with an autistic disorder whose IQ is at the lower end of the scale.[38] Tests of nonverbal intelligence, such as Raven's progressive matrices, may be more accurate in this group.[38] Interestingly, as Binet found, it was the full scale IQ that was the best predictor of educational outcome, and not any of the subscales.

MEMORY

Memory is universal in adaptive systems. Muscles remember previous contractions and atrophy or hypertrophy accordingly, for example. The term 'memory', if used without further specification, generally refers, however, to systems in the brain that store previous brain states. There are often considered to be three types: short-term memory and the two commonly recognized types of long-term memory, procedural or implicit memory and declarative or explicit memory. Procedural memory stores sensorimotor procedures.. It is the reason that 'once learned, never forgotten' holds true for motor skills, like riding a horse. Declarative memory is partly a repository of facts, names, facial identities, colours, and so on: sometimes termed 'semantic memory' because, at least in principle, all of them can be named and therefore interrogated by an effort of will although not always successfully. Declarative memories may also be episodic memories. These can be evoked into conscious awareness, and this can sometimes be achieved deliberately, but episodic memories cannot be immediately accessed. Talking about some time in the past is a common way of evoking episodic memory. It will often bring to mind images or events that one had 'forgotten'. Recall results in strengthening of the memory. This may be akin to the process of 'reconsolidation' that occurs after years of some memories being laid down. Episodic memories that are not re-evoked gradually weaken. Episodic memories have a kind of time stamp, or at least an index of their temporal order that is also reinforced by rehearsal.[39] 'Didn't we buy the car, just after that holiday?' people will say, and 'That must have been 1982 because it was the same year that your father died.'

As the example illustrates autobiographical memory contains a large episodic element (of course, there is a declarative element too, like one's name, address, phone number, date of birth and so on).

Procedural memory is stored as a result of changes in networks involving cerebral cortex and cerebellum. Declarative memories may be widely stored in the brain, but hippocampal and temporal lobe function is crucial to this. One possible reason is that the hippocampus is required to index what is being remembered so that it can be recalled and that the less effective the indexing, the less well the memory will be recalled or 'consolidated'. Consolidation occurs particularly during sleep, with slow wave sleep having a special role. Consolidation involves an emotional element of 'working through' that may particularly occur during REM sleep. Failure to work through emotionally has been thought to be a factor in post-traumatic flashbacks. Unconsolidated memories, even if stored, cannot be recalled and have a limited role as memory. Consolidated memories are sometimes known as long-term memories, or 'remote' memories. However, 'long term' is usually used by psychologists for any memories that are not 'short term', including recent memory traces that have yet to be consolidated.

Short-term memory is often used to refer to those perceptions, thoughts or experiences that linger in attention, possibly because they are actively rehearsed, for example by repeating a phone number over and over. Once attention switches they may disappear without leaving a trace. Short-term memories may be close to perceived experience (so close sometimes that they are termed flash bulb memories) but may also be elaborated or altered. For example, it is generally accepted that only seven items can, on average, be held in short-term memory, but apparent memory capacity can be exceeded by 'chunking' items into commonly occurring superordinate items that can be held as a single item. For example, area codes in phone numbers may be so familiar that they can be held as one item rather than the four or five digits of which they are composed. Short-term memory that has been subject to cognitive reworking is often called working memory, although that is also sometimes used for the process of creating this elaborated memory.

Short-term memories may leave a memory trace or recent memory behind that is a candidate for becoming more permanently stored through the consolidation process. It is often possible to choose to retain a memory trace, although not always possible to do this successfully. This kind of retained memory can be recalled within minutes or hours. Clinicians term this process 'registration', psychologists and neuroscientists, 'encoding'. It requires intact prefrontal cortex, most likely the ventrolateral PFC, with the left PFC being required to be intact for semantic encoding, and the right for episodic encoding.[40] Episodic memory traces, although they cannot be recalled consciously, are demonstrable in 'priming' studies, in which a response time is influenced by the subject's previous stimulus exposure.

If declarative and procedural memories are stored semi-permanently, and so correspond to some degree to the data stored on the hard drive of a computer, then the third type of memory, working memory, is much more like rapid access memory, or RAM. It has strong links with what a person is paying attention to, and will be considered below, in the section on attention.

There is a fourth type of memory that is not usually considered in discussions of memory. I have coined the term 'emotional flavour' for this.[41] This is the changing emotional tone that is associated with images, words, experiences and other 'emotors'. There is evidence that this type of memory is stored in secondary sensory cortex.[42]

Recall is achieved by using tags which are attached to particular memories. Most memories are multiply tagged. Words, for example, can be recalled via their synonyms, their antonyms, and a less deliberative reach for meaning. But particular words may also be evoked by emotional tags, or even by situational tags. People on holiday in France find that French words come back to them that they had forgotten that they knew. One tag that is often missing is age of first memorization. 'Haziness' of the memory is a kind of proxy, but very recent memories can be hazy, and false memories are usually hazy too, which may give them a meretricious appearance of verisimilitude.

Testing
Clinical tests focus on assessing declarative memory, especially in relation to those elements that are particularly concerned with pre-frontal function (short-term memory and memory

traces). History taking indirectly assesses the episodic elements as well as the declarative elements of autobiographical memory.

Relation to ASD

Hypermnesis, or an unusual memory ability, is often commented on by friends or relatives describing someone with an ASD. This may be limited to a particular special interest, or to the ability to recall the past in great detail, or to an ability to remember routes, which may be linked to an aversion to changing them. It has been suggested that this greater storage capacity is because memorization does not involve activating so much association cortex,[43] which would be consistent with the reduced number of memory 'tags' that many people with an ASD seem to have. Another, and more likely, explanation is that repeated rehearsal of facts increases the number that can be easily recalled. This would fit with the clinical link between obsessive repetition of facts and hypermnesis that is reported in individual cases. There is evidence that an increased efficiency of one kind of memory may be achieved at the expense of another. For example, London taxi drivers who have an exceptional memory for London streets and places and a larger than average posterior hippocampus, have a smaller than average anterior hippocampus and a lower than average memory for figures. The two volumes were inversely correlated: the better the navigation ability, the worse the memory for figures. The former fell after retirement, and the latter increased.[44]

A particular example of hypermnesis is the ability to remember exact dates. People with ASD with this ability will often give the appearance of having an excellent autobiographic memory, but their memory for episodes may be markedly deficient. There is a lack of narrative to the autobiography that is part of a general problem of narrative underpinnings of identity or 'self hood' that is common in people with an ASD. It is possible that this impairment in episodic memory is related to the lack of narrative rehearsal with other people of the stories of events. One of the reasons that many people with ASD dislike social occasions, and chat, is that much of it is taken up with stories about the past, often beginning with some statement like 'it's really changed this place or it's hardly changed this place, I remember when we were all here last year'.

A further consequence of a lack of narrative may be that past autobiographical memories are not randomly accessible. Ask most people what it was like to be seven years old, and they will be able to recall some feelings, some facts about where they lived, some images of their school, and so on. People with an ASD may not be able to do this. Their memory store is more like that of a computer that is backed up to tape. To get to one item in the store, it is necessary to start at the beginning and work forwards.

Case example

> Damien was detained in a special hospital after killing a school acquaintance as an experiment. He was very isolated, but the ward staff noticed that he seemed to keep himself busy. He told me that he 'sang through his life' on a regular basis. It took three days, and he had to sing a particular song for each period of his life. These had to be in autobiographical order. If he missed one, which sometimes happened because the staff insisted he did something else, he could not pick up the sequence where he had

previously stopped, but had to start again from the beginning. He could start again where he left off if he chose to stop, for example in order to sleep. But if he left one out, he could not sing it out of order, either, but had to start again.

Another person with Asperger syndrome said that his mind was 'over-focused' but 'disconnected from other people'. He could remember exact dates, what his father said, current events and so on but did not have a narrative about his father in memory with which he could have accessed his memory store. He could not remember his mother because to do so meant 'going back through her death' as if her memories could only be accessed on a single dimension of historical time.

Autobiographical memory

One possible explanation for the lack of random access is that autobiographical memory is normally tagged narratively and emotionally. Autobiography can therefore be accessed through current relationships, which are evocative of past ones, and through emotions,[45] or context.[46] There is also some evidence that autobiographical memory decays unless it is refreshed by talking to people about the past, or reminiscing. So people with ASD who are socially isolated may not be refreshing their autobiographical memory often enough to maintain it.

It has been suggested that the lack of memory 'tags' or associations between memories may reduce the frequency of false memories in people with an AS.[47]

Procedural learning is often slower in people with an ASD.[48] This may be part of a larger problem in imitation since much human learning involves other people as demonstrators or instructors. Human intervention may actually reduce the performance of people with an ASD, who learn better from computer feedback,[49] or trial and error with impersonal feedback.

This is probably the reason that it is the child with an ASD who best knows how to work the TV remote control. The child has already pressed all of the buttons, and worked out what each of them does. It may also be the reason why parents often say that their child with an ASD 'learnt overnight' how to ride a bike, or how to walk: they have not shown these skills off to admiring parents as neurotypical infants do. Inconspicuous imitation may play a part in this kind of learning, but not guided imitation.

EXECUTIVE FUNCTION

The use of the word 'executive' to apply to mental functions under conscious control can be attributed to Posner,[50] but it has been the work of Shallice and Baddeley which developed it as a separable function,[51, 52] possibly corresponding to a particular area or area of the brain. Like working memory, with which it is closely linked, it has become an accepted cognitive capacity, but there is a lack of consistency in its assessment and significance. Executive function is independent of IQ, but has many similar features to IQ, including the widespread nature of its influence on cognitive processes, and the apparent involvement of dorsolateral PFC and anterior cingulate cortex in both capacities. There is an overlap with motivation or what used to be called volition. Friedman *et al.* have suggested that executive function is, like intelligence, made up of several different capacities which, because they share a common heritability, are usually closely correlated but can, in some circumstances, be separated.[53] She and her co-authors further suggest, like others,[54] that there are three fundamental capacities: inhibiting pre-potent responses, working memory, and shifting attention between tasks. These same capacities are already apparent in pre-schoolers.[55]

Dysexecutive syndrome has become established as one of the consequences of ADHD and of chronic schizophrenia, but has yet to be recognized as a disorder in its own right. Clinical experience indicates that it may occur on its own as a specific developmental disorder, however, and that it accounts for many of the otherwise unexplained difficulties that people with an ASD may have living on their own.

Relation to ASD

Executive dysfunction is not found in every person with ASD.[56] The inhibition of prepotent responses may be more impaired than other executive functions.[54] Executive impairment may sometimes be found in family members of people with an ASD.[57] However, it does occur in the group where ASD and ADHD overlap,[58] and can be associated with other developmental disorders,[59] such as an impaired ability in interpreting facial expressions,[60, 61] and language disorders.[62] This overlapping group is discussed in Chapter 16, along with some of the consequences for health and quality of life in having an executive dysfunction.

Working memory

'Working memory' is based on the short-term memory that is more like the random-access memory of a computer than it is to other memory stores, such as declarative, procedural or episodic memory, which are themselves more like the various methods of more permanent data storage available to computers. RAM is volatile and constantly overwritten, and so is working memory. It is, according to one of the psychologists who coined the term, more like a scratch pad than a book.[63] It is likely that there are two separate equivalents of RAM, one for words or digits, and one for visual or spatial configurations. Baddeley attributed these to a constantly repeated sub-vocal phrase or phonological loop, and to a scene where the mind's eye scans and re-scans the visuospatial sketchpad.[63] These two subsystems are also present in modern computers, which have motherboards with two chips, one for number-crunching with its own RAM and the other a graphics chip for video processing, which also has RAM.

Working memory differs from short-term memory in that working memories are worked over, and are not just passive sensory impressions. Memories of images, for example, may include only those elements of a sensory impression that received attention (see also the section on attention). Elements of short-term memory may also be amalgamated in working memory, enabling it to escape the seven item limit, mentioned in the memory section.

Working memory is required not only for preparing memories for more permanent storage, but also for recall and for many other cognitive tasks, such as parsing phrases[64, 65] (see later section on language), language learning,[66] mental arithmetic (see later section on dyscalculia) and geometry (see later section on topographical disorientation), following instructions, returning to a task after an interruption, 'multitasking' (actually switching attention from one task to another, but maintaining a 'tab' on each task to mark progress so that switching goes back to the point of the task that had been previously reached), tracking changes on a blackboard, and planning (see later section on dysexecutive syndrome).

Although the existence of working memory is now accepted, there remains much debate about it. It is often difficult to demonstrate the impact of changes in working memory in other 'transfer' tasks that might be expected to be affected.

Women are generally better than men at spatial working memory tasks, and at object localization.[67]

Impairments in working memory may be more consequential than was once thought, and may affect a wide range of psychological functions. So-called personality disorder traits may, for example, be correlated with working memory impairment,[68] perhaps because working memory impairment leads to social difficulties that are attributed to 'personality disorder'.

Case example

William was 20 and had been living with his girlfriend and their child for about six months. She managed his money, prompted him about self-care, and intervened when they were in company if she felt that he was saying something inappropriate. He returned this care with genuine affection and on the whole they were getting on much better than his mother, who had looked after him before, expected. However, William did continue to upset his girlfriend by his occasional late hours and his inability to keep his promises about when he would come back home. William explained what would happen. He liked to go out in the evening, and would keep an eye on his watch so that he got home on time. But if he met an old friend and the friend suggested that they go somewhere else, it was as if he was being carried along into a different world and he no longer remembered about his girlfriend and could not recall any promises that he had made. All that belonged to a different time and place.

Testing

One problem in current understanding of working memory is that the tests of it are not consistent, and so no clearly identified capacity has been established. Digit span, a widely used clinical test of short-term memory, seems an obvious simple measure of verbal working memory, but reduced working memory in cerebellar dysfunction is associated with normal digit span.[69] This may be because working memory requires not only storage but also 'concurrent processing'.[70] Reverse digit span, in which the testee has to report the digits back but in reverse order, may be a better clinical test of 'working memory' therefore.

Size sequencing does not rely strongly on verbal instructions, and is particularly suitable for testing people with an ASD. In this test, sequences of shapes of different size are presented on a screen and test subjects have to touch them one by one in order of size, with stars of one colour being touched in increasing size order and stars of another colour in decreasing size order. The length of the sequence which can be correctly sized in this way is a measure of working memory.[71]

Treatment

Practice can improve memory, even working memory, but the gains are often small for a considerable effort in practice. Once working memory impairment has been discovered, it is often helpful to identify how it might affect a particular client, since the effects can be surprisingly variable. Once this has been done, possible work-arounds might be explored, which can include the use of personal organizers, notebooks, or simply list writing. Homework diaries may be helpful for school children. Project planning programmes, diaries, calendars on mobile phones, personal organizers or computers can be helpful.

Many people with working memory deficits have compensated for them without explicitly recognizing them by developing routines. Children may, for example, take all their books to school, every day, whether or not they are relevant to their lessons for that day.

Relation to ASD

A sub-population of people with ASD have reduced working memory.[72] Clinical experience suggests that it is those who overlap in their clinical symptoms with people with ADHD who have particular verbal working memory impairments although that was not supported in one study.[73] Verbal working memory is also reduced in people with learning disabilities, and particularly those who have been delayed in language acquisition,[74] but only under 'high language processing loads', that is when the task is presented in elaborate language. It is possible, therefore, that reduced working memory, and its consequences, are likely to be shown mainly or only in those people with an ASD who also have had language delay with consequent persistent but normally unnoticed impaired language processing.

Spatial working memory may also be reduced in people with an ASD,[75] but clinical experience is that there is a sub-population of people with an ASD who have higher than average spatial working memory capacity.

Relation to ADHD

A deficit in working memory is a consistent finding in ADHD.[76]

Inhibition of prepotent responses

Prepotent responses are those that have been created by habit. Giving a participant in a study the same stimulus and asking them to make the same response repeatedly will create a habit of responding. Giving a new stimulus, one that should, according to a previous instruction, lead to no response, may in fact be followed by the old response simply because the habit has been created to respond in that way. The old response is described as a 'prepotent' one because it asserts itself when no response is required. Correct performance of this task, which is sometimes called a Go–No Go task for obvious reasons, requires that the prepotent response is inhibited. Groman et al. reviewed a wide range of evidence for deficits in response inhibition being the cause of a wide range of ADHD symptoms, including the disposition to drug misuse.[77] One possible explanation of the failure of response inhibition is that there is a preference for immediate reward or an intolerance of a delay between a response and its dopamine-mediated reward or reinforcement,[78, 79] or both.[80]

Reactive control of behaviour first appears at the end of the first year of life, as demonstrated by the development of 'detour reaching' in an object reaching task, in which an infant learns not to try to reach for a visible toy in an open glass box by trying to get at it through the top, glassed over side, but reaching round for the open side.[81]

Temperamental factors also influence response inhibition, or 'control' as it is often termed in the related research on temperament or personality. Some authors, but not all,[82] distinguish effortful control involving lateral prefrontal cortex from reactive control. Effortful control is particularly involved when a frequent, overlearned or reflexive stimulus has to be inhibited (see Stroop test on the following page). Reactive control is called on, particularly, when infrequent stimuli are being processed, and involves anterior cingulate.[83] Reactive control applies particularly to stimulus conflict, for example 'double bind' utterances, in which the emotional content conflicts with the emotion with which that content is communicated.[84]

Impulsivity is a complex behaviour, but the inhibition of motor responses, including prepotent responses, is a major contributor. Or to put it another way, impulsivity is about 'not knowing when to stop' or that 'no' means 'no'. One review concludes that response inhibition (this review probably focused on effortful control) might be the explanation for impulsivity in conditions as diverse as obsessive compulsive disorder, compulsive hair pulling (trichotillomania), the repeated use of illicit drugs, as well as ADHD.[85] Effortful control is influenced by adrenergic agents,[85] but reactive control by serotininergic drugs.[86]

Effortful control is also involved in error detection. People with ADHD make more errors, but are less aware of them on tasks which demand control.[87]

Network dysfunction

The cerebellum's role in procedural learning and therefore in generating prepotent responses is modulated by a dorsolateral PFC cerebellum network,[88] with the dorsolateral PFC providing inhibition. Dorsolateral and ventrolateral PFC are themselves networked with anterior cingulate in a network that detects novelty and inhibits prepotent responding.[89]

In people with ADHD, the novelty network's ability to inhibit cerebellum seems to be reduced. In people with an ASD, the novelty network does not seem to be fully connected, but inhibition is passed on to premotor cortex and prepotent inhibition may be unimpaired behaviourally.[90]

Neuropsychological and imaging studies have shown that attention deficit hyperactivity disorder is associated with alterations in prefrontal cortex and its connections to striatum and cerebellum. Research in animals, in combination with observations of patients with cortical lesions, has shown that the PFC is critical for the regulation of behaviour, attention and affect using representational knowledge. The PFC is important for sustaining attention over a delay, inhibiting distraction and dividing attention, while more posterior cortical areas are essential for perception and the allocation of attentional resources. The PFC in the right hemisphere is especially important for behavioural inhibition. Lesions to the PFC produce a profile of distractibility, forgetfulness, impulsivity, poor planning and locomotor hyperactivity.

Testing

A commonly used measure of effortful control is the Stroop colour test of which there are several variants. An illustration of the original, colour naming test is shown in Figure 7.1.[91] In the original test the word 'red' is coloured green. Subjects are asked to name the colour of the font, which means effortfully controlling the tendency (for readers of English) to say 'red' (in the example below the correct response is, of course, 'black').

Figure 7.1 Item from Stroop colour test
Source: Adapted from Stroop, 1935.

The Wisconsin Card Sort test requires that the testee makes piles of cards based on matching criteria that are learnt through trial and error. The matching criteria are changed during the course of the test, and the rapidity with which the testee 'shifts sets', that is stops applying the old rule in a perseverative manner, but learns and applies the new one is a measure of 'frontal lobe function' more generally. Naming as many animals as possible beginning with 'P' is a bedside test, not requiring any equipment. Most people, having suggested a few animal names, like 'penguin' and 'parrot', find that these names keep coming back into their head. To be able to think up new names, these previous examples must be suppressed, for example '... Penguin? Parrot? No, I've already said them so NOT Penguin and NOT Parrot... AH, Pangolin.' Non-repeating number generation,[92] which is a variant of the animals beginning with 'P' task, may be more heavily dependent on working memory.

Treatment

Monkeys with PFC lesion can be trained to inhibit prepotent responses if these lead, after a delay, to a reward.[93] But no effective training regimes have been proven to be effective in people. The stimulant drugs, methylphenidate and amphetamine, that are effective in people with ADHD do seem to have their effect partly because they increase the capacity to effortfully control prepotent responses. They probably do this because they are both sympathomimetic and dopaminomimetic, and are therefore able to stimulate alpha2A-adrenoceptors and dopamine D1-receptors in the PFC. Alpha2A-adrenoceptors carry signal, and D1 neurons reduce noise by exciting GABAergic inhibitory interneurons.[94] In people with ADHD, methylphenidate increases D1 neuronal activation and therefore increases lateral PFC inhibition of incoming stimuli, and so increases its inhibition over prepotent responses. In people without ADHD, methylphenidate decreases inhibition,[95] and has its customary stimulant effect, which includes the distractibility shown normally during increased arousal.

Relation to ASD and ADHD

In younger children with ADHD, impaired effortful control is correlated with inattention, and impaired reactive control with hyperactivity. Impaired reactive control is also linked to anxiety proneness, and as such is influenced by familial environment and parenting styles. In older children reactive control continues to be linked to hyperactivity, but impaired effortful control is linked to both inattention and hyperactivity,[96] suggesting that top-down processes become more important in adolescence, a period when top-down processes are becoming more salient across the board with the maturation of the prefrontal cortex.[90]

Children with ASD show more false positive responses on memory tests compared to neurotypical children, an unusual pattern of response since it means that these children over-complied with the task, finding more matches with stimuli to which they had been previously exposed than there actually were. Their reduced performance was correlated with reduced theta power relative to other frequencies in frontal midline EEG, indicative of reduced anterior cingulate activity.[97]

Attention shifting and attentional maintenance

The best analogy for conscious attention remains the torch beam in a dark room. We can turn the torch hither and thither, and what it lights on is known to us, that is, it occupies our attention. But as soon as the beam moves away our attention shifts with it. All of the objects in the dark room outside the torch beam can only be known to us 'pre-attentively'. A sudden noise, a breath, or apparently nothing other than an impulse, may cause us to swing the torch to try to bring whatever it was into attention. The torch analogy is particularly relevant to visual attention, our primary modality.

Developmental psychologists differentiate between this exogenous capture of attention, and the endogenous control of attention by an effort of will. Endogenous attention develops during the first year of life. Both it and exogenous attention develop over subsequent years. The two types of attention may interact. We may suppress distracting noise and listen with 'bated breath'. We may also focus attention on sounds, tastes, touches, proprioception and gastric sensation or internal stimuli such as an emotion or pain.[98] Endogenous control may also involve widening or narrowing an attentional focus, or switching attention.

Endogenous attention has developed to adult levels by the age of six years, but endogenous attention continues to develop at least until the age of 11 years[99] with better strategies for dealing with complex stimuli perhaps involving what Broadbent called filtering, and the development of more complex search strategies. In social situations, pointing and gazing are also used by other people and possibly apes to switch other people's attention,[100] and so alter what is committed to memory. People with ASD are as likely to have their attention shifted in this way as neurotypicals.[100]

There are many sources of preattentive information, which orientate or alert. Intrinsic experiences that may claim attention include emotion and pain.[101] Visual information may be fed to the prefrontal area by the superior colliculus, which receives visual input from the lateral geniculate before the occipital cortex does. The prefrontal cortex, temporal cortex and the amygdala receive information about faces and about sounds before it is consciously available (see Chapter 6 for more examples).

Not only are there stimuli that may claim our attention, but also some of the things in our attention may be aversive. Focusing attention on maths problems, on angry or fearful faces, or on worrying thoughts may require effort. Clearly for the effective use of attention, some process or processes are required to maintain attention effortfully, and to filter out inconsequential stimuli or distractions but to switch attention to present priority stimuli. Too little of the former, and a person is seen as being distractible. Too little of the latter, and they are inattentive or over-absorbed. Both are potentially catastrophic errors.

Exogenous attention must overcome endogenous inattention in these situations, and this effortful process requires inhibition of an endogenous tendency to shift attention. This can be considered to be one of a generic class of response inhibitions that draws on dopaminergic reward networks, and which will be discussed below.

Treatment

Abnormal patterns of brain activity in people with ADHD may be partly normalized after taking methylphenidate.[102] For example, activation in basal ganglia may be increased during attention tasks by taking methylphenidate. However, these were adolescents who also had dyslexia, which may have had an independent effect. Although methylphenidate altered activation, it did not improve task performance.[103]

Although methylphenidate and other drugs acting on the dopamine and monamine systems in frontal areas clearly produce benefit in ADHD (this is discussed in more detail in Chapter 9) and are reported by observers to reduce inattentiveness, the effects of stimulants on distractibility is mixed, at least in monkeys.[104]

Relation to ASD and ADHD

People with ASD and also people with ADHD may have dysexecutive problems as a result of a disorder of attention shifting, but for quite opposite reasons. People with typical Asperger syndrome have an abnormally high threshold for attention shifts,[105] and are therefore 'rigid' in their attention whereas people with ADHD have an abnormally low threshold and are therefore distractible.

The network for attention shifting involves anterior cingulate, lateral PFC and caudate nucleus (to whose rostral head the lateral PFC projects),[106] with a secondary network within the basal ganglia itself, including the pars compacta of the substantia nigra, comprising dopaminergic interneurons which presumably modulate the responsiveness of the caudate.[107] There may be overlaps between this network, and the inhibition of prepotent response network, which also involves the caudate nucleus.[108]

People with ADHD have reduced activation of anterior cingulate and prefrontal cortex, and more activation of basal ganglia (e.g. caudate nucleus) and, perhaps more surprisingly, cerebellum on Stroop tests.

The cerebellum has also been implicated in the speed of reorientation of attention.[109] Orienting speed in children with cerebellar hypoplasia and autism has been found to be reduced in one other study.[110]

REPETITION AND PURSUIT OF SAMENESS: TICS, STEREOTYPIES, OBSESSIONS AND COMPULSIONS

Repetitive behaviour occurs not only in ASD but also in neurotypical children, and children with intellectual disability. It is more common in boys.[111] Factor analysis suggests that there are two components: a higher level 'insistence on sameness' and a lower level of repetitive behaviours, such as motor stereotypies or a preference for repeated sensory stimulation:[112] these are sometimes termed 'stimming' behaviours, short for stimulating. One reason for this name is that these behaviours are similar to comfort behaviours, and their frequency has been experimentally ameliorated by serotinergic agents, which reduce anxiety, and oxytocin, which increases 'security'. Repetition is not a universal characteristic. In my clinics, patient's parents were interviewed in detail about development. These questions included two on routines: whether or not the patient resisted changes in routine, and whether or not they made up routines of their own (see Table 7.2). More patients resisted change to routines than made them up. There was little difference in the use of routines between the autistic group and the Asperger group (the Asperger group did not have significant language or cognitive delay), and while some patients lost their routines as they got older, this was not true of many. However, there were still over 10 per cent of people meeting all the other criteria for autistic disorder who had never shown an unusual adherence to routines (see Table 7.2).

Table 7.2 Prevalence of routines in clinic series

	No. of patients	Percentage having routines	
		At some time	At the time of examination
Autistic disorder	97	87.4%	73.1%
Asperger syndrome	213	83.7%	71.6%

Nor is stereotypy universal. In the same series of patients, parents were asked whether or not the patient had shown any one of six different stereotypies (flicking, tiptoe walking, flapping, spinning, jumping or rocking). Around 73 per cent of the Asperger group had shown at least one of these behaviours at some time, and 83 per cent of the autistic disorder group had. Clearly there are people with ASD who do not show stereotypies. However, both stereotypy and repetition may be very prominent features, with resistance to change and repeated questioning contributing substantially to the burden of living with ASD.

Repetitive behaviours also occur in intellectual disability, although not as frequently in autism,[113] and they are associated with social isolation[114, 115] and anxiety. This suggests that repetition is not fundamental to autism. Further evidence for this is the fact that repetitive behaviours tend to worsen as people with ASD get older.[116] However, there is a familial association between ASD and obsessive compulsive disorder, and people with OCD have social impairments which are similar to, although much milder than, those of people with autism. Repetitive behaviour is also more common when there is overlap between ASD, tic disorder and ADHD, all of which are associated with an increase in childhood anxiety.[117]

It is possible that the tendency to repetition, as opposed to the tendency to distraction or impulsive activity, is the reflection of a distinct network, which may be activated by the social isolation and anxiety associated with autism, but which may also be affected in dysfunction of the social brain, just as attention, language and other networks are affected. If there is a distinct network, it would be expected that stereotypies might sometimes occur in the absence of other abnormalities, and this has been reported.[118] I discuss the possibility of this network further in Chapter 5.

My own clinical experience has led me to believe that the common thread in all children whom parents and professionals suspect of having an ASD is a dysfunction of their social brain, and a reduction of their social intelligence. The most reliable symptom of this dysfunction is an abnormality of nonverbal communication, and in Chapter 8 I consider nonverbal communication, its assessment and its impact.

MOTOR COORDINATION AND TOPOGRAPHICAL ORIENTATION

Clumsiness is the term that most people apply when someone bumps into things or people, drops things, or breaks things. There is a presumption that clumsiness is something that can be amended by sufficient attention, and that it involves actions, potentially under conscious control even if often habitual. So it excludes movement impairment due to muscle disorder or neuromotor control. Clumsiness is sometimes attributed to a lack of coordination. At first sight, there would seem to be several obviously distinct types of clumsiness, but studies rarely support the distinctions that appeal to clinicians.[119] Clumsiness is negatively correlated with intelligence.[120]

Ataxia

Gross movements can be carried out smoothly only if the remainder of the body acts as a stable platform. Dealing with problems of shifting weight, balance and compensatory postural change relies on intact cerebellar function. Movement disorders of cerebellar origin are called 'ataxias'. Ataxia is associated with abnormal wide-based gait, impaired balance, intention tremor, over- or under-shoot when reaching for something (dysmetria), jerky eye tracking, 'bad' writing, and slurred or 'scanning' speech ('dysarthria'). Intention tremor, dysdiachokinesis and instability on standing can easily be assessed in a clinical interview (see Chapter 10) and are specific signs of ataxia. Ataxia may be secondary to dorsal column or vestibular disease, or due to a lesion in the cerebellum.

Dystonias and dyskinesias

The basal ganglia are nuclei of grey matter in the forebrain, but derived from the older central part. They are highly interlinked, although the fact that the system serves very different functions suggests that there is a functional differentiation that is not apparent. Traffic through the ganglia acts as control loops on the cerebral cortex: one excitatory running from cortex, to striatum to globus pallidum, to thalamus, and back to cortex, and the other inhibitory, as a result of an additional superimposed loop running from the globus pallidum to the subthalamic nucleus before returning to the pallidum and then on to the thalamus and the cortex. The function of these loops is modulated by further excitatory and inhibitory circuits.

Feedback loops were the first devices invented to act as control systems to enable machines to track moving objects.[121] It is therefore understandable that the function of the basal ganglia was originally thought to be that of a control system for movement. Indeed, some of the disorders that occur from basal ganglia damage such as ballismus do look like a failure of smoothing.

However, one part of the striatum, the nucleus accumbens, is the 'reward centre' of the brain. Treatment of Parkinson's disease increases the activity of this centre, and this may lead to impulsivity and addictive behaviour. The reward aspects of the basal ganglia may also be linked to its association with motivation, and also with the initiation of activity. It is likely that the role of the basal ganglia in movement is part of a wider role that remains unclear.

There are suggestive links with ASD. People with an ASD sometimes show choreiform movements. 'Foreign language syndrome',[122] in which people are reported to change their accent from their native one to a foreign one following stroke or head injury, has been attributed to basal ganglia damage although also to cerebellar lesions. 'Foreign accent syndrome' may also occur in ASD, or as an apparently isolated developmental disorder.[123] However, it is premature to speculate about the role of the basal ganglia in the movement disorder of ASD.

The binding of C11-cocaine to dopamine transporters in nucleus accumbens is reduced in people with ADHD compared to neurotypicals, suggesting that the reduced dopamine transport that affects attention systems in ADHD may also adversely affect the reward system, and therefore motivation, too.

Dyspraxia

Dyspraxia is a disorder of purposive movement that affects a wide range of coordinated movement. Dyspraxia may develop following right hemisphere lesions, but may also occur in childhood. Developmental dyspraxia remains a poorly defined condition, possibly because there is considerable overlap with other developmental disorders. It is estimated to affect between 5 and 8 per cent of the general population.[124] The clinical impression is one of heterogeneity, and different children may have different profiles of functional handicap. The common feature remains uncertain, but one strong hypothesis is that dyspraxia is a disorder of movement planning,[125] based partly on maps of the body and the space around it.[126] Reduced visual working memory may also contribute. Some kinds of dyspraxia seem to involve errors of timing particularly.[127]

Functional deficits include impaired fine movement control, for example of the fingers, leading to problems with laces or buttons, and 'bad' writing; poor eye–hand coordination ('visuomotor problems') leading to reduced performance in ball games and sometimes, therefore, shaming at school; and visuospatial errors or errors of spatial awareness with impaired estimation of the body in space and of objects in the immediate space round the body.[128]

Attempts to classify dyspraxia into functional types, such as the constructional apraxia that is associated with a problem in building with blocks in younger children, have not proved successful. Nor is the distinction between ideational apraxia (a failure to make plans) and ideomotor apraxia (a failure to carry them out) useful in clinical practice.

There are some specific dyspraxias that are of such impact that it is worth singling them out. Speech dyspraxia has been discussed in Chapter 5. Writing apraxia results in handwriting being disorganized, or very slow, sometimes so slow as to amount to agraphia. Tension over the performance of writing may lead to 'writer's cramp', with antagonistic muscles being activated simultaneously leading to pain and muscle hypoxia.

Ideomotor and ideational dyspraxia

Impairment in copying complex movements is often called ideomotor dyspraxia. It provides information about a person's ability to organize movements in space and to sequence them, and is a sensitive test of dyspraxia.

Asking someone to demonstrate a movement – for example, to show how they would light a match – is sometimes termed 'ideational' dyspraxia, although it might equally be called a test of procedural memory, demonstrating the close links between dyspraxia, practice and memory.

Testing

Paradoxically there are many people with an ASD who have superior topographical memories, and can recognize a route if they have been along it once before, even after a long time. There may also be some people with an ASD who have excellent fine motor coordination.

There are no tests of motor function that have been particularly standardized for use in ASD (but see clinical testing in Chapter 10); however, the Bruininks-Oseretsky test and the Movement Assessment Battery for Children are widely used in clinical practice.[129] The Bruininks-Oseretsky test dates back to the 1920s, but has been revised repeatedly since then. It includes 46 items, and takes about an hour to complete.[130] It does differentiate incoordination in children with ASD from that of children with developmental dyspraxia and children with ADHD.[130, 131] The Movement Assessment Battery for Children scores correlated in one study of children with AS with core symptom scores.[132]

Simple clinical tests, suitable for older children and adults, are discussed in Chapter 10.

Treatment

Intensive motor training has been proposed as a treatment for ASD for many years. No evidence exists to support one of the most popular of these methods.[133] It must be assumed that the others may have no specific effects, until there is evidence to prove otherwise.

Relation to ASD

Clumsiness is a particular feature in some people with AS, particularly those with marked nonverbal expressive impairment. This suggests that the impairment of nonverbal expression may be linked to a more general problem in motor control, possibly due to a lack of connectivity between areas of the brain involved in motor control, such as cerebral cortex and cerebellum.[134] However, there is no simple correlation between dyspraxia, disorders of perception of movement and impaired imitation.[135]

There is evidence that motor control is generally impaired, in at least a subgroup of people with an ASD. A case review study showed that 75 per cent of 'high functioning' people with an ASD had motor impairment.[136] Studies of children with an ASD showed poorer performance on standardized motor assessments compared to neurotypical age peers,[137] with correlations between the severity of ASD symptoms and the severity of motor impairment in children,[138, 139] and in adolescents and young adults.[140] There is a higher than normal incidence of ASD in people with neuromuscular disorders, too.[141] My clinical experience is that dyspraxia is more likely to be linked to ASD if there is no language or speech impairment, and DSM-IV suggests that dyspraxia is more common in AS than in the other ASDs. Evidence from one study suggests that there is no difference in gross motor performance between AS and autistic disorder,[142] but that AS is more likely to be associated with 'motor clumsiness' and autistic disorder with 'abnormal posturing'.[143] Direct testing shows that the later movements in a complex movement are more impaired than the early elements in people with an ASD.[144]

Between 50 and 60 per cent of children with developmental dyspraxia have a co-morbid attention deficit disorder with hyperactivity and learning disorders.[145] Dyspraxia in ADHD may be more a consequence of disordered motor timing,[146] and in ASD more likely to be linked to disorders of planning and the creation of spatial maps.

Dyspraxia correlates with reduced white matter volume in both cerebral hemispheres in neurotypical children and in children with ADHD, but in children with ASD it is a marker of *increased* white matter in the left hemisphere.[147]

People with an ASD plan movements as do neurotypicals, but have difficulty in adjusting these plans to account for unexpected change, for example in the target of the movement.[148]

Topographical disorientation

Topographical disorientation, or not being able to retrace a familiar route, may result from lesions in a variety of cerebral areas, but may also occur as a developmental disorder that, like dyspraxia, is likely to involve a failure to create a mental map,[149] perhaps due to a failure to memorize cues while navigating. It may result from not attending to these cues, not perceiving the cues accurately or not storing cues in a cognitive map. Constructing a cognitive map normally requires activation of the hippocampus and restrosplenial cortex, lesions of both of which may lead to topographical disorientation.[150] Topographical disorientation may also occur as an isolated developmental disorder,[151] but it is also associated with ASD.

It may be disabling if it is severe enough for a person to get lost even one block from their house, or in a department store. Topographical disorientation may be associated with right–left disorientation.

Part 2

CLINICAL ASPECTS OF ASD

Chapter 8

THE AUTISTIC SYNDROME

CASE HISTORY: BEN

Ben is the only child of two university graduates, one of whom is a mental health professional, who has taken early retirement due to stress. His father was 35 and his mother 32 when he was born. His mother had a show of blood when she was 28 weeks pregnant, which required no specific treatment, and she spent the last two weeks of her pregnancy on bed rest because of increasing blood pressure and ankle swelling. Ben was born after a prolonged second stage of labour and required forceps delivery. There was concern about his foetal heart rate, and a Caesarean section was considered. His parents were worried that Ben had prominent marks of the forceps after birth, and have wondered ever since whether his brain was damaged during his extraction. He was also jaundiced.

Ben was a very placid baby, and his parents were pleased that he was so little trouble. His mother's mother did say that he seemed unusually placid, and was worried that he did not mould when she picked him up, but her worries did not crystallize. His parents now say that they did not really know what to expect, as Ben was their only child. So when Ben did not sit up at the expected age, and seemed late in walking, they were a bit worried, but not too much. His father, anyway, had had similar problems. Ben did not seem to relate to them, which was more worrying, but they attributed this to their overly high expectations. He loved to be in his rocker, and showed an early interest in shapes and puzzles, which would amuse him for long periods without seeming to need any input from anyone else. He shuffled rather than crawled, and when he started to walk, at 15 months, he seemed to learn the skill overnight as if not needing to practise.

The district nurse did not think that there were any specific developmental problems, but did comment on her inability to get Ben's attention. He seemed to look at everything but her. He did not babble, but the nurse said that every baby was different and that he would catch up.

When Ben was walking, he needed close supervision as he would bump into things, or walk close to holes or obstacles. Later on, he was delayed in his awareness of cars and their dangers. He never needed affection as other children do, but would hang round his mother, 'getting under her feet' as she put it. The only way to deal with him was to give him a new puzzle, which would absorb him completely, until he had finished it. When he started to read, which he did early, he could similarly get absorbed in a book, and later Lego and particular videos, some of which he would watch over and over again.

Ben went to playgroup, but was asked to leave after a few weeks. Organizers said that he just sat, not interacting with the other children, except if he saw a puzzle that he wanted, in which case he would go over and take it, whether or not another child was using it. The reason for his exclusion was that he had scratched another child who had resisted this.

His parents were, by this time, sure that Ben was not developing like other children. He had occasionally seemed to dislike cuddling or other displays of affection. They were particularly concerned because Ben was still not speaking at the age of three, although they thought that he could understand whatever they said to him. Their general practitioner (GP) reassured them that Ben could still catch up, and his father was willing to go along with this. His mother was not, and there was some tension between Ben's parents as a result. His father said that his mother was mollycoddling Ben, and making him worse. Ben was referred to a speech and language therapist, but by the time that the appointment came through, some six months later, Ben was speaking. His words were garbled, and only his parents could easily understand him, but the speech and language therapist thought that this would resolve spontaneously and Ben was not given a follow-up appointment.

Ben was a worry to his first teachers at primary school. He did not sit still in the classroom, he immediately went to the puzzle corner whatever the lesson, and if left alone, would just sit there for the whole day, interspersed with periods of twirling or rushing round the classroom. He would distract other pupils by tapping or scratching while he was doing the puzzles, but if he was asked to stop, he would do it more. He did not engage with the other pupils except with one other boy, who rushed round with him. His parents were by now sure that there was something wrong with Ben, but his school reports suggested that it was just about settling in. Matters at school improved when two of the girls in his class began to approach Ben and involve him in games in which they would push him around and say that he was their baby. This seemed to quieten Ben, who became much less hyperactive when with the girls. He would even allow them to put some of their clothes on him to make him look more like a baby, and in fact Ben was not aware of the ridiculous impression he made, as he had little self-awareness then, and continued to have little as he got older.

The school became concerned about Ben's continuing lack of academic progress. He was not reading or writing more than his own name at the age of eight, and a referral to the school's community paediatrician was made. She concluded that there was no physical abnormality, but suggested that Ben had attention deficit hyperactivity disorder although, she said, she was not an expert and could not be sure. Ben was started on methylphenidate, and there was an improvement in his attention in class, although he was still struggling to read and write. Ben's arithmetic was, however, ahead of his age, and he drew better than most of the class. Ben also enjoyed music, and had an excellent memory for tunes. His parents arranged piano lessons, and with the help of the methylphenidate, Ben became a competent pianist.

It may have been from this time that Ben began to be teased and then physically bullied, which became the pattern of his life at school. His parents were unaware of this until after, although they did sometimes notice that he came home with torn clothes, or with spittle on his clothing. The one time that it came to their attention was when Ben retaliated, hitting another boy with a sharp stone, and causing bleeding.

There was a school inquiry and his parents attended a meeting with the head teacher, at which they found out about the previous bullying that Ben had experienced.

His parents were by this time feeling rather bullied by Ben, although they would not put it that way as they felt Ben could not help himself. Ben had developed so many routines at home that his parents felt that their own lives were being dictated by them. He spent up to an hour in the bathroom every morning using up a great quantity of soap, and would use so much lavatory paper that the lavatory would get blocked. Ben became so agitated at changes of routine that if his tea was not ready when he expected it, or if there were a guest and he could not shower at the time he expected, he would bang things, and sometimes scream with frustration. He had lashed out once or twice at his mother, too, on occasions like this. Holidays were becoming more and more difficult because of all the change that they entailed, and because Ben's behaviour in public was becoming so eccentric. One particular problem was that he was fascinated with younger girls and would come up to them and stare into their faces or even touch their hair, causing considerable alarm to their parents.

After the incident with the stone, Ben was referred to the child and adolescent mental health team who carried out a further multidisciplinary assessment. Ben's intelligence was tested, and he was found to have an IQ within the normal range. A speech and language assessment showed that Ben had problems understanding what other people said, and in working out why they had said it. He covered this up by reacting as if he did understand or feigning indifference. His parents remembered that Ben would sometimes tell them fantastic stories, for example that he had fathered a baby, which he seemed to believe, and they had worked out that these were stories that other children told him as a tease and then elaborated because Ben was credulous enough to believe them. The speech and language therapist said that Ben had 'semantic pragmatic disorder' and his parents welcomed this because it seemed to make sense of some of Ben's lack of proper engagement with the social world, his being in the world but not of it, as they said. No official diagnosis was given but special education was recommended, and Ben went to a special school for children with learning difficulties, rather than going on to secondary school.

His parents were concerned that the attack that Ben made, and his behaviour towards little girls, showed a lack of awareness of other people. He seemed to be unaware when they were upset, or that they might feel better if he showed remorse and tried to change. He seemed opaque to them. They found it difficult to tell what he was feeling as his face gave no clue, and his speech problem had not cleared up as the speech and language therapist had predicted. In fact, not only was his speech still so rapid as to be difficult to follow, but also it was oddly accented. Other children in the neighbourhood would often mimic him, and mimic his walk, which was also idiosyncratic. His parents felt that these children's parents were also dismissive of Ben, although they said nothing, and this made his mother feel alone with her problems. The only positive feature of this period was that Ben and his father seemed to have become much closer. They shared an interest in computers, and would spend long periods playing computer games with each other.

Ben rarely mentioned his feelings, but his parents noticed that he became more restless when he had experienced some kind of social rejection. He would often tell one of his weirdly disturbing stories on these occasions. Over the years, they became better at recognizing that Ben had an anxiety disorder, whose severity came and went.

His interest in young girls, which had become a kind of fixation, became more or less overt depending on his anxiety level. When his anxiety was bad, he might go up and touch girls in public places, and had sometimes asked to see their private parts. His parents did not think that Ben's interest was sexual precisely, but he was aware how shocking other people found it and he sometimes wanted to have that kind of impact on others, especially when he felt that he had been marginalized or made ineffectual in some way. His parents also thought that the period at primary school when Ben had been 'adopted' by the girls in his class had been the time when he was most accepted and happiest. It was almost as if Ben was trying to recreate that intimacy again.

Ben settled into special school, although he still remained aloof from his fellow pupils. At 16 he was referred to a general psychiatrist, who made a diagnosis of Asperger syndrome with associated ADHD and expressive language disorder. The psychiatrist referred Ben to a counsellor, and recommended that the methylphenidate be continued.

Ben went on from school to college, where he stayed in different courses for five years. He showed an aptitude for computers, mainly demonstrated by his ability to find paedophile sites, and an ability in art, but the college did not think that he could fit into work, even sheltered work.

Ben was interviewed at several residential colleges. In three he was asked to stay for a week's assessment, but he refused to stay at two, telling his parents that he did not like the people. They knew that once Ben had made up his mind like that, they would not be able to change it, and so did not pressurize him. At the third, something happened, although his parents were not told what it was, and Ben came home early. He was not offered a place at any of the colleges, and so he continued to live at home, attending a day centre for people with learning difficulties, and several non-statutory projects, again mainly for people with learning difficulties. There were no specialized services for people with Asperger syndrome locally who could cope with Ben's mixture of special needs. A community care assessment recognized that Ben did have special needs, but considered that they could be met within the learning difficulties services.

There were occasional crises in the day centre, mainly associated with staff changes, and once or twice with other attenders bullying Ben. During one particularly difficult period Ben several times rang up the emergency services, and also began to make random calls to people he found in the phone book. Ben's GP noted that Ben was losing weight, sleeping badly, and was repeatedly asking his parents questions. She diagnosed a recurrence of his anxiety state, and prescribed fluoxetine that, after a delay of three weeks, resulted in an improvement. His parents also put a lock on the phone.

His parents thought that Ben was stagnating, and that he could have been helped to develop his skills more, and to become more socially integrated. But they also thought that little more was available in their locality, and that it was best just to accept the situation. Ben reached the age of 30 with little change, although his father, now aged 65, became increasingly concerned about the future, and what would happen to Ben when his parents were no longer there.

DIFFERENTIATING DEVELOPMENTAL DISORDER AND MENTAL ILLNESS

The links between schizophrenia, schizoid personality and autism have continued to be close. For a number of years, childhood autism was known as childhood schizophrenia, and there are still some clinicians who diagnose 'childhood schizophrenia' in children who other paediatricians and child psychiatrists consider to have an autism spectrum disorder,[1] or who meet criteria for ASD when fully assessed.[2] Research suggests that up to a half of children who meet criteria for childhood schizophrenia also have an ASD and that these cases have a shared genotype.[3] When an autism spectrum disorder is diagnosed in adulthood, the differentiation from schizophrenia remains a difficult one for the inexperienced clinician. The commonest previous diagnoses of men diagnosed as having Asperger syndrome is schizophrenia, even in the absence of any history of positive symptoms. Clinical experience is that the commonest previous diagnosis in women with Asperger syndrome is 'borderline personality disorder'.

Schizoid symptoms are symptoms of an emotional unease in relationships. For many years, autistic disorder was also thought to be the consequence of emotional trauma or poor parenting, leading to long-term unease in relationships manifesting as autistic disorder. This in turn led to a focus on psychoanalytic treatment as the treatment of choice, and on a culture of family blame. There is a possibility, discussed in Chapter 11, that severe deprivation may cause autistic disorder, although it seems likely that this is a very rare happening, and that there must be a diathesis towards autism for this to occur.

There are many reasons for rejecting an emotional explanation for any of the ASDs (with the possible rare exceptions considered above), which include all of the evidence of different brain development and hereditary predisposition that has already been considered. There is also considerable evidence that the families of people with an ASD are unusually caring. But the main reason for rejecting the emotional and relationship explanation of autistic disorder and the other ASDs is that the fundamental problem is clearly one of social interaction – the nuts and bolts of daily social living which affect relations with strangers as much as relationships with people who matter emotionally. Possible explanations for this no longer refer to emotions about other people, but to the brain's ability to communicate with other brains.

The current ignorance about what frontostriatal networks do means that there can be no precise specification of the psychological disorder or disorders that underlie ASD, although the fundamental impairments of ADHD do seem to be nearer being clarified than those of ASD. The diagnoses of all of the ASDs, with the exception of Rett syndrome, are therefore based, like the diagnoses of schizophrenia or the so-called personality disorders, on a 'syndrome' that is a description of characteristics that are manifest in a population of people with the disorder much more frequently than they are manifest in the relevant, non-affected population. Individual symptoms and signs, if they bear a family resemblance to the syndrome, are taken to be symptoms and signs of that syndrome. Wing and Gould's triad of social impairments was derived from a population study of young residents of Camberwell,[4] a district in South London, selected from the register of children in receipt of special education. Identified impairments in each of the triad – of social interaction, of communication, and of activities and interests – provides the currently dominant syndrome of ASD (see Figure 8.1).

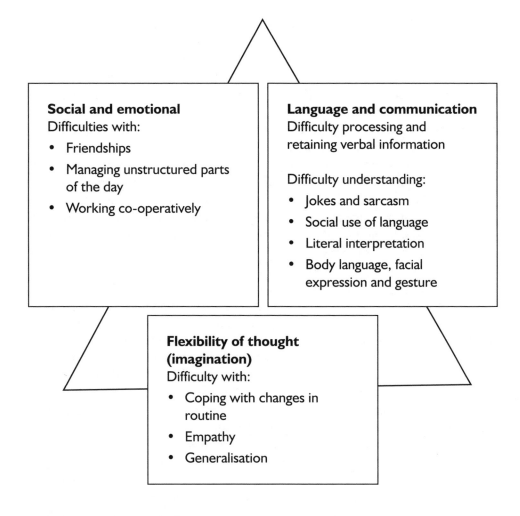

Figure 8.1 The triad of social impairments
Source: Reproduced with kind permission from the National Autistic Society, 2011.

DIAGNOSTIC CRITERIA

Setting the scene

The ASDs are conditions in which there is no sharp distinction between normality and pathology. This is recognized in the term 'autism spectrum disorders', which as well as meaning that there are no clear boundaries between identified disorders on the spectrum, for example between autistic disorder and Asperger syndrome, is usually interpreted to mean that those considered to have the disorder are simply those whose scores on some underlying dimension or variable are more extreme than the rest of the population. Asperger's own descriptions of the syndrome that he described are heterogeneous and overlap those of Kanner,[5] as he recognized himself.

Statistical attempts have been made to define clusters or subgroupings[6] but the clusters that emerge in one study do not correspond to those that emerge in others.[7, 8, 9] Intelligence strongly influences cluster membership, and is more important an influence on outcome than other cluster variables,[9] as is a global measure of ability.[10] Prior *et al.* conclude that it may be just as useful to describe where people with ASD fit on a continuum of ability, as to assign them to a cluster, [10] and there is strong evidence for a single, continuously distributed factor of this kind, with curves of the same shape for boys and for girls, but with the mean being higher for boys than for girls.[11, 12, 13, 14] (See the Distribution of Social Responsiveness Scale in Constantino and Todd, 2003.)

There are many conditions recognized in the clinical sciences of this kind, including hypertension, intellectual disability and body weight.

People who are overweight or obese suffer physically, personally and socially from their condition. Some consider themselves to have a disorder, but others reject this, arguing against what they take to be 'over-medicalization' or 'pathologization' of human variation. On the other hand, some airlines charge more for people over a certain weight, on the basis that they will require two seats, orthopaedic units withhold knee replacements to people above a certain 'body mass index' on the basis that their prosthesis will not last given the mechanical stress of their body weight on it, and epidemiologists can compute the amount of years lost in life expectancy given a particular level of body weight. People who have higher than normal body weights may argue that these practices are inappropriately or unethically discriminatory, but there is unequivocal evidence that normal functioning can be impaired by obesity, even if the sufferers themselves reject the notion that they are abnormal.

Making a diagnosis has ethical implications, as people who recognize that they are bit on the heavy side but would resist being diagnosed as 'obese' would be some of the first to argue. There is a view in the community of people with Asperger syndrome that pathologizing Asperger syndrome is wrong, and that it should simply be considered to be a 'difference'. These ethical issues are considered further in the Appendix.

Categorical diagnosis is necessary administratively as binary decisions have to be made, for example whether or not someone should be eligible for special educational support, or for disability payments from the state. Socially, too, categories are required. Someone coming home from a clinic, and telling a family member that 'The doctor thought I had some traits of Asperger syndrome,' is likely to be asked crossly, 'So what does that mean? Do you have it, or don't you?' Categories are required even if the cut off between normal and abnormal is arbitrary – as it is for mild hypertension, intellectual disability or body weight. So long as those concerned are aware of the arbitrary nature of any particular threshold for diagnosis, this need not present a problem. A greater problem for the diagnosis of the ASDs is that the underlying functional dimensions remain unclarified. For that reason, cut-offs cannot be precisely specified, but are based on a shared social intuition in the examining psychiatrist. So, for example, DSM-IV-TR criteria include phrases like 'appropriate to developmental level, marked impairment, and apparently inflexible'. Even frequency terms, such as 'persistent', are likely to be affected by the salience placed on the item. It takes only three offences for someone to be considered by the courts a 'persistent offender', but a great many more problems to be overcome for someone to be praised by a manager for being 'persistent'. For this reason, total symptom scores are useful in providing a measure of diagnostic certainty, but cannot be used in place of dimensional variables to measure severity or predict outcome (see later section, on dimensions of disorder in ASD).

Historical preoccupation with language

It has been thought in the past that autism was a disorder of language, and although it is now clear that any disorder of language is an independent impairment on top of the fundamental autistic syndrome, diagnosis has remained inappropriately focused on speech. This may be because the examination of speech is more highly developed than the examination of nonverbal communication. One consequence of this overemphasis on verbal communication is that children and young people with impaired nonverbal communication but unimpaired speech will be under-diagnosed.

Practically useful criteria for ASD

The most widely accepted international diagnostic systems, the *International Classification of Diseases* (the tenth edition, ICD-10, is the most recent at the time of writing) published by the World Health Organization,[15] and the *Diagnostic and Statistical Manual* (the fourth edition, with a textual revision, DSM-IV-TR, is the most recent available at the time of writing, although drafts of the fifth revision are also available) of the American Psychiatric Association.[16] Both incorporate the triad of social impairments, specifying three symptom groups: 'qualitative impairments in social interaction', 'qualitative impairments in communication', and 'restricted repetitive and stereotyped patterns of behaviour, interests, and activities' (expected, at the time of writing, to be reduced in the fifth edition of the *Diagnostic and Statistical Manual* (DSM-V) to two, with the amalgamation of impairments of communication and social interaction). However, there are considerable overlaps between these categories. For example, nonverbal behaviours like eye gaze and gesture are considered to be a means to regulate social interaction, and are placed in group A, impairments in social interaction, but could as easily and appropriately be placed in group B, qualitative impairments in communication.

Individual items lack, on the face of it, correlation with other items within each of the scales. 'Failure to develop peer relationships', listed as an impairment of social interaction, could be attributable to emotional difficulties and not to problems in social interaction. 'Relative failure to initiate or sustain conversational interchange', an item of qualitative abnormality in communication, could equally well apply both to children with impaired social use of speech, typical of an ASD, and to people with language impairments. 'Pretend play' or 'spontaneous make-believe' is listed as an abnormality of communication, although it may not involve any kind of communication.

The category of restricted, repetitive or stereotyped patterns is useful in differentiating people with an ASD who have learning difficulties from other people with an equal degree of learning difficulty with no ASD;[17] it is much less useful in Asperger syndrome.

DSM-IV-TR Asperger criteria reproduce those of autistic disorder minus group B, the speech and language items. The provisos that there should be no significant language and cognitive delay, and that there should be significant impairments of functioning are also added, as are additional diagnostic exceptions, including that no other ASD should be diagnosable. Since group B contains items that would be fulfilled by people with pragmatic language problems, it is very rare for anyone for whom group A items are positive not to have at least one positive item in group B. As a result, it is almost impossible to receive a diagnosis of Asperger syndrome using DSM-IV-TR criteria (likely to be addressed in the DSM-V by including AS within ASD).[18]

External validity of an ASD diagnosis

Research diagnoses need to be reliable across research groups and across countries. Validity is a secondary consideration. Researchers therefore rely on standardized instruments to make their research comparable, coupled with 'diagnostic' algorithms.

In clinical practice, although reliability is important, validity is more important still. External validation is provided by the utility of a diagnosis in facilitating the correct understanding of their condition by the patient or client, by their carers, and by relevant others, such as employers or teachers. A valid clinical diagnosis should also correctly indicate which treatments are useful, and which unhelpful. Prognostic value is another measure of external validity: for example, the social outcome of Rett syndrome is worse than that of autistic disorder,[19] which is worse than that of Asperger syndrome.[20] Predicting this outcome at an early stage is important for carers, particularly.

DSM-IV-TR criteria for autistic disorder have been successfully incorporated into clinical practice in one study in New South Wales, Australia, which is likely to reflect the practice of experienced clinicians elsewhere; but New South Wales clinicians use their own criteria rather than DSM-IV-TR for other ASD diagnoses, including Asperger syndrome.[21] One possible reason for this is that there is no scientific evidence that autistic disorder and Asperger syndrome can be separated by any criteria.[22, 23, 24, 25, 26] When differences are found, they can often be attributed to the fact that children with language impairment are included in the autistic disorder group and excluded from the Asperger group.[27]

It is carers who have driven the diagnosis of Asperger syndrome, rather than the scientific community. Asperger lectured in the UK in 1970, and the syndrome described by him was given early prominence.[28, 29, 30] It has therefore become well known to carers in the UK, and in those countries where there are influential UK-trained clinicians such as Australia. In the US,[31] and countries influenced by the US, more prominence was given to Kanner's opposition to the overlap between the ASDs and Kanner's own formulation of children with autistic disorder who 'go far' in social outcome[32] – the group now known as high functioning. Carers have therefore tended to use this latter term, although Asperger syndrome is also becoming increasingly popular.

Carers are much less concerned about developmental trajectories, and much more about current and future functioning. The fact that one person with an ASD had language delay, or even cognitive delay, and another did not, is much less important than their current level of functioning. Their carers might want to say that each has Asperger syndrome, and in meeting them, a clinician might also think that they are very similar, too. What makes them similar, and different from a person whom a carer will often accept has 'autism', is related to social function and intelligence. But it is not simply a matter of IQ, or even social adaptation. In my experience, the criterion that is most used by people with an ASD and their carers to distinguish autistic disorder from AS comes closest to what UK law recognizes to be 'capacity' or 'competence',[33] that is the extent to which a person wants, and is able, to make decisions on their own behalf. People with Asperger syndrome have, as the title of a booklet published by the UK National Autistic Society indicates, a 'Mind of their own'.[34] Self-awareness and therefore awareness of difference from other people is, clinical experience suggests, the most practical discriminator of Kanner and Asperger syndrome.

Although there is no accepted *sine qua non* criterion of ASD, several psychological impairments have been suggested to be fundamental on the basis of research rather than epidemiology.[35] One, central coherence,[36] is cognitive. The others, joint attention,[37] interbrain connection bandwidth,[38] and theory of mind (Baron-Cohen: but since modified by him to be two dimensions, empathy and systematizing),[39] all are linked to nonverbal communication with, in the case of theory of mind, an additional cognitive element. Impaired nonverbal communicative competence is therefore, on the basis of current thinking, the closest to a necessary criterion for an ASD diagnosis. Nonverbal communicative impairment may or may not involve impaired expression, as well as impaired interpretation. There are clinical reasons for considering this an important distinction (see Chapter 6).

Considering DSM-IV-TR or ICD-10 autistic disorder to be a single disorder leads to difficulty when all of the criteria are present for the diagnosis of autistic disorder, but the symptoms are clearly secondary to another named disorder, for example fragile X syndrome or Rett syndrome. Currently DSM-IV-TR precludes autistic disorder and Rett syndrome being concurrent diagnoses, but this is clinically unhelpful. DSM-IV-TR's listed criteria also exclude a diagnosis of Asperger disorder when schizophrenia has been diagnosed (this is now glossed in the text revision allowing a diagnosis of schizophrenia if there is a break between the onset of the ASD symptoms and the positive symptoms of schizophrenia), although clinicians are aware that young people with known Asperger syndrome may develop schizophrenia in adolescence as frequently as neurotypicals do. For this reason, it is more useful to think of autistic disorder as 'autistic syndrome', as reflected in the title of this chapter, and to prefer ICD-10's retention of 'Asperger's syndrome' over the 'Asperger disorder' of DSM-IV-TR.

AUTISTIC SYNDROME

Autism spectrum condition, autistic spectrum disorder, and autism spectrum disorder are all terms that illustrate the difficulty of separating out the subtypes currently given their own codings in DSM-IV or ICD-10. My use of autistic syndrome subsumes this notion of the spectrum of disorder, and indeed the spectrum of degrees of neurotypicality into which the autism spectrum itself fits. My use of the term autistic syndrome is also intended to emphasize that co-morbidity is the rule rather than the exception in the ASDs, and that it makes little clinical sense to reserve a diagnosis of ASD for people who do not have some other named condition, such as Rett or Prader-Willi syndromes. Recognizing these co-morbidities is important, however, because they may have a substantial impact on the course and prognosis of the autistic syndrome. It is becoming recognized that 'complex' autism spectrum disorder may have a worse prognosis than 'essential' autism spectrum disorder, for example.

The subtypes of autism spectrum disorder currently used have limited predictiveness since a child meeting autistic disorder criteria may grow into an adult with Asperger syndrome (or much more rarely, vice versa). But these categories are useful guides to the experience and likely difficulties of a person with an autism spectrum disorder. So for the clinician it is more useful to focus on the profile of a person's difficulties at the time of the assessment, rather than relying on historical information as DSM-IV and ICD-10 requires the clinician to do.

Figure 8.2 shows a diagnostic flow chart based on this kind of contemporaneous or ahistorical approach to diagnosis.

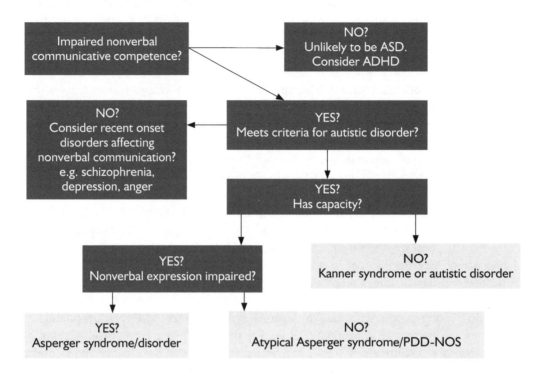

Figure 8.2 Recommended diagnostic flow chart

DIMENSIONS OF DISORDER IN ASD

An alternative approach to assessment of ASD is to look for dimensions of dysfunction, much as a physician assessing a patient with pneumonia may assess blood oxygen saturation, antibiotic sensitivity of the pathogen, and X-ray lung appearance as potentially independently variable impacts of the pneumonia, each of which may need to be considered independently when considering treatment.

Georgiades *et al.*[40] factor analysed developmental information about 209 children with ASD, and found that three factors accounted for 50 per cent of the variance: social and communicative behaviours, inflexible language and behaviour, and repetitive sensory and motor behaviour. In 2009, two factor analyses of developmental symptoms in large populations of people with an ASD, a two rather than a three factor solution provided the best fit, but the two factors were similar to those found by Georgiades *et al.* – one loading on social and communication items, and one on repetitive and restricted behaviour items.[41, 42]

Whether the autistic syndrome will continue to be defined as being the conjunction of three subsyndromes, and whether these subsyndromes can be considered to be single dimensions, or whether the autistic syndrome will be restricted to one or more of the subsyndromes is not clear. It is likely that genetic research will play a larger part in determining this, since disorders will be classified increasingly by genotype and not phenotype. It has been suggested that each of the three elements of the triad might be the product of a different genotype,[43] and that each corresponds to a potentially independently heritable component of the phenotype, or 'endophenotype'.[44] ADHD, executive impairment, speech and language impairment, and others to be discussed later, may all be endophenotypes that can contribute to the expression of ASD in any particular person with ASD.

EARLY RECOGNITION OF THE AUTISTIC SYNDROME

There is growing awareness among healthcare staff of the symptoms and signs of ASD, but it is still likely to be a parent who first suspects an ASD.[45] Parents often report that these first concerns are minimized by health professionals, who may imply that parents are exaggeratedly preoccupied with trivial differences. Parents find it difficult to specify exactly what their concerns are, which might explain the health professionals' unwillingness to 'label'; 18 months is the age at which parents commonly become sure that their child has a problem, although there may have been worries or comments made by relatives or friends previously.[46]

There has been no naturalistic study of the specificity or sensitivity of parental concerns in relation to formal diagnosis, although the completion of screening questionnaires by parents leads to a significant false positive rate with positive predictive values of 0.63–0.68.[47] Professionals may also have high false positive rates using screening tools in the first two years.[48] This is because there is considerable variation up until the age of three in the developmental trajectories of different infants. Diagnosis of typical autistic syndrome may be possible after the age of two, and can usually be made reliably after the age of three,[49] and many diagnostic services now aim to be able to make a definite diagnosis then. The diagnosis of other autism spectrum conditions may be suspected at that age, but can often not be made reliably until later.

SCREENING FOR THE AUTISTIC SYNDROME

Variations in diagnostic frequency between areas (see Chapter 9) partly reflect variations in self- and carer-recognition of the disorder. Poverty and being from a minority ethnic group are associated with low recognition in the US, and probably elsewhere. Children, adolescents and adults whose ASD is unrecognized may be denied appropriate intervention, and may be exposed to avoidable experiences of being shamed by bullying or stigma,[50] which can lead to long-term emotional harm. One way to avoid this might be to screen for ASD in the general population.

Screening is 'the presumptive identification of unrecognized disease or defect by the application of tests, examinations, or other procedures which can be applied rapidly.'[51] In conditions in which there is a continuous distribution of impairment that a cut-off must be applied, some people who consider themselves to be well will be labelled as being impaired. As a result, screening has potential adverse consequences. Furthermore, there is a much reduced compliance with interventions which are recommended following identification through screening than interventions recommended to people seeking help.

Screening has been developed mainly in relation to infants, partly because developmental screening at this age is already well established. There is also the hope that early ascertainment leads to earlier intervention, and this may mean better prognosis,[52] although evaluation of routine evaluation has yet to be done.[53] At least four English-language screening measures for use in the infant population to screen for ASD (level 1 screeners) have been developed.[54] There are additional measures that can be used by a clinician to estimate the likelihood of autism being present (level 2 screeners).[55]

The original Checklist for Autism in Toddlers (CHAT), or its two subsequently expanded and modified versions,[56, 57, 58] have been rigorously tested as level 1 screeners. The specificity of the CHAT and its modified form is much higher than its sensitivity, particularly for children with Asperger syndrome and for infants with marked developmental delays.[59] The lack of sensitivity may be a general problem facing questionnaire methods at this age, partly because of the difficulty in putting the quality of development at this age into words, and partly because developmental trajectories may be particularly variable at this age,[60] with some children meeting diagnostic criteria for ASD at the age of two, but no longer meeting them at four years.[61] However, the receiver operating characteristics of level 1 screeners may be a problem at any age, in that it may be possible to achieve either high specificity or high sensitivity, but not both, given the lack of knowledge of the primary impairment in ASD, and the failings of diagnostic algorithms for ASD.

Parents report that primary care physicians often reassure them that their children 'will grow out of it'. This may be because primary care physicians lack a method of determining which children should be referred for specialist assessment. A screening measure may assist with this. Pierce *et al.* tested the acceptability of the Communication and Symbolic Behavior Scales Developmental Profile Infant-Toddler Checklist at a one-year well baby assessment.[62] The checklist is completed by parents (estimated time five minutes, although no information is provided in the paper about non-literate or non-English-speaking parents) and reviewed by the paediatrician (estimated time after a brief training is two minutes). One hundred and thirty seven paediatricians with offices in San Diego county were involved in the study, and 10,479 checklists were handed out, and infants scoring positively referred to the authors' clinic for a fuller diagnostic assessment. The positive predictive value of the procedure is reported in the evaluation as 0.75 with only 5 out of 32 infants diagnosed as having an ASD no longer meeting diagnostic criteria at follow-up. Many of the paediatricians decided to continue to use the screening after the end of the study.

However, of the 1318 in which screening indicated possible ASD, only 346 were referred and of these only 208 got to the clinic and only 184 families completed all of the diagnostic interviews, some of which were extended with up to six interviews taking place per child. So, although the study is suggestive that screening might be incorporated into routine practice in the future, it indicates that at best only half of the at risk children are likely to be assessed – and this proportion will be much less if infants whose parents were not motivated to complete the checklist and take them to a paediatrician are included. Nor does the screening technique seem sensitive enough to pick up infants with Asperger syndrome: in fact, the checklist picked up more children with intellectual disability than children with ASD.

Red flags

Experienced clinicians use a 'family resemblance' approach to complex diagnoses, rather than relying on checklists. However, thinking of the possibility of an ASD is a first step to deciding whether one is present and unless a parent asks about this, which they may, something needs to tip the clinician's thoughts in this direction. A simple list of possible indicators of ASD, or 'red flags', is one way of doing this. Suggested red flags include a phase of regression in development, a parent reporting that their child lived in a world of his or her own, and delayed understanding of speech in the absence of hearing impairment.[63] The Child Neurology Society and American Academy of Neurology suggested specific behaviours with time limits,[64] but these were strongly biased towards language, and did not reflect recent research based on high risk studies,[65] or on studies of family videos[66, 67] which emphasize lack of emotional regulation, reduced joint attention, and reduced bids for attention. Watson *et al.* summarize the behaviours that parents of 38 children with an ASD, 40 neurotypical children, and 15 children with global development endorsed on a new structured questionnaire, the First Year Inventory, as being present when their child was aged one year.[68] The children with ASD had more symptoms than either comparison group, particularly in social orienting and receptive communication cluster, social affective engagement clusters, and the reactivity cluster (see Table 8.1). Both the children with an ASD and the children with global developmental delay had more impairments in imitation, expressive communication, sensory processing, and repetitive play or behaviour, indicating that these problems are not specific to ASD.[68]

Although the red flag approach has been mainly applied in infancy and early childhood, it is potentially applicable to every age group, and in the later age-specific chapters, a proposed 'red flag' list will be included.

Table 8.1 Features of early development that distinguish, highly significantly, between children with an ASD and typically developing infants, or infants with global developmental delay

Did your baby turn or look at you when you called baby's name?
Did your baby seem to have trouble hearing?
When you pointed to something interesting, did your baby turn to look at it?
Did your baby look at people when they began talking, even when they were not talking directly to your baby?
Did your baby look up from playing with a favourite toy if you showed him or her a different toy?
Did your baby seem interested in other babies his or her age?
When you said 'Where's [a familiar person or object]' without pointing or showing, would your baby look at the person or object named?
What did you typically have to do to get your baby to turn towards you?

Source: Adapted from Watson, Baranek, *et al.*, 2007.

Table 8.2 Criteria for implementing screening

The condition should be an important health problem.
There should be a treatment for the condition.
Facilities for diagnosis and treatment should be available.
There should be a latent stage of the disease.
There should be a test or examination for the condition.
The test should be acceptable to the population.
The natural history of the disease should be adequately understood.
There should be an agreed policy on who to treat.
The total cost of finding a case should be economically balanced in relation to medical expenditure as a whole.

IS SCREENING CURRENTLY WORTHWHILE?

Screening does not always improve health, and a WHO report suggests that ten criteria should be met before screening is implemented (see Table 8.2).[69] ASD currently fails several of these, and in the UK it has been concluded that there is little public health value in screening,[70] although in the US, it is recommended that all two-year-olds are screened for ASD (see Chapter 11 for details).

SURVEILLANCE

Case finding should be a continuous process, not just a 'once and for all' project. Surveillance is the term used to focus on people at high risk of having an ASD, for example those with a strong family history, or those who show a red flag. Surveillance is defined in guidelines produced jointly by the Council on Children with Disabilities, the Section on Developmental Behavioral Pediatrics, the Bright Futures Steering Committee and the Medical Home Initiatives for Children with Special Needs Project Advisory Committee in terms that are no different from those of a clinical assessment:

> eliciting and attending to the parent's concern (or in later life, this could be the spouse's concern or, of course, the person's own concern), documenting and maintaining a developing history, making accurate observations of the child (person affected), identifying the risk and protective factors, and maintaining an accurate record and documenting the process and findings.[71]

The American Academy of Pediatrics (AAP) has developed a surveillance flow chart (see the Surveillance and Screening Algorithm in Johnson, Myer, *et al.*, 2007).

The AAP flow chart incorporates the routine use of a screening tool although, as noted above, the receiver operating characteristics of current tools is not high enough to make these reliable diagnostically.

Effective surveillance relies on a prior assessment at which a red flag, or risk factor, might be identified. In the UK, some authorities are giving up on developmental checks for every child and this is likely to reduce the effectiveness of surveillance.[72] Surveillance in older children and adults relies on consultations with primary health care providers being used to elicit more general concerns, and the uncovering of unsuspected red flags.

DIFFERENTIAL DIAGNOSIS

Much discussion is given in clinical meetings to whether or not the child or adult in question has an ASD, or some other disorder. This question would normally mean, can the affected person's difficulties by explained best by ASD or by another disorder? Acquired impairment in nonverbal expression may be caused in adolescence by schizophrenia, and in adulthood by right hemisphere infarction or other damage, and by Parkinsonism, but in middle childhood acquiring persistent, selective (that is not attributable to a general sensorimotor disorder) impairment of nonverbal expression is vanishingly rare. So there are few situations where differential diagnosis *per se* is an issue, once it has been established that the autistic syndrome is present.

Discussions of differential diagnosis often involve considering whether or not other conditions are present, and this kind of discussion is of greater importance in assessing people with an ASD, for many of them may have associated neurodevelopmental disorders and a few may also have a known physical disorder that could be linked to the cause of their ASD.

Although attention will be given to differential diagnosis in Chapter 17 on adolescence and adulthood, more attention will be given to the assessment of associated conditions, and to the search for possible aetiology.

Differential diagnosis in the conventional sense does apply where the hypothesized disorder of nonverbal communication is in nonverbal interpretation, rather than directly observable nonverbal expression as is the case for atypical ASD.

INVESTIGATION

There are no specific investigations that will establish the presence or absence of an ASD, but investigation may be appropriate to investigate the presence and importance of co-morbid conditions. Investigations will vary with clinical presentation and with age group. They are considered in Chapters 12 to 17.

Routine karyotyping is not currently recommended, because the yields of recognized syndromes are low, although the presence of macrocephaly in older children and adults may increase the yield. This may change when conditioned specific gene chip arrays become widely available.

Recent guidelines have not recommended routine MRI, either, but improvements in MRI technique may justify a low threshold for imaging. For example, in one study of people with an ASD but no other named syndrome, it was found that $^{33}/_{69}$ (48%) MRI scans showed some abnormality: most usually temporal lobe abnormalities, a white matter signal abnormality ($^{16}/_{69}$), or substantial dilation of Virchow-Robin perivascular spaces surrounding blood vessels as they enter the brain ($^{12}/_{69}$).[73]

The requirements for more formal psychometric testing, speech and language assessment, imaging, and laboratory tests will also vary with age group as well as clinical presentation. This will be discussed in more detail in later sections, as will the necessity of involving a multidisciplinary team in these assessments.

Chapter 9

PRESENTATION, PREVALENCE, TREATMENT AND COURSE OF THE AUTISM SPECTRUM DISORDERS

PRESENTATION

Presenting symptoms of the ASDs

There is considerable variation in the clinical picture of the ASDs. There may be patterns of symptoms that point to specific aetiologies, as in Rett syndrome, or to specific outcomes, as in disintegrative psychosis (see Chapter 12 for a description), but these are rare. The causes for many cases of ASD are unknown. If abnormalities are found on investigation, an association with distinctive symptoms is the exception rather than the rule. Nor are there distinct phenotypes, corresponding to different clusters of symptoms or syndromes, although there is some evidence for the separation of social and communicative symptoms, and non-social symptoms like resistance to change, stereotypies, and fascination with repetitive sensory stimulation as discussed in Chapter 8.

Heterogeneity is increased because many factors that are probably independent of the primary impairment influence its expression. These include age and developmental level, intelligence, the presence or absence of specific language impairments, the presence or absence of physical disorders and impairments such as epilepsy, the presence or absence of associated neurodevelopmental syndromes like ADHD or dysexecutive syndrome, familial, psychosocial and cultural factors that impinge on development and therefore on the primary impairment.

Experienced clinicians do develop an intuitive sense that there are patterns of symptoms, much as one can sometimes glance at a stranger's face and think that they resemble someone else that one knows. But it is often difficult to categorize what constitutes the similarity in the pattern, and as in the analogy of making the acquaintance of a stranger, the better one knows the person, the more the resemblance with others fades.

Childhood and adolescence present young people with common challenges linked to social transitions, such as starting at or leaving school. Children or young people may develop an acute increase in symptoms at these stages, and children who 'break down' at a particular stage often have similarities with other children or young people who also break down at this stage. Chapters 12–17 have therefore been organized according to age at first presentation rather than clinical subtype as a means of reducing some of the symptom heterogeneity.

Attention deficit hyperactivity disorder

ADHD, too, is a heterogeneous disorder, and a distinction is often made between the inattentive type, the hyperactive/impulsive type, and the combined type. The combined type refers to the presence of both hyperactivity and of inattentiveness, but hyperactivity/impulsivity almost never occurs in the absence of inattentiveness except in very young children,[1] and ADHD combined and ADHD hyperactive/impulsive types can probably be assumed to be identical. The subtypes appear to share a degree of genetic risk, but also to have some separable variation.[2, 3] Most longitudinal studies suggest that both subtypes occur in adults as often as children, but clinical experience is that inattentive and dysexecutive symptoms affect adults more than impulsive/hyperactive ones.[4, 2] Hyperactivity may not persist into adulthood, but impulsivity does, although its manifestations may be more subtle and therefore overlooked.[5] Dysexecutive symptoms also become more prominent as children pass into adolescence. Inattentiveness is more likely to be associated with distress in adolescents.

There is no generally accepted diagnostic algorithm that can be used for the diagnosis of ADHD, and no pathognomonic signs of it. Indeed, it is easy to fake ADHD symptoms[6] presumably because ADHD symptoms are experienced by everyone when they are unusually fatigued.

The DSM-IV ADHD diagnostic guidelines have proven to be useful both in research and clinical settings. They require either the presence of a sufficient number of symptoms of inattention, or the presence of a sufficient number of hyperactivity and impulsivity symptoms. Hyperactivity manifests similarly in both children and adults, although it is rarer than the latter. The two items from the DSM-IV guidelines that have been found to be sufficiently common to be used in a screening questionnaire for hyperactivity (the Adult ADHD Self-Report Scale or ASRS)[7] are:

- How often do you fidget or squirm with your hands or feet when you have to sit down for a long time?

- How often do you feel overly active and compelled to do things, like you were driven by a motor?

Impulsivity in DSM-IV is assessed by symptoms of children not being able to contain themselves, as manifested by butting into conversations, not being able to wait in turn, or blurting out the answers to questions before the question is finished. Adult impulsivity rarely expresses itself so overtly, and is harder to assess clinically. Risk-taking and decision-making that prioritizes short-term gains over potential long-term losses may be an indication.

Inattentiveness also becomes more subtle. In children with ADHD this may be expressed by 'carelessness' or being easily 'distracted', to use the terms used by DSM-IV, but these symptoms may not apply to adults.[8] Three features of inattentiveness at all ages are the failure to maintain an attentional focus in the face of distraction, an apparent unwillingness or inability to devote cognitive effort to a sustained task, and an impaired ability to anticipate task requirements by organizing materials ahead of time. Four of the six questions from the ASRS cover these areas,[7] and could be used in children as well as adults:

- How often do you have trouble wrapping up the final details of a project, once the challenging parts have been done?

- How often do you have difficulty getting things in order when you have to do a task that requires organization?

- How often do you have problems remembering appointments or obligations?

- When you have a task that requires a lot of thought, how often do you avoid or delay getting started?

Language impairment

Language impairment independently contributes to a poorer outcome in people with an ASD.[9] Children with both language impairment and autistic syndrome are more likely to be socially withdrawn than children with autistic syndrome alone, although learning difficulty may also influence this association, and to have more severe autistic symptoms.[10] In one comparison of 58 people with AS and 39 with autistic disorder,[11] the latter being defined as showing language or cognitive delay, or both, 79 per cent of those with AS were rated as 'active but odd' and 82 per cent of those with autistic disorder were 'aloof and passive', using the criteria and terminology for social withdrawal developed by Wing and Gould.[12]

Delay in speech understanding, as reported by parents, is a simple measure of language impairment which correlates well with speech level estimated by direct testing (see Chapter 5), and with joint attention.

PREVALENCE

Rates of ASD

A meta-analysis of prevalence studies of ASD found 40 that met inclusion criteria.[13] The mean prevalence was calculated weighting for study numbers, and the 95 per cent confidence interval calculated using the odds ratio method. The prevalences were 7.1 per 10,000 for 'typical autism' (95 per cent confidence interval from a lower prevalence of 1.6 per 10,000 to a higher of 30.6 per 10,000) and for all ASDs, 20.0 per 10,000, with 95 per cent confidence interval of 4.9 per 10,000 to 82.1 per 10,000. The authors conclude that the age of the sample, whether it was rural or urban, and the diagnostic criteria used all affected the rates.[13]

A series of well-designed studies using well standardized diagnostic criteria and a wide variety of urban and rural settings has been conducted in various US sites under the auspices of the Centers for Disease Control and Prevention. The mean prevalence rate in eight-year-olds over 14 sites, involving 407,578 children, was 1 in 150 for all ASDs using DSM-IV-TR criteria.[14] This is higher than the mean of all the studies considered in the Williams *et al.* meta-analysis,[13] but well within their confidence interval. Only children known to health or educational services were considered, and variations in prevalence between sites may have reflected the extent to which children's problems were ascertained by these primary services. The measured prevalence may therefore be an underestimate but 1 in 150 is currently the prevalence figure that is most widely accepted, for example by the National Autistic Society of the UK.

Further analysis of these data indicates that ascertainment is systematically lower in people with generalized learning disabilities and an autism spectrum disorder, and when the child being assessed is from a minority ethnic group.[15] Rates from studies using parent ascertainment are lower, although this may be an artefact of the means of collection.[16]

Are there at risk populations?

The once popular view that ASD was a 'middle class disease' reflects the current situation of higher ascertainment in middle class communities. Very little evidence has come to light to challenge Lotter's conclusion in the 1960s that autism is equally prevalent in every culture and every ethnic group.[17] This is reminiscent of Kraepelin's conclusion about schizophrenia,[18] although evidence is now accumulating that schizophrenia is more common among African Americans and native Americans, and in the children of African Caribbean immigrants to the UK.[19] It has been suggested that ASD may also be higher in recent immigrants and this is borne out by Keen *et al.*, who looked at a clinic population and found that children of mothers who had migrated to the UK from outside Europe were over-represented in the children diagnosed with ASD; mothers who considered themselves to be black, especially if they were from the Caribbean, were most likely to have children with an ASD.[20]

Rates of specific AS subtypes

Although rates have been published for people with Asperger syndrome, the lack of diagnostic consensus means that these should be treated with caution. In one large Finnish study, involving 5484 eight-year-old children, four different criteria were used and there was good agreement between the prevalence rates using DSM-IV criteria (1 in 400), ICD-10 (1 in 370), and criteria developed by Gillberg and Gillberg (1 in 345). However, using criteria developed by a Canadian group, Szatmari *et al.*, the estimated prevalence was almost half of these figures (1 in 625).[21]

A large study (27,749 children aged 5 to 16 in the base population) in Montreal,[22] by a team led by one of the most experienced epidemiologists of child mental health, found a similar prevalence of ASD to the Centers for Disease Control and Prevention studies (1 in 154 children), but with an unexpectedly low proportion of them being thought to meet criteria of PDD-NOS (1 in 305 children) and lower figures for prevalence of autistic disorder (1 in 463 children) and for Asperger syndrome (1 in 990 children). Given the current lack of validity for Asperger syndrome and PDD-NOS diagnostic criteria, attempting to obtain accurate figures for the prevalence of ASD subtypes is probably premature.[22]

Rates of ADHD

ADHD prevalence estimates have been as variable as those of ASD, with some asserting that ADHD was a cultural determined diagnosis, and even that it was the way that white Americans chose to pathologize black American children. European psychiatrists, particularly, have suggested in the past that ADHD is an overused diagnosis in the US. One meta-analysis of surveys of children and young people aged 18 years or under has shown that there is considerable variation in rates, but that was attributable to different diagnostic criteria being used with the inclusion of a criterion of impairment being of particular impact, and to the course of information. Although geographic region in which the study was carried out did influence prevalence rates, there were no differences between Europe and the US, only differences between the Middle East and Africa on one hand, and North and South America, Europe, Oceania and Asia on the other.[23]

The pooled rate for young people, based on 171,756 individuals in 102 studies, was 5.29 per cent.

Rates in different age groups

It is generally assumed that ASDs are unremitting and that rates do not therefore change with age. However, two surveys have suggested that there may be a fall in prevalence with falling age.[24, 25] This may reflect a spurious ascertainment bias due to the reliance on people with ASD on people close to them to participate in community activities, including answering research questionnaires. There may also be a differential mortality in that as people age, they are more likely to lose the support of their parents, who are themselves at increased risk of disability or death.

Since parents remain the main carers for most people with ASD throughout their lifetime,[25] the unavailability of this care as they get older may mean that many people with an ASD who have no alternative care become socially isolated and neglected, and may possibly die earlier as a result. This may contribute to a fall in prevalence. However, there is also evidence that some symptoms of ASD may remit with age,[26] with social symptoms remitting more than communication-related symptoms, and with these remitting more than repetitive symptoms.[27] It has been estimated that up to a quarter of people with an ASD may recover,[28] as both Asperger and Kanner reported had occurred in some of their patients. These findings are consistent with a follow-up of adolescents and adults with an autism spectrum disorder, which showed that there was improvement in symptoms of autism over the 4.5 year follow-up period, and that older (over the age of 30) participants had fewer 'maladaptive behaviours' than adolescents.[29] This 'improvement' may be one facet of the general tendency of men to acquire more social skills over the life span or, to put it another way, the substantial delay of acquisition of social skills in men compared to women.[30]

Rates of ADHD fall more sharply with age, but ADHD does not normally remit in adolescence, as was once thought. However, the pattern of symptoms may change. A recent US study of 4175 adolescents led to an estimated rate of 1.2 per cent in adolescents[31] using DSM-IV criteria, but another larger study, part of the WHO world mental health survey initiative, found a pooled rate of 3.4 per cent in respondents aged from 18 to 44 years in ten countries (total number of respondents was 11,422) with an apparently lower prevalence in low income countries (1.9%) than in high income countries (4.2%).[32] The authors note that a minority of cases meeting research criteria of ADHD had been diagnosed as having the condition, but many had received diagnoses for co-morbid conditions, most frequently anxiety and mood disorders, and substance abuse. Although criticisms can be made of the study design,[33] the overall result – that a substantial proportion of children with ADHD continue to have ADHD symptoms in adulthood – seems incontrovertible.

Gender differences in rates

Rates in men and boys of both ASD and ADHD have always exceeded rates in girls and women, but the ratios have dropped in parallel with the apparently increasing prevalence. This, too, may reflect the broadening of criteria. In a survey of adolescents and adults in Sheffield,[34] the ratio of males to females in nearly half of the sample who had never previously been diagnosed was 1.9:1, but the ratio in the group who had previously been diagnosed was 6.6:1. Another interpretation of this finding may be that women with an ASD are more able to assimilate despite their social difficulties, and therefore are less likely to seek – or to be referred – for diagnosis. Girls with an ASD are often reported to be more likely to have an intellectual disability than boys with an ASD,[35] but this may reflect the bias towards ascertainment in males of many current diagnostic criteria. Prevalence rates in males in a meta-analysis were 10 per cent and in females, 4.5 per cent, giving a ratio of 2.2:1,[36] which is not dissimilar to the rate found in the Sheffield survey,[25] and much lower than the male to female ratios of prevalence reported in previous studies.

Rett syndrome is an X-linked disorder and so very rarely found in live-born males, since the mutation is almost always fatal in the male foetus in the absence of a normal MECP2 gene on another X chromosome. Other X-linked disorders associated with non-fatal mutations and associated with an increased incident of ASD may increase the male to female ratio.

Rates of Kanner syndrome in intellectual disability

The presence or absence of the autistic syndrome is a reliable indicator of an ASD in people with intellectual disability (ID),[37] but there is underdiagnosis of ASD in this group, particularly in adolescence and adulthood. One epidemiological study of adolescents attempted to overcome some of the difficulties by using consensus diagnoses made by clinicians with experience in the dual diagnosis. The rate of intellectual disability was 7.1 per 1000 and of ASD and ID was 2.0 per 1000. ASD therefore occurred in 28 per cent of those with ID, with a non-significantly greater prevalence in those with severe ID, and a lower male to female ratio (2:1) compared to the 2.8:1 ratio of males to female in the mild group. Less than a half of people with ASD had a previous diagnosis.[38]

Has there been an increase in prevalence?

There has undoubtedly been an increase in the ascertained prevalence of recognized autism spectrum disorders. Diagnoses are being made earlier,[39] and so lifetime prevalence is spuriously increased by earlier age of diagnosis, and the inclusion of younger age cohorts in the total of children diagnosed, but annual prevalence in older age groups has also increased, although it is difficult to compare surveys because differences in location (Japan versus the US, for example), age group surveyed, and diagnostic criteria have a substantial impact on reported rates.[40] Some have suggested that this reflects a true increase in prevalence and points to an environmental aetiology, with exposure to vaccines or toxins often being incriminated. However, expert opinion is strongly against there being a 'real' increase. Fombonne,[41] like many other experts, attributes the increase to more active case ascertainment and broadening diagnostic criteria rather that to a true increase in prevalence. Fombonne estimates the increase to have been about four or five times since the early 1970s; Wazana estimates it to be an apparent eleven-fold increase,[42] but even so finds that small changes in criteria and case ascertainment could explain this.

Broadening the diagnostic criteria has particularly increased detection rates in women, and in people who do not have additional learning difficulties. In the Brick Township study 51 per cent of the children with an autism spectrum disorder who were tested had an IQ in the normal range,[43] compared to Wing's finding that almost all of her cases had a learning difficulty.[44] Some proportion of this change may also be attributable to diagnostic substitution. The rise in administrative determinations of autism is paralleled by a fall in the rates of unspecified educational needs or learning difficulties, at least in British Columbia,[45] and in California.[46]

There has been a similar increase in the rates of diagnosed ADHD as in the rates of diagnosed ASD: an almost fourfold increase in the US between 1989 and 2000,[47] and some have argued for a toxic explanation for ADHD too, usually pointing the finger at food additives. But, as in ASD, the apparently increased prevalence could reflect changing diagnostic criteria and better ascertainment, and not a real change in prevalence.

TREATMENT

ASD management changes according to the age and previous history of the person whose condition is being investigated or treated.[48] However, there are some general principles, which will be considered here. Further discussion of age specific management is to be found in the chapters relating to age at first presentation (Chapters 12–17).

Many, many treatments have been developed for ASD, ranging from coercive interventions that could have been applied at the height of the popularity of hydrotherapy and Romantic psychiatry in the early nineteenth century to self-control using fMRI feedback. One difficulty is that many of them have been shown to be effective in at least one study or in at least one clinician's or educator's practice, although rarely in placebo-controlled randomized controlled trials.[49] One reason for this may be that a new method of intervention has the non-specific benefits of introducing new hope. But another, and perhaps more substantial reason, is that many interventions provide a structure for carers or professionals to interact with a person with ASD over a longer period of time than is normally comfortable if there is no structure. So great is this problem that one autism charity in the UK has spent considerable funding to create an online database of interventions (112 at the time of writing) which are being progressively graded according to the number of studies that show positive benefit and the number that show harm, with an additional rating between 1 and 3 of harm.[50]

Diagnosis

Having a diagnosis is often considered to be of little value in itself, being but a step to treatment. However, having a diagnosis is also a stepping stone towards personal and informal change that may have a therapeutic impact. In particular, it often means that there is a shift from moral to medical discourse. Instead of a person being blamed for failings, or blaming him- or herself, he or she may receive practical help or emotional support for their 'handicap'. Not everyone who meets the criteria for a diagnosis of ASD will want this reaction, and it may be important to check with them whether or not having a diagnosis will be welcome. Getting a diagnosis remains one of the most highly valued interventions by parents and, in later life, by adults.

Information

Providing information, like giving a diagnosis, is not treatment, but it has a substantial impact even so. Diagnosis may be the key to obtaining information, and parents increasingly turn to the internet for it,[51] although this may be because professionals do not provide information themselves. In one survey less than half of the professionals making the diagnosis provided further information and nearly 20 per cent gave neither information nor a possible course of further information.[52]

Training

Diagnosis not only is helpful to parents and people with a diagnosis, but also may orientate and inform professional carers. The value of diagnosis will, however, depend on the knowledge of those carers. Computer-assisted learning (CAL) packages have been shown to increase this in a study of nursery nurses,[53] and may be an alternative to sending staff on training courses or providing in-house training.

Early intervention

One principle of the treatment of ASD at every age is that the impact of the condition is a combination of the condition itself and of the social distance that the condition causes. In infancy this may be crucial since much of cognitive and emotional development requires social interaction. It has been argued that the disconnections in the brain that are putatively the cause of ASD may be restored if sufficient over-learning occurs at a sufficiently young age.[54] So there has been considerable emphasis on finding methods for early reliable diagnosis and then intervening with infants so as to get them back on a developmental track. These early interventions are considered in the chapter on infants and young children (Chapter 12). But the same principles apply to older age groups, too. One model that can be applied to adults that incorporates this perspective is 'crisis intervention' (see Chapter 17).

Focused remediation

Even if early intervention is not successful, or not applied, and social impairments become obstacles to social adaptation, there is the possibility that intensive training in one particular area of social adaptation will, through over-learning or the development of alternative skills or 'work arounds', overcome that particular difficulty. Two fundamental deficits in the ASDs are of imitation and of social orientating (see Chapters 5 and 6). Increasing either of these could potentially have widespread impact on social interaction from infancy onwards. Empathy, or its lack, has a particular impact on peer relationships in the early teenage years, and also begins then to create family strains. Empathy training has therefore been a focus of remediation in the early teens particularly. Social skills are needed at every stage of development, but their lack has a conspicuous impact on adolescents' ability to access social and public settings independently. Social skills training has a long history in the treatment of psychological difficulties in adolescents and adults,[55] and has been applied more recently to helping people with ASD. Paid employment is a source of personal satisfaction, belonging, future social relationships and, of course, money;[56] it may also improve social functioning.[57]

Although there are many projects that provide programmes of focused remediation, many of them citing anecdotal experience of considerable improvement, there is a lack of rigorously evaluated evidence for all of them,[58] and this should be kept in mind when recommending them.

Enhancing imitation, social orientation and communication

Although there are training methods that purport to increase imitation and others to make social orientation more accurate, it is difficult to see how the two can be distinguished since the only imitation that is important is the imitation of socially salient and relevant actions by others, and that requires that the child orientates preferentially to these actions. Conversely, the direction of orientation is often signalled socially by imitation as in the exchange of looks, eye contact, reciprocal smiling, and so on. However, one mother of a 21-month-old infant was able to increase her child's joint attention by imitating the child.[59]

Behavioural interventions targeting core symptoms

The prototype of behavioural interventions is applied behaviour analysis. These interventions are aimed at enhancing communication. The method identifies a range of key skills or actions to reinforce, with a particular emphasis on communication. Key skills are broken down into components whose frequency is first increased and then joined with linked skills through a backward chaining process. There have been several systematic reviews of evaluations of ABA and other similar methods that conclude that some, but not all, children benefit and that the studies may have methodological weaknesses, with no long-term studies having been conducted.[60, 61, 62]

Early intensive behavioural interventions: applied behaviour analysis

Early intensive behavioural interventions claim to be even more effective. One of the most widely used approaches is named after its originator, Lovaas. Clinical reports suggest that when there is benefit it may be substantial, but meta-analyses of outcome studies are less positive.[61] Although there is evidence for the Lovaas method,[63] it may not be superior to less intensive applied behaviour analysis (ABA) methods.[62]

Applied behaviour analyses, such as the Lovaas method, couples careful analysis of a child's individual responses to social situations with a method to reshape the child's responses towards being more social, and less idiosyncratic. The very earliest methods, such as those introduced by Lovaas, used aversive methods, including electrical stimulation, to discourage idiosyncratic responses. Another controversial issue was the reliance on food rewards, which could be both demeaning and unhealthy. These unethical methods have left a lingering taint on applied behaviour analysis, even though they have now been abandoned. Shaping nowadays involves positive reinforcement of social responses, and the rewards are within the range of normal affectionate or playful social interaction, including music, participating in the child's special interests, or, where appropriate, tickling and physical stimulation. One of the main differences now between the Lovaas and other ABA approaches is the amount of carer time that is prescribed for the method. The Lovaas method may require so many hours of interaction with the child that a team of helpers is required.

The pressure on parents is more intense the more intensive the method, and this may make the most intensive methods counter-productive.[64]

Other behavioural methods

Applied behavioural methods may be used for other than core symptoms, most often challenging behaviours, self-harm, and other actions by the person with ASD which may be considered by them, and are usually considered by others, to be undesirable.[65, 66] It is not clear whether these interventions have more or less success for the target behaviour in people with ASD than they do when used on neurotypicals.

Empathy training

Various methods of empathy training, including role-plays, computer-assisted learning,[67] or computer games, are designed to improve participants' recognition of facial expressions, and so increase affective empathy. One potential drawback is that they may train deliberate interpretation of facial expression, but this is likely to be independent of the reflexive response to face expression that results in emotional contagion and affective empathy. It is this rapid response that seems to be particularly error-prone in people with an ASD.[68]

Empty talk and thought 'bubbles' added to drawings or photographs of a social interaction have been used to teach theory of mind.[69] The teacher or therapist and the person with ASD fill in the empty bubbles with what they think that the person in the social interaction was saying or thinking at the time. There is some evidence that theory of mind skills improve following the use of thought bubbles in training young people with ASD in a theory of mind task,[70] although in everyday life, deliberation is arguably an unusual means of taking in another person's perspective.[71] Thought bubbles have also been used in retraining people with right hemisphere damage in theory of mind skills, with some evidence of efficacy.[72]

In adults, there is some evidence that psychotherapy may increase empathy.[73]

Social skills training

Social skills training is ineffective in young children, for obvious reasons as skills are acquired in a partly deliberate process that very young children cannot emulate.[74] The application of social skills requires an ability to judge the appropriateness of the skills to the situation, and to link these social skills with the responses of others in the social setting. Most clinicians will have experienced visiting a school or home and being approached by a young person with an ASD who asks something along the lines of, 'I'm Sam. What's your name? How far have you come?' without waiting for an answer or, seemingly, knowing what next to say. This may be the consequence of training in which the young person was taught that it is polite to introduce oneself and to show an interest in another person, for example asking them their name. 'Generalizing', that is adapting social skills to different contexts, is a limitation on the value of social skills training.[75, 76] There is some evidence that social skills can be improved in the setting in which they are taught although more evaluation needs to be done.[77] Methods which have been positively evaluated include social stories, video modelling, video modelling interventions, social problem solving, pivotal response training,[78] scripting procedures, computer-based interventions including virtual reality environments, priming procedures, prompting procedures, and self-monitoring.[76] Social skills training may be carried out by professionals, or by parents in an extension of their natural role. Parents who receive training in training the social skills of their children have been shown to assist their 13–17-year-old children in friendship maintenance in comparison to waiting list controls, but the stability of these gains, long term, has not been investigated.[79]

In practice, many older adolescents and adults seem to acquire social skills by imitation of admired or respected others – such implicit learning not being impaired by ASD.[80]

Social stories

Social stories provide the most widely used method of social skills training in schools,[81] possibly because little special equipment is required, the method fits unobtrusively into the classroom,[82] teachers and others using social stories require only a short training, and the social stories can be varied to make them ecologically appropriate. Their use requires that learners have verbal intelligence above 70 or thereabouts.[83]

A wide range of social stories is available, many of them created by Carol Gray,[84] the school psychologist who originated the method, and now copyrighted by her but available for sale at the Gray Centre.[85]

Social story based interventions may have non-specific effects that, like other intervention methods in ASD, may be the result of teachers interacting more readily with pupils if they have a structure to facilitate this.[86, 87]

Floortime

Floortime has been developed by Greenspan and focuses on reinforcement through play.[88] An unusual and intriguing feature is that it involves peers and siblings more than other approaches.

Work preparation and interview training

The factors that influence access to, and continuation in, work for people with psychological difficulties are complex.[89] Employment is an important determinant of quality of life for people with an ASD,[90] and, as for neurotypicals, work provides valuable cognitive training.[91] But employment rates for people with ASD, and even for people with AS, have improved little since the 1980s.[92, 93] Much less is known about the effects of adult ADHD on employment, but clinical experience, and what outcome studies there are,[94] suggest that unemployment and under-attainment is more frequent,[95, 96] although the rates are probably substantially less than the majority of people with ASD who are unemployed.

Work preparation, including interview skills training, is most effective when it is combined with post-employment support in the context of an autism-informed work environment,[97] which takes account of the bullying that people with an ASD may receive.[98] One scheme that combines these elements (NAS Prospects) claims a 68 per cent employment rate over an eight-year period.[99]

Executive difficulties

Executive dysfunction, the severity of the core ASD social impairment, and interventions fostering over-reliance on support by others were each found to make an independent, negative contribution to employability, independent living, and relationship development in a systematic review.[100] However, a caveat should be entered here. There is a lack of consensus about what constitutes executive dysfunction (see Chapter 7). In one study, for example, executive dysfunction was considered to be reflected in reduced semantic fluency, reduced ability to divide auditory attention, and behavioural dysregulation.[101] Not surprisingly, given that these might be non-specific consequences of having an ASD, these dysfunctions were found to be associated with each of the triad of impairments. A further problem is that executive dysfunction, a core symptom of ADHD, may be a marker for the presence of that disorder and its association with reduced social adaptation a spurious association, with some other feature of ADHD being the contributory cause.

Clinical assessment suggests the failure to budget time and money, along with difficulty in making and remaking plans in response to changing circumstances, are common and disabling associates of ASD. These difficulties may only come to the fore when a person with ASD attempts to live independently.

There are rare cases in clinical practice of people whose main difficulties appear to be executive dysfunction in the absence of definite symptoms of either ADHD or ASD. One man known to me lost his job because his work had to be accounted for on a computerized system and he could not plan his performance sufficiently well to be able to keep up with this, and so occasionally resorted to fictitious clients to give himself more time to catch up. There was no history of either ADHD or ASD, and he was a high achiever. MRI scan was normal. It did, however, emerge that he had disturbed sleep, although he did not admit to daytime naps, and a sleep EEG led to a diagnosis of sleep apnoea and treatment with continuous positive airway pressure treatment at night, with some self-reported improvement. Sleep apnoea in children may also be associated with attention disorder and some executive dysfunction.[102]

Stimulant medication

Stimulant medication improves attention in people with ADHD but not executive function,[103] although there may be a small group who do benefit.[104] Even though stimulant medication may also result in an improvement in both ASD and ADHD symptoms in people who have the combined disorder, routine use of stimulants cannot be recommended.

Training

Increased time spent on budgeting and planning as the result of teaching self-management results in an improvement in executive functioning in people with ADHD.[105] Working memory, a foundation of executive functioning, can be increased by practice as shown by psychological testing and by increased blood flow in target areas,[106, 107] and a commercial product exists that makes increasing working memory 'fun' (Nintendo's Dr. Kawashima Brain trainer) although a survey conducted by the BBC suggests that brain trainer improvement does not generalize to other tests.[108] Training can be improved by providing immediate feedback on the results, enabling a person to shape even internal stimuli.[109, 110] Real time feeds from fMRI have been used to enable the people being scanned to increase blood flow in the right insula and these methods may be applied to other neurological systems in the future.[109]

Psychoeducation

Providing information not only about ASD itself, but also about what causes difficulties for a person with ASD, what form those difficulties take, and what can be done about them – among other things – can help carers, employers, teachers, therapists and others to respond more effectively to the needs of a person with ASD. Information giving may need to be combined with training, for example in clearer, more concrete, less metaphorical and less ambiguous communication. Packages of information giving, role-plays to increase empathy, and training are called 'psychoeducation' in other areas of psychiatry. Few evaluations of this approach in ASD exist. One showed a much better response in children and families where the target problem was an emotional one (reactive attachment disorder) than when it was an ASD.[111] Schools and families are both possible targets for a psychoeducational approach, and further evaluation would seem to be worthwhile.

Support for carers

Support for carers is an essential component of any intervention.

Dealing with anxiety

One likely model of deterioration in psychiatric disorder for which there is a genetic predisposition is that it is caused by an increase in 'stress', that is depression or anxiety. Some people may be more at risk because of functional variation in the gene for brain derived neurotrophic factor. Those homozygous for the valine allele show nearly 30 per cent more blood flow in brain areas concerned with processing emotion (orbitofrontal cortex, amygdala and hippocampus) than those heterozygotes who have both the valine and the methionine BDNF.[112] This genetic marker has been used to identify adolescents who are at genetic risk of ADHD by virtue of neuroregulin polymorphisms, and who may be at increased risk of developing conduct disorder in response to parental criticism.[113] People with ASD are particularly at risk of increased anxiety and anxiety disorder.[114]

Family intervention and the EE model

The understandably shocked and angry reaction of parents to the supposition that they might cause ASD has led to an excessive swing away from the impact on family factors on the course of the disorder. Working with carers has considerable advantages, however, if it can be carried out in a way that does not seem to lay the blame for having ASD at the parents' door. Parents often experience considerable burden as a result of having a child with an ASD and family intervention can help relieve unrealistic self-blame. It may reduce stigma. But, most importantly, working with parents or other full-time carers can result in one hour of work becoming many hours of therapeutic conduct for the child.[115] In clinical practice, the expressed emotion model of Leff and Vaughn can provide a useful method for capturing some of the family factors that can either impede or enhance development and social adaptation in ASD.[116] Expressed emotion provides three dimensions of family interaction that can be associated with increased relapse in depression or schizophrenia and that, in my clinical experience, can be linked to 'melt downs' and ultimately deterioration in ASD. These are 'critical comments', 'over-involvement' and 'hostility'. High expressed emotion in the parents of adolescents with bipolar disorder is associated with an increase in relapse rates that can be reduced by family intervention.[117, 118] Increased criticism of children with ADHD by their mothers leads to increased conduct problems,[119] and it seems likely that family intervention that reduces criticism may reduce the conduct problems associated with ASD, too.

Counselling or psychotherapy

Another approach to buffering the adverse impact of stress is personal counselling or psychotherapy. This approach, like family intervention, has suffered from the exaggerated claims made for its efficacy in the past.[120] Clearly, counselling or psychotherapy, however 'deep' or prolonged, cannot cure ASD. But there is growing clinical experience, and some research evidence, that practical counselling or psychotherapy can reduce stress and improve social adaptation.[121] Cognitive behavioural therapy is perhaps the most available 'practical' therapy currently available, and has been shown to be effective in reducing anxiety in children with ASD who have normal language ability, but there is no reason to assume that other methods of psychotherapy are any less effective so long as they have a problem-orientated focus.[122]

Group interventions

Although it has often been assumed that people with ASD cannot participate easily in groups, this may not be the case, and groups may provide an effective means of reducing social anxiety.[123]

Enablement

Heidegger famously argued that 'This entity which each of us is himself…we shall denote by the term "Dasein".'[124] He did not invent the term Dasein, which is commonly used in German to mean existence, but he was the first philosopher to take its literal meaning, 'being there', as the starting point of ontology. Because he thought that we are not normally conscious of ourselves as separate units, but as being located in a social and physical context, there are some things that we find 'ready to hand' about us. We are pre-figured to recognize and reach out for these. I have argued at some length that people with an ASD do not experience themselves as Daseins:[125] their consciousness of being for others (être pour autrui), to switch to a Sartrean term,[126] is weak compared to their consciousness of beings in themselves (être en soi). So people with an ASD may not find the social ready to hand. In particular, the normal levers of influence over others that are so taken for granted, levers that rely on an intuitive understanding of popularity and the ability to charm, persuade and negotiate, may be inaccessible. Most people with ASD, if they formulate the matter at all, feel themselves to have little influence over others, but yet to be greatly in thrall to others. Feeling powerless, and being powerless too, are a major source of emotional upset to many people with an ASD, and may also lead to exploitation, bullying and aggression. This kind of disability is best reversed by what is sometimes called 'empowerment' or 'enablement'. Enablement is not a treatment, although there are procedures that can foster enablement such as advocacy,[127] but a principle of treatment that is relevant to people with ASD at all ages, and at all levels of ability.

Treatment and Education of Autistic and related Children with a Communication Handicap (TEACCH)

The TEACCH programme sets out the principles of enabling people with an ASD with a main focus on those without language. It includes the use of shapes as cues to the use of environmental objects, for example to label the drawer with cutlery, or the cupboard with crockery.

Sensory integration

Sensory integration has become popular[128, 129] especially among occupational therapists.[130] It starts out from the assumption, made by many other treatment approaches that have claimed cure over the years, that autism is a response to pervasive anxiety. A further premise is that sensory input may cause this kind of anxiety. Past methods that have also started from this premise have included auditory integration training. Sensory integration presumes that the main deficit in handling sensation is not decoding frequency information, as in auditory integration training, but in combining different modalities, for which there is some evidence.[131] Synaesthesia is the term given for stimulation of one sensory modality resulting in a perception in that modality but also in another one (for example seeing purple lights when hearing the opening chords of Beethoven's Fifth Symphony). It is commonly reported by people with an ASD, although it is not known whether it is associated with ASD. Synaesthesia might be an obstacle to multisensory integration, although it is not known whether it does, in fact, result in clashes between sensory modalities. Some studies suggest that synaesthesia may be more common in neurotypicals than was once thought.[132] These theories often become enmeshed with related theories about hypersensitivity to sensation, and the presumption that ordinary levels of stimulus might be overwhelming to people with an ASD whose threshold is lower. There is a further presumption that ASD symptoms are a kind of natural response to these confusing or overwhelming sensory inputs. An alternative formulation is that challenging behaviour, rather than autism itself, may be a response to a failure of sensory integration. Many people find these hypotheses plausible, but there is little evidence for any of them. As with many similar theories, the inverse hypothesis may be as or even more plausible. So, rather than a failure of sensory integration causing anxiety, and therefore challenging behaviour, it may be the case[133] anxiety causes a failure of sensory integration. There is some evidence for this.

The possibility that the theory of an intervention is wrong, but that the intervention still works should not be discounted. Many important medical and psychological interventions have been introduced for flawed theoretical reasons, but still work. Some studies suggest that sensory integration may be effective.[134]

MEDICATION

Many psychotropic drugs are sedative and, in the short term, reduce anxiety. Since anxiety is very common in people with an ASD, then it is inevitable that there will be short-term improvement in this when many people with an ASD receive these medications for the first time. Reducing anxiety may seem to reduce some symptoms of ASD, for example insistence on routines, which are used to control anxiety. So medication may seem to parents, too, to be beneficial.

In the long term, sedative effects diminish as a result of drug tolerance, and larger doses buy sedation at the expense of cognitive blunting and behavioural inhibition. The side-effects of medication also accumulate with continued exposure. There is therefore little indication, and possibly significant contra-indication, to treating ASD with medication. Although many new chemical types of medication have been introduced, there is no evidence that these have enhanced effectiveness in ASD.[135]

It is theoretically unlikely that medication will ever be a successful treatment, unless a drug is found that will restore neuronal connectivity with sufficient specificity to the networks affected in ASD for it not to have harmful effects on other brain systems. It is therefore disturbing, indeed in my view unethical, that clinical trials continue to be conducted of off-licence applications of psychotropics in ASD that have similar effects to congeners of already familiar drugs. These trials can only create false expectations in parents, encourage doctors to expose children and young people to potential harm,[136] and foster profit-orientated rather than patient-orientated marketing by drug companies.

This is not to say that there are no therapeutic indications for medication in ASD. Stimulants have an important role in treating ADHD. Psychotropics, too, may be indicated for conditions that are co-morbid with ASD.

Many clinicians might also consider that the use of antipsychotics or anticonvulsants to reduce aggressive outburst and other challenging behaviour is indicated, even though repeated reviews do not find that the evidence convincingly supports this. In clinical practice, it has to be admitted, staff and carers may need the respite that is sometimes provided, albeit briefly, by the sedative effects of these drugs to regain optimism and reduce their own frustrations.

However, it seems likely that medication is overused. About 35 per cent of children with ASD in one very large US sample were receiving medication, and residence in a poorer state in the US increased the likelihood of prescription.[137] In another study, of US government benefit (Medicaid) claims for 60,641 children with an ASD diagnosis in 2001, 18 per cent of children aged less than two years were receiving medication, and 32 per cent of children younger than five years old. Over half (56%) of the total sample of children were receiving medication. The most commonly prescribed drug was an antipsychotic (in 31%), followed by an antidepressant (in 25%) or a stimulant (in 22%). The use of stimulants may be justified if there is an independent diagnosis of co-morbid ADHD, as may be the use of an antidepressant in older children who have developed depressive disorder (clinicians differ about the youngest age at which this can be diagnosed but good practice is that, even if it is diagnosed reliably in children, medication is not the first line of treatment). Children on medication were more likely to have other psychiatric diagnoses. There is no specific indication for the use of antipsychotics. Polypharmacy in psychiatry is to be avoided, yet in one study 20 per cent of children were prescribed three or more psychotropic drugs concurrently.[138] Older, male children were more likely to receive medication and this may reflect the increase in challenging behaviour in some older boys with ASD. Medication was more likely to be prescribed to children who were white, living in counties that were more than averagely white, living in urban areas, and were greater users of services and in foster care. Similar profiles have been shown to apply to the medicalization of ADHD, and may indicate that the pressure to prescribe comes from carers who adopt a medical model of behavioural difficulties.[138]

OTHER INTERVENTIONS THAT ARE MENTIONED IN LATER CHAPTERS

- Advice.
- Genetic counselling.
- Education.
- Occupational therapy.
- Care management.
- Social inclusion.
- Diet.
- Language therapy or alternative communication strategies.

COURSE

False assumptions about the course of ASDs

Many assumptions are made about the course of the ASDs for which there is little if any evidence, but which have a profound effect on the perception of these disorders in the public mind, and among professionals.

Having an ASD does not reduce life expectancy

Although it is often said that life expectancy is unchanged by having an autism spectrum disorder, there is evidence for increased mortality, particularly in childhood, and largely as a result of epilepsy,[139] with reduced life expectancy greatest in the most severely affected children with multiple neurological problems. In one study, there was a five times increased mortality in people with an ASD before the age of 50, compared to the general population. Women had a higher mortality than men, with epilepsy, medical disorders and accidents being the commonest causes of death.[140] A follow-up study of children into adulthood indicates that life expectancy continues to fall, partly as a result of epilepsy but with accidents and suicide also contributing.[141] However, this cohort may not be representative of ASD since it included children with disintegrative psychoses and with conditions categorized using ICD-9,[142] which may not all have been recognized in ICD-10 or DSM-IV as being ASDs. Furthermore, there was a high risk of developing schizophrenia in the cohort,[143] which is not found in other cohorts of people with an ASD, and schizophrenia is itself associated with an increased suicide rate.

ADHD is also associated with an increased risk of accident, particularly on the roads[144, 145] and may therefore be associated with an increase in deaths by accident, although mortality figures are not available. ADHD is also associated with an increased risk of substance misuse, which is itself associated with an excess mortality.

ASD is lifelong

Asperger and Kanner both considered that ASD could have a 'good outcome'.[146, 147] Asperger went further and said that the condition that he described normally had a good prognosis. Long-term follow-ups support this.[148] Seltzer *et al.* used the revised version of the Autism Diagnostic Interview (ADI-R) to assess 405 individuals with a diagnosis of ASD.[149] Although all of them had met diagnostic criteria for ASD in childhood, only 54.8 per cent met those criteria when they were examined. Although the communicative impairment persisted, there was improvement in reciprocal social interaction during adolescence, and in restricted and repetitive behaviour during adulthood.[149] Most clinicians know about their patients for a limited period of time, and habitually overestimate the duration of disorder, particularly as many people reinvent their pasts to support the present,[150] and so may increase the apparent duration of their difficulties. It is on this false premise of the invariant nature of interpersonal difficulties that the fiction of personality disorder has been created. Many specialist clinicians will also know of patients who had been diagnosed as having an ASD as a child, apparently made a good recovery, may even have married and had children, but then developed social impairment following a severe life stress. So there are few clinicians who would claim that ASD can remit completely, although many might argue that there are some whose ASD ceases to have a clinically significant impact. Probably for historical reasons only, ADHD has often been considered to be a childhood disorder that remits in adolescence. Although it is now recognized that many children with ADHD continue to have persistent symptoms after they reach adolescence and adulthood, it is still often assumed that a proportion remit. In the absence of definitive evidence, it would be more appropriate to consider that some children with ASD and some children with ADHD lose their disorder through remission, conceivably as a result of the final myelination of fibre tracts in the brain in the late teens; some children with ADHD and some children with ASD continue to have those disorders but make a successful adaptation to them so they function neurotypically; and that the remainder have persisting and significant differences from neurotypicality (other considerations apply as to whether this neuro-atypicality should be termed a disorder).

Intelligence does not change

Intelligence interacts with the autistic syndrome in that having an intellectual disability in addition to ASD predicts a worse prognosis. Fluid intelligence is assumed to be a capacity (see Chapter 7) which is independent of acquired knowledge and information, probably reflects the connectivity of key centres in the brain, and which remains stable up until the late teens, when it starts to decline albeit very gradually. However, I have often observed in reviewing IQ scores from tests carried out through a patient's childhood that there may be considerable variation, even when the same tests are used. This may reflect the circumstances of the test, whether or not the testee is depressed or anxious at the time of the test, and the relationship with the tester.

But there is good evidence that IQ is not stable in people with an ASD, perhaps because of the abnormal development of intracerebral connectivity that is emerging as the most likely cause of ASD. In one sample of infants, there was a subgroup in whom IQ fell during the first two years.[151] In another 19 month follow-up study of pre-schoolers with ASD and comparison groups of children with intellectual disability and neurotypical children, the IQ scores of almost all of the children in the comparison group remained the same, but a third of the children with an ASD increased their IQ scores by 15 points or more.[152] Finally, in a study of 41 people with an ASD whose first IQ test was performed at the average age of 7.2 years (the mean of the whole group) and for whom the mean follow-up duration was 32.5 years, half of the group had IQ scores that were either at least 15 points (1 standard deviation) higher or lower than they had been in childhood. Those with an improvement in their IQ were included among the half of the participants whose social function was rated as 'good' or 'very good' at follow-up.[153]

Social disability does not affect quality of life

The lifelong disability of ASD, mainly attributable to social adaptation, has been estimated to be 43,928 Disability Adjusted Life Years (DALY) in Spain in 2003, from which 33,797 years were lost due to Autistic Disorder and 10,131 were lost due to Asperger's Disorder and Autism Spectrum Disorder-Not Otherwise Specified.[154] Social adaptation is largely independent of the number or severity of ASD symptoms and of quality of life.[155] It is reflected in a lack of social contact, lack of employment, exclusion from community resources, restriction on travel, particularly on public transport, a reliance on carers for carrying out or monitoring everyday activities, like self-care or cooking, and an inability to live independently.

In one follow-up study, only a minority (26%) had a very restricted life, with no occupation or activity, and no friends.[156]

IQ predicts later social functioning,[157] with people with lower IQ having lower social functioning. An 'aloof' group (based on Wing and Gould's original description) have lower IQs than the 'active but odd' group,[158] which may also be a reflection of the link with sociability.[159] People with a diagnosis of Kanner syndrome have worse adult social adaptation[160] but this is probably due to the autistic syndrome and language impairment, each making an independent but additive contribution to social adaptation.[161] Future social outcome is also predicted by the number and quality of current peer relationships in childhood,[162, 163] but bullying may disrupt this association.

Quality of life in people with ASD and their carers

Quality of life in people with ASD is strongly influenced by personal distress and mental health, but quality of life in carers is linked to physical rather than emotional health.[164] In children, pragmatic impairment in speech is highly correlated with conduct and emotional difficulties whereas the latter are independent of specific language impairments.[165]

Quality of life is lower in young people with an ASD, and family burden higher, than in young people with ADHD.[166] In fact, in one large survey the burden of having a teenage child with an ASD was higher than having a child wih any other psychological disability.[167] Quality of life is also lower in more able people with Asperger syndrome than in less able people. This is likely to be linked to self-awareness, and the ability of people with Asperger syndrome to compare themselves unfavourably with others, and to entertain hopes which sometimes turn out to be unrealistic.

Clinical experience is that quality of life reflects engagement in life, and that this is often a reflection of investment in special interests, and of social inclusion. A substantial proportion of people with an ASD fall out with or lose close family members in their thirties and forties, and become socially isolated. Social withdrawal, which is often linked to social rejection either as a cause or a consequence, is linked to poor quality of life. Peak periods for this are the late teenage years, when school is over and college or employment is not available, and in middle age, when parents die or become alienated.

A past history of bullying is associated clinically with depression, social withdrawal and a perception of society as being unfriendly or hostile. The latter may contribute to demoralization in middle age.

Critical parenting style, similar to that described as high expressed emotion in the literature on schizophrenia, is clinically associated with shame proneness and with an unwillingness to accept advice or 'negativism'. The origins of this in adolescence are likely to be different from its origins in childhood. Early childhood negativism may be innate and is a predictor of oppositional defiant disorder in middle childhood, and possibly of conduct disorder in later childhood.

Burden

The findings of a large US survey of children and young people aged 3 to 17 were that children with developmental problems had 'lower self-esteem, more depression and anxiety, missed more school, and were less involved in sports and other community activities' than normally developing children. Their families 'experienced more difficulty in the areas of childcare, employment, parent–child relationships, and caregiver burden'.[168] The quality of life of mothers with a child with ASD is reduced below norms,[169] and as this study shows, this impact can be demonstrated using brief generic quality of life measures (in this study, the WHOQOL-BREF, the briefer 26-item version of the quality of life scale developed by the World Health Organization). There are many anecdotal reports of the strains (and also rewards) of having an ASD or of having a family member with an ASD, but there have been fewer systematic studies, and many of these have lacked comparison groups. So it is not possible to conclude whether or not ASD is more or less burdensome than other developmental disorders.

One large, controlled study suggests that it is. Mugno *et al.* interviewed one or both parents of 135 children or adolescents with a developmental disorder, and one or both parents of 48 normally developing children using the brief WHO quality of life measure.[170] The parents of children with an ASD reported significantly more impairment in physical activity, social relationships and overall quality of life than parents of neurotypical children, and their perceived quality of life was also lower than that of parents of children with cerebral palsy or learning difficulty (intellectual disability). Mothers were more affected than fathers, and there was a tendency for the parents of children with AS to have poorer quality of life than parents of children with other ASDs.[170] Having support less frequently than daily, unsupportive interactions with others, and having a child with disruptive behaviour are particularly related to increased burden.[171]

Follow-up studies indicate that burden continues to affect parents as well as people with ASD well into adult life.[172]

In my own clinic parents complete a questionnaire in which there is a question, 'What worries you most about your child's future?' The parents' reply is, overwhelmingly, 'The future' or 'What will happen after we are gone?'. Myers *et al.* posted an online questionnaire, which included the question, 'How has your child in the autism spectrum affected your life and your family's life?'[173] The replies from 493 were 'content analysed' into themes, and clusters. Not all of the themes were negative (see Table 9.1).

More intensive studies bear out these quantitative findings. A questionnaire study of 23 mothers and 19 fathers of children and young people with ASD aged from 3 to 18 confirmed other findings that mothers are more affected than fathers, but showed that this can be reduced by helpful support and information.[174]

One factor in burden is the extent to which objective burden is subjectively perceived as over-taxing. Becoming angry may be a mediating factor in this, since getting angry or irritable can lead to additional stressors: the 'stress proliferation' effect.[175] Positive re-framing and support are some of the most important factors in reducing burden.[176] Cognitive coping rather than emotional coping styles may be particularly beneficial for the parents of fractious young children with ASD.[177]

Quality of life is also impaired in people with ADHD, particularly in those who have both hyperactivity and impulsivity.[178]

Table 9.1 The impact of having a child with an ASD

Cluster 1: Stress	
Cluster 2: The child's behavior and the demands of the child's therapy and care	Difficulty dealing with child's behavior problems
	Time demands for care and therapies
	Sleep problems, exhaustion
	Struggles with schools and services
	New understanding regarding the world of disabilities
	Glad for child's autism, uniqueness would not change
Cluster 3: Impact on parents' personal well being, work lives, and marital relationship	Marital or couple strain
	Difficult emotions: grief, depression, guilt, blame
	Mother's and/or father's career/employment affected
	Enriched our lives, a blessing, love for this child
	Positive emotions: taught us compassion, tolerance, patience, joy
	Learned to appreciate the little things, slow down
	Spiritual life enriched
	Marriage enriched
Cluster 4: Impact on the family as a whole, including siblings and extended family	Siblings neglected, embarrassed, or hurt
	Financial strain
	Center of our lives
	Strained relations with extended family
	Positive family adjustment and support
	Positive impact on siblings
Cluster 5: Social isolation	Restrictions on where we can go and what we can do
	Lost friends, no social life
	Bad treatment by strangers

Source: Adapted from Myers, Makintosh, *et al.*, 2009 with permission from Elsevier.

Financial burden

ADHD children have a significantly higher probability of visiting a general practitioner (60.3% vs 37.4%) and a specialist (50.9% vs 12.9%); they also visit the emergency department significantly more often (26% vs 12.1%), and they are hospitalized significantly more often (14% vs 8.4%).[179]

Several economic studies of ASD have been made. They are not easily comparable. Some give estimates for populations, others for individuals. The apportionment of costs between individuals, families, third party payers and 'society' (that is the benefit or welfare system) varies according to the provision of medical and social benefits in any particular country. There is also variance introduced by the use of different economic models, and different cost assumptions.

The costs that are easiest to capture are the costs of medical care, and lost income due to reduced working days. A review of the medical costs of ADHD, extrapolated to unit costs prevailing in the US in 2004, concluded that:

> children with ADHD had higher annual medical costs than either matched controls (difference ranged from $503 to $1,343) or non-matched controls (difference ranged from $207 dollars to $1,560 dollars) without ADHD. Two studies of adult samples found similar results, with significantly higher annual medical costs among adults with ADHD (ranging from $4,929 dollars to $5,651 dollars) than among matched controls (ranging from $1,473 dollars to $2,771 dollars).[180a]

Other costs of ADHD mentioned, but not estimated in this review, include the costs of offending, of days of work lost to family members,[181] of increased health care costs to family members,[181] and the costs of accidents.[180]

The costs of ASD are even higher, according to one study of routinely captured databases of subscribers to employer-sponsored insurance schemes. Children and adolescents with an ASD each used $4110–6200 more medical care, on average, than neurotypical children and adolescents, that is 4.1–6.2 times greater than for the medical care costs of neurotypicals.[182] Another study of private insurers' records demonstrates that the cost is increasing more rapidly than the rate of inflation, 20.4 per cent or $4965 in 2000 to $5979 in 2004, after adjusting for inflation. When combined with rising ASD prevalence rates, this amounts to an real increase in total spending of 142.1 per cent over the five-year period.[183]

Social care costs may also be high, but are influenced by policy: they can be easily reduced by raising the threshold for case recognition and therefore rejecting applications for a service that would be accepted elsewhere.[184] A Swedish study using a postal questionnaire in one municipality estimated that the annual social cost to the municipality was 50,000 euros per child, mainly for education and social care. Parents spent 1000 hours in direct care of their children but did not incur additional financial costs.[185]

Adding in non-medical costs increases the estimate of the economic burden of ASD substantially. Montes and Halterman estimated that having a child with ASD in the family reduces family income by 14 per cent, as a result of lost days of work for the wage earner having to deal with child-related problems or alter their working day to accommodate their child's needs.[186] Ganz has estimated the total social and medical costs in the US for a hypothetical cohort of people with autism born in 2000 to be $3.2million per person.[187] Ganz concludes that:

> Although autism is typically thought of as a disorder of childhood, its costs can be felt well into adulthood. The substantial costs resulting from adult care and lost productivity of both individuals with autism and their parents have important implications for those aging members of the baby boom generation approaching retirement, including large financial burdens affecting not only those families but also potentially society in general.[187a]

Predictors of course
Language and IQ
IQ in early childhood does have predictive value, but it may not remain stable, and may not then be an accurate predictor of course.[188]

Complex versus idiopathic
Epilepsy may be an index of overall neurological impairment,[189] and has been included with other markers of abnormal brain development, including microcephaly and dysmorphic features, as a marker of a group of people with 'complex autism' who have worse outcomes.[190] Miles *et al.* suggest that this group may account for about 20 per cent of children diagnosed with autism, that the combination of microcephaly and dysmorphic physical signs may be the two best indicators of group membership (86% specificity and 34% sensitivity), and that members of the group are more likely to remain nonverbal, to have IQs below 55, and to have repeated epileptic seizures.[190] This group was less likely to have a family history of ASD.

Another feature of membership of this complex group may be a diagnosis of atypical autism or ASD-NOS. In one comparison of people with a diagnosis of ASD-NOS and people with a diagnosis of autistic disorder, the ASD-NOS group, matched for age and gender. There was a stronger family history of epilepsy, an earlier onset of epilepsy, more findings of neurological impairment, more abnormal background EEG activity, and more known genetic pathology in the ASD-NOS group.[191]

Children with early onset epilepsy associated with developmental impairment have an increased risk of global developmental delay, inattentiveness and autistic disorder.[192]

CONCLUSIONS
Distinct diagnostic categories of ASD remain administratively useful. Carers and people with an ASD may also find it useful to 'know what is wrong with them'. The temporal stability of diagnostic categories is good, particularly if the symptoms of an autistic syndrome are used as the principal critiera for all ASD diagnoses. Differentiation of Asperger syndrome and Kanner syndrome cannot be made using scientific criteria. Clinical experience is that the main differentiation is between people with an ASD who lack self-awareness and other-awareness,

and people who have it (the Asperger group) although other operational differentiations might be made, for example between 'aloof', 'passive', and 'active but odd'.[158]

Understanding the problems, thinking about intervention and prognostication are better based on domains of impairment or difference, which outcome research is starting to clarify. These include severity of nonverbal communicative impairment, language impairment, rigidity, IQ, medical burden, environmental factors and personal characteristics.

These factors interact, and are also influenced by age and gender. How these are expressed at different age groups is considered in Chapters 12–17 following Chapter 10, which considers clinical research that is relevant to the whole of the ASD spectrum.

Chapter 10

CLINICAL ASSESSMENT OF THE ASDs

THE GOAL OF CLINICAL ASSESSMENT

Clinical assessment is a process of exchange during which concerns that parents or people with an ASD have can be expressed, and responded to, as well as used to inform the assessment. Information given by the clinician may trigger memories in the person being assessed, and lead to new, and valuable, information being provided by the person with an ASD or a carer. This style of assessment not only is of more value to all parties, but also can sometimes obviate the need for further investigation or at least focus the investigations that do need to be performed.

Not everyone who is assessed will want to have a diagnosis. Assessment may be driven by third parties, who may be spouses, carers, employers or legal professionals. Older children, adolescents and adults who are capacitous should be asked why they have come to the assessment, and if it emerges that they do not wish to be 'labelled' with a diagnosis, or they are of the view that an ASD is not a disorder at all, this should be respected. This may mean that the assessment does not proceed, or that it is focused on a psychological problem identified by the client. If a reluctance to be diagnosed has adverse consequences for the client, which need to be spelt out.

It is not necessary for a primary provider to make a diagnosis, if a need for further, specialist assessment has been established. If the primary provider does not consider that further assessment is required, they are behoven to explain what is causing the concerns that are being presented, and if necessary, to rule out a diagnosis.

Specialist assessment should normally lead to diagnosis, unless the person being assessed does not wish for one, and it is a perennial source of frustration that it often does not. If a diagnosis of an ASD is not appropriate, then an alternative diagnosis should be provided, or pathology ruled out.

Providing a diagnosis should not be the only end point of assessment. Advice about what parents, other carers, or people with the ASD can do with the diagnosis, a profile of the strengths as well as disabilities of the particular person being diagnosed, advice to other agencies such as schools or workplaces where appropriate, recognition of the emotional difficulties associated with the ASD and also with receiving a diagnosis, and a prognosis should all be provided.

GUIDELINES

Guidelines for the diagnosis and management of ASD of children have been produced by the American Academy of Pediatrics (AAP), by the Scottish Intercollegiate Guidelines Network (SIGN), and by the UK National Autism Initiative: Screening and Assessment who have produced the National Autism Plan for Children, which focuses on the identification, assessment, diagnosis, and access to early interventions of pre-school and primary school age children with autism spectrum disorders (summarized and updated in Dover and Le Couteur).[1] The UK Royal College of Speech and Language Therapists includes a section on autism spectrum disorders in its 'Clinical Guidelines'. In the US, the National Institute on Deafness and Other Communication Disorders convened a working party on language development and disorder in young children with ASD which has recommended guidelines and criteria for evaluating children's speech between 12 and 48 months of age.[2] A draft guideline is in preparation by the National Institute for Health and Clinical Excellence in the UK due out in 2012. The Australian Government Department of Health and Ageing recommends 'A review of the research to identify the most effective models of practice in early intervention of children with autism spectrum disorders' as a guideline.[3] An 'autism exemplar' showing an exemplar of optimal assessment of 'George's autism spectrum disorder' has been produced by the UK Department of Education and Skills and Department of Health as part of the National Service Framework for children, young people and maternity services.

One reason for the multiplicity of guidelines is that the diagnosis of ASD continues to remain patchy: some areas even in developing countries achieve much higher ascertainment and earlier diagnosis than others.[4]

All of the guidelines mentioned above are based on the same international research base, but there are differences between them that reflect national customs, service arrangements and priorities. For example, the AAP recommends routine screening of all children in their second year for ASD, but the SIGN guidelines do not recommend population screening but a 'high level of vigilance'. The US guidelines specifically mention 'appropriate training' This is not mentioned in the SIGN guidelines, but it may be assumed.

In the UK, relevant bodies have now accepted that paediatricians, developmental neurologists (who may staff regional centres), and child and adolescent psychiatrists should all have training in the assessment and management of the ASDs. General psychiatrists and clinical psychologists receive some training, but not enough for them to be confident diagnosticians.

All of the guidelines recommend multidisciplinary assessment with particular emphasis on speech and language, and psychological assessment including the assessment of adaptive functioning, intellectual level, and any relevant neuropsychological assessment. However, both US and UK guidelines recognize that resource limitations may mean that only one professional may make the diagnosis, although in practice there are several referrals before a diagnosis is finally made: more than two in the UK,[5] and a mean of 3.5 in India.[6] In the US, the final diagnosis might be made by a speech and language therapist or a child psychologist as well as a medical practitioner, but in the UK it is more likely to be a medical practitioner (see Table 10.1) and in India, it is only made by a medical practitioner or a psychologist, of whom a tiny fraction are trained as child psychologists. Paediatricians are most likely to make the diagnosis in the UK or the US, and psychiatrists in India. Paediatric neurologists make more diagnoses than psychiatrists in the UK, but the reverse is true in the UK and India.

Table 10.1 Who diagnoses ASD in the US, UK and India

	Children diagnosed with an ASD by profession (%)	Children assessed for an ASD by profession (%)	Children diagnosed with an ASD by profession (%)
	US (Virginia)[1]	UK[2]	India[3]
Paediatrician	43	39.4	10.7
Psychologist	16	28.1	26.0
Neurologist	17	5.4	10.7
Primary care physician	1	53.3 (GP or health visitor)	0.5
Psychiatrist	6	26.9	28.5
Other	12	9.6	23.0 (team of doctors)
No answer or not known	64	17.9	

Source: 1) Rhoades, Scarpar, *et al.*, 2007; 2) Howlin and Moore, 1997; 3) Daley, 2004.

Many children with an ASD deploy auditory attention idiosyncratically, and may appear not to respond to sounds that other children regularly would respond to, giving the impression that they may be deaf. Since deafness is associated with delays in social interaction and in the development of theory of mind, it should be excluded early in the process of diagnosis.

WHO MAKES THE DIAGNOSIS?

Many parents will have suspected a developmental problem, perhaps even an ASD before any professional, and it usually the parent who first raises the concern about ASD.[7] Many parents' worries crystallize into a definite suspicion at about 11 months of life, although some put off recognizing the problem until there is clear-cut evidence of speech delay and the child is also showing unusual relations with peers, at or after the age of 17 months.[8]

Definitive evaluation may be performed by a primary care physician or other first-line professional with special training, and where the diagnosis is clear-cut. However, it is recommended that in most circumstances it is conducted in a series of steps, with some of the evaluations being conducted by other staff, and that a final diagnosis is made only following a review of all of the information obtained. Intervention does not need to wait on diagnosis: speech therapy may, for example, be indicated on the basis of functional deficits, irrespective of diagnosis.

THE SETTING FOR THE DIAGNOSIS

An assessment can be carried out in a person's home or residential setting, at school, in a clinic, or in a consulting room. However, the ideal setting is one which is on a domestic scale, comfortable, but also unfamiliar. A private office, appropriately set up, may often be the best. If children or people with severe learning difficulties are being assessed, there should be enough objects to elicit interest and exploratory activity, but they should not be breakable, dangerous, or be small enough to be swallowed. Since many people with ASD have associated physical limitations, there should be easy access for people in wheelchairs, and suitable toilet facilities should also be provided. Some children can become very active in the stress of an assessment, and the environment should be one in which the child can roam freely. The perimeter should also be secure, in case the person being assessed runs out. Administrative staff may need training so that they are not put out by the occasional person being assessed who behaves in an odd or unexpected manner.

In young children it is usually most appropriate to conduct the whole history and examination with the parents present so that all of the attention need not be on the child, although the child can intervene, and so that the child can be observed without it being too pointed. In older children and adults, it is my practice to spend time with them alone, and then to see an informant, asking them if they wish to be present. If they do – and almost all of them do – then I obtain consent about how much information should be shared with the other informant (usually a parent, but may also be a spouse, a friend or another family member). A simply physical examination can be conducted in this setting too, but more formal physical assessment is probably best carried out in a more clinical setting.

Where necessary, for example because of diagnostic uncertainty, observations should be conducted in several settings, for example children may be observed at home and at school, as well as in the consulting room. It is particularly useful to observe people with an ASD interacting with more than one person and interacting with a stranger and with someone with whom they are familiar.

HISTORY TAKING

A careful history should be the starting point for all detailed assessments, and should be taken wherever possible from both parents or carers. Fathers who are excluded, or exclude themselves, from diagnosis may end up disputing its value, and becoming alienated from the measures being taken to help their child, including those taken by the mother. An adequate medical and genetic history may require information from the grandparental generation. The history should cover information about the person's development and health, with a focus on features of ASD and associated or alternative conditions. History taking should also provide information about the family background and circumstances. It may not be possible to obtain much historical information about early development when assessing children who have been abandoned or adults who have moved countries or whose parents have died. Caregivers may not be available to provide a developmental history, and this possibility increases as the age of person being assessed increases. Some practitioners are unwilling to make a diagnosis of an ASD at all in these circumstances, which effectively debars diagnosis in most older adults. An alternative is to obtain collateral information from a third party using some of the same probes as are used to obtain developmental information, and to supplement this with a more than usually careful enquiry into alternative explanations of symptoms, particularly into the possibility of symptoms being secondary to schizophrenia developing in later childhood or adolescence.

An older child, an adolescent or an adult can often describe their own experience and the difficulties that they have with other people and a clinician who is familiar with ASD will often be able to tell how well a diagnosis of ASD can account for the reported experience and difficulty. Relevant information can be obtained from other family members, or from medical and social records. This is invaluable information which can sometimes make a developmental history redundant.

Whether or not a diagnosis can be made in the absence of any developmental information will depend on the quality of other information available, the presence or absence of overt signs of ASD, and the experience of the assessor.

Clinicians who do not usually enquire after development, or who may even think it inappropriate to interview a parent, cannot evade the requirement to obtain a developmental history in this particular group of patients. General psychiatrists, whose practice is limited to the assessment of adults, may need to evolve specific procedures for the assessment of people with ASD to encompass this.

History taking is an opportunity to find out about people as well as eliciting facts. Even very young children have temperamental characteristics that may influence their development, independently of any ASD. Parents or carers will also have temperaments that may affect their childcare, along with any specific worries, fears or beliefs about developmental disorders that may come from their own life experience. This kind of more general information emerges spontaneously in less structured interviews, and it is important that clinicians allow parents to digress onto areas that seem important to them, in order for some of this more personal information to emerge. Some facts, for example about development or medical history, may be collected ahead of the clinical interview by using questionnaires.

DEVELOPMENTAL HISTORY

The use of recognized semi-structured instruments is recommended in all of the guidelines. The UK National Autism Plan for children recommends the use of the Diagnostic Interview for Social and Communication Disorders (DISCO) or of the ADI-R, the revised version of the Autism Diagnostic Interview.[9, 10] These are also recommended for use in adults,[11] although many clinicians recognize that the ADI-R scoring algorithm may be set too high to pick up some people who would be judged clinically to have AS. The DISCO is the more comprehensive, recent instrument and may be the more useful clinically,[12] although it can be extremely time-consuming. It includes both a historical element and a plan for structured observations. The DISCO may be especially useful in the more able.

The ADI-R is often paired with the Autism Diagnostic Observation Scale. The ADI-R includes 93 questions focusing on quality of social interaction, communication and language, and repetitive or stereotyped activity, but with some additional questions, for example on self-injury. It may take up to three hours to complete, and normally takes an hour and a half. Parents' or carers' answers are coded on a pre-provided scheme, and item scores assigned to them, leading to an overall score in each of the three main areas. A scoring algorithm enables these scores to be combined, and the likelihood of an ASD diagnosis estimated. Training is recommended, but training courses are not widely available and last three days. ADI-R scores tend to drop from infancy to age seven,[13, 14] but whether this is because symptoms change, or are overestimated in the younger age group, is unclear. The ADI-R is less effective than direct observation in some younger children with other developmental delays.[15]

The ADI-R and similar semi-structured interview or assessment schedules may be of particular value to inexperienced clinicians, and their use probably increases diagnostic concordance between different centres. However, they have primarily been developed for research, and they do not have the flexibility or speed of an expert clinical assessment. Ascertainment of the likely diagnosis using an algorithm based on information obtained using the ADI-R and ADOS did concord with clinical diagnosis in one study by experts in the research instruments,[16] but the validity of research instruments in a wider range of clinical settings needs investigation. The cut-offs that are appropriate for research may not be appropriate for clinical diagnosis. Using predetermined algorithms may not be appropriate in clinical settings where the most up-to-date information needs to be used,[17] since algorithms become outdated.[18] Thus an evaluation has shown that the ADI-R algorithm may over-emphasize repetitive or stereotyped activity.[13] Clinical judgement allows for fuzzy set classification that can pick up on family resemblances that procedural algorithms cannot.[19] Standardized instruments should therefore be used with caution and should supplement, but not substitute for, clinical judgement.

Whether ADI or another research instrument is used, or the clinician uses his or her own structured inquiry certain areas should always be inquired into (see Boxes 10.1 and 10.2).

Box 10.1 Delays in relevant milestones

Delays reaching the following milestones may indicate that further inquiry is required:

- Being interested in you and other people
- Responding to you
- Understanding speech
- Using speech
- Coordination, e.g. riding a bike, dressing himself
- Eye hand skill, e.g. throwing or catching a ball
- Fine movement, e.g. modelling, or building with blocks
- Spatial awareness, e.g. moving in small spaces without knocking things over
- Finding his way and going from A to B
- Calculating and using numbers
- Reading and spelling
- Joining in with other children and playing with other children

---

Box 10.2 Unusual features of development

(Only if the behaviour is more frequent than occasional should the feature be considered to be present.)

Empathy e.g. *Has he ever seemed to dislike cuddling or other displays of affection? Or, Has he ever seemed to take no notice of other people being upset, pleased or otherwise emotional?*

Nonverbal expression e.g. *Was his voice ever flat, monotonous or mechanical? Or, Have you ever had difficulty telling what he was feeling from his facial expressions?*

Speech e.g. *Has he ever repeated words like a parrot? Or, Did he have unusual difficulty with personal pronouns like 'you' and 'I'?*

Imitation e.g. *Has he had difficulty copying movements or actions?*

Social play or activity e.g. *Did he seem to be unusually restricted in his play?*

Attentional deficits e.g. *Have people ever thought that he was deaf (even though he was found not to be)?*

Routines e.g. *Has he ever seemed unduly distressed if the daily routine changed? Or, Has he ever had food fads?*

'Stimming' e.g. *Has he ever flapped his hands or arms? Or, Was he ever fascinated by particular sensations of touch?*

Suggestive idiosyncrasies e.g. *Have any sounds ever upset him? Or, Has he ever had an unusually narrow or engrossing interest?*

OTHER ASPECTS OF FAMILY HISTORY TAKING

Seeing families together can provide much more than just developmental information. Getting a sense of the circumstances of the family, its emotional climate, and the opinions of each family member is extremely useful. Meeting with families is not just about 'taking' a history either, but about an exchange of information, even in the first few minutes. Often valuable information is better obtained by telling the family what a person with an ASD might do in particular situations, and having the family either look blank, or say, 'Yes, he's just like that. Why only yesterday…'

The other important item of structured family history that is important to obtain systematically is the medical (and sometimes social and psychological) history of other family members. ASD is highly heritable, as are conditions that are associated with it, which include bipolar and other affective disorders, epilepsy, and what is sometimes termed, 'the broad autistic phenotype' (see Box 10.3). It is important to enquire about schizophrenia, partly because older people may have had mania misdiagnosed as schizophrenia, and partly because having a relative with schizophrenia will have influenced family attitudes to ASD. Because family history influences attitudes as well as biology, it is important to extend it to kin, to stepfamilies, and to adopted siblings. Family history can also provide clues of hereditary chromosomal disorders, which may be the cause of ASD in the proband. Guidelines for taking a family history preparatory to genetic counselling are available.[20]

Box 10.3 Family history

Enquire broadly but do not overlook, in other family members:

- ASD
- the broad autism phenotype: dyslexia, speech delay, obsessive compulsive disorder[21]
- bipolar disorder
- anxiety and depression, particularly in parents
- epilepsy
- tuberous sclerosis or other hereditary disorder linked with ASD
- learning difficulty in males (suggesting fragile X)
- other conditions affecting more than one family member.

STRUCTURED OBSERVATION AND EXAMINATION

The history should be combined with an examination, covering mental and physical status, as well as development. The first phase of the examination is observation. The guidelines recommend that this should be structured, and the UK guidelines recommend the use of the Autism Diagnostic Observation Schedule (ADOS) for this purpose. The current 'generic' version of the ADOS, ADOS-G,[22] is an amalgamation of the original ADOS,[23] and an amended version for use with people with speech below the three-year-old level, the Pre-Linguistic Diagnostic Observation Scale (PL-ADOS).[24] The ADOS-G provides standard activities designed to test competencies that are relevant to a diagnosis of ASD by eliciting behaviour that can be scored according to the level of competency shown. There are four modules, graded according to developmental stage. Module 1 activities are appropriate to children who do not consistently use phrase speech, module 2 for those who use phrase speech but are not verbally fluent, module 3 for children whose speech is fluent, and module 4 activities for adolescents and adults with fluent speech. Module 1 activities include the examiner using the child's name, and noting the response according to a rating scale. Module 3 activities will include, instead, the examiner playing a game with a child. The ADOS scoring system also allows for unstructured interactions to be rated.

The ratings for each activity are cumulated, and the likely diagnosis follows from whether or not the aggregate score is above threshold (slightly higher for autistic disorder than for other ASDs). The ADOS usually takes 30–45 minutes to administer.

The ADOS-G is not suitable for children under two years (although a revised version is in preparation), for younger children with other developmental syndromes, such as trisomy 21,[25] nor for people with sensory or motor impairments. ADOS scores in adolescence and adults may drop below threshold,[26] and it may be less useful for an older or more able group. Other observational schedules have been developed for assessing infants, for example the Autism Observation Scale for Infants,[27] although none is sufficiently reliable for use in definitive diagnosis, and they are not intended to be.

The value of the ADOS in assessing adults will depend on its ability to differentiate impairments due to ASD from similar impairments due to adult-onset psychiatric disorders, such as the negative symptoms of schizophrenia or the flattened affect of a person who is markedly depressed, or intoxicated. This has not been evaluated and the ADOS cannot therefore be recommended as a routine measure until it has.

Observation of a person with an ASD needs to be structured and therefore systematic. This requires the examiner to 'bracket off' his or her intersubjective involvement in the encounter – an involvement that may be of great value at other times in the assessment – so that the communications of the person being assessed are under scrutiny, independent of their meaning.[28] The ADOS prescribes activities that provoke this kind of scrutiny. If the ADOS or a similar instrument is not used, the examiner needs to develop his or her own structure. It is often best to make observations unobtrusively, following a plan in which specific kinds of behaviours and actions are considered separately and sequentially.

NONVERBAL EXPRESSION

As part of this structured assessment, nonverbal communication should be observed systematically. One good method for doing this is to focus on 'channels' of communication: voice prosody, gaze behaviour, posture and postural shifts, gesture and whether or not it is integrated with conversation and is other directed, and facial expression. People with a typical ASD will have a lack of expressiveness in all of these channels, which may be more apparent in some rather than others. The more severely affected will have additional, idiosyncratic expressions (see Table 10.2).

Care should be taken to account for emotional states, particular anxiety, shyness or shame, and anger, that may temporarily suppress nonverbal expressiveness and lead the observer to assume that nonverbal competence is impaired on the basis of an atypical nonverbal performance.

NONVERBAL INTERPRETATION

Impairments in the interpretation of other people's nonverbal expressions are probably common in individuals with an ASD,[29] affecting their ability to identify other people's emotions, age and identity. It is very difficult to detect whether or not another person is unable to accurately perceive nonverbal cues, since this inability can be inferred only from their behaviour, and it is common for people to suppress what they know about another person's feelings in order to carry out some unempathic action.

Impairments in nonverbal interpretation are particularly likely to occur when there is more than one person in a social interaction and when other people are physically present, and therefore providing nonverbal cues in every channel. People with a problem in nonverbal interpretation may be much more comfortable, and apparently unimpaired, in phone conversations and even more comfortable in internet-mediated communication with a paucity of nonverbal cues.

Ambiguous or blended expressions may also be more difficult to interpret for people with an ASD.

Table 10.2 Nonverbal expression in people with ASD channel by channel

Channel	Lack of expression	Altered expression
Voice	Reduced prosody: Monotonous voice, staccato speech, lack of variation in softness or hardness of speaking	Idiosyncratic rises and falls of pitch, especially over end of phrases ('dominant'); Uneven emphasis; unusual accent e.g. French accent in lifelong English speaker; extreme variations in rhythm leading to 'cluttering' or long unexpected pauses
Gaze	Gaze not used to bring home a point, to signal listening, to accompany other nonverbal expressions	Staring, gaze avoidance, looking just past the eyes of the other person, looking mainly when speaking
Posture	Few or no shifts, no postural imitation	Posture uncomfortable, or open: full face, legs apart; threatening posture, such as arms akimbo
Gesture	Lack of other-directed gesture (gestures towards the other person); gestures which are adventitious to effortful speech production, or which are self-regulating, stroking, tapping or twirling movements normal or increased. Conventional gestures normal in frequency	Gestures occur, but are not linked to speech or to gaze, and seem to hang in space, 'on their own'
Facial expression	Lack of involuntary expression, particularly in the brow, but conventional expressions, such as social smiles, present or even exaggerated	Facial grimacing: may overlap with tics

Nonverbal interpretative impairment may lead to people feeling confused when with people or finding it hard to look at people in the face. There is a suggestion here that a lack of the normal facial scan path which takes in the eyes, and the nasolabial folds only, may lead to more general face scanning and, consequently, too much facial information, particularly looking at people's eyes, or, for those people who have trained themselves to look at other people's eyes, being unable to take in what they see. People will often describe groups of other people as being more difficult or more aversive, presumably because they provide more complexity of nonverbal cues to be interpreted. Sometimes a person may describe a difficulty in using other people's facial expression to disambiguate a potentially hostile remark from a joke; telling when people are joking and when they are serious is a common complaint in people with Asperger syndrome. People with more severe difficulties in face recognition may have difficulty in recognizing facial identity. Increasingly, people with this difficulty describe themselves as having prosopagnosia or 'face-blindness' and a proportion maybe do have selective prosopagnosia but in people with an autism spectrum disorder the difficulty is likely to extend to other channels of communication, including recognizing a person's voice or footfall. It is likely that people who are severely affected by an ASD may also have even grosser difficulties in using nonverbal cues, such that they are unable to recognize identity or gender, but the evidence suggests that these are deficits that occur only in association with the most severe deficits in the interpretation of emotions in people with ASD, although studies provide evidence for a possible dissociation between these deficits.[30]

Age judgements sometimes assume clinical significance in people with an ASD accused of having underage sex, whose legal advisors may question whether or not the person concerned had the capacity to make an accurate judgement about the other person's age. It is, of course, sensible to test this directly in such cases but in my experience age discrimination is unlikely to be a problem, in the absence of a specific prosopagnosic syndrome in all but people who are the most severely affected by their ASD.

Direct testing of the ability of people with an ASD to interpret photographs or film clips of emotional faces or scenes can provide clear evidence of their ability in this area, but is often difficult to arrange. The most useful clinical measure is what parents or other people close to the person with an ASD report about that person's ability to register and respond to other people's emotional expression.

SPEECH AND LANGUAGE

The assessment of nonverbal communication can be usefully coupled with an assessment of language (Box 10.4). This may be done by observation or by combining observation with questions for parents or carers. Schedules for the latter are commercially available (available methods are reviewed by Dockrell,[31] and some have been standardized in people with an ASD, for example the CCC–2).[32] Language impairment makes an independent contribution to prognosis in ASD and needs to be assessed independently of other speech disorders, which do not, since they are an intrinsic element of the autistic syndrome. Narrative or discourse impairment is potentially a separate feature, as is sociolinguistic impairment (see Box 10.4). It has been suggested that the former reflects theory of mind impairment.[33] However, it is quite likely that the reversed relationship applies and that theory of mind impairment is a consequence of discourse impairment, and that the latter is, in turn, a consequence of a lack of conversational experience.

Interest in others, the way others are responded to – which may range from smelling or touching impersonally to sociable relating or even over familiar responses – and activity levels can also be observed. Finally, the use of stereotypic movements or vocalizations, touching rituals, and other repetitive activities can often be observed even in the space of a clinical interview if the child is observed repeatedly throughout.

The ADOS uses provocative activities or scenarios to elicit actions, and it is important that if the ADOS or a similar instrument is not used, that some kind of challenge – for example, asking the child to complete a simple task or asking an adult to describe a recent emotionally fraught social interaction – is provided. If the child is seen with parents, the spontaneous demands of the situation may be enough provocation for an expert observer, and no additional tasks may be required.

Box 10.4 Domains of speech and language assessment

Speech errors in:

- **Sociolinguistics** indicate narrative impairment. Commonest example is incorrect use of 'shifters' such as 'he', 'you', 'here' and 'there'.

- **Coherence** indicate narrative impairment. Examples include 'flight of ideas', presumption of listener's knowledge, e.g. reference to new characters or topics without introduction and outside of context.

- **Syntax (grammar)** indicate language impairment with the exception of abnormal use of shifters. Examples include wrong word order, irregular words regularized (e.g. baddest instead of worst), verbs omitted, duplication of words (e.g. 'a great lot').

- **Semantics (word meaning)** may indicate language or speech impairment. Common examples are neologisms.

- **Initiation** indicates a pragmatic impairment, probably linked to narrative impairments and a part of the autistic syndrome. Examples include taking conversation over, keeping on talking when others are bored.

- **Flexibility of language** may be used to hide language impairment, or may be a reflection of stereotypy. Examples include use of catchphrases, television advertising, proverbs, or repetition of common greetings such as 'You all right then?' but repeated after questions or other conversational demands.

- **Use of context** indicate a pragmatic impairment, probably linked to narrative impairments and a part of the autistic syndrome. Examples include referring to a clinician by their first name on first meeting, asking intimate questions, offering confidential but irrelevant information, making carelessly insulting remarks such as 'How fat are you?' or 'Do you think that white people smell bad?'

- **Speech interpretation (verbal working memory)** indicate reduced verbal working memory. Complex sentences in which subordinate calls are embedded load verbal working memory, as do long sentences. People with reduced verbal working memory may fail to understand them.

ASSESSING CO-MORBIDITY, ASSOCIATED CONDITIONS, SOCIAL RESPONSES AND PERSONAL REACTIONS

Whatever the presenting symptoms, a systematic overview of the features of the primary impairment, secondary developmental consequences, co-morbid disorders, and any emotional consequences of social or familial reactions to the disorder needs to be undertaken. For many of these factors, the assessor will be trying to determine exactly what the psychological impairment is, usually by careful questioning rather than by direct examination, but will also be estimating the functional consequences of the impairment.

Many people with an ASD will have co-morbid disorders and these are discussed in the ensuing chapters. Anticipating which of these is the most common and extending the assessment to include them is almost as important as assessing the autistic syndrome itself.

SOCIAL COMPETENCE

Iarocci *et al.* suggest that 'social competence entails the development of appropriate strategic processes (i.e. tools) and resources to tackle the social demands of a particular task in a given context'.[34] Eisenberg *et al.* provide a detailed review of what the tools might be. They include assertiveness (in order to actually undertake the social initiatives that one plans); perspective-taking (cognitive empathy) and having developed narratives about people and social situations; and sympathy or compassion, that is a wish to relieve the distress of other people.[35] Surprisingly, there is little evidence that emotional contagion or affective empathy – which is discussed in the next section – has a direct bearing on social competence.[35] Parents and carers most often complain about a lack of response to their emotions, not a lack of awareness of them. They may say, 'I'm sure he knows when I'm upset, but he just ignores it.' Or sometimes, 'I'm sure he can tell if I'm angry, but it's as if he doesn't know what to do. So he just goes on as if nothing was the matter.' Impaired affective empathy is more important in situations, like intimacy, in which a person is expected to know what someone is feeling without words having to be said.

Empathy

As noted in Chapter 6, empathy is the end result of interacting neurological and psychological processes. It is not an isolated capacity, either, but influenced by the other factors that make up social competence. It is therefore a multidimensional construct, based on affective and cognitive components. Empathy is one foundation of our understanding of other people, and therefore of prosocial behaviour, such as solicitude or persuasiveness. However, the willingness to engage in persuasion or to show care is determined by an evaluation of whether or not the situation, or the other person merits it. Empathy in older children and adults can be turned on, or off, by a more general process of appraisal or narrative. So in war the 'other side' may be appraised as not being truly human, and not therefore worthy of empathy. On the other hand, meeting an enemy and finding out about their fondness for children may change that appraisal so that this particular enemy is seen as being 'like one of us' and therefore someone to be empathized with.

Impairments in affective empathy,[36, 37] and in cognitive empathy,[38] have been reported in ASD (see also Chapter 6). Neurotypicals may also appraise people with an ASD as lacking human feelings, and therefore to be an outsider with whom there can be no empathic link. Parents consider that their children with ADHD are also lacking in empathy, but this may result more from a cognitive than an affective impairment.[39]

Empathy has to be distinguished from sympathy (Greek συμπάθεια (sympatheia), Latin compassion) which in its modern usage means concern or compassion for another person. Many people who lack empathy show sympathy. There are many violent people who can be callous to their victims and yet be tearful if they see a news item about a child who has been harmed. Contrarily, many people who are normally empathic suppress and have no sympathy for someone who, they feel, has forfeited their right to sympathy. Sympathy can be readily assessed by probing attitudes or emotional reactions to stories or events. Empathy is more difficult to assess. One question to a close informant that may disclose a lack of empathy is 'Has he/she ever seemed not able to pick up the signs of other people being upset, pleased or otherwise emotional?' When I ask parents this question, I often ask them to imagine a situation in which they have been upset, but about something not connected with their child. Did their child pick up this upset? Did their child react? How might one of their other children (if they have any) have reacted? I also contrast their response to this question with that to a question about sympathy or concern: 'Has he/she ever seemed to take no notice of other people being upset, pleased or otherwise emotional?'

A lack of empathy may be apparent in a person's difficulty in persuasion, charm, seduction, making excuses, negotiation or conflict resolution, all of which require knowing how another person is feeling and thinking in order to be able to more effectively influence it. People who lack empathy may make friendships, but often fail to maintain them, possibly because they lack a sense of what is needed to maintain them. They may also not realize when their friend expects them to be loyal or supportive.

People who lack empathy are vulnerable to exploitation, partly because they are often isolated and also because they often experience themselves as lacking in social impact. An unscrupulous flatterer who pretends an interest or who appears to take notice may quickly find themselves in a position of trust that they can abuse to their own advantage.

Assessing empathy
Situational and dispositional empathy
Empathy is assumed to be a capacity – sometimes termed dispositional empathy – that is not expressed in every situation, since it can be selectively suppressed. High situational empathy may be an indication of high dispositional empathy, but it may also be the result of training in how to deal with a particular situation. Low situational empathy may not indicate low dispositional empathy, either, since it may be suppressed towards those particular people, or in that particular situation. Situational empathy is easier to estimate in the clinical setting than dispositional empathy, however.

Measuring empathy
Report
Situational empathy may be estimated from self-reported feelings or reactions in imagined situations, in responses to narratives, and during experimental simulations.[40] Self-report, even structured by questionnaires, may not be a reliable measure of empathy.[41] Despite this, many studies of empathy rely on self-report, often in the form of questionnaires, many of them purporting to measure dispositional empathy.

Other informants
In the clinical setting information about empathy is often most usefully obtained from another informant, typically from a mother when the empathy of a young person is at issue. Spouses, too, may provide useful information, but when two people are in conflict they will readily attribute a lack of sympathy in the other person to be due to an incapacity and not, as is too often the case, the coldness that comes from anger or dislike.

Dadds *et al.* have developed a 23 item questionnaire for parents to rate the empathy of their children.[42] It has items that are specific to affective empathy and to cognitive empathy, and items that are common to both (see Table 10.3).

Table 10.3 Selected items from the Griffiths Empathy Measure (chosen for their greatest factor loadings)

	Loading on affective empathy factor	Loading on cognitive empathy factor
'My child gets upset when another person is acting upset'	0.8	—
'My child rarely understands why other people cry'	—	0.8
'My child gets sad to see a child with no one to play with'	0.5	0.5

Source: Dadds, Hunter *et al.*, 2008.

The results of one study are that callous and unemotional adolescent girls who behave antisocially have reduced cognitive, but not affective, empathy. Boys who were similarly callous and antisocial had reduced affective empathy, but acquired cognitive empathy in adolescence.[43] So a history of callousness and antisocial behaviour may be an indication of a lack of empathy, but clinicians often put too much weight on the link between antisocial behaviour and empathy in the absence of callousness. More than usual frequency of antisocial behaviour may simply be an expression of social disadvantage, that is intelligence and socioeconomic status,[44] without any implications for personality.

There are many other consequences of a lack of empathy, many of them affecting the unempathic person themselves rather than causing harm or difficulty to others.[45] This is because empathy is a basis for many social skills, both in their acquisition and in their performance. So people who lack empathy are readily exploited, avoid conflict and so feel socially powerless, and cannot charm or seduce others, and so are often isolated. All of these may be apparent in the history. Another characteristic expression of a lack of empathy is a normal rate of making friends but a very low rate of maintenance. It is enough to seem attractive, interesting, or even just available to make a friend. Maintaining a friendship requires following what have been called the 'rules of friendship',[46] many of which turn on knowing what the friend is feeling and thinking without them having to say.

Criminal damage (to keep in or gain recognition in a gang), social isolation, stealing to give 'friends' money or food, inviting people home who are very recent acquaintances, or accepting sexual propositions from strangers may all be pointers to a lack of empathy as much as antisocial behaviour.

Scales for dispositional empathy

The scale with the strongest research base is the Interpersonal Reactivity Index (IRI).[47] This has a factor structure which has been interpreted as meaning that it assesses four components of empathic response: perspective taking, fantasy, empathic concern and personal distress.

The IRI has been modified for children.[48, 49] The IRI fails to pick up the empathy deficits in people with AS.[50]

A study of the factor structure of the Empathizing Quotient (considered under Testing below) illustrates this, and provides some useful pointers to the complexities of clinical assessment. Muncer and Ling suggest that the three factors can be labelled cognitive empathy, social skills and emotional reactivity.[51, 52] The five items loading on the cognitive empathy factor are shown in Table 10.4.

Table 10.4 Self-report items that may be used to estimate cognitive empathy (with loadings on a factor of cognitive empathy)

I can tune into how someone else feels rapidly and intuitively (0.71)
I am good at predicting how someone will feel (0.65)
I am quick to spot when someone in a group is feeling awkward or uncomfortable (0.6)
I can sense if I am intruding, even if the other person does not tell me (0.49)
I can easily work out what another person might want to talk about (0.59)

Simple clinical assessment of empathy often involves asking how someone reacts in a particular situation. A lack of reaction may indicate one of the items in Table 10.4, but it might also indicate that the person would have endorsed 'I find it hard to know what to do in a social situation' or 'I find it difficult to explain to others things that I understand easily, when they do not understand it first time.' Muncer and Ling consider these items to be indicative of a lack of social skill rather than a lack of empathy.[51] A lack of response may also indicate a lack of emotional reactivity, and the person concerned may also have endorsed 'seeing people cry does not really upset me' (one of the items that Muncer and Ling found to load most highly on the emotional reactivity factor): here the problem is not empathic accuracy, but empathic sensitivity. These and other factors, including the level of anxiety in the room,[53] which may influence the expression of empathy, have to be taken into account in any clinical assessment.

Testing

Tests have been widely used in research settings to measure emotion recognition, a key component of affective empathy, and theory of mind. The tests of theory of mind that have been used in research settings include tests based on play materials such as dolls or sweets, computerized versions of these tests, and paper-based tests. None of them are being used routinely in clinical assessment and they lack the psychometric evaluation that would be needed before they could be routinely introduced.

The Reading the Mind in the Eyes test has become one of the most commonly used research methods, and may be of value clinically. However, it has been criticized for not being naturalistic and other video-based tests have been developed as an alternative.[54]

Rating physiological reactions

Physiological reactions, such as facial, gestural or vocal response or autonomic changes, such as the galvanic skin response or heart rate changes, may also be rated. Although these ratings can be more objective, they are only indirect measures of feelings. Simulations have been used to test the empathy of clinicians,[55] or sexual offenders (who were asked to write letters to victims),[56] but have been little used in people with ASD.

Neuroimaging

Neuroimaging may provide a means of directly testing empathy in that the brain areas that are active during empathic responding are beginning to be reliably known. However, the neurological substrate of empathy in the brain may be as complex as the interlinked psychological processes that lead to an empathic response. For example, activity in the subgenual cingulate cortex is associated with empathic concern, but not compassion.[57] It has been suggested that affective empathy can be distinguished from cognitive empathy by activation of limbic and paralimbic areas including the thalamus (presumably mediating an emotional feeling), the fusiform gyrus (presumably concerned with interpretation of facial and possibly bodily expression), and the inferior parietal lobule (presumably mediating the self–other distinction).[58] The design of this fMRI ensured that brain areas that were activated during both affective and cognitive empathy were not included in the contrast. So, for this reason presumably, superior temporal sulcus activation was not included as an association of affective empathy, although other studies do implicate it.

Clinical assessment

Empathy, or its absence, is normally only overtly demonstrated in exceptional circumstances and it is unlikely that these will arise during a clinical assessment. A clinical interviewer may suspect a lack of empathy from the descriptions that a person gives of other people who are close to them; if this is the case, the examiner should check whether the interviewee feels positively or negatively towards the person he or she describes, since empathy is routinely suspended when a person feels negatively towards somebody else. A crude assessment of empathy can be made by presenting a situation, and asking how a person might react. The value of this is limited by the extent to which the person being asked to speculate knows themselves and is willing to divulge their knowledge. A more reliable method might be to ask an informant how a person would react in such a situation. For example, I routinely ask mothers to say how their son or daughter might react if their son or daughter came upon their mother being upset if the upset had nothing to do with the son or daughter. Mothers, in answering this question, will often distinguish between gross upset, such as tears or shouting, and subtle upset, such as a change in demeanour or a slight change in facial expression. They will also sometimes distinguish between the child perceiving the distress and acting on it, since some mothers will say of their children: 'I think he knows when I'm upset but he doesn't know what to do and so he simply ignores it.' There is also the situation in which the child is perceived as being aware of upset and in some way relishing it when the mother might say 'He takes pleasure in winding me up.'

Nonverbal inexpressiveness and prosocial competence

In schizophrenia, reduced impaired nonverbal expressivity is the major contributor to reduced social, or prosocial, competence,[59] probably because social competence requires interactants to give each other nonverbal signals of interest, turn-taking, and so on. Nonverbal inexpressiveness may be equally important in ASD, too. Its assessment has already been considered.

Other contributors to prosocial competence

Flexibility, affecting the ability to take turns and to shift ideas, has been suggested to be one aspect of social competence that is particularly affected in ASD,[60] but there has been, as Cotugno notes, surprisingly little research into the relative importance of the hypothesized contributors to social competence.[60]

COGNITIVE STYLE

In a comparison of neurotypical children aged 7 to 12 years with children of the same age with either ADHD or ASD, reduced vigilance (or attention) and reduced response inhibition were found in the children with ADHD and many of the children with ASD (presumably those who had ADHD in addition).[61] These are likely to be traits that underlie what clinicians often term 'impulsivity'. In the same study, children with ASD and ADHD both had working memory deficits compared to the neurotypicals, which were greater in the children with ASD than in the children with ADHD.[61] Working memory deficits (see also Chapter 7) are probably linked to some of the specific developmental disorders considered below, and their clinical assessment will be considered there.

Visuospatial reasoning

Visuospatial reasoning is exemplified by the intelligence that is tested by Raven's Progressive Matrices, and requires 'perceptual processing and comparison of complex arrays, analogical reasoning, and relational reasoning'.[62a] In childhood, visuospatial reasoning draws on an extended network, but in adults it is primarily associated with frontoparietal connections.[62] One study suggests that a relative strength in visuospatial reasoning may be a reflection of persisting language difficulties in some people with ASD,[63] and that it is weakness in propositional reasoning rather than strength in visuospatial reasoning that differentiates the two groups. This does not accord with the experience of many people with Asperger syndrome, and so the matter may need further investigation.

Case example

> A 20-year-old man with AS described himself as a visuospatial thinker. On the WAIS, his verbal IQ was 76 but his performance IQ was 87. On the Wechsler memory scale, his verbal memory index was 62, and his nonverbal memory index was 95. Several male members of his family had, like him, been delayed in developing speech.

Testing visuospatial reasoning

Whatever the explanation for it, visuospatial reasoning is a strength of the reasoning of many people with AS, and assessment provides a measure of this strength. Raven's Progressive Matrices does not require special training to administer, and is probably the best measure. If a WISC or WAIS has previously been administered, the matrix reasoning score (only in the fourth edition) or the block design score might provide an estimate of visuospatial reasoning, too.[64, 63]

Over-focused attention

Another cognitive style commonly attributed to people with an ASD is a disposition to focus intensively on one thing, to the exclusion of all else. In early childhood, this may result in children being suspected of being deaf because they ignore their parents calling their names, or trying to get their attention in other ways, when they are engrossed in something. Although it has been suggested that over-focused attention can be explained by an inability to divide attention between competing targets – for example selecting one shape out of several being presented on a screen – tests of divided attention show slower responding in people with an ASD, but not significantly slower, except for participants who are on medication.[65]

Impulsivity

Clinicians often regard impulsivity as one of the important differentiators between ADHD and ASD. There is some research evidence for this. Impulsivity is not, from the psychologist's point of view, a single construct but the ability to inhibit an immediate response to a stimulus is an important component.[66] In a comparison of children with ADHD, with ASD, and with no ASD, both of the groups with ASD had executive difficulties but of different kinds. The ADHD were not markedly impaired in their ability to plan or initiate an action, but were markedly impaired in response inhibition and therefore were markedly impulsive. The ASD children had the inverse of these difficulties: no lack of response inhibition, but difficulties in planning or initiating responses.[67] However, response inhibition deficits were shown by children with ASD as well as those with ADHD in another study that required a sustained response,[68] suggesting that under some circumstances people with ASD might be impulsive, too.

Systematizing

Baron-Cohen has observed a greater frequency of people with ASD in the physical sciences,[69] and this has led him to conclude that there are two fundamental cognitive styles, 'systematizing' and 'empathizing'.[70] Systematizing is:

> the drive to analyze, explore, and construct a system. The systemizer intuitively figures out how things work, or extracts the underlying rules that govern the behaviour of a system. This is done in order to understand and predict the system, or to invent a new one.[70a]

Empathizing is also a 'drive', but in this case the:

> drive to identify another person's emotions and thoughts, and to respond to them with an appropriate emotion. Empathizing does not entail just the cold calculation of what someone else thinks and feels… Psychopaths can do that much. Empathizing…is done in order to understand another person, to predict their behavior, and connect or resonate with them emotionally.[70b]

Baron-Cohen argues that men are more systematizing than empathizing, and women vice versa. Similarly, physical scientists are more systematizing than artists, and vice versa, and men with ASD are even more systematizing than neurotypical men.[71] The theory therefore fits with the theory that ASD is the consequence of an 'extreme form of the male brain'.[72]

So far, there has been little independent investigation of the systematizing and empathizing cognitive styles although Baron-Cohen et al. have developed scales to measure each style,[73, 74] and have conducted several empirical studies using them. The empathy quotient was lower in men than women in one survey and lower in both men and women with ASD than neurotypicals in another.[74] This is consistent with clinical observations, which have already been discussed.

It is more contentious whether or not systematizing (or 'systemizing' as Baron-Cohen terms it) is a specific cognitive style, and whether it is one that is particularly associated with ASD. Baron-Cohen and his colleagues have repeated their two surveys in children using parental ratings rather than self-report, and find the same pattern of boys systematizing more and empathizing less than girls, and both boys and girls with ASD systematizing more and empathizing even less than neurotypical boys.[75] This result is not inconsistent with one reached on the basis of his own observations by Erik Erikson in the early 1960s, who observed children playing in the laboratory and noted that boys' play was dominated by movement, construction and rules (their favourite doll was a policeman) whereas girls' play was dominated by the creation of interiors, of a lack of movement, and of artistic expression (their favourite piece of furniture was a piano).[76] Whether or not these are the effects of testosterone or sexually dimorphic developments in the brain, or the consequence of gender identity assignment is as uncertain now as it was in Erikson's time.

It is equally unclear whether the increased systematization observed in people with an ASD is primary, is the result of selection bias in the sample, or is a consequence of the impairments in social interaction that the disorder typically brings. Many clinicians believe that people with an ASD try to find the rules of social interaction that they can learn, and so obtain a kind of learnt social intelligence. Perhaps this is the spur to a systematizing tendency.

Testing

The systemizing quotient has been used only in research up to now, and no clinically validated means of assessment exist. However, both the empathy quotient and the systematizing quotient are available for download from the website of the Autism Research Centre at Cambridge and are free to use for those clinicians who will find them helpful.[77]

Rigidity and inflexibility

Cognitive inflexibility is regularly commented on as a fundamental component of ASD, but it is hard to demonstrate in controlled tests, possibly because people with ASD may not always be inflexible.[78] Difficulty in disengaging from a previous task might also explain some of the functional inflexibility that is noticed in everyday functioning, particularly if it is combined with a lack of explicit instruction about task shifting.[79] This tendency, often called 'repetitiveness', is also shown by people with frontal lobe lesions, in whom it is usually termed 'perseveration' although perseveration may occur in association with lesions in other areas of the brain.[80] Perseverative errors include logoclonus, repeating the previously uttered syllable, and palilalia, repeating previously uttered syllables, words or phrases. Both palilalia and logoclonus are common in the speech of people with an ASD.

Many people with ASD focus on detail at the expense of the 'bottom line' or the 'wider picture'. People with an ASD perform better on the Embedded Figures Test than age- and IQ-matched neurotypicals,[81] and this 'field independence' is usually taken to indicate an inability to see the wood for the trees,[82] as the English (and Chinese) expression has it. Another way of expressing this is that people with ASD show more rapid perceptual responses that are not diverted by attention to context.[83] Field independence has been taken to be evidence of poor central coherence, Frith's more general psychological explanation of the difficulties in cognition and social cognition in ASD.[84] In one study, the frequency of repetitive behaviour, along with age and IQ, correlated with the speed of completion of the Embedded Figures Test by 29 children with AS, suggestion that weak central coherence and inflexibility may be facets of a single cognitive style,[85] although central coherence and 'mental shifting' were found to be independent in another study.[86] Some of the children with AS included in this study did not show characteristics of weak central coherence, leading the authors to conclude that this cognitive style was not universal in ASD.[86]

Routines and rituals

Perseverative responding may be linked to behavioural traits that are often seen as characteristic of ASD. These include resistance to change, the repetition of particular behavioural sequences as in the routines that may preface or follow everyday actions or the rituals that may surround transitions like going to bed or having a meal. There is considerable overlap between these routines and those of people with obsessive compulsive disorder (possible differentiata are discussed in Chapter 13). Like them, they become more intense and interfering – at least to other people – when a person is anxious, which may be a coping strategy against anxiety.[87] It is not clear whether routines and rituals are an intrinsic part of ASD or a nonspecific response to anxiety (this is discussed in more detail in Chapter 8). Repetition and stereotypy (repetitive movements) are just as frequently resorted to by neurotypicals with a learning disability as by people with an ASD.[88]

Inflexibility or 'insistence on sameness' and a tendency towards repetition make an independent contribution to symptoms like food fads, routines, special interests and resistance to change,[89] but only inflexibility is also to be found in fathers, suggesting that there may be an independent, hereditary contribution from this factor to the autism spectrum.[89]

Special interests may have a strong ritual element, with an internal pressure to complete 'full' collections, or to maintain the orderliness of collected objects. Although often particularly associated with Asperger syndrome, they occur in up to a third of young children, and are more common in boys.[90]

In the clinic, one meets occasional people who have all of the other symptoms of an ASD but who do not have inflexibility. Often, they have been exposed to considerable change during their childhood, such as frequent parental moves of home, suggesting that inflexibility may also be absent from their parents.

Peters-Scheffer *et al.* have suggested one approach to the assessment of inflexibility and repetition.[91] They ask patients or informants what the reaction would be to 16 scenarios (see Table 10.5 on the following page, to which I have added an additional item, shown last in the table, and modified the wording) providing a score from 0 to 34.[91]

Sensory behaviour

Boyd *et al.* used a questionnaire for parents and structured observations to record repetitive behaviour and unusual sensory behaviour in children with autism and a comparison group of children with other developmental delays.[92] Like other clinicians and researchers whose work they review, their factor analysis suggests three separable factors: hypersensitivity, hyposensitivity and sensation seeking.[92]

Hypersensitivity

A substantial number of people with an ASD complain of hyperaesthesia (extreme sensitivity to stimulation): they see colours more brightly (and may see colours linked with other sensations, synaesthesia), hear sounds more loudly, or are exquisitely sensitive to touch. There is disagreement about whether the auditory or visual threshold is lower, or whether it is that low level stimuli are not 'gated out', to use Broadbent's term.[93] There is evidence both ways.[94, 95, 96] Clinical experience is that once a low level perception becomes the focus of attention, it becomes subjectively louder, and more obtrusive. Clinical difficulties arise when the sensation is one that is inescapable. Many foods when mashed together have a slimy taste that may not only become abhorrent to a person with ASD, but also be detectable in more and more subtle manifestations, and therefore in more and more foods, leading to a more and more restricted diet. Hypersensitivity to touch may mean that only certain fabrics can be worn, or that new clothes that are stiff or scratchy cannot be tolerated. Hyperacusis (extremely sensitive hearing) may focus on father's voice, a particular pitch of a child's voice, or the sound of vacuum cleaners or ice-cream van ring tones.

In Boyd *et al.*'s study, hypersensitivity and repetition were significantly associated, suggesting either a common basis in anxiety or that both reflected a problem in attention shifting.[92]

Table 10.5 Assessing rigidity

To what extent is each of the following situations a problem for the person?	Severity of the problem		
	No (0)	Mild (1)	Severe (2)
A commonly used object is misplaced and cannot be found			
A planned event is delayed or cancelled with little warning because of unforeseen circumstances			
The person is required to move from their current location			
An object in the environment is not its usual or expected place			
The person wants something that is unavailable			
Something that the person wants to use breaks or is unavailable			
The usual routine is altered, e.g. a parent takes a new route home from school			
An unexpected interaction occurs with another person, e.g. a stranger starts a conversation			
The person becomes momentarily separated from his or her family or group			
Materials runs out, bringing an activity to an end unexpectedly			
Another person is doing something annoying, e.g. making a noise			
Objects or materials are not replaced at the end of an activity			
A new object, item or person is present			
An activity is interrupted before the person was able to finish the task			
A new activity is introduced into the person's routine			
Another person tries to use a favourite possession			
Someone interrupts the person when they are speaking, and does not allow them to complete what they were saying			

Source: Test adapted from Peters-Scheffer, Didden, *et al.*, 2008 (with an additional item) with permission from Elsevier.

Hyposensitivity

Hyposensitivity, or an apparent lack of feeling or at least lack of response to inferred feelings, seems to be the inverse of hypersensitivity, but both may occur in the same child. A child who cannot bear to wear wool, and can feel that even a wool mixture is scratching them through an inner layer of cotton clothing, may not react to pain and may have been investigated for deafness for apparently not responding to their name being spoken. Idiosyncratic attention deployment may provide an explanation for both hyper- and hyposensitivity.

Sensory seeking

Sensory seeking is the third group of sensory behaviours identified by Boyd et al.[92] The sensations that are sought are often repetitive or rhythmic, and once an appropriate source of sensation is found, a person may become rapt by it, a state similar to the fascination with which a person with an ASD may read a book about dinosaurs, or study a car mechanics manual for the Renault 4. Rhythmic sensations include whirling objects, like washing machines; flashing or flickering lights, like fires, diamond rings, or the flicker of sunlight; and rocking. Sometimes the sensations may be deliberately produced by rocking oneself, whirling round and round; flicking one's hands near the eyes; biting or tapping; or headbanging. There is therefore a close link between these stereotyped self-stimulating or 'stimming' behaviours and passive sensory seeking. Indeed, one possible common origin is that these are not anxiety-related but reward-related, self-grooming. In mouse models of ASD, self-grooming is reduced by a reduction of increased repetitive self-grooming in ASD mouse models by metabotropic 5 glutamate receptor antagonism,[97] and there are current trials of this drug in children.

SPECIFIC DEVELOPMENTAL SYNDROMES

Dysexecutive syndrome, dyslexia, dyscalculia and other, rarer, specific developmental disorders are more common in children with ADHD,[98] and probably in children with both ASD and ADHD. This is surprising as some of these disorders, for example dyscalculia,[99] are apparently localized: in the case of dyscalculia to the intraparietal sulcus.[99] One possible explanation is that there is often widespread neurological involvement in the ASDs. This may be particularly so when the risk of pregnancy complications and postnatal infection is high.[100] Another possibility is that specific developmental disorders,[101] like the ASDs, may result from impairments in connections between brain areas.

There may be a particular association of specific developmental syndromes and ADHD specifically, rather than ASD. It is possible that this is because connections between cerebellum and frontal lobe may be particularly important in both ADHD and these other specific developmental disorders. Some evidence of this comes from an unusual case in which an incapacity indistinguishable from that resulting from a combination of ADHD and a specific developmental disorder was acquired following an infarct in the territory of the right cerebellar artery and hypoperfusion in the left prefrontal cortex, suggesting a lesion in the fronto-cerebellar network.[102] The 58-year-old man affected developed a transcortical sensory aphasia, dyslexia and dysgraphia, along with persistent dysexecutive syndrome and an inability to divide his attention, and so switch between tasks.

Testing

Clinicians should take an educational history in everyone with an ASD, but especially in those who have ADHD symptoms, and wherever possible consult with teachers or see school reports. It should not be assumed that reading or mathematics delays are simply the result of intellectual disability.

If more detailed assessment is required, an educational psychologist can best provide this.

TEMPERAMENT

Many anecdotal reports support a link between ASD and anxiety, and also an association with a more general tendency to withdraw from social contact. In one of the few experimental studies, informants were asked to rate the personalities of adult relatives of people with ASD and people with trisomy 21 using a personality questionnaire. The relatives of people with ASD were more likely to be anxious, impulsive, aloof, shy, over-sensitive, irritable or eccentric. However, there were different patterns in male and female relatives, and in parents and siblings. Factor analysis of the scores resulted in three factors that the authors called 'withdrawn', 'difficult', and 'tense'. Tenseness was thought to be secondary to the strains of living with someone with an ASD, but 'withdrawn' and 'difficult' were thought to be linked to an ASD diathesis.[103]

Withdrawal

Withdrawal from social contact with others is a leading symptom of depression, but usually disappears once the depression remits. It is characteristic of the 'schizoidia' described by Bleuler, and the schizoid personality originally described by Fairbairn, and taken up by Klein.[104] Schizoidia has followed a rambling path since, which has now forked into schizotypal and schizoid, without either taking on any more definition (but see Chapters 8 and 17). There is an association between some schizoid traits and some traits that are conventionally associated with ASD,[105] especially emotional detachment and introspection,[106] and it has been suggested in the past that schizoid personality in childhood and AS are one and the same condition.[107]

Fairbairn's original concept of schizoid 'personality' was that it was a kind of protection against emotional vulnerability linked to extreme shame-proneness.[108]

Social withdrawal is a common complication of ASD in adolescence, quite often leading to the failure of therapeutic initiatives. It is also associated with raised levels of anxiety, depression and loneliness.[109] It is therefore important to assess. However, often adolescents who are withdrawn have become so, sometimes as a result of bullying or other emotional disappointments, many of them creating shame-proneness or low self-esteem, and social withdrawal is more often a reaction rather than a trait.

It is essential to ask about social contacts in every assessment of someone with Asperger syndrome. Table 10.6 provides some useful questions for older children, upwards.

Table 10.6 Probes about social withdrawal

Social integration
How often do you go out? To the pub? Shopping? Elsewhere? Do you belong to any clubs, e.g. cubs or scouts? Do you play any team sports? Do you talk to the neighbours?
Peer relations
Do you have friends? Do you go to parties (birthday parties in younger people)? (If appropriate) have you ever had a sexual relationship? (If appropriate) have you ever worked? (If appropriate) where do you go and who are you with during lunch hours/breaks? Do people visit you at home, or do you go to other people's houses? How often do you ring people up, or do they ring you? Who do you text/SMS? Do you get together with other people over the internet?
Family contact
Do you have your own room at home? How much of your time do you spend in there? Do you watch television with the family? Do you eat with your family? What do you do if a family members comes round to visit?

Anxiety

Anxiety is such a prominent feature of ASD that some psychologists have suggested in the past that ASD is caused by anxiety. One, no longer current, hypothesis was that ASD was caused by an insuperable approach/avoidance conflict provoked by anxiety (see attachment disorder in Chapter 12, on infancy). There are three other possible explanations for the association (these are discussed in more detail in Chapter 15, on adolescents): that anxiety reduces coping, allowing mild and previously unregarded symptoms of ASD to emerge; that anxiety and ASD are genetically linked,[110, 111, 112] or that ASD falling below the threshold for diagnosis may still result in social impairment enough to cause anxiety, for which there is some evidence.[113] Children with OCD and social phobia are at an increased risk of being bullied if they have additional symptoms of social impairment,[114] possibly because these children have undiagnosed ASD.

Anxiety is increased by family conflict with people with AS being especially sensitive, and less able to deal with conflict than neurotypical children.[115]

ASSESSMENT OF CO-MORBID DISORDER

In addition to the developmental disorders associated with ASD itself, and those associated with linked neurodevelopmental conditions, individuals with ASD are more at risk of having co-morbid psychiatric and medical conditions. In one study of consecutive children presenting to an autism diagnostic centre, children had sleep disorders, epilepsy, food intolerance, gastrointestinal dysfunction, mood disorder, and aggressive and self-injurious behaviours. Sleep, mood and gut disorders often went together, as did mood disorder and aggression or self-injury.[116] Assessment of a person with an ASD therefore needs to encompass these common co-morbid conditions.

PSYCHIATRIC DISORDER IN THE CONTEXT OF ASD
Examples of concrete thinking and the diagnosis of psychosis

Concrete description may increase the risk of misdiagnosis with schizophrenia. One man in his twenties was obsessed by the thought that he might be shot in the street, or possibly set on fire. When his anxiety was very high, he sometimes heard shots when he was out, and had vivid pictures of flames that seemed so clear to him that he thought that he must have seen these images. Another man, who had marked hyperaesthesiae of his legs, sometimes described them as his mother touching him at a distance, and got up from his chair and struck her on at least one occasion because he assumed that she had done so, even though she was sitting some distance away. A third man described himself as hearing two voices in his head, God and the devil, who had noisy arguments. On closer questioning, he said that one voice was that of a former headmaster and the other that of his father. When he was in doubt about what to do, he would ask each of these two what they would advise and sometimes, instead of knowing what to do, he became even more conflicted and imagined them as arguing with each other. One had been good to him, so he thought of that voice as God, and the other, not good to him – so he thought of that voice as the devil.

Many people with ASD, when asked, 'Can other people put thoughts into your mind?' will say, 'Yes.' But on closer questioning, they say that these thoughts are put into their heads by what people say.

An important decision in the management of someone with an ASD, but particularly an adolescent, is whether their experiences are attributable to a disorder and, if it is, whether a psychiatric illness, independent of their autism, should be diagnosed.

There is particular difficulty in the differential diagnosis of psychosis in autistic people because the negative symptoms of schizophrenia are not easily distinguishable from some autistic symptoms (but see above), and because the behaviour and beliefs of autistic people may be eccentric and unexpected without the supervention of illness:

Case examples

The following have been previously reported:[117]

- Subject 29 saw strange flickering lights in the air at times.
- Subject 39 saw rainbows.
- Subject 8 thought that he saw other people's faces altering.
- Subject 1 hoarded faeces in a pot under his bed.
- Subject 25 thought that he was really asleep (in a 'missage') between two periods of existence ('boating lines'). He was only aware because a witch had made him have a bad dream.

- Subject 4 saw television pictures of a fire in which a mother and daughter had been burnt to death, and laughed.

- Subject 19 thought that he had seen spaceships landing, and said that aliens had come out of them and talked to him.

- Subject 33 believed that he had been forcibly taken away from a heavenly home by the people who called themselves his parents but were not. He had believed that he was not properly alive and that he would turn into a skeleton overnight. He had also and may still have believed that he was in contact with the Holy Ghost at night time.

- Mr M heard voices, but these were recollections of two of his teachers.

- Ms L heard her grandmother telling her not to eat chocolate, but this was a vivid memory of what her grandmother actually used to say.

It was decided that these were not symptoms of psychosis because they had antecedents throughout the person's childhood, and because they were put forward as explanations of why living seemed so painful and so unsettling although put in an unusually concrete and idiosyncratic way. In several a depressive disorder probably made the experiences more certain and more vivid, however.

Other phenomena had the elation and self-referential quality of hypomania, the passivity of schizophrenia, or an element of confusion, and so were attributed to a functional psychosis or confusional state.[118]

- Subject 2's mood and weight appeared to go up and down on a regular basis although repeated examination of his mental state did not confirm a consistent variation in that. He had a long-standing idea that he may have tipped off the Israelis to raid Entebbe airport because he had talked to a fellow patient about the possibility of a rescue mission. He required emergency admission in an acutely disturbed state following his discharge from hospital where he had been a day patient for several years. He had become convinced that he may have been responsible for a terrorist bombing because he had overheard two Irishmen talking the day before it happened. He was mute for a few days after admission; it subsequently emerged that he had been convinced that Irish members of staff were undercover agents for the IRA. There was some sleep disturbance but no change in appetite. He had mild flight of ideas, and his mood was predominantly apprehensive. There was no evidence of hallucinations or other abnormal beliefs. Diagnosis: reactive psychosis.

- Subject 9 had, for several years, experienced intense depression alternating with moods of euphoria and grandiosity during which he slept less, was irritable, disinhibited and quick to assume that others were doing him harm. He had had a variety of suspicious delusions which disappeared as his sleep and irritability improved. During an elated period he had increased energy, wrote copiously, and his letters and speech became verbose and full of puns. Diagnosis: bipolar disorder.

- Subject 28 had long-standing fluid and all encompassing ideas of persecution. At any one time he was carrying on litigation with previous psychiatrists, the Official Solicitor, the Patents Office and others. He initiated these actions because he felt that he had been slighted or unfairly treated: there was always a basis in some actual incident but his complaint was founded on an unreasonable expectation of special treatment or understanding based on an exaggerated view of his own importance. He believed that he had inside political knowledge and mentioned contact with various VIPs, especially Russian diplomats, although disarmingly admitted that this might have only amounted to seeing them in shops. He thought that a file was kept on him at the Home Office, that his movements may have been monitored, and occasionally mentioned that he had been marked down for assassination by an Eastern European country. His reason for thinking this was that he had been struck by an umbrella carried by a red-headed man, and some days before, a Bulgarian diplomat had been murdered by a ricin-tipped umbrella being jabbed into him (at the time of the examination this was a speculative and slightly incredible news story, although it has since been proved). His symptoms were best treated by a combination of a neuroleptic and an antidepressant. He had periods when he seemed dejected which he 'treated' by giving himself electric shocks. At other times he was full of plans for new inventions and became much more active. Diagnosis: paranoid state.

- Subject 35 first became ill aged 16 when he expressed the belief that other people were talking about him. Although this belief had persisted, there had never been any definite evidence of hallucinations as these phenomena occurred only when other people were present. He had had recurrent episodes of depression since then, often associated with an increase in comments by other people which had an accusatory character, for example that he was to be castrated because he had been trifling with other people's daughters' affections. He had made two serious suicide attempts and had also hit himself during episodes, saying that he 'deserved to be dead because he was the wickedest man in the world'. On one occasion, he had said that he would commit suicide unless the government put the time back to Greenwich Mean Time so that it became darker earlier and he could see the stars to learn more about astronomy. He did in fact attempt to do so subsequently. Diagnosis: manic-depressive psychosis, depressed type.

- Subject 46 had episodes of stress-related behavioural disturbance associated with self-harm, feelings of panic and weeping. Hallucinations and passivity experiences were noted in the medical records but they were subsequently denied by the subject whose mother also could not confirm them. Repeated EEGs eventually demonstrated evidence of temporal lobe epilepsy, and the episodes ceased after anticonvulsants were begun. Diagnosis: temporal lobe epilepsy with acute confusional states.

- Subject 52 had had several episodes since he was 15 of excitement, irritability and insomnia. During the most recent episode he was euphoric at times and tearful at others, had pressure of speech, increased thought rate, was socially disinhibited and had some grandiose ideas. Second person auditory hallucinations were noted.

He made a complete recovery with neuroleptic treatment. Diagnosis: bipolar disorder.

- Subject 79 was first diagnosed as schizophrenic at the age of 13 when he 'had the impression' that his mother was a witch and was controlling his actions. He also believed that his sex had changed and that there was a foetus inside him although he would never give birth to it. He was noted to have a vigorous fantasy life which he found more pleasurable than contact with the outside world. At the time of the study, when he was 18, he said that he 'had developed delusions but no hallucinations'. The delusions were, he explained, that he thought that people were against him and that they kept an eye on him whenever he was out for a walk. They were conspiring against him to make him feel inferior. Diagnosis: schizophrenia.

Hallucinoses

Assessing perception may be complicated by the reification of experience discussed previously. Perceptual illusions include flashing lights, shapes falling through the air, tactile sensations, or thoughts that are spoken aloud in the person's own voice. Careful assessment of these experiences should be undertaken before a diagnosis of a hallucination is made. Sometimes hallucinations are really a kind of attribution, but one made in a state of puzzlement about the world. For example, an adolescent girl with autism was drawing at home with her parents, but was then distracted by the television. When she looked down at her drawing again she could not remember what she had been drawing and said, 'I didn't draw that. He [a boy she went to school with who was harassing her] came and did it.' Her parents could see that there was nothing new on the page, and a psychiatrist to whom this story was recounted presumed that this was a visual hallucination. But it was not something that Laura had seen despite the evidence to the contrary, but an explanation for something that she could not account for in terms that she did not find particularly unrealistic. In her world, people probably seemed to come and go unexpectedly in any case.

Delusions

The concrete thoughts described previously may suggest delusions and, as for suspected hallucinations, call for extra careful enquiry before a definite diagnosis is made.

Thought disorder

Speech disorder may be misinterpreted as thought disorder, particularly when it involves a pragmatic difficulty and the person with an ASD talks in a rambling, and lengthy way, jumping from topic to topic, and referring to personal details that are meaningless to the clinician. The clang associations of some people with schizophrenia do not occur, in that the clinician never gains the feeling that the course of the utterance is dictated merely by the assonances of syllables, independent of their meaning. The greatest differential diagnostic difficulty may be with the flight of ideas characteristic of hypomania, the only difference often being the lack of resolute grandiosity or superiority characteristic of the utterances of someone with hypomania.

Anxiety and depression

The somatic symptoms of anxiety or depressive disorder are no different in people with an ASD than they are in neurotypicals. However, the feeling content of the mood disorder may not be volunteered. People with an ASD may also lack a sense that they have anything to complain of, and so may not draw clinical attention to their symptoms. The presenting symptom may therefore be a physical one, as in somatized depression, a worsening of their ASD symptoms, or a loss of their capacity to think clearly and so solve interpersonal problems. So far as other people are concerned mood disorder can present as irritability or aggression, withdrawal, lack of self-care, regression with the appearance of challenging behaviour, or a change in sleep or appetite.

Clinical assessment should be as for neurotypicals but with particular attention to change in behaviour, to autonomic symptoms, and to symptoms of cognitive function like speed of thought, concentration and memory.

Screening measures for anxiety and depression may be used to augment assessments. The GAD-7 (for anxiety) and the PHQ-9 (for depression) have been widely used in primary care settings and can be self-administered or completed by an informant (see Tables 10.7 and Table 10.8). They are free to use, and have been used to assess people with ASD in general practice.[119]

Table 10.7 Quick anxiety self-report

GAD-7				
Over the last 2 weeks, how often have you been bothered by the following problems? (Use ✓ to indicate your answer)	**Not at all**	**Several days**	**More than half the days**	**Nearly every day**
1. Feeling nervous, anxious or on edge				
2. Not being able to stop or control your worrying				
3. Worrying too much about different things				
4. Trouble relaxing				
5. Being so restless that it is hard to sit still				
6. Becoming easily annoyed or irritable				
7. Feeling afraid as if something awful might happen				

Source: Reproduced from Spitzer, Kroenke, *et al.*, 2006 with permission from PHQ Screeners.

Table 10.8 Quick self-report assessment of depression

PHQ-9				
Over the last 2 weeks, how often have you been bothered by the following problems? (Use ✓ to indicate your answer)	Not at all	Several days	More than half the days	Nearly every day
1. Little interest or pleasure in doing things	0	1	2	3
2. Feeling down, depressed or hopeless	0	1	2	3
3. Trouble falling or staying asleep, or sleeping too much	0	1	2	3
4. Feeling tired or having little energy	0	1	2	3
5. Poor appetite or overeating	0	1	2	3
6. Feeling bad about yourself – or that you are a failure or have let yourself or your family down	0	1	2	3
7. Trouble concentrating on things, such as reading the newspaper or watching television	0	1	2	3
8. Moving or speaking so slowly that other people could have noticed? Or the opposite – being so fidgety or restless that you have been moving around a lot more than usual	0	1	2	3
9. Thoughts that you would be better off dead or of hurting yourself in some way	0	1	2	3

If you checked off *any* problems, how *difficult* have these problems made it for you to do your work, take care of things at home, or get along with other people?

Not at all difficult	Somewhat difficult	Very difficult	Extremely difficult
☐	☐	☐	☐

Source: Reproduced from Kroenke, Spitzer, *et al.*, 2001 with permission from PHQ Screeners.

Anxiety-related disorders
Social phobia

Many people with an ASD avoid groups of people especially in unstructured social situations. Sometimes this is attributed to 'not knowing how to chat', at other times to the confusion that comes from the multiple interactions between people in a group. However, there is often an element of fear, too: either a fear of being negatively evaluated, or even just a fear of standing out in some way. Fears like this may grow imperceptibly from childhood shyness or social avoidance, or may develop in early adolescence, and be associated with a fear of performing in public at school – answering questions in class, for example. The fear may extend to hours or days before an anticipated social event – anticipatory anxiety – and elaborate preparations to cover up. There may be an association with a kind of body dysmorphic disorder in that fears may centre on some perceived blemish like anxiety, or easy and unusually extensive blushing, or tremor. Avoidance of social situations because of this social phobia may be a cause of disability, affecting attendance or performance at job interviews, for example, or at parties where people make new friends. It may be a considerable source of distress. Social phobia is particularly common in association with ASD in adolescence and is worth screening for if it is not volunteered. A simple screening test (the mini-SPIN) has been developed by Connor et al. (see Table 10.9).[120] A cut-off score of 19 has been reported to distinguish neurotypicals with and without social phobia.[120]

Table 10.9 The mini-SPIN: Screening for social phobia

'Fear of embarrassment causes me to avoid doing things or speaking to people'					
Not at all					Extremely
0	1	2	3	4	5
'I avoid activities in which I am the center of attention'					
Not at all					Extremely
0	1	2	3	4	5
'Being embarrassed or looking stupid are among my worst fears'					
Not at all					Extremely
0	1	2	3	4	5

Source: Connor, Davidson, *et al.*, 2000.

Table 10.10 Screening questions for OCD in young people

1. Do you wash or clean a lot?
2. Do you check things a lot?
3. Is there any thought that keeps bothering you that you would like to get rid of but cannot?
4. Do your daily activities take a long time to finish? (e.g. getting ready for school)
5. Are you concerned about putting things in a special order or are you very upset by mess?
6. Do these problems trouble you?

Source: MacNeill, Lopes, *et al.*, 2009.

Obsessive compulsive disorder

There is an increased risk of obsessive compulsive disorder in people with an ASD, in people with ADHD, and of ASD in people with an OCD. This is distinct from the phenomenological overlap between rituals and compulsions, particularly those in children with OCD who may not resist them so strongly. OCD is a manifestation of anxiety and makes an independent contribution to the burden of having ASD. It is therefore important to identify and, if appropriate, treat it. The Yale-Brown Obsessive-Compulsive Scale, or its childhood version, has been validated for use in people with an ASD.

OCD may be particularly likely to be missed in children and young teens, and MacNeill et al. suggest that a six-item screen may be useful (see Table 10.10).[121]

Panic disorder

Panic disorder may be particularly associated with situational phobias such as agoraphobia or social phobia.[122] Its key element is a fear of dying or loss of control, and a physical sensation that supports this such as becoming light-headed or dissociating. Extreme panic may lead to cataplexy,[123] or to 'freezing',[124] in those who are susceptible to this response to strong emotion, it is presumably this that links the condition to the one that the ancients attributed to the consequences of Pan blowing his pipes. Panic disorder is not particularly associated with ASD in my clinical experience, although it may follow from contact with terminal illness or death in early adolescence.

Disorders specific to childhood

Oppositional and conduct disorder

Difficult and challenging behaviour, leading to a diagnosis of oppositional or conduct disorder, is substantially more common in children with ADHD, and therefore in children with ASD and ADHD. Whether this amounts to co-morbidity, or is a reflection of an increased risk of struggles over autonomy and social influence, both of which may be problematic in people with an ASD, will depend on the extent to which these disorders are taken to be medical conditions rather than social ones.

Attachment disorders

In an important review of attachment disorder, Rutter et al. distinguish between patterns of attachment based on 'security' and patterns based on 'disorganization'.[125] The latter was originally recognized by Main (reviewed by her in 1996)[126] as being separate to the three main types described by Ainsworth et al.,[127] and named by them: secure, insecure/avoidant, and insecure/resistant. Rutter et al. provide considerable evidence that 'security' and 'disorganization' are orthogonal dimensions of children's relating.[125]

Security and ASD

'Security' is provided in many infant mammals by the physical proximity of an attachment figure, typically a mother. Infant animals or humans tend to range away from their mothers, and if startled will vocalize and move towards them. Mothers recognize the specific fear vocalization of their infant and move towards them. Only mothers, or carers, who are bonded or attached to the infant will do this, and maternal oxytocin levels when first viewing, touching or smelling their infant play an important role in making this bond happen.

A considerable literature about attachment, its frustration, and the role of oxytocin and the other known social neuropeptide, vasopressin,[128] has grown up (see Chapter 11).

Insecure attachment has regularly been linked to ASD and to ADHD. The hypothesized causal direction has sometimes been that developmental disorder leads to insecure attachment,[129] and sometimes the reverse, that insecure attachment can lead to ASD or ADHD. A third hypothesis is that insecure attachment and developmental disorder are both consequences of some common cause.

Oxytocin or vasopressin transmission alteration is an intriguing possible candidate as a cause of both insecure attachment, and of ASD,[130] as they are known to be associated with attachment.[131] Polymorphisms in OXTR, the gene for the oxytocin receptor, are associated with ASD[132] and, in neurotypicals, with emotional loneliness, emotionality and IQ.[133] Oxytocin snuff administration increases male empathizing in both neurotypicals and in people with an ASD. However other evidence points towards these hormones having a more general role as emotional switches as oxytocin snuff also increases envy and Schadenfreude.[134]

There is little evidence for a statistical association between security of attachment and ASD. This was assumed by the charismatic Bruno Bettelheim, whose now discredited work has left a lasting impression that there is such a link.[135] But the evidence does not support it. In a review of 16 other studies, children with autistic disorders and intellectual disability were found to be slightly less likely to be securely attached than their age peers, but other children with an ASD were found to be as likely to be securely attached.[136] The association of severe autistic disorder with insecure attachment is more likely to be explained on the basis that a multiplicity of communication deficits obstructs the process of attachment, rather than that insecurity causes this type of ASD – although insecure attachment obviously may affect children with ASD as much as it affects neurotypical children. Secure attachment in a study of adults also occurred with the same frequency as in a 'general clinical sample'.[137] Other relevant evidence has come from studies of children brought up from early infancy in under-resourced orphanages where they had no consistent carer and where they were separated from their mothers. However, Rutter et al., who have conducted a considerable amount of research on both ASD and institutional rearing, conclude on the basis of a review of the evidence (summarized in their article) that attachment security is much harder to assess, and possibly less valid, after the age of three or four, when children show less urgency about being reunited with their parents after a separation (the paradigm used in the Strange Situation Test).[125] Children may also switch from one attachment style to another during infancy and early childhood, making it less likely that there is an attachment 'style'. Finally, although there is a correlation between mother's sensitivity to distress in their children and the child's security, it is a weak one.

Rutter et al. conclude that security should not be routinely assessed in clinical practice 'because it is only satisfactorily valid in the first 2–3 years and because security/insecurity is of quite limited psychopathological significance' and it should not be used to assess social relationships in autism 'because social functioning in autism is not conceptualised in terms of insecurity'.[125]

Separation anxiety and ASD

Beyond the age of three or four years, normally developing children show much less response to parents after separation, a fact that makes it harder to assess their behaviour and so determine attachment style. Children have longer and longer periods away from parents – at school, or on visits – after this age, normally without marked separation anxiety. However, anxiety persists in some children, including some children with ASD, and in people with ASD and intellectual disability it may persist into adolescence or adulthood. The relationship between attachment style and separation anxiety in ASD in older children has not been studied, but separation anxiety is more likely to be an expression of overall anxiety levels than of any particular characteristic of early development.[138]

Reactive attachment disorder

Reactive attachment disorder has previously been attributed to emotional abuse or neglect. It may lead to a predominantly inhibited or a predominantly disinhibited pattern of behaviour. Inhibited reactive attachment disorder, at least in follow-up studies of orphanage-reared children, remits after the child moves to a suitable adoptive home, but disinhibited attachment persists.[125] Rutter *et al.* argue that there is an inherent impairment in the child preventing them from selectively prioritizing some relationships and thus recognizing appropriate 'attachment figures' or, to avoid restricting the important relationship to security, to appropriate caring figures.[125] It has been speculated that disinhibited reactive attachment may be a prodrome of ADHD, and some evidence exists for the first signs of ADHD being present at the age of three in some children.[139]

Rutter *et al.* distinguish disinhibited reactive attachment from the 'deviant social reciprocity of autism',[125] but in practice the distinction between atypical autism and disinhibited reactive attachment disorder may be difficult to make.

Assessing parenting

A forensic issue that is often posed to child psychiatrists is whether a child with impaired social relationships and a mother at the end of her tether, is impaired because of mother's over-arousal – which may often be associated with breaks in the relationship with the child, or other family difficulties – or whether the child has an innate ASD that is contributing to mother's relationship difficulties. The conclusion from Rutter's review must be that security of attachment is not a useful way of looking at this problem, but that a broader conception of formative social relationship to include 'disorganization' or the selectivity of attachments is much more useful.[125]

Children with inhibited reactive attachment respond well to a change to a suitable, stable and caring environment and this pattern of relating strongly suggests that parenting does play a part. Psychoeducation for parents can also reduce the severity of reactive attachment disorder.[140]

Disorganized attachment disorder seems to be more likely to be a problem originating in the child's ability to attach selectively to a main, and reliable, carer. It has been suggested that it is an early manifestation of ADHD.[141] Although little definite is known as yet about the aetiology of disorganized attachment, it is premature to assume that it is the consequence of dysfunctional parenting, or to assume that fostering will solve the problem.

Assessment of relationship security

There are two generally accepted research measures for assessing attachment styles: the Strange Situation Paradigm (SSP) in children and the Adult Attachment Interview (AAI).[142] Neither can be considered to be valid tools in clinical assessment.[125]

INTELLECTUAL DISABILITY

Intellectual disability is, like the disability of ASD, a socio-medical judgement about whether a person's social or personal functioning is impaired by reduced intelligence. The UK General Medical Council was once asked to determine whether a doctor with a measured intelligence of 80 was intellectually disabled, and therefore not fit to practise. The cut-off point for intellectual disability is generally taken to be an IQ of 70 as measured on an appropriate test. But when it comes to an intellectual activity like medical practice, where convention has it that a student is expected to have an IQ of over 115 to graduate, does 80 constitute a sufficient impairment that amounts to a disability to practise? In other circumstances, even an IQ of 70 may not constitute a disability. However, although intellectual disability is a clinical judgement, it has to be based on an accurate estimate of IQ.

Clinicians may sometimes get an idea about intelligence from speed of grasp or from the complexity of ideas that an interviewee uses. But informal assessment of intelligence is notoriously unreliable, because it is so readily affected by prejudice, by education, by culture, by the use of language, and by the rapport between the interviewer and the interviewee. Nonverbal intelligence is often difficult to estimate at interview, and may be much higher than conversational skill suggests. In people with an ASD who have a special interest, the nature of this can be a useful guide to intelligence. The special interests of people with lower than average intelligence may simply be to collect and carry round ordinary objects, such as pebbles. Average intelligence is more likely to be associated with a special interest involving collecting informative materials, like timetables or maps, and listing or rote learning facts. People of more than average intelligence often like to collect concepts or ideas by memorizing them, and are often expert in their own field of interest.

Intellectual disability may add to the disability of ASD. So if there is any question about its presence, formal assessments of IQ need to be carried out. Conventional tests, such as the WAIS or the WISC, are as valid in people with ASD who have language as they are in the normal population. Performance components of these tests may be used in people with ASD who have no useful language.

FAMILY OR RELATIONSHIP FACTORS

Negative assessments of family factors, to which ASD used to be attributed, were routine during the 1970s but standardized family measures were not developed specifically to assess these. The evidence against family factors has become so strong that there has been no incentive to develop particular measures or even to systematically examine family functioning. Measures developed for any family, such as the Family Environment Scale, have not been shown to be scored differently when applied to the families of children with ASD than when applied to the children of neurotypicals.[143] One measure developed for schizophrenia, that of expressed emotion (see Chapter 9), may be applicable in the families of people with an

ASD to assess factors that may be creating emotional strain, leading to exacerbation of the secondary disability.

PHYSICAL ASSESSMENT

There are no anatomical abnormalities that are characteristic of uncomplicated ASD, with the possible exception of macrocephaly in children, but a substantial minority of people with an ASD have, in addition, a genetic condition (see Chapter 11 for chromosomal disorders, and Chapter 12 for named syndromes) that does have a characteristic anatomy. Physical examination, with an assessment of the skin, examination of the heart, and a simple neurological examination should normally be carried out on a person who is suspected of having an ASD, but who has not had a previous physical assessment. Microcephaly or macrocephaly are indicators of the presence of many of these genetic conditions, and head measurement should routinely be included in the assessment of children newly presenting with an ASD. Miles *et al.* estimate that the combination of microcephaly and soft signs has an 87 per cent specificity, although only a 47 per cent sensitivity, for complex ASD or ASD in which there is no family history.[144]

The requirements (and arrangements) for a physical examination will vary depending on age, and will be considered in the appropriate section in later chapters. Even if a formal physical examination is not carried out, careful observation throughout the assessment may identify signs of dyspraxia, including unusual gait,[145] and dysmorphia. Facial asymmetry is not an uncommon finding, and may indicate underlying frontal lobe asymmetry.[146] Facial dysmorphia may be an important clue to the presence of a named syndrome. There are anthropometric measures that can be used to determine the likely identity of the syndrome,[147] but familiarity with the characteristic facies (characteristic facial appearance) is the best method of detection, and it is unlikely that few clinicians who are not practising clinical geneticists will obtain this. Many dysmorphic syndromes are not yet genetically characterized, but if a person has an obviously unusual facies, particularly if it is associated with other indications of dysmorphia such as accessory toes or a branchial cyst and there is little resemblance to other family members, then a referral to a clinical geneticist may be indicated.

Assessment of the physical condition should include a medical examination in young children, and if there is any indication in the history suggestive of a related physical disorder. Head size, skin lesions and dysmorphia may all be indications of 'complex ASD' secondary to a rare or a named syndrome and should form part of a physical examination.

Head circumference

Head size should be measured at its largest circumference, usually above the ears and midway between the eyebrows and the hairline in the front, and over the occipital prominence at the back. A clean, unworn or disposable tape made for this purpose should be used,[148] and a standard procedure followed, for example that extant at Great Ormond Street Hospital in London. Height and weight should also be measured and noted down at the same time on centile charts (special charts exist for children with achondroplasia) using the child's decimal age. Head circumference stops increasing in the early teens, and later adolescent and adult head circumferences can be noted on the final age band of the child centile chart.

The procedure for adults is described in the *Handbook of Physical Measurements*.[149]

Table 10.11 Skin appearance characteristic of some physical disorders associated with ASD

Tuberous sclerosis	Periungual fibromata	Smooth firm papules emerging after puberty from skin folds
	Angio-fibromas	Papules containing leashes of blood vessels which may be white or skin coloured, occurring in nasolabial folds, on cheeks and on chin. May become nearly confluent by puberty, but do not increase thereafter. May be mistaken for acne vulgaris
	Shagreen patches	Soft, flesh coloured plaques often in lumbosacral area that are slightly raised and may resemble untanned leather or pigskin with large pores (the openings of enlarged hair follicles)
	Café au lait spots	Flat areas of reddish brown pigmentation up to 2 cm long
	White macules	Ovoid or shaped like ash leaves, hypopigmented areas that may be present at birth and therefore may be the earliest signs of TS. Count 3 or more as likely to be abnormal (1 or 2 normal in a neonate). White macules fluoresce in ultraviolet (UV) light at the 365 nm wavelength. A source of UV, such as a Wood's lamp, should be used to examine the skin if no macules are visible
Tuberous sclerosis and neurofibromatosis	Café au lait spots	Irregular splashes of hyperpigmentation
Neurofibromatosis	Freckling in moist skin areas	
	Soft nodules or tumours under the skin	Fibromas due to overgrowth of Schwann cells adjacent to nerves and spreading to surrounding tissue
Hypomelanosis of Ito	Patchy hypopigmentation of skin along Blaschko lines	Swirls of skin pigmentation, particularly in girls, preceded by blisters, then warty papules, then hyperpigmentation, and finally hypopigmentation, depigmentation of the iris, and nests of abnormally primitive cells in the brain May also be associated with strabismus and scoliosis (see also Chapter 12)

Note: For a visual representation of these physical disorders please see www.dermatlas.com/derm and search for the relevant disorder.

Skin examination

The skin should be examined for the neurocutaneous features of tuberous sclerosis, neurofibromatosis and hypomelanosis. The parent or the person with an ASD should be asked if they have noticed any odd patches on their skin to guide the search. Roughening ('shagreen patches') hypopigmented spots or swirls, hyperpigmented 'café au lait' spots, or angiofibromatosis nodules are all relevant (see Table 10.11 and Figure 10.1).

Dysmorphia facies

The parts of the face that are often included in descriptions of dysmorphic facies are shown in Figure 10.1.

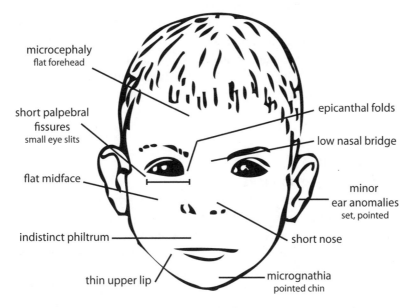

Figure 10.1 Face of a child with foetal alcohol syndrome showing some of the common anomalies in facial development (dysmorphias)

Other possible dysmorphic features of the face include an increased distance between the eyes ('hypertelorism'), or a slant in the transverse axis of the orbit (Mongolian or antiMongolian slant).

Other dysmorphic non-facial features

Other features include webbing of the digits, extra digits, flexion deformity of the interphalangeal joints ('camptodactyly'), adventitious nipples, abnormal fingerprints (with fewer loops and more whorls), and reduced palmar creases (the fusion of the 'heart' and the 'head' lines leading to a single deep palmar 'transverse' or 'simian' line is particularly associated with rare genetic syndromes). Reference texts (some with CDs of images) exist to help clinicians to identify genetic syndromes by reference to specific dysmorphic characteristics. No software exists to analyse faces although this may be developed in the future.

Motor function: clumsiness and topographical disorientation

Clumsiness is particularly associated with Asperger syndrome (see Chapter 7). Full assessment of motor function is best carried out by suitably trained and experienced occupational or physiotherapists, whose contribution may not only include simply providing information about ability levels but also, at least in the future, will provide information about clinical useful subtypes of ASD.[150]

Useful information about functional impairment can often be obtained by focused history taking, for example about asking about performance in sport, bicycle riding, or car driving. Dyspraxia can be tested by asking someone to repeat a complex, meaningless gesture; by testing eye–hand coordination by throwing a ball of paper backwards and forwards; by the standard neurological finger–nose test (the patient touching the tip of the examiner's finger with the index finger of their dominant hand and then the tip of their nose, and then the examiner's finger, which will have been moved, and so on); or by standing on one foot with the eyes open (in children) or closed (in adults).[151] If cerebellar dysfunction is suspected, for example by an inability to rapidly supinate and pronate the wrist (dysdiadochokinesis), the latter test can be preceded by simply asking a person to stand still with their feet together and their eyes closed. Swaying, which may be severe enough to force the person to take a step, is an indication of ataxia.

Sensory abnormalities
Abnormal sensory responses

People with an ASD may experience both hyper- and hypoacusis, and this may continue throughout life.[152] It may be due to altered higher level processing of sensation, for example its representation in sensory cortex, which may be altered in ASD,[153] or in focusing attention. It may also be due to differences in the sense organs themselves or in their first level of processing, that is true differences in acuity. There is some evidence of the latter.[154] Infants with marked sensory symptoms (either hyper- or hypoacusis) are likely to be unhappy or distressed,[155] compared with those who have few sensory difficulties. Other studies have suggested that the altered sensitivity is central. In one study, children with an ASD had heightened pain sensation but normal temperature sense, and heightened vibration sense but normal light touch sense.[156] Since light touch and vibration are carried by the same nerve fibres, and temperature and pain are also carried together, but in a different group of smaller fibres, this suggests that the differential sensitivity occurs at central level, where temperature and pain, light touch and vibration, are discriminated.

In clinical practice, where hyperacuity is causing distress or behavioural problems, testing is rarely of value, often failing to confirm a low sensory threshold. Systematic assessments, such as the Infant Toddler Sensory Profile,[157] are however used by occupational therapists and others if a comprehensive assessment is required. A 60-item questionnaire for adults to report sensory responses has been developed: the Adult/Adolescent Sensory Profile (AASP).[158]

Hyperaesthesia, or heightened sensitivity to touch, may occur in association with other developmental disorders such as ADHD as well as depression, and may also occur as an isolated symptom in neurotypical children or adults.[159]

Insensitivity to pain may also be shown by people with an ASD and may lead to a failure to spot surgical emergencies. In my own experience, I have failed to diagnose a greenstick fracture in a girl with ASD who had no abnormal movement in her arm, and did not appear to feel pain over the swelling that turned out to overlie the fracture. Another of my patients had acute torsion of the testis for several hours before even complaining of pain.

Hypoacusis may indicate sensory impairment and should be tested in the usual way, by simple tests of hearing (hearing the tick of a watch, or the hum of a tuning fork), vision, using standard charts, or sensation by mapping light touch sensitivity. A possible impairment should lead to referral to the appropriate hospital department or clinic for standardized testing so long as the person with ASD consents and is willing to participate in the assessment. There is no indication for testing someone against their will, but there is sometimes doubt that the testee is responding accurately. Some assessment of this can be made by observing a person's spontaneous actions in a setting in which they have to respond to sensory input. Hearing can also be tested using evoked potential responses as a proxy of having heard the test stimulus.

The range of altered sensation in ASD is shown in Table 10.12.

Table 10.12 Altered sensation in ASD

Sensory modality	Heightened	Diminished
Taste	Food fads: aversion to foods with prominent textures, such as 'slimy foods', dislike of blended tastes so meat must be separated from vegetables on plate	
Hearing	Aversion or distress to loud or high pitched sounds; possibly fascination by particular soft or soothing sounds. Rage when hearing particular sounds like father's breathing, brass bands, ice-cream vans	Reduced attentiveness to others, difficulty in echoing spaces, or where there are lots of different conversational strands
Sight	Distress in environments where there are particular colours or combinations of colours; problems with bright, fluorescent lights. Fascinations with flashing lights	Flapping in front of eyes, hitting eyes
Proprioception and vestibular stimulation		Toleration of heights, fast movement (e.g. fairground rides)
Touch	Aversion to certain textures such as wool, 'constriction', new clothes or starched clothes. Fascination with smoothness or silkiness. May carry around a 'silky'	Unawareness of cuts or bruises

SLEEP PROBLEMS

Sleep is often affected in people with an ASD, with sleep delay and reduced sleep efficiency (i.e. more waking) being characteristic. Sleep latency is a persistent complaint in people with ASD.[160, 161] Some people with ASD report that they do not feel ready to go to bed at a particular time (although others may have a ritual about exactly when they go to bed).

One very self-aware student thought that his ideal day length was about 30 hours, and if he could go to bed when he felt tired, he slept well, although often for 10 or 12 hours. Following a sleep like that, he would not feel tired again for about 20 hours, but this meant that he would sometimes be sleeping at night, and sometimes in the day. As a student, he could study at home in this rhythm, but not attend lectures or tutorials, or fit in with his girlfriend's routine.

There is research evidence to support the hypothesis that some people with an ASD are not on the 23.5 hour rhythm that governs much of the endocrine status of neurotypicals. Altered expression in 15 genes concerned with circadian rhythm has been found in those with severe ASD compared to neurotypicals,[162] along with altered expressivity in 20 genes that may be associated with androgen sensitivity. Pineal melatonin secretion is linked to, and possibly controls, the circadian rhythm,[163] and people with ASD typically have low levels of melatonin when compared to neurotypical controls, although not always when compared to people with intellectual disability.[164] Polymorphisms in the gene encoding acetylserotonin O-methyltransferase (ASMT), the enzyme involved in the last step of melatonin synthesis which is located on chromosome 22, confer a high risk of ASD.[165] In support of the association of sleep disturbance and severity, the greatest sleep disturbances (reported on a questionnaire in another study)[166] were found in the children with ASD who also had epilepsy. Although the evidence that the circadian rhythm is disturbed in people with ASD, and that is the cause of their sleep disturbance, treatment with melatonin is only rarely effective in my experience.

Sleep disturbance may become a source of concern for carers, affect daytime behaviour in younger children,[167] and lead to compensatory daytime sleep in older children and adolescents that may interfere with the activities of daily life. Short sleep is associated with late bedtimes, obesity, and emotional lability in children.[168]

Sleep may be additionally affected by co-morbid conditions, with ADHD being the most common. People with an ASD who have marked insomnia or parasomnia merit careful assessment partly because this may indicate the presence of a treatable co-morbid disorder.

Impact on sleep of co-morbid disorders
ADHD

Contrary to expectation, sleep disturbance affects only a minority (36%) of pre-schoolers as reported by their parents, and an even smaller number of these children have sleep abnormalities of sufficient severity to be demonstrable in the sleep laboratory.[169] However, as the children get older, sleep duration shortens with a particular loss of REM sleep.[170] There is an increased rate of ADHD in obese children, and a proportion of children with ADHD who are overweight report snoring and increased waking during the night, which is confirmed on polysomnography.[171] There are greater dips in pO_2 (oxygen available to the blood) in this group too,[171] compared to neurotypicals and other children with ADHD. Perceived insomnia, sleep terrors, nightmares, restless legs and bruxism are also more common in adolescents with ADHD,[172] particularly if there is an additional problem of anxiety.[173] The frequency of sleep disturbance was not influenced by the prescription of methylphenidate in the latter study,[173] but in other studies, sleep latency has been found to be increased in children taking methylphenidate.[174, 175] Children with the inattentive subtype of ADHD were not found to have sleep difficulties in this latter study,[175] and sleep disorder was noted to be more severe in hyperactive and combined types of ADHD in another.[172]

Anxiety

Sleep disturbance is a sensitive indication of mood disorder in children.[176] Anxiety may worsen sleep latency and frequent waking. In adolescents, this may be concealed by staying up later, and then sleeping in. This tactic may be adopted to reduce REM sleep, which can often be associated with anxiety dreams, although in the long run it can lead to REM pressure and an increase in anxiety dreams. Those antidepressants that suppress REM may be helpful, although they may also increase REM-sleep-related 'behaviour disorder'.[177, 178]

Depression

Depression in people with an ASD has identical somatic symptoms to depression in neurotypicals. Recent onset early morning waking may therefore be an indication of depression.

Bipolar disorder

People with an ASD are at greater risk of bipolar disorder. Early morning waking may be the earliest indication of this, particularly of the hypomanic phase of the disorder. Sleep disturbance may be one of the earliest means of differentiating bipolar disorder and ADHD,[179] may be an indication of future frank BPD in those at genetic risk,[180] and is a sensitive sign of impending relapse in many people with established BPD.

Assessment

Self-report, parental report in children and laboratory measurement may all be used to provide information about sleep, although with differential emphasis. Self-report provides the best information about wakefulness during the night and the following day, parental report often focuses on behaviour disturbance attributed to poor sleep, and laboratory measures about the quantity of different sleep stages.[181]

There is rarely an indication for laboratory measurement in clinical practice, but if this is performed then actigraphy (measuring movement) can be conducted at home, but polysomnography, that is simultaneous, poly channel EEG, electrocardiogram (ECG) and electromyogram (EMG) recording before and during sleep with video recording to measure sleep movements requires the attachment of many more recording leads. It can be carried out at home,[182] but may, in addition, require sleeping in a sleep laboratory, with all the attendant disruption to sleep that this may cause. Polysomnography also requires trained personnel to interpret the EEG recordings so that sleep stages and their duration can be marked.

More structured information about sleep can be provided by giving parents or older children diaries to complete, or by using questionnaires such as the Children's Sleep Habits Questionnaire.[183]

Coda: is there an alternative to clinical assessment?

The brains of people with an ASD are different from neurotypicals, as has been discussed in detail in Chapters 1 and 2. This difference is unlikely to be localized, since it is most likely to be due to a difference in connectivity. New methods of neuroimaging that can visualize white matter are being developed, but are not widespread or cheap. However, Murphy *et al.* have argued that connectivity can be inferred from biomarkers, of which two are available now, or so it is argued. These are the proportional volume of connected areas of the brain, especially if information about how these proportions change during development, and the relative concentrations of transmitters such as serotonin, dopamine and glutamate.[184]

Murphy *et al.* use a trained neural network, instantiated on a computer, to make the assignment.[184] However, training neural networks is open to the same problems as training people: the training criterion has to be correct, and the number of instances where this criterion is applicable has to be large enough.[185] Computer aided diagnosis is becoming increasingly important in medicine, but it remains an aid to diagnosis, rather than a replacement for it.[186] One, and probably ineluctable, reason for this is that diagnoses are classifications of whole person function. ASD is only a disorder because of its functional effects and although the function of the brain may be strongly correlated with personal and social functioning, there is no one-to-one correspondence except, that is, for the epiphenomenalist.

Chapter 11

AETIOLOGY OF THE AUTISM SPECTRUM DISORDERS

INTRODUCTION

There are very many conditions that have been found to be associated with the ASDs (see Table 11.1) and some of these are discussed in more detail in this chapter. Findings from clinical associations and epidemiology, including genetic epidemiology, are mixed together because there is no method for determining currently which are chance findings, which are consequences of some other, unknown, factor that is independently causing the ASD, and which will turn out to really be causes. A few apparent causes of ASD may turn out to be consequences. For example, for many years I have been asking parents whether or not their child had a circumcision for medical reasons. This was because there seemed to be a disproportionate number of children who had had that operation in my first cases. The rate has continued to be high, but it occurred to me after some time that comfort behaviour in infants with an ASD might include handling the penis, leading to an increased risk of inflammation, and that may be the explanation for this apparent association. Better knowledge than we currently have about the developmental pathways that lead to the ASDs will be required to determine what are truly causes.

The likelihood of medical conditions being associated with an ASD increases by a factor of up to nine when AS is compared to autistic disorder associated with intellectual disability.[1] One possible explanation of this is that this kind of 'complex' autistic disorder is the consequence of more genes being inoperative or genes of larger effect being inoperative than in Asperger syndrome, and these genes having an effect on non-neural as well as on neural tissue.

The classification that I have used for aetiological factors reflects the likely onset of the presumed aetiological factor, or its first clinical presentation, if that is not known. This may not be the time at which its effects on the child first manifest. For example, girls with defective MECP2 genes from conception develop symptoms of Rett syndrome only after the first few months of life.

Table 11.1 Rare syndromes associated with autism spectrum disorders and ADHD

Trigonocephaly with compression of the frontal lobes[2]
Mucopolysaccharidosis (Sanfilippo syndrome)[3, 4]
Cohen syndrome (a connective tissue disorder)[5]
Goldenhar syndrome[6]
West syndrome, especially where there is paroxysmal EEG frontal focus in infancy[7]
In-vitro fertilization by intracytoplasmic sperm injection[8]
Facial-port wine stain syndrome[9]
Very low birthweight[10]
Mitochondrial disorder[11]
Oculoauriculovertebral spectrum[12] including CHARGE syndrome (Coloboma, Heart Defect, Atresia Choanae, Retarded Growth and Development, Genital Hypoplasia, Ear Anomalies/ Deafness)[13, 12]
Macrocephaly[14] including megaloencephalies such as Sotos syndrome,[15] personal observation
Pachydermodactyly[16]
Congenital viral infections e.g. cytomegalovirus (CMV) infection[17] and congenital rubella
Brain folate deficiency,[18] creatine deficiency[19]
Moebius syndrome[20] although possibly not in the absence of learning disability[21]
Infantile spasms and bilateral temporal hypometabolism,[22] infantile encephalopathy[23]
*Neurofibromatosis type 1[24]
*Cerebral palsy[25, 26]
Sensory impairments[27] esp. congenital amaurosis,[28] retinopathy of prematurity[29] and possibly other causes of congenital blindness (personal observation). Idiopathic nystagmus,[30] personal observation
Muscle disorders, such as infantile hypotonia;[31] myotonic,[32] (personal observation) and other dystrophies[33] including Duchenne muscular dystrophy[34] and *Becker muscular dystrophy[35]
Tuberous sclerosis[36]
Hypomelanosis of Ito[37] and another hypomelanotic disorder, oculocutaneous syndrome with alibinism[38]
Inborn metabolic errors, e.g. errors in purine or pyrimidine metabolism,[39] Schindler disease (N-acteyl glucosaminidase deficiency),[40] biotinidase deficiency,[41] aminoacidurias,[42] e.g. phenylketonuria,[43] steroid sulfatase deficiency,[44] aminoacidurias,[42] e.g. phenylketonuria,[43] succinic semialdehyde dehydrogenase,[45] D-glyceric aciduria,[42] L-2-Hydroxyglutaric aciduria[46]
Infantile hydrocephalus[47]

Down syndrome[48]
Disorders of X chromosome including fragile X syndrome,[49] deletion of sulfatase and neuroligin genes,[44] *Turner syndrome where X chromosome is of maternal origin;[50] ring X chromosome;[51] *Aarskog syndrome,[52] *X-linked ichthyosis[44]
Cerebellar hypoplasias,[53] e.g. juvenile dentatorubral-pallidoluysian atrophy[54]
Agenesis of the corpus callosum[55]
Cowden syndrome[56]
Chromosome 22q13 deletion (Phelan-Macdiarmid) syndrome

*Also associated with ADHD

FACTORS PRESENT AT CONCEPTION
Biological sex

Many more boys and men are diagnosed with an ASD than girls or women. Male to female ratios are lower in previously undiagnosed adolescents and adults with an ASD who are identified in community surveys,[57] and it has been suggested by some that the reported excess of males is an artefact of preferential diagnosis in men. However, although this may be a part explanation, it seems unlikely to be the full explanation. Other frontostriatal disorders in which the connections between prefrontal cortex and the remainder of the brain are abnormal – Tourette syndrome, ADHD, and process or early onset schizophrenia, for example – are also more common in males. This led Geschwind and Galaburda to propose that the excess of males is caused by an increase in foetal testosterone, preventing the synaptic pruning that is normal during embryogenesis.[58] In one series, the male to female ratio in those with 'idiopathic autism' – those who had normal brain MRIs and no physical anomalies on examination – was much higher at 23:1.[59]

Females with ASD are reported in several studies to be more likely to have intellectual disability or epilepsy than males, suggesting that complex ASD may show a lower male to female sex ratio and that, conversely, the highest ratio of males to female ratio occurs in essential ASD. This could be attributed to X-linked recessive polymorphisms that are only penetrant in males, but also be attributable to testosterone, whose synthetic enzyme and receptor protein are both located on the Y chromosome.

The evidence for sexual dimorphism in the human brain is strong, and continues to accumulate.[60] There is also strong evidence that foetally produced testosterone plays an important part in creating this dimorphism, either directly or through hereditary differences in the androgen receptor. Tandem repeats (defined in Chapter 3) of CAG within the gene of this receptor lead to polyglutamine chains within the receptor whose length determines its receptivity.

Sexual dimorphism of the brain may be one cause of gender differences in behaviour after birth[61] although neuroscientists have been criticized for too readily arguing from brain findings to observed behaviour.[62]

One theory of ASD, the extreme male brain theory, is that foetuses that have been exposed to particularly high levels of testosterone are likely to go on to develop ASD. This view has been put particularly strongly by Baron-Cohen and his group who argue that: 1) male and female brains differ; 2) the difference can be attributed to testosterone levels in utero; 3) the difference has psychological implications that can be tested using measures of what he terms 'systemizing' and 'empathizing'; and 4) ASD is the result of an extreme variant of the male brain in which systemizing ability is particularly high, and empathizing particularly low. Points 1, 3 and 4 have been considered in recent reviews by Yamasue *et al.*[63] and also Baron-Cohen *et al.*[64]

Reduced empathizing in men is a crucial step in the extreme male brain theory. However, there are other possible explanations for this, of which one of the strongest is the oxytocin theory, based on differences in the nonapeptide hormones, oxytocin and vasopressin, between men and women.[65]

Oxytocin snuff increases social perception and empathizing performance in women[66] and in men,[67] including men with an ASD,[68] suggesting that the reduced empathizing in these two groups is due to structural brain changes, as suggested by the testosterone exposure theory, but functional differences.

A quite different explanation of better empathizing in women is provided by feminism and queer theory. Women are, at least in patriarchal societies, brought up to avoid direct confrontation with men. Women have, if they are to succeed in this, to be especially skilled at reading the signs of anger in the face. Another group, who have to be alert to hostility or rejection in the male face, are gay men, who are still subject to 'gay bashing' even in the least homophobic societies. If it were socialization and not the Y chromosome, or testosterone in the womb, that reduced men's ability to read facial cues, then gay men would be expected to be no better than other men at reading emotions in the face. But in fact, they are significantly better than heterosexual men at face recognition memory, and also at other cognitive tasks where women often show superiority over men. This and similar studies may, however, be confounded by laterality.[69]

The possible contribution of testosterone and oxytocin to the aetiology of ASD is discussed later in this chapter.

Heritability

Estimates of the contribution of heredity to the ASDs can be made from twin studies. Using a broad measure of ASD (Childhood Autism Rating Scale scores), heritability rates of 0.73 for boys and 0.87 in girls were found in one study.[70] In another study, of 277 twin pairs, the concordance rate in monozygotic twins was 88 per cent and for dizygotic twins was 31 per cent, and the concordance rate in MZ girl twins was higher than that in boys at 100 per cent. MZ concordant twins were more likely to have AS, and also bipolar disorder.[71] Similar although lower results were found in a community twin study in Europe.[72] Lower estimates of heritability are reported in a 2011 twin study,[73] mainly due to much higher rates of concordance in dizygotic twins, indicating that shared environment was more important than found in earlier studies (contributing to 58% of the variance), with proportionately lower estimates of heritability (38%) that were much the same when either narrow or broader ASD diagnostic criteria were used and much the same, too, in male and female twins.

The heritability of ADHD, again using a continuous self-report measure but this time the Conner's questionnaire, was estimated to be of the same order of magnitude in a large UK twin study: 0.88 for hyperactive-impulsive scores, and 0.79 for inattentive scores.[74]

The heritability shared between autistic traits and ADHD is also of the same order of magnitude, 0.72.[75]

High heritability means, in practice, that only about one in two people with AS have an affected family member, usually in the male line.[76] My clinical experience is that a far higher proportion has a sporadic ASD, that is the number of newly diagnosed individuals with a family history is substantially less than half. Iacobini et al. followed up children born to families who already had at least two children with an ASD.[77] These new additions had a 0.46 risk of developing an ASD (subject to sampling bias) if they were boys, but the risk was only 0.15 if they were girls.[78] The authors conclude that girls have some protective factor that reduces the penetrance of that autism genotype to a third, but that the genotype itself is dominant and almost fully penetrant in boys. However, these strongly familial cases of ASD, in which almost all of the males in a family are affected, make a disproportionate contribution to the heritability estimates of the whole population of people with ASD, meaning that sporadic cases can still be in the majority without much reducing heritability estimates. Sporadic cases, occurring in simplex families, may be the consequence of CNVs that are not inherited from parents, may be the consequence of some other biological effect on brain development, or be explained by a two-factor theory of ASD: that a genetic predisposition and a subsequent event or environmental factor are both required.

Genetic causes of ASD

The genetic contribution to ASD is consistent with the increased risk in children of older fathers, and mothers.[79] This risk is not specific to ASD but extends to schizophrenia and, more widely, to impaired social functioning in the absence of known disorder conditions.[80] Modelling suggests that increasing father's age makes an independent contribution in conceptions where the mother is younger than 30, but in older mothers the risk is entirely accounted for by maternal age at conception, with each year of age adding further risk.[81] Shelton et al. estimate that the tendency of Californians to have older children has increased the risk of their having a child with ASD by 4.6 per cent.[81] However, it should be noted that this inference is based on cross-sectional associations, and it may also be possible that an increasing prevalence of ASD has resulted in later marriages and therefore later conceptions.

Family history

Some reported associations in the family history may be consequences of caring for someone with an ASD, known to increase the risk of maternal depression.[82] Others may be the consequence of the family member having a degree of the index disorder in the proband, for example mothers of children with ADHD who also have ADHD themselves have an increased risk of alcohol abuse.[83] The relationship between these factors may be even more complex since drinking during pregnancy may increase the risk of ADHD developing.

Family history may be relevant to understanding the clinical picture in ASD in that it can provide information about relevant co-morbidity. Anxiety disorders have an increased prevalence in all of the ASDs (see Chapter 10), and have themselves a strong hereditary component,[84] and possibly, too, an increased transgenerational transmission because of parenting styles.

Record linkage studies suggest an association between parental schizophrenia and having a child with autism,[85] but these data, although numerous, are open to selection bias, as children with autism were identified through hospital records. Parental diagnosis was also based on hospital records and not confirmed by research assessment.

Bipolar disorder

Bipolar disorder, which may be genetically linked to schizophrenia,[86, 87] occurs more commonly in my clinic population than expected by chance, and family history studies suggest a non-random association.[88] A link with bipolar disorder is more reliably established and there is an increased risk of bipolar disorder in people with an ASD too, particularly those who do not have an autistic disorder.[89]

Genetic association of ASD and ADHD

There is an increased risk of ASD traits in siblings of children with ADHD,[90] and, as has been mentioned in earlier chapters, siblings and parents (fathers in the case of ASD, both parents in the case of ADHD) of probands with ASD have psychological impairments similar to those of the proband, suggesting that ASD traits are more widely distributed in families and not confined to diagnosed individuals.

Wider ASD phenotype

Dyslexia and language delay have been considered in the past to be part of a wider autistic phenotype,[91] on the basis that these were increased in prevalence in the family members of probands with an ASD. The wider ASD phenotype may include lack of affection, social difficulties and lack of friends, reduced play or shared interests, language delay and speech abnormalities, dyslexia, repetitive behaviour, circumscribed interests, rigidity and, possibly, anxiety proneness.[92] Even this list does not include the increasing number of cognitive and communicative abnormalities, many of them discussed in previous chapters, which are more common in siblings or parents, too, abnormal attention to eyes being one of the earliest discoverable.[93] Up to now, there has been no redefinition of the wider ASD phenotype to take these into account, although social cognition would seem to be central to it.[94] One proxy measure might be the Social Responsiveness Scale, which correlates with a standard symptom measure of autism spectrum disorder.[95] Total scores on this scale are distributed leptokurtotically with no trough between the mean and the most extreme score. The genetics of ASD would therefore be similar to those of intellectual disability,[96] and of hypertension.[97]

Another approach to the wider phenotype has been to include siblings, fathers or parents in tests that have been shown to have non-neurotypical results in individuals with ASD. Impairments of smooth eye tracking have been consistently reported in family members of a person with a frontostriatal disorder, such as schizophrenia or ASD. Mosconi et al.[98] report, for example, that saccadic eye movements (when the gaze 'jumps' to a new target of attention) are more likely to fall short and to require conscious correction in first-degree relatives of people with autism than in the relatives of neurotypical controls.[98] The ASD relatives also showed more executive difficulties.[98]

It is less clear whether there are one or two wider ADHD genotypes. Some twin studies suggest that there are two: inattentiveness, and inattentiveness with overactivity.[99]

Sources of genetic variation

Genes may also be activated, or repressed, as a result of environmental change and its effects on cell proteins ('epigenesis').

One answer to the complexity of these interacting genetic effects has been to try to scan the whole human genome in people with an ASD and compare it to the human genomes on file (so far, only belonging to a few exceptional individuals, who may or may not be typical of the general population) or to use a control group. This is most usually done using commercially available gene 'chips' or micro-arrays that are coated with up to a million different oligonucleotides, which bind the denatured (i.e. uncoiled) strand of interest. The cost and complexity of this work has meant that only a few international teams are able to carry it out, for example the International Molecular Genetic Study of Autism Consortium.[100] Some genome wide scans have found more CNVs on the long arm (q) of chromosome 7 (7q) and the 11–13 region of the long arm of 15 (15q11–13) in people with ASDs compared to controls. But there are many other candidate areas.[101] Chromosome 7 (see Table 11.1) has also been implicated in some cases of Tourette syndrome,[102] and Williams syndrome is reliably associated with heterozygous deletions in 7q11.23, involving genes that code proteins involved in the formation of cytoskeletal microtubules. There has been little success in finding a specific gene, or gene product, that might be responsible for autism. Particular attention has been paid to those genes which are involved in controlling cell migration,[103, 104] or in coding for transmitter transporter proteins, such as the serotonin transporter,[105] but the results from different laboratories are contradictory. It has been speculated that several genes may be involved, some of which may be epistatic.

Attention deficit disorder is also heritable,[106] but genome scans again implicate multiple chromosomes,[107, 108] and as in the case of autism, it has been difficult to identify which of the genes affected by the chromosomal abnormalities are responsible for the development of the ADHD. Environmental factors may also have more of an effect in ADHD in increasing symptoms severity, and in complicating the effects of the disorder, for example via oppositional and conduct symptoms.[109]

Chromosome disorders

Chromosome 1

The MARK1 gene is located in 1q41–q42, encodes a kinase regulating microtubular transport in neurons, and is over-expressed in human prefrontal cortex and cerebellum. SNPs in this gene are increased in ASD kindreds but the relative risk is low (1.8).[110] The NTRK1 (neurotrophic tyrosine kinase receptor, type 1) gene encodes a neurotrophic tyrosine kinase receptor located on cell membranes that is the site for neurotrophin, or nerve growth cell factor, binding which leads to neuronal differentiation, possibly specifically sensory neuronal differentiation. Polymorphisms of NTRK1 are associated with ASD traits.[111]

Chromosome 2

The gene for GAD1, a gene for one isomer of glutamate decarboxylase, the enzyme responsible for converting glutamate to GABA, is located on 2q31. A rare haplotype may be associated with ASD,[112] but the main association might be with risk for ADHD; 2q32 contains two homeodomain genes, DLX1 and DLX2, that code for transcription factors that are crucial to the development of GABAergic cortical interneurons. SNPs in these genes are associated with an increased risk of ASD;[113, 114] 2q31-q33 also contains the SLC25A12 gene, which encodes a mitochondrial aspartate/glutamate carrier that may be particularly important in the metabolism of highly active neurons. There are SLC25A12 gradients in other mammals in ventral temporal and lateral prefrontal areas at mid-gestation that coincide with the development of gyri and sulci, and the gene may then be active in modelling connections between brain areas. SLC25A12 is expressed more strongly in dorsolateral prefrontal cortex (Brodmann area 46) in people with an ASD, and an association between SNPs in the gene and ASD has been reported.[115] A deletion in the region around the osteodystrophy gene in 2q37.3 has also been found in a person with osteodystrophy and ASD.[116]

Several homeobox genes are located in chromosome 2. Homeobox genes are phylogenetically linked to segmentation, and determine embryological development in the midline. HOXA abnormalities cause Bosley-Salih-Alorainy syndrome,[117] which is associated with ASD, but HOXA polymorphisms have not been associated with an increased risk of ASD on screening tests. A particular allele of the HOXA1 gene, G218, is associated with more rapid head growth and therefore head circumference in neurotypical children, although not with final head circumference,[118] and with reduced cerebellar volume,[119] in neurotypical children. The same allele is associated with more rapid head growth in ASD.[120]

Chromosome 3

A genome wide scan of seven affected males from several generations of a single family identified SNPs in common between the affected members in 3q13.2-q13.31 and 3q26.31-q27.3.[121]

Chromosome 7

Deletion of the LIM-kinase gene,[122] which is adjacent to the elastin gene in a region of 1–2 megabases on 7q11.23, results in Williams syndrome (discussed in more detail later in this chapter), which confers a risk of ASD. Other deletions in this area lead to visuoconstructive problems.[122] Deletions of the elastin gene itself lead to connective tissue abnormalities, resulting in reduced visual acuity, supravalvular aortic stenosis, and a susceptibility to hernia. Although the deletion is sporadic, usually occurring during meiosis, it is heritable as a recessive gene.

Deletion in the 7q31.1 region, in or near the FOXP2 gene, may lead to language impairment and it has been speculated that deletions in an adjacent gene may also be associated with ASD.[123] The MET gene for a transmembrane tyrosine kinase is also in 7q31. This is an oncogene, active in immune function, organ repair, and the development of cerebral cortex and cerebellum. There is an association between one allele of the promoter region, and ASD.[124] Particular SNPs in this gene are associated with ASD.[125]

UBE2H, a gene for an ubiquitin-dependent proteolytic ligase, is located in region 7q32. (Another gene for a ubiquitin-dependent ligase, UBE3A2q, is on chromosome 15 and is inactivated in Angelman syndrome.) An SNP in one of the seven exons of this gene (a substitution of adenonine for guanine), was found in a subgroup of people with an ASD.[126]

There is also a homeobox gene in 7q, EN2 (engrailed 2, so called because of its effects on fruit fly markings), that influences the embryological development of midbrain, including cerebellum. SNPs in the intron, or noncoding, region of EN2 have been reported to be associated with ASD, but in Han Chinese appear to have a protective effect being associated with a reduced incidence.[127]

Chromosome 8

Polymorphisms of CYP11B1, a gene coding for one of a cytochrome enzymes, in the P450 family, have been linked to subclinical autistic traits.[111] The gene is located at 8q22. Alterations in the CYP11B1 protein results in conformational change in steroid 11β-hydroxylase and reduced activity of this enzyme. Steroid 11β-hydroxylase is one of five enzymes involved in the synthesis of cortisol and aldosterone from cholesterol in the adrenal cortex, and mutations in CYP11B1 result in hypertrophy of the adrenal cortex (congenital adrenal hyperplasia), but reduced secretion of mineralo- and glucocorticosteroids, and increased secretion of androgenic hormones.[128]

I have seen two patients with congenital adrenal hyperplasia who I have diagnosed with an ASD, although it has to be said, the clinical picture of neither of them was typical. Baron-Cohen's 'extreme male brain' theory of autism (see earlier in this chapter) suggests that congenital adrenal hyperplasia is linked to ASD through the oversecretion of adrenal androgens in utero leading to hypervirilization of the foetal brain but it is also claimed that high androstenadione levels persist in older children.[129] Androstenadione is a precursor of sex hormones, including testosterone, and other glucocorticoids.

Chromosome 10

The PTEN (phosphatase and tensin homologue) gene is located on chromosome 10. PTEN phosphorylates lipids on signalling pathways have growth suppressing and tumour suppressing functions, and possibly a direct signalling function.[130] The gene is involved in controlling neuronal and synaptic function.[131] Copy number variations (CNVs) on chromosome 10 are associated with an increased risk of ASD.[132] Mutations in the PTEN gene lead to Cowden's syndrome, in which hamartomata and malignant tumours develop in breast, thyroid, endometrium, brain, skin and mucosa. There is often macrocephaly.[133]

Chromosome 11

CNVs in the 11p12–13 section, in which neurexin genes are present, has been reported to be associated with an increased risk of ASD.[134] Linkage to other regions of chromosome 11 have also been found.[135, 136, 137] The gene for contactin-associated protein-like 2 (CNTNAP2), a member of the neurexin superfamily, was also found to be associated with increased risk of ASD in a separate study.[138] Other studies suggest linkage in the Chromosome 11 is the site of a gene coding for a D4 receptor (dopamine receptor) that is linked to an increased risk of dyslexia.[139]

Chromosome 12

Long CNVs of the atrophin1 gene cause a cerebellar disorder, dentatorubral-pallidoluysian atrophy, which may lead to myoclonic epilepsy and ASD if it develops in childhood.[140] SNPs on a restricted region of 12q have also been found to be linked to ASD.[141] The gene for neurotrophin 3 is located on the long arm of chromosome 12, too, and some but not all studies have suggested a link between this neurotrophin, which is involved with the development of dopaminergic neurons, and ASD.[142]

Chromosome 13

Interstitial deletions on chromosome 13 have been reported in cases of ASD.[143, 144] A frameshift variation in the mRNA coded by the SLITRK1 gene in 13q31.1 is associated with Tourette syndrome.[145]

Chromosome 14

There is one case report of a ring on chromosome 14 being associated with coloboma of the eye and ASD.[146]

Chromosome 15

The chromosome region 15q11q13 is known for its instability.[147] Deletions, duplications or other reading errors in this region should, one study recommends, be suspected in a child with hypotonia, dysmorphia, language delay,[148] ASD, and later onset refractory seizures.[147] Prader-Willi and Angelman syndromes are associated with either duplicated or deleted genes in the region 15q11-13. Prader-Willi syndrome (the result of maternal imprinting with two copies of the maternal chromosome) is associated with an increased risk of ASD and also of bipolar disorder and cycloid psychosis.[149, 150] The lack of expression of one gene in this section, at marker FLJ33332, may be a particular risk factor for psychosis in PWS.[151] Microdeletions within 15q13.3 are also associated with ASD, intellectual disability, seizures, dysmorphic features and psychosis, but in the absence of Prader-Willi symptoms.[152]

Chromosome 16

The short arm of chromosome 16, 16p, is rich in genes, including one gene (tuberous sclerosis disease 2, TSC2), whose impairment is associated with the development of tuberous sclerosis. There is a link between ASD and this region,[153] possibly in the area coding a protein kinase.[154]

A small proportion of children with ASD had a deletion, or duplication, of approximately 600,000 base pairs on 16p11.2.[155, 156] CNVs occur at this locus that do not lead to ASD, and some are compatible with a normal phenotype.[157] Duplications may be more benign than deletions.[158] Children with ADHD, compared to siblings, have SNPs in 16q23.[159] Other studies also link ADHD with 16q SNPs.[160] An adjacent area, 16q13, has been found to have CNVs associated with ASD.[161] A norepinephrine transporter gene is located at 16q12.2.[162]

Chromosome 17

There are several case studies of abnormalities in chromosome 17 and ASD.[163, 164] In one of these,[164] ASD is associated with neurofibromatosis type 1. Some linkage studies implicate 17q11-q21,[165] a region also implicated in schizophrenia.[166]

Chromosome 18
Inattentiveness in ADHD may be linked to abnormalities of 18q.[167]

Chromosome 20
A genome wide scan of seven affected males from several generations of a single family identified SNPs in common between the affected members in 20q11.21–q13.12.[168]

Chromosome 21
Down syndrome is associated with trisomy of 21,[169, 170] and is associated with an increased risk of developing ASD (discussed in more detail later in Chapter 12, in the section on named syndromes).

Chromosome 22
Deletions at 22q11.2 lead to velocardiofacial syndrome (di George syndrome).[171] Micro-deletions in this region may have subclinical effects and may be inherited.[172] Velocardiofacial syndrome is associated with an increased risk of autism (discussed in more detail later in Chapter 12, in the section on named syndromes) and with an increased risk of ADHD, schizophrenia and bipolar disorder.[173] The gene SHANK3 (also known as ProSAP2) is located at 22q13. It is a binding partner of neuroligins, which contributes to the structural organization of dendritic spines, and mutations can result in ASD and in language disorders.[174]

Chromosome 23
The two chromosomes 23 are the sex chromosomes. They are homologous in XX women, but heterologous in XY men as the Y chromosome has lost much of its chromatid.

Unisomy and polysomy of the sex chromosomes
Turner syndrome (X0), Klinefelter syndrome (XXY) and XYY syndrome are all associated with learning disability and an increased risk of ASD. They are discussed in more detail later in Chapter 12, in the section on named syndromes. XYY syndrome is associated with a high risk of ADHD.[175]

Specific genes
Other genes on the X chromosome with polymorphisms associated with ASD include the Aristaless related homeobox gene, ARX, which, like other genes implicated in ASD such as PTEN and MECP2, is responsible for controlling the transcription of other genes.[176] ARX mutations are associated with epilepsy, often myoclonic or of infantile onset (West syndrome), ataxia, dystonia, intellectual disability and ASD.[177] ARX mutations may also be linked to alpha-thalassaemia.[178]

Fragile X syndrome (discussed in more detail later in Chapter 12, in the section on named syndromes) is caused by silencing of the FMR1 gene at Xq27.3 on the X chromosome. Silencing normally occurs through methylation and is triggered by an expansion of a repeating CGG duplication within the gene.

X-linked ichthyosis and Rett syndrome are also discussed in more detail later in Chapter 12, in the section on named syndromes.

X-linked adrenoleukodystrophy (X-ALD or Schilder's disease), first described in 1923 as the cause of a neurodegenerative disorder, was thought to be fatal until 1976, when it became apparent that there could be less penetrant presentations of disorder including an ADHD-like disorder and a disorder mimicking multiple sclerosis. The prevalence may be similar to that of phenylketonuria, affecting 1 in 17,000. Although most women are carriers, a few may also have symptoms. The absent gene (ABCD1) lies at Xq28 (see Chapter 3). It codes for a protein that is involved in the transport into peroxyisosomes of very long chain fatty acids. In the absence of this protein very long chain fatty acid accumulate, with particular damage produced to the adrenal cortex (sometimes leading to Addison's disease) and to myelin. There is a possibility that if detected early, a diet low in very long chain fatty acids may slow disease progression.[179]

Other rare X-linked conditions associated with ASD are Borjeson-Forssman-Lehmann syndrome,[180] Danon disease,[181] and disorders of the TSPAN7/TM4SF2 gene.[182]

Rare syndromes

There are numerous case reports of rare syndromes in conjunction with an ASD. Some of these are likely to have occurred together by chance, some may be of aetiological significance. Artigas-Pallares *et al.* list the following: Angelman syndrome, Prader-Willi syndrome, 15q11-q13 duplication, fragile X syndrome, fragile X premutation, deletion of chromosome 2q, XYY syndrome, Smith-Lemli-Opitz syndrome, Apert syndrome, mutations in the ARX gene, De Lange syndrome, Smith-Magenis syndrome, Williams syndrome, Rett syndrome, Noonan syndrome, Down syndrome, velocardiofacial syndrome, myotonic dystrophy, Steinert disease, tuberous sclerosis, Duchenne's disease, Timothy syndrome, 10p terminal deletion, Cowden syndrome, 45, X/46, XY mosaicism, Myhre syndrome, Sotos syndrome, Cohen syndrome, Goldenhar syndrome, Joubert syndrome, Lujan-Fryns syndrome, Moebius syndrome, hypomelanosis of Ito, neurofibromatosis type 1, CHARGE syndrome and HEADD syndrome (Hypotonia, Epilepsy, Autism and Developmental Delay).[183]

Some of these conditions are discussed in more detail in Chapter 12.

Since this list was compiled additional reports have been published, and a more complete list is shown in Table 11.1 on page 262.

Tuberous sclerosis and neurofibromatosis are relatively common syndromes and have been thought to provide information about the possible causes of ASD. They are therefore considered below. Selected other named syndromes are considered in Chapter 12 on infancy and early childhood, since they are most likely to be diagnosed then. Details of all of these conditions can be found on numerous websites, include those of the National Human Genome Resource Centre of the US National Institute of Health,[184] the Online Mendelian Inheritance in Man site created by Johns Hopkins University,[185] the Genetics and Rare Diseases Information Centre,[186] and the Gene Reviews developed by the University of Washington.[187]

INTRA-UTERINE FACTORS

Growing evidence suggests that some mothers, who do not themselves have ASD traits, may be less able to protect a foetus from teratological effects. One particular allele of the glutathione S-transferase P1 gene (GSTP1), for example, was more likely to be found in mothers of children with ASD than in other female family members.[188]

The impact of intra-uterine factors depends on timing. In a meta-analysis of 64 studies of prenatal factors, parental age and being firstborn were significant risk factors, although the latter is probably attributed to the stoppage effect: parents deciding not to have more children if their firstborn has an ASD.[189] No other factors emerged as significant according to the authors, although they ruled out some significant results, such as bleeding in pregnancy and toxaemia, because of heterogeneity of effect size.[189]

Maternal stress

Although maternal stress during pregnancy is associated with later ADHD in their offspring, the correlation disappears if shared genetic factors are taken into account.[190]

Placental insufficiency

Placental insufficiency is the most common reason for intra-uterine growth restriction (IUGR) or prematurity, that is children being small for their due date. IUGR is associated with increased risks of reduced verbal working memory,[191] intellectual disability and ASD,[192] and ADHD.[193] It is not the weight at birth itself that increases the ADHD risk, but the reduced weight for gestational age.[193] Placental insufficiency may result in the diversion of foetal blood to the brain (the 'brain sparing effect') and so an increase in flow in the ratio of cerebral artery to umbilical flow can be used, paradoxically, as a measure of placental insufficiency. In a large study of children in whom these flows had been estimated in utero by ultrasound, there was a correlation between placental insufficiency and emotional problems, somatic complaints, and ADHD.[194]

Placental insufficiency may be caused by abruptio placentae, and present as uterine bleeding, which is itself associated with an increased risk of ASD.[195] Other causes are gestational diabetes, and pre-eclampsia. Following a systematic review in 2009, the authors concluded that bleeding and diabetes were possible causes of ASD, but that pre-eclampsia was not.[189]

Hormones and brain development
Nonapeptide hormones

Oxytocin and vasopressin are both nonapeptides with multiple physiological functions. Oxytocin was first discovered because of its effects on uterine smooth muscle. A burst of oxytocin shortly after birth leads to uterine contraction and the release of the placenta, so minimizing blood loss, as well as contracting the milk ducts in the breast leading to the let down reflex. Vasopressin, also known as anti-diuretic hormone, modulates glomerular filtration rate and therefore plays a part in blood pressure control. There are receptors in the medial amygdala nuclei for both, activation of which affects amygdalar control over the hypothalamus.[196] Failure of vasopressin synthesis, for example in diabetes insipidus, has not been noted to be associated with ASD,[197] although I have observed one case. Female mammals have an oxytocin surge before copulation, and male mammals a vasopressin surge, which is thought to suppress the normal male threat response that close contact with another conspecific would otherwise engender, and therefore enable copulation. Orgasm produces further surges.

The importance of nonapeptides is reflected in their evolutionary ancestry. They are made use of as transmitters by every vertebrate taxon, and a predecessor polypeptide even occurs in the mollusc, Lymnaea stagnalis, where, like the nonapeptides in human endocrinology, it binds to a G protein coupled receptor in both neural and gonadal tissue, and influences male copulatory behaviour.[197] In human beings, like in other mammals, the control of copulation has extended to a more extended role in reproduction and thence to nurturance – hence the role of these hormones in attachment that was briefly discussed earlier in this chapter on factors present at conception. The divergence of two lineages of nonapeptides, one of which is particularly important in male reproductive behaviour and the other in female, is already present in fish. The 'female' nonapeptide, oxytocin or its equivalent, has been the one that has been most studied in relation to ASD, both because of the possible protective effect of female gender against ASD and because childcare and attachment is a model of socialization.

The American prairie vole has become a widely used model of oxytocin's effects because, unlike its genetic cousins, the meadow and montane voles, it forms enduring pair bonds; both male and female voles play a part in the care of pups, and it is a communal living rather than an isolated animal, with pup care being shared out between families. The prairie vole also has much denser concentrations of oyxtocin receptors in the brain, particularly in female prairie voles, than either of its cousins.

Oxytocin reduces amygdala activation by threat and increases trust.[198] People with ASD who inhaled oxytocin in one experiment spent more time looking at the eyes of virtual opponents in a game, and were more likely to play cooperatively.[199] Oxytocin also increases gaze to the eye area of angry faces, a condition in which gaze is usually avoided, presumably for fear of confrontation.[200] Interestingly, testosterone reduces trust, at least in some women,[201] and this seems a readily reversible effect as it varies during the menstrual cycle.

However, there are theoretical reasons to consider that oxytocin may not always have a benign effect. By suppressing the amygdalar response to fear, it may reduce violence inhibition (see Chapter 2) and therefore increase the risk of an attack on another person being prolonged. There are currently too many gaps in the understanding of nonapeptides[197] to be able to hypothesize about their role in ASD. Although the prairie vole has more oxytocin receptors overall, these are particularly prevalent in the nucleus accumbens (the reward centre). Prairie voles have fewer receptors in the amygdala than meadow voles and oxytocin may, in meadow voles, predispose to a lack of violence inhibition.

Although there has been considerable speculation that nonapeptide levels may be low, leading to ASD, there is little evidence for this, nor is there evidence for the presence of less active isomers, altered receptor numbers or polymorphisms in the very short area (17 kilobases) on the short arm of chromosome 3 (3p25.3) where the gene for the oxytocin receptor lies.[202]

Androgen

In humans, the default brain is female. However, the expression of one or more Y chromosomes, however many X chromosomes there may be, allows the sex-determining region of the Y chromosome (the SRY gene) to be transcribed, leading to the production of testis-determining factor (TDF) and the differentiation of the uncommitted gonad to become the testis which, from the sixth week of gestation on, begins to secrete testosterone as it lacks the aromatase present in the ovary that converts testosterone to oestradiol. Testosterone levels vary under the influence of luteinizing hormone, which is released from the anterior pituitary in response to gonadotropin releasing hormone (GnRH), that is another peptide produced in the hypothalamus but not, unlike the nonapeptides, released into the general blood circulation but into a local 'portal' system. Even before the higher level control of testosterone is established, there is enough circulating to alter the development of various tissues, including the brain, into a masculine pattern so long as androgen receptors are present. There is a rare genetic condition (androgen insensitivity) in which, although a testis develops and produces testosterone, the androgen receptor is less sensitive to it. If the receptor is very insensitive, the affected person develops as an anatomical female, although lacking an ovary and so not menstruating.

The most common cause of androgen insensitivity syndrome, which may be partial or complete, is a mutation in the androgen receptor gene. Low copy numbers produce partial haploinsufficiency. Although testosterone usually provides about 90 per cent of the androgenic effect of circulating steroids, overgrowth of the adrenal cortex, or congenital adrenal hyperplasia, may lead to high levels of circulating androgens, mainly androstenedione, even in XX individuals who lack a testis. These androgens may be enough to stimulate tissue androgen receptors sufficiently that they develop some male characteristics.

The most common cause of hyperplasia is lack of an enzyme, 21-hydroxylase that converts cortisone to cortisol. Since it is cortisol that mainly inhibits the production of adrenocorticotropin (ACTH), people with a 21-hydroxylase deficiency have high levels of circulating ACTH, and therefore high levels of steroid synthesis, despite high levels of cortisol precursors, including androstenedione. There may be varying degrees of vulval development, and the clitoris may be large enough to seem like a small penis. Women with congenital adrenal hyperplasia (CAH) are often brought up as women, but are said to have a psychology that is more male than women who were exposed to lower levels of androgen in pregnancy. However, since their genital morphology is often atypical – sometimes called an 'intersex condition' – their upbringing may not be the same as that of other girls and it cannot be assumed that their psychology is purely a consequence of exposure *in utero* to androgens.

One effect of intra-uterine androgen exposure is to increase the length of the index finger (second digit). Women who were not so exposed typically have a shorter index finger compared to their ring finger (the fourth digit) and men have a longer one,[203] although there is considerable variance and the ratio is not a specific predictor of an individual's exposure.[204] This '2D:4D ratio', which in most men is less than 1 and most women greater than 1, is used as a proxy of embryonic virilization. It is not an entirely accurate measure.[205] Other recent studies have used direct assays of testosterone in the amniotic fluid;[206] acne or masculine play in girls;[207] and post- partum levels of steroid precursors.[208] Foetal testosterone measured in amniotic fluid taken for other reasons correlates with the number of symptoms of ASD reported by mothers at later follow-up.[209] There are also lower 2D:4D ratios in young men with ADHD compared with non-ADHD if conscientiousness is controlled for,[210] although the difference between ASD and the control children could not be attributed to the 2D:4D ratio.[211]

Several of these studies have been carried out by the same group, and report an increase in ASD symptoms rather than an increase in diagnosis. One potential confounder is that the measures used for these symptoms may be biased towards the expression of ASD in males, and away from its expression in females. On balance, the evidence is intriguing but not conclusive at the time of writing.[212, 213]

Infections

Rubella and cytomegalovirus infections are associated with widespread effects on embryological development, including the development of ASD.[214, 215] Cytomegalovirus infection may be overlooked.[216]

Teratology
Foetal alcohol

Maternal drinking above a safe level exposes the foetus to alcohol levels that causes widespread effects including a characteristic facies. White matter in the brain is reduced,[217] and CNS abnormalities, including microcephaly, deafness and visual impairment, may be produced. Foetal alcohol syndrome is frequently unrecognized. It is associated with intellectual disability.[218] However, an often reported association with ADHD may be spurious.[219] Children with foetal alcohol syndrome may have difficulties in peer relationships, but they do not have the characteristic impairment of nonverbal communication or other characteristic symptoms seen in ASD.[220]

Valproate and other antiepileptic drugs

In utero exposure to several antiepileptic drugs is associated with an increased risk of neural tube deficits, but in utero exposure to sodium valproate seems to be particularly teratogenic.[221] Mouse studies suggest that there is a gestational age when the foetus is most vulnerable. It has been suggested that this is as early as four to six weeks of gestation for the ASDs.[222]

Valproate exposure in utero is associated with speech and language disorder, and ASD,[223] possibly due to abnormal dendritic pruning, and cell migration occurs in rats exposed in utero to sodium valproate.[224, 225]

Other factors

Children born to heroin dependent mothers have an increased risk of ADHD, even when adopted,[226] suggesting the intra-uterine exposure to heroin may have a teratogenic effect.

PERINATAL FACTORS

Cognitive impairment and behavioural problems, but not ASD, may follow from even mild episodes of hypoxia after the perinatal period in children.[227] Follow-up studies of children born with low Apgar scores suggest that there is an increased risk not only of ASD,[228] but also of cognitive and executive deficits,[229] in this group. Intrapartum hypoxia may be a risk factor for ASD,[230] but it is difficult to establish definitely as many factors, including some in the foetus,[231] such as breech presentation,[232] may delay labour and increase the risk of hypoxia. Nor is there strong evidence of perinatal factors, other than low birth weight, increasing the risk of ADHD.[233] Babies born at 28 weeks do, however, have a substantially increased risk of later ASD, which can be predicted by their overall scores on scales of maturation in the first 12 hours after birth.[234]

Severe hyperbilirubinaemia has been found to be associated with an increased risk of ADHD,[235] and moderate or severe neonatal hyperbilirubinaemia with ASD,[195] although the later association was possibly confined to atypical ASD or pervasive disorder not otherwise specified,[236] a condition that overlaps with ADHD. However, other studies of hyperbilirubinaemia have not found an association with ASD.[236] Another study of a variety of perinatal factors found only breech birth to be predictive of later development of ASD.[232]

Neonatal jaundice

My clinical experience is that neonatal jaundice is more common in ASD, and that the impact of severe neonatal jaundice may be underestimated.[237] Estimates of the incidence of neonatal hyperbilirubinaemia in the NICE guidelines published in 2010 are that about 650,000 babies are born in England and Wales each year, 300,000 develop visible jaundice, 1 in every 650–1000 babies develops a serum bilirubin concentration >427 µmol/l and about one in 10,000 has a concentration of more than 500 µmol/l.2 8.[238] These bilirubin concentrations refer to the total of conjugated and unconjugated bilirubin, but only unconjugated bilirubin crosses the blood–brain barrier. If enough crosses, significant toxicity to the brain occurs, leading to kernicterus. Kernicterus particularly affects basal ganglia and cranial nerve nuclei, leading to long-term choreathetosis, deafness, and forced upward gaze. It occurs in about 1 in 17 babies with a serum bilirubin concentration >340 µmol/l and perhaps one in seven with a concentration more than 500 µmol/l. Babies at risk of jaundice, or clinically jaundiced babies, should have their bilirubins estimated used a transcutaneous bilirubinometer, backed up by a serum bilirubin estimation if the bilirubinometer shows yellowing suggestive of a serum bilirubin higher than 250 µmol/l. The infant's skin should be exposed to light, preferably blue (phototherapy), if the bilirubin is at this level or above.[239] In rare cases where phototherapy fails, exchange transfusion may be needed.

POSTNATAL FACTORS

Establishing that a condition is more often associated with an ASD than with no ASD is a straightforward matter of epidemiology, requiring attention to the selection bias of using clinic samples and other potential sources of error. Selection biases are substantially increased if publicity increases reporting, as happened with the reports that MMR (measles, mumps and rubella) vaccination caused ASD. Retrospective bias may increase reporting, with parents recalling episodes in their child's history that fit with newly described conditions apparently associated with ASD.

However, even if an association is found, it may not be possible to determine if it is a causal one. Spurious associations may be due to genetic linkage, or to the ASD causing the associated condition and not the other way round. Having a child with an ASD may alter the family environment, and lead to unusual behaviour in the child which can increase the risk of infections or other conditions that may be interpreted as causes.

Currently, it seems very unlikely that there are any systemic disorders, other than those leading to irreversible changes in the developing brain, that cause autism. However, there are many associated conditions that contribute to the overall symptoms of a particular person with an ASD, and even if it seems unlikely that these are causes of ASD, they are also considered in this section.

Psychological events

Retrospective ascertainment bias often leads people to attributing something with an insidious onset to a memorable moment, and that may lead people to misattribute cause to whatever made that moment memorable. Parents may report that an ASD began from a vaccination, from the birth of a sibling, or from a hospital admission because these events stood out. However, in the case of hospital admission, it is likely that such a sudden change of routine might so worsen the condition of a child with ASD that mild symptoms which may have been overlooked become overt.

For many years, ASD was considered to be entirely psychogenic, with the emotional distance of the mother or principal carer being considered to be the most likely explanation. The only empirical support for this explanation has come from studies of unusually extreme neglect (see next section), and this cannot be considered a viable explanation for children under ordinary circumstances, even ordinary circumstances of poor or neglectful parenting, although it may need to be considered when parental or carer neglect is at a level that would be considered criminal in most developed countries.

Psychological factors do, as in any other groups of people, have emotional consequences for people with an ASD, whether or not they have other learning disabilities and may result in a worsening of symptoms or in challenging behaviour.[240] For children with ADHD, this may make the difference between clinically significant disorder and sub-threshold disorder, as epigenetic effects seem to be particularly important.[241]

Evidence from orphans

The significance of studies of children who have been placed in neglected, and neglectful, orphanages in Romania and Russia has been considered in the Introduction. Some of these children may have had an ASD, leading to them being placed in the orphanage. Social withdrawal, loss of communication and stereotypies are commonly observed in these children and there is overlap with the symptoms of ASD, leading to the one group of researchers calling this 'quasi-autism'. A proportion of these children have an ASD: 9 per cent in one study,[242] and 8 per cent in another.[243] There were as many girls in these 'quasi-autistic' children as boys.[244] A quarter of these children had lost their ASD by the age of 11 in the Rutter *et al.* study,[242] suggesting that ASD might in these cases have been psychogenic or, alternatively, that some children with an ASD genotype can develop overt ASD in adverse psychosocial conditions but lose it again when these conditions improve. A further alternative is that institutionalization may suppress the contagion of emotion that is neurotypical,[245] leading to a condition similar to that of the child with an ASD who is disconnected from emotional contagion.

Language delays and ADHD are more persistent, particularly in girls, in children who have been of low weight at birth, or were in long-term care.[246] Some children are persistently less good at theory of mind tasks, and there is a risk of developing emotional disorders during adolescence, although this appears to be independent of these other factors.[247, 248] Many children who were adopted from these severely emotionally and cognitively deprived environments showed disinhibited attachment and this has persisted throughout a five-year follow-up period, although reduced in intensity.[242]

Postnatal conditions having a recognized predilection for the brain
Epilepsy
Epileptoid personality
Older textbooks described an 'epileptoid personality', which was variously thought to be the cause of epilepsy, the consequence of disordered electrical conduction in the brain, or the consequence of repeated head injuries or hypoxia. Dostoevsky was sometimes given as an example of a person with epileptoid personality, when the concept still had credence. At least some reported cases of so-called epileptoid personality may have been people with an ASD who had epilepsy.

Childhood epilepsy, particularly petit mal epilepsy, may spontaneously remit in the early teens.

Electroencephalography
It is estimated that approximately one-half of all seizures in people with epilepsy are not caused by paroxysmal electrical waves in the brain, even though they are indistinguishable phenomenologically from seizures that are. These pseudo-seizures may sometimes occur in people who never suffer from electrical paroxysms. Since anticonvulsant drugs are effective only against the electrical discharge, a diagnosis of epilepsy normally requires supportive evidence about the brain's electrical activity, which can be obtained from an encephalogram (EEG). EEG interpretation is difficult. A single recording may show evidence of resting instability from which the likelihood of paroxysms can be inferred, but to record a paroxysm taking place normally requires continuous recording. Methods for doing this, and criteria for interpreting EEGs, can be found described in standard textbooks.

Classification of the epilepsies
Epilepsies with onset in early childhood are classified according to the age of onset (infantile spasms), the nature of the provoking stimulus (febrile convulsions), or associated clinical and EEG features (Landau-Kleffner syndrome, Lennox Gastaut syndrome, myoclonic-astatic

epilepsy). Children with febrile convulsions have no higher risk of seizures except when they are febrile than any other child, and grow out of their susceptibility in middle childhood. Unless they suffer ill effects during a seizure, which is rare, their development is normal and no treatment for epilepsy is required, only treatment of fever. Febrile convulsions are not therefore normally considered to be an epilepsy.

All of the other infantile onset epilepsies are associated with abnormal child development.[249]

Epilepsies with later onset are classified according to the type of seizure that most commonly occurs. The first seizure most commonly occurs in middle childhood, at around the age of eight years, or in adolescence. Epilepsy with onset in adulthood is suggestive of stimulant misuse, exposure to epileptogenic drugs, including many of the psychotropics, or newly developing brain disease, such as neoplasm or an ischaemic lesion.

Course

Minor seizures of childhood often remit. Idiopathic epilepsy may also remit. Both occur spontaneously and there are few predictors.

Treatment

Seizure frequency can be increased by tiredness, by worry, or by emotional turmoil. Practical advice and counselling are the foundations of treatment. Epilepsy can sometimes be triggered, for example by flashing lights, and people with epilepsy can learn how to avoid these triggers as much as possible once they know them. Driving is contra-indicated if a person has epilepsy, or indeed any sudden and involuntary losses of consciousness, and in some countries professionals may have a duty to inform the appropriate authorities, if the patient is not willing to do so. There are numerous drug treatments; although monotherapy is recommended, many people with unstable epilepsy are taking several drugs. Drug treatment should normally be left to an epileptologist, at least until a stable regime has been established, as should decisions about stopping medication.

Physical treatments, such as continuous vagal nerve stimulation or neurosurgery, may be considered in the most intractable epilepsies. One open label study of vagal nerve stimulation for epilepsy in children with autism has not shown an effect.[250] Ketogenic diets have also been recommended, both for epilepsy and for autism (see dietary treatments later).

Many people with ASD are unaware of what professional help is available to them. They may be content to continue on outdated drugs or drug regimes for longer than is necessary. Both of the original two anticonvulsants are now considered to have too many side-effects to be used unless there are exceptional circumstances. Phenobarbitone may impair concentration, and therefore has a negative effect on learning. Phenytoin may cause gum hypertrophy leading to altered appearance, and possible stigmatization. People still on these drugs should therefore be encouraged to seek a specialist review, unless one has taken place recently. People with uncontrolled seizures should also be assisted to seek further advice and treatment.

Sometimes patients and their carers have not been told, or do not remember, the information that they have been given about epilepsy. It is therefore good practice to ask about this, and if necessary provide further information or direct carers to an information resource such as the website of the British Epilepsy Association.[251] Two simple facts that are often overlooked is that enuresis, and sometimes encopresis, almost always occur during a grand mal seizure, and that seizures occur more frequently at night. Even though it is good caring not to blame someone for wetting the bed, it may help fortify a carer's resolution not to get cross, if they are aware that bed-wetting in a person with epilepsy may be an involuntary symptom of poor epilepsy control.

Relation to ASD

Epilepsy, ADHD[252] and ASD occur together more often than would be expected by chance. It is estimated that between 20 and 30 per cent of people with an ASD have at least one seizure with onset after early childhood, and the rates of spike and wave abnormalities may be even higher,[253] especially over the superior temporal cortex and adjacent peri Sylvian areas.[254] Spike and wave may predict epilepsy developing later. There may be only one seizure, and no more. This is most likely in late childhood.

The commonest epilepsies associated with ASD are those in which partial and generalized seizures are mixed (61% in one sample),[255] particularly those with symptoms suggestive of a temporal lobe focus. Intellectual disability and lower social maturity increase the association of ASD and epilepsy, [255] as does receptive language impairment.[256]

Epilepsy with onset after infancy does not cause ASD, or vice versa,[257] but there are likely to be overlaps in the networks subserving both.[258] Treatment of ASD with antipsychotics, many of which are epileptogenic, may increase epilepsy risk.

Early childhood onset epilepsy is discussed in Chapter 13.

Meningitis and encephalitis

Intracranial infections may cause ASD.[259]

Hypothalamic hamartoma

Hypothalamic hamartomata in infancy may be associated with the development of ASD,[260] and with intractable epilepsy. Controlling the epilepsy may improve the ASD symptoms. In one case, surgical removal of the hamartoma, which was associated with paroxysmal giggling and possibly seizure activity, resulted in an improvement in the ASD.[261]

It has been suggested that hamartomas, macrocephaly and an increased risk of ASD result from mutations that activate the mTOR/P13K pathway and dysregulation of cellular and synaptic growth rates; mTOR or rapamycin controls protein synthesis and therefore cell growth by modulating serine/threonine kinase.[262] A lack of rapamycin allows cell overgrowth and the formation of knots of hyperplastic cells in tissues, such as the brain, the skin, the kidney and elsewhere. These 'hamartomata' are termed tubers in tuberous sclerosis and neurofibromata in neurofibromatosis. TSC1/TSC2, NF1, or PTEN reportedly all impact on the mTOR pathway and mutations in them can produce cell overgrowth and macrocephaly.[263] Mutations in TSC1 or TSC2 cause tuberous (tuberose) sclerosis. Mutations in NF1 cause neurofibromatosis.

Tuberous sclerosis

Frequency
There are between seven and twelve cases per 100,000.

Heredity
Tuberous sclerosis (TS) is inherited as an autosomal dominant, but there is partial prevalence.

Genetic cause
Tuberous sclerosis is the result of defects in one of two genes, TSC1 (encoding hamartin) located on the long arm of chromosome 9, or TSC2 (encoding tuberin) located on the long arm of chromosome 16. Two-thirds of these defects arise as spontaneous mutations.[264] These genes encode proteins that regulate cell growth, and suppress tumour formation.

Appearance
Characteristic skin appearances are shown in Table 11.1 on page 262; alternatively, they can be viewed in several online sites, including the very useful dermatology atlas.[265] Characteristic radiological appearances include tubers (harmartia) in the CNS, and in the kidneys (these are most likely to have a cystic appearance).

Intelligence
About half of people with TS have mild or more severe intellectual disability.

Clinical features
Epilepsy occurs in almost 100 per cent of people with TS. However, the most common presentation is during investigation for renal or neurological symptoms, or sometimes in the dermatology clinic.

Investigations
Diagnosis relies on careful skin examination, and the application of a checklist of symptoms. Genetic diagnosis is not currently possible in routine practice.

Psychiatric symptoms
In one study of 241 children and adults with tuberous sclerosis complex (TSC), 30 per cent had ADHD, 28 per cent had conduct disorder, 27 per cent had a history of mood disorder symptoms and another 27 per cent had anxiety disorder symptoms. These symptoms were influenced by age, gender, genetic mutation, seizure history, surgical history, cognitive impairment, features of autism or autism spectrum disorder, and neurological manifestations of TSC.[266]

Association with the ASDs
Autism may occur in as many as 20 per cent of people with tuberous sclerosis and there is also a greater than chance risk of ADHD in association with the condition.[267, 268, 269] Although every somatic cell has two copies of every gene, one copy may become inactivated during

cell division. When this happens in a cell which is heterozygous for the inactivated TSC1 or TSC2 gene, and it is the functioning gene that is inactivated, hamartin or tuberin production ceases and the cell continues to divide unchecked, leading to the formation of 'tubers'. Tubers may occur in any tissue, and may occur at different stages of development, although cerebral tubers develop only before birth.[270] Bolton *et al.* looked at the risk of autism and the location of cerebral tumours, and found that autism develops only if there are bilateral temporal tubers, with the occurrence of infantile spasms adding to the risk,[271] although these findings have been questioned.

Neurofibromatosis

Frequency
Neurofibromatosis type 1 (NF1) 1 per 3300[272] and neurofibromatosis type 2 (NF2) 1 in 60,000.[272]

Heredity
The altered gene is inherited as an autosomal dominant, but 50 per cent of cases are estimated to result from a *de novo* mutation.

Genetic cause
Neurofibromatosis is the result of a lack of control on the growth of tissues derived from the neural crest: this includes not only neurons, but also Schwann cells, melanocytes and some fibroblasts.

Neurofibromatosis type 1 (von Recklinghausen's disease) results from a deficit of neurofibromin production due to a mutation of the gene at 17q11.2. Type 2 results from impaired production of myelin, encoded by a gene at 22q12.

Appearance
The most common reason for presentation in early childhood in one series were café au lait spots.[273] Other cutaneous appearances are shown in Chapter 10.

Intelligence
There is deficit in working memory.[274]

Clinical features
One-third of the children in one series had macrocephaly.[275] Type 2 is more likely to present with symptoms of an acoustic neuroma.

Investigations
Genetic tests are not currently available.

Association with the ASDs
There is a substantial increased risk of developing ASD if a person also has neurofibromatosis.[276]

Macrocephaly

Larger than average head circumference is a common feature of ASD: it is one feature that has been used to distinguish ASD following severe psychosocial deprivation ('quasi-autism') from other kinds.[242] Along with hypotonia, it may be a marker for disorders of the genes regulating the expression of other genes.

A study of 241 children and young people with an ASD aged 3 to 16 with no known genetic syndrome confirmed that their average head circumference, from front to back, was greater than average.[277] Macrocephaly was associated with more social impairment, but with less language or motor impairment. There was a subgroup of young people with the largest heads who also had proportionately large bodies, suggesting that, for them, macrocephaly was an expression of a more general macrosomia,[277] a phenomenon also reported in a Dutch sample.[278] Macrocephaly is a symptom of a number of conditions associated with ASD, including organic aminoacidurias, leukodystrophies, and lipid storage diseases.[279]

Macrocephaly is associated with a larger than average corpus callosum, with thickening particularly in the median area. Normocephalic individuals with an ASD have a corpus callosum that is smaller than average at its caudal end (the genu), but this is not the case for the macrocephalic individuals with an ASD.[280] Children with an ASD and macrocephaly are more likely to have PTEN mutations.[281] Macrosomia, obesity, macrocephaly and ocular abnormality have been suggested to comprise a genetic syndrome associated with ASD.[282]

In a community-based study, 9 per cent of eight-year-olds were considered to have macrocephaly.[283] One study suggests that there are two populations: children who are born with macrocephaly and children who develop it early in life.[284]

Macrocephaly has been found to be variously associated with AS,[284] with higher performance than verbal intelligence,[285] with hyperlexia (associated with performance IQ/verbal IQ (see Chapter 7) discrepancy in favour of performance IQ),[286] and difficulties in global processing or 'seeing the wood for the trees'.[287]

Hydrocephalus

The most common cause of extreme macrocephaly is hydrocephalus, in which the ventricular system is enlarged disproportionately to the volume of brain tissue. There is, however, no association between hydrocephalus and ASD, and the macrocephaly in ASD is associated with a disproportionate decrease in ventricular volume.[288] Normal pressure hydrocephalus is associated with inattentiveness but not the full ADHD syndrome.[289]

Disorders affecting sensory function in early childhood

Selective orientation to social stimuli may be an important precursor for normal social development that is missing in many people with an ASD (see Chapter 5). So it might be expected that deaf-blind children, for example children with CHARGE syndrome, are more at risk of developing an ASD. If that is so, then any condition affecting sensory development, particularly visual development, might increase the risk of ASD. Alternatively, it might be that CHARGE syndrome increases the risk of ASD because of one of its other, widespread, embryological impairments. In one survey of 14 children with CHARGE syndrome (all of whom were deaf, and 10 of whom were also visually impaired), language was more delayed than in children with other developmental disorders associated with autism (Williams syndrome, Down syndrome and Prader-Willi syndrome) and they had more symptoms of ASD, including being more socially withdrawn, more lacking in interest in social contact, less attention seeking from others, and manifested reduced seeking of attention from others, more need to maintain order, and more hyperactivity.[290] However, they did not show expressive speech impairments, other than delay, and did not have motor stereotypies, or narrow and restricted interests.[290] Children in another study of CHARGE syndrome were less likely to have ASD symptoms if they were not deaf-blind.[291]

Congenital blindness

Visually impaired children and adolescents have an increased risk of ASD with a prevalence in one survey of 12 per cent. The young people with an ASD in this sample were more likely to have severe visual impairment, cerebral palsy and intellectual disability than those without an ASD in the sample.[292] Children with congenital nystagmus who may have normal visual acuity but cannot maintain visual fixation are also at increased risk of developing AS. I have diagnosed AS in three adults with congenital nystagmus over the years, and another two have been reported.[293]

Hearing impairment

In one large Finnish study of children and young people with an ASD, 8.6 per cent had a hearing impairment and 3.7 per cent had severe visual impairment. However, the sample may not have been representative, as 12.3 per cent had an additional genetic syndrome.[294] There are no particular features of ASD in deaf people which might suggest that there is a particular association.[295] Although deafness, and delayed speech, are associated with delay in theory of mind development, it seems to be the level of conversational interaction rather than the deafness that produces this effect.

Apparent deafness in children with an ASD may be a consequence of anomalous auditory responses, and a consequence of attentional orientation, rather than raised auditory threshold.

Disorders affecting mobility
Dystrophies

Myotonic dystrophy type 1 (DM1) is the most frequent inherited neuromuscular disorder, and is associated with a high frequency of ASD, ADHD, and a lower frequency of Tourette syndrome. It is inherited as an autosomal dominant and is due to an expansion of a cytosine-thymine-guanine nucleotide (CTG) (see Chapter 3) triplet in the DMPK gene which codes for dystrophin. The more the repeat, the earlier the onset of the disorder, the lower the level of dystrophin and the greater the prevalence of ASD.[296] Intellectual disability is often present, particularly if the mutation is maternally derived.[297]

Of the registrants with neuromuscular disorder on a regional database, 9 out of 82 had co-morbid ASD.[298] In a sample of 351 boys or men with Duchenne muscular dystrophy, the parent-reported prevalence of ADHD was 11.7 per cent, of OCD was 4.8 per cent, and of an ASD was 3.1 per cent.[299]

Myotonic dystrophy type 1 (DM1) is an autosomal dominant disorder, caused by an expansion of a CTG triplet repeat in the DMPK gene. The aims of one study by Ekstrom *et al.* were to classify a cohort of children with DM1, to describe their neuropsychiatric problems and cognitive level, to estimate the size of the CTG expansion, and to correlate the molecular findings with the neuropsychiatric problems;[296] 57 children and adolescents (26 females; 31 males) with DM1 (CTG repeats >40) were included in the study. The following instruments were used: Autism Diagnostic Interview-Revised (ADI-R), 5–15, Griffiths Mental Development Scales and the Wechsler Scales. Based on age at onset and presenting symptoms, the children were divided into four DM1 groups: severe congenital (n = 19), mild congenital (n = 18), childhood (n = 18), and classical DM1 (n = 2). Nearly half (49%) had an autism spectrum disorder (ASD) and autistic disorder was the most common diagnosis present in 35 per cent of the subjects; 86 per cent of the individuals with DM1 had intellectual disability or mental retardation (MR), most of them moderate or severe MR. ASD was significantly correlated with the DM1 form; the more severe the form of DM1, the higher the frequency of ASD. The frequency of ASD increased with increasing CTG repeat expansions. ASD and/or other neuropsychiatric disorders such as attention deficit hyperactivity disorder and Tourette syndrome were found in 54 per cent of the total DM1 group. In conclusion, awareness of ASD co-morbidity in DM1 is essential. Further studies are warranted to elucidate the molecular aetiology causing neurodevelopmental symptoms such as ASD and MR in DM1.[296]

Duchenne and Becker muscular dystrophy are allelic X-linked disorders causing progressive muscle weakness in males. Duchenne muscular dystrophy is caused by absence of dystrophin in muscle and brain; boys with Duchenne muscular dystrophy have a static cognitive impairment with mean Wechsler Full Scale IQ approximately one standard deviation below the mean. Less is known of the cognitive profile of males with Becker muscular dystrophy, which is associated with variable alterations in the amount or size of the dystrophin protein. Patients with Becker muscular dystrophy demonstrate a less homogeneous cognitive phenotype than that seen in Duchenne muscular dystrophy. Males with Becker muscular dystrophy have a high incidence of learning difficulties. Autism and behavioural and attention problems are also more common in Becker muscular dystrophy than in the general population.[300]

Leukodystrophy
Two people with ASD and neuroaxonal dystrophy have been reported.[301]

Mitochondrial disorders
There are case reports of disorders in the mitochrondial cytochrome oxidase system leading to myopathies and associated with ASD. One resulted from a DNA SNP leading to a mutated, and presumably therefore ineffective, tRNA.[302]

Connective tissue disorders
The prevalence of neuropsychiatric symptoms in systemic lupus erythematosus varies between 37 and 95 per cent; cognitive dysfunction, mood disorder, and anxiety syndromes are especially frequent. In Sjoegren syndrome, cognitive dysfunction is combined with frontal

executive disorder and attention deficit. Memory impairment, frontal executive dysfunction and personality changes have been reported in Behçet's disease. Classic polyarteritis nodosa, the Churg-Strauss syndrome and Wegener's granulomatosis may be associated with cognitive changes due to inflammatory encephalopathy. Cranial arteritis belongs to the treatable causes of dementia. In primary angiitis of the CNS, small-vessel disease presents more frequently with encephalopathy.[303]

Joint hypermobility syndrome or ligamentous laxity

Increased 'flexibility' at the joints is associated with many chromosomal disorders including Down syndrome.[304] There is genetic overlap with Ehlers-Danlos and with Marfan syndrome, language delay in 14 per cent of one series, and lifelong. Tantam *et al.* reported three cases in association with Asperger syndrome.[305]

Metabolic disorders

Disorders of glutamate,[306] cholinergic,[307, 308] and GABAergic[309] transmission have been implicated in autism. In one study, glutamic acid, phenylalanine, asparagine, tyrosine, alanine and lysine were higher than control values in people with ASD and their siblings and parents.[310] However, there was no control for diet, and the sample was not random. It seems unlikely that abnormal biochemistry is the consequence of a systemic disorder of metabolism, although this has sometimes been suggested, for example reduced cholesterol bio-synthesis,[311] and sulphation defects.[312] However, the evidence for these associations remains inconclusive, too.

Phenylketonuria is associated with an increased risk of ASD, although the prevalence is very low.[43] There is an association between nucleic acid metabolic disorders and ASD, and a link with aminoacidurias,[313, 314] but this may be accounted for by a common genetic link with the gene whose mutation is causing the ASD, or because of a teratological effect.

Adenylsuccinate lyase deficiency can lead to ADHD. The clinical features are similar to those of Angelman syndrome and may be a result of an accumulation of succinylpurines in the developing embryo. Some organic aminoacidurias, such as L-2-hydroxyglutaric aciduria (L-2-HGA),[315] and maple syrup disease,[316] interfere with myelination, therefore causing leukodystrophies which may particularly affect intracerebral tracts. Their symptoms include not only ASD, but also impaired speech development, and learning difficulty.

Metabolic disorders are rare in clinical practice,[317] and it is unlikely that postnatal treatment will reverse the embryological effects.

Many associations between autism (and less often other ASDs) and metabolic disorders have been reported since autism was first described. Some of these associations have been suggested by responses to interventions, often undertaken by parents and usually involving one or a small group of affected children. Examples are treatment with vitamins, sometimes in larger than usual doses, fenfluramine, biopterin, calcium and secretin. Many other associations have been suggested on the basis of response to exclusion diets. Examples are gluten-free and casein-free diets, both of which are reported by many parents to be of benefit (although empirical research does not support this,[318] reduced exposure to food dyes or other food additives, reduced exposure to foods presumed to be containing heavy metals, and diet or other methods to reduce the population of commensal Candida species in the gut.

There is insufficient evidence to know whether or not these interventions are effective, and many parents who try their children out on diets or vitamins do not report improvement. However, others report dramatic improvement. There may be two explanations for this: that placebo effects are particularly large in the treatment of autism, or that there are subpopulations of children with autism who do have specific metabolic abnormalities. There are known metabolic causes for autism, although they are rare in a clinic sample.

Endocrine disorders

Thyroid

There is some suggestion that thyroid dysfunction in mothers may be associated with an increased risk of ASD in children. Event transient low thyroid hormone may affect neuronal migration.[319]

Miscellaneous disorders

The apparent rise in ASD prevalence has led to the emergence of several popular hypotheses about aetiology, which have gained ground despite being based on little hard scientific evidence. Some of these, despite not being sustained in the original form in which they were proposed, have continued to be supported simply by changing the nature of their presumed action. The MMR hypothesis is an example. Although the original formulation of this – that vaccination with a combined measles, mumps and rubella vaccine led to a measles encephalitis and that led to autism – has been extensively investigated and is not upheld,[320] many parents are still refusing vaccination for their children on the basis that MMR is hazardous, citing three possible sources of this hazard.[321] These are that the attenuated measles virus has sufficient virulence to infect the gut endothelial cells, widening the junctions between enterocytes and allowing the absorption of proteins that cause encephalopathy; that the preservative in vaccines is toxic to the brain, with thimerosal, an ethylmercury salt, being thought to be particularly toxic; and that combined vaccines like MMR overtax the immune system, allowing the development of autoimmune disorders.

'Leaky gut' and ASD

Widening of the junction between enterocytes increases the permeability of the mucosal lining of the intestine. Increased permeability results from Crohn's disease, gluten enteropathy, trauma, and non-steroidal anti-inflammatory drugs, like aspirin. A number of ill-defined medical conditions, such as myalgic encephalopathy, have been attributed to 'leaky gut' syndrome, a condition in which an increased permeability of the intestine is assumed to have allowed entry into the bloodstream of substances with toxic effects on the brain, although the latter is itself protected by a barrier. Unusual peptides may be found in the urine of people with autism and some scientists have argued that they are degradation products of polypeptides absorbed from food or bacterial by-products that would normally be excluded if the intestine was not 'leaky'. If this were so, it would be expected that reducing intestinal permeability would decrease these peptides. However, one study of children with autism on gluten-free diets showed a non-significant improvement in their condition, but no change in urinary peptides.[322] It is further assumed that these peptides or their precursors have an effect on the brain, perhaps acting as endogenous opioids, but there has been no direct evidence for this.

Gastrointestinal symptoms

Gut neural plexus and CNS tissue are both derived from neuroderm, and the possibility that there is a link between bowel and brain pathology has some face validity. Gut-active hormones may double up as transmitters – secretin and cholecystokinin are both examples. Finally, the gut acts as a barrier to substances that may otherwise pass the blood–brain barrier and disrupt the function of intracranial contents – tyramine is an example.

All of these different functions of the gut have been the basis for a number of different speculations about gut-related causes of ASD. These are themselves based on a probably spurious raised prevalence of gastrointestinal symptoms in ASD. This has been based on anecdotal reports. The prevalence has probably been an overestimate because of selection bias as case series of children presenting to gastro-enterology clinics have often provided the basis for reports.[323] This may be the explanation, too, for the finding of nonspecific bowel pathology in children with an ASD based on biopsy findings.[324]

In clinical practice, encopresis with overflow is not uncommon in children with an ASD, probably reflecting emotional or family strains, as it does in children without ASD. These impressions are consistent with research findings. In one series, there was no correlation between gut symptoms – mainly either constipation or diarrhoea – and autistic symptoms or adaptive functioning, but there was a correlation with irritability, anxiety and social withdrawal.[325]

Enteropathy is, according to the 'leaky gut' hypothesis, a possible cause of toxin absorption. One consequence of the 'leaky gut' hypothesis is that more attention has been paid to the bowel symptoms that many children with ASD have.

Many parents report that their children with ASD also have gastrointestinal symptoms, such as diarrhoea and bulky or offensive stools. But an alternative explanation of the link between autism and gastrointestinal symptoms has been proposed by Campbell *et al.*, who have found an increase in the C-allele of tyrosine kinase, a MET receptor which is expressed in temporal cortex and in gut, in families where there is a history of gastrointestinal disorder and ASD, but not in families where the two conditions may occur separately, but do not co-occur.[326]

An argument against the association between ASD and enteropathy being, as Campbell *et al.* suggest, spurious is that the urine of people with an ASD show unusual peptides that are not only active in the CNS, but also not normally present.[326] However, these findings, too, appear to be spurious.[327]

Casein and gluten enteropathy are most often implicated as causes of any supposed enteropathy in ASD. There are a few case reports of untreated enteritis, specifically gluten enteropathy, causing an ASD, which remits when a gluten-free diet is instituted.[328] A review of the literature suggests that such cases are very rare, and that response to gluten-free diets (see Chapter 12) is most often attributable to placebo effects.[329]

Environmental toxins

Mercury

Although thimerosal in vaccines is considered safe, and not likely to be a cause of ASD, by licensing authorities, studies of mercury and ASD that the concerns about vaccines stimulate have led to some reports suggesting a link between other environmental sources of mercury and ASD.[330, 331, 332] However, the balance of evidence continues to be against toxicity being a common cause of ASD.

Lead

Lead has been used in petrol as an anti-knocking agent, in paint, and in plumbing. Paint containing lead persists on the surfaces of public buildings in many parts of the world since it offers better weather proofing for lower cost. Exposure to lead is a risk factor for ADHD.[333] Exposure to other low level toxins that increase ADHD risk, such as nitrogen dioxide or persistent organic pollutants,[334] and other industrial chemicals,[335] may be higher in families with low incomes or social status.[336]

'E numbers'

E numbers is the slang term given to the miscellaneous group of food additives that have been given a 'European number' by the European Food Safety Authority. Equivalent international numbers have the prefix INS. Considerable anecdotal evidence supports a commonly held view that some food additives can exacerbate the motor over-activity and impulsivity of children with ADHD and possibly ASD, and this has led to changes in food safety regulations, even though there is no convincing scientific evidence of these effects.[337]

Organophosphorus insecticides

Dimethyl thiophosphate is a metabolite of the pesticide, dimethyl alkylphosphate (DMAP). Children with detectable levels of dimethyl thiophosphate are twice as likely to have ADHD as children with undetectable levels. However, this may be a spurious association since longitudinal data are not available.[338]

Autoimmune disorder and ASD

There is an increased risk of ASD in the children of mothers with autoimmune disorders,[339, 340] although it has not been found in all studies.[341] Children with an ASD have frequently been found to have high levels of circulating mast cells, whose increase is often a marker for an autoimmune disorder.[342] An increase in antibodies to antigens in temporal cortex has been reported.[343] The siblings of children with ASD have also been reported to have abnormalities of their immune system.[344]

Some investigators have concluded that autism is associated with an autoimmune response to dietary protein,[345] or an increase in autoantibodies specific to the brain.[345] Another group has demonstrated significantly low levels of platelet–endothelial adhesion molecules in autism, which likely plays a role in the immune system as a marker for inflammatory changes.[345] Chez *et al.* showed an elevation of cerebral spinal fluid tumor necrosis factor α in patients with autism.[346]

Sydenham's chorea

A long recognized complication of streptococcal sore throat in pre-teens has been the development of a time-limited chorea often associated with behavioural changes.[347] This 'Sydenham's chorea' has been suspected to be more widespread than previously thought, and has been renamed PANDAS (Paediatric Autoimmune Neuropsychiatric Disorders Associated with Streptococcal infection). PANDAS is diagnosed on the clinical presentation of anxiety, a relapsing and remitting course, a history of beta-haemolytic streptococcal infection, with raised anti-Streptolysin O titres[348] features of ADHD, obsessive compulsive disorder, and Tourette syndrome.[349] It is speculated that the ADHD in these children is a consequence of an autoimmune response to an antigen present in nerve cells – possibly in caudate nucleus[350] – and Streptococcus cell wall.

Chapter 12

PRESENTATION IN INFANCY AND EARLY CHILDHOOD (THE PRE-SCHOOL YEARS)

RELEVANT DEVELOPMENTAL CHALLENGES

Developmental checks focus on four areas of development in the first year of life: social, language, truncal coordination, and eye–hand coordination. Although all may be affected in ASD, it is delayed social development that is fundamental. Some of the key milestones are shown in Table 12.1.

Table 12.1 Key developmental milestones in social and communicative behaviour

Month	Social and communicative behaviours
1	Looks and follows object moving in front of him/her in range of 45 degrees; quietens when a voice is heard; cries to express displeasure; makes throaty sounds; looks intently at parents when they talk to him/her
2	Follows dangling objects with eyes; visually searches for sounds; makes noises other than crying; cries become distinctive (wet, hungry, etc.); vocalizes to familiar voices; social smile demonstrated in response to various stimuli
3	Locates sound by turning head and looking in the same direction; squeals, coos, babbles and chuckles; 'talks' when spoken to; recognizes faces, voices, and objects; smiles when he/she sees familiar people, and engages in play with them; shows awareness to strange situations
4	Makes consonant sounds; laughs; enjoys being rocked, bounced or swung
5	Watches objects that are dropped; says 'ah-goo' or similar vowel–consonant combinations; smiles at mirror image; gets upset if you take a toy away; can tell family and strangers apart; begins to discover parts of his/her body
6	Turns head from side to side and then looks up or down; prefers more complex visual stimuli; says one syllable sounds like 'ma', 'mu', 'da' and 'di'; recognizes parents
7	Responds to name; awareness of depth and space begin; has taste preferences; 'talks' when others are talking
8	Reaches for toys that are out of reach; listens selectively to familiar words; begins combining syllables like 'mama' and 'dada' but does not attach a meaning; understands the word 'no' (but does not always obey it!); dislikes nappy (diaper) change and being dressed
9	Responds to simple verbal commands; comprehends 'no, no'; increased interest in pleasing parents; puts arms in front of face to avoid having it washed
10	Comprehends 'bye-bye'; says 'dada' or 'mama' with meaning; says one other word beside 'mama' and 'dada' (hi, bye, no, go); waves bye; object permanence begins to develop; repeats actions that attract attention; plays interactive games such a 'pat-a-cake'; enjoys being read to and follows pictures in books
11	Rolls a ball when asked; becomes excited when a task is mastered; acts frustrated when restricted; shakes head for 'no'
12	Turns pages in a book; follows rapidly moving objects; says three or more words other than 'mama' or 'dada'; comprehends the meaning of several words; repeats the same words over and over again; imitates sounds, such as the sounds that dogs and cats make; recognizes objects by name; understands simple verbal commands; shows affection; shows independence in familiar surrounding; clings to parents in strange situation; searches for object where it was last seen

18	Says 8–10 words you can understand; looks at a person who is talking to him/her; asks specifically for his/her mother or father; uses 'hi,' 'bye' and 'please,' with reminders; protests when frustrated; asks for something by pointing or by using one word; direct another's attention to an object or action; becomes anxious when separated from parent(s); seeks attention; brings toys to share with parent; acts out a familiar activity in play (as in pretending to take a bath); plays alone on the floor with toys; competes with other children for toys; recognizes him/herself in the mirror or in pictures; seems selfish at times
24	Has a vocabulary of several hundred words; uses 2–3 word sentences; says names of toys; interacts with peers; asks for information about an object (asks, 'Shoe?' while pointing to shoe box); hums or tries to sing, listens to short rhymes; likes to imitate parents; sometimes gets angry and has temper tantrums; is shy with strangers; comforts a distressed friend or parent; takes turns in play with other children; treats a doll or stuffed animal as though it were alive; applies pretend action to others (as in pretending to feed a doll); shows awareness of parental approval or disapproval for his/her actions; refers to self by name and uses 'me' and 'mine'; verbalizes desires and feelings ('I want cookie'); laughs at silly labelling of objects and events (as in calling a nose an ear); enjoys looking at one book over and over; points to eyes, ears or nose when you ask

Source: Adapted from Centers for Disease Control and Prevention; National Network for Child Care.

FIRST SUSPICIONS OF ASD

Parents report unusual gaze and emotional expressions from the age of six months in children who go on to be diagnosed as having an ASD. However, these observations are usually put down to normal variation and not to a developmental problem, and it is only after 11 months, and sometimes not until 17 months, when children are expected to start playing interactively with other children, that parents might think that there is definitely something wrong.[1] Parental observations are more sensitive than objective measurement. So these developmental differences become apparent on home videos from about one year onwards.[2] In an earlier study, the same group found that the main differences between home videos of infants who were to be diagnosed as having ASD, normally developing infants, and infants with language or developmental delay, were that the infants with ASD had less peer interest, averted their gaze more, and made fewer anticipatory postures.[3]

Box 12.1 Red flags leading to a suspicion of an ASD in infants

- Gaze does not indicate expected emotional or social contact with carer.
- Fewer or no apparent bids to engage carer's attention to infant or to what infant is interested in.
- Infant vocalization does not seem to be a response to interaction with carer.
- Reduced or absent indication by infant that carer is recognized.

Source: Adapted from AAP guidelines in Johnson, Myers, *et al.*, 2007.

RED FLAGS

There are a variety of proposed red flags, some more specific than others.[4] The most recent guidelines from the American Academy of Pediatrics (AAP) suggest taking particular account of nonverbal communication particularly in children in their first year of life (see Box 12.1). The AAP recommends that every child be screened for 'red flags' of ASDbetween 18 and 24 months.

DIAGNOSTIC CRITERIA

The principles and criteria of diagnosis have been considered in previous chapters. Both international diagnostic manuals are biased towards diagnosis in childhood, and need little modification for them to be immediately applicable to this group (but see also Box 12.2). Diagnosis by experienced psychiatrists at age two years has good specificity and acceptable sensitivity for autistic disorder, although not for Asperger syndrome,[5, 6, 7, 8] so long as psychiatrists are experienced with children of this age and take account of their general level of development.

Box 12.2 Modification of DSM-IV criteria to make them more specific to infancy

Qualitative abnormalities in communication

- Delay or lack of development of spoken language that is not accompanied by an attempt to compensate through the use of gesture or mime.
- A lack of babbling.
- A lack of pointing to express interest or a lack of spontaneous pointing.
- Odd speech patterns, words or phrases, echolalia, unusual tone and pitch.

Qualitative abnormalities in social interaction

- Poor eye contact.
- Failure to follow gaze.
- Limited social smiling – does the child spontaneously smile in greeting?
- Limited imitation of others (also seen in play) – for example, pretends to mow lawn.
- Poor use of gestures – for example, shakes head, nods, waves and claps.
- Failure to show an interest.
- Does the child show things of interest – for example, brings toys to parent?
- Does the child respond to others' emotions?
- Limited pretend and imaginative play.
- Limited social play – for example, peekaboo, pat-a-cake.

Restricted and repetitive interests and behaviours

- Repetitive play – for example, lining up cars.
- Unusual interests, interest in non-functional elements of play material.
- Oversensitivity to household noises.
- Extreme adverse reaction to change in routine.
- Motor mannerisms or stereotyped behaviour – for example, hand flapping.
- Sensory hypo/hypersensitivity.

Source: Adapted from Dover and Le Couteur, 2007.

Case history: David

David was born after a long and difficult labour. At birth, he was jaundiced but did not require specific treatment for this. He was slow to feed, seeming to need to be taught to suck at the breast. Other than that, he was an easy baby. Unusually placid, his mother thought when she looked back. At the time, she was just grateful that she could recover from the birth without too many demands from David. However, she did note that David seemed heavier than other babies because he did not mould to her when he was picked up and because he was quite a floppy baby. David was able to sit and to walk at the expected age, but he did not babble and did not speak. When he wanted something, he would take his mother's hand and pull her towards whatever it was that he wanted.

David's family were told by family and professionals alike that David would talk 'when he was ready' but by the time that David was two years old, his parents were worried that this might not be true. His parents were also more aware that it was difficult to engage David's attention. Sometimes, his parents wondered if he was deaf, because he could just ignore them if he were absorbed in something. At two, David was becoming increasingly absorbed in a few fascinations: the washing machine spinning, a particular mobile which flashed in the sun, jigsaw puzzles which he liked to do over and over again. The latter were a surprise to his parents. David seemed able to manage puzzles that would normally defeat older children, and he could do this just as easily if the pieces were upside down as when they were picture side up.

If David was interrupted in one of these fascinations he would become distressed and bite himself, or bang his head. One day, when one of the puzzle pieces was lost, David seemed to shut off and became absorbed in rhythmically pressing his eye. This became a regular habit after that, along with other stereotyped movements such as flapping with excitement or rocking with anxiety.

By the age of five, his parents had become more aware of David's limits. They knew that he would have a temper tantrum if something unexpected happened during the day, and tried to avoid this. They accepted that they could not easily contact David by looking at him or by asking him questions, but had discovered that David was aware of them even when he did not seem to signal it. He liked to listen to music with his mother, and he liked to rock with her in time to music although he resisted being hugged. They were impressed by David's ability to recognize tunes, and had bought him a keyboard to see if he would be willing to play himself. David's parents had developed a system of toileting that generally resulted in David being continent, and he had stopped using nappies (diapers) at the age of four, even at night. David was still not speaking, but did use some nonverbal signs such as waving.

Their family doctor had told them that 'David was a bit slow' and that 'they would have to accept it'. When they asked about autism, the doctor said that he was 'not an expert in that kind of thing', but did not think that a referral to a paediatrician was necessary. It was better, the doctor said, just to accept David as he was, and not try to label him. The parents did not press the matter as David was due to attend an assessment centre to see what type of special education he would need.

David clearly has an autistic disorder. His is the most commonly recognized presentation: that of a child with language delay who shows 'islands of ability', which indicate that his problem cannot be simply attributed to generalized learning difficulty. Autism like David's can be detected at the age of 18 months by a combination of abnormal pointing, lack of pretend play, and failure to use gaze to monitor another person's attention shifts.[9] Despite the reliability of this early detection – in the Baron-Cohen *et al.* study there were no false negatives, and only two false positives out of twelve – there is usually considerable delay in the diagnosis of autism. In a survey by Howlin and Asgharian, it was not until five and a half that the diagnosis was confirmed.[10]

David has had little time to develop a personality of his own, although his parents experienced him as having a strong and distinctive character. His life has, as yet, been untouched by few of the life events that will later on shape him. He is only just beginning on the phase of life when he has to make social relationships outside his family, social relationships which will largely depend on how he reacts to others, because his new acquaintances will not make the allowances for him that his parents have. David does have a characteristic temperament, however, which affects the expression of his autism. Even as a newborn, he reacted to the world around him, which must seem incomprehensible to a baby with autism, by passive withdrawal, which his mother experienced as placidity. Other children with autism are reported by their mothers to be constantly fretful and incapable of being soothed. Both David and these other children are unable to benefit from the comfort of contact with their parents, but David withdrew and the other children complained. Crying may be an indication of vigour,[11] and the willingess to make demands on others. David's lack of vigour may reduce his determination to make a place for himself in a hostile, social world in the future.

PRESENTING SYMPTOMS

Primary impairment or difference

Experienced mothers, or grandmothers, may become aware early on of the infant's lack of moulding or social interaction. Since many families with a child with autism do not go on to have more children, children with an ASD are more likely to be firstborn than neurotypical children. Their parents are therefore more likely to be inexperienced. So they may only become aware of the primary impairment in their child when his or her failure to communicate becomes explicit in a delay in speaking. Other parents may make so many adjustments to their baby that it is only when the infant goes to playgroup and mixes with other children that the child's social difficulties become overt.

The expression of the primary impairment does not differ between girls or boys, although boys may show more repetitive activities and girls more communicative difficulties.[12]

Secondary disability or idiosyncrasy

Secondary disability in infancy is related to impaired social interaction between infant and main carer, which can lead to problems in feeding and emotional regulation. Infants with ASD may fail to thrive, may have difficulty in sucking and taking to the breast, and may regurgitate food for longer than average. Settling at night and sleeping through the night may be more of a problem, too, with girls seeming more anxious and having more difficulty in sleeping than boys.[13]

Attachment security (see Chapter 10) is established at a later age, after the period when the infant has begun to be anxious about strangers. The obstacles to full social interaction with the mother increase the risk of the relationship between mother and child being more fraught, and a reduction in attachment security can therefore be expected at this later age. Studies of toddlers with an ASD suggest that secure attachment is not impossible, but is less likely than in neurotypicals when the child has intellectual disability in addition.[14] However, some of this effect may be exaggerated by the inapplicability of the Strange Situation Test to observations of children with an ASD. Using a Q-sort method of assessing attachment and an altered set of criterion behaviours may be more accurate.[15] Secure attachment is more likely if the mother understands the child's difficulties, and if the child has received a diagnosis and post-diagnosis information.[16]

Tertiary handicap or altered life style

There is little information about the long-term impact of social reactions to infants and toddlers on their adjustment to their ASD. One factor that may be relevant is the impact of ASD on spontaneous conversation between the child and family members, and later, with peers. One important element of these conversations is the discussion of the motives, justification, or hopes of other people. It is not known whether or not a lack of such conversations contributes to later deficits in social competence and in theory of mind.

DIFFERENTIAL DIAGNOSIS AND ASSOCIATED CONDITIONS

See section on differential diagnosis in Chapter 8.

Speech and language disorder

If, as suggested in Chapter 8, impaired nonverbal communication is taken to be a fundamental symptom of ASD, then a speech and language disorder should rarely be confused with an ASD. Parental reports of social interaction and of nonverbal communication have been found to clearly differentiate children with an ASD from those with receptive language impairment.[17] However, a lack of nonverbal expression may be a normal reaction in a frightened child to a stranger and may superficially resemble ASD, and this may complicate observational assessments, in the absence of detailed information from parents. This may even be true in a child whose verbal communication may be impaired because of hearing difficulties, or even because they are being assessed in a foreign and little understood language. This is brought home by two apparently similar cases reported by Snyder *et al.*: one with an ASD, and one a Spanish-speaking child assessed in an English-speaking school setting, and in English.[18] Nonverbal communication must therefore be observed in several settings if necessary, and less weight should be placed on a lack of expressiveness than on unusual or idiosyncratic expression. Assessment should take place wherever possible in language that is familiar to the child: in a hearing impaired child, this might require the mediation of a suitable signer. Children without speech should be assessed in familiar surroundings, or observed interacting with people with whom they are familiar.

Speech and language disorder as an associated condition

Speech and language disorders are characteristic of autistic disorder, but there has been considerable debate about whether or not they are comparable to the speech and language disorders that may occur as an independent developmental disorder, in which case they would be a condition associated with the ASD, or whether there is a specific autistic-type speech and language disorder. The evidence for each of these positions is discussed in Chapter 7.

There is considerable evidence that verbal IQ, the acquisition of speech before the age of five years, and other proxies of having a speech and language disorder are associated with a worse outcome for a child with an ASD. It is possible that the presence of a speech and language disorder is simply a proxy measure of some more fundamental factor that leads to poorer outcome: that speech and language disorder is, in other words, a confounder. But given the social difficulties that can arise for children who have only speech and language impairment, it seems more likely that speech and language disorder is an 'associated condition' that makes its own partly independent contribution to the social impairment of a person with an ASD. If this is so, then careful and independent assessment of the speech and language disorder, and of other associated conditions, should be carried out and specific remediation provided, if it is available.

Hyperlexia

A proportion of infants with ASD read early, some being described as reading before they can talk. A few of these children show symptoms of hyperlexia,[19] that is forced attention to the written word with pressure to read even when other tasks are more urgent. Children with an ASD who have advanced reading ages may have normal or reduced comprehension ages,[20] that is they have grasped the principles of producing speech from seeing letters, but without fully processing the semantic content.

Attachment disorder

The study of those rare children who have been brought up 'ferally',[21, 22, 23] or by parents who have excluded them from social contact, or who have been severely deprived in institutions have confirmed that a proportion, but only a proportion, may have what Rutter *et al.* have termed 'quasi-autism'.[24] The view that ASD may more generally be caused by occult or everyday neglect, or neglect coupled with abuse, was once widely held.[25, 26] The high heritability of ASD has gainsaid these assumptions, and it is a rare child psychiatrist who would maintain that an ASD could be caused solely by neglect, and be cured, as Bettelheim maintained, by care. But it is still recognized that children who are socially deprived may develop a psychological disorder, and that a particular category of attachment disorders are more likely to be caused in this way (see also Chapter 10).

Reactive attachment disorder may be the main differential diagnosis to ASD in children with a disturbed or disrupted upbringing, and it is not uncommon in care proceedings for experts to differ on whether or not a child has an attachment disorder, in which case the expert is likely to attribute this to parenting failure and to be advocating local authority care, or whether the child has an ASD, in which case any failings in the parent or parents are likely to be seen as understandable in the face of having a troubled child. Which view the judge in the family court goes with may determine whether the child remains in the care of the parent, or is removed into the care of the state.

Children with reactive attachment disorder may be intermittently non-communicative, and during these periods their nonverbal expressiveness may dwindle. However, these states are socially, situationally and emotionally reactive, and changes in the child's mood result in changes in expressiveness, contrary to ASD.

The aetiology of reactive attachment disorder is not fully understood. It may affect only one child in a sibship, and that may not be the only or even the least abused or neglected sibling. Distractibility and impulsivity is a feature of disinhibited reactive attachment disorder, suggesting a possible link with ADHD. Delayed speech, and speech and language difficulties, may also overlap. Reactive attachment disorder is rare and no follow-up studies have been performed of sporadic children diagnosed with this condition, but there are follow-ups of children who had previously been in Eastern European orphanages and they have many symptoms of ADHD and speech and language disorder,[27] suggesting disinhibited reactive attachment disorder may be an early manifestation of a hereditary diathesis. The manifestations of an ADHD diathesis are known to be influenced by social environment,[28] as is speech and language development. Children with reactive attachment disorder often behave oppositionally, even in early childhood, as do many older children with ADHD.[29]

Oppositional behaviour in children with reactive attachment disorder may be seen as provocative, or done to punish or wind up someone else. Cruelty to animals or other children may have this quality, for example. However, sometimes the cruelty, or what seems like a deliberate negation of adult authority, seems more likely to be due to a lack of awareness in the child of the impact of his or her actions: to a lack of empathy. Opposition normally involves empathy, if only to know how best to oppose. This kind of apparently oppositional behaviour betokens a lack of empathy that is characteristic of children with atypical ASD or 'PDD not otherwise specified' (see Chapter 16). It is therefore possible that as these children get older, features of an impairment of nonverbal interpretation may become more overt and a diagnosis of an atypical ASD may be made.

Attachment disorder as an associated condition

Children with an ASD are no more or less likely to be securely attached than neurotypical children unless they have an intellectual disability in addition,[14] but whether or not they are more likely to show disorganized attachment (see Chapter 11) has not been examined. Children with an ASD who show 'disorganized' attachment use symbolic play less than children with ASD and organized attachment,[30] but it is unclear whether this is because disorganized attachment is an additional contributor to the impairments of a child with an ASD, or a reflection of ASD severity. Nor was there a difference in this study between securely and insecurely attached children in their symbolic play. Inability of mothers to accept a diagnosis of ASD has been associated with disorganized attachment in one study,[31] suggesting that there is a maternal contribution to this pattern of attachment.

Distinction from intellectual disability

Children with intellectual disability are delayed in speaking and understanding language, and may be delayed in social understanding, too. But they are equally delayed in all other areas of their development, unlike children with an ASD who show specific delays in socialization and communication. Communication difficulties in particular may cause frustration if they are out of proportion to intellectual ability. Care staff with little knowledge of ASD may sometimes infer from this frustration that a child who is being treated as having intellectual disability actually has an ASD, either in addition or as the sole explanation for their communication problems, since the behaviour of children with an ASD may be more challenging than their peers, whether or not they have intellectual disability.[32]

Detailed assessment will disclose evidence of the autistic syndrome in people with intellectual disability and ASD, in that social and communicative impairments will be out of proportion to other intellectually related skills. However, people with intellectual disabilities who are also deaf and blind present particular assessment difficulties in that their communication may also be impaired by their reduced perception. In one study of ten people with intellectual disability who were also deaf-blind, five people had a consensus clinical diagnosis of an ASD and five did not. Comparisons indicated that 'openness for contact', 'reciprocity/joint attention' and 'communicative signals/functions' discriminated significantly between the ASD and the non-ASD group.[33] This indicates, as other studies have done, that the most important clinical differentiation is that of the kind of reflexive nonverbal communication described in Chapter 6 as 'interbraining'.

Intellectual disability as an associated condition

Half of all children with an ASD have an intellectual disability, and 8 per cent of children with an intellectual disability have an ASD.[34] But although there is a strong genetic correlation between conventional ratings of ASD and IQ, this is confined to speech and language impairments, and repetitive behaviour. Impaired nonverbal communication and social impairment have no genetic correlation with intelligence.[34]

Recognized syndromes associated with ASD often presenting in infancy

An increasing number of syndromes are described which have particular skin, organ and psychological characteristics that include an increased risk of ASD. Most of these syndromes were originally described by particular individuals who have lent their names to the conditions: as a result they are often collectively known as named syndromes, although they include a few that are not eponymous, such as fragile X syndrome. The genetics of an increasing number of these disorders are known, and it is likely that they will all prove to be of hereditary origin. Some hereditary causes of ASD have already been considered in Chapter 10.

The place of named syndromes in the classification of ASD has been confused. Rett syndrome is given as an alternative diagnosis to autism spectrum disorder, although there are cases of Rett syndrome that do not have marked ASD features. Morever, it seems likely that there are many other 'complex' cases of ASD, currently diagnosed as autistic disorder, which will turn out to be endophenotypes of genetic disorders, for example ASD in associated with Klinefelter syndrome, which is particularly associated with a lack of conversational skills, and 22q11 deletion syndrome, associated with stereotypies, interest in part objects, and language delay.[35]

Rett syndrome, although a separate disorder in ICD-10 and DSM-IV, will be considered here as a named syndrome.

The association of rare syndromes with ASD can be interpreted to mean that the cause of the rare syndrome also causes ASD, although it may be that in a few cases the ASD is a consequence of the physical manifestations of the rare syndrome. Visual impairment is a particular example of a symptom that may disrupt the early process of shared attention and pave the way to the development of an ASD.[36]

More and more rare syndromes are associated with known genetic abnormalities, but a few are associated with teratological effects of drugs, such as alcohol or valproate exposure, and some are of unknown aetiology.

Genetic disorders
Sotos syndrome
Frequency
The syndrome occurs in approximately 1 in 14,000 births.

Heredity
If the cause is a deleted gene, this is inherited as an autosomal dominant, but almost all cases are sporadic, resulting from a new mutation.

Genetic cause
A proportion of Sotos syndrome cases have a mutation in the NSD1 gene at 5q35, typically small deletions, leading to haploinsufficiency of this gene.[37] If the deletion extends to the neighbouring gene, SLC34A1, infantile hypercalcaemia and nephrocalcinosis may also occur.[38]

Appearance
The facial features are particularly apparent in childhood: they include malar flushing, sparse frontotemporal hair, high bossed forehead, downslanting palpebral fissures, a long narrow face, and a prominent narrow jaw. The head is sometimes said to resemble an inverted pear. Puberty is precocious and although children with Sotos syndrome are unusually tall, adults are of average size.

Intelligence
Intelligence is rarely normal, and is usually in the mild to moderately severe intellectually disabled range.

Clinical features
Children with Sotos syndrome are floppy as infants and continue to be hypotonic, have more rapid growth leading to larger than average bodies and heads, advanced bone age, and early puberty. The cerebral cortex is enlarged on MRI.

Investigations

Overgrowth syndromes present as a precociously large body size and increased skull circumference (either measure greater than two standard deviations above the mean for the sex and age group). In infancy, this may be caused by gestational diabetes in the mother, which needs investigation, or one of several syndromes of which Sotos is one. The latter include Beckwith-Wiedemman, Weaver, Simpson-Golabi-Behmel, Perlman and Bannayan-Riley-Ruvalcaba. Sotos like these other syndromes may be associated with the VACTERYL syndrome: Vertebral spine anomalies; Atresias in the gut (notably oesophageal atresia); Congenital heart lesions; TracheoEsophageal defects; Renal and urinary tract anomalies; and Limb lesions.[39]

A CNV in the NSD1 gene can be detected in 80 to 90 per cent,[40] and molecular genetic testing should be performed, along with the appropriate investigations for VACTERYL and other linked anomalies.

Association with the ASDs

Case reports suggest an association with ASD,[41, 42] although expressive speech impairment may be more common.[43] Cases of Sotos syndrome not associated with NDS1 mutations have more developmental symptoms, including ADHD.[44] It seems likely that the genetic disorder leading to ASD is not the result of NSD1 mutation, but another as yet unknown gene mutation, for example the one causing Cole-Hughes syndrome, which is a familial macrocephaly associated with Sotos syndrome and obesity.[45]

Williams-van Beuren syndrome

Frequency

The syndrome occurs in 1 in 20,000 births.

Heredity

Although the deleted gene may be inherited as an autosomal dominant, most cases are sporadic.

Genetic cause

Deletion of the LIM kinase1 gene in 7q11.23 causes Williams-van Beuren syndrome. Duplication in the area may cause a similar syndrome,[46] although with more features of ASD. The LIM kinase 1 gene is adjacent to other genes of considerable effect, which may influence the clinical picture. These include the elastin gene, which is often affected by the deletion, a gene for visuoconstructive processing, and a gene that may be implicated in ASD.[47]

Appearance

Physical features might include stellate iris, bulging eyes, low set nose and mouth, nose broad at the tip, flat cheeks, smooth philtrum, wide mouth, and dental malocclusion.

Intelligence

Intelligence is rarely normal, and is usually in the mild to moderate range of intellectual disability.

Clinical features

If the elastin gene is involved, the child may be born with supravalvular aortic stenosis, leading to a heart murmur at birth and the onset of hypertension in adolescence. Young children have hyperextensible joints, but joints become more than usually rigid as the child gets older. Umbilical and inguinal hernias are common. The eyes may be crossed (strabismus) and hypermetropic (long-sighted). Gastrointestinal problems are common, including constipation and vomiting in infancy, and pain in adulthood. Some of these complaints may be secondary to hypercalcaemia, which occurs in 20 per cent. Hypothyroidism may also occur. Recurrent ear infections may occur. Children may be enuretic until a late age. The bladder may have diverticuli leading to chronic urinary infection and eventually renal disease.

Investigations

Hypercalcaemia is most prominent in infancy. Later in life, the calcium to creatinine ratio is a more useful screening test. Cardiac function should be assessed, and blood pressure in older children and adults.

Association with the ASDs

There is a deficit in visuoconstructive learning if a gene adjacent to LIM kinase is involved. Children with Williams-van Beuren syndrome learn best with materials presented auditorily. Most children with Williams-van Beuren syndrome have ADHD. A minority (perhaps 10%) have ASD, but most children with Williams-van Beuren syndrome are unusually socially outgoing, approaching others and wanting to share with them.[48] This is because, although people with Williams-van Beuren syndrome can rank faces in terms of approachability (a smiling face being universally considered the most approachable),[49] they lack anxiety in response to unfamiliar faces, possibly because of an alteration in serotinergic signalling affecting the pathway between the prefrontal cortex and the amygdala.[50]

One of the most striking features of Williams-van Beuren syndrome is therefore a lack of stranger anxiety, and this can lead to an unexpected sociability, since social approach is unhindered by neurotypical social inhibition and prejudice.[51] It also results in a lack of avoidance of other-directed gaze,[52] which may be linked to the increased ability of children with Williams-van Beuren to interpret facial expressions.

Prader-Willi syndrome

Frequency

Between 1 in 10,000 and 1 in 25,000 neonates have Prader-Willi syndrome.

Heredity

Infants with the condition, like infants with many other genetic disorders, are hypotonic.

Genetic cause

About 1 per cent of the human genome is imprinted, which means that in imprinted regions, one chromatid is silenced, often by methylation of the DNA in its double helix. This occurs after the embryo has begun to develop, and results in either the maternally derived or the paternally derived DNA being expressed in these regions. The region on the long arm of chromosome 15, 15q11-13, is imprinted. It is a particularly unstable region, subject to a range of different mutations. If a mutation that leads to altered activity of the gene occurs on the paternally derived chromosome is paired with a maternally imprinted chromosome, Prader-Willi syndrome results. If it is the maternally derived chromosome that is mutated and the paternally imprinted chromosome that is imprinted, Angelman syndrome (see below) results. Duplication of the maternally derived genes in this section (maternal uniparental disomy) is a cause of Prader-Willi syndrome which is less common than a deletion in the paternally derived chromosome, but results in the same effect.

At least two and possibly more genes have to be affected for the full Prader-Willi syndrome to result.

Appearance

In later life, the most prominent feature in untreated people is short stature, hyperphagia and obesity. As with many other genetic disorders, the most prominent effect in infancy is hypotonia.

Other suggestive features are a long face, with a prominent nose, and an absent philtrum between the nose and the mouth.

Intelligence

Estimates vary about what proportion of people with Prader-Willi syndrome are of normal intelligence, but it is likely that half or more meet the standard criteria for intellectual disability.

Clinical features

The most frequent presentation is learning disability, but rarely people with Prader-Willi may present with endocrine disorders, obesity or a psychiatric disorder. Hypogonadism in boys results in bilateral undescended testes. The surge of androgen secretion by the adrenal cortex that normally occurs between the ages of six and eight years, and precedes sex hormone secretion by the gonads, occurs earlier and may lead in girls to the early development of sexual hair and increased sebaceous sweat that may be attributed to precocious puberty.

Growth hormones level are low, too, and supplements are now routinely given. Obesity may lead to type 2 diabetes.

These abnormalities point to hypothalamic abnormalities, and the characteristic hyperphagia of Prader-Willi syndrome was once attributed to this. However, attention has now turned to an impairment in the intrinsic gastric hormones that signal satiety,[53] such as ghrelin.[54]

People with Prader-Willi syndrome have an increased risk of OCD and ASD, and characteristically an increased risk of atypical, cycloid or affective psychoses. Psychosis is much more likely when both chromatids at the 15q11-13 locus are maternally derived (maternal uniparental disomy, or mUPD).[55]

Investigations

Genetic tests are now widely available. Large deletions in chromosome 15 may be detectable by microscopy, and the possibility of doing so is increased by using appropriate fluorescently tagged reagents (fluorescence in situ hybridization, or FISH testing). However, a DNA methylation test is the most reliable, detecting over 90 per cent of cases.

Association with the ASDs

No community-based prevalence studies have been carried out, but a review of 12 case series led Veltman *et al.* to suggest that the rate of ASD in Prader-Willi syndrome was of the order of 25 per cent, with a higher risk in those whose Prader-Willi was due to mUPD.[56]

Angelman syndrome

Angelman syndrome is much less likely to be associated with an ASD: Veltman *et al.* estimate the risk to be 2 per cent.[56]

22q deletion syndromes

Velocardiofacial syndrome

Frequency

Up to 1 in 4000 of live births may be affected by velocardiofacial syndrome, although the frequency in the US has been estimated to be twice this. Velocardiofacial syndrome may account for nearly 10 per cent of cases of cleft palate.

Heredity

All but a very small proportion (perhaps of the order of 5–10%) of cases have no family history, with the disorder arising in them as a new mutation.

Genetic cause

Deletions and other derangements in 22q11.2 cause velocardiofacial syndrome. The heart defects may be attributable to an inactive TBX gene, but the inactive section is longer: of the order of three megabases. Duplication may increase the risk of ASD.[57] Genes in this region influence the development of frontostriatal and cerebellar-cortical networks,[58] and depending on which network is affected, and the knock-on effects on brain area, different cognitive impairments come to the fore.

Appearance

There is no characteristic facies.

Intelligence

There is often a slight reduction in intelligence, with performance IQ being particularly affected. Expressive speech and language impairment is also common.

Clinical features

Velocardiofacial syndrome is associated with abnormal development of the pharyngeal arch, leading to defects in parathyroid, thymus, and the part of the heart derived from the conotruncal contribution. Although the manifestations are variable, approximately 75 per cent of people with velocardiofacial syndrome have cardia symptoms, which include an interrupted aortic arch (the most common), truncus arteriosus, and Fallot's tetralogy.

Maldevelopment of the palate may cause speech and feeding difficulties.

Maldevelopment of the eye causes ophthalmic problems in the majority.

The combination of conotruncal cardiac anomaly, hypoparathyroidism with hypocalcaemia, and thymic dysplasia leading to immune dysfunction is termed 'di George syndrome'. People with velocardiofacial syndrome who have a small jaw, a U-shaped palatal cleft, and a rearward or downward displacement of the tongue are said to have 'Pierre-Robin syndrome'.

There may be an overlap with symptoms of CHARGE syndrome.

Investigations

The mutation can be detected on FISH testing.

Association with the ASDs

ASD may occur in 50 per cent of people with velocardiofacial syndrome.[59] There is a high incidence of psychosis, with about 25 per cent of adults with velocardiofacial syndrome developing schizophrenia. Where there is a duplication in relevant area, 22qDS, there is a significant positive correlation between severity of (i) schizotypy score and grey matter volume of the temporo-occipital regions and the corpus striatum; (ii) emotional problems and grey matter volume of frontostriatal regions; and (iii) social behavioural difficulties and grey matter in frontostriatal regions. Frontostriatal and cerebellar-cortical networks are affected.[58]

Children with velocardiofacial syndrome and ASD have larger right amygdala volumes.[60]

Phelan-McDermid syndrome

Frequency

There are no accurate estimates of its frequency, although it is probably rare.

Heredity

Phelan-McDermid syndrome may be inherited but the ratio of hereditary to de novo cases is not known.

Genetic cause

Phelan-McDermid syndrome is due to a deletion in and around the telomere of chromosome 22, at 22q13, most often involving the paternally derived chromosome. The effects of Phelan-McDermid syndrome have been attributed to haploinsufficiency of the SHANK3 that is within 220Kbases of the telomere. SHANK3 gene products are involved in the formation of glutamate receptors, and the development of synapses and dendrites.

Appearance

Some people with Phelan-McDermid syndrome may have ptosis, an elongated head (dolichocephaly) and prominent ears.

Intelligence

Nothing is known.

Clinical features

Absent or severely delayed speech is almost universal, as is hypotonia. Increased pain tolerance is common, as are large hands and ears.

Investigations

FISH tests are available.

Association with the ASDs

Up to now all of the cases of Phelan-McDermid syndrome that have been described meet criteria for an ASD, with cases where there is a deletion meeting criteria for an autistic disorder, and one case with a duplication in this area meeting criteria for AS.[61]

Smith-Lemli-Opitz syndrome

Frequency

Smith-Lemli-Opitz (SLO) syndrome occurs in 1 in 20,000–40,000 live births. One person in 220 might be a carrier. The carrier frequency is highest in Northern and Central Europeans and rare in Africans and Asians. Diagnosis is more common in males.

Heredity

The disease is inherited as a Mendelian recessive, although some SNPs in the gene may lead to reduced function and so variable penetrance.

Genetic cause

The disease is caused by defects in both alleles of the gene for 7-dehydrocholesterol reductase (DHCR7) at chromosome 11q12-13. Cholesterol is a precursor of myelin formation, and is therefore required for the development of fibre tracts in the brain. It is also a precursor in the synthesis of sex steroids, and so hypogonadism with low testosterone or oestrogen is a feature of SLO. Some of the other developmental features may be to the absence of cell membrane sterol, another lipid that has cholesterol in its synthetic pathway.

Appearance

Microcephaly with reduced distance between the eyes, ptosis in 50 per cent, down slanting palpebral fissures, short stature, polydactyly, cleft palate, malformed genitals (only observable in boys) including hypospadias, cryptorchidism, micropenis, hypoplastic scrotum, and microurethra, webbing between the second and third digits in 90 per cent, low set and posteriorly rotated ears, retrognathia, and a short nose with a depressed nasal bridge and upturned nostrils.

Associated clinical features

Moderate to severe intellectual disability, failure to thrive, hypotonia, cleft palate in about 50 per cent, cardiac and associated vasculature defects in a third, pyloric stenosis, Hirschsprung's disease and urinary tract anomalies in two-thirds, including hydronephrosis, renal cystic dysplasia, renal duplication, renal agenesis and reflux.

Twenty per cent of infants with SLO die within the first year of life.

Investigations

Assay of 7-dehydrocholesterol, which is raised.

Association with the ASDs

It is estimated that 75 per cent of people with SLOS have an ASD.[62]

Smith-Magenis syndrome

Frequency

It is estimated to affect 1 in 25,000 live births.

Heredity

There is rarely a family history.

Genetic cause

Mutations in 17p11.2, and particularly inactivation through deletion or by a CNV of the retinoic acid induced 1 gene (RAI1), which is required for RNA transcription from DNA.

Appearance

The face may appear broad with a flattening of the middle of the face and of the bridge of the nose. The face is likely to be square in shape, with deep-set eyes, a prominent lower jaw, and a downturned mouth with a prominent upper lip.

Intelligence

In one study 75 per cent of children had an intellectual disability.[63]

Clinical features

Short stature, scoliosis, and visual and hearing problems are all associated, as is hoarse voice. Hearing may be part of a more general VIIIth nerve disorder, with hyperacusis and vestibular disturbances also reported. However, many of the characteristic features are behavioural with an overlap with many symptoms of ADHD and ASD.

Disrupted sleep is a characteristic feature, due to a reversal of the circadian rhythm. Impulsivity, anxiety, temper tantrums and inattentiveness are common, as are repeated self-injury, such as skin picking or self-biting, repeated self-hugging and tics, compulsive finger licking, and flipping printed pages. Over 90 per cent of children with Smith-Magenis syndrome have speech delay.

Investigations
A specific FISH test is available.

Association with the ASDs
Children with Smith-Magenis syndrome may be diagnosed as having an ASD or ADHD, including disorders in socialization. They rarely have as many symptoms as do children with ASD, however, and do not have communication impairments.[64]

Down syndrome
Frequency
Down syndrome occurs in about 1 in 650–1000 live births. The frequency increases with maternal age.

Heredity
About 2–3 per cent of Down syndrome cases are hereditary. The asymptomatic parent, who may be father or mother, has a translocation of the long arm of chromosome 21 onto another chromosome, often chromosome 14, and this makes non-dysjunction and therefore duplication of the long arm more likely, leading a high proportion of affected children.

Genetic cause
There are three copies of chromosome 21 or a part of the chromosome, due to a failure to segregate one copy of the chromosome to each gamete during meiosis. One gamete has none, and is nonviable. Another has two, resulting in the fertilized egg having three. Several genes are over-expressed and have been implicated in causing the characteristic phenotype. Of interest for the risk of autism is that several of these genes regulate the expression of the MECP2 gene, leading to the under-expression of this gene: also implicated in Rett syndrome (see below).

Appearance
The appearance of children with Down syndrome is characteristic, and led to the commonly used term 'Mongol' for this group of children. The term has now been dropped because of its pejorative connotations.

Intelligence
Trisomy 21 is almost always associated with an intellectual disability.

Clinical features
Trisomy 21 is associated with a wide range of physical symptoms, affecting a variable proportion. They include symptoms of congenital heart disease, thyroid disease, disorders of the bowel wall (leading to Hirschsprung's disease), infertility, visual impairment due to

lack of synchronization of extra-ocular muscles, otitis media that may lead to deafness, and ligamentous laxity. Leukaemia is also more common, but solid tumours are less common than in the general population.

Neuropsychiatric complications include receptive language disorders with impaired short-term verbal memory and reduced explicit memory, and presenile dementia of Alzheimer type.[65]

Investigations

In many cases, the additional chromosome can be observed on microscopy. Diagnosis in utero can be made using cells obtained by amniocentesis or chorionic villus sampling, but these tests carry some risks and are normally indicated only if ultrasound appearances of the foetus suggests trisomy 21 or if there is an indication from maternal age or some other risk factor.

Association with the ASDs

The view that ASD was rare in Down syndrome has now been replaced by clinical experience that it is likely to be more common. However, there are few epidemiological data. One study, carried out using questionnaires in special schools in a city in Brazil, suggested that 15 per cent of people with Down may also have an ASD. Interestingly, this study also found a ratio of affected boys to girls of less than two, with an equal ratio in boys and girls who did not meet criteria for an autistic disorder.[66]

X-linked disorders

Rett syndrome

Frequency

Rett syndrome is estimated to affect 1 girl born in every 10,000–15,000.

Heredity

It is estimated that less than 1 per cent of cases are hereditary.

Genetic cause

Rett syndrome is caused by an abnormality of the methyl CpG binding protein (MECP2) gene, located on the X chromosome. Girls who are homozygous for this mutant gene and boys who have the mutant gene on their single X chromosome usually die in infancy. MECP2 binds reversibly to a DNA section that encodes nerve growth factor, which regulates neuronal growth.[67] MECP2 is only normally expressed during infancy, and is probably mainly concerned in the pruning and development of synapses during early infancy. Affected girls only show signs some months after birth with one of the early signs being deceleration in head growth.[68] This corresponds to a reduction in dendrite formation with smaller, less well-connected neurons in brain areas whose known functions correspond to the typical symptoms of Rett syndrome. Failed pruning leads to an increase in glutaminergic synapses, especially of the N-methyl-D-glutamate (NMDA) type, in early childhood, but numbers eventually fall to lower than normal levels in later childhood. Glutamate is an excitatory transmitter, and these changes are consistent with symptomatic evidence of brain excitation, including epilepsy in children with Rett syndrome.[69] Missense (especially the p.R133C type) or late truncating mutations in the MECP2 gene may allow partial expression leading to a high functioning form of Rett syndrome (Zappella variant).[70]

Appearance

There are no specific facial features, but as a girl with Rett syndrome gets older, her head can be seen to have grown more slowly than her peers, and she is likely to have marked incoordination, including a wide-based gait.

Intelligence

It may be difficult to test intelligence formally, but girls with known Rett syndrome have intellectual disability that affects all types of learning.

Clinical features

Rett syndrome results from a mutation in the gene encoding the methyl-CpG binding protein 2 (MECP2), which functions as a transcriptional repressor on the X chromosome. Inactivation of the gene by the mutation results in an increase in protein transcription, which affects differentiating neurons, whose dendritic arborization and axonal projections is impaired. The reduction in dendritic development mainly affects rostral grey matter, in the prefrontal, posterior-frontal and anterior-temporal regions,[71] accounting for the clinical picture of Rett syndrome.[72]

Rett syndrome is classified as an ASD in DSM-IV because many girls with the condition meet ASD criteria. However, the main features of the condition are a profound regression in motor abilities in the first year of life, affecting the hands particularly, and often preceded by stereotyped movements with the hands. Many girls with Rett syndrome lose truncal coordination and as a result develop a scoliosis. They become unable to walk, and any speech that they have developed is lost. Fits occur in a substantial minority.

Case history: Paula

Paula was an unusually easy baby. She liked to be cuddled, unlike a baby with autism, but when she was put down she was happy to lie without stimulation, just crooning to herself. Her mother noticed that she seemed to be momentarily inattentive, and that Paula's mouth occasionally twitched, but neither of these observations gave cause for concern. At nine months, Paula was noted not to be growing as quickly as expected, and one or two people had commented on her rather small head. Her movements could also be jerky. But she was a smiley, friendly baby who related well to her mother and father, and to her siblings. She also passed her developmental checks. She was beginning by the age of 12 months to use occasional words, could reach for objects, and was just beginning to use a spoon. But then Paula seemed to come to a stop.

Her younger sister was born when Paula was 15 months old, and Paula seemed to react to this badly. She became irritable, and cried a lot. She also stopped being able to chew food, and had to go back to being fed with purée. She developed odd movements of continually touching her mouth with her fingers, and had difficulty in using her fingers. Her parents and the doctor were inclined to see this as an emotional response to her sister's birth at first, but when Paula could not manage to hold food in her mouth and developed odd, hand-washing movements which were obviously involuntary, they realized it was more serious. Paula became increasingly unable to control her muscles. She had difficulty in walking and feeding, and could not care for herself. The involuntary movements got much worse. They could affect her whole body, but particularly affected her mouth and hands. The latter often seemed to come together involuntarily in her midline, even in the middle of Paula trying to do something. Paula lost the ability to communicate to others with her loss of motor control, and she was unable to gesture, make appropriate facial expressions, or form words. However, her mother was sure that Paula was still trying to relate. She seemed calmer when with people whom she knew and would sometimes smile apparently completely normally during a social interaction. Paula by this time could not control her tongue and had great difficulty in feeding. Her respiratory control also seemed to be affected, and she was having alternate hyperventilatory and apnoeic spells. Paula also had frequent absence attacks but, although an EEG was abnormal, she had no seizures.

Investigations
A FISH test for the MECP2 mutation is definitive.

Association with the ASDs
There are many similarities in the presentation of Rett syndrome and ASD of other causes. There is particular overlap when the MECP2 is not completely haploinsufficient, in which case there may be a later onset and less severe regression and movement disorder. These girls may gradually redevelop motor skills, and be able to walk again and to develop some verbal ability. Mild Rett syndrome may therefore be mistaken for an ASD of unknown aetiology at first,[73] although nearly a quarter of these more mildly affected girls may not have an ASD.[70] Boys with partial expression of the MECP2 gene may also survive and are likely to be diagnosed as having an ASD without their Rett syndrome being suspected. Later in life it may be difficult to distinguish girls with more severe Rett syndrome from girls with profound intellectual disability of unknown aetiology, many of whom also have symptoms of an ASD.[74]

Turner syndrome
Frequency
Turner syndrome occurs in 1 in 2500 live births.

Heredity
Women with Turner syndrome are infertile.

Genetic cause
Turner syndrome results from the failure to transmit one X chromosome to the foetus leading to a 45, X0 karyotype, although why this happens is unknown. The effects partly depend on whether the remaining X chromosome is of maternal or paternal (as it is in 75%) origin. It is speculated that the X chromosome has a gene, or genes, probably in the Xp22.3 segment,[75] not found on the Y chromosome, that affects development of elements of the

social brain, including amygdala and orbitofrontal cortex. About 15 per cent of genes on the inactivated X chromosome escape inactivation, mainly those on the short arm. It is thought that these genes include those at Xp22.3, and that the action of these genes and those on the homologous X chromosome are both required for haplosufficiency.[75] Some researchers have argued that, as men have only one X chromosome, they are, like women with Turner syndrome, haploinsufficient for this gene compared to neurotypical women and so have a Turner-like underdevelopment of the social brain. Neurotypical men have larger amygdala than neurotypical women, and women with Turner syndrome have even larger amygdala.[76] Women with Turner syndrome also have increased orbitofrontal grey matter,[76] and smaller hippocampi[77] than the average, and they have reduced prefrontal functioning (see below) that resembles ADHD. ADHD is much more common (18 times more common according to one study[78] in girls with Turner syndrome than in neurotypical girls.

Appearance
People with Turner syndrome are female, usually short, and about one-third have skin folds on their neck (webbed neck).

Intelligence
Most affected girls and women are of normal intelligence, but nonverbal intelligence may be reduced.

Clinical features
Slowed growth becomes apparent from the age of five years, but can now be reversed by the prescription of growth hormone. The ovaries involute before birth in most women with Turner syndrome, and there is no puberty unless, as is usually the case nowadays, sex hormone supplementation is used. There is an association with heart defects, especially coarctation of the aorta, lymphoedema, skeletal abnormalities and kidney disorder.

Investigations
Turner syndrome, due to the missing X chromosome, can be detected on routine karyotyping.

Association with the ASDs
Women with Turner syndrome have executive impairment, hyperactive and impulsive symptoms of ADHD, and a lack of empathy for others, with consequent difficulties in social relationships.[78] These symptoms are those of atypical AS (see Chapter 16). Four cases of ASD and Turner syndrome have been reported.[79]

Impaired face reading,[80] especially in reading fear in faces,[76] is common, as is impaired eye direction estimation.[80] Reduced performance in detecting fear in faces is correlated with orbitofrontal PFC hypertrophy.[76]

There is a substantially increased risk of ADHD.[78]

316 Autism Spectrum Disorders Through the Life Span

Klinefelter syndrome

Frequency
It is estimated that 1 in 500 boys are born with an extra X chromosome, and that it is clinically significant in 1 in 1000.

Heredity
Klinefelter syndrome arises as a *de novo* mutation.

Genetic cause
One or more additional X chromosomes cause the syndrome, hence 'XXY' syndrome.

Appearance
Men with Klinefelter syndrome may appear no different from an XY male, although there is reduced testosterone, possibly because of reduced testicular volume, and increased FSH (follicle stimulating hormone) and LH (luteinizing hormone) levels that leads to gynaecomastia in one-third. Men with aneuploidy of the sex chromosomes, including XXY, tend to be taller than average.

Intelligence
Intelligence is unaffected.

Clinical features
Clinical features may be minimal. Some neoplasms are more common.[81]

Investigations
Investigation includes the examination of chromosome preparations under the light microscope.

Association with the ASDs
There is an increased risk of language delay, reading difficulty,[82] and in disorders of social interaction. Screening with ASD inventories suggests that all of the symptoms of an ASD are present in a higher proportion of people with Klinefelter syndrome than in the general population.[83]

Fragile X syndrome

Frequency
Fragile X syndrome is the most frequent hereditary cause of intellectual disability, affecting 1 in 3600 male births, and 1 in 4000–6000 female births. The premutation may be present in 1 in 2000 men and in as many as 1 in 260 women.

Heredity
Fragile X syndrome is most often inherited from a mother with the premutation.

Genetic cause

Fragile X syndrome is caused by inactivation of the FMR1 gene at Xq27.3. In 1 per cent of cases this may be caused by an SNP, but in 99 per cent it is due to a copy number variation in the promoter region of FMR1. This region functions to stop gene transcription by a tandem repeat of a repeat cytosine-guanine-guanine base triplet up to 55 base pairs long. However the repeat may increase (the premutation) with each generation ('anticipation') until it becomes so long (over 200 triplet repeats) that it is methylated and the gene becomes inactive (mutation). The methylation of such a long segment alters the appearance of the chromosome under the light microscope which appears thinned or 'fragile' at this point.

As women have a homologous chromosome, they are much less likely than men to lack an effective copy of FMR1, and so the full fragile X syndrome is much rarer in women than in men. However, the permutation state, in which there has been some expansion of the repeating section does not lead to methylation and is more likely to occur in women who are, effectively, carriers.

FMRP, the protein that FMR1 codes for, is widespread in cells, and binds to RNA resulting in an increase or decrease in its ability to translate to protein. The absence of FMRP decreases the concentration of superoxide dismutase 1, which, it has been speculated, might account for the sleep disorders, anxiety and ASD in people with Fragile X syndrome.[84] In mice with FMR1 genes knocked out there is also down-regulation of MECP and WNT2.[85] WNT2 expression is not linked to ASD[86, 87] despite an earlier report,[88] but MECP2 clearly is (see Rett syndrome earlier in this chapter).

Appearance

People with fragile X syndrome often have prominent ears, a long face, a high arched palate as a consequence of the vertically lengthened maxilla, hyperextensible joints and low muscle tone. Men with the condition may have large testes.

Intelligence

Some degree of intellectual disability is common, although this may be aggravated by the executive problems considered below as well as slow processing speed.

Clinical features

Social anxiety is common, as are executive difficulties that are often out of proportion to working memory impairments, although these may be present. The executive disorder may be present in people with the premutation too, and seems to worsen as the person gets older. People with fragile X syndrome are prone to develop an ASD.

Premutations may be associated with mild intellectual disability and a reduction in the number of viable oocytes leading to a premature menarche at a younger age than 40 years. Both premutations and full mutations increase risk of late onset cerebellar ataxia associated with tremor.

Investigations

A DNA probe for the cytosine-guanine-guanine nucleotide (CGG) tagged with a fluorescent or radioactive ligand is available commercially. This is used in two ways: to bind directly to a

DNA strand in which the chromatin has been exposed to a DNA polymerase that augments the length of the tandem repeat (PCR, or polymerase chain reaction) or by the less sensitive and more time-consuming Southern blot analysis. The advantage of the latter is that it more readily distinguishes mutations from premutations. Southern blot analysis uses restriction fragments of DNA, created by snipping the chromatin at various points using restriction enzymes that are separated by in an agar gel by gravity, blotted onto a nylon film, and then labelled with the DNA probe.

Association with the ASDs

The symptom profile of ASD in fragile X is indistinguishable from ASD of unknown aetiology.[89] In one study, 50 per cent of boys with fragile X syndrome, and 20 per cent of girls had an ASD.[90] The figures were 67 per cent and 23 per cent respectively in another study, and much lower in a premutation group, 14 per cent and 5 per cent, respectively.[91] Self-injury in the first series was common, occurring in 58 per cent of boys and 17 per cent of girls.[90] Compulsive behaviour occurred in 72 per cent of boys and 55 per cent of girls and did not appear to be associated with self-injurious behaviour. Girls who showed compulsive behaviour had lower levels of FMRP than girls who did not, and boys with autistic symptoms had lowered levels of cortisol.[90] A smaller proportion of people with the premutation have an ASD.

It is possible that there is most similarity with atypical ASD, since face reading seems to be a particular problem in people with fragile X syndrome.

X-linked ichthyosis

Frequency

X-linked ichthyosis affects 1 in 2000–6000 male births, although only a proportion of these will have polymorphisms in adjacent genes that confer an increased risk of developmental disorder.

Heredity

X-linked ichthyosis is most commonly inherited from a carrier mother.

Genetic cause

X-linked ichthyosis is caused by haploinsufficiency of the gene at Xp22.3 for a steroid sulfatase enzyme (aryl sulfatase).

Appearance

The appearance of scaly skin on extensor surfaces, particularly the neck, trunk and legs, is characteristic.

Intelligence

Intellectual disability may occur occasionally.

Clinical features

The involvement of adjacent genes may lead to short stature or hypogonadism. Female carriers who are otherwise asymptomatic may have difficulties in labour.

Investigations

Reduced steroid sulfatase levels in blood is the definitive test. Linked polymorphisms may be detected using DNA probes (see section above, Fragile X syndrome, Investigation).

Association with the ASDs

Boys with X-linked ichthyosis have an increased risk (70%) of ADHD and an increased risk of AS, too, if the neuroligin gene (NG4) adjacent to steroid (aryl) sulphatase gene is also affected,[92] although complete deletion of the neuroligin gene is incompatible with normal development.[93] Reduced leukocyte steroid sulfatase activity in adults is associated with metachromatic leukodystrophy, a dementing disorder.[94]

Other rare genetic disorders associated with autism

The following disorders are all reportedly associated with an increased risk of ASD.

Hypomelanosis of Ito (also known as incontentia melanosis achromians) is attributed to chromosomal mosaicism in which bands of hypopigmentation or other skin conditions along Blaschko's lines correspond to a chromosome abnormality affecting the skin cells in that dermatome, possibly often trisomy 13. Extracutaneous abnormalities occur in 75 per cent of affected people, usually involving the brain. About 60 per cent have an intellectual disability, and 50 per cent seizures, which may be difficult to control. It is estimated that 10 per cent of people with hypomelanosis have an ASD.[95] The mosaicism occurs after fertilization.

Moebius syndrome is associated with abnormal development of the brain stem, associated with facial nerve paralysis and other cranial nerve abnormalities. Chromosome 13 impairment has also been suggested, but not supported in case series.[96]

CHARGE (coloboma, heart anomaly, choanal atresia, retardation, genital and ear anomalies) syndrome may be associated with mutations in the chromodomain helicase DNA-binding protein 7 (CHD7) at 7q21.11,[97] and possibly also mutations in 8q12.1. It is commonly associated with severe visual and auditory impairment.

Goldenhar syndrome is an occasional familial disorder of development of the first branchial arch leading to coloboma of the upper eyelid, and changes in the shape of the face, of the pinnae of the ear, and of the jaw, which are often greater on one side than on the other (oculoauriculovertebral dysplasia),[97] but 1p22.2-p31.1 is a candidate region for ASD, with a deletion there causing a similar clinical picture in one reported case[98] (I have also seen one case in my own practice).

Disintegrative disorder

Currently disintegrative disorder is considered to be a pervasive developmental disorder distinct from ASD, but it is proposed that it will be re-classified as a type of ASD. However, its aetiology is in many cases not known, and it seems safer to consider that the disintegrative disorders are a heterogeneous group of conditions, many of which predispose to an ASD.

Case history: Tom

Tom's father is a teacher and his mother a general practitioner. They were therefore well able to observe Tom's development during his early years, and they are sure that it was normal until he was three years old, when he seemed to become dreamier and more withdrawn. His interests also became narrower and he became fascinated with a locomotive from a series of books about anthropomorphic railway vehicles. After the age of three, there was a transient loss of language, and a gradual loss of nonverbal expression, with the appearance of facial grimacing and unusual rhythms and changes of pitch in his speech. These symptoms are particularly bad when Tom seems anxious. After the age of three, Tom looked at his parents increasingly less often, and developed new symptoms suggestive of autism, including motor stereotypies, unusual sensory behaviours, dislike of change, and impaired nonverbal communication. This now included a lack of expressive gaze, grimacing, and abnormalities of voice prosody with a loss of rhythmic tonal variation in his voice, especially when he was anxious. As well as apparently losing some skills, Tom did not develop other skills at the same rate as he was doing until the age of three. At the age of 14, Tom had a marked lack of social awareness, continued to use the same approaches, requesting physical affection that he may have done when he was three or four, had the language of an 11-year-old, and the self-care ability of a five-year-old.

When Tom was examined by an experienced paediatrician at the age of six, he was thought to be normal. After a lapse of time, he was diagnosed as having Asperger syndrome, and by the time that he was 14, the picture was identical to that of a more able person with autism.

Tom had his first epileptic seizure at the age of five, and from the first, his fits were difficult to control, despite the full range of treatments being tried. He had regular absence attacks during the day as well as the occasional grand mal seizure. MRI showed minor hippocampal abnormalities only, and urine amino acids and chromosome studies were normal. Tom was double jointed, and bruised easily, but the significance of this is unknown, although ligamentous laxity has previously been reported in association with Asperger syndrome and epilepsy.[99]

Tom's long period of normal development and his progressive deterioration with a failure to acquire new skills is unlike the development of most children with an ASD. All the evidence points to autism being the consequence of an abnormality of brain development, and not a consequence of psychosocial factors. Even if the latter was sometimes the cause – which I think is extremely unlikely – there was nothing in Tom's history or that of his family to suggest that such a cause was operative in his case. The association with the later development of epilepsy adds weight to the overall impression that Tom's brain was normal at birth but then suffered some insult during his development. Epilepsy could be a consequence of this insult, or could itself be the insult. Uncontrolled epilepsy in childhood, Landau-Kleffner syndrome, can present with absence attacks. Its onset is usually after the age of three years, and a waking EEG may be normal. The epilepsy tends to remit in adolescence, and after that the autistic symptoms may improve. This suggests that autistic symptoms may be the consequence of reversible impairment caused by repeated, abnormal electrical activity. Further support for this comes from the introduction of new antiepileptics which have enabled the control of previously intractable seizures in some children with tuberous sclerosis and autism. The autistic symptoms in these children diminish when seizure frequency is reduced[100] although this may be the result of the even greater reduction of language agnosia associated with Landau-Kleffner syndrome.[101]

Kolvin's distinction between ASD with an age of onset under three years, schizophrenia with an onset over 5 years, and a median group of psychoses with onset between three and five has stood the test of time.[102] The middle group includes children first described by Heller as having demential infantilis,[103] to distinguish them from the patients that Kraepelin termed dementia praecox, a condition later subsumed in Bleuler's group of schizophrenias. De Sanctis had described a dementia praecocissima three years before reporting three children aged six, seven and ten,[104] and then reported a child of three that De Sanctis considered had catatonia.[105]

Disintegrative psychoses develop after a period of normal or near normal development until at least the second year of life. Careful analysis of a home movie of one boy who developed characteristic disintegrative regression in the second year of his life confirmed this pattern, with a sharp reduction in pointing, social gaze and spontaneous language, and an increase in repetitive behaviour preceding the regression.[106] Disintegrative disorders of childhood – sometimes called Heller syndrome – are rare. Fombonne estimates a prevalence of 1.7 per 100,000 children.[107] The condition is probably a heterogeneous presentation of several different disorders. In the past, there is likely to have been a greater admixture of encephalopathic causes. The end result may be very similar to ASD in the context of intellectual disability. In a series of 18 cases, 17 showed nonverbal communicative impairments, and all of them met criteria for either autistic disorder or PDD not otherwise specified, except for the age of onset.[108] As with Lennox-Gastaut syndrome, language may be more severely impaired following the regression and there may be a greater degree of auditory impairment.[109] Two children at four and a half years and diagnosed as having childhood disintegrative disorder with an acute onset of behavioural regression have been described in a study in which there was a response to prednisolone,[110] but both showed EEG abnormalities and the first had tonic clonic seizures.

Childhood disintegrative disorder was assumed to have a worse prognosis than ASD in the past, possibly because individuals with more severe organic pathology were included in older series. In some modern series there are still more medical complications in the disintegrative group and a tendency for them to have a worse outcome,[111] but other series, albeit more short term, do not find this.[109]

The next edition of the *Diagnostic and Statistical Manual* (DSM-V) is expected to re-classify disintegrative disorder as a variant of ASD. How successful this will be remains to be seen. However, DSM-V will probably allow for the syndrome of ASD to be diagnosed in association with a rare syndrome as a secondary diagnosis and those disintegrative disorders that appear to be associated with childhood epilepsy may be distinguished from ASD of unknown aetiology by an appropriate secondary diagnosis.

Multidisciplinary involvement

Which specialist is responsible for the diagnosis may vary between areas, depending on the experience available. However, a range of professionals have skills to contribute to the infant with an ASD, and his or her family. In the UK, health visitors may provide support but specialist health visitors can make a particular contribution. The general practitioner or family doctor is an important link person. Family support workers can provide essential advice and practical help, and may work closely with non-statutory authorities. If the primary diagnostician has not already arranged for further investigations these will need to be chosen and organized either by a paediatric neurologist or by a paediatrician who may be hospital or community based. If the child has marked dyspraxia, movement therapists or physiotherapists may be able to provide an exercise programme to be carried out at home.

Investigation

The general guidelines for assessment have been discussed in Chapter 10. Diagnosis in infancy and early childhood may be particularly demanding because all parties have less experience of the child, there has been little or no opportunity to see how the child is at school or with peers, and congenital disorders may not have declared themselves fully. Developmental plasticity in infancy has also to be taken into account. Good practice guidelines for every assessment are shown in Box 12.3, which is adapted from the UK National Autism Plan for Children and Dover and Le Couteur.[112]

Box 12.3 What should be done in assessing an infant for an ASD?

- Take a careful, ASD relevant, developmental history.
- Have at least one experienced professional involved in the assessment.
- Make structured observations in more than one setting.
- Independently assess:
    physical condition
    cognitive function
    communication
    motor skills
    areas of distress or concern.
- Make and communicate a diagnosis.
- Plan any supplementary investigations or assessments.

Many of the steps shown in Box 12.3 have already been considered in detail in Chapter 11, including the assessment of areas of distress or concern which in infants or toddlers are commonly related to sensation, for example an intolerance of particular noises or routines.

Supplementary assessment and investigation

Miles *et al.* analysed a clinical series of 260 children with an autistic disorder, of whom 5 per cent had microcephaly and 16 per cent had significant physical abnormalities.[113] They termed this the 'complex autism' group, and compared them to the remaining 'essential autism' group. The complex group composed 20 per cent of their patients, and had poorer outcomes, lower IQs, more seizures, more abnormal EEGs, and more brain MRI abnormalities. The male to female ratio was lower in the complex group, too, and they were less likely to have a family history of ASD. Surprisingly, the essential group were more likely to have an episode of developmental regression.[113]

Battaglia and Carey exhaustively investigated 85 patients with an ASD selected out of a clinical series of 236, partly on the basis that they had received a comprehensive diagnostic evaluation, including an ADI-R and ADOS. About 11 per cent of the children and adolescents involved were found to have an additional disorder on the basis of their history and routine physical examination, but only another seven co-morbid disorders were found on the further tests: one child had an abnormal karyotype on high resolution banding, and another had fragile X premutation. Two children had MRI abnormalities, one had previously unsuspected Landau-Kleffner syndrome on EEG, and one had bilateral sensorineural hearing loss demonstrated by abnormal brainstem evoked potentials. No child had a metabolic abnormality. Battaglia and Carey conclude that audiometry, EEG and a genetic screen are worth carrying out routinely, but not MRI.[114] Given Miles et al.'s findings,[113] MRI may be worthwhile in children with complex autism, too.[114]

On the basis that infants and pre-schoolers newly diagnosed with an ASD with complex features such as epilepsy, microcephaly or macrocephaly, dysmorphic facial features and intellectual disability are more likely to have demonstrable abnormalities on MRI or EEG, it makes sense to restrict MRI screening to this group.

Quantitative serum amino acid estimation and urinalysis for organic acids are not indicated on a routine basis, but are indicated if the child is failing to thrive, is lethargic or vomiting, or has a sustained developmental regression. Thyroid function tests should be performed only if there are clinical signs of hypothyroidism such as slow growth, a large tongue, dry skin and hair, and floppy joints.

The current UK and US guidelines are that karyotyping and molecular testing for the repeated CGG base sequence is indicated only if there is a clinical suspicion that a fragile X mutation or premutations are present.[112]

Semi-automated genomic analyses using DNA microarrays are likely to become cheaper and more accessible, enabling more routine screening for a wider range of known genetic polymorphisms. These guidelines are therefore likely to change in the next few years.

Facilitating collaboration between healthcare providers and carers

The health department of New York State publishes guidelines for parents about questions to ask of health providers (Box 12.4). These questions are equally applicable to doctors, psychologists and other statutory providers, and are a useful basis for collaborative working.

Box 12.4 Parent intervention guide: Questions to ask providers

The following are questions that may be helpful to parents when interviewing potential intervention providers.

1. What kinds of intervention, therapy, and services do you provide?

2. Do you have a particular philosophy for working with children with autism/PDD?

3. How many hours per week do these services require, and how much of this is one-on-one time with the child?

4. How would you describe a typical day or session?

5. What experience do the teachers and/or therapists have in working with children with autism?

6. What experience does the person who supervises the program have? How closely does the program supervisor work with the therapists, teachers, and parents?

7. What kinds of ongoing training do your full and part time staffs participate in?

8. Are parents involved with planning as part of the intervention team?

9. Do you provide a parent training program?

10. How much and what kinds of involvement are expected of parents and family members?

11. Are parents welcome to participate in or observe therapy and/or group sessions?

12. What techniques do you use to manage difficult behaviors?

13. Do you ever use physical aversive techniques or any physically intrusive procedures? If yes, please describe them.

14. Please describe your program for communication and language development. Do you use a picture communication system, sign language, other kinds of communication systems, or all of these?

15. Are there opportunities for integration with typical and/or higher functioning children?

16. How do you evaluate the child's progress, and how often?

17. How do you keep parents informed of the child's progress?

Source: Reproduced from New York State Department of Health, 2005 with permission.

Treatment

Treatment evaluations in ASD present the same problems as evaluations of psychotherapy or education: there is likely to be spontaneous improvement irrespective of the treatment, and non-specific factors such as increasing interaction may be more important than the specific factors that the researchers value. Moreover, parents who are given hope, greater understanding of their children's difficulties, and an example of how to interact with their child may feel empowered and enabled, even if the treatment itself is based on a false hypothesis about causation (which almost all of the treatments for ASD up to the present time have been).

Psychological interventions

The most influential people in the lives of most young children with an ASD are their family members, and particularly their parents. Supporting, assisting and working with parents is therefore the basis for all interviews. It may be surprisingly difficult to achieve. Services might consider turning to mediation when conflicts arise, since they can turn into battles about who really cares about the child with an ASD. Support groups, advocates and non-statutory services can all play an important part.

Specific interventions have been considered in Chapter 9. There is some evidence that, at least in some children, some of the strategies considered there – if applied early – can increase IQ. Two meta-analyses of studies of early intervention behavioural analysis (by the 'Lovaas method') led to the conclusion that although IQ was increased, the impact on language and social impairment was more limited, and the change was not statistically significant in many studies.[115, 116] Some of the improvement could also have been due to maturation as the comparison groups were sometimes inadequate controls.

Child-centred responding

The Lovaas and other behavioural methods attempt to instil behaviour by reinforcement, shaping the child to behave more as the adult thinks is appropriate. An alternative approach is for adults to shape their behaviour to fit the child in order to increase social orientation. In one small study, singing, responding to the child's focus of attention, repeating a routine or simply repeating, and imitating the child all increased social attention.[117] In another, again very small study, three pre-schoolers and their mothers participated in an 11-week programme, teaching the mothers to follow the children's lead, promote children's participation in routines, and model language at the children's level. Mothers made more verbal responses to their children's activity at the end of ten weeks, and the children's vocabulary and the rate at which they initiated social interactions also increased.[118] A similar approach, but focusing on the mother imitating her child, has been applied to an intensive single case study of a six-month intervention, starting when the child was 21 months old. There was an increase in joint attention, but this may have been secondary to the mother's increased positive feelings about her child.[119]

Early start programmes

Early start programmes, such as the Earlybird project of the UK National Autistic Society,[120] provide information and practical help to parents, as well as ideas about increasing parental responsiveness. A review of clinical evidence for early interventions concluded that there was insufficient evidence that any of them were effective.[121] However, they are highly valued by parents.

Increasing parents' responsiveness to children with ASD

Training parents in responsiveness to their children with ASD may be combined with child-centred interventions, for example behavioural training, and may increase its effectiveness, and reduce the amount of professional contact required,[122] although there may be a substantial time commitment for parents instead. The Son-Rise approach is particularly demanding and as a result parents may not implement it as prescribed.[123] A much simpler child-responsive approach, 'Floortime', has been developed by Greenspan and others.[124] It is described as a technique for an adult to follow the emotions of a child with an ASD.

Increasing joint attention bids to which a child with autistic disorder is exposed accelerates language learning.[125]

Postdiagnostic support

It is important for someone in the diagnostic team to provide information and also to invite parents to ask questions, and clarify their own understanding about the implications of diagnosis. Genetic counselling might need to be provided at this stage, too, as well as information about practical help that the family can receive in the form of benefits, respite care, holiday and play schemes, playgroups and support networks.

Carter et al. followed up 143 mothers of toddlers with an ASD, 77 per cent of them boys.[126] They found that the mothers were at substantial risk of developing anxiety and depression, particularly if their child had additional challenging behaviour and if they were anxious about their own mothering ability and angry that fate had dealt them this problem to deal with. Lack of support from a partner – who may even deny that there is a problem, or seek to blame it on the mother – increases the risk of depression. Depression risk continued to be raised for the two years of the follow-up, although individual rather than group scores did change over this period.[126]

Being angry or hostile towards a child increases the risk of challenging behaviour, and the risk of feeling defeated and hopeless. Avoiding this kind of vicious circle is particularly important in carers who are already highly stressed, as are the mothers of children with an ASD.

Home support

Health visitors in the UK combine a public health role with support to individual families, with the former often having to take precedence over the latter.[127] The Portage scheme, developed in the US, has been taken up in many areas, and provides specialist home support to families of people with a range of developmental disorders. There is no published evidence of efficacy,[121] but this may reflect the difficulty in capturing what parents value in this and other early interventions.

Diet

Despite the absence of evidence for autoimmune disorder as a cause of ASD, many parents try an elimination diet and some report benefit. It may be that changing a child's diet is something that is completely under the parents' control and therefore offers an opportunity for them to feel that they can do something about their child's condition. It is unwise to oppose a parent who wishes to undertake this investigation for themselves, unless the diet is such an extreme one that the child's health might be harmed. In one survey, a majority of parents who embarked on a gluten-free or casein-free diet for their child reported some improvement (to put this in context, 10 out of 16 educational or behavioural therapies resulted in the parents reporting improvement in 70 per cent of participating children).[128] However, parents may welcome even-handed advice from a healthcare professional before they embark on this step; this should include a discussion of the placebo effect, and its size in autism interventions, which is considerable, especially if there is a cost attached to the intervention,[128] as there is in adopting a completely different diet.

Elimination diets are effective except in those children who have independently diagnosed coeliac disease or lactose intolerance.

Drugs
There are no drugs that are effective in ASD. The treatment of co-morbid disorder does not arise at this age.

Issues
The significance of regression
Most ASDs are considered to be lifelong disorders, beginning at birth. But a period of apparently normal development followed by a loss of previously achieved communicative ability is reported in 22 per cent[129] to 41 per cent of children,[130] who later meet diagnostic criteria for an ASD. If the regression occurs after the age of three, then childhood disintegrative disorder should be diagnosed according to DSM-IV and ICD-10, but this is an arbitrary cut-off point.

These children may have somewhat more severe ASD symptoms compared to children with onset at birth, especially in repetitive behaviour and communication.[129] Regression may occur in association with a named condition such as Rett syndrome or Landau-Kleffner syndrome (see next section), but a neurological explanation may often not be found with present methods of investigation. Regression in social skills is more frequent than regression in language.[130]

On balance, there seems to be little reason for distinguishing ASD with regressive onset before 18 months, and that with regressive onset after 24 months, although there may be other grounds for distinguishing particular cases, for example the extent to which neurological symptoms including epilepsy are evident. The outcome of regression is variable but when it occurs, it is probably an indication that the ASD is a complex rather than an essential one.

Regression may occur, as De Sanctis reported at any age of childhood or adolescence.[131] With older age, a diagnosis of schizophrenia is more likely than with ASD, but there may be no positive symptoms. Frontotemporal dementia may be the explanation in a proportion of these cases,[132, 133] but the aetiology of this is unknown.

Electrical status epilepticus during slow wave sleep

Children who develop epilepsy associated with electrical status epilepticus during sleep regress behaviourally. Those with the Landau-Kleffner syndrome subtype show particular regression in their language skills, but other subtypes of the disorder may lead to more global regression.[134] However, the loss of skills does not particularly affect nonverbal communication and so can be differentiated from the regression in autism.[135, 136, 137] The pattern is also different from disintegrative psychosis.

Does epilepsy cause autism?

About 80 per cent of infantile onset epilepsies are due to West syndrome in which there are runs of a single clonic jerk following by tonic stiffness. These have been descriptively named jack-knife seizures or salaam attacks. They are most common on waking, usually begin some months after birth and last throughout early childhood, but then remit. The affected infant may have been diagnosed as having brain disease before the onset of the epilepsy, but this is not so in a minority. The onset is associated with an arrest or even a regression in development. The EEG shows a disorganized high voltage 'hypsarrythmic' pattern. Vigbatrin is the treatment of first choice, following by ACTH or prednisolone.

One in five infants with epilepsy have atonic or drop attacks, too, and their EEGs show rapid spike and wave bursts interspersed by slowing. The epilepsy of children with this Lennox-Gastaut syndrome does not remit spontaneously, but persists into adulthood. Other rarer infantile onset epilepsies include myoclonic epilepsies caused by mitochrondriopathy. Both conditions are difficult to treat, but valproate may be the treatment of first choice followed by corticosteroids.[138] Infection is a rare cause of infantile epilepsy,[139] as are biotinidase deficiency, phenylketonuria and pyridoxine deficiency, and these are treatable by biotine, a low phenylalanine diet and pyridoxine respectively.[137] The regression associated with infantile epilepsy may particularly affect social interaction and social communication, leading to an ASD.[140] Opinion is divided as to whether effective treatment of infantile epilepsy, if it is possible, can prevent the ASD developing. If the epilepsy is a manifestation of an underlying brain disease, then suppressing it is unlikely to affect the incidence of an ASD. But if, as seems likely in some cases, the repeated seizures are sufficient to affect brain function, then treatment may be of preventative value. No definite evidence is available either way.[141]

Children with ASD and intellectual disability are much more likely to have epilepsy, to have a lower male to female ratio, and greater intellectual disability, but it is likely that the epilepsy is a marker for a more severe brain disorder rather than itself causing the ASD.[142, 143]

Chapter 13

PRESENTATION OF ASPERGER SYNDROME IN MIDDLE CHILDHOOD

RELEVANT DEVELOPMENTAL CHALLENGES

Havighurst[1] itemized the developmental tasks for children between the ages of 6 and 12. Those that are particularly relevant to ASD include: learning physical skills necessary for ordinary games; learning to get along with age mates; achieving personal independence; and developing attitudes towards social groups and institutions. Unstructured play provides all of these challenges and is one of the principal settings in which ASD can be diagnosed in this age group, as well as providing a possible means of therapy for the emotional consequences of having an ASD.

Play and socializing with peers
What is play?
Play has been defined as:

> a seemingly 'non-serious' variant of functional behavior. Playful behaviours resemble serious behaviors but participants are typically more concerned with the behaviors themselves (i.e., 'means') rather than the function (i.e., 'ends') of the behavior. Playful behaviors are also typically more exaggerated than their functional counterparts and the components of functional behavioral routines are often re-arranged in play. [2]

Play is rewarding to the children and other juvenile mammals that spontaneously indulge in it, is creative, unstructured (unlike games), requires energy and concentration, and is often social. Play assists in the development of operant skills, imagination, and social skills. It is the latter two that are of most relevance to ASD.

Development of play
Sensorimotor play, enjoying the sensation or use of objects begins early in the first year of life. Functional play begins at approximately 14 months of age, when models which resemble objects are used as the represented objects would be: miniature cups are put on miniature saucers, or spoons are used to feed a doll. Pretend play, in which objects being played with have an 'as if' relation to what they represent, begins at about the age of two years (but see Chapter 12 for factors that influence the onset of pretend play and its link with theory of mind). This kind of play might be carried out with other children, but they are not required for playing to take place. Play from this point on is intertwined with story-telling or narrative,[3] but at this age the child's narrative may be embellished or extended by contributions from others, but is essentially a story told by one person. Play at this age is influenced more by the security of the relationship of the child and her or his main carer, than by a diagnosis of ASD,[4] – although having an ASD may influence the child's ability to form a trusting relationship with the mother.[5] The requirement for a playmate, or social play – and the development of joint narratives or scripted enactments in play – begins from about the age of five years.

From this age, play is socially constructed with a joint narrative in the context of which opportunities for cooperation and conflict are generated that accelerate the development of prosocial competence, enhance the child's sympathy by increasing the child's awareness of others and prompt the development of a systematic morality.[6] Interactive play also begins to create playmates and exclude peers who are not interesting or who are too difficult to play with. Excluded children may be excluded further by teasing or bullying.

Towards the end of the UK primary school period (ages 10 years onwards), boys' and girls' play becomes increasingly differentiated and gender identities begin to figure in it.[7] Since identity formation is impaired in people with an ASD (see Chapter 14) it is possible that this may present a further obstacle to social interaction for people with an ASD.

How play differs in autism

Pretend or imaginative play has often been supposed to be impaired in ASD, but more able people with ASD often have highly developed imaginations, just as they may have a strong sense of humour.[8] Many children with an ASD have imaginary friends. Some write short stories or poems, and draw or paint. However, play in even very intelligent children with an ASD is not interactive. Children with an ASD do play if they allow themselves to be used, or if they can impose their game on other people. Since younger children are more compliant, and older children may make a patronizing effort to do so, children with an ASD at this age may often gravitate away from their peers who expect interaction, either to being alone or to being with younger or older children. As a result there are fewer stimuli for play, and many fewer opportunities for interactive play, and so it seems that the child with an ASD lacks the ability to play. This may be further reinforced by the intrinsic pleasure of repetition. So what play that does occur is often inflexible.

Children with ADHD also begin to have difficulties in interactive play in primary school, but this seems to be due to their aggressiveness and anxiety, and possibly their unwillingness to defer the pleasures of playing until the denouement of the game.

It has been suggested that interactive play may have benefits for children with an ASD, and for people with ADHD, but there have been few studies. One, using Lego plastic bricks as the medium for interactive play, showed improvement in social skills in participants with ADHD.[9] Small-scale interventions to increase play, often using neurotypical mentors,[10] have shown some success.[11, 12] Video modelling increases social initiation,[13] and reciprocal play with social imitation.[14] Encouraging children to put what they observe in play training into words may also facilitate future playing.[15]

Learning challenges

Middle childhood is the period in many world cultures when children are expected to acquire intellectual skills and knowledge. Depending on the culture, they may also be expected to acquire motor skills and the ability to complete motor tasks successfully: from dressing themselves, washing and toileting to bicycle riding and hunting, agricultural tasks, and even manufacture. Middle childhood is therefore the period when mild to moderate learning difficulties and specific developmental problems that affect this learning, such as dyspraxia, dyscalculia and dyslexia, emerge as disabilities.

The statistical discovery that there is a general factor of intelligence was an important one in the history of psychometrics.[16] But it has had damaging consequences. It suggested that this general factor accounted for most of the important cognitive differences between people. Musical and mathematical abilities were always exceptions to this, not least because there were people, often suffering from autism, whose abilities in these areas seemed to be discrepant with their measured intelligence.

Ranking people on a general factor of intelligence has possible consequences far beyond predicting who will do well at school or college. The noxious ethical implications of such a ranking have precipitated a backlash against the presumption that ability and success are linked to IQ. (I shall not consider the divisions of IQ that have been proposed, for example into fluid and crystallized intelligence.) One argument against the value of IQ as a predictor of social or occupational achievement is that IQ is a measure of brain, and not mental, functioning.

Mental functioning is influenced by reaction time, possibly a reflection of intelligence, and by knowledge, whose acquisition is a consequence of IQ, but is also determined by personal factors like motivation, focus and confidence. Psychiatrists specializing in learning disability have long been familiar with these ideas, and regularly consider personality and social support in their assessment of a person with a learning disability.

The importance of the general factor of intelligence in determining life adjustment diminishes as intelligence increases. Indeed, some have argued that success at specific occupations or activities may require a minimum IQ but the degree of success may depend on other cognitive factors. The tournament rank of chess masters does not, for example, correlate with their IQ, but it may be assumed that all chess masters will have an IQ above a certain threshold. One reason for this may be that general intelligence is a reflection of processes such as memory store or speed of processing which affect all other cognitive processes only so long as they are limiting. If there is enough computational power then more specific cognitive abilities may limit performance. It would follow that a person with a low IQ would be more likely to have uniformly impaired performance on all of the sub-tests that constitute the commonly used measures of general intelligence, but that as IQ rose, some more sub-test scores would become discrepant. And this is borne out in studies.[17]

The threshold at which general intelligence affects function will also vary from function to function. A computer analogy might illustrate this point. To process three-dimensional images on my computer, I need a certain amount of memory and a certain speed of central processing unit, but beyond that my computer's ability to produce these images will depend on its graphics card. The computer's ability to communicate will depend on its CPU and memory but only if it is a very old one with an outdated chip and little RAM. For most computers, it will be the specification of the modem that determines the rate and reliability of electronic communication.

Communication by people is similarly much less affected by general intelligence than are other cognitive abilities. The boundary between profound and severe intellectual disability, conventionally put at an IQ of 50, roughly corresponds to the threshold above which speech is usually developed. Nonverbal communication requires an even lower threshold of general cognitive power for its development.

Moderate to severe intellectual disability affects all aspects of development, as well as communication, and is usually apparent in early childhood, resulting in much greater dependence on parental care than is the case for normally developing peers. Having an autistic disorder increases this disability, but the communication disorder that is specific to ASD may be less apparent. Impaired nonverbal communication is more salient in older more able children and specific intellectual difficulties may also become apparent for the first time.[18]

Social demand

In addition to the interactive demands of play, and the cognitive demands of learning, middle childhood is a period when children have to move outside the informal organization of family life and adapt to, and eventually internalize, the structures of their society. Structure can be defined 'as comprising those cultural or normative patterns that define the expectations of agents hold about each other's behaviour and that organize their enduring relations with each other.'[19]

These patterns are sometimes formalized, but may also be unspoken. Discerning the unspoken ones, and generalizing them to other situations, is a particular challenge for people with an ASD, presumably because they require the same kind of simulation task that underlies theory of mind. Less able people with an ASD may fall back on explicit rules or repetitive structures. For example, children at one school for people with autism were encouraged to take a walk in the formal garden at lunchtimes, and many of them took the opportunity do this. Each would walk in a circular path around the central fountain, carefully spacing themselves so that there was an equal distance between each of them.

More able people with an ASD may try to emulate unspoken rules by developing their own set of explicit procedures or regulations. Maintaining these, knowing when they apply, and repairing social relations when mistakes are made is cognitively tiring and may be compensated for by withdrawing into idiosyncratically structured activity at home.

Social structure and identity have a reciprocal relationship. Identity is expressed within social structure, but social structures and the roles and enactments that make up the structures also shape identity. With increasing age, a child shifts away from behaviour that is defined by social structure and the child's biology, and more to actions that are expressive of identity. This further challenge for people with an ASD is discussed in Chapter 14.

First suspicions of ASDs presenting in middle childhood

Parents, even if they consider that their child is different, may be reluctant to concede this at first, and even after they do, professionals may resist 'labelling' the child. The variability of infant development may justify this reluctance in more able children with an ASD, such as those with Asperger syndrome. Part of the difficulty may be that the assessment of nonverbal communication remains unstandardized. The variability of the social situations in which children may find themselves also contributes. Many parents have told me that they first attributed their child's shyness to being an only child, or to having spent some time abroad, or being brought up in a village with few other children of his or her own age. The difficulty in the assessment of socialization and nonverbal communication is in contrast to the clear and universal nature of motor and language milestones, although even they may be affected by special circumstances, such as the child being in a family whose language is not that of the surrounding culture.

Because motor milestones are much more standardized, many children who are later diagnosed as having AS are diagnosed as having dyspraxia as pre-schoolers.

With school come some of the socialization challenges described above, and a diagnosis can usually be made reliably even in children with mild ASD. Diagnosis also becomes of much more practical importance since schooling has a significant impact on the prognosis of ASD, as discussed below.

Two syndromes of previously undiagnosed ASD may present after the child first goes to school: these are AS and autistic disorder in the context of a diagnosed intellectual disability. Primary school may also provide the first strong evidence that a child has an ADHD.

ASPERGER SYNDROME PRESENTING IN MIDDLE CHILDHOOD

It is estimated that about 40 per cent of children with an ASD in mainstream primary school in the UK neither have a diagnosis nor are they recognized as having a special educational need.[20] Diagnosis therefore remains an important intervention in this group.

Red flags for Asperger syndrome presenting in middle childhood

The red flag approach, that is using concerns as triggers for further investigation of the ASDs, has rarely been extended beyond infancy. Box 13.1 lists red flags for Asperger syndrome presenting in middle childhood and is based on my own clinical experience.

Box 13.1 Red flags for Asperger syndrome presenting in middle childhood

- Incoordinated child with an unusual manner.
- Does not fit in to classroom routine, but has routines of his or her own.
- Has unexpected areas of knowledge or interest, for example dinosaurs or the *Guinness Book of Records*.
- Isolated: alone in playground, no 'true' friends at school, does not meet classmates outside school.

SCREENING

Screening tools such as the Childhood Autism Screening Test (CAST) have been developed specifically for use in this age group.[21] (See general issues about screening in Chapter 8.)

Case history: Josh

Josh was born following an uneventful pregnancy, with no birth complications; indeed his parents did not suspect that Josh had any particular problems until he was aged three. At that time, he was noted at the playgroup to panic when he was asked to do things which would make him stand out, such as ringing the bell, and when he first began to go to infants' school he was noted to be very anxious. His family moved house, and he began at a new infants' school. Shortly after his grandfather died, Josh was noted to 'retreat', even within the family. He made no friends at primary school, but was accepted by his classmates. The school's and his parents' concerns were mainly with his studies, rather than with his social isolation or his tendency to anxiety. He was referred to an educational psychologist at the age of six, who diagnosed him to have reduced visual working memory, slightly below average performance IQ, and slightly above average verbal IQ. On re-testing two years later, his visual working memory was nearly normal, but his verbal working memory was now reported to be reduced. The psychologist also noted him to be a sensitive child who seemed under a lot of stress, but this was attributed to his academic difficulties. He was treated by his GP for regular headaches, for gastrointestinal problems, and for fainting spells, all of which led to him missing days of school. He was investigated for petit mal epilepsy; although there were no definite EEG findings he was treated with anticonvulsants for a year, but these were discontinued because there had been no change. For a short time he received antiepileptics but without any effect. At seven, he was seen by a research psychologist who diagnosed dyslexia, and he began to receive additional tuition from a retired special needs teacher, arranged by his parents. His family were not so concerned about his lack of involvement in family gatherings as his father, now a successful accountant, had been very shy as a child. Other family members sometimes commented on the fact that Josh would often go upstairs to his room when they visited, and one family member hinted at autism, although there was no family history of this. Josh had a number of food fads which bothered his mother, but she managed to give him enough of a balanced diet. He was very studious and took a particular interest in natural history, having an encyclopaedic knowledge of bats. He would sometimes sit in the garden – which was large and enclosed – to observe them until late at night. The diagnosis of Asperger syndrome was not made until much later, in his late teens, after he had suffered extreme bullying at his private secondary school, following which he developed symptoms of social phobia and obsessive compulsive disorder.

In retrospect, as a child, and on direct questioning, his parents agreed that Josh frequently:

- seemed to dislike cuddling or other displays of affection
- had difficulty in copying movement or actions
- used catch phrases in a peculiar way
- had difficulty with his words and would muddle them or put them in the wrong order
- rocked either sitting or standing up, but has now stopped
- frequently became absorbed looking at an object from every angle or with unusual intensity
- seemed to be fascinated by particular sensations of touch
- was upset by sounds
- seemed unduly distressed if his daily routine changed
- made up special routines of his own
- had food fads
- was fascinated by one particular object
- had an unusually narrow and engrossing interest

and that:

- others frequently found difficulty in telling what he was feeling from his facial expressions
- his movements seemed aimless or purposeless.

SYMPTOMS OF ASPERGER SYNDROME PRESENTING IN MIDDLE CHILDHOOD

Primary impairment or difference

Nonverbal communication, particularly reflexive communication 'interbrain' (see Chapter 6), is rarely the subject for spontaneous reflection. Carers may be concerned that they cannot tell what their child is feeling, for example if he or she is in pain. Towards the end of middle childhood, fathers may find it frustrating not to see their child showing anxiety or remorse at being told off. But parents often accept a lack of nonverbal responsivity as being within the normal range. These difficulties are attributed to their child's personality, and not to a disorder. A lack of responsiveness to other people's nonverbal communication, and the consequent lack of empathy, may be a cause of distress but again is rarely attributed to disorder. One mother told me, for example, that her son was 'evil', and that she had seen it in his eyes from when he was aged seven.

Repetitiveness and routine

Not every person with an ASD shows resistance to change, which may represent an overlapping syndrome rather than being a fundamental characteristic of ASD (as discussed in Chapter 9). Symptoms of resistance to change include: upset and even screaming if a new route is taken to school or the times of bathing or meals are changed; needing to know beforehand what meals are being prepared; fury or distress if belongings are moved, or even if someone has gone into the bedroom; insistence on watching particular television programmes; repeatedly watching the same DVDs or videos; having problems with holidays or staying in other people's houses; rituals at bedtimes, for example laying out clothes in a certain order, or using particular dishes or cutlery at meal times; rituals around bathing that may take an hour or more and resemble obsessional slowness; rituals around toilet cleanliness which often lead to excessive use of paper and blocked lavatories; making lists for pleasure; obsessions such as counting, or making sure that objects of interest are present in multiples of two and not odd numbers; and asking repetitive questions.

There are behaviours that may be linked to resistance to change in that they involve highly predictable stimulation, for example watching things spin, watching flashing lights, or stimulating oneself by spinning, flapping or whirling objects. All of these may become particularly noticeable in middle childhood.

Resistance to change activities are apparently soothing because of their repetition. However, they may also have other functions.

Some are playful exercises of cognitive skill: for example making lists, or memorizing games, like memorizing car number plates.

Others involve what Freud called 'undoing'. These are activities that confer mastery over a feared stimulus. Unexpected noise, which is particularly frightening to infants with Asperger syndrome, may become the basis for a fascination in middle childhood. Steam trains, which whoosh in a frightening and unexpected way when one is standing next to them, are an example. Infants with autism may be phobic of them, but the same child may collect models of them, books about them, and may plan journeys on them with pleasure in middle childhood (and as an adolescent may develop a lifelong passion for model railways).

Altered sensory acuity may also influence behaviour. Faddy eating, leading to restricted diet, is common to children with ASD once they have been weaned.[22] Many children with food fads seem particularly sensitive to, and disgusted by, gustatory sensations that are 'slimey'. So they will not eat mashed potatoes or purées. Others do not want change, and so eat the same foods over and over again. Children with an ASD often find blends difficult. They are, as their parents say, very 'black and white'. Food tastes must therefore be kept separate. Either vegetables are never eaten with meat at all, or if they are eaten, they must be served on separate plates, or on one plate with a clear division between the two, and eaten separately.

Resistance to change, and what Baron-Cohen has termed 'systemization',[20] appear to be linked in that both co-occur in a number of conditions including anorexia nervosa during the fasting phase, ASD and obsessive compulsive personality disorder (formerly anankastic personality disorder).[23] One link between the two is that systemization may be, like repetition, a means of reducing anxiety and one that relies on explicit procedures – sometimes called cognitive coping – rather than intuitive reactions, or affective coping. Affective coping might involve telling oneself 'life's too short' or 'tomorrow's another day': but this seems unacceptable to a person with ASD who wants a determination to be made of who or what is at fault, and the fault rectified.

Collecting, hoarding or memorizing (a kind of cognitive collecting) are systemizing activities, as are some computer and handheld device games. Some psychiatrists consider that hoarding is an atypical manifestation of OCD.

The complexity of repetitive activities is a measure of intelligence. Highly intelligent people with AS may have the routine of extracting the factors of new numbers that interest them, whereas less intelligent people with Asperger syndrome may simply try to remember them.

Secondary disability

Secondary disabilities in middle childhood may be the consequence of lost development, of being out of dialogue, or of anxiety.

Lost development

Substantial amounts of social learning occur without explicit instruction, for example through modelling. This learning requires an orientation to social happenings that are considered to be salient by others, and this requires social orientation, which is reduced in people with an ASD (see Chapter 5). Modelling rests on involuntary imitation, which is also reduced in ASD.[24] In one study, reduced imitation from memory and differences in reward learning in four-year-olds with an ASD were predictive of their social and communicative development (as estimated by their scores on the Vineland Social Maturity Scale) two and a half years later.[25] One might simply say that reflexive social learning requires adequate bandwidth of the 'interbrain connection' discussed in Chapter 5, and this is lacking in ASD.

Where ASD is associated with a speech or language impairment, further loss of social learning may result from the inability of the person with an ASD to participate fully in family discourse about the intentions, motives or emotions of other people. This may lead to a reduction in the richness of emotional scripts that guide affective processing,[26] and may contribute to the 'alexithymia' that has been observed in people with an ASD, and to the absence of emotional narrative in dreams,[27] which is a feature of alexithymia in other conditions.[28]

Being out of dialogue

Dialogue with adults, like play, contributes to the development of reciprocity and social awareness,[3] but makes a more specific contribution to the developing child's narrative theory of mind and to the development of values and morality. Children with autistic disorder may be unable to participate in social discourse because of their lack of language, but children with AS can, and do. However, the ability of people with AS to take account of the discourse context – for example, the needs of other participants for relevant background – and of a listener's attention is reduced.[29] This ability may stem from a mismatch between mother and child in movement synchrony, and to the mother's discourse about the child emphasizing the differences between the child and other neurotypical children.[30]

School age children with ASD are less competent at producing narrative than their neurotypical peers, for example not knowing how to emphasize a 'high point' of the narrative,[31] which may be both cause and consequence of a lack of self-awareness. Lack of practice at dialogue in infancy is likely to contribute to these more pervasive narrative difficulties during school age.

Narrative deficits may reach further than is apparent. One study has suggested that narrative about typical social events may underly the difficulties that children with AS have in ceremonials such as birthday parties.[32] In later life, similar difficulties arise in relation to mourning ceremonials, with the consequence that people with an ASD are experienced as lacking in sympathy for others.

Anxiety

Anxiety and depression are rare in pre-schoolers, but their incidence increases as childhood progresses.[33] There may be a genetic contribution to this in that polymorphisms of the COMT gene may be more associated with social phobia,[34] although a study of over 3000 twins aged eight or nine years found that although both ASD and anxiety proneness were heritable, there was only a small shared inheritance.[35]

Anxiety is common in children with ASDs,[36] however, and so must be mainly due to situation. The most likely candidate is the uncertainty of the social environment for anyone who, like the child with an ASD, has to try to understand it 'from outside' rather than knowing it from within.

The average age of onset of generalized anxiety in children is eight and a half years,[37] although social anxiety – shyness – may develop earlier. Somatic symptoms are a common feature, and may be the main presentation, of anxiety in children. These include headaches, tension, restlessness, gastrointestinal distress and heart palpitations. Gastrointestinal symptoms are particularly common in children with an ASD. Constipation and constipation with overflow faecal incontinence may be as common as the diarrhoea caused by gastrointestinal hurry that is more often associated with anxiety.

Anxiety is associated with social withdrawal and loneliness,[38] although the direction of these relationships is not known. The most likely direction, in my clinical experience, is that children experience exclusion, feeling anxious and alone, and they deal with this by denigrating other children from whom they withdraw, and then feel more anxiety and loneliness.

Tertiary handicap

Primary school makes demands on any child. The first school day may be the longest period that a child has been separated from their mother. The child has to meet new peers, and adjust to a new kind of social situation, the class. Timetabled activities may well be a new experience. Children also have to quickly pick up the ground rules of 'instruction' – listening out for key messages, remembering them and following them at appropriate times, and suppressing their own inclinations or habits if necessary. Children have to locate the toilet, and find out how to request to use it. Children who still need help with dressing or toileting need to ask for it, or make embarrassing blunders. The child needs to learn who is in authority, and who isn't; how to estimate the passage of time; when to talk, and when to be silent...it is a long list of demands.

Fitting in to this new structure can (as noted above) be a source of anxiety or cognitive demand and may lead to anxiety or a refusal to participate that increases social isolation and idiosyncrasy.

Every child experiences some of these demands. The greatest impact on emotional health is likely to be from those stresses that are particular to the individual child. These include the cognitive demands of learning on a child with specific developmental difficulties, for example in mathematics (these are discussed below) and the effects of being teased or bullied.

Bullying

Victimization is usually less severe in primary than it is in secondary school, but may still occur. The consequences, treatment and prevention of bullying are discussed in Chapter 4.

DIFFERENTIAL DIAGNOSIS FOR ASPERGER SYNDROME PRESENTING IN MIDDLE CHILDHOOD

Obsessive compulsive disorder

OCD is rare before the age of three. Boys are more frequently affected than girls (although this is not the case for adult onset OCD), and there is more likely to be an association with Tourette syndrome and other developmental disorders. In one study the mean age of diagnosis was ten years, but symptoms began at a mean age of five, and the full OCD syndrome was present from an average age of eight and a half years old.[39] There were many similarities between childhood onset and adult OCD in this study, and those differences that were present may have been the consequence of cognitive development or experiential preoccupations, such as the increase in obsessions, especially aggressive obsessions, in adolescence.

The repetitions, compulsions and stereotypies of children with anxiety, ADHD, and ASD in another series could not be distinguished, suggesting that all of these conditions may be associated with the same compulsive endophenotype. However, children with ASD had the autistic syndrome which the others did not.[40]

Although the phenomenon of OCD may overlap with the repetitive characteristics of ASD, it is unlikely to be mistaken for the social impairment in this condition. However children with obsessive compulsive personality disorder (OCDP) may also be 'sensitive' (see section on sensitivity below) and this may result in social impairment.

Associated conditions

ASD, ADHD and Tourette syndrome are common in children referred for treatment of OCD, and children who are co-morbid for the two disorders, particularly the children with ASD, have the most OCD symptoms.[41] Hoarding is a common behaviour in ASD and is the commonest symptom of childhood onset OCD, too.[41]

Citalopram prescription does not reduce OCD symptoms in children with ASD,[42] although it is effective in reducing anxiety in children with ADHD.[43] Drugs may have little place in treating repetitiveness.

Sensitivity

There are a number of childhood onset conditions that result in social anxiety and social avoidance. The most common is 'shyness'. Shyness and social phobia, or avoidant personality, differ in degree, but not qualitatively.[44, 45] The downcast look of the shy person, or their inability to meet direct gaze, suggests a possible link with ASD, but one study demonstrates that shy people scan faces in a neurotypical way rather than like a person with an ASD.[46] Shyness and social phobia is a context-bound behaviour. It is elicited by novel social situations, by the risk of negative social evaluation, and by impersonal attention.[47] It is not exhibited in relation to familiar people or to those who are not perceived as threatening, such as younger children. So, unlike ASD, the social inhibition and reduced nonverbal expressiveness are most marked in encounters with strangers, such as in the doctor's surgery, but disappear when the child is observed with family members or with friends.

Shyness has been attributed to an increased sensitivity to social cues, particularly negative ones, and especially to gaze. For this reason, internet-based virtual therapy seems particularly acceptable.[48] It is often associated with sensitivity to embarrassment and to disgust, as well as to social anxiety, possibly mediated by increased activation of insula and amygdala respectively.[49]

Shame sensitivity is associated with another so-called personality disorder, schizoid personality. Schizoid personality may differ from shyness and avoidant personality in extending to all social interactions, whether familiar or unfamiliar, and involving submissiveness and a lack of pleasure in social interaction.[50]

Anxiety sensitivity may also be a precursor of adolescent-onset schizophrenia with avoidant personality being diagnosed twice as often as schizoid personality disorder.[51]

Although a descriptive study of children with schizoid personality has suggested an overlap with ASD,[52] there have been no studies using current diagnostic criteria, focusing on nonverbal communication for ASD and recent criteria for schizoid personality, to ascertain whether there are two conditions.

Associated conditions

Sensitivity to anxiety is associated with ASD, and may predispose children with an ASD to developing anxiety-related disorders both in middle childhood and later in life.

Schizophrenia

Schizophrenia may appear before the age of 12 in a very small proportion of the total of people who develop schizophrenia. When it does, there is continuity with the adult illness. A research group at the US National Institute of Mental Health (NIMH) has been recruiting such cases throughout the US since 1992; so far it has recruited 320 possible cases of childhood onset schizophrenia, of whom 112 meet DSM-IV criteria. There is no evidence from this study that ASD and schizophrenia are overlapping conditions, nor that childhood onset schizophrenia has different symptoms from that of adult schizophrenia.[53]

'Simple schizophrenia', in which there are no positive symptoms but only negative ones, has not been described in childhood and is therefore only a differential diagnosis later in life.

As an associated condition

In a review of their own cases and those of a group at the University of California in Los Angeles (UCLA), the NIMH group has suggested that there is an increased risk of developing schizophrenia in middle childhood if a child already has an ASD,[53] although this remains a live issue.[54, 55] The onset they argue was typically three to five years after the onset of the ASD 'in the first five years of life'. The risk of developing schizophrenia in the UCLA sample was 1 per cent for children with autistic disorder, 2 per cent for children with AS, and 25 per cent for children with atypical autism (PDD-NOS). The principal feature of the diagnosis was 'failure to develop reciprocal social behaviour'.[53a] The diagnosis of atypical autism requires fewer symptoms than the other ASDs, and it may therefore be significant that it is by far the most common hypothesized antecedent ASD. The rarity of these conditions make research difficult, but these findings are not consistent with the frequency of schizophrenia reported in prospective studies of children with an ASD, and must therefore be considered to be unproven at the moment.

Other associated conditions

Leyfer *et al.* screened a series of 109 children with an ASD ('idiopathic autism') (average age 9 years, range 5 to 17 years), using a parent as the key informant for a rating scale based on the Kiddie SADS (Schedule of Affective Disorders and Schizophrenia for children).[56] Children with IQs less than 65 were excluded. They found that the majority had at least one other diagnosable condition (see Table 13.1).

Table 13.1 Conditions associated with ASD in middle childhood and adolescence

DSM-IV condition	Per cent affected
Specific phobia	44.3
Obsessive compulsive disorder	37.2
ADHD	30.6
Depression	12.8
Separation anxiety	11.9
Hypomania or mania	8.5
Social phobia	7.4
Oppositional defiant disorder	7.0
Generalized anxiety	2.4
Schizophrenia	0.0
Panic disorder	0.0

Source: Adapted from Leyfer, Folstein, *et al.*, 2006.

Attention deficit hyperactivity disorder

The diagnostic features of ADHD in children are distinctively different from those of ASD except that children with either condition may be socially isolated. When a child has ADHD alone, social isolation is often a symptom of the conflict with peers that ADHD symptoms may lead to. However, social isolation may also be a symptom of ADHD and ASD co-morbidity. Despite this, the diagnosis of one disorder often precludes assessment for the presence of the other.

Parents or professionals may resist making a diagnosis of ADHD before middle childhood, instead attributing ADHD symptoms to family problems or simply to 'boisterousness'. The formal diagnosis of a medical condition of ADHD may be entertained in middle childhood only when a child with ADHD becomes markedly disruptive in class, or becomes socially isolated because of an inability to share or to play with others without attempting to control the interaction.

ADHD and ASD often coexist,[57] and it is estimated that, after oppositional disorder, ASD is the most common condition premorbid with ADHD. About 70 per cent of children with ASD meet criteria for ADHD and so the diagnostic task is not so much to distinguish ADHD from ASD but to consider whether the diagnosis of only one, or both, are justified. As has been emphasized already, the presence or absence of the autistic syndrome, and particularly, the presence or absence of nonverbal communicative impairment, is the mark of whether or not a diagnosis of ASD should be made. In older people with an ASD, nonverbal expression may normalize, although nonverbal interpretation may continue to be impaired. This can present special diagnostic difficulty (see Chapter 14), but in this age group nonverbal expressiveness and associated impaired social interaction are reliable markers of ASD.

Box 13.2 Red flags for ADHD

- Seems unable to give full attention to anything except computer games.
- Can't concentrate on anything for long except for computer games.
- Can't remember instructions or lists without writing them down.
- Interrupts what people are doing or when people are talking, and blurts things out.
- Always in trouble at school for disrupting the class, for not doing homework, for fighting, or for daydreaming and being easily discouraged.
- Can't sit still, ants in the pants.
- Getting into mischief constantly or being anxious and shy.

Dyspraxia

Many children who are ultimately diagnosed as having AS are first diagnosed as having developmental dyspraxia, and then as having dyslexia. This may reflect the changing challenges for development at different ages that bring different developmental strengths and weaknesses into salience.

Dyspraxia particularly affects balance and gait, and movement rhythm,[58] suggesting cerebellar involvement. Similar difficulties have been reported in ADHD. However, ideomotor dyspraxia is also more common in people with an ASD, suggesting a cerebral basis for some of the dyspraxia.[59] Studies of dyspraxia,[60, 61, 62, 63] including my own,[64] have persistently failed to identify the precise nature of the difficulty. Gross motor coordination, throwing and catching are almost always affected, but fine movements may be either poor or good. A few children may meet all of the criteria for an ASD, but have normal coordination. Having a language disorder is more likely in these circumstances, but not universal.

One reason for the difficulty in pinning down the dyspractic impairment is that movement is a performance that is shaped by imitation of others. People with an ASD may make efficient movements that are not socially appropriate performances, and may therefore seem clumsy even when they are not.

Dyspraxia affects children's participation in games and sports and may be a source of disability in itself. It may also be one of the first reasons that children get bullied as suggested by a common epithet thrown at young children with an ASD, 'spastic'.

Specific writing dyspraxia may also occur in association with ASD. In this condition, writing which is anyway often poorly formed as a result of dyspraxia seems especially hard hit, with the child apparently being unable to form letters at all, even though letters are recognized.

Dyslexia

Dyslexia is also more common in children with an ASD, particularly those who also have ADHD.[65] It too is an independent cause of disability, particularly when spelling difficulties are mistakenly attributed to a lack of effort, or 'laziness' or 'stupidity'.

Irlen's syndrome

Although the primary disorder in dyslexia is phonological, reading difficulties may also be caused by the physical problems of focusing on the printed page. Some of these may be corrected by glasses, but other difficulties are not orthoptic but produced by the apparent jumpiness of the text due to impaired eye movement control. This phenomenon is often known as Irlen's syndrome. In about one-third of children with Irlen's syndrome, letter discrimination and therefore reading can be improved by the use of yellow light or yellow paper.[66]

Dyscalculia

Dyscalculia may occur more commonly in children with an ASD and, like dyslexia, it appears to be most common in children with the kind of atypical ASD that has a strong overlap with ADHD. The actual prevalence in people with ASD is unknown, as is the prevalence of dyslexia.

Dyscalculia, dyslexia and dyspraxia may all occur independently of autism, and also in association with ADHD or OCD, but in the absence of autism. This suggests that there may be a number of different developmental disorders caused by associated centres or networks in the brain that can be affected separately or in clusters with different composition.

Visuospatial tasks

People with an ASD tend to out-perform neurotypical children detecting visually simple elements or patterns; they have superior abilities in mapping, for example in recognizing landmarks and in detecting the similarity between maps and features on the ground.[67]

Savant skills

Up to 10 per cent of people with ASD may develop superior skills in specific areas – 'savant' skills – that are markedly above what might be expected given their other skills.[68] Savants who have normal or superior IQs may have exceptional skills that may make them celebrated. There may be a link between savant skills and synaesthesia. Savants may attract suspicion and may conceal their abilities. The possible aetiology of savant skills is discussed in Chapter 4.

Anxiety disorders

The increased risk of some anxiety-related disorders such as OCD has already been considered. Generalized anxiety disorder may also begin in middle childhood, and is more common in children with an ASD, although the main age of onset is after 11. Specific phobias may also begin in middle childhood. As well as the fear of loud noises already mentioned, common fears include needles, crowds,[56] asking for things in shops, dogs, and travelling on the bus. Some of these situations are actually threatening to people with an ASD: dogs make social demands and may become fierce if not handled correctly, shop assistants become impatient and cross, and bullying often happens on buses. Other anxiety-related conditions include school refusal, somatization, attachment disorder, selective mutism, enuresis and encopresis. The latter three occur together more commonly than expected by chance.[69]

Attachment disorders and separation anxiety

The distinction between secure and insecure attachment, and organized or disorganized attachment has been considered in Chapter 10. Reactive attachment disorders, in which attachment is disorganized were considered in Chapter 12. Insecure attachment, associated with separation anxiety, is more likely to become problematic in middle childhood, when periods of separation from a parent become a normal part of the child's routine. Separation anxiety, unlike other anxiety disorders in middle childhood, tends not to develop into other conditions in adolescence but persists as separation anxiety.[70] A link with the oxytocin gene has been suggested, although not proven.[71] It is the most common anxiety disorder in middle childhood.[72] Separation anxiety disorder is currently considered to be a differential diagnosis of ASD in international classifications, but this may hark back to a time when a psychogenic aetiology for ASD-like symptoms was still considered frequent. Although separation anxiety may occur in people with an ASD,[73] there is no evidence that it is more common than in the general population.

Selective mutism

Selective mutism, that is an unwillingness or inability to use speech in particular social contexts, is often considered to be a manifestation of social phobia,[49] but a significant minority of children with social phobia have underlying speech and language disorders.[45, 74] Although there is some evidence for communicative impairment in children with selective mutism, it is not clear whether there is an association with ASD.[75]

Interventions for selective mutism are described on the web pages of the American Speech-Language Hearing Association.[76]

Encopresis

In one study, 22 per cent of children with an ASD had additional gastrointestinal symptoms, mainly constipation and diarrhoea.[77] Constipation can become so severe that the child is encopretic, often secondarily having first achieved bowel control and then losing it again at the age of seven or thereabouts. This pattern of gastrointestinal symptoms is characteristic of an emotional disorder and in the study just cited was not associated with demographic characteristics, autism severity or adaptive functioning, but was associated with irritability, anxiety and social withdrawal.[77] Despite not being a core symptom of ASD, children with psychosomatic symptoms of anxiety such as these have a worse prognosis,[77] unless the anxiety is treated.

CAUSES OF ASD

The causes of ASD have been reviewed in Chapter 10. There are no specific causes that are more likely to result in an AS presentation in this age group, but it is less likely that the ASD will be complex, that is associated with epilepsy with a named syndrome, although this cannot be ruled out.

There are rare cases of children who appear to develop AS in this age group, in that their parents describe their development in infancy as having been normal. The most parsimonious explanation is that there were subtle impairments of social interaction and communication, but these did not obtrude into familial social relationships and so were disregarded.

MULTIDISCIPLINARY INVOLVEMENT

Multidisciplinary involvement with the child and the family are especially important during middle childhood, but may be particularly difficult to secure. The key professionals are teachers, especially the teacher with special responsibility for children with disabilities (known as the special educational needs coordinator, or SENCO, in the UK); educational psychologists; speech and language therapists; community paediatrician; and representation from the child and adolescent mental health team.

There are many obstacles in the way of joint working. Many educational psychologists and teachers are suspicious of diagnosis, and prefer to consider every child according to their particular needs. The Treaty of Salamanca, which established the right of every European child to attend their local school, has exacerbated this difficulty in that many educationalists extend the notion that every child should attend a 'normal school' to the notion that every child is 'normal'. Some schools undoubtedly resent the extra resources that are given to children with ASD, and may even imply to parents that, really, the problem is in the parents' inability to manage their children. Parents may suspect teachers of bullying, and teachers may suspect parents of over-involvement.

Educational psychologists have limited ability to influence funding, and may find themselves hamstrung by this, and also by a wish not to 'label' the child. Parents may assume that behavioural problems displayed by their children are an indication of the failure of the school, rather than being in any way their own or their child's responsibility. Child and adolescent mental health teams in the UK adopt a family-centred approach to mental health difficulties in middle childhood, and may sometimes seem to families to be implying that the problems are really those of parenting than of the child's ASD. Community paediatricians in the UK are often the most involved professionals, but their knowledge of ASD may be variable, and some services rely heavily on locum staff.

Teachers

Teachers know the children in their classes well, and may be able to provide a fresh perspective, even sometimes being the first to raise the possibility of Asperger syndrome. Children's attitudes may also influence the attitudes of other children, and influence whether or not a child with ASD is bullied. Some teachers are willing to accept that children with an ASD study in their own way, and can fit in with the child. Others are unwilling to do this, considering that children have to learn to fit in, and this may blunt these teachers' awareness of the child's strengths and weaknesses.

Teachers make formal assessments of learning and knowledge, but rarely make formal psychological assessments. However, a teacher-administered questionnaire – the Strengths and Difficulties Questionnaire – has been shown to be a useful screen for ASD as well as of the emotional difficulties resulting from ASD.[78] Ratings of teachers were also correlated with parents' ratings using the Autism Syndrome Screening Questionnaire. Simply giving teachers information about 'red flags' of ASD and asking them to nominate children with ASD results in over 93 per cent agreement with screening using a questionnaire, and takes the teachers only 15 minutes per child, compared to 3.5 to 5 hours per class for the application of one screening questionnaire (the Autism Syndrome Screening Questionnaire).[79] The Social Responsiveness Scale has also been recommended for use in the classroom,[80] as has a subset of items from the Developmental Behaviour Checklist.[81]

Speech and language therapists

Although DSM-IV and ICD-10 diagnoses of Asperger syndrome rule out speech and language disorder, in practice many children with high functioning ASD who may have escaped diagnosis until middle childhood do have speech and language difficulties. These are principally pragmatic,[78] but mild receptive language difficulties may also occur and may also have been missed previously. Speech and language therapists are able to identify these, and can also make excellent assessments of nonverbal communication. A routine speech and language assessment should therefore always be considered.

Educational psychologists

Educational psychologists can provide the most reliable picture of a child's cognitive strengths and weaknesses using psychometric tests. However, their belief in testing is variable and some may use the bare minimum of tests, including giving only a sample of sub-tests of one of the recognized batteries, such as the Wechsler Intelligence Scale for Children (WISC), and 'prorating' the scores. While this may be an appropriate technique for many children, the variability between subscores may make this an unreliable technique for children with an ASD.

Paediatricians

Identifiable causes of ASD in this age group are rare. Paediatricians may have a limited medical role to play, although many find themselves advising about managing behavioural or emotional problems.

Child and adolescent psychiatry team members

Knowledge about ASD may be variable within the different members of the child and adolescent psychiatry team, and teams may resist being involved or, if they are involved, contact is often lost again.

Child psychotherapists

Child psychotherapists have in the past been strongly influenced by psychoanalytic theory that has considered autism to be a psychological reaction in the child to emotional neglect by parents. Methods of treatment have therefore often focused on recovery, despite the lack of evidence that this is an achievable goal. There is growing evidence that psychotherapy or counselling may help children with an ASD overcome some of the emotional difficulties, and it is likely that there will be a growing role for this new generation of counsellors and child psychotherapists who are aiming to ameliorate emotional complications but not 'cure'.

INVESTIGATIONS

The investigations of AS in middle childhood should include educational and, if necessary, a psychological assessment of the additional cognitive difficulties discussed above.

INTERVENTIONS

Home based

As at every age, diagnosis may be the single most important intervention if it leads to greater understanding and greater ability to access additional resources.

Children in middle childhood who have AS and who have not yet been diagnosed may be the subject of conflict between parents, in that fathers may want to normalize their child's difficulties and mothers may wish to find a cause for it. Parental conflict may lead to a partnership break up that is preventable if both parents can be engaged and informed.

Parents may benefit from discussion of how much to tell siblings, family friends and members of the extended family about their child's difficulties. Openness is usually the best policy, and can be facilitated by having a diagnosis.

Children with AS are at increased risk of emotional disorders, and so need access to suitable services to assess and treat these. Parents may need advice about how to deal with any emotional or conduct problems that their child is presenting, in addition to their AS (these problems are dealt with more fully in Chapter 14). Family-based anxiety interventions using the principles of cognitive behavioural therapy have been shown to be effective in over two-thirds of children with an anxiety disorder in the context of ASD in one study.[82]

Health services

A minority of children with AS have associated health problems and so need paediatric services. When children do, special support may need to be available to make these services accessible, including giving the child as much information as possible about what to expect at the hospital. Staff should be willing to answer questions put by the child, some of which might be repetitive. Extra time may need to be set aside for the consultations, which should not be carried out by inexperienced staff.

A larger number of children with AS in this age group will need mental health services for the treatment of anxiety-related and other mental health disorders. Play therapy,[83] child psychotherapy and other psychological approaches have a long history of use with many anecdotal reports of success, but systematic evaluation has not been carried out.

School based

Most primary school teachers in one European national survey considered that children with AS should be educated in mainstream schools, but only one in ten thought that they had the resources to do so, and nearly nine out of ten thought that there should be greater collaboration between schools and mental health services in assisting these children. Nineteen out of twenty teachers wanted more in-service training about ASD.[84]

Parents often express dissatisfaction with the lack of recognition of what they see as their child's needs in mainstream school, and may press for special education for their child as a result. This lack of recognition may be the result of the combination of a lack of resources and a lack of awareness, both of which could be rectified by an increase in spending if local authorities could find the money. Lobbying by charities has been increasingly effective in pressurizing school authorities to spend more and in the UK this has resulted in an Autism Bill (2009). The provisions of this bill are summarized in Box 13.3.

Box 13.3 Provisions of UK Autism Bill (2009)*

Every local authority has the new duty to:

1. record and provide information on the number of children with autism

2. consider needs of children with autism in preparing a children and young people's plan, and in order to do this to have regard for the views of children and young people with autism, and their parents and carers, and make assessments of:

    1. the specific needs of children with autism in its area

    2. the services required to meet those needs

    3. the training requirements of staff employed or commissioned to enable these services to be delivered effectively

3. promote effective transition for young people with autism

4. recognize the needs of persons with autism

5. promote services and support for adults with autism and, so far as is reasonably practicable and consistent, promote independent living: that is enjoying the same choice, freedom, dignity, control and substantive opportunities as persons who are not disabled.

*Autism being defined as including all autism spectrum disorders, including Asperger syndrome.

Educational strategies for dealing with specific study difficulties

As a general principle, interventions work best when they are based on a careful appraisal of the needs of the particular child, and when teachers and parents plus any other specialist staff when appropriate, such as speech and language therapists, occupational therapists or educational psychologists, collaborate in devising interventions. An empirical stance is often the best for implementing strategies: avoiding ruling out possible interventions (unless they are unethical, clearly harmful, or clearly impractical) but evaluating them by simple before and after observations, and giving some attention to their long-term as well as short-term consequences.[85]

Bullying prevention

Teachers have a duty to provide an emotionally healthy environment in schools, as well as an environment that is conducive to learning, not least because emotional ill-health impairs learning. One important element in this is to minimize bullying and, if it occurs, to intervene quickly and effectively.

General principles for teaching children with an ASD

It is beyond the scope of this book to consider these in any detail, but some of the principles for teachers developed by Mike Connor are shown in Box 13.4.[86] Some school systems have issued handbooks and guidelines that may be consulted, for example the *Technical Assistance Manual on Autism for Kentucky Schools*, which comes with a checklist that teachers can use to monitor their ASD-appropriate teaching methods.[87] This is available in modified form on the OASIS@MAAP website.[88]

Education to reduce the primary impairment in AS

There are many school-based programmes for children with AS, some of which suggest that they can lead to 'cure'. There are many methodological difficulties in evaluating these, not least because of the non-specific effects of interventions, which may produce improvement through reduction in anxiety rather than a direct effect on the primary impairment.[89] A comprehensive US report concluded that:

> Studies have reported substantial changes in large numbers of children in intervention studies and longitudinal studies in which children received a variety of interventions. Even in the treatment studies that have shown the strongest gains, children's outcomes are variable...there does not appear to be a simple relationship between any particular intervention and 'recovery' from autistic spectrum disorders...gaps remain in addressing larger questions of the relationships between particular techniques, child characteristics and outcomes.[89a]

Box 13.4 Connor's guidelines for mainstream practice for teachers of children on the autistic spectrum

- Always try to look at the observed behaviour in terms of the function or meaning this behaviour has *for the pupil*.

- Providing a very clear structure and a set daily routine (including for play).

- Using clear and unambiguous language. Avoiding humour/irony, or phrases like 'my feet are killing me' or 'it's raining cats and dogs', which will cause bewilderment.

- Making clear (including with a firm 'No') which behaviours are unacceptable.

- Avoiding sentences like 'Would you like to do this?' or 'Why did you do that?'

- Addressing the child individually at all times.

- Providing warning of any impending change of routine, or switch of activity.

- Ensuring consistency of expectation among all staff, and avoiding any 'backing-down' once a reasonable and manageable target has been set.

- Recognizing that some change in manner or behaviour may reflect anxiety or stress (which may be triggered by a (minor) change to routine).

- Not taking apparently rude or aggressive behaviour personally and recognizing that the target for the child's anger may be unrelated to the source of that anger.

- Specific teaching of social rules/skills, such as turn-taking and social distance; and of gambits for initiating and maintaining conversation. Enhancing verbal expression (intonation) via drama, role-play, and audio- or video-taped feedback. (This kind of intervention, with individual debriefing afterwards, may be particularly relevant for senior school pupils.)

- Specific teaching, via photographs or video recordings, of how feelings are expressed and communicated, and how, therefore, they can be recognized.

- Protecting the child from teasing at free times, and providing peers with some insight into the needs of children on the autistic spectrum.

- Regular opportunity for simple conversation, with increasing use of 'how' and 'why' questions.

- The use of charts as a record of behavioural progress and a basis for reinforcement.

- Enhanced supervision during practical or physical activities.

Source: Adapted from Connor, 1999.

Lack of empathic responsiveness

People say that the face, or sometimes the eyes, is the mirror of the soul. A face expressive of positive feelings is taken to be an indication of trust or affection. Understandably, few people are willing to express negative feelings so openly, and therefore a lack of facial expression is taken to be an indication of negative feelings which are being suppressed. A lack of nonverbal expression is therefore often experienced by others as frightening or threatening. In close relationships it may also be experienced as withholding, uncaring, detached or unfeeling.

Debate continues about whether emotional feelings are the consequence of appraisals of arousal and of facial expression, or whether subjective feelings are the cause of facial expression and arousal. The evidence seems to be that both James and Cannon, and therefore both theories, were right.[90] Clinically, there is no lack of emotion in most people with Asperger syndrome, although they may sometimes have difficulty in naming it correctly,[91, 92] or in recognizing its build-up or origins.

So when a person with ASD does not evince any emotion for another person, it does not mean that they do not have any emotions for that person. Indeed, they may feel positively about the person. But the other person is most likely to interpret the lack of facial expression as an indication either of a lack of emotion or, more likely, that negative emotion is being suppressed.

Lack of emotional expressiveness may be one reason that people with an ASD can provoke an unexpected hostility in others, especially people in authority who may interpret it as a lack of proper regard for them, or even impertinence. It may lead to problems with teachers at school, bosses at work, or father figures in the home.

Clinical observation suggests that the inexpressiveness in face is particularly marked in the lower two-thirds, the part of the face that is least linked to language.[93] This contrasts with the reduction of facial expressivity in schizophrenia, which is particularly marked in the expression of emotion in the upper third of the face.[94]

Child based
However carefully family members, teachers and services work together, there may be some problems that children with an ASD may present that require intervention. Particular problems include irritability and aggression, narrowing of the behavioural repertoire, withdrawal and anxiety.

Irritability and aggression
Irritability and aggression are most likely to be due to anxiety, but may become sustained by the rewarding effects that they produce, although this is more likely to occur in older children, and so will be dealt with in Chapter 16. One study has shown a reduction in aggression following intensive group cognitive behavioural therapy plus a parental support group. There was a waiting list control group, and the therapeutically effective elements of the interventions could not be identified.[95]

Behavioural narrowing, inflexibility and rigidity
Many children with AS have some degree of narrowing of their behavioural repertoire, but this may become problematic if the child's health or welfare are affected, or if it imposes itself on family life. Narrowing includes dietary restriction due to food fads; longer and longer periods getting up and getting ready to go out; increasing time spent in repetitive activity; an intolerance of particular sensations manifested as sound aversion or an inability to wear

certain types of clothing; and an increase in repetitive questioning. Many of these behaviours are backed up by aggression if people do not go along with them.

It is often tempting to accommodate to these behaviours, particularly as these children seem so distressed about them. Some of them may be attributed to the ASD itself: for example, parents and people with ASD will both assume that it is a difference in the perceptual apparatus, 'hyperacusis', that makes noise or certain kinds of touch unpleasant. However, testing may not always find that children are more sensitive, and anxiety is the most likely explanation for the heightened sensation and not altered thresholds in the sense organs themselves.

Going along with the behavioural narrowing may increase it.[96]

Sensory overload

One theory about anxiety in ASD is that it is the consequence of having too much sensation, of sensory overload. Sensory overload occurs in hypokalaemia (low blood potassium),[97] possibly as a result of changes in peripheral receptors, and an increase in, and lack of selective attention to, human voices, which occurs in schizophrenia and may lead to hallucinations.[98]

In one study of 72 adolescents with ASD and 57 controls, four out of five adolescents with ASD had normal auditory discrimination, but one in five had hyperacusis with exceptional frequency discrimination skills.[99] None of the one in five had AS, since all had language delay. Members of this group had developed strategies for reducing sound stimulation. Increased visual discrimination compared to neurotypicals has also been demonstrated in adults with AS,[100] although in this case it was true of each of the adults tested rather than a minority.

Sensory integration

Sensory reduction, for example by the use of ear plugs or altering lighting, should be considered only if there is definite evidence of hyperaesthesia. The subjective experience of unpleasant stimulus may lead a person with an ASD to avoid important social situations, to destroy the course of the stimulation, or to coerce others into reducing their output. To answer this with confrontation or coercion increases the risk of violence, and also promotes coercive strategies over negotiated ones. A middle path between compliance and coercion has to be found, often by an unemotional discussion about how the various life styles of the family can be harmonized in practice. Dealing with the problems posed by sensory stimulation is one of the two main sources of stress for support workers applying behavioural methods at home.[101] Sensory overload is also one of the six main triggers for assault on staff by patients in mental health facilities.[102] Easy solutions are not to be expected.

Therapeutic measures to reduce the effects of sensory overload have been included in a package of therapies often termed 'sensory integration'. A precursor of sensory integration which focused on hearing, auditory integration, had strong anecdotal support, but systematic reviews did not provide unequivocal evidence for effectiveness.[103]

Most occupational therapists use sensory integration approaches when dealing with problem behaviours in people with an ASD, but there is little evidence for their effectiveness, and when compared to traditional methods using behavioural approaches, outcome is poorer.[104]

Anxiety and ASD in middle childhood

Anxiety disorders often make their first appearance in middle childhood. They may be symptoms of the ASD itself. A change of routine is a well-known cause of anxiety, but other causes might be ruminating about an unresolved and upsetting past incident, and grief. Many children with an ASD do not show grief, and it is sometimes assumed that they do not feel bereavement. In my clinical experience, this is not so. People with AS often grieve the loss of pets, even if they contributed to this, and the loss of a grandparent. But they may have difficulty in showing it at the time. Simple discussion may be enough to move the person with an ASD towards resolution, once the first step, of recognizing the grief, has been taken.

More established anxiety in neurotypical children can persist and may lead to adult psychiatric disorders. Cognitive behavioural interventions have been developed for children in middle childhood and have been shown to be effective in children across cultures.[105] Although other modalities of therapy have not been tested, there is no reason to consider that they would be less effective. Interventions of this kind have not been trialled in children with ASD, but anecdotal evidence suggests that counselling may help even young children if carried out by a counsellor with experience of working with children with an ASD. However, further research needs to be done.

Chapter 14

PRESENTATION OF KANNER SYNDROME IN MIDDLE CHILDHOOD

KANNER SYNDROME IN THE CONTEXT OF LEARNING DISABILITY

Box 14.1 Red flags for autistic disorder in the context of learning disability (Kanner syndrome)

- Unusually severe or persistent challenging behaviour.
- Islands of ability.
- Impaired nonverbal expression.
- No friends, makes few if any social overtures.

Diagnostic criteria for Kanner syndrome in the context of learning disability

International criteria are readily applicable to this age group but the criteria have to extend across the developmental range, and only some items are applicable to children with ASD and intellectual disability. I have summarized this in Box 14.2 (but see also Box 12.2 in Chapter 12).

> # Box 14.2 DSM-IV-TR Diagnostic criteria for autistic disorder adapted for school age children with co-morbid intellectual disability (and with diagnostic items reallocated to their appropriate headings)
>
> A. Qualitative impairment in social interaction
>
> 1. Failure to develop peer relationships
> 2. Discomfort with sharing toys, space, activity, or attention from an adult with another peer
> 3. Does not approach others with cooperative intent
>
> B. Qualitative impairment in communication (note A1 is shifted here)
>
> 1. Lack of gaze exchange, facial expression, and other nonverbal expression
> 2. Unawareness of proxemics
> 3. Absent speech, or speech but with syntactic and semantic errors
>
> C. Restrictive, repetitive and stereotyped behaviour (note B4 moved here)
>
> 1. No make believe play. Play dominated by collecting objects whose significance may escape others
> 2. May spend long periods apparently inactive
> 3. Eating, dressing, bathing routines.
> 4. Attracted to making repetitive movements which readily become stereotyped
> 5. Absorbed or fascinated by particular stimuli, objects, or parts of objects

Source: Adapted from American Psychiatric Association, 2001.

Case history: Derek

Derek's older brother had Asperger syndrome. Derek was born quickly, and was an avid feeder, but spent most of the rest of the day asleep. His mother thought of him as an easy baby at first, but she soon realized that he was not sitting up when he should and the health visitor raised the possibility that Derek might have learning difficulties at his one-year check. He could sit unaided at one year, but only shuffled during his second year, and could not walk or hold a spoon until he was over two years old. He spent most of his time, apparently contentedly, watching the mobile over his bed or rocking himself. His parents noticed that he liked music, and as he got older, they could interest him in some television programmes. By observing him carefully, they could tell when he wanted a drink, and which drinks he liked. He was adamant about not eating certain foods, but loved fruit.

By the age of five, it was clear that Derek would not be able to attend mainstream school. He had been fully assessed in the paediatric clinic, and no physical disorder had been found for his condition. The paediatrician said that there were some 'autistic features' but no formal diagnosis of an ASD had been made. He was attending speech and language therapy and his parents thought that there were words that he understood, but he was not using them to communicate himself. He had become interested in cars, and could recognize his parents' car just by the sound it made. He liked to look at pictures of cars, too, and recognized cars of the same make as his parents'. He would become excited if he saw a photograph of one in a book or magazine. Once, his father had a minor accident which left a dent in the back bumper. Derek noticed this immediately when next he went in the car, and walked over and pointed to it. At six, he was able to recognize routes on the road, and would be upset if his parents took him to school by a different route.

PRESENTING SYMPTOMS OF KANNER SYNDROME

Children with ASD and intellectual disability are more likely to be socially impaired, and to spend time in repetitive activity than IQ matched children with intellectual disability alone.[2]

Primary impairments of Kanner syndrome

The ASDs all have one primary impairment in common, the impairment in nonverbal communication that has been frequently alluded to, but it is more likely to be expressed in Kanner syndrome as anomalous communication, such as grimacing, sing-song voice prosody, gaze directed close to, but away from, the other person's eyes, and a lack of proxemic constancy with the person with ASD sometimes standing very close to or even touching another person, and sometimes standing unusually far away.

Intellectual disability and a language impairment are also primary, but independent, impairments. Both may be consequences of a failure in brain connectedness,[3] and it may be this that explains the association of the three impairments.

Speech and language

The severity of the language impairment in Kanner syndrome is proportionate to the cognitive impairment, but that is not so in intellectual disability in other syndromes, for example in Williams syndrome, where there may be a more mixed picture with some aspects of language being preserved.[4] Speech in children with Kanner syndrome is particularly likely to be characterized by echolalia or by abnormal use of referents, for example the misuse of personal pronouns that, because it may involve referring to oneself as 'you', is sometimes called pronominal reversal. In fact children are more likely to refer to themselves in the third person as 'he' or 'she' or to use their names.

Most children with Kanner syndrome do not use speech communicatively. A few may use catch phrases, although when this happens the meaning of the phrase may seem irrelevant to the situation. However, one conversational analysis led the authors to conclude that repetition may have some communicative significance,[5] and this may also be true of the use of catch phrases.

Nonverbal communication

Although nonverbal communication has been studied very little in intellectual disability, and often with little attention to the presence or absence of ASD,[6] there is evidence that although there is a link between intellectual and social disability, the two are also partly dependent. In a study of observer ratings of pleasure ('liking') and disgust ('disliking') 24 professional carers, with no particular training in rating nonverbal communication, reliably rank ordered three facial expressions provoked by liked or disliked stimuli by four different service users with profound intellectual disability.[7] This suggests that nonverbal communication is a more robust form of communication than speech, and is less affected by intellectual disability. This would be consistent with the use of nonverbal communication by many animal species which do not have the cognitive capacity to understand or use speech.

Although nonverbal communication may be less complex and expressive in people with an intellectual disability, it is not absent. In a study of ten people with intellectual disabilities who had been deaf and blind from birth, five people who had received a clinical diagnosis of ASD were compared to the other five who had not. Nonverbal communication rated as 'openness for contact', 'reciprocity/joint attention' and 'communicative signals/functions' discriminated significantly between the ASD and the non-ASD group.[8]

Nonverbal communication is as applicable to the diagnosis of ASD in the context of intellectual disability as it is in people with no intellectual difficulties.[9]

The interpretation of facial expression may be impaired in some children with intellectual disability,[10] but this is not a consistent finding as it is in ASD.

Repetitive behaviour

Repetitive behaviour is particularly prominent in people not only with ASD and learning difficulties, correlating with nonverbal IQ scores,[11, 12] but also with level of social adaptation (and with poor sleep). One possible explanation for this association is that the lack of awareness of the inhibitory feedback from other people that normally curtails repetition is absent. However, another possible explanation is that people with Kanner syndrome may have a kind of 'stimulus hunger', similar to that which drives some cage stereotypies in animals and the repeated self-injury in people, such as prisoners, kept in isolated and unrewarding circumstances. It has been suggested that it is an abnormality of forebrain dopamine that is responsible for this 'repetitive reward-seeking behaviour'.[13, 14, 15, 16, 17, 18, 19, 20]

Repetitive reward-seeking behaviour

Long-term studies of people with Parkinson's disease treated with L-dopa, a dopamine antagonist, and of cocaine users (cocaine is a dopamine receptor agonist),[21] have shown an increased risk of behaviours that are comparable to those shown by people with an ASD, particularly those with Kanner syndrome, and people with ADHD. These are sometimes termed 'dopamine dysregulation syndrome' or 'repetitive reward-seeking behaviours'. Repetitive reward-seeking behaviours,[22, 23] which include impulsive and appetitive behaviours, such as overeating; hypersexuality; 'punding' or prolonged, purposeless, stereotyped behaviour like hoarding objects, assembling then disassembling objects repeatedly, and lining objects up over and over, are associated with increased dopamine activity, and can be blocked by dopamine antagonists, such as antipsychotics. However, in mice given L-dopa, wild-type mice do not develop stereotypies (thought to be a model of human stereotypies), but dopamine deficient mice do, even when their overall dopamine levels are still lower than the wild-type mice.[24] This suggests that starting from a lower than normal level of dopamine-mediated neurotransmission is a risk factor for dopamine dysregulation syndrome, even though it is an increase in dopamine availability that actually causes them. One explanation is that a chronic reduction of D2/D3 activity in the reward system leads to long-term receptor loss or inactivation. So increasing dopamine transmission results in an excess of dopaminergic activity in the basal ganglia, but activity in other areas remains at levels below which reward would normally occur.[25] Parkinson's disease is associated with reduced activity in downstream areas through disconnection of prefrontal cortex; repeated cocaine use may reduce dopamine receptors through excitotoxic effects.

ASD and ADHD are both, probably, consequences of disconnection, and diffusion tensor imaging has confirmed that reduced activation of right anterior cingulate during an eye-tracking task was correlated with repetitive symptoms on the ADI-R.[26] Anterior cingulate dopamine activity is required for animals to undertake tasks that require the overcoming of obstacles to obtain reward.[27] Perigenual anterior cingulate is more active in people of higher social status, and gaining social status in primates is associated with an increase in dopamine.[28] Increased dopamine increases social extroversion, but reduced dopamine is associated with social avoidance and social phobia. Dopaminergic activation of nucleus accumbens, the 'reward centre', results in further activation of dopaminergic neurons leading to, among other things, an increase in grooming behaviour, social behaviour appropriate to a dominant animal, and the continuation of the rewarded behaviour.[29] Social housing for dominant macaques also increases D2 receptor numbers.[30] This leads to the possibility that social factors – submissiveness and a lack of social contact – may be enough to deplete dopamine receptors, and might contribute to the susceptibility to dopamine dysregulation syndrome and therefore – and this is a further speculation – to the repetitive reward-seeking syndrome seen in those people with ASD who are particularly isolated and lacking in social influence, who are likely to include people with Kanner syndrome. It is also possible that there is a genetic explanation for low dopamine levels, at least in some people with ASD, as an SNP in one of the genes encoding a dopamine receptor (DRD3) has been reported to be more common in at least some people with an ASD, suggesting that in these people, dopamine transport and therefore dopamine availability may be reduced.[31] Polymorphisms in another dopamine-related gene, that for the dopamine transport protein DAT1, have been shown to be associated with either an increased risk of social anxiety and tics, or a reduced risk of hyperactivity and language disorder in people with ASD,[32] and an increased risk of anxiety and depression in children with ADHD.[33] Dopamine availability is reduced in adults with ADHD, compared to controls, in the caudate and in the nucleus accumbens, the 'reward centre', as well as in the hypothalamus and mid-brain.[34]

Secondary disabilities of Kanner syndrome

Children with Kanner syndrome are even more likely to lose out on development and dialogue than children with Asperger syndrome, and as a result may often seem to live in their own world, in which other people may join them by adopting its rules, or emulating its behaviour, but the person with Kanner syndrome may be reluctant to enter the other person's subjective world. The difficulty in understanding the world around them may be exacerbated by dysexecutive syndrome.[35] Unless others are prepared to adapt to the person with Kanner syndrome, that person may be as socially isolated as if they were actually on their own.

Social approach

Children with Kanner syndrome are unlikely to make social approaches to others, although they may approach others to take things from them, or to hit them. Some children with Kanner syndrome will tolerate an approach from others, others will avoid this and, if it cannot be avoided, may try to dissuade the other person by spitting, violence, or other means.

Social approach always involves both threat and invitation. If the invitation cannot be reciprocated, the threat component is accentuated. Approaches that are more likely to include cues of submissiveness, such as a reduction of direct gaze, are less likely to be threatening, and more likely to elicit a response. Physical contact may also be perceived as threatening, and may be aversive to many people with autism, who reject normal cuddles or social touch. Prolonged enforced cuddling has been reported to lead, after a period of distress and attempts to escape, to quieting and apparently increased social contact, suggesting that the aversiveness of social approach is the obstacle to discovering its benefits.

Treating people as objects

If approach behaviour does occur, it may not be social but instrumental. A person's hand may be moved towards an object that the person with ASD wants, or a person's hair may be stroked as one might stroke the hair of a doll. Unless people respond to this as a person, and do not allow their body parts to be used, the person with Kanner syndrome may think of that body part as being something like property.

Case example

> Richard had developed a fascination with blond hair. He would want to stroke or fiddle with the hair of any woman in his vicinity if she was a blonde. He could do this to strangers on public transport and, more seriously, if the woman drew away, he would get angry and might hit them.

Treating objects as people

Stroking blond hair may be comparable to other common sensory pleasures for people with an ASD, which are pursued repetitively. Other examples include stroking velvet or silk. Many young children with an ASD become attached to an object that they carry everywhere with them; often this originated as an object with a particularly strong sensory 'flavour'. The attachment may derive from habit, from the ability of the object to give comfort, or from something more akin to attachment in the sense that people might use 'sentimental value'. Losing the object may cause distress that can be as severe as a bereavement, and can lead to lasting behavioural changes that are similar to grief.

One possible explanation for the intensity of the emotional investment in an object may be that people with an ASD lack an awareness of other people as being people and so emotional investment is not restricted to people. In slightly more able children, some objects clearly become friends and companions. They may be chosen for their sentimental value because, for example, they are reminders of the past.

Case example

> Louisa began to swallow pins at the age of ten. She had lived with her mother up until then, but had become too much of a handful and was now in a residential home. Her mother was a seamstress and Louisa liked to 'help' her stitching patterns together. When Louisa was younger, and was less intrusive, this had been pleasant for both mother and daughter. But as Louisa got older, and tried to emulate her mother, it became a struggle, especially as Louisa began to put pins in her mouth as she saw her mother do. Her mother held them between her lips, but Louisa was too clumsy for this. After she went into the home, Louisa seemed to change as if grieving her old way of life, but then she resumed her old habit of putting pins in her mouth as if trying to recall the pleasant times in the past. Probably without intending to do so, at least at first, Louisa swallowed a proportion of these pins, and sometimes required emergency surgery when one damaged her gut wall sufficiently to cause bleeding or perforation. Louisa's exposure to pins was carefully controlled, but she seemed to show a super-human ability to spot those that were lying on the floor. Staff knew that the ability to see anomalous detail is stronger in people with an ASD because there is reduced top-down suppression of detail in favour of the 'bigger picture', but still joked that Louisa certainly knew how to keep them on their toes or, more aggressively, that she could be clever enough when it suited her.

Tertiary handicap with Kanner syndrome
Institutionalization

People with intellectual disability, and particularly those with an ASD too, are at risk of atrophy of their social skills, and an increase in repetitive behaviour and resistance to change, if they are exposed to an undemanding, routine-bound environment in which there is little attention to individuality, and little opportunity for choice or decision-making. Little has been written recently on how to provide this.

Supported living at home

One of the main planks in preventing institutionalization has been to support children with Kanner syndrome to live in their own homes. Whether this is possible depends partly on intrinsic disability and partly on support. One study showed that the key elements of the latter are, first, emotional and practical support to parents, including respite care availability –

without it only being available for people having to 'jump through hoops';[36] second, physical accessibility to toilets and public buildings; and third, accessible transport.[37]

INVESTIGATIONS

Children with Kanner syndrome are more likely to have 'complex autism', and investigation is therefore more likely to discover a known aetiology. Although this is unlikely to be treatable, having this further information may assist in prognosis, and active investigation is therefore justified.

INTERVENTION

Children with Kanner syndrome have problems in learning, particularly in social learning, may suffer from anxiety in many social situations, and may lack the ability to obtain comfort from others or experience a sense of social influence over others. Additional problems that lower quality of life may include epilepsy, social isolation, bullying, and the pain or disability of any associated physical disorders.

General strategies for intervention in ASD have already been considered and some of the particular issues for children with Kanner syndrome will be considered here.

Communication

Symbol use most commonly develops in the context of a language or a stream of social intercommunication. Identifying tokens – words, gestures, expressions and so on – within such a continuum may be particularly difficult for people with ASD, but learning a referent for an already isolated token may be much easier. Various communication schemes for children with Kanner syndrome have been developed on this basis. For example, the Picture Exchange Communication System (PECS) uses pictures of items to indicate something that the child wants.[38] To get what they want the child simply presents the picture to a teacher or carer (at phase 1, but there is the possibility of building into more communicative exchanges up to phase 6). Iconic resemblance between the picture and what the child wants is important for the teacher, but iconicity does not matter to the child, only that previous conditioned learning has associated that picture with a desired reward.[39] An attempt has been made to provide a tactile PECS system for children with autism and visual impairment.[40] The use of PECS increases social approach, but only while it is available. It does not increase the use of language, or alter autistic symptoms.[41]

Other symbol-based treatment methods are the visual supports that are part of the Treatment and Education of Autistic and related Children with a Communication Handicap (TEACCH) programmes and the use of simplified sign languages such as Makaton. Many of these methods have been evaluated as if they are potentially curative and so focused on enduring change in the primary impairment of ASD,[42] but a more important consequence of them may be to increase children's control, including their control over their own learning.

Social behaviour

A particular difficulty in helping anyone with an ASD is the risk that there are no rewards in prosocial behaviour. This is unlikely to happen in children whose carers are responsive to them, but if this fails, and the child discovers that they can have an impact through threat, then asocial behaviour may become more rewarding to the child than prosocial behaviour.

Challenging behaviour

Many of the ways that people behave can challenge others. What sets 'challenging behaviour' apart is that it has a negative impact on carers,[43] and that it appears to be devoid of context because it is partly self-reinforcing, akin to addictive behaviour. Self-reinforcement may be through the primary release of tension, perhaps most applicable to self-injurious behaviour, or by means of the increase of social dominance that follows from the negative impact of the behaviour on others.

Matson and Rivet suggest, on the basis of a case control study of 161 adults with ASD, intellectual disability and challenging behaviour, that four categories of challenging behaviour can usefully be distinguished. These are aggression (including aggression to others and damage to property), stereotypy, self-injury and disruptive behaviour (mainly running away). All of these were more frequent in the adults with ASD than the controls. These categories also apply to school age children with Kanner syndrome.[44]

Organic causes of challenging behaviour are rare, although it has been suggested that missed cases of phenylketonuria may present in this way, and that changing to a low phenylalanine diet can result in improvement in the learning disability and ASD, as well as an improvement in challenging behaviour. However, with a national screening programme in place this is likely to be rare.[45]

Challenging behaviour is often minimized by those not in the front line, or staff may be blamed. Negative responses to challenging behaviour, whether directed towards the challenging person or to their carers is never helpful. If mistakes are being made they should be identified, and dealt with. Challenging behaviour may be stereotyped and relatively unresponsive to the immediate environment but a new episode of challenging behaviour should never be dismissed in that way. Possible factors might include recent distress, often linked to some change, or frustration. Abuse may trigger challenging behaviour and should not be ignored,[46] although should not be assumed either. Challenging behaviour that is not repetitive in people with intellectual disabilities may be more responsive to the care environment than is apparent. In one study (not specifically of ASD) adults with intellectual disability, the risk factors for challenging behaviour were also factors that made caring more difficult: lower intellectual level, visual impairment and urinary incontinence. Having a severe physical disability or Down syndrome made for less challenging behaviour – perhaps because carers were more forgiving of the burdens of care placed on them by their charges. This may also have been why caring for groups of people, where the burdens would be cumulative, and being cared for by paid rather than family carers were also risk factors for challenging behaviours in this study.[47]

Families dealing with a child with challenging behaviour are more stressed if the child is, as a result, excluded from day services, if respite care cannot be provided, and if there is no expert support available.[48]

There has been little research into the intentions behind challenging behaviour, or its meaning. Most research has focused, instead, on suppressing it. Providing alternative means of dealing with problems before the challenging behaviour begins may also be neglected, although training in alternative methods of expression has been shown to reduce challenging behaviour.[49]

Simple measures, such as the treatment of anxiety or depression if it is present, and ensuring a good night's sleep where possible,[50] should be considered.

Most studies of intervention have been of single cases but positive reinforcement of alternative behaviours in situations which might formerly have evoked challenging behaviour is a consistently effective intervention, as is the careful analysis of the antecedents to the behaviour and its consequences, and a change in the reinforcement provided by the behaviour itself or by the consequences of it.

Drug treatment is often considered when aggression is a prominent feature, but an expert review concluded that it is of limited value, and is ineffective in the long term.[51] The same team concluded that it was not cost-effective.[52]

Repetitive challenging behaviour

There is much less knowledge about how to treat repetitive challenging behaviour,[53] although these may become lifelong.[2] Behavioural methods have included attempting to control the patient's whole environment in 'token economies' in which patients may lose tokens for challenging behaviours, and earn them for previously defined appropriate behaviours. But these methods break down if patients are not motivated by the rewards. Staff often find these milieu ethically challenging too, because the loss of rewards may be experienced as being punitive.

An alternative approach is to consider that these repeated challenging behaviours are a kind of stereotypy, with a basis in altered neurochemistry. This may be particularly applicable to repeated self-injury.[54]

Stereotypies are more common in children with Kanner syndrome than in children with intellectual disability alone. They are also more common in girls. The presence of ASD increases the likelihood of hand and finger stereotypies, and of reduced nonverbal IQ of postural stereotypies, such as rocking.[55] This suggests a possible distinction between them, with finger movements perhaps being linked to grooming.

Drug treatment has often involved the use of antipsychotics. Their effects may be uncertain if the repetitive challenging behaviour is a kind of repetitive reward-seeking behaviour as transient increases of dopamine, blocked by antipsychotics, cause this on the foundation of long-term dopamine depletion in nucleus accumbens. Antipsychotics might be expected to make the latter worse, and to have a negative effect in the long term. An alternative strategy may be to treat with methylphenidate, for whose efficacy there is some evidence.[56]

The use of methylphenidate is also consistent with the hypothesis that stereotyped challenging behaviour is an expression of ADHD in the context of Kanner syndrome.

Schooling

Most European countries are parties to the Salamanca Declaration that asserts the right of every child to attend their local school, and to experience 'normalization'. This policy has had mixed results for children with Asperger syndrome, but its success for children with Kanner syndrome may require the investment of an unrealistic level of resource. Most parents prefer their child with Kanner syndrome to attend a special school.[57] There have been few studies of special education for children with Kanner syndrome. One, actually a study of TEACCH, showed improvements in motor control, social adaptation and communication in special residential schooling and in a specialist programme, but not following inclusion in mainstream school.[58]

Parents' opinions

There are no treatments for the primary impairment in ASD currently although some, such as applied behaviour analysis, target early consequences of the primary impairment. Others, like drug treatments, have a place in treating a particular complication in a few children with an ASD. Reports of the efficacy of treatment may therefore be misleading if considered over the whole population of children with an ASD, without specifying the target of the intervention.

However, a survey of 479 parents who were mainly parents of children with autism (average age 8.3 years, and 80.2% boys) did provide information about what parents had tried, and what they thought worked, to give two crude league tables of the popularity of different treatments (see Tables 14.1 and 14.2).[59]

Table 14.1 Physical treatment by order of preference

Type of medication	Ratio of improved to no effect or worse	Number of children trying this treatment (% of sample)
Miscellaneous gastrointestinal medications	4.00	10 (2%)
Miscellaneous herbal medication	3.33	13 (2.7%)
Atypical antipsychotics	2.08	80 (16.7%)
Anxiolytics	2.00	12 (2.5%)
Stimulants	1.80	172 (35.9%)
Mood stabilizers	1.80	70 (14.6%)
Chelation	1.60	32 (6.7%)
Gluten-free and or casein-free diet	1.52	155 (32.4%)
Antidepressants	1.31	136 (28.4%)
Other diets	1.19	54 (11.3%)
Miscellaneous other medications	1.17	13 (2.7%)

Source: Adapted from Goin-Kochel, Mackintosh, *et al.*, 2004.

Table 14.2 Other interventions by order of preference

Type of intervention	Ratio of improved to no effect or worse	Number of children trying this treatment (% of sample)
Applied behaviour analysis (ABA)	3.76	225 (47.0%)
Social skills training	3.05	244 (50.9%)
Picture Exchange Communication System (PECS)	2.88	231 (48.2%)
TEACCH	2.86	88 (18.4%)
Positive behavioural support	2.82	233 (48.6%)
Sensory integration	2.79	255 (53.2%)
Occupational therapy	2.77	361 (75.4%)
Physical therapy	2.68	146 (30.5%)
Speech therapy	2.53	403 (84.1%)
Early intervention services	2.39	331 (69.1%)
Social stories	2.33	197 (41.1%)
Floortime	2.10	129 (26.9%)
Options programme	2.00	21 (4.4%)
Music therapy	1.72	129 (26.9%)
Auditory integration therapy	1.52	88 (18.4%)
Neurofeedback	0.67	16 (3.3%)

Source: Adpated from Goin-Kochel, Mackintosh, *et al.,* 2004.

ISSUES

Abuse

The physical or sexual abuse of young people with ASD is under-investigated. In one survey of children in mental health settings in the community, one in five were reported to have experienced physical abuse, and one in six were reported to have experienced sexual abuse.[60] Rates are probably higher for children in residential care where 61 per cent have been reported in one study to have been 'severely maltreated by a careprovider',[61] although the rates in this latter study were lower in the children who were more socially disabled. Reported rates of children in schools are lower, but these might be underestimates.

The risk of abuse may be no greater for children with an ASD than for children with uncomplicated intellectual disability,[60] but discovering and investigating abuse may be more difficult. Children with an ASD are unlikely to complain about abuse, may misread social situations and so may misunderstand abuse as harmless behaviour, or consider appropriate limit-setting as abuse. Children with an ASD may also be more suggestible than other children and less likely to have the capacity to give evidence in legal proceedings.

The symptoms that are alerts to sexual abuse in neurotypical children are also increased in children with an ASD who have been abused. These include sexual acting out behaviour and running away.[60]

There is no evidence about the specific needs of children with an ASD in order to protect them against abuse or to remedy any emotional difficulties that may result from being abused.

Chapter 15

PRESENTATION OF ASPERGER SYNDROME IN LATER CHILDHOOD AND ADOLESCENCE

RELEVANT DEVELOPMENTAL CHALLENGES

It has been argued that adolescence is a modern Western development, providing extended financial and emotional parenting in exchange for the child's willingness to be educated for a longer period to perform the more complex occupational roles needed by society. There are obviously social advantages in this, but there is also a communal disadvantage if adolescence continues at the expense of remaining economically dependent or postponing caring for others.

Having recognized that adolescence may be a significant stage only in Westernized cultures, every culture must deal with the biological universals of puberty and the development of an adult body,[1] including a fully myelinated brain, that typically occur between the ages of 11 and 18. Many cultures make the transition from childhood with a rite of passage, and some include a period of instruction in gender roles. People in Western cultures often have a normative view of adolescence that does not recognize the multiplicity of paths to adulthood. According to this view, adolescence is when people make lasting friendships, make choices that determine their sexuality often for many subsequent years, arrive at a body shape that will provide the basic armature of their physique until osteoporosis or accident alters it, and make – or consciously defer – choices about occupation.[2]

Knowing what kind of person one is and what one wants for oneself ('identity') and having the emotional commitment and resources to be able to shape events accordingly ('agency') have been proposed as 'key factors that shape the life course',[3] and that the end of childhood coincides with their rapid development.

Agency

Agency begins with the experience that an effect has occurred because one has caused it, but generalizes into a capacity: that one could bring about an effect if one chose to. It has been suggested that agency involves not only a feeling,[4] but also a belief, for example the belief in self-efficacy first identified by Bandura.[5]

The feeling of agency does not require the observation that a willed action leads to an intended consequence. Reward at the time that an action is initiated increases the efficiency of the action,[6] and unconscious actions may, if they lead to desirable consequences, contribute to the perception of agency.[4] So, the feeling of agency may be a consequence of an experience of positive affirmation of actions and may be based on a wide range of outcomes that are perceived as having been desirable, even if these were not consciously planned.

A belief in self-efficacy is, by contrast, based on conscious effort and the past experience, and future expectation, that it will produce the desired outcome. Acquiring a sense of self-efficacy is influenced by not only the innate capacity to bring about an outcome, but also the value that others place on the outcomes that one does bring about. There are close links, therefore, between social efficacy and shame: if what one does is denigrated, shame is the emotion that may ensue and reduced self-efficacy is the belief. On the other hand, 'mastery experiences' in which a child is rewarded for what they can achieve, and the use of 'positive persuasion' or encouragement, are associated with an increase in self-efficacy.

It has been suggested that there is a particular 'social self-efficacy' and that is needed for making friends, pursuing romantic relationships, social assertiveness, performance in public situations, groups or parties, and giving or receiving help. One might add resolving interpersonal conflict to this list. Reduced social self-efficacy is associated with loneliness and depression,[7] and social anxiety.

Both types of agency, unconscious and conscious, rely on prefrontal lobe activation.

Agency and capacity

Agency can also be interpreted as the capacity to make choices.[8] It therefore is an important contribution to 'competence' or 'capacity' to consent and make judgements about medical and social care. From the age of 14 UK law assumes that a young person may be competent to give or withhold consent. Competence, or capacity, is assumed from the age of 16 unless there is strong evidence to set it aside. The presumption of capacity is intended to protect the rights of the patient, but it may sometimes go against the patient's interest. This may occur when a person with an ASD is more able to recount facts than to understand the need to put those facts in context, and to influence how others will perceive those facts. People with ASD are also less able to withstand persuasiveness by others, and may have a long-standing tendency to go along with others wherever possible. People with an ADHD are more likely than other offenders to have made a false confession;[9] anecdotal reports suggest that people with an ASD are also at increased risk of making false confessions as a result of friendly but persistent interrogation.

False confession

This lack of ability for self-presentation and self-protection may lead people with an ASD to overestimate their own capacity to consent, leaving them vulnerable not only in police interviews but also in clinical ones. Consent to disclosure may be given too easily by patients whose interests are not served thereby. It is therefore good practice to accept the withholding of consent, without over-persuasion to change the person's mind, and to ensure even more carefully than usual that consent is fully informed. Assuming apparent capacity may not always be in the interests of the person with ASD.[10]

The perception of oneself as an agent may rest on the ability to narrate a life story that seems to have a plot extending into the future. Narrating a life story may involve internal reflection, perhaps conducted by means of the inner speech that Vygotsky described.[11] It might also involve exactly those conversations – chatting or small talk – that many people with ASD find otiose and difficult. There is evidence that recounting the past to another person, if it allows for commentary and rethinking, also changes autobiographical memory. This may increase the sense of agency or purposefulness in life. People who lack a sense of agency, for example those who have been sexually abused, may conversely be unable to recall biographical events and may also have a reduced connectedness in their narrative of unemotional and unrelated personal experience in the present. Activation of the default network during day or night dreaming may also subserve the consolidation of memory, possibly involving this kind of autobiographical memory. The evidence points to the orbitofrontal PFC as being one of the neural substrates of narrative, along with theory of mind and autobiographical capacity. This may be less active in many cognitive tasks in people with an ASD than in neurotypicals (see Chapter 2), particularly in people with co-morbid ADHD.

It is theoretically likely that having a weak personal narrative would impair the ability to recall both other people's actions and one's own intentions, and increase vulnerability to subscribing to another person's narrative, especially if their authority or simply their confidence gives them hegemony. In experimental paradigms children with ASD are more susceptible to false memory, more often involving omitting facts rather than embellishing them.[12] In another study, the more impaired their theory of mind, the more suggestible they were.[13]

Autonomy

Choice and control are both necessary for autonomy. Choice presupposes an understanding of what is possible, as well as the consequences of what is possible. Adulthood increases the range of what is possible, partly because society grants powers to adults that it does not to children, and partly because of the development through adolescence of the executive functions and of the frontal lobes that subserve these functions. Control similarly relies on access to powers granted by others, as well as to internal resources to which the frontal lobes and their development make a key contribution.

Many people with ASD find decision-making difficult. One reason sometimes given by people with an ASD is similar to that given by people with OCD, that they are inhibited by the fear of making the wrong decision and regretting it afterwards. Another, and more fundamental reason given sometimes is that no emotion attaches to the decision, and so if there are no rational grounds for preferring one choice over another, a decision seems impossible. Most people making decisions do not have this difficulty, but without thinking ascribe a value and an emotional flavour to each possible choice, struggling only when there is a clash between the two, such as when a well-cut, body-hugging top which looks highly desirable is valued as looking disreputable when worn to work.

The inability to make decisions when rational criteria do not apply may contribute to perseverative decisions, with people with an ASD seeking to replace articles that they already have rather than buying something different or novel. It may also contribute to the inability of people with an ASD to say 'who they are': to have a consciousness of their own agency, as an autonomous person driven by particular and invariant values, with passions for and against practices, people, foods, activities, and so on.

People with ADHD may also lack autonomy, although for different reasons. They do not lack a knowledge of their own personal values, and have a normal emotional reaction to experience resulting in further experience acquiring a normal degree of emotional flavour. Moreover, their decision-making may be unusually rapid and decisive, or impulsive, with no demonstrable impairment under laboratory conditions. However, in real life conditions, the lability of decisions, and their ability to be driven by immediate rather than long-term concerns, leads to deficits in decision-making and therefore to the ability to demonstrate autonomy, for example in self-guided study at college.[14, 15] The deficit may be linked to a lack of synergy between cerebellum and frontal lobe.[16]

Identity

That we remain the same person from birth to death is so taken for granted that it seems apodeictically true, although philosophers have questioned it (e.g. Parfit).[17] However, what is it that remains the same? Not our body shapes, nor our cells, as they change. Our DNA is an obvious answer, although the invariance of a person's identity was taken for granted before the discovery of DNA. The invariance of identity is usually based on three foundations: a sense of personal continuity; personal identity, or those characteristics that are considered typical of a person by others, or by themselves; and social identity, that is those ascriptions that identify a person from his or her name, passport number, job title, and so on.

Personal identity has gradually taken on a different emphasis, less on secular aspects of psychological identity and more on what, at any moment, distinguishes one particular person from another. More often than not the distinctive characteristics of a person are a consequence of their particular circumstances, and if not that, their innate temperament or the events that they have experienced. These factors, though, are formative, and not directly expressed, and it is what is expressed that constitutes identity. So, personal identity has the further connotation of being a construction or performance, and has taken on the connotation of what makes each of us distinctly 'me' and, paradoxically, not identical to anyone else.

Identity, like a new logo or a new brand name, comes into its own only if other people recognize it. So, creating an identity has two sides: making something unique, and distinct from anyone else, and having this identity accepted as an identity by others. Identities may therefore be more or less deliberate, and more or less accepted by others. The former is often termed personal identity, and the latter social identity. Social identities shape the recognition of ill-health, coping and being able to call on social support in ill-health, and overcoming ill-health.[18]

One simple way to consider this kind of identity is as the story that we would tell about what makes us 'us', and the extent to which that story or narrative would be shared by others. The process of identity construction accelerates after childhood, and one reason for this is that conversations with friends increasingly turn on this kind of self-definition,[19] but it is based on conversations with mothers or other close carers. Neurotypical children can extract information about social emotions from discussions about facts, but people with ASD require narratives for theory of mind development.[20]

Identity and ASD

People with an ASD are disinclined to tell stories about people, preferring stories about facts or connections between facts. They are, anyway, less likely to have the close friendships in which narratives about identity occur. So they are doubly handicapped in the process of identity creation.

A created, inhabited identity is something that many people with an ASD aspire to: many of my patients have bitterly bewailed not having a 'personality' and others have said that they feel that they are constantly playing a role or 'masquerading'.[21]

Some people with an ASD identify with places rather than people. Others identify with physical objects, and these provide them with an identity. One person collected books on mountaineering, although he was scared of heights, and books on aviation, although he couldn't fly. Another identified with steam. He had made very good progress in a residential placement after leaving school, but the placement had changed hands, and he could not get on with the new staff. He gave up college, began to get aggressive with staff, and was eventually required to leave. It was the same for steam, he once explained to me. It had been a popular source of motive power, and steam engines had driven boats, cars, lorries, trains and buses. Then the internal combustion engine came along and steam engines were dumped. It was so unfair, he said. This man's books on steam were in a special shelf in his room. One day, redecoration was required and the steam books had to be removed. He was beside himself. 'They are my power,' he said.

Some people inhabit an identity that others give them – the class joker for example, or the troublemaker. Identities of this kind may result in the person with an ASD acting against their own interests Others identify with another person, quite often someone who is on the fringes of society. One 13-year-old girl with AS tried to borrow books on Jack the Ripper from the school library, saying that she thought he was great and wanted to read as much as possible about him and be like him if possible.

Religious organizations, cults and institutions of every kind offer 'off the peg' identities that a person with an ASD may adopt by accepting the associated ideology. Drama, too, may be attractive to people with an ASD as may role-play games, sports like worldwide wrestling, or films such as *Star Wars* or *Star Trek* that provide easily differentiable identities which do not have to be tested against real world criteria for a sustainable identity.

The internet now provides opportunity to create identities that, like *Star Wars* characters, do not have to be realistic or even grounded in a physical universe. Although some people have become immersed in the internet in this way, the intensity of the social interaction that follows is off-putting to many who prefer the social distance of texting or using discussion forums.

Social competence: self-promotion and persuasion

The narrative skill that goes into constructing a plausible identity also makes a contribution to social competence.

The self-presentational behaviour of 43 six- to twelve-year-old children with high-functioning autism spectrum disorders (HFASD) and normal intelligence and 43 matched comparisons was investigated. Children were prompted to describe themselves twice, first in a baseline condition and then in a condition where they were asked to convince others to select them for a desirable activity (self-promotion). Even after controlling for theory of mind skills, children with HFASD used fewer positive self-statements at baseline, and were less goal directed during self-promotion than comparison children. Children with HFASD alter their self-presentation when seeking personal gain, but do this less strategically and convincingly than typically developing children.[22]

Negotiating in this sense, like persuading, charming, soothing, inflaming and leading, requires good prefrontal lobe function that some people with an ASD lack.[23] Cooperators who are willing to enter into compromises are rewarded by others, unlike non-cooperators.[24] Aggression offers an alternative means of persuasion to negotiation, but undermines group cooperation, and since aggressors cannot control themselves, must be controlled by socially sanctioned aggression, or punishment. Knowing when punishment might follow, and being influenced by that knowledge, is another developmental challenge.[25] Unsanctioned aggression undermines cooperation, as does unbridled sexuality. Maintaining codes of sexual conduct, and punishing deviators, is as important to society as punishing other kinds of antisocial acts.

Sexual identity

Sexuality offers a different opportunity to create a strong identity. Some people with an ASD may define themselves primarily as sexual beings. This is difficult for heterosexual men, who have to overcome the obstacle of initiating a relationship with a woman, although some define themselves through their emotional investment in the world of the 'working girl'. Homosexual men may find an identity in the gay world. Women are, in my experience, less likely to use their sexuality as an identity.

For those men whose sexuality is mainly auto-erotic, fetishes may provide a kind of identity. Fetishes that I have come across are conserving bodily waste (in jars under the bed), dressing in nappies, identifying with animals, paedophilia, stealing women's underwear or asking women intimate medical details over the telephone. One person said that this kind of identity came from connecting with other people and was not the same as having a real, intrinsic identity.

Gender identity disorder is another expression of the search for identity that is affected by ASD symptoms.[26] Reported cases are rare,[27, 28] although frequency in my own practice (three to date, two born male, and one born female) suggests that this kind of gender confusion is either under-reported, or that the association with an ASD is undetected. Gender identity may revert to being consistent with chromosomal sexuality in adulthood.[29]

Identity and theory of mind

Mason *et al.* assessed narrative comprehension and the ability to make narrative inferences in three domains: narratives of intent, narratives of emotions, and narratives about physical causality.[30] The tasks were performed while the participants, people with an ASD and a neurotypical control group, were in a scanner. People with the ASD showed greater right hemisphere activation during the narrative comprehension tasks, suggesting that they had a degree of language impairment. The right temporo-parietal area, which Mason *et al.* consider to be specific to theory of mind (but see Chapter 6), was activated in the neurotypicals only during the narrative of intent task, but activated equally in all three narrative tasks in the participants with an ASD. The authors conclude that narrative use and theory of mind are closely linked, and that both are disrupted by a lack of connectivity in people with an ASD.[30]

Hypoconnectivity has already been considered as a possible explanation for the aetiology of ASD (see Chapter 10), but the findings of Mason *et al.* leave open whether the hypoconnectivity that they describe is neurological, for example due to white matter defects, or linguistic – words, or rather utterances, themselves provide connections in the mind.[30]

It seems likely that both are involved and that a lack of narrative practice leads to a reduction in theory of mind, just as the failure to develop a theory of mind leads to reduced narrative competence. It follows that lacking a sense of personal identity may be coupled with a lack of a clear grasp of other people's identity or, to put it the other way round, lacking a theory of mind is to lack a theory not only of other people's minds, but also of one's own.

Other people's identity

Some people with AS may be aware of not being able to retain an image of someone else, even someone very close to them, when they are not physically present. There are a number of characteristic actions of people with an ASD that suggest this too: repetitive questions, for example, are rarely intended to evoke an answer – often any realistic answer is dismissed as being too conditional – but may serve to create a kind of contact between questioner and questioned. Some people with an ASD will follow a carer around (mothers sometimes say, 'he hardly leaves me alone even in the toilet'). Although this is often interpreted as a kind of separation anxiety, it is a response not merely to physical separation but to the cessation of interaction – as if, once discourse with another person ceases, that person ceases to exist.

The difficulties that people with an ASD have in maintaining friendships may be linked to the lack of a story, theory of mind, or simulation (each of these terms has been used) about the friend. Friends know when to text each other. They have a sense of how long the delay is since the last contact, or of key happenings in the other person's life that merit contact. People with an ASD are rarely able to do this. In fact, any task that requires knowledge of another person's identity – choosing a card or present for them – is challenging, and many people with an ASD simply ignore them.

Memorialization

A coping strategy that people with an ASD may use to hold on to another person's identity is to memorialize it. Many people with Asperger syndrome have interests like Manfred Mann's music, or the top ten in the 1960s, which are the interests that their parents had when they were the same age as their child is now. These interests, now that we are in the twenty-first century, are eccentric. They do not develop out of the person with Asperger syndrome's identification with their peer group, or with their parents, whose own interests have often moved on quite considerably. They are a kind of unthinking mimicry, or memorialization, of their parents.

PRESENTING SYMPTOMS

Primary impairment or difference

Although the diagnosis of AS is most often made at the onset of adolescence,[31] it is rare for the primary impairment to present for the first time then as difficulties with making friends, difficulty in social interactions, taking language concretely, and a lack of empathy will have been evident from middle childhood, if not before (but see also Chapter 14). One exception to this may be the interpretation of others' nonverbal expressions. Neurotypical children may vary considerably in their interpersonal sensitivity and a lack of awareness of other people's feelings or unspoken thoughts may not be a cause for concern in middle childhood, becoming problematic only in adolescence (this presentation of 'atypical AS' is discussed specifically in Chapter 16). When the first intimations of impaired nonverbal communication occur post childhood, it is not because they have first developed then, but because they have been overlooked. This may happen if the nonverbal impairment is mild or if the person with an ASD has a restricted social circle who have become adapted to his or her communication style, and him or her to them. School difficulties may sometimes be attributed to another, co-occurring neurodevelopmental problem, such as dyslexia.

Although some symptoms of autistic disorder persist irrespective of social circumstances, a person with AS may make such a good adjustment to a particular life style and group of acquaintances or family members, that their communication difficulties and tendency towards repetitiveness falls below the threshold of eccentricity or disability. It may only be when there is a change in circumstances requiring a greater degree of social adaptation that the person seems to be disabled by an autistic syndrome. It may be anxiety that mediates between the change and the apparent increase in symptoms. Changes may occur at any time in a person's life, for example as a result of bereavement or of the birth of children, but changes also occur at common social transitions, that from childhood to adolescence and from there to adulthood is particularly taxing for many.

Extreme reactions: to change or for no apparent reason

Changes in the school curriculum, the pressure of examinations, or the shock of leaving school may occasionally lead to an increase of repetitive activity to a paralysing degree, or to behavioural regression, which may include the re-emergence of incontinence, hoarding behaviour, aggressive outbursts, and a loss of skills such as self-care, timekeeping or language. Some adolescents may show the reversal of the sleep–waking cycle that is often found in adolescent depression and may describe themselves as feeling low or hopeless. Others may sleep more throughout the day and night. Indiscriminate binge-eating may occur, and hypersexuality. The clinical picture can vary from obvious depression to something more like precocious dementia. There may be considerable similarities with Klein-Levin syndrome,[32] which has been reported in young men.[33] In my clinical experience, extreme constipation may also occur in people with AS, with hypersomnia and hyperphagia, too.

Klein-Levin syndrome may be episodic but other deteriorations in adolescence may be progressive or at least non-remitting. In two cases known to me, the cause of the deterioration was probable abuse in a care home, but a cause may not always be found: schizophrenia and an organic disorder are among the differential diagnoses (see differential diagnosis later).

Secondary disability or idiosyncrasy

Some of the challenges, and benefits, of adolescence have already been considered. Enduring friendship groups coalesce in early adolescence. Young people decide who they like, and who they dislike.[34] In one study, young people with AS in mainstream school were more likely to like others, and more likely to perceive themselves as not being liked than neurotypicals. Liking increases reward,[35] and counteracts depression.

People with an ASD either are not part of friendship groups or become members of a group whose membership criterion is that the members were not able to, or did not want to, join any other group. Loneliness intensifies for many young people with an ASD and may be its presenting characteristic. At the same time people with an ASD may not be satisfied with just blaming this on others and may have to take on the usually discomforting truth that they are different. Conflicts are more likely to develop in friendship groups than in the looser aggregates of earlier childhood, and conflict resolution skills are important in maintaining friendships. Young people often learn these conflict management skills by dealing with these early conflicts and this is another area that people with an ASD may miss out on.

People with an ASD are less likely to be chosen by, or to successfully choose, a sexual partner. Adolescents typically begin to imagine a future for themselves and having a partner often forms part of this. Not being able to find one may become an obstacle to achieving this desirable future and this causes distress, not least because adolescents measure themselves against working towards these goals.[36]

Full participation in activities outside the school and the home often relies on friends. So the pattern of social exclusion that is created in school may be extended into the community in the absence of friends to act as allies in community exploration.

Tertiary handicap or altered life style

The effects of bullying: 'low self-esteem' or shame proneness

Thomas Scheff has suggested that self-esteem is not just threatened by shame, it is no more and no less than shame proneness.[37] Bullying and marginalization are potent causes of shame proneness, to which there may be a variety of responses by the person with an ASD,[38] including behavioural inhibition and avoidance of shame, explosive response to any hint of shaming or humiliation, or by becoming a bully oneself.[39]

Behavioural inhibition increases the risk of anxiety and depression. Sensitive rejection of any hint of humiliation may lead to adolescents rejecting any kind of discipline or even advice, and may sometimes result in the complete breakdown of relations with the disciplining parent, usually the father (see also the discussion of schizoid 'personality disorder' in Chapter 16).

Stigma

People with AS compare themselves unfavourably with other pupils in mainstream schools, although this may not be caused by explicit bullying, it is a reflection of their inability to fit in. Twenty pupils from four secondary schools in the UK were interviewed in one study, and many referred to themselves dismissively as having a 'bad brain' or being 'retarded'.[40]

The effects of parenting

Adolescence is often a time of conflict with parents. Parents' conflict coping styles resurface in conflicts with their adolescent children and how these conflicts are dealt with may increase the risk of aggression or misconduct ('externalizing behaviour'), with fathers making demands from which the child withdraws and mothers getting into mutual recriminations being particularly likely to increase externalizing behaviour.[41]

People with an ASD are much less likely than neurotypicals to be able to deal with conflict by negotiation or compromise, and therefore more likely to respond with withdrawal or hostility. Maternal hostility and paternal demand are therefore particularly unhelpful conflict strategies on the part of parents of children with an ASD. Maternal warmth and praise are, on the other hand, more likely to lead to a reduction of externalizing behaviour and of mood disorder ('internalizing behaviour'), an increase in social reciprocity, and a reduction in repetitive behaviour.[42] However, it should be noted that how parents react depends a lot on their children's previous behaviour, with previous challenges to the parent by the child biasing mothers towards hostility.[43]

DIAGNOSIS

Many of the key diagnostic characteristics of ASD are in areas that adolescents are self-conscious about. 'Do you have good friends?', 'Are you ever bullied?', 'Do you get on well with other people?', 'Are you having any problems with your studies?' are all questions that may have a strong social desirability bias. They may therefore be answered in the negative, and information from a carer may be essential. Adolescents may also have learnt to overcome, or at least minimize, some of their communication deficits. Language difficulties may be concealed by stock answers like 'If you say so.' Adolescents may have taught themselves to look at others, or not to grimace. An opportunity should therefore be created for unobtrusive observation when the adolescent with possible ASD is not trying to create an impression. Seeing a family together may provide this opportunity.

If a diagnosis has not been made in childhood, it may be because the nonverbal impairment is subtle, and so more protracted observation may be required. This may mean seeing a person again, at a later appointment.

DIFFERENTIAL DIAGNOSIS

There is greater divergence between the repetitive and the communicative symptoms of ASD after childhood. The risk of psychosis and of mood disorder also increases, as does the misuse of alcohol and drugs. All of these may be included in the differential diagnosis, and among the associated conditions that may have a pathoplastic effect.

Differential diagnosis of communicative disorder

Schizophrenia

The most difficult differential diagnosis is with schizophrenia, especially in those rare cases where positive psychotic symptoms are not reported. Kolvin suggested that an age of onset after the age of five was indicative of schizophrenia,[44] but this may be difficult to apply to adolescents with more subtle ASD in whom a sufficiently detailed early childhood history may not be available. The negative symptoms that may precede the onset of overt schizophrenia may also be difficult to distinguish from an ASD. In one record linkage study, 15-year-olds completed a prodromal screening scale and records of first episodes of psychosis were followed up some years later; 94 per cent of those who had developed schizophrenia and had been previously included in the population survey had answered positively to five negative syndrome items in the survey, indicating that the negative symptoms were part of a schizophrenia prodrome.[45]

High risk of schizophrenia may be associated with delayed milestones,[46] reduced ability to interpret voice prosody and facial expression.[47] Prodromal symptoms of schizophrenia overlap with those of 'schizotypal personality disorder' (see Chapter 16) and symptoms of this are moderately correlated with scores on screening questionnaires for ASD, such as the autism spectrum questionnaire.[48] Finally, the development of positive psychotic symptoms may not always augur schizophrenia as brief psychotic disorders are more common in people with an ASD than in the general population (see associated conditions, below).

A careful history is often the best method of making a diagnosis since an onset of the autistic syndrome before the age of four is a clear indication of ASD, and a change in social functioning after the age of 13 points to schizophrenia. However, people with AS may not have overt symptoms until the age of seven, and at that age children at risk for developing schizophrenia may be avoiding social contact because of their developing anxiety and timidity. Social decline from the age of 11 may also be due to AS and its provocation by the increased demands of secondary school.

Although reduced nonverbal expressiveness is one of the negative signs of schizophrenia, the idiosyncratic features of nonverbal communication in ASD, which seem to be anomalous attempts at social engagement such as staring, close approach, touching, grimacing, loud speech, and an unusual intonation patter, are not found early on in schizophrenia,[49] although such symptoms may be observable in people with schizophrenia who have lived for long periods in institutional settings.

It is sometimes not possible to make a definitive diagnosis; and in these circumstances regular follow-up is advisable so that early treatment of any positive psychotic symptoms that may develop can be treated early.

Speech and language impairment

Mild language impairment may be overlooked, especially as a person with mild language impairment, such as an empathy impairment, may conceal it to avoid being singled out, criticized or shamed. Suggestive symptoms are that complex sentences, especially those involving grammatical tropes such as conditionals that require long phrases to be held in memory, are not understood. Sequences of instructions may also be a problem, and the person with a mild language impairment may remember only the first or the last instruction.

As is so often the case with subtle neuropsychological impairments, the misunderstandings or failed instructions that result are likely to be attributed to moral failings, to lack of attentiveness or to lack of interest or commitment, rather than to cognitive factors. Mild language impairment may therefore have a disproportionately disabling effect because of the hostility with which other people respond to what they consider to be bad behaviour in the disabled person.

Adolescents or adults who have an unsuspected speech or language impairment may also be misdiagnosed as having an ASD. Their speech and language impairment may have led to the same social rejection and consequent emotional difficulties as ASD and their presentation may therefore resemble ASD. General psychiatrists are also much less likely to recognize speech and language disorders than child psychiatrists or psychologists, and are less aware of their pervasive effects. Adults with severe hearing impairment who have little spoken language may provide a related challenge.

Although resistance to change, special interests and the presence of routines are all suggestive of an ASD, these may also occur in some socially isolated young people with high anxiety, so the most reliable diagnostic criterion is whether or not impaired nonverbal expression is present.

Case example

A young adult had been in care since the age of eight years, having had a previously abusive upbringing. He was of mixed race and had been bullied about this. He had been aggressive at school and to foster parents, and had also threatened to harm himself, and this had led to changes of school and of foster placement. He was effectively excluded from school from the age of 14. He had been diagnosed as having severe learning difficulties and autistic disorder. On examination he was withdrawn at first, but gradually became more emotionally expressive, and this was mirrored in his eyes and his face. A simple test of motor coordination demonstrated that he was better coordinated than the average. He was living alone, and his daily living skills were sufficient for this with minimal support. His speech was, however, dysfluent throughout the interview, he had word-finding difficulties, and he could not understand complex sentences. Psychometry showed him to have a verbal IQ of 78, a performance IQ of 88, and a reading accuracy of a child half his age. Referral to a speech and language therapist confirmed that he had a receptive language disorder.

Speech and language disorders and ASD occur together more than might be expected by chance. Often therefore the differential diagnosis is not so much distinguishing between two aetiological distinct categories but determining which of them are functionally significant. This has prognostic value. Whitehouse *et al.* followed children diagnosed as having specific language impairment, pragmatic language impairment and ASD into adulthood.[50] All of the affected adults had problems in social relationships, but these were greatest in the pragmatically impaired and in the ASD group. The ASD group had lower levels of independence and greater difficulty in finding work than the other two groups. The specific language impaired and the ASD group went less far in education and were less likely to be in a profession than the pragmatically impaired group, and the specific language impaired group were employed in jobs requiring less use of language and literacy.[50]

Anxiety disorders

Anxiety disorders leading to phobic avoidance of going out may, in combination with fearful parenting, become chronic with the socially isolated adolescent becoming increasingly unskilled socially, or unempathic towards family members. Parents may be fearful because they have another child with a disabling disorder, or because there is conflict between them with one parent being forced into a more and more protective stance and the other into withdrawal from childcare. Sometimes one of the parents may themselves have an ASD, but the affected young person will have had a normal social development earlier in life and has a normal range of nonverbal expressiveness on examination, making this diagnosis inapplicable to them.

The young person may regress, may become indifferent to the welfare of other family members, or behave in an eccentric fashion, all increasing the fears of at least one parent that there is a serious illness at work. Loss of energy may complicate the situation, as myalgic encephalitis may be diagnosed. The family doctor may be drawn in, and may share the family's criticism of services, only to be dismissed by the family as not doing enough.

Although the core of this problem is often social phobia, and can have its origins in some earlier medical history that has set the young person apart from his or her peers, the avoidance may be inconsistent. One young person said, for example, that what he feared was the loss of control that he felt outside the house.

There may be considerable pressure to make a diagnosis of an ASD, parents sometimes arguing that all of the other doctors are 'useless, and never know what's wrong, or at least never tell us'. But a spurious diagnosis is not the answer. Often the problem requires simultaneous work with the parents and with the young person, sometimes together but usually separately. This may be difficult to set up because these families are often 'enmeshed'.

Distinction from neurodegenerative disorders

Disintegrative psychosis may rarely occur in late childhood, when the picture resembles a frontal lobe dementia and would, until the 2000s, have been diagnosed as schizophrenia simplex. I have seen approximately one person like this in every hundred that I have been asked to assess for an ASD, and so the condition may be less rare than is assumed. Detailed investigation, including MRI, is usually negative.

Case example

Hubert had developed normally until the age of 10. He went to his local primary school, and enjoyed football. He was very attached to the family dog, and when the dog died, Hubert stopped talking. This was attributed to selective mutism at first, but then Hubert became incoordinated, and began soiling. Hubert seemed less able to understand what was said to him, he started to pinch people, and would often run off, not coming back for several hours. He was admitted to hospital with a presumed diagnosis of schizophrenia, and remained in hospital for the next 15 years. Positive psychotic symptoms were never observed. Hubert's conditions stabilized. He continued to live in his own world, but he had a simple understanding of what others said to him, and had his favourites and his enemies among the ward population. He continued to be mute, but his face was expressive. He would convey his attention by his gaze, and he could use gestures to communicate feeling. After a few years in hospital, Hubert regained his continence, although he would occasionally urinate in public. He would sometimes run small errands for the nursing staff so long as he was given the exact money and he was asked to fetch only one item. Neurological examination by successive psychiatric registrars was unremarkable, as were standard laboratory investigations. CT scanning was introduced towards the end of Hubert's stay in hospital but it was not possible to obtain informed consent from him and no scan was performed.

Differential diagnosis of repetitive behaviour

The repetitive symptoms of ASD can also be found in adolescents with ADHD or with anxiety disorder (both of them are discussed below). What differentiates these conditions from ASD are the impairments in communication and socialization.[51]

Differential diagnosis of social impairment
Schizoidia and alexithymia

The distinction between the suppression of fellow feeling, and a failure of emotional contagion, can best be made in an extended case example, based on several clients, with some identifying information changed:

Thank you very much for asking me to see Mr X who suffers, as you say, from recurrent depression for which he is receiving CBT and an SSRI antidepressant. He has recently wondered whether he has Asperger Syndrome, and that is why he was referred to this service. Mr X has written me several long and helpful letters describing his experience and although he was unable to obtain a developmental history from his elderly parents, he has also described his own development, including his earliest memories in detail and since the appointment, and at my request, his wife has kindly completed the developmental questionnaire based on his current behaviour.

I do not think Mr X has Asperger Syndrome or indeed any neurodevelopmental disorder, but he does have an emotional detachment from other people, indeed an abhorrence of emotional entanglement with other people, coupled with an intense interest in and concern about his own inner life, that is often described as 'schizoid'. Although there may be a temperamental, and therefore biological, contribution to this, I think that the problem is principally emotional, arising from a deeply engrained fear of, and sensitivity to, humiliation by other people that leads to a preference for social isolation over social involvement. Mr X describes what he feels in one of his letters as follows:

> Ultimately I don't see any point in 'needing' the affirmation of others. What if they go away? What if someone who has provided this 'support' starts to criticise instead? Any reliance on external factors is vulnerable to implosion due to factors beyond your control and I see no sense in entrusting your wellbeing to those who may well damage or abuse it. Internal self-sufficiency is logically the only truly reliable method of maintaining the integrity of yourself.

Mr X also refers to the fear of abandonment that some theorists consider to be related to this kind of emotional detachment, too.

Regrettably in this area there are no clear cut boundaries or categories and Mr X does have some symptoms that suggest he has an unusual degree of pleasure in repetitive activities, sometimes called obsessionality. He spends the evening alone, often on his computer, but has had the intermittent although passionate interest in collecting cards relating to the game Magic: The Gathering. He began this in 1991 and estimates he has collected over thirty thousand cards since then. He also ruminates about incidents in the past when he has felt humiliated and imagines corrective memories in which he takes action that avoids the humiliation or defeat. He gets some relief from stereotypies and describes in one letter, when he is at a party trying to escape into a garden building where he can be on his own, but while there he often engages in stereotypical behaviour such as picking stones out of pebble dash walls or breaking twigs repetitively.

Although one can speculate that these ritualistic behaviours have the function of relieving distress, Mr X says that he does not feel distress. Indeed, Mr X is often cut off from spontaneous emotions. For example, he said that if he were to hear his daughter cry in the next room he would not feel an immediate emotional demand to go to her side, but would think over whether or not he needed to go to her. In people with Asperger Syndrome, this disconnect may be due to the absence or dysfunction of a neural circuit or a neural network but the cutting off from emotion in people who are schizoid is probably attributable to a higher level process of emotional suppression, leading to a lack of awareness of the emotion but not a lack of emotion.

Mr X described having tactile aversions as a child which affected the clothes he was able to wear without feeling chaffed by them and always felt at a distance from other people, even as a toddler. These sensitivities are also reported by people with an ASD but are not specific to ASD. He may also have had some degree of developmental dyspraxia that might have increased his marginalisation.

People who are schizoid may apparently lack an emotional response to other people, possibly as a result of the suppression of the normal, involuntary sympathetic emotional response by force of habit but over the years. This may become so successful that the emotion itself disappears from awareness. Empathy suppression may occur in non-schizoid people too. For example, it has been noted often that men in war may be unfeeling about their own or other's wounds, even though they may be emotionally overwhelmed by these experiences if they had occurred in civilian life. The cost of suppressing empathy is that it may lead to an emptying out of most feelings, including feelings of happiness or pleasure and this can pave the way for depression. I think this is likely to be the reason for Mr X's tendency to depression over the years.

People with schizoid personality do not lack a cognitive understanding of other people's problems and Mr X described often dealing with another person's distress by providing a solution. Solution focused reactions to distress are more often used by men with women more often dealing with problems by emotional focused methods. Although he lacks emotional expressiveness when I met him, I did not think Mr X was impaired in his emotional expression, as people with Asperger Syndrome are, but that he habitually avoided pro-social feelings in social interactions. This would not preclude him getting angry with other people but would prevent him from expressing emotions that may lead to more emotional entanglement. That Mr X is well able to manage the nuts and bolts of social interaction is apparent from his ability to 'woo' people. His wife describes feeling almost betrayed by the intensity of his focus on her during their courtship and his apparent neglect of her since. Mr X describes this as follows. He is quoting from two psychoanalysts, Guntrip and Horney, and says:

> This again echoes my experience of enjoying frequent sexual activity in the early stages of a (non-committed) relationship with a relatively distant partner, which suddenly crashes to negligible activity; certainly with both wives this has roughly coincided with the agreement to marry; and I can identify with the concept of sex being 'too intimate for a permanent relationship'.

Mr X goes on to say:

> We [his wife and himself] have also discussed the possibility of me attending swingers' clubs or websites as this appeals to me on the basis of its unconventional nature, less emotional involvement and the prospect of less predictable, more adventurous sexual activity.

Although it is often speculated that schizoid personality disorder is entirely a consequence of parenting experience, there may be biological or constitutional factors, too. Mr X remembers that he may have had some degree of jaundice after birth, although this is unlikely to have been at a level known to be associated with altered brain development and he describes the male members of his family having similar problems to himself, both his father and at least one of his brothers. His father, now aged 88, has never been diagnosed with depression but had symptoms similar to those of Mr X and is described by Mr X as having problems in mixing and rarely speaking outside the family. Mr X's memory of his father is that he would spend long periods in the shed and so not interacting with his children. Mr X has had no contact with his brother Steven, now aged 55, for the last ten years but does keep in contact with Andrew, now aged 50, who is divorced, works as a teacher and has had CBT for depression himself.

So far as I know, there is little definite evidence that psychotherapy is successful in treating schizoid personality disorder, but in my clinical experience it is the only treatment that is likely to be effective than approaches such as existential therapy or psychoanalytic psychotherapy. The latter are available in Leeds and I would recommend, if Mr X were willing and able to attend, a referral to the NHS Psychotherapy Department in Leeds, or if Mr X can afford that, to a private psychotherapist.

I have not arranged to see Mr X again but would be happy to do so if funding were available and he or his wife wish me to see him, either alone or with his wife.

ASSOCIATED PROBLEMS
Psychiatric disorders
Surveys of psychiatric disorder co-morbid with ASD are at an early stage. Samples are often convenience, clinic-based ones, with variable inclusion criteria, variable lengths of follow-up and variable types of ascertainment. The community-based survey by Seedat et al. is an exception.[52] They report on a community-based sample of 112 ten- to fourteen-year-old children with ASD assessed using a standardized parent report questionnaire for three-month prevalence of psychiatric disorder.[52] They found that 70 per cent of the children had at least one more additional disorder, and 41 per cent had two or more (84% if one diagnosis was ADHD) (see Table 15.1). Anxiety and mood disorders were even higher in another smaller study.[53]

Hutton et al. conducted a follow-up study to at least the age of 21 years of 135 individuals with an autism spectrum disorder diagnosed in childhood and an IQ of over 30.[54] The study is distinctive in its large size, low attrition rate and use of systematic interviews to obtain clinical information. Questionnaires completed by caregivers asked about the development of new psychiatric disorders. For the 39 individuals with a possible new disorder, a detailed psychiatric assessment was undertaken through parental interview. Of all participants, 16 per cent developed a definite new psychiatric disorder. A further 6 per cent developed a possible new disorder. Five individuals developed an obsessive compulsive disorder and/or catatonia; eight developed an affective disorder with marked obsessional features; three developed complex affective disorders; four developed more straightforward affective disorders; one was a bipolar disorder; and one developed an acute anxiety state complicated by alcohol excess. There was no case of schizophrenia.[55] I have previously reported information obtained about psychiatric history from a personal series of people referred to an assessment clinic,[56] and, in a second series, reported information from a community sample of family and participant reports about previous psychiatric diagnoses.[57] The former sample is biased towards the inclusion of more able individuals, and the second explicitly excluded children younger than 13, and anyone with intellectual disability. Hofvander et al. also report on a clinic sample biased towards Asperger syndrome.[58] The results of each of the foregoing studies is summarized in Table 15.2.

Table 15.1 Three month prevalence per 100 children aged 10–14 of selected psychiatric disorders

Disorder	Percentage affected (95% confidence interval)
Social anxiety	29.2 (13.2% to 45.1%)
ADHD	28.2 (13.3% to 43%)
Oppositional defiant disorder	28.1 (13.9% to 42.2%)
Enuresis	9.0
Tic disorder	3.9
Encopresis	11.0
Tourette Syndrome	6.6
Trichotillomania	4.8

Source: Seedat, Scott, *et al.*, 2009.

Table 15.2 Percentage of late adolescents and adults with an ASD who have developed a named psychiatric disorder

Disorder	Hutton *et al.* N=135	Tantam clinic sample N=490	Balfe *et al.* N=78	Hofvander *et al.* N=122	Weighted mean (%)
ADHD				43	43.0
Anxiety	16	42	47	50	39.4
Panic disorder			30		28.4
Depression		25	30		17.7
Obsessive compulsive disorder	4	14			9.0
Substance misuse		4		16	4.7
Somatoform disorder			41	5	4.6
Bipolar disorder	1	3.2		8	3.3
Brief psychosis		3.4		2	2.3
Schizophrenia		3		3	2.2
Eating disorder				5	0.7
Catatonia		1			0.6
Delusional disorder				1	0.2

The comparison of these four series shows some similarities, particularly between the two clinical series of my own (Balfe *et al.*), and Hofvander *et al.* Both of us found a high and comparable prevalence of anxiety, and this high prevalence was also found in the community sample. The community sample reported a high incidence of body dysmorphic disorder, although this may have been below clinical significance. There are also some distinctive features: a high incidence of eating disorders in the Swedish and French series,[58] a high incidence of body dysmorphic disorder in the community sample, although many of these cases may have been subclinical. There was a high incidence of OCD in the Hutton *et al.* sample, but never as the primary co-morbid disorder. Hutton *et al.* also reported that many of their cases of affective disorder were 'complex affective disorders'.[54]

The diagnosis of psychiatric disorders complicating ASD is rarely difficult once it is given conscious consideration, but it may easily go unlooked for and therefore unrecognized. Sometimes people with an ASD may describe their inner experience so concretely that it can sound psychotic even when not (see Chapter 10). Often the account of symptoms is unvarnished because people with an ASD do not do the 'face work' that neurotypicals do to explain away or justify abnormal experience,[59] although many people with ASD may simply deny it. Finally, the emotional content usually associated with abnormal experience may be lacking as it is in people with long-term psychosomatic disorders or substance abuse, who are sometimes said to have 'alexithymia'. People with ASD may also score high on scales of 'alexithymia' or the ability to put words to feelings,[60] a trait also reported in some of their parents.[61]

There are considerable differences between the series of young teenagers (Table 15.1) and the four series of older teenagers (Table 15.2), indicating the switch from child to adult nosologies during adolescence. This may be an artefact in part. It is possible, for example, that unacceptable or antisocial behaviour is attributed to oppositional defiant or conduct disorder in childhood and reattributed to antisocial personality disorder in adulthood.

The co-morbidity of ADHD and ASD is discussed more fully in Chapter 16.

Developmental staging of psychiatric disorder

Why different psychiatric disorders have different ages of onset has not been systematically studied. Biological factors play a part. The development of what are now termed very late onset psychoses – the paranoid states of middle age – is linked to age-related hearing deterioration and, in some cases, to cognitive deterioration. My clinical impression is that changes in psychosocial identity, and therefore changes in the concerns that are most salient to an individual, also play a part. Table 15.3 shows the predominant disorders at different ages in my clinic. The table summarizes tendencies only, and there are many exceptions. Alcohol misuse may begin in the early teens, especially in those young people who also have ADHD, and social phobia may develop after the teenage years, although this is rare and usually follows some additional stigmatizing event, for example one of my patients, who set fire to himself because he had been rejected in love, suffered facial scarring as a result.

Table 15.3 Disorder by characteristic age of onset in a clinic population

Age range in years	Disorder
11–13	Surge of anxiety-related problems including OCD, body dysmorphic disorder, panic disorder
14–16	Secondary depression, social phobia
>16	Progressive social withdrawal sometimes attributed to schizophrenia
>17	Bipolar disorder Brief 'cycloid' psychoses Non-psychotic hallucinoses
>18	Catatonia
>25	Paranoid states
>35	Social withdrawal, isolation, relationship disrepair, 'anomie', alcohol misuse

Not fitting in

Adolescence is the age when fitting in is particularly important. Fitting in, or rather not fitting in, is one of the key themes of life for people with ASD.[62] A key existential question for many of those adolescents with ASD who have the capacity to reflect on themselves is why they cannot fit in. If they think that it is other people's fault, this can lead to 'externalizing' symptoms. If they conclude that it is their own, this can lead to 'internalizing' ones. It is not clear what determines these locus of control judgements, although having an ADHD increases the likelihood of having an external locus of control. This is particularly discussed in Chapter 16. Having an avoidant, timid or inhibited temperament increases internal locus of control.

Psychosis

Brief psychosis

Schizophrenia is probably no more common in ASD than in the general population, but there is an increased risk of schizopheniform psychoses, whose florid 'positive' symptoms of psychosis may include those symptoms in the first rank for a diagnosis of schizophrenia. Unlike most cases of schizophrenia, these symptoms may remit completely and over a short period with medication, and do not relapse once the medication has been withdrawn following remission. Brief psychoses, probably of a comparable kind, have been described under a variety of terms and are currently much more commonly reported in the developing world.[63] They are classified in ICD-10 as 'acute, transient psychoses' but this is a heterogeneous grouping.[64] The psychoses associated with ASD are often associated with intense anxiety and therefore most approximate the cycloid psychoses described by Kleist,[65] which may form a subset of the 'acute, transient psychoses'.[66] Atypical brief psychoses are also associated with Prader-Willi syndrome.[67]

Catatonia

Catatonia is another psychosis that, like brief psychosis, does not fit easily into Kraepelin's dichotomy of schizophrenia and affective psychosis. The risk of developing catatonia and of brief psychosis may be increased following brain inflammation such as an encephalitis. Brief psychosis has been linked to cerebral malaria and to temporal lobe epilepsy,[68] and catatonia has been linked to encephalitis lethargica. Catatonia, Tourette syndrome,[69] and autism have some symptoms in common, particularly perseverative and echo phenomena, and tics.[70, 71] There may be an increased risk of developing catatonia in ASD,[72, 73, 74, 75, 76] and in ADHD.[77]

Catatonia may be complicated by a dysautonomia, and this 'lethal catatonia' may overlap in symptoms with the malignant hyperpyrexia of the hyperserotinergic syndrome and the neuroleptic malignant syndrome. It can be fatal unless treated.[78]

Catatonia in ASD may be particularly associated with language impairment[79] and has to be differentiated from depression or mania, which may also lead to stupor. Immobility and slowness are probably more common in the catatonia associated with ASD than that associated with ADHD and Tourette. The treatment of catatonia has been revolutionized by the use of benzodiazepines as the first-line treatment, although antipsychotics may also be used; a combination of olanzepine and amantadine was successful in one case where lorazepam was not.[80] ECT may still be recommended by some psychiatrists.[70]

Effective treatment of catatonia in ASD usually requires an activity programme in addition to physical treatment.

Anxiety

The world is often described as uncertain, unpredictable or troubling by many people with an ASD. Adolescents with ASD often become distrustful of other people during adolescence, too, so being with other people often has an undercurrent of threat. This might be enough to explain the strong association between ASD and anxiety but, in fact, there are many more demonstrated or proven reasons for the association, which are discussed in Chapter 8.

Specific anxiety disorders

Body dysmorphic disorder

Body dysmorphic disorder often has its onset in early adolescence, at the time that self-consciousness emerges in an adult form, and is accordingly sensitive and easily derailed. Body dysmorphic disorder, or a distressing preoccupation with the size or shape of a particular bodily part, may make sense of the social rejection that a young person with ASD may experience. It involves a fixed idea, sometimes almost of delusional intensity, to which people with an ASD may be especially vulnerable given their reliance on thinking as a means of coping. It may be triggered by comparisons with others: one person with AS for example became determined to have a rhinoplasty because his nose looked unattractive after watching *Grease*, a film about teenage mating rituals. Body dysmorphic disorder often remits spontaneously.

Generalized anxiety disorder

Generalized anxiety disorder may be mistakenly attributed to mood swings, and often remains unrecognized.

Panic disorder

Panic disorder is probably not increased in people with ASD. A trigger in adolescence may be seeing someone who is dead or dying, which leads to a preoccupation with the possibility of dying oneself and a hypochrondriacal sensitivity to bodily functioning linked to the perception that these might be the presentiments of imminent death. A hereditary disposition to panic disorder is a marker for a response to SSRIs.

Obsessive compulsive disorder

Obsessive compulsive disorder was once thought to occur more commonly in people who had an 'anankastic' personality, now called obsessive compulsive personality. But the latter does not seem to be either a homogeneous or a stable condition. There is stronger evidence for an endophenotype, marked by a reduction of grey matter volume in the orbitofrontal cortex, and consequent dysfunction of frontostriatal networks. This leads to reduced inhibition of motor behaviour, and greater perseveration. However, in some circumstances, there may be a failure to inhibit impulsive actions, too.[81] The endophenotype of OCD surprisingly overlaps with that of ADHD, and clinic samples of people with OCD have higher than average scores of ASD and ADHD screening tests.[82] The endophenotype may also overlap with that of Tourette syndrome, and in another clinic study, ASD traits were raised in young people with OCD, with ADHD, and with Tourette syndrome (especially in girls).[83]

There may be some overlap between this endophenotype and the endophenotype of rigidity in ASD that is only weakly correlated with the social and communicative impairments of the condition.[84] There is some evidence that some people with familial OCD have ASD, or at least social impairments that are suggestive of ASD.[85] The routines of people with an ASD may be as compulsive as routines in people with uncomplicated OCD, but are not resisted although they may be perceived as ego alien.[86] Routines in children with OCD may not be resisted either, and there may be greater difficulty in differentiating them from routines on this basis, although routines in children with OCD are more likely to be motivated by undoing some perceived threat and therefore involve decontamination, guarding against harming others, or checking, compared to children with ASD; routines in children with ASD are more likely to be motivated by collecting and repetition compared to children with OCD.[87]

Life events, particularly traumatic ones, increase the risk of developing OCD,[88] but only a minority of episodes of OCD are associated with a life event, possibly because change in everyday habits is a more important precipitant that may not show up as an event.

Obsessive compulsive disorder has a lifetime prevalence of 2–3 per cent in the general population, and tends to run in families, with a 5–7 times greater risk in the first degree relatives of probands compare to the relatives of controls.[89]

The relation between the endophenotype and obsessive compulsive personality still needs clarification, but is likely to include a tendency to repetition and repetitive activities, made worse by anxiety. How this leads to the counting and touching rituals and the tendency to prefer routine to varied activity, associated with both OCD and ASD, is not clear. Nor is the part that is played by events in precipitating overt OCD, although in one study of MZ twins discordant for OCD, the affected MZ twin had experienced more life events, particularly sexual abuse, than the unaffected one and also had lower birth weight, worse school performance, and a greater tendency to anxiety and depression.[90]

Overt OCD, once it develops, seems to be an interfering, burdensome condition, unlike the tendency to check, to be orderly, or to be clean and tidy that may have preceded it, all of which traits may be considered desirable in both ASD and OCD. Interference, 'ego alien' content, and compulsiveness are the main differentiata of routines and rituals in people with ASD who have not developed additional OCD, and those who have.

OCD symptoms have been subdivided into reactive (checking and fears of contamination leading to washing) and autogenous (fears of doing harm).[91] Obsessions or compulsive thoughts may fall into either group. There is little evidence that these subtypes are different in people with both ASD and OCD, although folie de doute – an intolerance and overpreoccupation with small but ineradicable risks – is particularly common in this mixed group.[83]

Although the phenomenon of OCD in people with and without ASD has not been formally investigated, there are some clinical clues that suggests a difference. For example, obsessions to ward off harm are often intended to ward off the harm of other people rather than the person with ASD themselves. For example, one man with ASD developed obsessions after his father died, and he became convinced that his father had become the devil. He thought that as 666 was the devil's number, he could protect his mother from going to hell like his father by avoiding ever using the number '6'. So he would count 1, 2, 3, 4, 5, 5+1, 7...

Hoarding, obsessions and ruminations

Hoarding is often considered to be a subtype of OCD, but is less clearly associated with anxiety and responds less well to treatments for anxiety such as CBT or SSRIs than OCD. Pure obsessions and ruminations also respond less well to behavioural or pharmacological treatment, and may be considered to be a kind of hoarding of thoughts that a person cannot bring themselves to 'throw away'. About 4 per cent in a community sample were reported to be hoarders, and hoarding was found to occur at a younger age than OCD symptoms, to be more likely to be associated with alcohol dependence, physical abuse as a young person and parental psychopathology, as well as having experience of previous break-ins.[92] A minority of hoarders keep valueless objects and find the act of selecting what may be thrown away to be anxiety-provoking. Sometimes there is the fear that something thrown away 'may have come in useful', but sometimes the fear seems to be without content. Rarely people who hoard may be unable to judge value, and may throw away items of high monetary value, but retain junk. This subgroup is more likely to show repetitive or perseverative behaviour, and throwing away may be possible only after a ritual has been performed.[93] Lesions around the anterior cingulate and orbitofrontal cortex are associated with an increased risk of hoarding.[94] It has sometimes been suggested that this is because a person with such a lesion may not be able to separate the valuable from the value-less. However, it may also reflect abnormally reduced disgust at the accumulation of trash that is such a feature of hoarding.

There are a growing number of agencies dedicated to working with people who hoard to 'declutter' their chosen environment, supporting them while they throw away redundant belongings.

Ruminations are recurrent thoughts that may become insistent and troublesome. They are often emotionally charged. They include worries, in which the emotional tinge is anxiety and the time orientation is to the future, and thoughts that make one 'cringe' that are tinctured with embarrassment or shame so intense that they may be described as flashbacks, which may become recurrent in people who are sensitive to social evaluation, for example because of social phobia.[95] Cringing thoughts are about the past, and may include an element of wishing the past to be different. Obsessional ruminations about the past often involve a mental attempt to change or undo some event.[96] Ruminations in ASD are also about the past, and also involve a wish to change it, but usually to change how someone else behaved and they are associated with anger. They are similar to the ruminations of people with 'paranoia litigans' who think recurrently of having someone 'eat their words'. Incompleteness itself conduces to rumination, and it is often unfinished business in people with Asperger syndrome that is the focus of ruminations. Ruminations may revive buried emotions, and if the emotion is anger, this may lead to unexpected rage. For example, one young man had been told off by his father and sent out of the room. While he was in his bedroom, he had thought of effective rejoinders to his father's criticisms, but when he went downstairs to deliver them, his father had developed chest pain and was on his way to hospital where he died. This had been five years before, but he continued to hear his father's voice in his head saying that he was a 'waste of space', and this phrase and his reply – along the lines that space is never got rid of, so can never be wasted – would go round and round in his head until he flew into a rage and punched the door or the wall, or broke one of his favourite belongings.

Ruminations may be associated with depression, but may also lead to it.

Depression

Depression is less common than anxiety in adolescence in people with an ASD, but may develop as a result of unremitting anxiety, or in response to a loss or a defeat. It is often associated with suicidal thoughts, but deliberate self-harm and suicide may be less common in people with Asperger syndrome, although self-injury as a repetitive behaviour is more common in people with intellectual disability who have an ASD than it is in those with an intellectual disability but no ASD.

Grief

Grief is an idiosyncratic set of emotions, and may not be easily recognizable to others. Mourning rituals may canalize it in culturally appropriate directions, but these may not be known to people with an ASD, who often upset close relatives by an apparent lack of grief response. However, clinical experience suggests that depression following a loss may occur in people with an ASD and this is consistent with the ability of people with ASD to make close relationships and secure attachments (see Chapter 10 for a review). Young people with an ASD may become particularly attached to a grandparent, and so are often exposed to bereavement in their early teens.

Defeat

People with an ASD are particularly prone to defeat when the social world challenges their hope and expectation that other people are, like them, bound by justice or fairness.

Case examples

A young and isolated man with undiagnosed Asperger syndrome met a young woman through the internet. They got on well, and planned to get married. He was 19, but she said that she was 18 and his family did not doubt it. She seemed much more worldly wise than their son. She initiated sex, and although he was anxious about this, he felt that having a sexual partner was something to be proud of. He also enjoyed planning their wedding, and they spent many happy hours doing this. It was only when he was arrested and interviewed by the police that he discovered that the girl was 14. The police took the view that he was just pretending that he did not know, and in the interrogation tried to take the line that they, and him, were men of the world who were willing to bend a few rules. He did not understand why they could not see how shocked and angry he was that he had been duped. He told them that he would never break the law in this or any other way, and that he felt terrible that he had done so, but that it was not intended. The police prosecuted him anyway, and the first psychiatrist who interviewed him assumed that he was simply being disingenuous. The young man began to sleep less and less, lost his appetite and hardly ate and, although he continued to go to work, worked more and more slowly and made more mistakes until he was asked to take time off, which he refused at first to do. He thought that killing himself was the only way out, and started to ask other people what methods would work.

Another young man had formed the habit of swimming at the local pool at 8 o'clock every morning. He enjoyed it as it was very quiet then, and his family approved of him taking exercise. The council said that the pool was underused and planned to close it. He wrote numerous letters of protest, but the pool was closed. He became less and less active, until he was so retarded in his movements that he hardly moved or spoke at all, and was admitted to an adolescent unit, which treated him for schizophrenia.

A third young man identified strongly with clockwork. He wore two watches to avoid the wear and tear to their mechanism of having to change them from Greenwich Mean Time (GMT) to British Summer Time (BST) once a year, and then back to GMT six months later. One watch was set to GMT, and one to BST so neither had to be changed. He became so concerned over the situation of other clocks and watches (this was before the digital era) that he wrote to the government asking for the cessation of BST. He was told that this could not be changed, and he became increasingly self-preoccupied, eventually travelling to Greenwich and walking into the Thames with the intention of killing himself and for his death to be a kind of protest.

Hypomania and mania

Bipolar disorder is one of the few ASD-related conditions that is more common in people with AS or atypical AS than those with autistic disorder.[97, 98] There is an increase in bipolar disorder in relatives of people with ASD. The diagnostic criteria are the same as in neurotypicals except that the content of the thoughts may be linked to special interests, and without the usual grandiosity, sexual excitement, or religious fervour that is more usual in neurotypicals.

Case example

> Fervoured elation was obviously gripping an 18-year-old man, who welcomed me into the day room, and asked me if I had come to find out what he had discovered. I said that I had, and he told me that he had solved all his problems: an extension of the bus that he usually took to work from his mother's house, which would now go on to his aunt's and his grandmother's. He could see every stop in his mind's eye, and was rehearsing them with delight.

Caution

'Mood swings' are a characteristic feature of bipolar disorder, but these swings have a long period, up to months or years. Even so-called 'rapid cycling' mood disorder has a period of days. However, changes of mood within a day are also often described as mood swings. Careful enquiry usually reveals these as fluctuating levels of anxiety, which should be treated accordingly and not with anticonvulsants or lithium.

Temper tantrums or rages may occur in hypomania, when people are disinhibited, but these are rare: in a series of young people (up to the age of 12) admitted for tantrums, over one-third were previously diagnosed as having bipolar disorder, but less than 10 per cent were still so diagnosed after extensive evaluation.[99] The use of treatments for bipolar disorder may be effective in reducing aggression, but only if the person has a bipolar disorder; and since this is unlikely but anticonvulsants are used widely, it follows that many of these prescriptions are unnecessary.

Treatment

Young people with and without ASD respond to the same treatments as adults for bipolar disorder. This includes not only medication,[100] but also psychological treatments focusing on prophylaxis,[101] particularly the prevention of sleep deprivation.

Epilepsy

Idiopathic epilepsy may begin in epilepsy, but childhood onset epilepsy may remit. There are rare instances of a brief run of seizures in boys between the ages of 13 and 14 which do not require treatment (benign focal seizures of adolescence).[102] Epilepsy is a marker of complex ASD, as noted in earlier chapters: in consequence children with ASD and epilepsy are more likely to have other neurological or medical problems, more motor difficulties and more developmental delay; there is a lower ratio of boys to girls, and they have less object fascination and less gaze aversion; they also receive later diagnoses. Children with epilepsy and ASD are also more likely to behave in challenging ways.[103] Treatment of epilepsy has a complex effect on challenging behaviour. Some anticonvulsants, such as levetiracetam, may worsen it.[104]

Drug misuse

Drug misuse is less common in people with AS than in their peers, but there is an increased risk if there is co-morbid ADHD.

Sleep disorder

Sleep disorder may worsen social adjustment in adolescence, and an abnormality in the circadian rhythm (see Chapter 10) may contribute to this. Melatonin may work through its impact on this rhythm: at least, there is evidence that it can reduce sleep latency and nocturnal waking, increasing total sleep time as a result.[105] It may also be effective in children with ADHD,[106] although it should be noted that it is not effective in neurotypical children with sleep disturbance.

Eating disorders

Abstaining anorexics perform significantly less well than peers on empathy and theory of mind tasks when underweight,[107] but their performance normalizes once they have achieved normal weight.[108] The reduction in theory of mind may be an effect of starvation on frontostriatal function. There is no evidence that anorexia nervosa is more common in people with an ASD,[109] and bulimia nervosa may be less common.

Anger, aggression, violence and other behavioural problems

This topic is dealt with in Chapter 16, and also see the section on anger in Chapter 4.

Sexual disorders

People with an ASD may be unaware of sexual convention, and may behave publicly in a sexual way that is only seemly in private. Usually matter-of-fact counselling is enough to deal with this difficulty, but occasionally if a person with an ASD realizes that others are troubled or perturbed by their sexual behaviour, then they may use it as a form of coercion and the more that others comment adversely on it, the more it might persist. Public masturbation may be a reflection of 'stimulus hunger' and can be a consequence of institutionalization. It may also be a symptom of an affective disorder. Specifically sexual disorders are also considered in Chapter 16.

INVESTIGATIONS

Further investigation of a person with newly diagnosed ASD is indicated if there is evidence of a genetic syndrome; if the history or physical examination suggests a known aetiology; or to obtain evidence of any additional, related neurocognitive difficulties. A medical and psychiatric history should be undertaken, independently of the developmental history, to screen for possible aetiology.

Head circumference is a simple investigation that may provide evidence of a genetic syndrome, and may be worth undertaking.

It is my practice to include a screening tool for ADHD, and also for dysexecutive syndrome. The latter is extracted from the UK criteria for the award of disability living allowance, which focuses on independent living skills, and therefore provides a useful guide to executive function in practice.

If there is no indication in the history or physical examination of a neurological lesion, routine MRI or EEG are probably not indicated.

Neuropsychological assessment often contributes to an overall understanding, and may be of value in identifying academic difficulties, but is not routinely indicated. It may be useful if advice about education is being sought, or for the rare situation in which frontal lobe impairment and atypical ASD are to be distinguished (see Chapter 16).

MANAGEMENT
Primary impairment or difference
Impression management
Many people with AS become more aware of their appearance to others, and some try to remedy this, for example by trying to look others in the eye, trying to smile more frequently, or improving their gait, for example by swinging their arms. Although there have been no studies of movement training, drama training and participation in theatre is often valued by people with AS and may help in impression management.

Interview skills training
The impression that a person with AS makes at an interview, or even before the interview in their initial contacts with a prospective employer, has a disproportionate effect on their future since it may make all the difference between obtaining appropriate work, or being unemployed. Interview skills training often forms part of employment training schemes, although it has not been formally evaluated.

Prosocial competence
The cognitive elements of social competence, which include perspective-taking, may be augmented by explicit instruction about antecedent factors. One small study demonstrated an improvement in three school attenders with autism using teacher guidance to relevant cues.[110]

Empathy training
Empathy is key to social success in adolescence (see Chapter 6). Empathy training is widely used in professional training, and in offender rehabilitation. The lack of empathy in AS is partly based in the failure to read facial expressions, and training in emotion recognition, often using a computer, has been shown to be effective. However, adolescents with Asperger syndrome may find rich multimedia virtual environments, that neurotypical adolescents prefer, confusing. Attention may also be an issue.[111] Generalization from successful training to new social situations is a limitation on the efficacy of empathy training programmes.[112] A further limitation is that young people may be reluctant to accept that they have a deficit in this area.

Physical treatment

There is no convincing evidence that diet, drugs, vitamins or any other physical intervention has any direct benefit on ASD, although all of these may have a substantial placebo effect on any associated anxiety. Drug treatment may be indicated for a definite co-morbid condition, although psychological management may be the first preferred approach.

Secondary disability or idiosyncrasy
Emotional support

Counselling or psychotherapy is increasingly widely used to assist people with ASD overcome anxiety-related disorders and depression. I have been supervising a counselling service since 1997 and it has become a highly valued service, although formal evaluation has yet to take place.

Therapeutic counsellors working with people with AS often have to widen their role compared to their counterparts working with neurotypicals to include providing advice, sexual counselling, benefit counselling, and even careers counselling.

Although cognitive behavioural approaches are often advocated, there is no evidence that they are superior, and their reliance on introspection and homework may be stressful to some people with AS. The most effective counselling is provided by counsellors who are experienced in AS, and how people with AS think and feel. The modality is unimportant so long as it is one with which the person with AS is comfortable. Perhaps the single most effective therapeutic interventions are to be able to take the person with AS as they are, the ability to translate other people's behaviour and responses to them, and to 'back-translate' their behaviour as to how it would appear to other people, and to deal with concrete predicaments such as, 'If you say "hello" to someone outside a building, and then you meet them again by chance inside the building, do you say anything and, if so, what?'

Social integration

A narrative study of 18 young people with ASD highlighted their social and emotional isolation. They recommended the following to be of value in reducing this: peer groups based on shared interests or in structured groups (Scouts, religious groups, motor rallying, war re-enactments, role-play games, and Taikwondo are all examples that have helped my patients); communication training; and trying oneself to overcome anxiety, for example through spiritual practice or going to church, mosque, temple or synagogue, or through physical activity.[113]

Social groups for people with AS are also becoming widespread. These may be either face-to-face or virtual. Face-to-face groups may be led by professionals, or may be informal, peer support groups. Virtual groups may be structured by an activity, such as a role-play game, or may simply be meeting places. There is an Asperger island on the multi-user domain, Second Life.

Social skills training

Social skills training is considered in general in Chapter 9. Laugeson *et al.* have developed and evaluated an approach specifically for adolescents. They used a manualized parent-assisted social skills intervention to improve friendship quality and social skills among teens 13–17 years of age with ASD, and compared it with a waiting list control group. Targeted skills included conversational skills, peer entry and exiting skills, developing friendship networks, good sportsmanship, good host behaviour during get-togethers, changing bad reputations, and handling teasing, bullying and arguments. Results revealed, in comparison with the control group, that the treatment group significantly improved their knowledge of social skills, increased frequency of hosted get-togethers, and improved overall social skills as reported by parents. Possibly due to poor return rate of questionnaires, social skills improvement reported by teachers was not significant. Future research should provide follow-up data to test the durability of treatment.[114]

Academic support

Whether or not a person with ASD may require academic support will often depend on any associated developmental disorders that they have. Young people with dyslexia may benefit from using a laptop computer for note-keeping, and in examinations. Some students also benefit from having a note-taker in examinations.

Additional teaching support may be of value in the classroom, or access to a learning resource. Special tutorial arrangements may have to be made in university or college. Many universities now publish guidance about supporting students with dyslexia and with an ASD.

Support for carers

Adolescents with AS provide many challenges to carers, whose responses may, in turn, exert considerable influence over the young person and the impact of their difficulties. Support and information for carers may increase the chances that this influence is beneficial.

Tertiary handicap or altered life style

Bullying, victimization and inclusion are potent causes of emotional difficulty in adolescence, and may continue into adulthood. Exclusion at school may lead on to social exclusion in later life.

Mentoring of a pupil or college student with Asperger syndrome by a neurotypical peer has proved to be an effective method of preventing bullying.

Transition planning

The transition from school to work or college requires adjustment to substantial changes in routine that may be highly stressful to many people with AS. In the UK, transition at 16 also coincides, still, with the transfer from child to adult services. Many young people with AS are lost to care at this point. Planning for transition is now a legal requirement in the UK under the Autism Bill (2009), bringing young people with AS into line with the legal protection provided for other young people with disabilities. Arrangements will differ in other countries, some of whom may have child and adolescent services up to the age of 18 or even 21, thus filling the 'black hole' that many young people with AS fall into in the UK.

ISSUES

Normalization and mainstream education

Young people with ASD may learn by mimicking others, but they may learn deviant roles by this method, too. In fact many young people who are vulnerable by virtue of their lack of self-confidence may imitate challenging behaviour that they see in others. Special schools, inpatient units, and day centres may all offer unhelpful role models to people with an ASD and this possible adverse effect should always be offset against any possible benefits.

Mainstream school does provide the greatest educational opportunity for most young people with AS, and the greatest opportunity, too, to learn social skills through mimicry and practice. However, too many people with AS are, effectively, bullied out of school. This happens either because they become phobic, or because they fight back against the bullies (and indeed other young people more generally) and are then excluded.

Simply placing a young person with AS in mainstream school is not normalization unless active steps are taken to facilitate the young person's inclusion, too.

PRESENTATION OF ATYPICAL ASPERGER SYNDROME, OFTEN WITH ADHD, IN LATE CHILDHOOD AND ADOLESCENCE (SECONDARY SCHOOL AND COLLEGE)

RELEVANT DEVELOPMENTAL CHALLENGES

Belonging, giving and taking

Social inclusion is normally automatic for neurotypical children. They are connected to their parents by ties of blood, by bonds of attachment, and by the interbrain connection. Finding a place in the absence of some of these ties is one of the childhood challenges for people with an ASD. As childhood goes on, children develop ties to their peers and these can conflict with family ties. But a new conflict also develops, between a developing sense of self-determination or autonomy and a continuing investment in interpersonal relationship. This involves making up one's own mind, indeed it is effectively about developing an independent mind with personal values and beliefs. Having a mind of one's own, going one's own way, creates a dilemma. It leads to a person wanting things for themselves, but having to find ways to persuade others to give them. Belonging in adolescence involves knowing what to take, and what to give in exchange; this is in the context of physical maturity with a peak in fluid intelligence and in untutored strength.

Self-control
Emotional regulation
Being able to master one's own impulses and desires is a requirement if one is to have a relationship with other people that allows for all parties to obtain sufficient rewards to offset the costs of social relationship. Emotional regulation makes an important contribution to the development of prosocial competence considered in Chapter 15, and may be specifically delayed in people with ADHD.[1] In addition to the personal consequences of impaired social competence considered in Chapter 15, emotional dysregulation may increase intermittent dysphoria directly and may also lead to the dyscontrol of negative emotions towards others. ADHD is associated with a substantially increased risk of rage in children, presumably for this reason.[2]

Consequences
Self-control is advantageous not only because it avoids adverse social consequences of thoughtless actions, but also because it is required to achieve desirable long-term goals. Self-control is particularly impaired in people with combined type ADHD,[3] possibly because of reduced inhibition of prepotent impulses by lateral PFC,[4] mediated by dopamine.[5] Children with ASD alone, not complicated by ADHD, may also show reduced self-control but the reasons may be exogenous rather than endogenous, that is due to the absence of a peer group to reinforce inner resolve. This may explain why, unexpectedly, therapy to enhance social interaction also leads on to increased self-control.[6]

WHO ARE THE ATYPICAL GROUP?
DSM-IV includes Pervasive Developmental Disorders Not Otherwise Specified (PDD-NOS) in the PDDs, and includes atypical autism within it. It is a residual diagnosis, to be made when other diagnostic criteria are not met, but the signs of PDD are present. ICD-10 also has a category of PDD unspecified (F84.9), but in addition allows for a diagnosis of other PDD (F84.8), atypical autism (F84.3), which is most likely to apply to children with no language, and overactive disorder associated with mental retardation and stereotyped movements (F84.4). Overactive disorder in children with IQs in the severely handicapped range is distinguished because those who drafted this section of ICD-10 thought that these children were made worse by stimulants, and became underactive as they got older.

Most clinicians meet young people who have social and communicative impairments characteristic of ASD but have a later age of onset than is specified in diagnostic criteria, or do not show the rigid or repetitive behaviours that are required by these criteria. Sometimes the absence of key symptoms is due to a lack of an informant or of records for the crucial infancy period. Occasionally there will be cases where a reliable history of social and communicative impairment is available, but with no evidence of the other developmental criteria being met. These young people often have difficulties and needs that are similar to young people who do meet all the ASD criteria, and most clinicians consider that this justifies including them in an atypical or not other specified group.

Adolescents with developmental histories of an ASD and a clear history of ADHD often present a distinctive picture in adolescence. In one study over a half of participants with atypical autism had ADHD, but only one-third with typical Asperger syndrome had ADHD.[7] One of the characteristics of this atypical picture is that, although there may be some impairment of nonverbal communication, the main impairment is in face-reading and other tasks involving the interpretation of other people's facial expressions. Combined with this, these young people also seem to have less ability to recall what other people's faces would look like, and what their expression would be. They lack what theory of mind adherents might term a simulation of the other person, or what psychoanalytic psychotherapists have for a long time called, a stable internal object. My clinical experience is that this group face different problems during adolescence, and require different understanding and management. They are more likely to have additional specific developmental disorders such as dyscalculia, dyslexia, the dysexecutive syndrome associated with their ADHD, working memory impairment, and expressive language disorder. These children fit with the combination of Voeller's type 1 and type 2 of social incompetence in children.[8] Doris Lessing in her novel *The Fifth Child* (1989) provides a non-clinical description,[9] and in the follow-up, *Ben, in the World* (2000), comes to the conclusion that 'fifth children' are a different race of human beings, relicts from a former time – although it is equally plausible that they may be the future.[10]

Red flags

Some of the comments made by family members and others about an adolescent with atypical Asperger syndrome are shown as 'red flags' in Box 16.1. I have included an additional red flag that is more appropriate to the educational psychologist, and one for a juvenile offending team or child and adolescent mental health team member. These are all drawn from my own clinical experience, and require validating in an independent sample.

Box 16.1 Possible red flags for atypical Asperger syndrome

- Claims acquaintances to be friends, but friendships short-lived.
- Exploited by others, and may react with anger or with denial to this.
- Always in trouble at school for 'silly' things: cheek, forgetting homework, not bringing in things needed for lesson.
- Lacks awareness of family members' feelings.
- 'Immature'.
- Tells 'tall stories' that can easily be found out.
- Has several co-occurring developmental disorders including ADHD, but also dyslexia and dyscalculia.
- Motiveless arson or assaults on strangers.

Forensic considerations

Many people with atypical AS may first come to attention through the police or the juvenile court system. I shall therefore deal in detail with forensic issues in the final section of this chapter. I shall consider not only atypical Asperger syndrome, but also other ASDs, and their forensic implications.

SCREENING

Although general population screening for ASD is not indicated, screening of at risk populations may be. Since half or more of young people with an ASD meet criteria for ADHD, too[11] and a similar proportion of young people with ADHD meet ASD criteria,[12] screening young people with ASD for ADHD and young people with ADHD for ASD is likely to be much more worthwhile. Screening measures for ADHD in young people with ASD have not been evaluated clinically, although the six item WHO ADHD self-report scale has been used successfully for several years in my clinic; it has been translated into a number of European languages, and has excellent performance against clinical diagnosis in adults.[13] It is suitable for older adolescents, and can be used by parents to rate younger adolescents. Measures that have been used in research include the Conners questionnaire.[12] Computer-based assessments of vigilance and response inhibition have been used in diagnosis.[14] They may also be helpful in training attention in children[15, 16] and have the potential for use in training adolescents, particularly as they can be incorporated into a conventional gaming environment. Computer-based assessments have also been used to evaluate the impact of stimulant medication.[17]

Case example

A man of 21 spent most of his free time with lads of 14 because, he said, he felt most at ease with them. He had many acquaintances, but had difficulty in keeping them as friends. He had a long history of being exploited, for money or for favours, by these acquaintances and avoided going out in the daytime in case he met one of them, who would then pick on him. He said that he had always had difficulty telling if he could trust someone by looking at their face, or telling when someone was being serious or making a joke, by listening to their voice. This sometimes caused offence, and also made it easy for people to wind him up, which they often did. He had learnt to combine several channels of communication together and could now tell if someone was lying, but he was lost when he had to rely on voice cues alone, and in consequence never answered his phone if it rang. He did use the phone for texting, though, and this was his preferred method of communication. He was very aware of the bone structure of faces, he said, and he grouped faces into a relatively small number of fundamental structures. He could easily mix up the identities of people who had similar bone structures, and sometimes did make misidentifications among his acquaintances for this reason. He denied lacking empathy because, he said, he cared about other people, although he admitted that he often found it difficult to know how other people would react and often said things that others found too blunt, and sometimes even offensive. His mother said she thought that he knew what she was feeling, but sometimes did not seem to know how to react to her, and so blanked out her upset. He admitted that sometimes if someone was upset, he would simply ignore it and carry on as if they weren't. His mother said that he would try to respond if she told him what was wrong (usually), but 'You don't always want to have to tell people what you're feeling, do you? Sometimes, you want them to know you well enough to work it out for themselves.'

DIAGNOSIS

The principles of diagnosis are set out in Chapter 8. In a clinical setting, it is rarely possible to test nonverbal interpretation directly, so this needs to be assessed indirectly using the reports of other informants about empathy.

PRESENTING SYMPTOMS

Primary impairment or difference

Adolescents with atypical AS will often have a history of impairment in nonverbal expression, but this commonly remits during childhood leaving an impairment of nonverbal interpretation that cannot be observed directly. The effects are apparent in a lack of empathy, or rather an age-inappropriate lack of awareness of other people that is often attributed to 'immaturity'.[18] As illustrated in the case example, the lack of awareness of nonverbal cues may sometimes appear to be based on an inability to recognize expressions – sometimes severe enough to extend to prosopagnosia – but it is complicated by the restricted repertoire of appropriate emotional responses to a person in distress, which may lead to the cues simply being ignored. Face processing in people with atypical AS may require a more painstaking strategy than the privileged method that neurotypical adolescents can apply.[19] Inattentiveness attributable to ADHD may interfere with this painstaking strategy and further reduce the ability to put a name to an expression.[20]

Empathy and prosocial competence

Children with ADHD who do not have ASD may be too restless and impulsive to resolve conflicts with their peers, and from the age of seven or thereabouts face increasing marginalization that they may worsen by trying to overcome it by coercing others. Children with ADHD who are bullied are particularly likely to become bullies themselves. Those children with atypical AS have further difficulties because their empathy makes negotiated resolution to conflict particularly difficult. By the time that they reach adolescence, children with atypical AS are often marginalized, and lacking in the power to influence others or the social competence to persuade others. As social competence becomes an important determinant of group membership and popularity in early adolescence, many young people with atypical AS experience loneliness or a sense of personal inefficacy. They may deal with the latter by creating outrage: by doing or saying things that are so upsetting to others that a strong – and therefore easily read – reaction from them is guaranteed. Such outrageous behaviour has been attributed to 'demand avoidance syndrome', but the clinical evidence is that if anything it leads not only to greater demands but also to notoriety, which is a kind of power.

Empathy and aggression

Constitutionally reduced empathy is often perceived as a risk factor for aggression or violence, although there is little evidence for this. However, an inability to read faces may mean that there is a reduction in violence inhibition and so aggression may be inappropriately fierce or prolonged. Violence disinhibition in animals is increased by previous victories in agonistic encounters, and is associated with more rapid progression to violence, the choice of more dangerous attack methods, and indiscriminate violence including attacks on more vulnerable others.[21] Rats who show this kind of disinhibited aggression are impaired in their communication with other rats, and show lower 5HT and dopamine levels in the brain, levels that in human beings would be associated with anxiety-proneness, reward hunger and ADHD.[22]

Empathy and social gaffes

Many people with low empathy report making remarks that others find upsetting or offensive, often without intending to do so. Sometimes these remarks develop from a gradually more and more inappropriate conversation, in which the person with atypical AS has missed a growing discomfort on their audience's face(s). Sometimes the remark is an indication of a failure of anticipation of the likely response, and therefore a failure of the simulation of the other person. But sometimes the remark is exactly the one that the person has been trying to suppress, for example saying to someone who is overweight, 'Why are you so fat?' Such 'ironic errors' are a consequence of low effortful control in the face of high reactive control.[23]

Effortful control and other consequences of ADHD

Some of the primary impairments in people with atypical AS are probably attributable to their associated ADHD. The primary impairments in ADHD are not well characterized. The DSM-IV division into inattentive and hyperactive subtypes does not correspond well to clinical outcome, to aetiology, or to underlying neuropsychology. Neuropsychological attempts (see Chapter 10) to differentiate working memory, executive function, error control and attentive orienting have so far failed because of the overlapping nature of each of these impairments.

Clinical experience is that people with atypical ASD may have varying degrees of control over prepotent responses; they may lack persistence in cognitively demanding tasks; they may have problems in shifting attention away and then back again to where they left off; and they may have problems in budgeting time and money, and in planning ahead, including seeing longer-term consequences. Executive syndrome is the consequence of a blend of these impairments along with a disposition to anxiety. Working memory impairment may underly many of them.

Effortful control corresponds loosely to Freud's super-ego in that it provides the means for suppressing first responses, and replacing them with more considered – and usually more socially acceptable alternatives. Sympathy – that is care or concern for others' suffering – is for example more correlated with effortful control than it is with impulsivity.[24]

The confounding effect of anxiety

Hyperactivity in young children is as much of a feature in ASD as it is in ADHD. It is likely that it is closely related to anxiety-proneness and may, in some children, be the leading symptom of an anxiety disorder. It may lead to impulsivity but due to a failure of bottom-up or reactive dyscontrol, probably associated with serotinergic neurons and the anterior cingulate, rather than the top-down effortful control that is mediated by noradrenergic and dopaminergic neurons in dorsolateral prefrontal cortex.

Impulsivity in adolescence is of a different kind, and linked to top-down control failure, although that may itself be influenced by strategies learnt from parents and others at an earlier phase of life, and when dealing with anxiety.

Cognitive persistence

Giving up on cognitively demanding tasks may be linked to a lack of effortful control, and is also one explanation of the lack of sustained attention that people with atypical AS and ADHD give to unrewarding tasks. It may not always be obvious that this is a problem, as many young people with ADHD do give sustained, even exclusive, attention to tasks like computer games that provide immediate rewards as well as long-term ones. It is persistence at those tasks that are not in any way rewarding in the short term, such as filing correspondence, dealing with a difficult letter, or contacting someone by phone via a succession of intermediaries that tests persistence.

Attention shifting

Distractibility, like hyperactivity, is particularly a problem of anxiety and not fundamental to ADHD. The fundamental problem is rather that of being able to shift attention and then return it to the same place. This is not tested in tasks that engross the attention. So the ability to concentrate on something to the exclusion of all else is not a test, any more than is the absence of fleeting attention. The impairment is probably not even in attention at all, but in something analogous to putting pins in a map. The pins enable a person using the map to examine the area around the destination and then the area around the start, and then the route in between without having to search the map each time to find these places. The pins act like putting a finger on the last word being read in a book, or drawing a line under the point reached in a recipe: they enable attention to be moved backwards and forwards without any of the concurrent tasks that are being attended to one after the other having to be begun again. People with AS and ADHD become angry, or refuse to respond to attention bids when they are doing something, or if they do shift their attention, have to restart what they were doing all over again. So when they are reading, and if they have some degree of speech and language impairment, they may have to read a sentence or a paragraph afresh if they have not understood it because they cannot pick out the word or phrase that puzzles them.

Lists, budgets and plans

This is the task most clearly related to working memory. Keeping lists in mind means being able to shuffle them. Suppose I go shopping and want to buy: lemons, soap, sugar, self-raising flour. I remember the list in that order, but the lemons are near the exit, and the soap near the entrance. I can buy the soap, and then re-order my list, so that it now reads: soap (got already), lemons, sugar, and self-raising flour, and then I go to the next item on the list – lemons – and look for them. Or I keep the list in the same order, but walk backwards and forwards around the shop (or from one shop to another) buying the items in the order that I first remember them. Moving items around as one moves items in random access memory in the computer or on a disk is much more flexible than moving items on sequential, tape-based memory, where the list has to be changed and then re-encoded from the beginning. A person with AS or ADHD who cannot easily move items around has, however, to re-encode the whole list. When it comes to budgeting time or money, this makes dealing with unpredicted changes or bottlenecks difficult, if not impossible. Plans, too, cannot be altered to fit circumstances or left conditional on circumstances.

Case example

Malcolm's family reported that Malcolm had difficulty in picking up conversational cues and would often interrupt conversations, had difficulties in adjusting his conversation to that of other people and so would turn the conversation back to topics of special interest to him, and showed a lack of empathy. He would become upset if this was pointed out, and seemed to be unaware of his lack of contact with others. Malcolm had a similar lack of self-awareness about his inability to follow instructions or agreements. For example, if he arranged to meet someone he would be in the assigned spot at the assigned time sometimes. But if he saw something he wanted to investigate he would do so, and lose all track of time. Nor would he think to contact the person he was supposed to meet. However, he would come to the meeting place at some much later time and wait for the person to show up there. He could not cook or do his washing unless he was constantly supervised because he would become derailed in these activities, too. For example, if he was cooking something on the stove and he found that it required carrots, he would go in search of them. But, if he did not find them, he would forget about the cooking and go off to do something else, leaving the pan on the stove to burn.

Problems with time budgeting

Problems with time budgeting may be associated with an impaired awareness of the passage of time, often associated with a lack of intuition about time intervals, so that a person has little sense of what ten minutes or an hour means subjectively. This difficulty may be associated with problems in reading clocks, particularly analogue clocks, whose interpretation is based on the image of time as the length of an arc.

Although distractability of this kind is most obviously related to working memory impairment, it may also be able to turn search rules into inner language.[25]

Secondary disability or idiosyncrasy

ASD other than atypical AS/PDD-NOS has its impact on socialization early on, as described in the previous chapters. Atypical AS does affect socialization, but leaves some of the interbrain connection intact so that it is only with the increase in prosocial competence in later childhood that its effects become most notable. One of these is the difficulty in dealing with interpersonal conflict that is an early feature of the socialization of boys. Boys with atypical AS find it hard to share, or to compromise. This affects other boys' willingness to play with them and often leads to social isolation in later childhood and adolescence. This alienation affects relations with family members, and may lead to an unwillingness to cooperate with parental authority and a label of oppositional disorder or theft from and deception of parents leading to a label of conduct disorder. However, these are not inevitable or even typical developmental courses for people with atypical AS, who may instead go out of their way to be liked and accepted. Some may adopt roles that accept or even exaggerate denigration by others in order to be accepted: some turn their social ineptitude into buffoonery and become the class joker. Others take on dares from other pupils at school, even knowing that this will get themselves into trouble.

Later in life, people with an atypical AS may see themselves as having given in to peer pressure, and this may be a source of shame and low self-esteem.

Tertiary handicap or altered life style

Because it is not apparent that impaired nonverbal interpretation is a disability it is often perceived as a fault, due to a lack of respect, a lack of attention, or a kind of slight. This can result in understandable but unwarranted emotional reactions in others

Lack of the ability to interpret faces may open people with atypical AS to exploitation by people they erroneously trust. It may result in a lack of 'street smarts' that may lead people into dangerous situations in which men get mugged, or women get sexually assaulted, or people get caught up in criminal activity without having formed an intention to do so.

Box 16.2 Indications of possible prosopagnosia

- Difficulty recognizing people, even if you know them well.
- Being unsure if you have already met someone that day.
- Getting confused watching films because you are unsure which characters are which.
- Being confused if someone changes their hairstyle, or is dressed differently to usual.
- Trouble telling if someone is joking.
- Being unsure how to react when someone is emotional.
- Feeling that other people do not take one seriously.

DIFFERENTIAL DIAGNOSIS

Distinction from mixed educational difficulties

If ascertainment is first made at school, then the presenting features may be the combination of educational difficulties attributable to several specific developmental disorders. ASD and ADHD should be looked for in these children, and if a disorder of nonverbal interpretation is found in the absence of impaired nonverbal expressiveness, the most appropriate diagnosis would be atypical AS.

Distinction from adjustment reactions

Young people with atypical AS may have considerable difficulties in establishing an identity. Indeed their identity may sometimes seem to have been borrowed piecemeal from people around them. They may be so passive in social relationships, and yet so keen to have them, that their lives are driven by casual encounters and they seem to be without direction but yet unpredictable. The level of disorganization is of a kind that does not suggest schizophrenia but either what some clinicians term 'personality disorder', often the abused category of 'borderline personality' if the person with atypical AS is a girl, or an adjustment reaction. Very occasionally when this kind of disorganization occurs in the absence of a significant lack of empathy, a definite diagnosis cannot be made.

Distinction from antisocial personality disorder

Conduct disorder in children is assumed to be the precursor of antisocial 'personality disorder',[26] or antisocial psychopathy, sometimes simply referred to as psychopathy or, by Cleckley, as sociopathy.[27] The validity of attributing antisocial behaviour to a disorder is questionable and it is a worrying reflection of the politicization of Western psychiatry that it is rarely questioned.

Much of what has been written in this chapter about atypical AS may also be claimed by those who believe that there is a disorder termed 'conduct disorder'. I have argued elsewhere that antisocial personality disorder is not associated with a primary, generalized lack of empathy, but with the suppression of an intact, reflexive empathic response. Some evidence is provided by a study of adolescents labelled as having a conduct disorder, who were divided into two groups depending on whether their conduct problems began in childhood or in adolescence. Those who had problems before the age of ten years had impaired recognition of all facial expressions of emotion tested, those who had later onset of conduct problems were only insensitive to fear.[28] Another study also found impaired fear recognition in adolescents with 'callous-unemotional' traits, although children with antisocial behaviour were impaired in anger recognition, but not in fear recognition.[29]

Empathy, as noted in Chapter 6, may be suppressed. So even though their emotional apparatus is intact,[30] the adolescent may become impervious to particular emotions leading to corresponding behavioural dyscontrol.[31] As the victim's fear acts as an inhibitor of violence, so turning off the perception of this leads to increased violence and callous and unemotional traits. Other people's anger may similarly act as a brake on oppositional, disruptive or antisocial behaviour – but if the response to this is turned off, more disruptive behaviour ensues. Both callous and disruptive behaviour are more frequent in adolescents with atypical AS whose ability to read anger or fear in other people's faces is also impaired. But this is outweighed by the handicap of being unable to read emotions across the board, and by the early onset of these difficulties causing (as noted above) marginalization and often social impotence.

Other studies of adolescents who offend indicate that they are a heterogeneous group. Gauthier et al. gathered information from offenders themselves and from informants, and concluded that some conduct problems are due to impulsive aggression and some premeditated.[32] Adolescents who were anxiety-prone and socially detached were impulsively aggressive. Adolescents who were highly extrovert but self-centred, unpopular, and lacking in concern for others went in for premeditated aggression.[32] The former group are likely to have contained at least some adolescents with atypical AS, the latter group are more like those typified as antisocial or psychopathic. Another study of disruptive adolescent boys came to a comparable conclusion, although this time there were three and not two subtypes, and the methods were different. Some 293 clinicians 'randomly' selected outpatients in their care between the ages of 14 and 18; 138 young men were selected, of whom 71 had offended or had a history of disruptive behaviour. Of the 71, 28 were considered 'psychopathic', 17 were 'impulsively delinquent' and 22 were 'social outcasts'.[33]

Green et al. compared 20 young people, 11–19-year-olds, referred to an adolescent unit who were diagnosed with AS (both typical and atypical groups) with 20 referred in the same age group with conduct disorder.[34] Both groups have equal levels of depression, suicidal thoughts, temper tantrums and defiance, but the AS group had, in addition, severely impaired social functioning, high anxiety and OCD symptoms.[34] This further supports a distinction between young people with ASD and conduct problems, and those without.

Distinction from frontal lobe epilepsy

Frontal lobe syndrome most commonly follows from injury,[35] which may occur either at the front or the back of the head, since rapid deceleration of the head may lead to the brain swinging forwards and crushing the orbital poles ('contra-coup injury'). Although it may sometimes complicate a developmental disorder, there is rarely any doubt about the diagnosis.

Frontal lobe syndrome may also develop as a result of frontal lobe epilepsy which may be as common as temporal lobe epilepsy but is less often diagnosed, possibly because fits often occur solely at night.[36]

Untreated frontal lobe epilepsy can result in disruptive or oppositional behaviour with a lack of empathy, very similar to ADHD and atypical ASD. Treated frontal lobe epilepsy may leave a frontal lobe syndrome (*International Classification of Diseases*, F07.0 Organic personality disorder, nonspecific). Lateral prefrontal lobe impairment results in an 'executive dysfunction syndrome',[37] whose symptoms include those described under 'primary impairments' above and medial prefrontal involvement that results in a lack of empathy as well as passivity (abulia, as it may be called by neurologists), lack of self-awareness, lack of empathy, and lack of emotional responsiveness.[38]

Case example

Eric had a chaotic childhood, and several of his family members had special educational needs, as he did himself. There was no known familial disorder, however. Despite these difficulties, Eric fitted in well, and made friends at school until he was aged 11, when he became disruptive in class and got into fights, especially with girls to whom he could be particularly spiteful. He was frequently excluded from school. His mother reported that he had begun to wet the bed at night and he was having turns, although the description was not typical of epilepsy but of a kind of posturing, and he was not having fits during the day. At first this was considered to be part of a mixed emotional and conduct disorder, but eventually an EEG was performed, which was normal. He was admitted to a paediatric unit for observation, and nocturnal fits were observed and a 24-hour EEG showed spike and wave activity. He did not respond to first or second line drugs, but did to topiramate, following which his episodes of aggression disappeared and he was able to get work. However, he avoided unstructured social situations, could not maintain a relationship with a girl, lived in a clean, tidy, but emotionally cold environment on his own, and spent all of his spare time watching television or playing computer games.

Turner syndrome

The phenotype of Turner syndrome corresponds closely to that of atypical AS.

ASSOCIATED PROBLEMS
ADHD

As already noted, very many, if not all, of those with atypical AS have ADHD in addition. Some of the contributions of ADHD have therefore been included in the primary impairments section (above). Although it is now accepted that as many as 50 per cent of children with ADHD have persisting symptoms throughout adolescence and into adulthood, there may be a change in symptom profile which is not well characterized. Hyperactivity may lessen or may be replaced by inactivity, although thoughts often continue to be racing or to flit from one topic to another. The dysexecutive symptoms often come more to the fore in adolescence, too, partly because more executive ability is expected of adolescents than it is of children. Keeping things tidy, paying bills, managing money, and preparing for the next day may all become problems. Cooking, doing the chores, or using the washing machine may all be disrupted by distractions, leading to dishes burning, jobs left half done, or the washing getting unloaded still soaking wet.

Projects may be begun with enthusiasm, but then left unfinished. In adulthood, houses may have floors up, doors off, or holes in the wall because an ambitious project has been started, but not completed because an unexpected pinch point in the project timeline has not been circumvented.

The diagnosis of ADHD in adolescence is helped by a systematic inquiry about the full profile of symptoms, and this can be assisted by the use of a schedule to be completed both by the person themselves and by an informant. A useful guide to diagnosis and management is provided by Weiss and Murray.[39]

Tourette syndrome

Tourette syndrome, ADHD and ASD are independently associated with an increased risk of anxiety, and these risks are add together when these disorders co-occur.[40] Co-morbid ADHD increases the risk of anxiety, difficult behaviour and social impairment.[41] Copralalia (swearing) or making rude gestures occur in only one-fifth of young people with Tourette syndrome.[42]

Case example

A 13-year-old boy with tics was diagnosed with Tourette syndrome, and during the assessment at a specialist centre, a history of attentional problems at school led to a further diagnosis of ADHD. Stimulant medication was initially thought to be contra-indicated for fear of exacerbating his tics, although this risk is theoretical rather than actual.[43] He was started on methylphenidate, but his conduct deteriorated. He would fly into rages outside home, developed hyperaesthesia when exposed to water despite having previously been in the habit of taking a daily shower, and became disinhibitedly aggressive towards family members. His parents became both highly anxious about him, and rather frightened of him but he, a previously affectionate child, seemed unaware of this. A diagnosis of 'atypical AS' was made and the aggression redefined as an expression of anxiety. His aggression diminished over a period of months without any additional treatment, and he successfully made the transition from home to a residential school.

Anxiety disorders

Anxiety disorders are more common in atypical AS, and generalized anxiety disorder contributes to the mood fluctuations that bother many people with ADHD and with atypical ASD. The same range of anxiety disorders occurs in atypical as in typical ASD, although people with atypical AS and ADHD are more likely to self-medicate to 'treat' them. Anxiety disorders probably contribute to the irritability of some people with atypical AS, and a proportion of people with atypical AS learn (perhaps through modelling on parents) to blame others for their anxiety and so externalize it rather than experience it for themselves.

Shaming

Shame – the anxiety that goes with the impulse to hide from the negative valuation of others because it is shared by oneself – is a potent source of anxiety in people with ASD. Fending off shame is a potent motive in people with atypical ASD, and one cause of aggression. In an interesting intervention with a large cohort (405) of neurotypical adolescents, the participants were given a writing assignment: half to write about the values that they held to be important (termed a self-affirmation assignment) and half just asked to write something. The self-affirmation task was designed to reduce 'narcissist's aggression', that is aggression by shame-prone individuals and in fact produced a reduction in aggression in the self-affirmation group that lasted for a school week.[44]

Substance misuse

People with atypical AS are, like other people with ADHD, drawn to substance misuse. In my clinical experience, the substance most often misused is the one that is most used by their acquaintances. There is no particular preference for amphetamine, even though this may be expected to have a therapeutic effect. Cannabis and alcohol are used by almost everyone, but are less often the principal drug of abuse, and clinical experience suggests that these are used no more frequently than they are by other young people with social difficulties. Alcohol may have a disinhibiting effect on aggression.

Specific developmental disorders

Dyslexia, dyscalculia and disorders of speech and language are all more common in people with atypical AS,[45] and contribute to the overall disability associated with the disorder. They have been discussed fully in previous chapters (especially Chapter 10). Narrative ability may also be impaired.[46]

AETIOLOGY

Temporoparietal networks play a key role in nonverbal communication (see Chapter 6 for a review) and an increasing number of neurobiological studies suggest that this area functions differently in people with ASD compared to neurotypicals, and also compared to people with ADHD.[47] However, there are a substantial number of studies that implicate prefrontal cortex in cognitive empathy (see Chapter 2), with orbitofrontal cortex having a special role. Studies of theory of mind, particularly those of narrative theory of mind, show reduced activation in PFC in both ADHD and ASD. One possible explanation is that medial PFC provides a 'cache' or store of social knowledge that is drawn on in determining a course of action that is appropriate to the situation and to others involved in the action. I have put forward one possible explanation of how knowledge is 'cached', based on the analogy of caching internet pages for searching with an offline computer. I have suggested that social events and narratives about them are filed in the PFC, possibly particularly in the orbitofrontal area.[48] Although this sounds complex, it might simply mean that patterns of activation in networks link to groups of neurons in prefrontal cortex whose interconnectivity is thereby reconfigured so that it has a local correspondence to the wider network of centres with which it is linked. Local networks would be created by the brain activations that correspond to others' response to an action, so that the PFC would contain a kind of reduced history of past actions and others' reactions. Planning a future action might involve activating this history, and benefiting from the past reactions of others, which might then modify the plans for future actions. A similar model has been put forward independently by researchers in the cognitive neuroscience section of the US National Institute of Neurological Disorders and Stroke.[49]

If one or both of these models are approximately correct, it would suggest that one kind of lack of empathy or of forethought about emotional consequences would be produced by the failure of the PFC to furnish a sufficiently detailed or accurate record of past social and emotional encounters, which would fit with the report of many people with atypical AS that once someone is no longer physically present, it is as if they have disappeared altogether, and it is impossible to think how they would react.

There is some evidence that the association of ADHD, ASD and other neurodevelopmental problems represents a heritable subtype of both disorders,[50, 51] which would be consistent with a disorder affecting connectivity in prefrontal cortex.

INVESTIGATIONS

Investigations in ASD have been considered in Chapter 10. There are no investigations that are specific to atypical AS in adolescence beyond those that are indicated by clinical suspicion of associated disorders, or of frontal lobe impairment.

The immaturity of people with atypical AS may sometimes be hard to differentiate from reduced social intelligence as the consequence of a general impairment of intelligence. Psychometry is therefore especially valuable in this condition, especially if it is combined with tests of frontal lobe function, and a formal assessment of face reading and of executive function is desirable. There is no gold standard of tests in either of these areas. A commercial package (Mind Reading) has been developed as a training, and can also be used for testing.

There are also sets of facial expressions online,[52] which can be used to create a test battery.[53] The Reading the Mind in the Eyes test may also be useful in detecting empathy impairments in children with ADHD as well as ASD.[54] Tests developed for assessing frontal lobe damage and face recognition may also be suitable, although results in the normal range may be misleading.[55]

TREATMENT

The intermingling of symptoms of ADHD and atypical ASD in many people with this condition means that both need to be addressed in planning treatment. In addition, educational assistance for any specific developmental disorders affecting schooling, and general advice, support or, where appropriate, counselling are as important as for typical ASD (see Chapter 15).

ADHD is, as noted above, a disorder of both top-down and bottom-up control. The bottom-up element, which accounts for hyperactivity in early childhood, is closely linked to anxiety and anxiety proneness, and is therefore susceptible to environmental influence,[56] particularly to parenting styles. Negative comments increase anxiety, and reduce control. External repression may also foster the young person developing an external locus of control, and therefore increase the likelihood that adolescent emotional problems will be externalized.

Guidelines about the treatment of ADHD do not always mention co-morbid ASD and may focus on medication.[57] A more recent publication (September 2008) by the UK National Institute for Health and Clinical Excellence reviews the evidence base for behavioural treatment (e.g. time out), parent training using an established method like the Webster-Stratten approach, cognitive behavioural therapy often based around self-talk, social skills training, family therapy, and parent support groups.[58] The review concludes that there is insufficient evidence to recommend psychological treatment in adolescence. An earlier technology assessment document, cited in the guidelines, on the management of conduct disorders gives advice about the principles of parent-training/education approaches. Although it makes clear that these are applicable to children, and that there is no evidence for their value in adolescents, NICE recommends that a group psychoeducational package may also be of benefit to the parents of adolescents, and provide some principles that might be of value to anyone planning group interventions for adolescents with atypical AS (Box 16.3).

NICE recommends that young people with ADHD are offered social skills training, and a cognitively orientated approach that is similar to the coaching that is often advocated in the US. The American Academy of Child and Adolescent Psychiatry (AACAP) has also published guidelines about ADHD,[59] but their conclusion is that there is no evidence to support social skills training , although the NICE recommendations may be based more on teaching children self-reflectiveness in social situations (see Box 16.4) rather than social skills *per* se.

Box 16.3 Guidelines for parent psychoeducation groups for young people with ADHD

- Be structured with a curriculum informed by principles of social learning theory.
- Include relationship-enhancing strategies.
- Offer a sufficient number of sessions, with an optimum of 8–12.
- Enable parents to identify their own parenting objectives.
- Incorporate role-play during sessions, as well as homework.
- Delivered by appropriately trained and skilled facilitators who are supervised, and have access to necessary ongoing professional development, and are able to engage in a productive therapeutic alliance with parents.
- Adhere to a manual.
- Involve both of the parents or all carers.

Source: NICE, 2008.

Box 16.4 Teaching planning from 'Think Aloud' programme

1. What is the problem?
2. What is my plan?
3. Do I use my plan?
4. How did I do?

Source: Camp and Bash, 1981, cited in NICE, 2008.

Medication

Medication continues to be the first-line treatment of ADHD in children and adults,[58] although there are limitations to the approach: some young people have serious side-effects, including (with amphetaminics) anorexia, sleep disturbance and reduced growth in younger children (although this seems to be less of a problem in practice than theory would suggest). Benefits, too, may be limited, because children are unwilling to take medication. This unwillingness may be reinforced by the stigma attached to children using stimulations, and by the ethical or cultural objections to medication.

Amphetaminic drugs remain the most widely prescribed and the most reliable drugs, although there are many alternatives including an SSRI originally developed as an antidepressant (atomoxetine). These drugs all seem to be effective on both noradrenergic and dopaminergic endings,[60] although alpha 2a noradrenergic agonists, with no dopaminergic activity, have also been used – most recently the selective agonist, guanfacine, which may, in theory, be more useful for those young people who also have tic disorders,[61] although, in practice, tics do not seem to be made worse by methylphenidate.[62]

The abuse potential of methylphenidate continues to be of concern in adolescents (it can produce a rush if crushed and insufflated as a snuff), although there is little evidence for this being a major problem.[63] Slow-release preparations may be preferred since they have less abuse potential. Slow-release preparations also reduce the frequency of offset effects and the number of tablets that have to be taken (which may reduce compliance), although slow-release preparations can be less effective.[64] Various formulations of methylphenidate are currently being trialled to try to improve the bio-availability of the active drug, and increase its duration of action.

It has already been noted that ADHD involves several distinct neural networks, and affects several overlapping neuropsychological functions. But there is a lot still to learn about the former, and also about the neurochemistry. So it is not surprising that it is unclear which of the symptoms of ADHD change the most in response to stimulants. There is evidence that most of the symptoms benefit to some degree: hyperactivity and impulsivity, organization, time management and planning all seem to improve on methylphenidate,[65] and adults benefit as much as children.[66]

Long-term efficacy

There is a theoretical risk that long-term use of amphetaminics might down-regulate dopamine receptors, as long-term use of cocaine does. There has been no evidence of this so far,[67] although misuse seems to increase in young adults. Long-term follow-up of children on methylphenidate who continue to take it into adulthood demonstrate a reduction in substance misuse and fewer difficulties in everyday life, compared to those who discontinued medication. However, this was a small, naturalistic study, and there was no reduction in either offending or alcohol misuse in the group who continued on medication.[68] Medication has been shown to reduce the risk of road traffic accident in adolescents with ADHD, presumably as a result of reducing risk-taking symptoms.[69] This may be one reason why health economists consider methylphenidate a cost-effective treatment option, with cost-effectiveness ratios ranging from $15,509 to $27,766 per quality-adjusted life year (QALY) gained.[70]

Use in atypical ASD

Methylphenidate is effective in reducing ADHD symptoms when they occur in association with atypical ASD,[71] and in a study of children up to the age of 13, there was an improvement in attention to another person in a social task, with more initiations of interaction and more evidence of emotion regulation.[72] This result, if confirmed in other studies (there were a considerable number of drop-outs in this one), suggests that treating the ADHD symptoms may have a beneficial knock-on effect on social interaction and therefore reduce social impairment.

ISSUES

Forensic problems

A minority of people with an ASD present forensic problems, but those that do can be particularly difficult to deal with. There are several reasons for this. People with an ASD may take the view that neurotypicals are all of a piece, and therefore revenge on any one is equivalent to revenge on any other. The lack of emotional self-awareness combined with reduced nonverbal expressiveness may make it hard to know if a person with an ASD is getting 'wound up'. Finally, a lack of empathy may mean that aggression or antisocial conduct, once begun, is not inhibited by distress or fear in the victim. Offending, if it occurs, is much more likely to be against the person than against property, and more likely to involve an assault than a fraud or a deceit.

In a case note review of a consecutive series of 1100 clinical attenders with ASD, I found that 53 per cent had reported to me that they had been interviewed by the police concerning violence against a person (not all of these interviews had led to a prosecution), and that 12 per cent reported an interview about an alleged sexual offence (again, not all of these had led to further action). Interviews about property offences were much less common and this is the reverse of the situation in the general population in which offences against the person are much less than a third as commonly reported in British Crime Surveys as are property offences, even when the most common offence, of taking and driving away a vehicle, is excluded.

ASD and ADHD are also over-represented in adolescents in residential units. Anckarsa *et al.* analysed 130 consecutive referrals to two Swedish psychiatric units over one year. The average age of these young people was 16.2 years, 66 per cent met DSM-IV criteria of at least one psychiatric disorder, and 53 per cent had a neurodevelopmental disorder; the most common (in 39%) was ADHD, and the second most common (in 15%) was ASD.[73] People with an ASD are also over-represented in UK special hospitals.[74] One group has argued, on the basis of a literature review of a small number of cases, that people with ASD rarely commit crimes unless they also have another psychiatric disorder,[75] but this does not take account of the high incidence of psychiatric disorder in offenders. Nor is it consistent with the role of ASD symptoms in paving the way to offending in that minority of people with ASD who do offend. Many clinicians consider that a childhood history of ADHD increases the risk of offending in adolescence, but a recent record linkage study in Norway challenges this view[76] although the population studies, of children who are inpatients, may not be representative of the general population of children with ADHD.

Violence and threats of violence

It is usual in neurotypicals for the risk of violence to increase predictably with increasing indications that arousal is heightening. Threats of violence in this scenario are an indication of a certain level of arousal, and there is an expectation that they will not lead to violence without further provocation. One of the difficulties in working with aggression in people with an ASD is that there may be very little warning, nor sense of mounting rehearsal leading to violence. Threats may be delivered simply as warnings, and given in an unemotional and emotionally neutral way. Violence if it occurs is often seen as justified by a person with AS and one reason may be that they gave warnings that were ignored. For this reason, people with an ASD may make no attempt to conceal their part in violence, even if it is criminal. This may be one difference between them and neurotypical offenders.

Many people with AS may express regret but not remorse or shame for violence, since they will have usually considered it carefully. Even those people with atypical AS who may react impulsively often do so in the belief that other people have treated them unfairly and that their actions are justified.

Neurotypicals may be lumped together, so that aggression against one is almost as good as against another. For this reason, revenge violence – getting back at someone, a common reason for aggression in ASD – may be targeted on someone who is unlikely to retaliate rather than the actual provoker of the vengefulness.

Grievances or unfairness are the most common causes of violence, although habitual violence may not require much justification but be maintained by the outrage that it produces. Some grievances might be shared by anyone, but some are more idiosyncratic. Noise intolerance may create a grievance against ice-cream vans; trains leaving early may create a grievance against station staff; and being attracted to a girl may create a sense of grievance against the girl in question.

Predisposition
The disposition to violence is, in neurotypicals, influenced by culture, group membership and family environment. There have been no specific studies in people with an ASD, but it is likely that comparable factors influence violence disposition, although with the factors mentioned previously in this chapter that influence emotional self-regulation and the likelihood of externalizing distress.

Risk assessment
Risk assessment, as in other areas of psychiatry, should involve a combination of actuarial (drug misuse, previous offending) and clinical (thoughts of violence, violent fantasies) assessments, but their predictive value has not been tested and is likely to be lower than in neurotypicals since 'warning signs' are less likely to be present.

Violence and special interests
Special interests occur in about one-third of neurotypical children, and are more common in boys.[77] The special interests of people with an ASD are not only circumscribed and the subject of considerable investment of time and other resources, but also they are pursued asocially or, more rarely, antisocially. Some people with Asperger syndrome identify strongly with violent offenders or people who have distinguished themselves by violence in other ways, such as in military actions. They may admire their power or their determination. They may identify with the hostility that such people receive from society and think that this is comparable to the hostility they themselves have experienced. Worldwide Wrestling is a particular interest of many people with Asperger syndrome in the UK. Occasionally, these interests can lead to a person emulating one of the people that they identify with and committing an offence as a result.

Violence may itself be a special interest. For example, one male child strangled a school friend and said that he was interested to know if he could; a young woman put ground glass in a baby's food to see what would happen (the baby survived); a middle-aged man sent letter bombs to judges, probation offices and others as a result of a fascination with the work of the family courts, but also his admiration of the Unabomber; and a young man strangled a young female relative apparently because of a sexual interest in bondage.

However, these acts are often complex and more neurotypical motives like jealousy can often be uncovered. The man who sent the letter bombs had been traumatized by a difficult family divorce for which he wholeheartedly blamed his father, and had been scandalized that the judge in the family court seemed to conclude that there were faults on both sides.

Case example

Peter identified with an English mercenary who had staged an attempted coup in Equatorial Guinea and planned to do the same himself. He bought equipment and drew maps, but his lack of money led him to a series of ill-judged decisions to mug someone, and during the mugging repeatedly and ferociously stabbed her to death. It was alleged by the prosecution that there had been a sexual element in this attack and computer records showed that Peter had actually visited pornographic sites, including those that depicted sexual violence. Watching violent films is something that attracts some young men with Asperger syndrome and has been cited as one of the factors leading to murder or serious assault in other cases.

Sexual crimes may flow from a fetishistic interest. Blond hair, for example, may be particularly fascinating to some people with Asperger syndrome who start off by liking to touch it and may be permitted to do so when they are younger, but then continue to have the interest to touch the blond hair of strangers long after they are of an age when it is no longer suitable to do so. Rebuffs may lead to aggression or to a preoccupation with blond hair and covert or coercive ways of getting to touch it.

Fascination with fire

Some people with an ASD who experience a sense of social impotence go through a period of fascination with fires, and some set small or harmless fires. When more serious fire-setting takes place, the person with an ASD may be less likely than most neurotypicals to consider the risk to others who may be using the building or involved in putting out the fire.

Unreciprocated attachment to others

It is not unusual for adolescents with an ASD – most usually typical rather than atypical AS – to form one-sided attachments to others. Young men are more likely to do this than young women, reversing the trend in neurotypicals, but it is often a teacher or care worker who is the object of the attachment. Because the young person may not be able to empathize, the relationship can progress in their mind to the point where they may feel that they have an established relationship with the other person, and be justified in making demands on that person or in feeling jealous if they find out that the person has a partner already.[78] This can sometimes lead to apparently inexplicable anger with the other person, to notes or terse troubling communications, and sometimes to stalking.

Stalking

The largest group of stalkers are jilted lovers, and people with an ASD are unlikely to be in this group, but another group of stalkers form one-sided or 'predatory' attachments, often to celebrities or people with whom the stalker has had no personal contact. Stalkers like this present a threat to the person being stalked.[79] People with an ASD who stalk are often carrying on a one-sided relationship with a person that they have known, although stalking of ex-partners and of strangers may also occur. How dangerous stalkers with ASD are to their victims is not known, but whether or not they are, considerable distress is caused by this behaviour.

Very often the victims of stalking are unwilling to confront the stalker, but on the one occasion that I have come across when the victim did turn and speak to her stalker, and made clear that although she did not want to do him any harm, she did not want any kind of romantic relationship either, the stalking stopped. Professionals may be reluctant to be confrontational on the victim's behalf, but that can also be a successful approach, although it may take some time for the stalker to accept what the professional is saying.

Since the risk of assault on the victim by the stalker is significantly increased, steps should always be taken to safeguard the person being stalked as well as dealing with the stalker.

Several people with an ASD that I have assessed have also kidnapped women of their acquaintance. The kidnaps have not resulted in sexual assault, and may have been motivated by the desire to have a woman to themselves rather than by any specific sexual desire or fantasy. This does not, understandably, make the kidnapping any less frightening.

Stranger violence

Violence towards strangers is rare, especially when committed by a solitary person and with no hope of gain. A person who commits such an act should be carefully assessed, as such attacks may indicate psychosis, as well as ASD. In ASD the motive may be that the aggression is displaced from someone else, or that it is incidental to some plan. Occasionally, it is simply inexplicable. A common feature of all of these situations is that violence is not perceived as horrific or abhorrent. It is likely that this abnormal response to violence is not itself due to Asperger syndrome, although the bullying that a person with AS has experienced may contribute.

Homicide and attempted homicide

Homicide in AS has been little studied. In the ten cases that I have personally examined, the most common motives were to redress what the person with ASD thought of as a wrong, or to ingratiate oneself with or impress a friend or would-be friend.

In people with atypical AS and ADHD, violence in the context of alcohol or drug use may be reminiscent of the utilization behaviour first described by Lhermitte,[81, 82] suggesting that there is an element of frontal lobe impairment.

Case example

A young man with ADHD was out with friends and they were approached by two strangers, a man and a woman, who asked the way, and then shared a cigarette with them. He then went off to drink with some girls and had sex with one of them. Later, he met the strangers again by chance, this time when he was with other friends, one of whom knocked the male stranger down and began to kick him. The young man with ADHD simply followed suit, but continued kicking and stamping until both the man and the woman were dead.

It has been suggested that serial homicides may be committed by people with ASD, and one US murderer (Jeffrey Dahmer) has been speculated to have this diagnosis.[83]

Violence at home

Familiarity breeds contempt, as the old adage says, and many people with an ASD can be aggressive with family members, often apparently displacing frustration with others on to family members, who are unlikely to retaliate. One reason that this situation may escalate is that the family member feels the need to try to talk about the aggression, and engage in discussion, which leaves the person with ASD feeling deskilled and even more angry.

'If it is at all safe to do so, walk away and say you will come back when he or she has calmed down (and then do so)' is my regular advice.

Justice versus understanding

People with ASD like the law courts and God, live by justice and not by give and take. As they do not want to take (or perhaps do not always recognize it when they are taking), why should they give? Giving and taking is, anyway, not based on a calculus but something much more mysterious connected to social influence. In the novel *Bonfire of the Vanities*, Thomas Wolfe calls this the 'favour bank'.[84] The preference of language-based, categorical rules or procedures of justice over the interbrain-based favour bank may also reflect what some people with AS call their 'black and white' thinking.

Case example

'Black and white' thinking can sometimes lead to aggression: one young man repeatedly smacked his five-year-old cousin because the cousin had pushed his three-year-old sister. This man wanted to teach his cousin not to hurt others, but clearly the way he did that was disproportionate and likely to have had an effect that was the opposite of the one intended.

Harassment

The search for justice can sometimes lead people with an ASD to harass others, often without realizing that they are doing so. Harassment is increasingly possible using electronic means, and some people with an ASD who have particular skills in this area may use hacks or the creation of malware as a kind of virtual violence. However, some high profile hackers with AS seem to be motivated more by a wish to be accepted or admired by others than in pursuit of a vengeful motive.

Protest

Protest may be a variant of harassment. One man wrote repeated abusive letters to particular companies that he believed had lied about polluting a local river with effluent. The letters were so unpleasant that he was arrested, but he carried on and was re-arrested and charged, following which he began a campaign against the police and the courts for injustice, leading to further offences of public disorder or obstruction (he was picketing) and further charges. This man had strong political opinions, as do some others with AS, but he also became over-preoccupied with his campaign, which gradually took over his life.

Offences against property

Criminal damage is a catch-all charge that can be applied to people with an ASD who have a temper tantrum and break or damage public property because they happen to be in the street and not at home.

Other property offences are rarely committed by people with a typical ASD. People with atypical AS may commit property offences apparently to impress others or at the instigation of others, however. Burglaries, petty arson offences, and even taking and driving away motor vehicles (although most often as the passenger rather than the driver) are all charges that some of my patients have been convicted of, but they have rarely if ever profited by these crimes. Successful crime, like other social activities in adolescence, requires social competence.

Paraphilias and sexual offending

A few people with an ASD may indecently expose themselves, but this offence has lost much of its impact, and offenders are rarely reported to the police, let alone prosecuted.

Sexual assaults or rapes are rarely committed by adolescents with ASD, in my experience. The most common sexual offence committed by people with an ASD in my clinical experience is linked to a fetish (see below). However, in one series of rapists in forensic services, six had ADHD and seven had dyslexia (four with a dual diagnosis). Two had also murdered, one more than once.[85] There had been no investigation for an ASD, but this study does suggest that some rapists might have atypical ASD, and that this should at least be assessed.

Paraphilias

Much of what used to be called deviant sexuality is no longer considered harmful or bad, and some is no longer considered particularly deviant either. However, some paraphilias do create obstacles to close relationships and can cause embarrassment, particularly if not enacted discreetly.

Sexual fetishes

There are many theories about the development of sexual object choice. None is fully satisfactory. Undoing some sexually related shame is one theory that has good clinical support, especially in transvestism. Some people with ASD may cross-dress[86] and others may enjoy wearing nappies. Sexual preferences and sexual behaviour are socially shaped, and may be more chaotic in people with an ASD.[87, 88, 89] Increased sexual drive may increase sexually inappropriate behaviour, but antiandrogens, while they may be used, have little place.

Sexual identity

Some people with an ASD are excessively homophobic, but that is often because they find their identity in stereotypes. People with an ASD are more likely to be bisexual than the general population,[90] and this suggests that most have a less established sexual identity that may reflect the lack of a clear-cut personal identity, which has been mentioned in Chapter 4. A homosexual orientation may have advantages for men with an ASD who are relieved of the need to make the first sexual move, and who may also be able to engage in sexual contact with a minimum of demand for intimacy. Women may find same sex relationships more protective, and other women more accepting of their ASD than men would be. Many people with an ASD do not wish to have children, either because they are concerned about possible genetic transmission of their condition or because they do not feel ready to have a child depend on them. However, another possible reason for preferring same sex relationships is that they can provide an identity.

Paedophilia

Paedophilia, too, may provide an identity. It may also be attractive because people with an ASD may look back to the past as a golden time, and because they may feel more comfortable socializing with younger people. Some people with ASD may think of themselves as much younger than they are.

Case example

John was a bright 16-year-old, the son of professional parents. He felt more at home with younger children, and liked the company of much younger girls particularly. His parents often received complaints from neighbours that John was being inappropriate with their eight-year-old daughter after John had told her that he really, really liked her and that he wanted to go somewhere alone where they could play. The daughter saw a sexual threat in this that was not understood by John. One reason that it was not understood was that John could not really understand sexuality. He had been told by Tracy, a 14-year-old girl who frequented the local park, that she was pregnant by him, after she had kissed John for a dare. The more Tracy teased him, the more confused John became, and the more satisfaction Tracy seemed to get.

John could not pick up information about sexuality in bits and pieces, as other children do, because he did not have the social scaffolding to organize it, and to know what to believe and what to disbelieve. Nor did giving him rules solve the problem. When he was told that he should not talk to eight-year-old girls, John would say that he was expected to talk to them in some circumstances and, anyway, he did not mean anything bad. It was other people who saw the badness, not him, and so it was they who were at fault. When John was told that it was not possible to get pregnant through kissing someone, he would say that Tracy had told him that she was pregnant and she should know.

Paedophile images are easy to find on the internet, and looking at these may be all the contact with children that a person with an ASD needs, although that still constitutes an offence and the images may be of a violent or grossly unpleasant nature, which suggests a potential for acting out sexual fantasies in the future. There may be other more troubling manifestations of paedophilia. Young children may be approached and inappropriately touched, often in obvious public ways. Some boys with an atypical AS may seduce younger children into sexual activity that is kept secret.

Sexual regression

Adolescents with an ASD who become depressed may regress, leading to an increase in masturbation, sexual play with faeces, drawing crude diagrams, the open use of pornography, and the use of foreign objects in masturbation. The priority is to treat the mood disorder, rather than to suppress the sexual behaviour so long as that is not causing risk.

Cries for help

Other young people in distress may externalize it. Some ring ChildLine, making up a story about being abused. Others randomly phone people, or ring the emergency services.

Victimization

For every one offender with ASD, there are many who are victims: 90 per cent of people with AS say that they have been bullied.[91] Many people with an ASD, of both sexes, have been sexually assaulted in care, prison or health care settings. Women are at greater risk of being abused by men in relationships. People with atypical AS are particularly at risk because they take more risks.

Case examples

A young woman with atypical Asperger syndrome was at constant loggerheads with her parents, who accused her of being ungrateful and of never listening to them. Her father tried to lock her in her room, but she got out through the window. She met some people who said that they would be her friends, and she said she wanted to go to live with them. Her parents felt that they had no choice, but were concerned that she did not keep in contact. When they saw her in the street she seemed unwell, but refused to speak to them. She was always accompanied. Later she said that she was being kept a near prisoner by some men who had raped her and that she had seen other women being physically attacked. Her parents were never sure if this had happened. She managed to get away and came home, but then met up with a former boyfriend and ran away with him. The police picked her up trying to cash a cheque that had been stolen by the boyfriend. They had been living in a squat, which the police found to be in a derelict state. Someone had lit a fire in it. She was taken to a place of safety (a hospital) by the police using their powers under the Mental Health Act as she refused to go home to her parents.

Alan was targeted by a 12-year-old girl from his neighbourhood who said she loved him. He gave her money regularly although he never touched her or asked her for any sexual favours. When all his money was gone, she taunted him, and disappeared. He now regularly goes into the nearest town, and walks round till the early hours to try to spot her, although he never does.

A particularly tragic example of victimization is the dual homicide and suicide, in which a parent, usually a mother, kills her child with an ASD and then kills herself. Such cases are on the rise.[92]

Chapter 17

THE PRESENTATION AND CONSEQUENCES OF ASPERGER SYNDROME IN ADULTHOOD

CHALLENGES IN ASSESSING ADULTS

Obtaining detailed information about early development may present challenges when assessing adults, but a greater difficulty is that development itself becomes less and less like a single trajectory as people get older.

Developmental milestones, including social development, in infancy are strongly influenced by biological development. Norms for social development exist, and an infant who falls substantially behind them can be objectively determined to be socially impaired. In middle childhood, children are assessed regularly in many developmental areas, including socialization, and school reports provide a measure of social impairment. Parents and families also judge children's development according to family norms. Professionals do not need to rely on their own prejudices about what constitutes normal social development to be able to determine whether the social impairment criterion is met.

Adolescents develop in different directions, and whether or not they are impaired is more complex than it is for children, although school attendance, finishing the final school examinations, socializing with peers, making and keeping out of trouble are tasks that most Westernized adolescents shoulder. But adulthood is often considered the end or the fulfilment of development. If people can be said to continue to develop, then it has to be accepted that they may do so in quite different directions, and with quite different emphases. The social development of an anchorite cannot readily be compared with that of the chief executive of a large advertising business. Moreover, there is no independent arbiter of social performance, as there is for children. Adult children reject their parents' judgements about their maturity or adult social adjustment and may withhold evidence from parents about their social adjustment. So parents cannot be relied on. Some parents would prefer to gloss over any social difficulties that an adult child might be having, in any case. Partners or spouses can provide valuable sources of information, but may become biased if there is conflict – as there may often be, since partner dissatisfaction is one trigger for an assessment.

The clinician may have to rely on the person being assessed to judge whether or not they are socially impaired, effectively making the diagnosis partly contingent on the lack of bias of the client or patient. Although this is rare in medicine, it is perhaps not so very unusual.

For example, how incapacitating arthritis is may depend more on the patient's history than on an objective display of signs of pain or limitations of movement on the particular day of the examination. This kind of bias towards reporting severe social impairment occasionally crops up in assessing people who believe that they have AS, too, and may be one reason that clinicians are reluctant to accept unsupported evidence from the person seeking a diagnosis. Normally, there is another informant: if not a parent, a spouse, a sibling, another family member, a long-term friend, an employer, a landlord, an advocate, even a child (I have interviewed all of these). There may be some objective evidence, too, for example a person's CV: although, as doctored CVs are not uncommon, people should be asked for the one that shows all of their jobs, even any short-lived ones, and any from which they were sacked. Facts from the personal history are useful, too. A person who says that they are socially impaired, but is chair of their local Rotary club, a trade union organizer having had a previous career in sales, and has been married for 20 years with four children has some explaining to do if he or she claims to be socially impaired.

These comments apply only to the impact of the autistic syndrome, not to whether or not it is present. The latter is a matter for the opinion of the assessing clinicians.

RELEVANT DEVELOPMENTAL CHALLENGES
Adaptation
The developmental paradigm may apply only weakly to adults, but it cannot be entirely dispensed with. Most adults have a notion of what benefits and duties adults can expect, and also what skills adults should have acquired to justify these benefits and carry out these duties. So the normative elements of the developmental paradigm do still apply to a degree in adulthood. Moreover, there are developmental transitions in adulthood as there are in previous phases of life. These transitions create change and make greater demands on social and communicative competence, both of which are anxiety provoking for people with an ASD. Since anxiety aggravates social impairment, these transitions create dips in social functioning for people with an ASD and referrals for assessment and advice increase as a result. So the ages at which referral for assessment occurs can be used as a marker of transitions (see Table 17.1).

There are two periods in adulthood in which assessments or reassessments peak in my clinical experience: early adulthood (in the West more likely to be early twenties than mid teens, as it might be in Africa) and late thirties and early forties. The latter peak may be partly explained by the age of fathers when their sons are first diagnosed, since it is not unusual for fathers to recognize some of their own difficulties in the picture of ASD that is painted during their son's assessment. However, this peak is often associated with marital difficulties and with work difficulties. Spouses may say:

> I was so determined to make the relationship work that I turned a blind eye to how different he/she was, and anyway in the early years, the only women I met were mothers and we just talked about the children. Now they are at secondary school, and I see the difficulties that he/she has with them, and now that some of the ardour of our relationship has cooled, and I realize how little he/she actually knows me, I realize that there is a lot missing in our relationship. And I've begun to have more confidence that it's not me, but him/her.

Table 17.1 Transitions between life stages marked by an excess of referrals for ASD assessment in the later stages

Age (years if not otherwise specified)	Nature of transition
0–3 months	Birth and individuation
9–12 months	Relating to non-intimates, reaching out to others socially
12–18 months	Conversation
2–4	Relating to peers, play
7–9	School rules, games with peers, learning from teaching
10–13	Pre-puberty, transition to secondary school, in-groups and out-groups
14–16	Formal examinations, first work, sexual relationships
14–21	Work as obligation, developing partnerships
14–30	Adult responsibilities, caring for family members, responsibility for a home, financial independence, marriage or committed partnership, conscientious acquisition of skill
35–50	Partnerships fuelled less by passion, and more by closeness, work relies less on technical ability and more on working with others, parents no longer able to provide support, serious health problems become more likely, loneliness cannot be filled so easily by casual relationships. More life has been lived than there is to live, hope gives way to regret or satisfaction
At any age	Change and loss
At any age	Unresolvable past conflict

Employers may communicate their opinions by increasing the frequency of reviews, by moving the employee sideways on more than one occasion, by suggesting counselling or coaching, or by sending the employee on courses. Often, the employee has reached the point when a move to a management rather than an operational post would be expected, but a lack of personnel skills has blocked this. Sometimes more junior employees are appointed over the employee's head, creating bitterness. Typically feedback from the employer is non-specific and couched in careful and unemphatic language that the employee fails to recognize as a warning. Suspension over a trivial matter, or even dismissal, may sometimes follow with little further warning, and come as a shock to the employee with an ASD who has not been 'reading the signs'.

Bereavement can occur at any age, and its impact is both emotional and practical. The practical consequences of bereavement may include loss of practical support or of assistance, change in accommodation, or loss of income, and it is these practical changes and demands that often have the most consequences for a person with AS. These consequences are similar to those that might follow a transition, and bereavement has therefore been included in the table as a kind of transition, too, but one occurring at any age.

Change of status is, for many people, a transition that demands as much emotional work as bereavement. But few adults with AS are concerned with, or even much aware of, social status. Few people with Asperger syndrome believe in a just world. So the loss of the security that may follow trauma or abuse is not a danger to many adults with AS.[1] Few people with AS are, anyway, concerned about the future. But many are very concerned about the past. Ruminations and recriminations about past conflicts can undermine people with AS as much as traumas may undermine neurotypicals.

Case example

> Damien was once told by a teacher at school that he was 'not a good European'. He fumed about this for some weeks, and then took out a subscription to a newspaper called *The European*. He said that he did not always understand it, but at least he was proving the teacher wrong. The newspaper failed after several years, and Damien was once again confronted with the unfairness of the teacher's assertion. But there was nothing he could do to put the record straight as the teacher had died. He thought about the false accusation every day, and would sometimes feel the injustice so keenly that he would work himself up into a rage, and have to break something.

Fulfilment of duties

Another way of looking at adulthood is that it is the fulfilment of development. This can be seen in two ways. One kind of fulfilment is that an adult is now qualified to take up an adult's duties. Arnett concluded from a literature review that US adolescents thought that adults had three main duties: first, accepting responsibility for oneself; second, making one's own decisions; and third, being financially independent. Marriage and relationship stability were not considered to be a duty.[2]

Many people with an ASD, including many people with an AS, do not carry out one or more of these duties, but then neither do many neurotypicals. Should this be considered an impairment? To consider life up to adulthood as a kind of training, and adulthood as a kind of employment, conflicts with the spiritual or political values of many adults. Ten years on from Arnett, another meta-analysis, this time of 94 studies of adolescents' rankings of the importance of different life goals, placed more emphasis on achievement. The three most important life goals were considered to be completing education, getting a good job, and having close relationships.[3] These goals are likely to coincide with what many parents think of when they want their children to have a good start in adult life. When I interview parents, I always ask what worries the parents most about their child, and not getting a job or not getting married or having a partner are commonly cited by the parents of children with AS.

The parents of adolescents most often worry about how their child would manage without them, that is, whether their child can live independently. The parents of adults often worry that their child is not happy or fulfilled.

Independence is the goal of early adulthood, but fulfilment becomes a more important goal in later life. Dissatisfaction with a lack of independence, or remaining dependent, is most likely to be associated with the peak of referrals of young adults. A lack of fulfilment is more relevant to the peak of referrals in middle to later adulthood.

Independence

Independent living requires an adequate income, but much more besides. It means dealing with bills, with correspondence, and with any neighbours, independently. It means shopping for oneself, doing the household chores, eating and sleeping healthily, going to the doctors when necessary, keeping appointments, accessing community facilities, and being able to travel. Depending on the environment, it might also mean knowing how to keep warm or cool; knowing where to get clean water; how to dispose of rubbish; how to mend broken household objects; how to deal with common dangers, including dangerous animals; and how to keep up one's spirits.

The definition of independent living provided in a recent UK interdepartmental government report identifies capacities that constitute independence,[4] but the ones proposed are most relevant to what is required from society rather than what is required of the person with ASD. However, the report goes on to focus on the transition from adolescence and adulthood, and identifies several steps that young people need to take in transition, reverting to the acquisition of statuses, such as the independent use of transport, appropriate accommodation, and permanent employment (or education and training towards that end).[4]

Independent living requires executive skills and personal care skills.

Executive skills

Executive dysfunction is common in adults with AS.[5] Problems with time budgeting may interfere with work attendance, medical care, and maintaining the right benefit status. Problems with budgeting money may lead to periods of overspending followed by lack of food, inability to afford taxis or other means of transport, and the inability to pay bills. The result may be emergency intervention by families, and eventually the decision that a person is unable to live independently, although in other respects they are succeeding. Spending nights on the computer without thinking of when work starts the following day may also interfere with work performance.

Personal care skills

Many people with Asperger syndrome are reluctant to change their clothes, partly perhaps as a general resistance to change, partly because certain clothes become emotionally important, and partly because certain clothes are known not to irritate because of constriction or a scratchy texture, to which many people with Asperger syndrome are particularly averse. Other people with Asperger syndrome may dislike washing or bathing because of its intrinsic inconvenience or because it inevitably leads to a series of rituals which are time-consuming and potentially anxiety provoking if not completed satisfactorily. One way or another, self-care can be problematic to many people with Asperger syndrome who may need reminding about it on a regular basis, unless they can establish a routine which takes care of it.

The issue of self-care may be a general problem in self-monitoring, leading to people with Asperger syndrome being unable to see the figure they cut in other people's eyes, and as a result sometimes dressing incongruously or saying bizarre things without realizing that they are being in any way eccentric. This lack of self-monitoring or self-awareness lies at the cusp between people with high functioning autism or Asperger syndrome and people who are more severely affected. Occasionally, a person crosses over this cusp during development and experiences the pain that self-awareness can bring.

Case example

James had a fascination with aerodynamics and worked constantly to improve the fairings that he would fix to the front of his bike to reduce drag and increase efficiency. One day, cycling around his neighbourhood with his latest fairing design sticking out from the front of his bike, he caught a glimpse of a person staring at him open-mouthed and for the very first time realized that there was, in that expression, an element of derision. He experienced shame for the first time and this anxiety did not then diminish but persisted; it grew the more he could picture other occasions when he had seen similar facial expressions as he went by. Greater self-awareness may explain why people with Asperger syndrome may be less severely impaired than people with autistic disorder, but have a much reduced quality of life in comparison.

Other obstacles to work
Interview skills
Being a good interviewee requires empathy with the interviewer(s). It also requires a socially acceptable degree of self-aggrandisment, and a demonstration of obedience to the culture of the organization by wearing appropriate clothes and showing appropriate deference. All of these may be difficult for people with AS. Interview skills training often forms part of employment preparation nowadays, but, like social skills training, this may not generalize readily from the training setting to the actual interview.

Exploitation and bullying
Bullying has been considered already in this book (see Chapter 4) but it is important to note here that people with AS may be bullied out of work. Even if there is no overt bullying, the lack of assertiveness characteristic of many people with typical AS may mean that they are given less rewarding work. In one US study of adults with disability, a greater proportion of people with ASD were employed than were employed from most other disabled groups, but the ASD group worked fewer hours and received lower wages than other groups. They also required more support.[6]

Accidents

Adults with AS who have persistent dyspraxia may have more breakages in assembly jobs than neurotypical workers. If they have ADHD too, they may have more accidents, as well as more days off sick. In a large (more than 8500 workers) survey, workers with ADHD had a 4–5 per cent reduction in work performance compared to other workers, and their risk of sickness absence and workplace accidental injury was doubled.[7]

Independent living and emotional resilience

Living independently requires the executive skills already mentioned, plus the practical skills for self-care, although these can be supplemented by using services, such as ready meals from supermarkets. Emotional self-sufficiency is also required and may be harder to achieve. For people with atypical AS, problems may arise from acquaintances who take advantage of the accommodation to crash out, deal in drugs, get drunk, or otherwise abuse their host's involuntary hospitality.

Transport

Getting a car and gaining a driving licence marks, for many young people, the first substantive step into adulthood. It means an incremental step in independence, and therefore choice and control. It also makes employment more practical, opens up the use of more distant community resources, and plays its part, too, in courtship. Even if a young person does not have enough money to buy a car, the first train or plane journey, or the first time a taxi is hired, may have something of the same significance.

The ability to use transport is influenced by practical factors, such as previous experience, the local availability of transport, and disposable income. International transport may also be influenced by the availability of passports or visas. But using transport also requires organization – knowing which bus to take, for example, when it goes, and where it leaves from – and the confidence to deal with the unexpected.

Case examples

> Solomon had typical Asperger syndrome and topographical disorientation. He got a holiday job (he was studying archaeology at university) working with a survey firm. His team was late completing a job one day, and rather than taking him home, dropped him off at a railway station some 20 miles away. 'You can get a direct train from there,' his boss said, 'they're pretty frequent and you're well before the last train goes.' Solomon was so anxious he could hardly speak, but he was too ashamed to say that he had no idea which platform to go to, or how he could tell which his train was. He did not want to ask anyone at the station, either. He thought that they would laugh at him. All he could think of to do was to ring his mother, who did come and pick him up after something of a wait. It was mortifying. Solomon knew that if he went to work the following day, and he was asked if he got home all right, he would be too ashamed to tell them the truth. So he called in sick, and did not go back to work. In fact, he still had not found another job, five years later, when he was seen for an assessment and his Asperger syndrome was confirmed.

Robert was staying with his grandmother, and it was normal for her to walk with him to the bus stop for the bus that took him to the day centre. He had done the journey many times before, but always panicked beforehand a little bit. So she would take him to the stop well before the bus was due. One Thursday, she dropped him off as usual but, as she had some shopping to do, walked straight to the shops rather than going home. Robert waited, but the bus did not come. After waiting an hour at the stop, a man in uniform came over and asked him what he was waiting for. Robert did not know the number of the bus, or its destination, although he knew the colour and shape of the bus. So Robert just said, 'Bus'. But the man in the uniform said that the road ahead was closed, and that the bus had been diverted. It would not be stopping there that day. Robert panicked, and got angry with the man, who got angry back. Robert hit him, and the police were called. By the time that they arrived, Robert was saying that the man had made the buses stop deliberately. The police restrained him, and searched his pockets. They found his grandmother's phone number, but there was no answer. So they took Robert to the local mental health unit. Robert did not seem to understand when they explained that they were taking him to see a doctor, and he shrieked when they took him into the strange building. He did not speak at all, and tried to hit several nurses who came to assist the policeman. A doctor was called, who prescribed intramuscular medication, which was given immediately under restraint and Robert was admitted compulsorily to the mental health unit.

Driving

A proportion of people with AS learn to drive, and clinical experience suggests that they drive safely, if cautiously. Less able people with an ASD may be prohibited from driving because of a lack of coordination, especially the hand–foot coordination and hand–eye coordination, that driving requires. Other people with an ASD may be unsafe because a special interest in something to be found on or near roads means that their attention could be fatally attracted to it, and away from the road. Yet other people with an ASD who would otherwise be safe drivers could not be trusted to manage a conflict with another driver that may result from an accident or a confrontation at a junction. If the licensing agency requires a report, it is normally safe to recommend that there is no medical contra-indication to a licence being given to a person with AS who would not have problems in the areas mentioned previously. However, co-morbidity may also be a contra-indication to the granting of a licence. ADHD and drug misuse, unstable bipolar disorder and active epilepsy may all reduce driving safety.

Many people with ADHD are drawn to driving as an escape, or as a means to the freedom of movement that is particularly attractive to them, and this applies to people with ASD and ADHD. But ADHD is associated with a substantially increased risk of accident, possibly as a result of inattention when driving becomes monotonous or tiring.[8] Methylphenidate use reduces the risk.[9, 10] Amphetamine use may also decrease risk but at a cost of a rebound increase when the effects wear off.[11]

Fulfilment of personal goals

In later life, many adults are more concerned with what makes a life 'meaningful' rather than successful. Health, happiness and spiritual wellbeing become more important life goals than income, status or reproductive success.

Health

Very little is known about the health status of older adults with AS, but there is a suspicion that without family carers, many may neglect their health and as a result may die earlier than the average.

Happiness

Some people with Asperger syndrome say that it has been their special interests that have made life worthwhile. Even though they recognize that the interests have sometimes been eccentric, quite often dismissed by other people as not leading to anything useful, and sometimes have taken up too much time, the passion with which they have been pursued and the engagement with the world (usually the physical and not the social world) that they provoked has made them fulfilling. Special interests may thus provide 'flow', seen by some psychologists as a key contributor to wellbeing and therefore happiness. Work or occupation may provide income and social contact, but may not provide flow.

Loss

Leaving work in mid-life may provide the opportunity to take up activities that do provide 'flow', and may be positive, but in most cases the opposite is true and losing a job leads to greater social isolation and inactivity. Ending a relationship may also be a positive development if the relationship was marred by conflict or dissatisfaction, but too often leads to isolation.

Case example

Steven had some money put by, had a large council flat, and a regular income, thanks to benefits. He thought that all he was lacking was a wife. He heard that one could travel to the Ukraine to find a wife through an agency, and that is what he did. He met Olga, and they married three weeks later. However, when she got back to Britain, she found living with Steven increasingly difficult. His home was a mess. He had stopped throwing things away some years before, and rarely cleaned in the kitchen or the bathroom. She took these tasks on, and even got a part-time job to supplement Steven's benefits. But instead of being grateful, Steven found it harder and harder to share his flat with someone else. It turned out that Olga was a qualified carer in the Ukraine, and she so impressed her employers in the local care home in which she worked that they gave her a full-time post. She told Steven that unless their relationship improved (he would often spend days not speaking to her), she would move out, but he made no attempt to change and she did move out. Steven began to drink heavily. He set fire inadvertently to the kitchen on two occasions when he forgot something on the stove, and he cut himself on three occasions, saying that he wanted to die. Olga felt that she had been duped by Steven into a marriage that amounted to a live-in carer role, but also that Steven had no one else. So she visited him most days to check on him, and once a week came over to clean up and make him a hot meal.

Had Steven not gone to the marriage agency in the Ukraine, his life would have remained empty, but he would not have been confronted with his own inability to make a close relationship. It was this that seemed to have floored him, and to make him feel that there was no place for him.

Relationships

Steven's experience illustrates the contribution of close relationships to wellbeing. Many would agree with Freud's contention that 'The communal life of human beings had, therefore, a two-fold foundation: the compulsion to work, which was created by external necessity, and the power of love'.[12] This of course presupposes that there is a communal life. This may not be the experience of many people with AS. Jones *et al.* conducted a thematic analysis of personal websites of people with AS and four main themes were identified: alienation, frustration, depression, and a pervasive sense of fear or apprehension.[13]

Few young adults with AS are completely alienated from the surrounding community, although alienation does seem to increase as people get older. Relationships are as important to many people with AS as neurotypicals,[14] although the actuality may not be as rewarding as the fantasy since adults with AS continue to feel 'different' even when in relationships.[15] For neurotypicals, starting a new close relationship was found to be the greatest source of happiness, and ending a close relationship the greatest source of unhappiness, in one survey.[16] What comes in between, when the initial peak of happiness has dwindled, constitutes the challenge of relationship, as Steven's difficulties illustrate.

The maintenance of close relationships requires that the negative aspects of relationships are dealt with as well as the positives.[17] 'Integration' – of learning, of emotions, and with people – is conducive to greater happiness when older,[18] as is empathy for others.[19] Continued satisfaction in close relationships may be increased by positive appraisals of and positive statements to the partner, and these strategies are also successful in defusing negativity over minor issues, but may increase the likelihood of relationship breakdown if applied to more major discontents, which need to be explored even at the cost of short-term increases in conflict and negativity.[20] Knowing when to avoid conflict, and when to engage with it, are important competencies in longer-term relationships, but they rely on social intuitions that may be lacking in people with Asperger syndrome. When people advise, 'don't sweat the small stuff', one has to know when stuff is 'small'. Accurate empathy is required for this.

Same sex couples may be more positive and less negative in their interaction, at least according to a small longitudinal study carried out by the Gottman Institute, but lesbian couples are more emotionally demonstrative than gay male couples.[21] This may account for the clinical observation that stable lesbian relationships seem more common than male partnerships in people with AS seen in the clinic.

Spiritual wellbeing

Some of the most fulfilled adults with AS that I have met have had a strong religious faith and are active participants in a faith community.

Ethics of diagnosis

Receiving a diagnosis of AS changes not only how a person sees themselves, but also how others see them.[22] The expectation is that these changes will be facilitative, but they may not always be so.[23]

It is rare in my experience for even adults with AS to seek out a diagnosis, and even rarer for people with ADHD or autistic disorder, unless there is someone in the background encouraging them. This may be a clinician who is puzzled, a spouse or partner, someone in the criminal justice or care system, or more rarely an employer.

Even highly intelligent adults may sometimes miss the possible social consequences of a diagnosis. So if the assessor knows, or suspects, the interests of a third party, these need to be dealt with, following the guidelines already discussed in Chapter 15 on adolescence.

Some particular issues arise in relation to referrals prompted by life partners, by legal professionals and by employers. Referral by a spouse or partner may be triggered by a failing relationship, and can be a prelude to separation or divorce, or to a realignment and improvement in the relationship. If the diagnosis will prove a pretext for a divorce, it might be helpful to anticipate this before the assessment. Some employers wish to make appropriate adjustments to the workplace, and providing a diagnosis can be of assistance to the client. Other employers may intend to use the diagnosis as the basis for redundancy on medical grounds. An assessment of a patient's ability to care for a child may be requested by a legal professional and a diagnosis of an ASD may work to the patient's disadvantage in these proceedings. Diagnosis may also be requested in criminal proceedings and may lead to an outcome that a few people with an ASD may regret – for example, it may lead to a medical disposal even if, as may happen, the person with an ASD may prefer a custodial one.

The inverse problem may also arise, that the assessor does not consider that there are grounds for a diagnosis, even though the person being assessed may be convinced that they have a diagnosis, and may even already be receiving a variety of benefits on the basis that they have an ASD diagnosis.

If there is any doubt about potential harm to the patient in reaching a diagnosis, it is wise to discuss these issues before beginning the diagnostic assessment. In legal cases it may also be necessary to explain the assessor's primary duty to the court, rather than to the client. In other situations, it may be possible to give the patient some discretion about whether or not a diagnosis is communicated to anyone other than the patient, but not when the opinion is being requested by a court or by a quasi-judicial tribunal, such as a professional registering body.

If a detailed assessment report is provided, some discussion should also take place about who might receive a copy of this, and who it should be shown to by the patient. It is good practice to provide a copy of this report to the patient, but it may be appropriate to advise the patient against showing the full report to parties whose interests may conflict with the patient, such as an employer engaged in a health or disciplinary procedure.

Case example

A 55-year-old laboratory scientist was medically qualified, but not practising in a clinical capacity. He was engaged in a disciplinary procedure with his employer who, he was claiming, had suppressed certain negative findings of a clinical trial, and who had counter-claimed that the doctor was in breach of his duty of confidentiality to the company. During a negotiation with managers over this allegation, the doctor became irate and abusive. He was suspended, and became depressed, leading to the referral for assessment. At the end of the interview, the assessor told the doctor that he had Asperger syndrome and asked him who he would like copies of the report to go to, and he said 'the company'. The assessor thought that this would weaken the doctor's position in relation to this whistleblowing, and increase the likelihood of a dismissal under the disciplinary proceedings. After some discussion, the doctor accepted this point, and the letter was sent only to the referrer and to the doctor himself.

In many jurisdictions, there is a duty to disclose a medical condition that might affect employment, and there is a corollary right, at least in the UK, to expect the employer to make appropriate allowances for a disability. But having a diagnosis does not automatically mean that an employer has the right to know it. No one would notify their employer that they have developed 'presbyopia' simply because they had started to require glasses for reading – unless, that is, their employment required a high level of visual acuity, in which case a person might be derelict in their duty to their employer not to inform them. Presbyacusis, leading to high frequency hearing loss, might be a different matter for anyone who has to perform in meetings, but few people would notify their employer about it. ASD may not have much more impact on work performance than one of these two conditions, and it may therefore be a matter of judgement whether a person is required to inform their employer. If it is their employer who is seeking the diagnosis, or if the person with an ASD wishes their employer to make adjustments for their condition (see below for what these might be), then the information must be given. But if the diagnosis is being sought for other reasons, the person giving the diagnosis may want to discuss with the person being given the diagnosis what the social implications might be, including whether an employer should be told. If there is doubt, it may be appropriate for the person to discuss the matter confidentially with an advocate in the workplace, for example an official in their trade union.

A related issue to fitness for employment is fitness to be a parent. It is not unusual for specialists to be asked for reports to family courts about a parent alleged to have an ASD with an instruction to comment on the parent's fitness to look after a child or children. In accepting these instructions, the specialist accepts the duty to comment on this, and in going along with the assessment, the parent implicitly consents to this assessment being made (sometimes, it is good practice for the specialist to explicitly draw this to the attention of the parent). But sometimes in a contested divorce or when a local authority is seeking a care order, to have an ASD may be presented to the judge as tantamount to being unfit. A specialist providing a report to the family courts must put the interests of the children above other considerations, and should provide an unbiased report. But this should include the arguments for, as well as against, the parent with ASD contributing to the child's upbringing. The specialist may also need to communicate the emotional suffering that a parent deprived of their children experiences. This is not the overriding consideration in such a case, but it is a consideration, and a person with an ASD may not be able to advocate for themselves and the court may assume that the parent has no feelings.

ASPERGER SYNDROME IN ADULTHOOD
Case history: Mr A

Mr A is a pharmacist in middle age who has been having increasing difficulties at work and at home. Two years ago, his son was diagnosed as having Asperger syndrome, and now attends a special school. He and his wife had put their long-standing marital conflicts down to the difficulties of bringing up their son but, after his wife began to read about Asperger syndrome, she realized that her husband also had Asperger problems. He lacked empathy, became absorbed in particular interests which he pursued irrespective of family demands, he was a loner, and he had a routine for everything which could not be broken. Mrs A had begun to discuss separation, and Mr A had himself referred to a specialist centre for diagnosis. He was noted to lack facial expression, and to have a monotonous voice. His answers to questions were long-winded, and he often digressed. Mr A was aware of this himself, and apologized for not getting to the point, but did not change his conversational behaviour and, in fact, seemed unable to change. Mr A's gaze did not at first seem abnormal, but the doctor examining him began to realize that Mr A was not responding to her social cues. The doctor became self-conscious about her own facial expressions because of this. She realized that Mr A was not responding to them, and probably that he was not really 'seeing them'. Once or twice the doctor make a slightly idiomatic remark that threw Mr A, although, after a hesitation, he seemed to be able to interpret what she had said.

When the doctor told Mr A that he had Asperger syndrome, he said that it explained a lot about his lifelong difficulties with other people. At follow-up, Mr A felt better in himself, but had been having more rows at work and at home. He said that now he knew that he had a disorder, he realized that he was doing the best he could as a pharmacist and as a husband. He thought that other people should recognize this, and not be so critical. In particular, Mr A thought that his wife should nag him less, and understand him more. He had told her so on a few occasions, and on two of these had become so threatening that his wife had called the police. Since then, Mr A had spent more and more time on the internet, mainly in contributing to a bulletin board. He considered himself one of the greatest fans of the Russian tennis player, Maria Sharapova. He collected minute information about her life, her activities and her matches.

Mr A's social adaptation is immeasurably greater than that of a person with autistic disorder such as David, who was described in Chapter 12. Mr A has gained a professional qualification and worked constantly since. He has married, and fathered a child. David, of course, is at the other end of his life, but it seems unlikely that he will achieve so much. Mr A's social adaptation, when looked at more closely, is not quite so felicitous. He has never made a friend, unless his fellow discussants on the Sharapova bulletin board can be counted as friends. His wife had been as lonely as Mr A when they first met, and they had come together in mutual relief at not being so alone. Mrs A had fallen pregnant, and the marriage seemed inevitable thereafter. Then there had been the years of working together to create a family. But when their son had begun to present his own difficulties, Mr and Mrs A took opposing views of what to do and the gulf between them had widened ever since.

David was worse when his routine changed. He liked to go out in the car. He hated loud or sudden noises. He liked one particular Beatles song, and had learnt to use the

CD player largely, it seemed, so that he could listen to this song repeatedly. However, it was not clear that David distinguished people from objects, or that he made any distinction between what a person does and what a person intends to do. He did consider that people were agents and not just causes, but he extended the agency to inanimate objects. On one occasion, David dropped a vase onto a tiled floor, and the vase smashed. David smacked the floor, as if to say, 'bad floor for smashing the vase'. David did not seem to have a category of person as agent, or indeed a category of person at all. He lacked, in other words, a 'theory of mind'. This lack applied to himself as well,[24] and David did not seem to have a sense of self. He would bang his face if he was frustrated, just as he could bang a toy or a machine – or his mother.

Mr A had a clear sense of himself. He knew what he liked, and what he wanted. He also had a theory of mind. He was aware of why he so infuriated his wife, and the assistants in the pharmacy where he worked. But, although he had the theory, this did not arise out of an emotional connectedness with others.

Case history: Miss G

Miss G described herself as living her life behind a pane of glass, but despite this, she believed that she understood people better than they understood themselves – possibly because she ignored the emotional ambiguities that other people often dwell on. She has difficulty in making small talk and as a result feels anxious about meeting people she knows who might engage in it. When she is out on the street, she worries that she might meet somebody who will recognize her and want to chat. In her most recent job, in a newsagents, she did not know how to respond when customers made conversation. She said: 'People catch me off guard and I don't know what my response should be.' 'I know what to do to be in their world but can't do it.' Miss G has had numerous jobs previously. They often started promisingly and people sometimes said that she would soon be in line for promotion (she has several A levels from sixth form college) but after a month, Miss G had become so anxious about making a mistake at work that she was regularly late and often missed days. After a few more weeks, she was generally asked to leave.

Miss G rarely used gesture and spoke in a somewhat monotonous voice. She had fleeting enthusiasms, most recently candle dipping. Miss G often became fascinated with a particular word or phrase, and would bring this into conversation even when it was not relevant. At the time that I met her, it was 'fandango'. She had some routines about food, for example never eating toast with butter, and was upset by change. When the packaging on her contraceptive pill was changed, she could not bring herself to take it for a month.

Miss G said that her first sexual relationship began at 14. She had slept with many men since then, not because she is attracted to them, she said, but because they want her. She has had only two long-term relationships, each one affected by Miss G's insecurity about her partner's feelings for her. She has regularly accused them of not caring for her, and this has eventually led to the relationship ending. Fears that she is not loved by her current boyfriend may, like worrying about making a mistake, also cause Miss G to burn herself.

Gender differences

Miss G and Mr A have the same impairment of nonverbal communication, but this similarity is not immediately obvious, particularly as they seem so different in their interest in other people. Mr A was, by his own lights, someone who was more interested in problems than people. His wife's talk of divorce worried him a lot, but more because of the changes that it would make in his life than that he would miss her. She was his only sexual partner, and sexuality had never been important to him. Miss G felt the same way about sex, but had gone along with other men's sexual desires in order to have a relationship with them, which made her feel accepted. She appeared to be much more confident than Mr A but was much more concerned about other people's opinions than he was. In the past, her frequent sexual relationships and her self-harm had been attributed to borderline personality disorder and it was true that she had the high emotional reactivity and ready startle often associated with a history of abuse. But her anxiety was related to her preoccupation about never fitting in, and her doomed attempts to overcome this.

PRESENTING SYMPTOMS

In community-based surveys of adults with either ID or normal intelligence,[25] about half of those meeting research criteria for a diagnosis of ASD will have received a diagnosis previously. The diagnosis is most likely to be missed in adults with Asperger syndrome. I shall therefore consider this diagnosis, and the requirements for making it, in people over the age of 18 in this chapter. The consequences of having AS may be different for adults than they are for younger people, and so I shall also consider how the impact of AS changes as people get older. The chapter will therefore be relevant to adults who have already been diagnosed with AS. A few adults may consider that the AS with which they were diagnosed as children has remitted. So this chapter will also consider 'un-diagnosis' criteria, that is what justifies the clinician in certifying that a person has recovered from the syndrome, which is often spoken of as being lifelong.

Primary impairment or difference
Communication

Nonverbal communication impairments may remain overt in adults, in which case a person may seem odd or eccentric, but this is by no means always the case. Many adults with AS may strive, more or less successfully, to conceal their eccentricities. Adults may school themselves to look at other people directly, and so overcome gaze avoidance, sometimes by developing a rather staring gaze. They may be advised to smile more, and since this fits in with a tendency to be compliant in many people with AS, people with AS may smile a lot more than usual and seem socially responsive and friendly in consequence. Finally, some people with AS may deliberately use gesture and facial expression, and can therefore seem to be almost theatrical in their demonstrativeness with a manner that seems the opposite of communicatively impaired. Careful, prolonged observation will indicate differences from the nonverbal expressiveness of neurotypicals. Deliberate, or posed, expressions have a subtly different quality to involuntary ones, which may be difficult to pin down explicitly but lead to a 'sense' in an observer that they are somehow false or put on. The physiological difference between an involuntary or 'Duchenne' smile and a social or deliberate smile, which may be perceived as being shallow or not genuine, is the closure of the eyes through contraction of the orbicularis oris, and the deepening of the cheek furrows by zygomaticus contraction.

Social anxiety, anger, iatrogenic Parkinsonism or Parkinson's disease may diminish facial expression, and also other channels of nonverbal communication, but this often diminishes as a person becomes less stressed.

Sometimes observations of nonverbal expressiveness can be supplemented by reports of what others have said. If other people do comment on impaired facial expression, it is usually critically and from the point of view of the observer, for example: 'I can never tell what he's thinking' or 'He never looks pleased.'

Impairment of nonverbal expression diminishes in adolescence in atypical Asperger syndrome, although the impairment of nonverbal interpretation does not. However, this latter impairment is usually overlooked in adults. Failure to detect social cues or a failure to show empathy are almost always attributed to motivational or characterological factors as a default. People may rarely complain that they find faces difficult to read, or more rarely still that they cannot recognize a person's face even when they know them well (a form of prosopagnosis). The best indication usually comes from an informant, who might say, 'I have to tell him when I'm upset' or 'He doesn't know how to react, unless I tell him what to do.'

Social interaction
Social interaction in children is developmentally driven. In adults, it is determined by emotion. The quality of social interaction is much less useful diagnostically in adults than it is in children.

Imagination
Imaginative play and imaginative language diminish with age,[26] and this may mean that the impaired social imagination that is so salient in many autistic children becomes a less overt difference in adulthood. Imagination also contributes to empathy and perspective taking, and impaired imagination is most often demonstrated in adults by the consequences of a lack of empathy.

This lack of empathy may also affect everyday social interaction. People with Asperger syndrome, even if they are able to manage task-focused interactions as well as anyone, may have difficulty in unstructured situations in which people share interests and sometimes personal information. Success in these unstructured social situations requires the imaginative projection of oneself into another person's world, and this is difficult for people with an ASD to do.

Repetition
Avoiding the new or the spontaneous, and cleaving to routines and repetition, is a trait that is probably independent of ASD, although it appears in the diagnostic criteria currently. If present in childhood, it tends to persist into adulthood, although the manifestations may

change and become less salient. Ordering cutlery in a particular way in the kitchen, placing CDs in a particular order, always using the same soap or buying the same jackets, all of these may be manifestations of repetitiveness that might be less salient in an adult than they would be in a child, since children are rarely in a position to prevent other people's interference with their routines.

Secondary disability or idiosyncrasy

A qualitative study with 16 'Aspie' participants concluded that adults with AS grapple with feeling different, trying to fit in, and also finding safe spaces.[15] The authors conclude that not fitting in leads to an uncomfortable degree of emotional freedom similar to the 'anomie' that results from having no social order or social regulation.[27] These turbulent emotions lead often to a person with AS feeling unsafe – although another reason may be the bullying and social exclusion that over 90 per cent of adults with AS have received.

Empathic accuracy about negative feelings is a predictor of relationship satisfaction,[28] and the avoidance of relationship breakdown.[29] Contrary to expectation, empathic accuracy in neurotypicals does not increase with relationship duration and appears to be fully developed by late adolescence, suggesting that it is a competence that is acquired in mid adolescence in neurotypicals. Empathy is reduced in many people with ASD (see Chapter 8) and this may be a contributor to the breakdown of close relationships that is often the presenting problem in adults not previously diagnosed as having an ASD.

People with AS have difficulty in empathizing with others. But possibly the greatest influence on balancing positive and negative is emotional regulation. This has two elements, an early prefrontally mediated appraisal element, and a later component involving the suppression of negative emotional responses.[30]

Appraisal is likely to be influenced by upbringing, by experience, and by personal reflection. The quality of relationships, and the experience of alienation or frustration, of an adult with AS is not an inevitable consequence of the AS itself, and may be open to change by further life experience or by psychotherapy or counselling, in a way that the primary impairment of AS is not.

Intimacy and power

Positive and negative feelings are one dimension of relationship that emerges from meta-analyses. Another is dominance or submission, that is the ability to influence others in directions preferred by oneself. Adults can exercise an authority, or legitimated power, in relationships which is normally denied younger people. One element of authority is the power to choose on behalf of others. This may lead to conflict, and in adulthood, the expectation is that this will be resolved by negotiation and persuasion[31] and not by mere coercion. Dealing with conflict is a key skill in assertiveness and persuasion, where potential conflicts need to be anticipated and headed off before they become disruptive. In one study of people with an ASD, a lack of close friendships, loneliness, and depressive symptoms were all linked to high levels of conflict and betrayal in past close relationships.[32]

People with ADHD are also more likely to be rejected by their peers, and to like others more than others like them.[33] People with ADHD are more likely to be involved in conflict, or at least in conflict that leads to higher than normal levels of negativity,[34] and adults with both ADHD and ASD may have particular difficulties both in exercising and in responding to authority.

Authority may be less important for getting one's own way than it is for claiming and keeping a valued place in the family, at work, or in society generally. The loss of place leads to what Weiss called 'social loneliness'.[35] The failure to achieve or hold on to authority may be a significant issue for adults with ADHD, who also have particular difficulty in recognizing, or accepting, the authority of others.

Tertiary handicap or altered life style

Adults cannot rely, as many younger people do, on nearly unconditional and unstinted family support. They are much more at risk of social isolation. Deviance is more likely to lead to rejection, too. Low popularity or high aggressiveness that led to social isolation as a child continue to affect adult social adjustment. Peer exclusion as a child predicts reduced academic achievement and job competence ten years later, and subsequent social withdrawal predicts a lack of intimate relationships.[36] The pattern of social disability is therefore particularly set in adolescence, but joblessness or a lack of romantic relationships as an adult also reduces the chances of finding work or of finding a romantic partner.

Independence in adults with AS

Very few studies have been conducted into social adjustment in adults with AS, although there are more in adults with intellectual disability. Howlin reviewed six follow-up studies of children, excluding two surveys of adults.[37, 38] There was no attempt at a systematic coverage of social adjustment,[39] since the studies included were so varied. Engström et al. extracted items from the Camberwell Assessment of Needs, a widely used but highly medically orientated checklist, and surveyed 16 adults with AS or HFASD.[40] Many of the adults with AS included in all of these studies were living on their own, and many were employed, although sometimes in sheltered settings, but they were almost all reliant on emotional and practical support from family members and on state benefits. Balfe et al., in a community-based sample of 77 adolescents and adults with AS in Sheffield, found lower levels of independence (Table 17.2).[25]

The report identifies some of the capacities that are problematic for many people with ASD, but excludes others, notably those that are connected with personal satisfaction and quality of life rather than the capacities that are linked to social performance.

Table 17.2 Level of independence found in the Sheffield survey

Paid work, unsupported	30%
Paid work, supported	6%
Living with parents	80%
Living independently	21%

Source: Balfe, Chen, *et al.*, 2005.

Enablement by society

The definition of independent living provided in a UK interdepartmental government report identifies capacities that constitute independence,[4] but the ones proposed are most relevant to the proposed three general capacities that constitute independence: choice, control, and accessing community resources. It is difficult to see how these might relate to surviving in a hostile environment, and it might be better to consider them duties of enablement by the community.

DIFFERENTIAL DIAGNOSIS

Frontotemporal dementia

Frontotemporal dementia may reduce cognitive empathy, and may lead to the 'moral insanity' first described by Prichard,[41] in which an awareness of the impact of actions and of their moral significance is reduced.[42] An early sign might be a preference for utilitarian morality over virtue ethics.[43] Frontotemporal dementia is likely to be a difficult differential diagnosis only if there is no developmental history available, and is unlikely in any case to be confused with typical AS, since frontotemporal dementia does not cause an impairment of nonverbal expressiveness.

Prosopagnosia

Right-sided stroke, when it affects non-dominant parietal areas, may produce an impairment of all of the channels of nonverbal communication. There will rarely be diagnostic confusion with AS because the deficit will have occurred suddenly in adulthood and will be associated with other impairments including right-sided paresis for which there may be a characteristic neglect. Developmental prosopagnosia may occur, although rarely, as a familial disorder.[44]

Personality disorder

Psychiatrists are divided about the nosological status of personality disorder. There are those who consider it a useful concept, but a sociocultural one, rather than a medical one. Others consider that personality disorder has the same status as other psychiatric diagnoses, including schizophrenia or dementia. These psychiatrists point to the neuroimaging studies that have been conducted in people with personality disorder, which purport to show findings that are specific to the diagnosis. Other psychiatrists, of whom I am one, consider that personality disorder is a 'category error' in which medicine is being inappropriately applied to social deviance or even to social difference. Given my viewpoint, my approach to the differential diagnosis of personality disorder may differ from some other psychiatrists. In clinical practice, I look independently for signs and symptoms of an ASD or ADHD, relying strongly on the presence or absence of impairments of nonverbal communication in the former, and the presence of impaired working memory with executive dysfunction and a reduced persistence in the latter.

'Bracketing off',[45] the presence or absence of ASD from the emotional quality of relationships, helps to reduce the complexity of the differential diagnosis. Complexity is, however, increased by the psychological consequences of the bullying and social exclusion that most people with an ASD experience from their peers. This leads to persistent shame proneness or low self-esteem, an assumption that others will be hostile, and sometimes a willingness to attack others before they can attack first. These reactions to maltreatment may themselves be misdiagnosed as personality disorder. One way of dealing with this is to use criteria for the assessment of social relationships that are less dependent on social exclusion.

Even among those psychiatrists who are committed to the use of personality disorder as a medical condition, there is disagreement as to the existence or otherwise of specific subtypes of personality disorder. The lumpers, who put all the categories together, have received considerable support from the revival of the term 'psychopath' and its non-specific application to anyone with any personality disorder diagnosis, irrespective of whether or not they show antisocial proclivities. Some of the worst consequences of using the term 'personality disorder' come from it being used as a sufficient diagnosis, without further specification. These consequences include an assumption that having this diagnosis means that the person cannot benefit from medical intervention – or, nowadays, from medical intervention not provided by a specially constituted team of 'specialists'. Another assumption is that any protest or dissent by a person with a diagnosis of personality disorder is a consequence of their diagnosis, and not to be taken as seriously as if made by someone without that diagnosis.

My own practice is to reformulate what other psychiatrists might call personality disorder in terms of managing interpersonal relationships, and the emotions that arise from them. Formulating the problem in this way may have some helpful explanatory value, and may also lead to the patient receiving the additional psychological resources that have been set aside in the UK and in other developed countries for people who have persisting strains in their relationships, including their relationships with strangers, with neighbours, and with community agencies.

My rule of thumb is not to refer to relationship difficulties of this kind unless I can tell the patient beforehand what I think, and they can tell me that to formulate it in this way is helpful.

'Personality disorder' in men
Schizoid personality, shame proneness and 'low self-esteem'
Schizoid personality has long been associated with a lack of empathy, and it has been argued that schizoid personality and Asperger syndrome are the same.[46] I have argued that the traits

of emotional detachment and introversion, which were described by Bleuler and Kretschmer as being the key characteristics of schizoid personality,[47, 48] do occur in people with Asperger syndrome, but are not universal.[49] They may also occur independently (see also Chapter 7 for an illustrative case history). Over the years, my clinical experience is that a sensitivity and consequent aversion to shame are key features both of schizoid personality – where the possibility of shame is averted by withdrawal – and in narcissistic personality where shame is dealt with by being brazen.[50] Shame proneness is often termed 'low self-esteem' or a severe 'lack of self-confidence'.

Case history: Harold

Harold was a fit man in his late thirties who seemed to vibrate with tension. His face seemed devoid of expression, although as the interview went on it became more expressive. His tone of voice and use of gaze were neutral, but did not strike the interviewer as odd or unusual in any way. Harold used gesture appropriately but minimally, and his posture was unexceptionable.

Harold did not want to talk about his parents, and had decided not to ask them to complete a developmental questionnaire. He felt too angry with both of them. He brusquely rejected the interviewer's statement that such developmental information would have been very useful. He described his father as a bully but said that his mother was far worse. She played 'mind games', at one moment being friendly, even so friendly that he wondered if she had sexually abused him, and at other times taking a delight in putting him down, or so it seemed to him. Harold went to school locally, and was sufficiently able to make up for a lack of study and get good enough grades in his school leaving examinations to attend university. He went to the local one, but could not stand the people there whom he thought stuck up and affected, and so he dropped out. He had discovered while at university that both drinking and smoking marijuana relaxed him in a way that nothing else had, and intoxication became the focus of his life. He made some acquaintances through both of these activities, but had no close friends. Girls came and went, but he did not want to become committed. Harold tried to work, but resented the authority structure that always seemed to be present in the workplace, and adjusted his life style so that he could survive on unemployment benefit. He felt, anyway, that he needed time 'to get his head together'. Neither crime nor hard drugs interested him. They would involve him too much with other people.

Harold spent a lot of time reading science fiction, and thinking about his place in the world. The only thing that he was sure about was that he did not want to have any contact with his parents, although he did maintain some contact with his sister. After several years without any particular goal, Harold thought that he should do something about his physical condition and took up jogging. Then someone in the local pub said that he was looking for a partner for a climb, and Harold said that he would give it a try. Over the next few years, climbing became an obsession. He gained a reputation as a fearless climber who would tackle anything, but who was also thought to be dangerous because he preferred to climb alone. Harold explained that other climbers were always competitive, and that this took away the purity of being in nature. Climbers always wanted someone to tell them how great they were, Harold said. He just wanted to climb. He didn't care what other people thought of his climbing. When asked what he enjoyed about climbing, Harold said that he never experienced enjoyment, but he did feel more at peace on the rocks than anywhere else.

To finance his climbing, Harold had to have a regular income and he took a menial job, which he had kept up to the time of being interviewed. He decided to move into a housing association flat that would give him a more reliable base. Soon after this, he began to go out with an older woman he met at work and, after a few years, moved in with her. The relationship was precarious because Harold had regular periods when he would say that life was pointless, and talked about suicide. His partner also said that Harold seemed unaware of her emotional needs. He resented her having friends round, and seemed happy never to meet anyone else. He had no friends of his own.

Things worked out well between them if she constantly adjusted to Harold, but he could never adjust to her. Harold, his partner thought, just did not seem to tune in to other people emotionally. Harold said that he could do so, but it exhausted him, as if he could do it only by a great effort. Harold also had a similar problem with sexuality: if he ejaculated during intercourse, he was subsequently overcome by a devastating feeling of emptiness, as if his life essence had been drained away. Masturbation did not have this effect, and Harold normally preferred this, although he recognized that he had a duty to try to satisfy his partner, too.

Harold meets DSM-IV criteria for schizoid personality: he is detached from others emotionally, he prefers his own company, he prefers solitary activities, he rarely experiences pleasure, avoids sexual activity with another person, has no friends other than his partner, does not want contact with other family members or other close relationships, and he seems cold. However, there are no other developmental features of ASD and Harold has none of the communicative problems in adulthood that are so prominent in other people diagnosed as having an ASD. Moreover, Harold's problem does really seem emotional, not only in the domain affected, but also in its origins. We expect an emotional problem to be a consequence of previous problematic relationships. If this were the consequence of a mild degree of ASD, then it would be expected that everyone with an ASD would also have a schizoid personality. But this is not true, just as it is not true that everyone with an ASD is socially isolated, or lacks friends.[51]

Harold has an inability, or an unwillingness, to make an emotional commitment to another person. Fairbairn, who made a detailed study of this condition, attributed it to upbringing,[52] as Harold did himself. Studies have supported this. For example, Torgersen *et al.* found that the heritability of schizoid personality disorder as defined by DSM-IV was 0.29, while that of personality disorders as a whole was over twice as much, at 0.6.[53]

Borderline and histrionic personality

Women with a diagnosis of borderline personality disorder do not normally have nonverbal impairment. If they do, it is likely that they have AS rather than borderline personality disorder. Adult women with AS are much less likely to be diagnosed as having schizoid personality as men, but much more likely to be diagnosed as having borderline personality disorder, as Miss G had been. The hyperarousal associated with borderline personality disorder is particularly associated with sexual abuse.[54] There has been no survey of the frequency of sexual abuse in a representative sample of people with ASD, but my clinical experience is that it is raised in both men and women, or rather it would be raised if they recognized that being used sexually, as Miss G was, was indeed a kind of *ab*-use. Sexual abuse seems particularly likely to lead to self-injury, again as it did in Miss G, and as it has in others of my patients. The appropriate diagnosis in them, and perhaps all of the other women with AS who are being pejoratively labelled and stigmatized as having 'borderline personalities', is that they have AS and a kind of PTSD following on from sexual abuse.

Amphetamine misuse

Little is known about the long-term effects of amphetamine misuse, but there is some suggestion that it may cause a reduction of face interpretation ability.[55] Some adults with ADHD who misuse amphetamine and have reduced empathy may not have ASD but may be suffering from the effects of the amphetamine. The developmental history in these latter cases will be purely of ADHD without ASD symptoms.

Paranoid states

Some adolescents with ASD and social phobia develop sensitive ideas of reference in adolescence or early adulthood, and a few may have more elaborate beliefs that others are harming them or conspiring against them.

Case example

> Mr R had a family history of drug-induced psychosis, and had one episode when he thought that he was being followed by a demon when he had been using cannabis. He subsequently often misinterpreted what others were saying, for example he had been at a bus station waiting for his girlfriend (his first, a Thai woman whom he had met at the age of 40), when he overheard a couple talking about an Arsenal football match. Mr R was sure that they were talking about him and that they had concluded that he was gay. He deduced this from their use of the word 'Arsenal', which he told me was 'arse-nal' and therefore a reference to sodomy.

There may have been other risk factors for suspiciousness in Mr R as well as his family history. He suffered from nocturnal panic, induced by lucid dreams, although these were successfully treated with citalopram. He was also addicted to internet gambling and this led to further sleep deprivation. However, there is other evidence that adolescents with AS are more inclined to feel that others are against them.[56] There is also evidence from an fMRI study comparing people with AS, people with paranoid schizophrenia, people with schizophrenia, and neurotypicals rating the trust worthiness of faces of similarities between people with AS and those with paranoid schizophrenia. These two groups had significantly reduced neural activation in the right amygdala and fusiform area than the neurotypicals and less activation of left ventrolateral prefrontal cortex during the task than either the neurotypicals or the group with other forms of schizophrenia.[57] Paranoid suspicions about others can be a cause of aggression.

There is no evidence that people with paranoid states have impaired nonverbal expression, but it may be difficult to make this judgement if someone is being treated with antipsychotics. The developmental history may therefore have to be relied on to make the differential diagnosis. Established paranoid states are rare in AS, and the differential diagnosis is an unusual one.

Covert positive schizophrenia
This is discussed in Chapter 15.

ASSOCIATED PROBLEMS
Developmental prosopagnosia
An inability to recognize who other people are from their faces may be associated with the reduced ability to read emotions in face, and can itself lead to substantial social anxiety, driven by the fear of offending other people or the embarrassment of not recognizing people who expect to be recognized.[58] Unusually, the social anxiety may be greater when meeting family members or good friends than when meeting new people: this is the reverse of social anxiety in the common social phobias.

Cognitive impairment
Word learning difficulties may continue into adulthood in people with AS who have a history of language impairment or ADHD.[59]

Psychiatric disorder
Psychiatric disorder in adults with AS has been little studied, and there are no data on community samples. People who are referred to a psychiatric assessment clinic may be expected to have more co-morbidity. In a study of 110 adults seen at a specialist clinic in the UK, 61 per cent had another, co-morbid disorder, and 24 per cent had two or more.[60] The level of anxiety and ADHD was lower and of schizophrenia higher than in the adolescent group reported in Table 5.2 in Chapter 15, but this is not consistent with results from my own clinic and further data are required.[60] Rates of depression were higher than the general population in the Spain et al. study, and about the same as those in adolescents.[60] In another clinic sample, the commonest type of depression was reported to meet criteria for bipolar disorder rather than major depression.[61]

Health problems
Hypercholesterolaemia has been reported in adults with AS,[62] but it is not clear whether this is linked to diet or life style. No medical disorders are definitely linked to uncomplicated AS otherwise, but adult obesity may be a consequence of co-morbid ADHD,[63] and this could also account for the hypercholesterolaemia reported by Dziobek et al.[62] Obesity may also be a complication of the antipsychotic medication that is sometimes prescribed to people with an ASD.

AETIOLOGY

Aetiology is discussed in Chapter 10. There is no aetiology that emerges in adulthood for the first time, although some people who have coped with previous life transitions without an explicit diagnosis of Asperger syndrome may break down at or after university, or even in mid-life, with their symptoms of AS becoming more manifest and therefore recognized for the first time.

INVESTIGATIONS

No investigations may be required in adults newly diagnosed with definite AS, but a neuropsychological investigation providing information about specific developmental disorders and executive function is often useful if vocational counselling, life-style counselling or employment counselling are planned. An IQ test has no diagnostic significance: verbal-performance mismatch is not typical of ASD,[64, 5] but the sub-test scores can provide useful information about a person's cognitive profile that can be applied to planning for the future. A work-based assessment may help if there are work-related difficulties. An assessment of everyday living skills may help in planning how to increase independence. Keeping a diary or using experience sampling may help in treatment planning. Assessment of family or couple interaction may sometimes be indicated.

If there is a strong family history of developmental disorder or if the person being assessed appears to have dysmorphic facies, then referral to a clinical genetics service for genetic investigation may be indicated. The increasing number of genes associated with ASD, the recognition of haploinsufficient cases in which the full phenotype is not expressed, and the unreliability of facial abnormalities as a marker of genetic abnormality may in the near future lead to increased referral for genetic screening, however, and the development of better clinical guidelines for when screening is likely to be of value.

Routine physical examination is not indicated if there is no history suggestive of a medical disorder, but there may be a case for measuring head circumference as a marker of possible genetic syndrome. A history of epilepsy is an indication for a physical examination, including an examination of the skin with and without ultraviolet illumination. Undiagnosed epilepsy should lead to referral to an epilepsy clinic. An MRI is indicated only if there is a suggestion in the history of a focal neurological disorder, if neurological examination is abnormal or if there is a strong suggestion of frontal lobe impairment.

INTERVENTIONS

Recognition

As at every age, recognition of AS is itself more often empowering than disabling. This is because developmental disorders are not, as some clinicians may tacitly think, created by diagnosis, but exert their effects whether or not they are recognized. This is true of

ADHD, too.[65] Recognition not only enables professional intervention, but also helps family and friends to have more realistic expectations, and the person with AS him- or herself to implement more effective 'work-arounds' for their condition. It also means that the person with AS is less likely to feel that they are blameworthy.

Advocacy and self-advocacy

Adults with AS may be disabled by their coping strategies. As already noted, social withdrawal is associated with reduced success in making intimate relationships, for example. One consequence of the diagnostic assessment is that the person with the diagnosis begins to think of different ways that they may deal with problematic situations in life, including the consequences of their AS. But disablement also imposes a duty on others to do what they can to enable. Advocacy, both by others and by oneself, is the term used for the process by which a person asserts their rights to be enabled. So one consequence of obtaining a diagnosis is that a person may have the right to advocate for their own enablement.

Advocates

Advocates are one kind of carer who may act as supporters in the advocacy process. People with AS may make good advocates for each other, but may be less good at dealing with any conflicts that may arise. Other related roles are buddy, mentor and befriender.

Peers

Befrienders do not bring specific expertise to their role, but act as surrogates for friends. An increasing number of adults with AS who cannot maintain peer friendships face to face are able to make them online, either through participation in fan groups, special interest groups, or multi-user games, all of which are likely to have attached discussion forums and chatrooms, but also in meeting places for people with AS, such as Second Life.

Assertiveness training

Problems with conflict resolution are a persistent difficulty for adults with AS. There has been no research into whether this can be resolved, but assertiveness training that is used to help people with emotional difficulties with conflict may be helpful for people with AS, too.

Care management

New arrangements in the UK mean that people with disabilities may directly employ their carers, or their caring agencies. On paper this is an excellent means of empowering them, but in practice it is difficult for many people with AS to see enough of the broad picture of their care to be able to see gaps where they occur, and to get an overall impression of the work of this or that agency. One advantage, though, is that it encourages more flexible care packages. Many people with AS may need only intermittent intervention and the direct employment of carers may make this kind of flexibility more likely.

Sheltered or supported accommodation

Independence in housing makes an important contribution to the quality of life of many young adults, although there is a growing trend for young adults to remain in the parental home or to return to it in later life, sometimes after a failed relationship.

It cannot be assumed that independent living is an appropriate goal for every person with an ASD.

For those who aspire to live independently, live-in care (sheltered accommodation) may sometimes be required but others may be able to manage with carers who visit (supported care). Sheltered care may be required because a person needs a level of supervision or monitoring, or because they are vulnerable to exploitation or bullying by their neighbours or acquaintances.

Employment

The UK National Autistic Society surveyed adults with ASD in 2001 and found that 6 per cent of more able and 2 per cent of less able were in full-time employment, with a further 4 per cent in part-time employment.[66] A more recent report, based on a small number of UK areas, but compiled by the prestigious UK National Audit Office concluded that the number in work could be substantially increased, and the number drawing benefit reduced, by work preparation and support, coupled with supported employment. This paper seems to have been written with little input from experienced workers in the field,[67] and may have given undue emphasis to the marginal changes produced by innovation rather than to the enduring effects of regular services. Many people with ASD, even people who are in other respects very able, are unlikely to be able to find or hold down a job.

Employment preparation and supported employment, particularly with the assistance of alternative employees who can work when a person with ASD is unable to, are excellent ideas on paper. Employment preparation has been shown to be effective over a long period in some areas,[68] but in others, schemes that have been begun have had to be closed because of a lack of employers.

Schemes rely on an adequate supply of employers willing to make the necessary adjustments. In some areas, where people with an ASD may have particular skills to offer, such as IT, certain schemes have worked well. But it is likely that opportunities for work will remain restricted for people who are markedly socially impaired with ASD. This is not to say that employment preparation and support should be abandoned. They are valuable for some people with an ASD who have worked and wish to return after a period of unemployment; they may also be appropriate for people with an ASD who have employable skills, but who lack interview skills or have difficulty in adjusting to new situations, both of which may act as barriers into work.

Crisis intervention

As already noted, adults with AS are vulnerable in transitions. Early intervention – including early recognition that there is a problem – is important and that means that someone recognizes the problem, and the potential for intervention. This is a challenge for services, who may 'know' about people who are actively engaged, but then forget about former clients. Counsellors or mental health workers who are experienced in dealing with the problems of people with an ASD may be best placed to help with these crises, but community teams can provide valuable assistance using their accustomed mix of assessment, psychological assistance, and medication if necessary, even without any direct experience of people with an ASD.

Treatment of associated conditions
ADHD
Treatment of any co-morbid ADHD should be considered if it is leading to functional difficulties. Amphetaminics are (in 2010) the treatments for which there is the best evidence of efficacy in adults. Although some adults with ADHD self-medicate, surprisingly few are drawn to illicit amphetamine. However, when they do use the drug, they may report an increase in attention that increases work functioning, suggesting that treatment would also have knock-on benefits. The risks of drug misuse may be greater in adults, and the treatment of choice may therefore be slow-release methylphenidate.

Other psychiatric disorders
The detection and treatment of co-morbid psychiatric disorder is particularly important in adults with AS, as the development of anxiety is often the factor that provokes breakdown during transitions.

As in neurotypicals, drug treatment is rarely the first choice in the anxiety disorders, and psychological intervention or therapeutic counselling should therefore be offered. Drug treatment may sometimes have to be combined with psychological treatment if the anxiety is so severe that it makes it impossible for a person to travel to appointments, to concentrate during appointments, or to make the behavioural changes that are necessary to consolidate treatment so that it has a long-term effect. The SSRIs continue to be the most useful first-line treatment. My clinical experience is that drug company claims that these have differential effects is not substantiated in practice, although they do differ in their side-effects and it is the latter that are most likely to determine the choice of medication.

The medical treatment of other psychiatric disorders should be along conventional lines, but much lower doses of drugs should be used if there is any suggestion of focal neurological abnormality since this may result in greater sensitivity to medication. Conventional doses in these circumstances may seem to be ineffective because they are, in effect, overdoses.

Counselling
Independent living and employment of carers
Independent living for older adolescents and for adults may offer an improved quality of life over living with the family of origin, but this should not be assumed. Independent living may entail considerable loneliness and empty hours. One reason that independent living may improve quality of life is the relationship with parents – who often remain the people who are most emotionally close – improves with an increase in distance and a decrease in sources of conflict.

Independent living can be augmented by assistance from carers that may be of a practical kind or may be a source of social support, either explicitly through befriending schemes or indirectly by providing companionship when using community facilities.

In the UK, people with an ASD, like other disabled people, may be given a budget for care that they manage themselves, acting as employers for their own carers.

Being an employer requires a social understanding not only of what can reasonably be expected of an employee but also of what the employee can expect of themself. Some people with an ASD may be too compliant in this situation, but others may be too exacting. Independent mediation may sometimes be called for and, in the case of people with ASD who have a series of caring agencies, each terminated with the breakdown of the employing relationship, counselling may be required to help work through scenarios with the person with an ASD so that they can develop a clearer sense of what they can, and cannot, reasonably expect.

Work

Similar issues may arise at work. A person with an ASD may be overly compliant, putting their own legitimate interests and concerns to one side and going along with bullying or exploitation, or they may become too exacting. Other work-related issues arise from the requirement to fit in with others, to socialize, and to allow the goals of the organization to govern time allocation.

Bullying has been considered already in a separate section. In some industries it may be entrenched in the culture with new apprentices being sent out for a 'pint of elbow grease' or given a pejorative nickname as soon as they start in the firm.

Exploitation may be more difficult to demonstrate. The least popular or the newest employees may be routinely given the least attractive task, the most weekend, evening or night work, or the least helpful foreman. However, people with an ASD may come to feel that they are continuing to be used to do tasks or duties that other employees would not only refuse, but also feel that they had the right to refuse. Part of the problem may be that in a business of any size, employees will have a reference group of other workers with whom they can rehearse grievances and find them either legitimized or pooh-poohed. A person with an ASD is unlikely to have a reference group and may therefore lack the encouragement that others have to make legitimate grievances known, or may err in the other direction, and earn a reputation for being sensitive or work-shy by complaining about employment practices that other workers accept.

A counsellor can, in this circumstance, be most helpful simply by acting as the representative of a hypothetical reference group.

Work-related socializing – saying 'Hi' to acquaintances, remembering confidences, being polite and non-confrontational in areas of close proximity like lifts and car parks, sharing in common areas like kitchens, fridges and open working spaces – all of these may be challenging for someone with an ASD who might not find the work itself challenging. A counsellor can be of most assistance by working through scenarios as they arise. Particular attention should be given to the natural but often self-destructive tendency for some people with an ASD to assume that others are being unfair or discriminating whenever a conflict or misunderstanding arises. One approach that may be fruitful is to consider not just procedures, but social and emotional 'rules' too. For example, Michael Argyle's rules of friendship include showing loyalty to friends and behaving reciprocally, such as giving a confidence in exchange for a confidence or vice versa, or buying the tea bags if one did not buy them previously.[69]

Individual counsellors may have their own 'rules'. The main contribution of the counsellor is not, however, the rule itself but how to apply them.

Socializing outside work may be one of the greatest challenges for people with an ASD who can manage to socialize in work. Although it may be tempting to avoid all such situations, counsellors may also help workers to consider a minimum number of attendances that will prevent them from becoming isolated within work and to select the easiest occasions to make up this minimum number.

Many people with Asperger syndrome may find it difficult to switch tasks, preferring to complete the one that they are working on to their satisfaction. Their employer may, however, want them to switch as new organizational demands arise and may, anyway, be willing to accept a quick fix rather than a detailed solution. Counsellors can do little to help what is, essentially, a clash of values but can prevent some of the worst impact of the conflict if, as may often happen, each side begins to stigmatize the other for their attitude.

People with Asperger syndrome may sometimes ask whether or not they should declare their condition at interview. There is no definitive answer and counsellors should avoid giving directive advice. The answer depends in some degree on how relevant the ASD is to the work being undertaken. If, at a later date, the employee advances their ASD as an explanation for their inability to carry out work that was in their job description or ask for reasonable adjustments to their working conditions to be made, the fact that they did not mention their ASD at interview may count against them (if, that is, they had a formal diagnosis at the time). However, employers cannot now, at least in the UK, require that potential employees volunteer their medical history.

Many developed countries have enacted legislation against discrimination in the workplace, including discrimination against people with an ASD. This may entail that employers make reasonable adjustments to accommodate workers with a disability, such as ramp access to buildings, toilets with fittings that make them usable by wheelchair users, and so on. Reasonable adjustments for people with cognitive or social impairments are more contentious. Counsellors may be involved as interim advocates while a client is negotiating with an employer about adjustment. They should encourage the person with an ASD to find a friend or advocate who can act in this capacity in the longer term, as there may be a conflict between helping a client to accept a situation emotionally and encouraging an employee to advocate robustly for an improvement in their working conditions.

Sexual satisfaction

Sexual satisfaction as an end in itself is neither giving in to evil, nor a cause for physical exhaustion, nor a prerequisite for good physical or mental health, although all of these positions have been held in the past. But it is still considered an almost indispensable element of a good quality life and, therefore, seeking sexual satisfaction, like the pursuit of happiness, can be considered to be a right. But both pursuits may adversely affect others and so the right to seek sexual satisfaction must be qualified by the impact of that search on others. It is not a licence to offend, assault or spread disease.

Although this may hardly need stating, parents and professional carers may find the topic of sexuality in a person with an ASD perturbing and it may be difficult to apply the same matter of fact principles that one would to a neurotypical adolescent or adult. One reason may be that a person with an ASD may have greater difficulty in imagining the impact of their sexual approaches or desires on others. Another may be that a person with an ASD may lack social intuition about what is, or is not, appropriate sexual expression in public. Finally, sexual desire may be directed towards carers or other people who are unlikely to requite it. Neurotypical adolescents may have an inner sense of their value in the sexual marketplace and may be willing to trim the expression of their sexual desires accordingly. It is painful to learn, but even more painful to be told, that one is aspiring to have a relationship that will never materialize.

Some people with an ASD seem willing and able to dispense with sexual desire in order to avoid these complexities. But many people with an ASD are able to find sexual satisfaction in relationship, and practical counselling and advice may help them to do so.[70] Peer relationships are particularly challenging for people with an ASD as may be having the responsibility to care for a child. So some people with an ASD may develop relationships with people much older or younger than themselves, or be drawn to homosexual rather than heterosexual relationships. Parents may find these sexual choices disappointing, even a reason for criticism, and this may increase the pressure on the person with an ASD and undermine the relationship. Counselling, or at least advice giving, may therefore need to extend to family members.

Genetic counselling

FISH reagents are becoming available for a wider range of genetic disorders associated with ASD. Many of these disorders may not be familial, in that they arise de novo in the individual who has them, but may be hereditary in that they can be passed on to future generations. However, some may be familial, although previous generations may have been affected without a diagnosis being made.

Investigation of a condition in an unsuspecting person may have implications for their own hopes to have a family, and also those of their siblings or even children, if the children are carriers. It is unethical to suppress the results of an investigation, and counselling should therefore precede genetic testing and take into account the likelihood of a positive genetic finding being made, along with its possible implications. Specialist training programmes exist for genetic counsellors, and most genetics clinics have a counselling service that will offer a pre-testing service.

Relationships and therapeutic counselling or psychotherapy

Relationship counselling and therapeutic counselling by people with Asperger syndrome and their spouses are increasingly in demand. Anecdotal evidence suggests that counsellors who have Aspie experience can provide valuable help to couples in finding emotionally satisfactory patterns of relationship and help individuals to find greater life satisfaction. However, there is a lack of research evidence.

More focused interviews include assertiveness training, focusing on conflict resolution, anxiety management and cognitive training, with a particular emphasis on executive problems.[71]

Many counsellors and psychotherapists are already using a mix of these interventions, based on the principles that have been pioneered in other groups, and modifying them for the more concrete and solution-focused orientation of people with an ASD. However, their efficacy has not been systematically evaluated.

ISSUES
Science
The genetics of ASD and other developmental disorders have been altered by two surprising consequences of the human genome project. The first was that the uniqueness of humanity is not reflected in our genome, which is surprisingly similar to our chimpanzee cousins. The second is that the genome is not a genetic code at all, but a complex and interacting biological system that yields a reliably working phenotype, but with considerable potential for adaptation. Add to this the significant epigenetic effects of early environment, and it is almost surprising that heredity is as reliable as it is.

This genetic diversity is expressed within a single genome by the unexpectedly high number of copy number variations and other polymorphisms. These polymorphisms become even more frequent in populations close to humanity's origin in east Africa.

The reduction in genetic diversity in more distant populations may be the result of small populations only having succeeded in migrating further afield, but may have also been a consequence of cultural control of phenotypic variation.

Functional imaging studies of ASD have led to a homologous conclusion to that of genetic studies. 'Silent' areas of the cortex persist, just as do introns in the genome filled with apparently meaningless repetitions, but the suspicion grows that these areas are hardly redundant. The frontal lobes of the brain used to be thought of as redundant, and neurosurgeons were willing to surgically ablate them less than a century ago. Neuroscientists now consider the frontal cortex, and particularly the pre-frontal cortex, to be essential substrates for many of the capacities that are thought of as uniquely human – empathy, for example. However, in another homology with the genome, fewer and fewer brain areas have unique psychological functions. Instead they are nodes on networks that interact with other networks, and it is the interaction and the brain's interaction with its environment, that corresponds most closely to psychological description.

Nature cannot afford to throw away and start again. Organisms cannot be taken offline the way that machines can. New developments are made by cobbling something new with something old, and making something different out of it.

Values
Understanding how diverse normality can be may be a challenge for health professionals, and part of the excitement of working with people with ASD will be that the science that underlies the medicine will be of this new and challenging kind. But another implication of the new

genetics is that diversity is not a mistake or a breakdown in an otherwise deterministic code, but built in. Phenotypic diversity is therefore the natural condition. Cultural factors such as sexual attraction for the average face or the alienation of individuals who are physically or psychologically different may play a much larger role in ensuring that identifiable human phenotypes exist.

If genetic stability is not natural, then neurotypicality may not be natural either, but a consequence of culture. Cultures come and go, perhaps not arbitrarily but in response to changing climate, population density and inventions. Within many Western cultures, the values and emotional responses shared by many 'neurotypical' individuals seem right and proper. In particular, the connectedness with other people on what I have called the interbrain seems to be one of the essences of humanity. Many of us might quote Donne, who wrote that no man is an island. But we should not assume that this is a natural condition of humanity, only that it is the most dominant expression of the human genome and the human brain at the moment.

Perhaps readers may not wish to reflect so deeply on the human condition. Some readers may think that the disadvantage that many people with an ASD labour under may be sufficient argument that ASD is a disability and that anyone with an ASD would exchange that state for neurotypicality if they could. But to come to this conclusion is to apply values: about wellbeing, about satisfaction, about – if this does not seem too rarefied – the purpose of living. Many people with ASD are preoccupied by these issues too, but from their different perspective. Their conclusions are as admissible as ours to the wider debate. Sometimes listening to our patients can illuminate our own concerns and turn a clinical encounter into a different kind of meeting, the kind that can sometimes also happen between two strangers who are for a short time taking nothing for granted and putting up no barriers of self-deception. Meeting with someone with ASD is more often like that, at least for me, than meeting with any of my other patients.

Strengths

This book has focused on impairments, like most medical textbooks. I have recognized that these impairments may sometimes not be as long-lasting as we assume, and that they may also be more situation dependent than we assume: more like dispositions, sometimes, than impairments at all.

Fortunately there is a growing literature written by people who take a different view. They may love, value or deeply respect someone with an ASD and wish to testify to that. They may be fascinated by the skill of someone with an ASD who has a mathematical, or computing, or physics genius. Indeed, they may argue that we need people with an ASD to make their special contributions to these areas. However, it is less often that people write about the plus side of social impairment and it is on this note that I will end. In an interesting study of Schadenfreude, Shamay-Tsoory concluded that people with an ASD did not rejoice over other's misfortunes, as neurotypicals are accustomed to do.[72] Life for a person with an ASD is not a zero-sum game. If everyone sticks to the rules, there is enough for everyone without competing, getting the better of anyone, charming anyone away from anyone else, or selling more than the next person just to show that one is a better business person.

Sartre argued that power relations are engendered by scarcity.[73] Trying to get a scarce resource almost always means beating someone else to it. However, combating cold, hunger and thirst may no longer be the drivers of civilization that they once were, at least not for the moment, and not in fortunate areas of the world. Our main driver may be almost the opposite: how to avoid the poisoning effects of greed or lust. Perhaps new ways of relating to others may be better at dealing with these effects than competition and struggle. In this respect, people with an ASD may have something to teach neurotypicals.

Appendix

ETHICS AND ASD

When referral is initiated by parents, as it often is even when the AS sufferer concerned is an adult, special care must be taken to safeguard the patient's right to a confidential assessment. It is often useful to negotiate with the patient how much parents should be involved before the assessment takes place – sometimes, even before an appointment is sent. It is, fortunately, rare for people with AS to prevent a parent, or a carer, from being involved. With the patient's permission, I obtain further information, particularly about early development, from a person other than the patient and I often take the opportunity of counselling parents or carers about AS. Parents may ask about the diagnosis, prognosis and treatment of an adolescent or an adult with AS, and may sometimes suggest that this information should be given to them alone, and not given to the AS sufferer.

My present position is that I ask permission of the person with AS to see their parents, and to discuss these matters with them, and that I further ask the patient whether or not they wish to have the same information that I give their parents about their condition. I also offer to send the AS sufferer a copy of my letter to the referring doctor. However, I am influenced by my own assumption that it may sometimes be harmful for a person with AS to perceive themselves as having a medical condition that is likely to be lifelong and for which there is no specific treatment. My approach is influenced by the values prevailing in the practice of medicine in the UK and may not be appropriate in other countries. However, clinicians do need to be clear how they solve the conflicting ethical demands of beneficence and autonomy.

Many people with ASD, although not all, are vulnerable to exploitation or coercion. This vulnerability can create ethical issues for services and for the criminal justice system,[1] and many of these are now dealt with in statute law or in codes of practice. Since these vary from one legislature to another, details have not been given in this book. The issues include taking appropriate measures to communicate with someone with an ASD to minimize unnecessarily coercive treatment (for example, by requiring trained staff to undertake assessments for compulsory detention to hospital); assessing capacity to give consent or to make decisions, and providing support to make such decisions; following appropriate guidelines for interviewing vulnerable witnesses in forensic contexts; providing witness support when appropriate in court or tribunal proceedings; recognizing the role that carers play as advocates; and minimizing false confessions.[2]

NOTES

PREFACE

1. Hong and Hong, 2000, p.157.
2. Tantam, 2009.
3. Kanner, Rodriguez, *et al.*, 1972.
4. Whitaker, 1985.

INTRODUCTION

1. Asperger, 1944.
2. Kanner, 1943.
3. Wing, 1981.
4. American Psychiatric Association, 2001. a) p.69.
5. Asperger, 1979.
6. De Sanctis, 1908.
7. Heller, 1908.
8. Barr, 1898.
9. Fitzgerald, 2005.
10. Hobson, 1995.
11. American Psychiatric Association, 1987.
12. World Health Organization, 1992.
13. Rimland, 1964.
14. Wing, 1996b.
15. Anderson, 2001.
16. Ritvo, Freeman, *et al.*, 1989.
17. Wing and Gould, 1979.
18. Wing, 1996a.
19. Bertrand, Mars, *et al.* 2001.
20. Brown, Freeman, *et al.*, 2001.
21. Breslau, Kessler, *et al.*, 1998.
22. Reiss, 2009.
23. Gater, Goldberg, *et al.*, 1997.
24. Baron-Cohen, 2000.
25. Guevara, Lozano, *et al.*, 2001.
26. Jarbrink and Knapp, 2001.
27. Shimabukuro, Grosse, *et al.*, 2008.
28. Jarbrink, McCrone, *et al.*, 2007.
29. Knapp, 1997.
30. Argyle and Henderson, 1984.
31. Goffman, 2001.
32. Bradshaw and Sheppard, 2000.
33. Bettelheim, 1973.
34. Eisenberg and Kanner, 1956.
35. Kanner and Eisenberg, 1957.
36. Burmeister, McInnis, *et al.*, 2008.
37. Geschwind, 2008.
38. Adolphs, Spezio, *et al.*, 2008.
39. Dalton, Nacewicz, *et al.*, 2007.
40. Ozgen, Hop, *et al.*, 2008.
41. Hallahan, Daly, *et al.*, 2009.
42. Hobbs, Kennedy, *et al.*,2007.
43. Mraz, Green, *et al.*, 2007.
44. Hazlett, Poe, *et al.*, 2005.
45. Ben, Kronfeld-Duenias, *et al.*, 2007.
46. Wang, Jiang, *et al.*, 2007.
47. Wolosin, Richardson, *et al.*, 2007.
48. Makris, Biederman, *et al.*, 2007.
49. McAlonan, Cheung, *et al.*, 2007.
50. Krain and Castellanos, 2006.
51. Valera, Faraone, *et al.*, 2006.
52. Brieber, Neufang, *et al.*, 2007.
53. Durston, Hulshoff, *et al.*, 2004.
54. Elia and Devoto, 2007.
55. Hoekstra, Bartels, *et al.*, 2007.
56. Chen, Zhou, *et al.*, 2008.
57. Nijmeijer, Hoekstra, *et al.*, 2009.
58. Van Essen, 2005.
59. Tantam, 2012.
60. Suomi, van der Horst, *et al.*, 2008.
61. Ross, 1967.
62. For a critical review, see Rutter, Kreppner, *et al.*, 2009.
63. Koren-Karie, Oppenheim, *et al.*, 2009.
64. Barnett, 1997.
65. Creak, 1972.
66. Favazza, 1977.
67. McNeil, Polloway, *et al.*, 1984.
68. Stevens, Sonuga-Barke, *et al.*, 2008.
69. Rutter, Andersen-Wood, *et al.*, 1999.
70. Hoksbergen, Laak, *et al.*, 2005.
71. Colvert, Rutter, *et al.*, 2008a.
72. Hobson, 2007.
73. Heinrichs and Domes, 2008.
74. Marazziti and Catena, 2008.
75. Woollett, Spiers, *et al.*, 2009.
76. Feinberg, 2008.
77. Isles and Wilkinson, 2008.
78. Guan, Haggarty, *et al.*, 2009.
79. Glaser, 2000.
80. Lim, Bielsky, *et al.*, 2005.

81. Rapin and Tuchman, 2008.
82. Anderson, 2007.
83. Tabelow, Piëch, *et al.*, 2009.
84. Ballerini, Cabibbo, *et al.*, 2008.
85. Hare, Camerer, *et al.*, 2009, p.646.
86. Poldrack, 2008.
87. Nagel, 1979.
88. Mar, 2004, p.1421.
89. Falk, 2009.

90. Yuan, 2009.
91. Fitzgerald, 2000.
92. Tantam, 2009.
93. Merritt, 2008.
94. Bilder, Sabb, *et al.*, 2009, p.30.
95. Tantam, 2002b.
96. Vygotsky, 1966.
97. Schwartz, Henderson, *et al.*, 2009.
98. Diewald and Mayer, 2003.

CHAPTER I NEUROLOGY OF THE SUPERFICIAL STRUCTURES OF THE BRAIN

1. Plessen, Bansal, *et al.*, 2006.
2. Barr, 2003.
3. Gazzaniga, 2000.
4. Grèzes, Frith, *et al.*, 2004.
5. Kingstone, Friesen, *et al.*, 2000.
6. Molina, Ruata, *et al.*, 1986.
7. Happé, Brownell, *et al.*, 1999.
8. Charbonneau, Scherzer, *et al.*, 2003.
9. Ozonoff and Miller, 1996.
10. Levin, Scheller, *et al.*, 1996.
11. Hendren, De Backer, *et al.*, 2000.
12. Filipek, 1999.
13. Reilly, Stiles, *et al.*, 1995.
14. Levin, Scheller, *et al.*, 1996.
15. Taylor, Neville, *et al.*, 1999.
16. Makris, Biederman, *et al.*, 2007.
17. Rizzolatti, Ferrari, *et al.*, 2006.
18. Hickock and Hauser, 2010.
19. Polezzi, Daum, *et al.*, 2008.
20. Leslie, Johnson-Frey, *et al.*, 2004.
21. Cheng, Lee, *et al.*, 2008.
22. Engell and Haxby, 2007.
23. Montgomery and Haxby, 2008.
24. Calder, Beaver, *et al.*, 2007.
25. Mosconi, Mack, *et al.*, 2005.
26. Gobbini, Koralek, *et al.*, 2007.
27. Shamay-Tsoory, Tibi-Elhanany, *et al.*, 2007.
28. Decety and Lamm, 2007.
29. Brieber, Neufang, *et al.*, 2007.
30. Vance, Silk, *et al.*, 2007.
31. Williams, Whiten, *et al.*, 2001.
32. Fan, Decety, *et al.*, 2010.
33. Campbell, Heywood, *et al.*, 1990.
34. Materna, Dicke, *et al.*, 2008.
35. Ferrari, Kohler, *et al.*, 2000.
36. Engell and Haxby, 2007.
37. Zahn, Moll, *et al.*, 2007.
38. Brewer amd Mogheker, 2002.
39. Ullman, 2001.
40. Hamann, 2001.
41. Elfgren, van Westen, *et al.*, 2006.
42. Kirwan and Stark, 2004.
43. Murray and Richmond, 2001.
44. Moran, Wig, *et al.*, 2004.
45. Bachevalier, Malkova, *et al.*, 2001.
46. Braun, Denault, *et al.*, 1994.

47. Cohen, David, *et al.*, 2009.
48. Boddaert, Chabane, *et al.*, 2004.
49. McAlonan, Cheung, *et al.*, 2005.
50. DeVito, Drost, *et al.*, 2007.
51. Friedman, Shaw, *et al.*, 2006.
52. Hazlett, Poe, *et al.*, 2006.
53. Rojas, Peterson, *et al.*, 2006.
54. Waiter, Williams, *et al.*, 2004.
55. Ito, Mori, *et al.*, 2005.
56. Murphy, Daly, *et al.*, 2006.
57. Gendry, Zilbovicius, *et al.*, 2005.
58. Bauman and Kemper, 2003.
59. Casanova, Buxhoeveden, *et al.*, 2003.
60. Casanova, Buxhoeveden, *et al.*, 2002.
61. Boddaert, Chabane, *et al.*, 2004.
62. Boelte, Uhlig, *et al.*, 2002.
63. Just, Cherhassky, *et al.*, 2004.
64. Pierce, Muller, *et al.*, 2001.
65. Pelphrey, Morris, *et al.*, 2007.
66. Falk, 2009.
67. McAlonan, Cheung, *et al.*, 2007.
68. Castellanos, Lee, *et al.*, 2002.
69. Brieber, Neufang, *et al.*, 2007.
70. Decety and Lamm, 2007.
71. Brun, Nicolson, *et al.*, 2009.
72. Ranta, Crocetti, *et al.*, 2009.
73. Hill, Inder, *et al.*, 2010.
74. Wood and Grafman, 2003.
75. Dumontheil, Burgess, *et al.*, 2008.
76. Akbarian, Chen, *et al.*, 2001.
77. Jabbi, Swart, *et al.*, 2007.
78. Morita, Hakura, *et al.*, 2008.
79. Chamberlain and Sahakian, 2007.
80. Brodmann, 1909.
81. Gibson, 1979.
82. Lhermitte, 1983.
83. Lorena, 2009.
84. Suzuki, Yamadori, *et al.*, 2000.
85. Martos-Perez and Ayuda-Pascual, 2003.
86. Murphy, Critchley, *et al.*, 2002, p.891.
87. Eslinger, Flaherty-Craig, *et al.*, 2004.
88. Arnsten, 2006.
89. Iacoboni, 2009.
90. Phan, Fitzgerald, *et al.*, 2005.
91. Fletcher, Happé, *et al.*, 1995.
92. Iacoboni, 2009.

93. D'Argembeau, Ruby, *et al.*, 2007.
94. Mundy, 2003.
95. Dichter, Felder, *et al.*, 2009.
96. Yamada, Hirao, *et al.* 2007.
97. Knight and Fuchs, 2007.
98. Hänsel and von Känel, 2008.
99. Williams, Waiter, *et al.*, 2005.
100. Lee, Josephs, *et al.*, 2006.
101. Phan, Fitzgerald, *et al.*, 2006.
102. Winston, O'Doherty, *et al.*, 2003.
103. Decety and Lamm, 2007.
104. Lee, Josephs, *et al.*, 2006.
105. Teasdale, Howard, *et al.*, 1999.
106. Decety and Chaminade, 2003.
107. Shamay-Tsoory, Tibi-Elhanany, *et al.*, 2007.
108. Damasio, 1996.
109. Damasio, Grabowski, *et al.*, 2000.
110. Dunn, Dalgleish, *et al.*, 2006.
111. Palminteri, Boraud, *et al.*, 2009.
112. Schippers, Roebroeck, *et al.*, 2010.
113. For a review, see Tantam, 2009.
114. Damasio, Grabowski, *et al.*, 1994.
115. Osaka, Otsuka, *et al.*, 2007.
116. Lough and Hodges, 2002.
117. Hopkins, Dywan, *et al.*, 2002.
118. Shamay-Tsoory, Tomer, *et al.*, 2003.
119. Di Martino and Castellanos, 2003.
120. Wang, Lee, *et al.*, 2007.
121. Boes, Bechara, *et al.*, 2009.
122. Bremner, Innis, *et al.*, 2000.
123. Lanius, Williamson, *et al.*, 2004.
124. Worthington, Witvliet, *et al.*, 2007.
125. Farrow, Zheng, *et al.*, 2001.
126. Knoch, Gianotti, *et al.*, 2006.
127. Boggio, Zaghi, *et al.*, 2009.
128. Cohen, Kaplan, *et al.*, 2004.
129. Stern, Owen, *et al.*, 2000.
130. Ramnani and Owen, 2004. a) p.184. b) p.194.
131. Raposo, Han, *et al.*, 2009.
132. Manoach, White, *et al.*, 2004.
133. Kennerley and Wallis, 2009.
134. Paulus, 2004.
135. Eshel, Nelson, *et al.*, 2007.
136. Taylor, Welsh, *et al.*, 2004.
137. Spence, Kaylor-Hughes, *et al.*, 2008.
138. Romanski, 2007.
139. Davies, 2007.
140. Sowell, Thompson, *et al.*, 2003.
141. Ernst, Kimes, *et al.*, 2003.
142. Schneider, Krick, *et al.*, 2010.
143. Fiehler, Burke, *et al.*, 2009.
144. Li, Delgado, *et al.*, 2011.
145. Hare, Camerer, *et al.*, 2009.
146. Buckley, Mansouri, *et al.*, 2009.
147. De Pisapia, Slomski, *et al.*, 2007.
148. Osaka, Otsuka, *et al.*, 2007.
149. Torriero, Oliveri, *et al.*, 2007.
150. Kubler, Dixon, *et al.*, 2006.
151. Wild, Erb, *et al.*, 2003.
152. Eippert, Veit, *et al.*, 2007.
153. Herrington, Mohanty, *et al.*, 2005.
154. Nunez, Casey, *et al.*, 2005.
155. Polezzi, Daum, *et al.*, 2008.
156. Knoch, Pascual-Leone, *et al.*, 2006.
157. Gaymard, François, *et al.*, 2003.
158. Stephens, Silbert, *et al.*, 2010.
159. Shackman, McMenamin, *et al.*, 2009.
160. Ragland, Gur, *et al.*, 2004.
161. Chaminade, Meltzoff, *et al.*, 2002.
162. Cahn and Polich, 2006.
163. Baron-Cohen, Ring, *et al.*, 2006.
164. Troiani, Ash, *et al.*, 2006.
165. Harrison, Brydon, *et al.*, 2009.
166. Kringelbach, de Araujo, *et al.*, 2008.
167. Qin, Hermans, *et al.*, 2009.
168. Montag, Schubert, *et al.*, 2008.
169. Ghika, 2008.
170. Mah, Arnold, *et al.*, 2004.
171. Eslinger and Biddle, 2000.
172. Narendran, Frankle, *et al.*, 2005.
173. Hirao, Miyata, *et al.*, 2008.
174. Salmond, Vargha-Khadem, *et al.*, 2007.
175. Luna, Minshew, *et al.*, 2002.
176. Takarae, Minshew, *et al.*, 2007.
177. Lepagnol-Bestel, Maussion, *et al.*, 2008.
178. Bonilha, Cendes, *et al.*, 2008.
179. Pescucci, Meloni, *et al.*, 2003.
180. Mukaetova-Ladinska, Arnold, *et al.*, 2004.
181. Sabbagh, Moulson, *et al.*, 2004.
182. Lee, Foss-Feig, *et al.*, 2007.
183. Reverberi, Toraldi, *et al.*, 2005.
184. Kaya, Karasalihoglu, *et al.*, 2002.
185. Spalletta, Pasini, *et al.*, 2001.
186. Hesslinger, Thiel, *et al.*, 2001.
187. Yeo, Hill, *et al.*, 2003.
188. Durston, Tottenham, *et al.*, 2003.
189. Makris, Biederman, *et al.*, 2007.
190. Barry, Clarke, *et al.*, 2003.
191. Berger, Kofman, *et al.*, 2007, p.286.
192. Viskontas, Possin, *et al.*, 2007.
193. Savic and Gulyash, 2000.
194. Shaw, Kabani, *et al.*, 2008.
195. Miyashita, Ichinohe, *et al.*, 2007.
196. Reilly, Stiles, *et al.*, 1995.
197. Burgess, Dumonthiel, *et al.*, 2007.
198. Vuilleumier, 2002.
199. Adolphs, 2001.
200. Eippert, Veit, *et al.*, 2007.
201. Christoff and Gabrieli, 2000.
202. Nitschke, Nelson, *et al.*, 2008.
203. Fairhall and Ishai, 2007.
204. Rolls, 2000.
205. Royet, Koenig, *et al.*, 1999.
206. Yamamoto, Oomura, *et al.*, 1984.
207. Tate, Bigler, *et al.*, 2007.
208. For an elaboration of this, see Tantam, 2009.
209. LoPresti, Schon, *et al.*, 2008.
210. Phan, Sripada, *et al.*, 2010.
211. Conty, N'Diaye, *et al.*, 2007.
212. Alia-Klein, Goldstein, *et al.*, 2007.
213. Tantam, 2003.
214. Vollm, Taylor, *et al.*, 2006.
215. Lamm, Nusbaum, *et al.*, 2007.
216. Emery, 2000.

217. Mah, Arnold, *et al.*, 2004.
218. Sturm, Rosen, *et al.*, 2006.
219. Viskontas, Possin, *et al.*, 2007.
220. Hornak, Bramham, *et al.*, 2003.
221. Weidenheim, Goodman, *et al.*, 2001.
222. Ashwin, Baron-Cohen, *et al.*, 2007.

223. Williams, Waiter, *et al.*, 2005.
224. Girgis, Minshew, *et al.*, 2007.
225. Ashwin, Baron-Cohen, *et al.*, 2007.
226. Gilbert, Bird, *et al.*, 2008.
227. Loveland, Bachevalier, *et al.*, 2008.

CHAPTER 2 THE CEREBELLUM AND DEEP STRUCTURES IN THE FOREBRAIN

1. Anderson, 2007.
2. Matano, Hirasaki, *et al.*, 1997.
3. Schmahmann, 2004. a) p.367.
4. Vygotsky, 1966.
5. Beblo, Driessen, *et al.*, 2006.
6. Lemon and Edgley 2010.
7. Hayakawa, Nakajima, *et al.*, 2002.
8. Takagi, Trillenberg, *et al.*, 2001.
9. Takagi, Tamargo, *et al.*, 2003.
10. Casey, 2005.
11. Sullivan, Harding, *et al.*, 2003.
12. Posner and Rothbart, 2007.
13. Grèzes, Frith, *et al.*, 2004.
14. Calvo-Merino, Grèzes, *et al.*, 2006.
15. Najib, Lorberbaum, *et al.*, 2004.
16. Singer, Seymour, *et al.*, 2004.
17. Allen and Courchesne, 1998, p.209.
18. Gaytan-Tocaven and Olvera-Cortes, 2004.
19. Bobee, Mariette, *et al.*, 2000.
20. Pascual, Verdu, *et al.*, 1999.
21. Pascual, Hervias, *et al.*, 1998.
22. Lancaster, Dietz, *et al.*, 2007.
23. Weissenbock, Hornig, *et al.*, 2000.
24. Thompson and Potter, 2000.
25. Kuemerle, Gulden, *et al.*, 2007.
26. Bartlett, Gharani, *et al.*, 2005.
27. Shi, Smith, *et al.*, 2009, p.116.
28. Sullivan, Harding, *et al.*, 2003.
29. Turner, Paradiso, *et al.*, 2007.
30. Bolduc and Limperopoulos, 2009.
31. Kumandas, Akcakus, *et al.*, 2004.
32. Takahashi, Farmer, *et al.*, 2005.
33. Steinlin, Styger, *et al.*, 1999.
34. Garrard, Martin, *et al.*, 2008.
35. Riva, 2000.
36. Torriero, Oliveri, *et al.*, 2007.
37. Baillieux, De Smet, *et al.*, 2006.
38. Riikonen, Salonen, *et al.*, 1999.
39. Elliott, Payne, *et al.*, 2008.
40. Vaurio, Riley, *et al.*, 2008.
41. Fagerlund, Heikkinen, *et al.*, 2006.
42. Courchesne, Yeung-Courchesne, *et al.*, 1988.
43. Akshoomoff, Lord, *et al.*, 2004.
44. Kaufmann, Cooper, *et al.*, 2003.
45. McAlonan, Cheung, *et al.*, 2005.
46. Bloss and Courchesne, 2007.
47. Fatemi, Halt, *et al.*, 2002.
48. Singer, Seymour, *et al.*, 2004.
49. Weber, Egelhoff, *et al.*, 2000.

50. Eluvathingal, Behen, *et al.*, 2006.
51. Belmonte and Carper, 2006.
52. Rinehart, Tonge, *et al.*, 2006b.
53. Yip, Soghomonian, *et al.*, 2007.
54. Yip, Soghomonian, *et al.*, 2008.
55. Yip, Soghomonian, *et al.*, 2009.
56. DeVito, Drost, *et al.*, 2007.
57. Cecil, DelBello, *et al.*, 2003.
58. Catani, Jones, *et al.*, 2008.
59. Yang, Lung, *et al.*, 2008.
60. Wills, Cabanlit, *et al.*, 2009.
61. Valera, Faraone, *et al.*, 2006.
62. Mackie, Shaw, *et al.*, 2007.
63. Durston, Hulshoff, *et al.*, 2004.
64. Halperin and Schulz, 2006.
65. Ashtari, Kumra, *et al.*, 2005.
66. Castellanos, Lee, *et al.*, 2002.
67. Jones, Hesselink, *et al.*, 2002.
68. Gläscher and Adolphs, 2003.
69. Zald, 2003.
70. Hamann, 2001.
71. Schaefer, Jackson, *et al.*, 2002.
72. Gray and McNaughton, 2000.
73. Brothers, 1990.
74. Adolphs, 2009.
75. Meyer-Lindenberg, 2008.
76. Swain, Lorberbaum, *et al.*, 2007.
77. De Bellis, Keshavan, *et al.*, 2002.
78. Hooker, Paller, *et al.*, 2003.
79. Gobbini and Haxby, 2006.
80. Amaral, Bauman, *et al.*, 2003.
81. Bar and Neta, 2007.
82. Whalen, Rauch, *et al.*, 1998.
83. Habel, Windischberger, *et al.*, 2007.
84. Bickart, Wright, *et al.*, 2011.
85. Anisman and McIntyre, 2002.
86. Prather, Lavenex, *et al.*, 2001.
87. Kalin, Shelton, *et al.*, 2001.
88. Amaral, Bauman, *et al.*, 2003.
89. Siebert, Markowitsch, *et al.*, 2003.
90. Wicks-Nelson and Israel, 2003.
91. Shaw, Lawrence, *et al.*, 2004.
92. Frith and Frith, 2003.
93. Sweeten, Posey, *et al.*, 2002.
94. Madsen, Hviid, *et al.*, 2002b.
95. Aylward, Minshew, *et al.*, 2002.
96. Howard, Cowell, *et al.*, 2000.
97. Abell, Krams, *et al.*, 1999.
98. Schumann, Barnes, *et al.*, 2009.

99. Mosconi, Cody-Hazlett, *et al.*, 2009.
100. Haznedar, Buchsbaum, *et al.*, 2000.
101. De Bellis, Casey, *et al.*, 2000.
102. Bauman and Kemper, 2003.
103. Plessen, Bansal, *et al.*, 2006.
104. Baron-Cohen, Ring, *et al.*, 2000.
105. Otsuka, Harada, *et al.*, 1999.
106. Mori, Hashimoto, *et al.*, 2001.
107. Gewirtz and Davis, 1997.
108. Ashwin, Baron-Cohen, *et al.*, 2007.
109. Bailey, Braeutigam, *et al.*, 2005.
110. Fajardo, Escobar, *et al.*, 2008.
111. Parr, Waller, *et al.*, 2005.
112. Marino, Butti, *et al.*, 2008.
113. Kennedy, Semendeferi, *et al.*, 2007.
114. Russo, Backus, *et al.*, 2002.
115. Maclean, 1990.
116. Le Doux, 1999.
117. Papez, 1937.
118. Le Doux, 1999.
119. Hodzic, Kaas, *et al.*, 2009.
120. Chaudhry, Parkinson, *et al.*, 2009.
121. Johnson, Raye, *et al.*, 2006.
122. Binder, Desai, *et al.*, 2009.
123. Hagan, Hoeft, *et al.*, 2008.
124. Orr, Weissman, *et al.*, 2009.
125. Tantam, 2003.
126. Costantini, Galati, *et al.*, 2008.
127. Decety, Michalska, *et al.*, 2008.
128. Kedia, Berthoz, *et al.*, 2008.
129. Fujiwara, Tobler, *et al.*, 2009.
130. Chiao, Harada, *et al.*, 2009.
131. Gao, Zhu, *et al.*, 2009.
132. McAlonan, Suckling, *et al.*, 2008.
133. Abraham, von Cramon, *et al.*, 2009.
134. Schiller, Freeman, *et al.*, 2009.
135. Gobbini, Koralek, *et al.*, 2007.
136. Mano, Harada, *et al.*, 2009.
137. Xiao, Qiu, *et al.*, 2009.
138. Nente, Carrillo-Mezo, *et al.*, 2007.
139. LaGraize, Labuda, *et al.*, 2004.
140. Hauber and Sommer, 2009.
141. Di Martino, Ross, *et al.*, 2009.
142. Di Martino, Shehzad, *et al.*, 2009.
143. Berger, Kofman, *et al.*, 2007.
144. Mundy, 2003.
145. Chiu, Kayali, *et al.*, 2008.
146. Thakkar, Polli, *et al.*, 2008.
147. Oner, Devrimci-Ozguven, *et al.*, 2007.
148. Murphy, Critchley, *et al.*, 2002.
149. O'Connell, Bellgrove, *et al.*, 2009.
150. Perlov, Alexandra, *et al.*, 2009.
151. Albrecht, Brandeis, *et al.*, 2008.
152. Kleinhans, Richards, *et al.*, 2008.
153. Naqvi and Bechara, 2009.
154. Craig, 2002.
155. Jabbi, Bastiaansen, *et al.*, 2008.
156. Craig, 2009.
157. Mizuhiki, Richmond, *et al.*, 2007.
158. Christensen, Boysen, *et al.*, 2005.
159. Nordahl, Dierker, *et al.*, 2007.
160. Schienle, Stark, *et al.*, 2002.
161. Di Martino, Ross, *et al.*, 2009.
162. Dichter and Belger, 2007.
163. Dichter and Belger, 2008.
164. Kana, Keller, *et al.*, 2007.
165. Zang, Jin, *et al.*, 2005.
166. Harley, Pope, *et al.*, 2009.
167. Whatmough, Chertkow, *et al.*, 2002.
168. Barton, Press, *et al.*, 2002.
169. Gauthier, Klaiman, *et al.*, 2009.
170. Hernandez, Metzger, *et al.*, 2009.
171. Pierce and Redcay, 2008.
172. Annaz, Karmiloff-Smith, *et al.*, 2009.
173. van Kooten, Palmen, *et al.*, 2008.
174. Pietz, Ebinger, *et al.*, 2003.

CHAPTER 3 INTERACTIONS IN GENES AND NEURONS

1. Muhle, Trentacoste, *et al.*, 2004.
2. Geschwind, 1970.
3. State, 2010.
4. Anatskaya and Vinogradov, 2010.
5. Lobo, 2008.
6. Crespi, 2008.
7. Canli, Qiu, *et al.*, 2006.
8. Gregory, Connelly, *et al.*, 2009.
9. Baieli, Pavone, *et al.*, 2003.
10. Gannett, 2010.
11. Pollard, Salama, *et al.*, 2006.
12. Piggot, Shirinyan, *et al.*, 2009.
13. Marco-Pallares, *et al.*, 2009.
14. Matthew, Valerie, *et al.*, 2010.
15. Zhang, Gao, *et al.*, 2007.
16. Ben-David, Granot-Hershkovitz, *et al.*, 2011.
17. Freeman, Perry, *et al.*, 2006.
18. Kegel, Bus, *et al.*, 2011.
19. Simon, Stollstorff, *et al.*, 2011.
20. Guilmatre, Dubourg, *et al.*, 2009.
21. Sanders, Ercan-Sencicek, *et al.*, 2011.
22. Levy, Ronemus, *et al.*, 2011.
23. Pinto, Pagnamenta, *et al.*, 2010.
24. Van de Lagemaat and Grant, 2010.
25. Sakai, Shaw, *et al.*, 2011.
26. Voineagu, Wang, *et al.*, 2001
27. Buxhoeveden and Casanova, 2002.
28. Banaclocha, 2007.
29. Casanova, 2008.
30. Bauman and Kemper, 2005.
31. Freitas, Fregni, *et al.*, 2009.
32. Casanova, 2006.
33. But see Casanova and Trippe, 2009.
34. Wang, Ramos, *et al.*, 2007.
35. Sallee, Lyne, *et al.*, 2009.
36. Bradshaw and Sheppard, 2000.
37. Meunier, Achard, *et al.*, 2009.
38. Perlbarg and Marrelec, 2008.
39. Helps, James, *et al.*, 2008.
40. Fair, Cohen, *et al.*, 2009.
41. Van den Heuvel and Hulshoff Pol, 2010.
42. Chiang, Barysheva, *et al.*, 2009.

43. Ciccarelli, Catani, *et al.*, 2008.
44. Fernandez-Miranda, Rhoton, *et al.*, 2008.
45. Mantini, Perrucci, *et al.*, 2007.
46. Hagmann, Cammoun, *et al.*, 2007.
47. Dosenbach, Nardos, *et al.*, 2010.
48. Doron and Gazzaniga, 2008.
49. Schmithorst, 2003.
50. Tepest, Jacobi, *et al.*, 2010.
51. Fair, Cohen, *et al.*, 2009.
52. Hagmann, Cammoun, *et al.*, 2008.
53. Schell-Apacik, Wagner, *et al.*, 2008.
54. Badaruddin, Andrews, *et al.*, 2007.
55. Zafeiriou, Ververi, *et al.*, 2008.
56. Bindu, Shehanaz, *et al.*, 2007.
57. Kesler, Reiss, *et al.*, 2008.
58. Peru, Beltramello, *et al.*, 2003.
59. Savazzi, Fabri, *et al.*, 2007.
60. Vidal, Nicolson, *et al.*, 2006.
61. Frazier, Hardan, *et al.*, 2009.
62. Alexander, Lee, *et al.*, 2007.
63. Noonan, Haist, *et al.*, 2009.
64. Keary, Minshew, *et al.*, 2009.
65. Keller, Kana, *et al.*, 2007.
66. Just, Cherkassky, *et al.*, 2007.
67. Hutchinson, Mathias, *et al.*, 2008.
68. Luders, Narr, *et al.*, 2009.
69. Makris, Buka, *et al.*, 2008.
70. Bluhm, Osuch, *et al.*, 2008.
71. Buckner, Andrews-Hanna, *et al.*, 2008.
72. Baron-Cohen, 2009.
73. Kana, Keller, *et al.*, 2009.
74. Ke, Tang, *et al.*, 2009.
75. Ke, Hong, *et al.*, 2008.
76. Kennedy and Courchesne, 2008a.
77. Di Martino, Shehzad, *et al.*, 2009.
78. Helps, James, *et al.*, 2008.
79. Uddin, Kelly, *et al.*, 2008.
80. Broyd, Demanuele, *et al.*, 2009.
81. Fransson, Skiöld, *et al.*, 2007.
82. Kennedy and Courchesne, 2008b.

CHAPTER 4 DEVELOPMENTAL, SOCIAL AND EMOTIONAL CONSIDERATIONS

1. Stevens, Sonuga-Barke, *et al.*, 2008.
2. Beverly, McGuinness, *et al.*, 2008.
3. Ornoy, 2003.
4. Zola, 1993.
5. Leiter, 2007.
6. Hughes, 2005.
7. Yianni-Coudurier, Darrou, *et al.*, 2008.
8. Miller, Nigg, *et al.*, 2009.
9. Olaniyan, dosReis, *et al.*, 2007.
10. dosReis, Butz, *et al.*, 2006.
11. Kanne, Christ, *et al.*, 2009.
12. Helt, Kelley, *et al.*, 2008. a) p.339.
13. Derks, Hudziak, *et al.*, 2008.
14. Matthew, 2008.
15. Ijichi, Ijichi, *et al.*, 2008.
16. Happé and Vital, 2009.
17. Snyder, 2009.
18. Rutherford, Richards, *et al.*, 2007.
19. Tantam, 2009.
20. Bellgrove, Hawi, *et al.*, 2005.
21. Guo, Tong, *et al.*, 2007.
22. Arcos-Burgos and Acosta, 2007.
23. Williams, Higgins, *et al.*, 2006.
24. Williams and Taylor, 2006.
25. Emerson and Hatton, 2007.
26. Bryson, Corrigan. *et al.*, 2008.
27. Chen, Liu, *et al.*, 2007.
28. Begeer, Bouk, *et al.*, 2009.
29. Anckarsater, Stahlberg, *et al.*, 2006.
30. Bryson, Zwaigenbaum, *et al.*, 2007.
31. Schwartz, Henderson, *et al.*, 2009.
32. Chick, Waterhouse, *et al.*, 1979.
33. Wolff, 1991.
34. Tantam, 1996a.
35. Tantam, 1988d.
36. Westen, Nakash, *et al.*, 2006.
37. Esterberg, Trotman, *et al.*, 2008.
38. Johnston and Ohan, 2005.
39. Pham, Carlson, *et al.*, 2010.
40. Chen, Seipp, *et al.*, 2008.
41. Pellegrini, 2008.
42. Bandura, 1977.
43. Gilbert, 1992.
44. Verte, Roeyers, *et al.*, 2003.
45. Hoza, Mrug, *et al.*, 2005.
46. Rorty, 1980.
47. Waal, 1989.
48. Hobbes, 1660.
49. Krysko and Rutherford, 2009.
50. Ravaja, Kauppinen, *et al.*, 2000.
51. Iacobini and Mazziotta, 2007.
52. Gomez, 2009.
53. Knauft, 1991.
54. Vigilant, 2007.
55. Wobber, Wrangham, *et al.*, 2010.
56. Pika and Zuberbuhler, 2007.
57. Insel, 2010.
58. Stuart, Levin-Silton, *et al.*, 2008.
59. Tantam, 1995.
60. Blair, 1995.
61. Leist and Dadds, 2009.
62. Carlson, Greenberg, *et al.*, 2010.
63. Leist and Dadds, 2009.
64. Tantam, 1995.
65. Jennes-Coussens, Magill-Evans, *et al.*, 2006.
66. Cederlund, Hagberg, *et al.*, 2008.
67. Hedley and Young, 2006.
68. Causton-Theoharis, Ashby, *et al.*, 2009.
69. Whitehouse, Durkin, *et al.*, 2009.
70. Hurt, Hoza, *et al.*, 2007.
71. Sebastian, Blakemore, *et al.*, 2009.
72. White and Roberson-Nay, 2009.

73. Bosch, 2002.
74. Twenge, Baumeister, *et al.*, 2007.
75. Cacioppo, Norris, *et al.*, 2009.
76. Weiss, 1973.
77. Bauminger, Solomon, *et al.*, 2008. a) p.1211.
78. Whitehouse, Watt, *et al.*, 2009.
79. Balfe, Chen, *et al.*, 2005.
80. Little, 2001.
81. Bejerot and Mortberg, 2009.
82. Naylor, Dawson, *et al.*, in press.
83. Wainscot, Naylor, *et al.*, 2008.
84. Balfe, Chen, *et al.*, 2005.
85. Williams, Chambers, *et al.*, 1996.
86. Muldoon, Schmid, *et al.*, 2009.
87. Sourander, Jensen, *et al.*, 2007.
88. Twemlow and Fonagy, 2005.
89. Schachter, Girardi, *et al.*, 2008.
90. Canino and Alegria, 2008.

91. Kurita, Koyama, *et al.*, 2005a.
92. Hedden, Ketay, *et al.*, 2008.
93. Gove, 1970.
94. Cohen, 1955.
95. Nietszche, 1968 (1888).
96. Frith and Frith, 1974.
97. Mechanic, 1982.
98. Bakare, Agomoh, *et al.*, 2009.
99. Merton, 1948.
100. Christensen and Rosenthal, 1982.
101. Dishion, McCord, *et al.*, 1999.
102. Bennett, Pitale, *et al.*, 2004.
103. Henderson, Zahka, *et al.*, 2009.
104. De Vries, Noens, *et al.*, 2010.
105. Tateno, Tateno, *et al.*, 2008.
106. Wolsko, Lardon, *et al.*, 2007.
107. Orsmond, Kuo, *et al.*, 2009.

CHAPTER 5 SOCIAL ORENTATION, COMMUNICATION AND LANGUAGE

1. Pierce, Conant, *et al.*, 2011.
2. Doi, Ueda, *et al.*, 2009.
3. Emery, 2000.
4. Birmingham and Kingstone, 2009.
5. Grossmann, Johnson, *et al.*, 2007.
6. Deak, Walden, *et al.*, 2008.
7. Blass and Camp, 2001.
8. Tantam, 2009.
9. Engell and Haxby, 2007.
10. Conty, N'Diaye, *et al.*, 2007.
11. Becchio, Pierno, *et al.*, 2007.
12. Tantam, 1992.
13. Itier and Batty, 2009.
14. Elsabbagh, Volein, *et al.*, 2009a.
15. Senju, Yaguchi, *et al.*, 2003.
16. Sasson, Tsuchiya, *et al.*, 2007.
17. For a review, see Tantam, 2009.
18. Bonato, Priftis, *et al.*, 2009.
19. Rutherford and Krysko, 2008.
20. Riby and Hancock, 2009a.
21. Liszkowski, Carpenter, *et al.*, 2007.
22. Henderson, Yoder, *et al.*, 2002.
23. Okamoto-Barth, Call, *et al.*, 2007.
24. Mundy, Sullivan, *et al.*, 2009.
25. Riby and Doherty, 2009.
26. Warreyn, Roeyers, *et al.*, 2007.
27. Warreyn, Roeyers, *et al.*, 2005.
28. Charman, 2003.
29. Mosconi, Steven, *et al.*, 2009.
30. Gomez, 2009.
31. Klin, Lin, *et al.*, 2009.
32. Siller, Sigman, *et al.*, 2008.
33. Scheeren and Stauder, 2008.
34. Shepherd, Klein, *et al.*, 2009.
35. Meltzoff and Moore, 1977.
36. Ferrari, Visalberghi, *et al.*, 2006.
37. Tantam, 1986.

38. Zentall and Akins 2001.
39. Ham, Corley, *et al.*, 2008.
40. Smith and Bryson 2007.
41. Moody, McIntosh, *et al.*, 2007.
42. Sonnby-Borgstroem, 2002a.
43. Stinear, Coxon, *et al.*, 2009.
44. Luo, Peng, *et al.*, 2004.
45. Lee, Dolan, *et al.*, 2008.
46. Gallese and Metzinger, 2003.
47. Buccino and Amore, 2008.
48. Dinstein, Thomas, *et al.*, 2008.
49. Clifford, Young, *et al.*, 2007.
50. Colombi, Liebal, *et al.*, 2009.
51. Fletcher-Watson, Leekam, *et al.*, 2009.
52. Rutherford and Towns, 2008.
53. Boraston, Corden, *et al.*, 2008.
54. Jones, Carr, *et al.*, 2008.
55. Merin, Young, *et al.*, 2007.
56. Senju, 2009.
57. De Giacomo, Portoghese, Kikuchi, *et al.*, 2009.
58. Vivanti, Nadig, *et al.*, 2008.
59. DeQuinzio, Townsend, *et al.*, 2007.
60. Haswell, Izawa, *et al.*, 2009.
61. Gallese, Rochat, *et al.*, 2009.
62. Rizzolatti, Fabbri-Destro, *et al.*, 2009.
63. Welsh, Ray, *et al.*, 2009.
64. Aitken, 2008.
65. Gernsbacher, Sauer, *et al.*, 2008.
66. Luyster, Kadlec, *et al.*, 2008.
67. Thurm, Lord, *et al.*, 2007.
68. Sanders, Ameral, *et al.*, 2009.
69. de Saussure, 1959.
70. Pelphrey and Carter, 2008.
71. Redcay, 2008.
72. Lancker Sidtis, 2007.
73. Kleinhans, Richards, *et al.*, 2008.
74. Koshino, Kana, *et al.*, 2008.

75. Meinhardt-Injac, Persike, *et al.*, 2010.
76. Martineau, Cochin, *et al.*, 2008.
77. Effron, Niedenthal, *et al.*, 2006.
78. Duquette, Michaud, *et al.*, 2008.
79. Gepner and Feron, 2009.
80. Moody, McIntosh, *et al.*, 2007.
81. Tardif, Laine, *et al.*, 2007.
82. Martineau, Cochin, *et al.*, 2008.
83. Oram Cardy, Flagg, *et al.*, 2008.
84. APA, 2001.
85. Miller, 2003.
86. Peirce, 1958.
87. Derrida, 1978.
88. The relationship between language and colour words is disputed. One school of thought has it that the words for colour are dictated by the visual system's ability to differentiate primary colours, but another is that we see those different colours that we have the words for: that in learning a word, we change our perceptions.
89. Chomsky, 1957.
90. Shannon, 1948.
91. Kravchenko, 2007.
92. Brentano, 1973 (1874).
93. McLuhan, 1962.
94. DeWall, Baumeister, *et al.*, 2008.
95. Lucarelli, 2008, p.35.
96. Bateson, Jackson, *et al.*, 1956.
97. Hans, 2003.
98. Miller, 1951.
99. Kertèsz, 2010.
100. For a detailed discussion of this and subsequent points in this section, see Tantam, 2009.
101. Buck and Ginsburg, 1997.
102. Tantam, 2009.
103. Senju, Maeda, *et al.*, 2007.
104. Wild, Erb, *et al.*, 2003.
105. Sonnby-Borgstrom, 2002a.
106. Vygotsky, 1966.
107. Gazzaniga, 2005.
108. Wallace, Silvers, *et al.*, 2009.
109. Satpute and Lieberman, 2006.
110. Havas, Glenberg, *et al.*, 2010.
111. Ekman, 1994.
112. Matsumoto and Willingham, 2009.
113. Ekman, 1969a.
114. Fonteneau and van der Lely, 2008.
115. Falcaro, Pickles, *et al.*, 2008.
116. Paul, Lancker-Sidtis, *et al.*, 2003.
117. Geschwind, 1970.
118. Snowling and Hayiou-Thomas, 2006.
119. Chein, Ravizza, *et al.*, 2007.
120. Zatorre and Gandour, 2008.
121. Nan, Friederici, *et al.*, 2009.
122. Leff, Iverson, *et al.*, 2009.
123. MacSweeney, Campbell, *et al.*, 2004.
124. Kertèsz, 2010.
125. Singleton and Tittle, 2000.
126. Malinowski, 1934.
127. Dunbar, 2004.
128. Whorf, 1972.
129. Hallett, 2001.
130. Rapin, 1996.
131. Gabrieli, 2009.
132. Lassus-Sangosse, N'guyen-Morel, *et al.*, 2008.
133. Rubinsten and Henik, 2009.
134. Rapin, Dunn, *et al.*, 2009.
135. Volden, Coolican, *et al.*, 2009.
136. Geurts and Embrechts, 2008.
137. Truss, 2003.
138. Young, Diehl, *et al.*, 2005.
139. van Santen, Prud'hommeaux, *et al.*, 2009.
140. Oller, Niyogic, *et al.*, 2010.
141. Viana, Beidel, *et al.*, 2009.
142. Kristensen and Oerbeck, 2006.
143. Rapin and Dunn, 2003.
144. Groen, Zwiers, *et al.*, 2008.
145. Williams, Botting, *et al.*, 2008.
146. Whitehouse, Barry, *et al.*, 2008.
147. Eigsti, Bennetto, *et al.*, 2007.
148. Eigsti and Bennetto, *et al.*, 2009.
149. Dominick, Davis, *et al.*, 2007.
150. Norbury and Bishop, 2003.
151. Garcia-Perez, Hobson, *et al.*, 2008.
152. Gabig, 2008.
153. Riches, Loucas, *et al.*, 2010.
154. Guo, Xu, *et al.*, 2007.
155. Fonteneau and van der Lely, 2008.
156. Smith, 2007.
157. Vasanta, 2005.
158. Bennett, Szatmari, *et al.*, 2008.
159. Loucas, Charman, *et al.*, 2008.
160. Stribling, Rae, *et al.*, 2007.
161. Dobbinson, Perkins, *et al.*, 2003.
162. McCann, Peppe, *et al.*, 2007.
163. Buschmann, Jooss, *et al.*, 2008.

CHAPTER 6 NONVERBAL COMMUNICATION, EMPATHY AND THEORY OF MIND

1. Charman, Taylor, *et al.*, 2005.
2. Chiang, Soong, *et al.*, 2008.
3. Kircher, Straube, *et al.*, 2009.
4. Casasanto and Jasmin, 2010.
5. Ekman and Friesen, 1969a.
6. Beattie, 1983.
7. Hubbard and Trauner, 2007.
8. Hamilton, 2008.
9. Aitken, 2008.
10. Decety and Meyer, 2008.
11. Nagy, 2008.
12. Ekman and Friesen, 1969.
13. McCann, Peppe, *et al.*, 2007.
14. Diehl, Bennetto, *et al.*, 2008.
15. Jarvinen-Pasley, Peppe, *et al.*, 2008.
16. McCann, Peppe, *et al.*, 2007.

17. Ham, Corley, *et al.*, 2008.
18. Reed, Beall, *et al.*, 2007.
19. Fletcher-Watson, Leekam, *et al.*, 2009.
20. Clifford and Dissanayake, 2008.
21. Nation and Penny, 2008.
22. Chen, Kono, *et al.*, 2006.
23. Agaliotis and Kalyva, 2008.
24. Knight and Fuchs, 2007.
25. Hietanen, Nummenmaa, *et al.*, 2006.
26. Thompson, Malloy, *et al.*, 2009.
27. Smith and Milne, 2009.
28. Sokhadze, Baruth, *et al.*, 2009.
29. Jarvinen-Pasley, Pasley, *et al.*, 2008.
30. Itier and Batty, 2009.
31. Tantam, 1991a.
32. Klin, Lin, *et al.*, 2009.
33. Kaiser, Delmolino, *et al.*, 2010.
34. Freitag, Konrad, *et al.*, 2008.
35. Decety and Lamm, 2007.
36. Kana, Keller, *et al.*, 2009.
37. Mooshagian, Iacoboni, *et al.*, 2009.
38. Chan, Mattingley, *et al.*, 2009.
39. Tantam, Monaghan, *et al.*, 1989.
40. Deruelle, Rondan, *et al.*, 2008.
41. Wong, Fung, *et al.*, 2009.
42. Conturo, Williams, *et al.*, 2008.
43. Kleinhans, Richards, *et al.*, 2008.
44. Harley, Pope, *et al.*, 2009.
45. Wilmer, Germine, *et al.*, 2010.
46. Montag, Gallinat, *et al.*, 2008.
47. Bölte, Feineis-Matthews, *et al.*, 2008.
48. Gillberg, 1992.
49. Shamay-Tsoory, Aharon-Peretz, *et al.*, 2009.
50. Carothers and Taylor, 2004.
51. Sabbagh, 2004.
52. Freud, 1932.
53. Zaki and Ochsner, 2009.
54. Preston and de Waal, 2002.
55. Hatfield, Cacioppo, *et al.*, 1994.
56. de Waal, 2008.
57. Hill, Rand, *et al.*, 2010.
58. Minio-Paluello, Baron-Cohen, *et al.*, 2009.
59. Field, Field, *et al.*, 2001.
60. Hadjikhani, Joseph, *et al.*, 2009.
61. Scambler, Hepburn, *et al.*, 2007.
62. Hermans, van Wingen, *et al.*, 2009.
63. Dadds, El Masry, *et al.*, 2008.
64. Becchio, Pierno, *et al.*, 2007.
65. Senju, Kikuchi, *et al.*, 2009.
66. Adolphs, Tranel, *et al.*, 1994.
67. Wiltermuth and Heath, 2009.
68. Goldie, 2003.
69. Lamm, Porges, *et al.*, 2008.
70. Moriguchi, Ohnishi, *et al.*, 2009.
71. Decety and Lamm, 2007.
72. Chiu, Kayali, *et al.*, 2008.
73. Morita, Itakura, *et al.*, 2008.
74. Gallup, 1970.
75. de Veer, Gallup, *et al.*, 2003.
76. Reiss and Marino, 2001.
77. Plotnik, de Waal, *et al.*, 2006.

78. Prior, Schwarz, *et al.*, 2008.
79. Garner, Meehan, *et al.*, 2003.
80. Morita, Itakura, *et al.*, 2008.
81. Morin and Michaud, 2007.
82. Lind and Bowler, 2009.
83. Williams and Happé, 2009.
84. Henderson, Zahka, *et al.*, 2009b.
85. Gunji, Inagaki, *et al.*, 2009.
86. Chiu, Kayali, *et al.*, 2008.
87. Silani, Bird, *et al.*, 2008.
88. Shamay-Tsoory, 2008.
89. Dadds, El Masry, *et al.*, 2008.
90. Spinella, 2002.
91. Vollm, Taylor, *et al.*, 2006.
92. Hubert, Wicker, *et al.*, 2009.
93. Vaish, Carpenter, *et al.*, 2009.
94. Premack and Woodruff, 1978. a) p.515.
95. Wittgenstein, 1958, p.178.
96. Wimmer and Perner, 1983.
97. Happé, 1994.
98. Senju, Southgate, *et al.*, 2009.
99. Porter, Coltheart, *et al.*, 2008.
100. Wimmer and Perner, 1983.
101. Baron-Cohen, Leslie, *et al.*, 1985.
102. Tager-Flusberg and Sullivan, 1994.
103. Kaland, Callesen, *et al.*, 2008.
104. Peterson, Wellman, *et al.*, 2005.
105. Pyers and Senghas, 2009.
106. Sodian and Thoermer, 2008.
107. Miniscalco, Hagberg, *et al.*, 2007.
108. Ziatas, Durkin, *et al.*, 2003.
109. Colvert, Rutter, *et al.*, 2008a.
110. Bedny, Pascual-Leone, *et al.*, 2009.
111. Frith and Frith, 2008.
112. Happé, 2003.
113. Johnson, Barnacz, *et al.*, 2005.
114. Goldman, 2008.
115. Morin and Michaud, 2007.
116. Happé, 1994.
117. Kaland, Moller-Nielsen, *et al.*, 2002.
118. Kaland, Callesen, *et al.*, 2008.
119. Mazza, De Risio, *et al.*, 2001.
120. Salter, Seigal, *et al.*, 2008.
121. Klin, 2000.
122. Gallagher, Happé, *et al.*, 2000.
123. Kaland, Callesen, *et al.*, 2008.
124. Zalla, Sav, *et al.*, 2009.
125. Warren, 1994.
126. Oberman and Ramachandran, 2007.
127. Adolphs, 2006.
128. Samson, Apperly, *et al.*, 2005.
129. D'Argembeau, Ruby, *et al.*, 2007.
130. Mitchell, Macrae, *et al.*, 2006.
131. Ferreira, Palmini, *et al.*, 2009.
132. Marton, Wiener, *et al.*, 2009.
133. Baron-Cohen, Campbell, *et al.*, 1995.
134. Tantam, 1992.
135. Ames and Jarrold, 2007.
136. Senju, Tojo, *et al.*, 2004.
137. Castelli, Frith, *et al.*, 2002.
138. Murphy, Brady, *et al.*, 2009.

139. Decety and Lamm, 2007.
140. Cohen, David, *et al.*, 2009.
141. Samson, Apperly, *et al.*, 2004.
142. Smith, Taylor, *et al.*, 2006.
143. Barnea-Goraly, Kwon, *et al.*, 2004.
144. Castelli, Happé, *et al.*, 2002.
145. Bateson, Jackson, *et al.*, 1956.
146. Demurie, De Corel, *et al.*, 2011.
147. Zaki, Hennigen, *et al.*, 2010.
148. Decety and Moriguchi, 2007.
149. Chauhan, Mathias, *et al.*, 2008.
150. Xu, Zuo, *et al.*, 2009.
151. Blais, Jack, *et al.*, 2008.
152. Knafo, Zahn-Waxler, *et al.*, 2009.

153. Hein and Singer, 2008.
154. Price, 2001.
155. Miller and Jansen-op-de-Haar, 1997.
156. Eisenberg, Fabes, *et al.*, 1996.
157. Miller and Jansen-op-de-Haar, 1997.
158. Eisenberg, Fabes,*et al.*, 1996.
159. Costantini, Galati, *et al.*, 2008.
160. Casasanto and Jasmin, 2010.
161. Bateson, Jackson, *et al.*, 1956.
162. Ruesch and Bateson, 1951.
163. Jolliffe, Farrington, *et al.*, 2004.
164. Brune, Abdel-Hamid, *et al.*, 2009.
165. Warden and Mackinnon 2003.
166. Twenge, Baumeister, *et al.*, 2007.

CHAPTER 7 NEUROPSYCHOLOGY OF ASD

1. Catani and ffytche, 2005.
2. Damasio and Maurer, 1978.
3. Just, Cherkassky, *et al.*, 2007.
4. Araque and Navarrete, 2010.
5. Dichter and Belger, 2007.
6. Victor Adams, personal communication.
7. Carroll, 1993.
8. Cattell, 1971.
9. Conway, Cowan, *et al.*, 2002.
10. Colom, Haier, *et al.*, 2003.
11. Haier, Colom, *et al.*, 2003.
12. Gläscher, Rudrauf, *et al.*, 2010, p.4705.
13. Rypma and Prabhakaran, 2003.
14. Neubauer and Fink, 2003.
15. Karama, Ad-Dab'bagh, *et al.*, 2003.
16. Yu, Lin, *et al.*, 2003.
17. Pierce and Courchesne, 2000.
18. Roux, Bruneau, *et al.*, 1997.
19. Schultz, Gauthier, *et al.*, 2000.
20. Zeidner, Roberts, *et al.*, 2008.
21. Zillmer, Ball, *et al.*, 1991.
22. Funnell and Pitchford, 2010.
23. Wechsler, 2003.
24. Wechsler, 2008.
25. Dawson, Soulieres, *et al.*, 2007.
26. Bello, Goharpey, *et al.*, 2008.
27. Ryburn, Anderson, *et al.*, 2009.
28. Quoted with some minor amendments from Rourke and Tsatsanis, 2000. p.232.
29. Rourke and Tsatsanis, 2000.
30. Panos, Porter, *et al.*, 2001.
31. Paul, Lancker-Sidtis, *et al.*, 2003.
32. Cunningham and Papero, 1997.
33. Weber, Franz, *et al.*, 1997.
34. Tantam, 1988c.
35. Goldstein, Allen, *et al.*, 2008.
36. Mayes and Calhoun, 2007.
37. Mayes and Calhoun, 2006.
38. Bölte, Dziobek, *et al.*, 2009.
39. Tendolkar, 2008.
40. Floel, Poeppel, *et al.*, 2004.
41. Tantam, 2003.
42. Sacco and Sacchetti, 2010.

43. Beversdorf, Smith, *et al.*, 2000.
44. Woollett, Spiers, *et al.*, 2009.
45. Beversdorf, Anderson, *et al.*, 1998.
46. Beversdorf, Narayanan, *et al.*, 2007.
47. Beversdorf, Smith, *et al.*, 2000.
48. Mostofsky, Reiss, *et al.*, 1998.
49. Labelle, 2003.
50. Posner and Petersen, 1990.
51. Shallice, 1982.
52. Baddeley and Wilson, 1988.
53. Friedman, Miyake, *et al.*, 2008.
54. Russo, Flanagan, *et al.*, 2007.
55. Garon, Bryson, *et al.*, 2008.
56. Bishop and Norbury, 2005.
57. Wong, Maybery, *et al.*, 2006.
58. Sinzig, Morsch, *et al.*, 2008.
59. Houghton, Douglas, *et al.*, 1999.
60. Cadesky, Mota, *et al.*, 2000.
61. Schachter, 2002.
62. Javorsky, 1996.
63. Baddeley and Hitch, 1974.
64. Fernell, Norrelgen, *et al.*, 2002.
65. Adams and Gathercole, 2000.
66. Cohen, Dehaene, *et al.*, 2000.
67. Evardone and Alexander, 2009.
68. Coolidge, Segal, *et al.*, 2009.
69. Justus, Ravizza, *et al.*, 2005.
70. Colom, Shih, *et al.*, 2006.
71. Gonigle-Chalmers, Bodner, *et al.*, 2008.
72. Barnard, Muldoon, *et al.*, 2008.
73. Sinzig, Morsch, *et al.*, 2008.
74. Isaki, Spaulding, *et al.*, 2008.
75. Luna, Doll, *et al.*, 2007.
76. Marchetta, Hurks, *et al.*, 2008.
77. Groman, James, *et al.*, 2009.
78. Johansen, Killeen, *et al.*, 2009.
79. Lincoln, Taylor, *et al.*, 2010.
80. Marco, Miranda, *et al.*, 2009.
81. Diamond, 2005.
82. MacDonald, 2008.
83. De Pisapia and Braver, 2006.
84. Wittfoth, Schroder, *et al.*, 2010.
85. Chamberlain and Sahakian, 2007.

86. Carver, Johnson, *et al.*, 2008.
87. O'Connell, Bellgrove, *et al.*, 2009.
88. Torriero, Oliveri, *et al.*, 2007.
89. Dias, Foxe, *et al.*, 2003.
90. Kana, Keller, *et al.*, 2007.
91. Stroop, 1935.
92. Estecio, Fett-Conte, *et al.*, 2002.
93. Chudasama, Kralik, *et al.*, 2007.
94. Arnsten, 2006.
95. Moll, Heinrich, *et al.*, 2003.
96. Martel, Nigg, *et al.*, 2009.
97. Chan, Han, *et al.*, 2011.
98. Henseler, Krüger, *et al.*, 2011.
99. Ames and Fletcher-Watson, 2010.
100. Freeth, Ropar, *et al.*, 2010.
101. Roy, Lebuis, *et al.*, 2011.
102. Zang, Jin, *et al.*, 2005.
103. Shafritz, Marchione, *et al.*, 2004.
104. Prendergast, Jackson, *et al.*, 1998.
105. Ambery, Russell, *et al.*, 2006.
106. Hedden and Gabrieli, 2010.
107. Hikosaka and Isoda, 2010.
108. Durston, van Belle, *et al.*, 2011.
109. Townsend, Westerfield, *et al.*, 2001.
110. Harris, Courchesne, *et al.*, 1999.
111. Lincoln, Searcy, *et al.*, 2007.
112. Mooney, Gray, *et al.*, 2009.
113. Bodfish, Symons, *et al.*, 2000.
114. Howlin and Asgharian, 1999.
115. Ridley, 1994.
116. Howlin, 1999.
117. Harris, Mahone, *et al.*, 2008.
118. Tan, Salgado, *et al.*, 1997.
119. Barnett, Koistra, *et al.*, 1998.
120. Ishijima and Kurita, 2007.
121. Wiener, 1948.
122. Coleman and Gurd, 2006.
123. Blumstein and Kurowski, 2006; Coleman and Gurd, 2006.
124. Goez and Zelnik, 2008.
125. Schmitz, Martineau, *et al.*, 2003.
126. Ladavas, 2002.
127. Kristensen and Oerbeck, 2006.
128. Scalais, Nuttin, *et al.*, 2005.
129. Henderson and Sugden, 1992.
130. Deitz, Kartin, *et al.*, 2007.
131. Dewey, Cantell, *et al.*, 2007.
132. Hilton, Wenke, *et al.*, 2007.
133. Bishop, 2007.
134. Mostofsky, Powell, *et al.*, 2009.
135. Freitag, Konrad, *et al.*, 2008.
136. Sturm, Fernell, *et al.*, 2004.
137. Jansiewicz, Goldberg, *et al.*, 2006.
138. Hilton, Wente, *et al.*, 2007.
139. Dziuk, Larson, *et al.*, 2007.
140. Freitag, Kleser, *et al.*, 2007.
141. Darke, Bushby, *et al.*, 2006.
142. Rinehart, Tonge, *et al.*, 2006a.
143. Rinehart, Bellgrove, *et al.*, 2006.
144. Schmitz, Martineau, *et al.*, 2003.
145. Goez and Zelnik, 2008.
146. Van Meel, Oosterlaan, *et al.*, 2005.
147. Mostofsky, Burgess, *et al.*, 2007.
148. Nazarali, Glazebrook, *et al.*, 2009.
149. Iaria, Bogod, *et al.*, 2009.
150. Alsaadi, Binder, *et al.*, 2000.
151. Iaria, Bogod, *et al.*, 2009.

CHAPTER 8 THE AUTISTIC SYNDROME

1. Addington, Gauthier, *et al.*, 2011.
2. Reaven, Hepburn, *et al.*, 2008.
3. Rapoport, Chavez, *et al.*, 2009.
4. Wing and Gould, 1979.
5. Marsden, Kalter, *et al.*, 1974.
6. Klin, Volkmar, *et al.*, 1995.
7. Eaves, Ho, *et al.*, 1994.
8. Prior, Eisenmajer, *et al.*, 1998.
9. Stevens, Fein, *et al.*, 2000.
10. Prior, Eisenmajer, *et al.*, 1998.
11. Constantino, Gruber, *et al.*, 2004.
12. Constantino and Todd, 2003.
13. Posserud, Lundervold, *et al.*, 2008.
14. Posserud, Lundervold, *et al.*, 2006.
15. World Health Organization, 1992.
16. American Psychiatric Association, 2001.
17. Matson, Wilkins, *et al.*, 2008.
18. Mayes, Calhoun, *et al.*, 2001.
19. Mount, Hastings, *et al.*, 2001.
20. Cederlund, Hagberg, *et al.*, 2008.
21. Williams, Tuck, *et al.*, 2008.
22. Kurita, 1997.
23. Ozonoff, South, *et al.*, 2000.
24. Schopler, Mesibov, *et al.*, 1998.
25. Witwer and Lecavalier, 2008.
26. Ring, Woodbury-Smith, *et al.*, 2008.
27. Ene, 1999.
28. Tantam, 1986.
29. Tantam, 1988b.
30. Wing, 1981.
31. Schopler, 1996.
32. Kanner, 1972.
33. Mental Capacity Act, 2005, c.6.
34. Tantam, 1988a.
35. For a review, see Tantam, 2009.
36. Frith and Happé, 1996.
37. Sigman, Mundy, *et al.*, 1986.
38. Tantam, 2009.
39. Baron-Cohen and Belmonte, 2005.
40. Georgiades, Szatmari, *et al.*, 2007.
41. Kamp-Becker, Ghahreman, *et al.*, 2009.
42. Snow, Lecavalier, *et al.*, 2009.
43. Happé and Ronald, 2008.
44. Geschwind, 2009.
45. English and Essex, 2001.
46. Howlin and Asgharian, 1999.

47. Eaves, Wingert, *et al.*, 2006.
48. Stone, McMahon, *et al.*, 2008.
49. Webb and Jones, 2009.
50. Farrugia, 2009.
51. Commission on Chronic Illness, 1957, p.45.
52. Landa, 2008.
53. Matson, Wilkins, *et al.*, 2001.
54. For a list, see Barbaro and Dissanayake, 2009.
55. For a review, see also Zwaigenbaum, Bryson, *et al.*, 2009.
56. Allison, Auciello, *et al.*, 2008.
57. Baron-Cohen, Allen, *et al.*, 1992.
58. Robins, 2001b.
59. For a detailed discussion of individual instruments and comments, see Barbaro and Dissanayake, 2009.
60. Oosterling, Swinkels, *et al.*, 2009.

61. Sutera, Pandey, *et al.*, 2007.
62. Pierce, Carter, *et al.*, 2011.
63. Barbaro and Dissanayake, 2009.
64. Filipek, Accardo, *et al.*, 1999.
65. Bryson, Zwaigenbaum, *et al.*, 2007.
66. Naber, Bakermans-Kranenburg, *et al.*, 2008.
67. Maestro, Muratori, *et al.*, 2005.
68. Watson, Baranek, *et al.*, 2007.
69. Wilson and Jungner, 1968.
70. National Initiative for Autism: Screening and Assessment, 2003.
71. Council on Children with Disabilities, Section on Developmental Behavioural Pediatrics, Bright Futures Steering Committee *et al.*, 2006, from Figure 1.
72. Tebruegge, Nandini, *et al.*, 2004.
73. Boddaert, Zilbovicius, *et al.*, 2009.

CHAPTER 9 PRESENTATION, PREVALENCE, TREATMENT AND COURSE OF THE AUTISM SPECTRUM DISORDERS

1. Riley, DuPaul, *et al.*, 2008.
2. Hurtig, Ebeling, *et al.*, 2007.
3. McLoughlin, Ronald, *et al.*, 2007.
4. Stavro, Ettenhofer, *et al.*, 2007.
5. Malloy-Diniz, Fuentes, *et al.*, 2007.
6. Harrison, Edwards, *et al.*, 2007.
7. Adler, Spencer, *et al.*, 2006.
8. Balint, Czobor, *et al.*, 2009.
9. Bennett, Szatmari, *et al.*, 2008.
10. Luyster, Kadlec, *et al.*, 2008.
11. Ghaziuddin, 2008.
12. Wing and Gould, 1979.
13. Williams, Higgins, *et al.*, 2006.
14. Levy, Giarelli, *et al.*, 2010.
15. Mandell, Wiggins, *et al.*, 2009.
16. Kogan, Blumberg, *et al.*, 2009.
17. Lotter, 1966.
18. Kraepelin, 1904.
19. Morgan, Charalambides, *et al.*, 2010.
20. Keen, Reid, *et al.*, 2010.
21. Mattila, Kielinen, *et al.*, 2007.
22. Fombonne, Zakarian, *et al.*, 2006.
23. Polanczyk, de Lima, *et al.*, 2007.
24. Yeargin-Allsopp, Rice, *et al.*, 2003.
25. Balfe, Chen, *et al.*, 2005.
26. Moss, Nair, *et al.*, 2007.
27. Fecteau, Mottron, *et al.*, 2003.
28. Helt, Kelley, *et al.*, 2008.
29. Shattuck, Seltzer, *et al.*, 2007.
30. Constantino, Abbacchi, *et al.*, 2009.
31. Roberts, Roberts, *et al.*, 2009.
32. Fayyad, de Graaf, *et al.*, 2007.
33. Thome, 2008.
34. Balfe, Tantam, *et al.*, 2011.
35. Liptak, Benzoni, *et al.*, 2008.
36. Autism and Developmental Disabilities Monitoring Network Surveillance Year 2000 Principal Investigations; Centers for Disease Control and Prevention, 2007.

37. Matson, Wilkins, *et al.*, 2008.
38. Bryson, Bradley, *et al.*, 2008.
39. Ouellette-Kuntz, Coo, *et al.*, 2007.
40. Williams, Higgins, *et al.*, 2006.
41. Fombonne, Simmons, *et al.*, 2003.
42. Wazana, Bresnahan, *et al.*, 2007.
43. Bertrand, Mars, *et al.*, 2001.
44. Wing, 1996a.
45. Coo, Ouellette-Kuntz, *et al.*, 2008.
46. Croen, Grether, *et al.*, 2002.
47. Mandell, Thompson, *et al.*, 2005.
48. Aman, 2005.
49. Seida, Ospina, *et al.*, 2009.
50. See Research Autism, 2011.
51. Plantin and Daneback, 2009.
52. Rhoades, Scarpa, *et al.*, 2007.
53. Chuthapisith, diMambro, *et al.*, 2009.
54. Altemeier and Altemeier, 2009.
55. Kurtz and Mueser, 2008.
56. Boardman, Grove, *et al.*, 2003.
57. Burns, Catty, *et al.*, 2009.
58. Dawson, 2009.
59. Wakako, Hiroshi, *et al.*, 2009.
60. Smith, Felce, *et al.*, 2002.
61. Howlin, Magiati, *et al.*, 2009.
62. Ospina, Krebs, *et al.*, 2008.
63. Reichow and Wolery, 2009.
64. Grindle, Kovshoff, *et al.*, 2009.
65. Kodak and Piazza, 2008.
66. Minshawi, 2008.
67. Golan and Baron-Cohen, 2006.
68. Clark, Winkielman, *et al.*, 2008.
69. Howlin, 1999.
70. Wellman, Baron-Cohen, *et al.*, 2002.
71. Rockwell, 2008.
72. Lundgren, Brownell, *et al.*, 2010.
73. Block-Lerner, Adair, *et al.*, 2007.
74. Bellini, Peters, *et al.*, 2007.
75. Bauminger 2007a.

76. Bellini and Peters, 2008.
77. Charman, 2011.
78. Coolican, Smith, *et al.*, 2010.
79. Laugeson, Frankel, *et al.*, 2009.
80. Nemeth, Balogh, *et al.*, 2010.
81. Hess, Morrier, *et al.*, 2008.
82. Chan and O'Reilly, 2008.
83. Quirmbach, Lincoln, *et al.*, 2009.
84. Gray, 2002.
85. See www.thegraycenter.org.
86. Ozdemir, 2008.
87. Crozier and Tincani, 2007.
88. Greenspan and Wieder, 2009.
89. McGurk, Mueser, *et al.*, 2009.
90. Jennes-Coussens, Magill-Evans, *et al.*, 2006.
91. Garcia-Villamisar and Hughes, 2007.
92. Tantam, 1988d.
93. Saldana, Alvarez, *et al.*, 2009.
94. Bernfort, Nordfeldt, *et al.*, 2008.
95. Biederman, Petty, *et al.*, 2008.
96. de Graaf, Kessler, *et al.*, 2008.
97. Lawer, Brusilovskiy, *et al.*, 2009.
98. Van Wieren, Reid, *et al.*, 2008.
99. Howlin, Alcock, *et al.*, 2005.
100. Hume, Loftin, *et al.*, 2009.
101. Kenworthy, Black, *et al.*, 2009.
102. Beebe, 2006.
103. Biederman, Seidman, *et al.*, 2008.
104. Kurscheidt, Peiler, *et al.*, 2008.
105. Solanto, Marks, *et al.*, 2008.
106. Hempel, Giesel, *et al.*, 2004.
107. Olesen, Westerberg, *et al.*, 2004.
108. See www.bbc.co.uk/labuk/results/braintestbritain/1_results_summary.html.
109. Caria, Veit, *et al.*, 2007.
110. Heinrich, Gevensleben, *et al.*, 2007.
111. Charman, Howlin, *et al.*, 2004.
112. Gasic, Smoller, *et al.*, 2009.
113. Sonuga-Barke, Lasky-Su, *et al.*, 2008.
114. White, Oswald, *et al.*, 2009.
115. Vismara, Colombi, *et al.*, 2009.
116. Leff and Vaughn, 1985.
117. Miklowitz, Axelson, *et al.*, 2008.
118. Miklowitz, Axelson, *et al.*, 2009.
119. Sonuga-Barke, Oades, *et al.*, 2009.
120. Tustin, 1972.
121. Tantam, 2002a.
122. Wood, Drahota, *et al.*, 2009.
123. Cotugno, 2009.
124. Heidegger, 1927, p.27.
125. Tantam, 2009.
126. Sartre, 1969.
127. National Autistic Society, 2007.
128. Wong, 2009.
129. Hess, Morrier, *et al.*, 2008.
130. Case-Smith and Arbesman, 2008.
131. Oberman and Ramachandran, 2008.
132. Parise and Spence, 2009.
133. Viaud-Delmon, Warusfel, *et al.*, 2006.
134. Fazlioglu and Baran, 2008.
135. Gringras, 2000.
136. Harrington, 2008.
137. Rosenberg, Mandell, *et al.*, 2010.
138. Mandell, Morales, *et al.*, 2008.
139. Fombonne, 2003.
140. Gillberg, Billstedt, *et al.*, 2009.
141. Mouridsen, Bronnum-Hansen, *et al.*, 2008.
142. WHO, 1977.
143. Mouridsen, Rich, *et al.*, 2008.
144. Brook and Boaz, 2006.
145. Reimer, D'Ambrosio, *et al.*, 2007.
146. Asperger, 1944.
147. Kanner, Rodriguez, *et al.*, 1972.
148. Farley, McMahon, *et al.*, 2009.
149. Seltzer, Krauss, *et al.*, 2003.
150. Berger and Kellner, 1964.
151. Bryson, Zwaigenbaum, *et al.*, 2007.
152. Dietz, Swinkels, *et al.*, 2007.
153. Farley, McMahon, *et al.*, 2009.
154. Sanchez-Valle, Posada, *et al.*, 2008.
155. Billstedt, Gillberg, *et al.*, 2005.
156. Cederlund, Hagberg, *et al.*, 2008.
157. Klin, Saulnier, *et al.*, 2007.
158. Wing and Gould, 1979.
159. Beglinger and Smith, 2005.
160. Cederlund, Hagberg, *et al.*, 2008.
161. Bennett, Szatmari, *et al.*, 2008.
162. McGovern and Sigman, 2005.
163. Tantam, 2000.
164. Allik, Larsson, *et al.*, 2006a.
165. Farmer and Oliver, 2005.
166. Lee, Harrington, *et al.*, 2008.
167. Constantine, Hudziak, *et al.*, 2003.
168. Blanchard, Gurka, *et al.*, 2006.
169. Shu, 2009.
170. Mugno, Ruta, *et al.*, 2007.
171. Pottie, Cohen, *et al.*, 2009.
172. Nyden, Myren, *et al.*, 2007.
173. Myers, Mackintosh, *et al.*, 2009.
174. Tehee, 2009.
175. Benson, 2009.
176. Pottie, 2009.
177. Smith, Seltzer, *et al.*, 2008.
178. Escobar, Hervas, *et al.*, 2008.
179. De Ridder and De Graeve, 2006.
180. Matza, Paramore, *et al.*, 2005. a) p.1.
181. Birnbaum, Kessler, *et al.*, 2005.
182. Shimabukuro, Grosse, *et al.*, 2008.
183. Leslie and Martin, 2007.
184. Bebbington and Beecham, 2007.
185. Jarbrink, 2007.
186. Montes and Halterman, 2008.
187. Ganz, 2007. a) p.343.
188. Farley, McMahon, *et al.*, 2009.
189. Turk, Bax, *et al.*, 2009.
190. Miles, Takahashi, *et al.*, 2005.
191. Parmeggiani, Posar, *et al.*, 2007.
192. Plioplys, Dunn, *et al.*, 2007.

CHAPTER 10 CLINICAL ASSESSMENT OF THE ASDs

1. Dover and Le Couteur, 2007.
2. Tager-Flusberg, Rogers, *et al.*, 2009.
3. Roberts and Prior, 2006.
4. Shattuck, Durkin, *et al.*, 2009.
5. Howlin and Moore, 1997.
6. Daley, 2004.
7. English and Essex, 2001.
8. Chawarska, Paul, *et al.*, 2007.
9. Lord, Rutter, *et al.*, 1994.
10. Le Couteur, Rutter, *et al.*, 1989.
11. Kan, Buitelaar, *et al.*, 2008.
12. Billstedt, Gillberg, *et al.*, 2007.
13. Kleinman, Ventola, *et al.*, 2008.
14. Moss, Magiati, *et al.*, 2008.
15. Gray, Tonge, *et al.*, 2008.
16. Le Couteur, Haden, *et al.*, 2008.
17. Boomsma, van Lang, *et al.*, 2008.
18. Gotham, Risi, *et al.*, 2008.
19. Tantam, 1988b.
20. Peay, Veach, *et al.*, 2008.
21. Cullen, Samuels, *et al.*, 2008.
22. Lord, Risi, *et al.*, 2000.
23. Lord, Rutter, *et al.*, 1989.
24. DiLavore, Lord, *et al.*, 1995.
25. Hepburn, Philofsky, *et al.*, 2008.
26. McGovern and Sigman, 2005.
27. Bryson, Zwaigenbaum, *et al.*, 2008.
28. Walker, 1995.
29. Golarai, Grill-Spector, *et al.*, 2006.
30. Deruelle, Rondan, *et al.*, 2008.
31. Dockrell, 2001.
32. Geurts and Embrechts, 2008.
33. Colle, Baron-Cohen, *et al.*, 2008.
34. Iarocci, *et al.*, 2007, p.113.
35. Eisenberg, Fabes, *et al.*, 2006.
36. McIntosh, Reichmann-Decker, *et al.*, 2006.
37. Minio-Paluello, Baron-Cohen, *et al.*, 2009.
38. Dziobek, Rogers, *et al.*, 2008.
39. Marton, Wiener, *et al.*, 2009.
40. Zhou, Valiente, *et al.*, 2003.
41. Hemmerdinger, Stoddart, *et al.*, 2007.
42. Dadds, Hunter, *et al.*, 2008.
43. Dadds, Hawes, *et al.*, 2009.
44. Jolliffe and Farrington, 2004.
45. Worthen, 2000.
46. Argyle and Henderson, 1984.
47. Davis and Kraus, 1997.
48. Litvack-Miller, 1993.
49. Litvack-Miller, McDougall, *et al.*, 1997.
50. Rogers, Dziobek, *et al.*, 2007.
51. Muncer and Ling, 2006.
52. Lawrence, Shaw, *et al.*, 2004.
53. Prehn-Kristensen, Wiesner, *et al.*, 2009.
54. Ickes, 1993.
55. Teherani, Hauer, *et al.*, 2008.
56. Webster and Beech, 2000.
57. Zahn, de Oliveira-Souza, *et al.*, 2009.
58. Nummenmaa, Hirvonen, *et al.*, 2008.
59. Brune, Abdel-Hamid, *et al.*, 2007.
60. Cotugno, 2009.
61. Corbett, Constantine, *et al.*, 2009.
62. Yamada, Hirao, *et al.*, 2007. a) p.1.
63. Sahyoun, Soulières, *et al.*, 2009.
64. Spek, Scholte, *et al.*, 2008
65. Bogte, Flamma, *et al.*, 2009.
66. Chamberlain and Sahakian, 2007.
67. Bramham, Ambery, *et al.*, 2009.
68. Johnson, Robertson, *et al.*, 2007.
69. Baron-Cohen, Wright, *et al.*, 1998.
70. Baron-Cohen, 2003. a) p.3. b) p.2.
71. Baron-Cohen, 2009.
72. Baron-Cohen and Hammer, 1997.
73. Baron-Cohen, Richler, *et al.*, 2003.
74. Baron-Cohen and Wheelwright, 2004.
75. Auyeung, Wheelwright, *et al.*, 2009.
76. Erikson, 1963.
77. http://autismresearchcentre.com.
78. Geurts, Corbett, *et al.*, 2009.
79. Van Eylen, Boets, *et al.*, 2011.
80. Annoni, Pegna, *et al.*, 1998.
81. Shah and Frith, 1983.
82. Rinehart, Bradshaw, *et al.*, 2000.
83. Keehn, Brenner, *et al.*, 2009.
84. Happé, Briskman, *et al.*, 2001.
85. Chen, Rodgers, *et al.*, 2009.
86. Berger, Aerts, *et al.*, 2002.
87. Joosten, Bundy, *et al.*, 2009.
88. Richler, Bishop, *et al.*, 2007.
89. Smith, Lang, *et al.*, 2009.
90. DeLoache, Simcock, *et al.*, 2007.
91. Peters-Scheffer, Didden, *et al.*, 2008.
92. Boyd, Baranek, *et al.*, 2010.
93. Broadbent, 1958.
94. Milne, Griffiths, *et al.*, 2009.
95. Bach and Dakin, 2009.
96. Ashwin, Ashwin, *et al.*, 2009.
97. Silverman, Turner, *et al.*, 2009.
98. Capano, Minden, *et al.*, 2008.
99. Rubinsten and Henik, 2009.
100. Karande, Satam, *et al.*, 2007.
101. Gabrieli, 2009.
102. Mariën, Baillieux, *et al.*, 2009.
103. Murphy, Bolton, *et al.*, 2000.
104. See Tantam, Berrios, *et al.*, 1996a for background and references.
105. Hurst, Nelson-Gray, *et al.*, 2007.
106. Tantam, 1988d.
107. Wolff, 2000.
108. Tantam, 1996a.
109. White, Oswald, *et al.*, 2009.
110. Freitag, Agelopoulos, *et al.*, 2009.
111. Gadow, Roohi, *et al.*, 2009.
112. Miller, Shen, *et al.*, 2009.
113. Kanne, Christ, *et al.*, 2009.
114. Bejerot and Mortberg 2009.
115. Kelly, Garnett, *et al.*, 2008.
116. Xue, Brimacombe, *et al.*, 2008.
117. Tantam, 1986.
118. These examples are reported in Tantam, 1986.
119. Spitzer, Williams, *et al.*, 1999.
120. Connor, Davidson, *et al.*, 2000.
121. MacNeil, Lopes, *et al.*, 2009.

122. Nardi, Lopes, *et al.*, 2009.
123. Flosnik, Cortese, *et al.*, 2009.
124. Lopes, Azevedo, *et al.*, 2009.
125. Rutter, Kreppner, *et al.*, 2009.
126. Main, 1996.
127. Ainsworth, Blehar, *et al.*, 1978.
128. Heinrichs and Domes, 2008.
129. Goursaud and Bachevalier, 2007.
130. Yamasue, Kuwabara, *et al.*, 2009.
131. Donaldson, Young, *et al.*, 2008.
132. Campbell, Datta, *et al.*, 2011.
133. Lucht, Barnow, *et al.*, 2009.
134. Shamay-Tsoory, Aharon-Peretz, *et al.*, 2009.
135. Bettelheim, 1967.
136. Rutgers, Bakermans-Kranenburg, *et al.*, 2004.
137. Taylor, Target, *et al.*, 2008.
138. Gillott and Standen, 2007.
139. Friedman-Weieneth, Harvey, *et al.*, 2007.
140. Charman, Howlin, *et al.*, 2004.
141. Franc, Maury, *et al.*, 2009.
142. George, Kaplan, *et al.*, 1985.
143. Koegel, Schreibman, *et al.*, 1983.
144. Miles, Takahashi, *et al.* 2005.
145. Esposito and Venuti, 2008.
146. Hammond, Forster-Gibson, *et al.*, 2008.
147. Butler, Allen, *et al.*, 1988.
148. Bartram, Rigby, *et al.*, 2005.
149. Hall, 2007.
150. Esposito, Venuti, *et al.*, 2009.
151. Weimer, Schatz, *et al.*, 2001.
152. Crane, Goddard, *et al.*, 2009.
153. Coskun, Varghese, *et al.*, 2009.
154. Ashwin, Ashwin, *et al.*, 2009.

155. Ben-Sasson, Cermak, *et al.*, 2008.
156. Cascio, McGlone, *et al.*, 2008.
157. Dunn, Myles, *et al.*, 2002.
158. Crane, Goddard, *et al.*, 2009.
159. Reynolds and Lane, 2008.
160. Allik, Larsson, *et al.*, 2008.
161. Allik, Larsson, *et al.*, 2006b.
162. Hu, Sarachana, *et al.*, 2009.
163. Pandi-Perumal, Srinivasan, *et al.*, 2007.
164. Hare, Jones, *et al.*, 2006.
165. Melke, Goubran, *et al.*, 2008.
166. Giannotti, Cortesi, *et al.*, 2008.
167. Goodlin-Jones, Tang, *et al.*, 2009.
168. Nixon, Thompson, *et al.*, 2008.
169. Goodlin-Jones, Waters, *et al.*, 2009.
170. Gruber, Xi, *et al.*, 2009.
171. Goraya, Cruz, *et al.*, 2009.
172. Silvestri, Gagliano, *et al.*, 2009.
173. Gau and Chiang, 2009.
174. Mayes, Calhoun, *et al.*, 2009.
175. Corkum, Panton, *et al.*, 2008.
176. Chorney, Detweiler, *et al.*, 2008.
177. Teman, Tippmann-Peikert, *et al.*, 2009.
178. Thomas, Bonanni, *et al.*, 2007.
179. Luckenbaugh, Findling, *et al.*, 2009.
180. Duffy, Alda, *et al.*, 2007.
181. Owens, Sangal, *et al.*, 2009.
182. Gruber, Xi, *et al.*, 2009.
183. Owens, Maxim, *et al.*, 2000.
184. Murphy, Beecham, *et al.*, 2011.
185. Sahiner, Chan, *et al.*, 2008.
186. Giger, Chan, *et al.*, 2008.

CHAPTER II AETIOLOGY OF THE AUTISM SPECTRUM DISORDERS

1. Chen, *et al.*, 2009.
2. Shimoji and Tomiyama, 2004.
3. Jabourian, Turpin, *et al.*, 2002.
4. Wolańczyk, Banaszkiewicz, *et al.*, 2000.
5. Howlin, 2001.
6. Landgren, 1992.
7. Kayaalp, 2007.
8. Knoester, Helmerhorst, *et al.*, 2007.
9. Orphanet, 2008.
10. Limperopoulos, Bassan, *et al.*, 2008.
11. Tsao and Mendell, 2007.
12. Johansson, Billstedt, *et al.*, 2007.
13. Hartshorne, Grialou, *et al.*, 2005.
14. Miles, Hadden, *et al.*, 2000.
15. Morrow, Whitman, *et al.*, 1990.
16. Woodrow and Burrows, 2003.
17. Yamashita, Fujimoto, *et al.*, 2003.
18. Moretti, Peters, *et al.*, 2008.
19. Newmeyer, Degrauw, *et al.*, 2007.
20. Strömland, Sjögreen, *et al.*, 2002.
21. Briegel, Schimek, *et al.*, 2009.
22. Chugani, Da Silva, *et al.*, 1996.
23. Badawi, Dixon, *et al.*, 2006.
24. Mbarek, Marouillat, *et al.*, 1999.

25. Nordin and Gillberg, 1996.
26. Kilincaslan and Mukaddes, 2009.
27. Fombonne, Du Mazaubrun, *et al.*, 1997.
28. Rogers and Newhart-Larson, 1989.
29. Janson, 1993.
30. Kumar, Sarvananthan, *et al.*, 2009.
31. Tantam, Evered, *et al.*, 1990.
32. Yoshimura, 1989.
33. Challman, Barbaresi, *et al.*, 2003.
34. Hendriksen and Vles, 2008.
35. Young, Barton, *et al.*, 2008.
36. Numin, Major, *et al.*, 2011.
37. Pascual-Castroviejo, Roche, *et al.*, 1998.
38. Bakare and Ikegwuonu, 2008.
39. Simmonds, Duley, *et al.*, 1997.
40. Blanchon, Gay, *et al.*, 2002.
41. Zaffanello, Zamboni, *et al.*, 2003.
42. Topcu, Saatci, *et al.*, 2002.
43. Baieli, Pavone, *et al.*, 2003.
44. Kent, Emerton, *et al.*, 2008.
45. Sacnacchal, Forget, *et al.*, 2003.
46. Zafeiriou, Ververi, *et al.*, 2008.
47. Fernell, Gillberg, *et al.*, 1991.
48. Kent, Evans, *et al.*, 1999.

49. Kaufmann, Cortell, *et al.*, 2004.
50. Donnelly, Wolpert, *et al.*, 2000.
51. El Abd, Patton, *et al.*, 1999.
52. Assumpcao, Santos, *et al.*, 1999.
53. Wassmer, Davies, *et al.*, 2003.
54. Licht and Lynch, 2002.
55. David, Wacharasindu, *et al.*, 1993.
56. Goffin, Heofsloot, *et al.*, 2001.
57. Balfe, Chen, *et al.*, 2005.
58. Geschwind and Galaburda, 1985.
59. Miles and Hillman, 2000.
60. Valla and Ceci, 2011.
61. Hines, 2010.
62. Fine, 2010.
63. Yamasue, Kuwabara, *et al.*, 2009.
64. Baron-Cohen, Lombardo, *et al.*, 2011.
65. Bora, Yucel, *et al.* 2009.
66. Riem, Bakermans-Kranenburg, *et al.*, 2011.
67. Bos, Panksepp, *et al.*, 2011.
68. Guastella, Einfeld, *et al.*, 2010.
69. Brewster, Mullin, *et al.*, 2011.
70. Taniai, Nishiyama, *et al.*, 2008.
71. Rosenberg, Law, *et al.*, 2009.
72. Hoekstra, Bartels, *et al.*, 2007.
73. Hallmayer, Cleveland, *et al.*, 2011.
74. Greven Rijsdijk, *et al.*, 2011.
75. Reiersen, Constantino, *et al.*, 2008.
76. Cederlund and Gillberg, 2004.
77. Zhao, Leotta, *et al.*, 2007.
78. Iacoboni and Mazziotta, 2007.
79. Reichenberg, Gross, *et al.*, 2006.
80. Weiser, Reichenberg, *et al.*, 2008.
81. Shelton, Tancredi, *et al.*, 2010.
82. Faraone and Biederman, 1997.
83. Weinstein, Apfel, *et al.*, 1998.
84. Segenreich, Fortes, *et al.*, 2009.
85. Daniels, Forssen, *et al.*, 2008.
86. O'Donovan, Craddock, *et al.*, 2009.
87. Craddock, O'Donovan, *et al.*, 2009.
88. Rosenberg, Law, *et al.*, 2009.
89. Bryson, Corrigan, *et al.*, 2008.
90. Nijmeijer, Hoekstra, *et al.*, 2009.
91. Folstein and Rutter, 1977.
92. Micali, Chakrabarti, *et al.*, 2004.
93. Elsabbagh, Volein, *et al.*, 2009b.
94. Losh, Adolphs, *et al.*, 2009.
95. Constantino, Davis, *et al.*, 2003.
96. Detterman, 1999.
97. Ruppert and Maisch, 2003.
98. Mosconi, Kay, *et al.*, 2010.
99. Neuman, Todd, *et al.*, 1999.
100. Maestrini, Pagnamenta, *et al.*, 2009.
101. Wassink and Piven, 2000.
102. Verkerk, Mathews, *et al.*, 2003.
103. Acosta and Pearl, 2003.
104. Keller and Persico, 2003.
105. Anderson, 2002.
106. Levy, Hay, *et al.*, 1997.
107. Fisher, Francks, *et al.*, 2002.
108. Ogdie, Fisher, *et al.*, 2004.
109. Buschgens, van Aken, *et al.*, 2008.
110. Maussion, Carayol, *et al.*, 2008.
111. Chakrabarti, Dudbridge, *et al.*, 2009.

112. Buttenschøn, Lauritsen, *et al.*, 2009.
113. Liu, Novosedlik, *et al.*, 2009.
114. Sugie, Sugie, *et al.*, 2009.
115. Lepagnol-Bestel, Maussion, *et al.*, 2008.
116. Smith, Escamilla, *et al.*, 2001.
117. Tischfield, Bosley, *et al.*, 2005.
118. Muscarella, Guarnieri, *et al.*, 2007.
119. Canu, Boccardi, *et al.*, 2009.
120. Conciatori, Stodgell, *et al.*, 2004.
121. Allen-Brady, Miller, *et al.*, 2008.
122. Mervis, Robinson, *et al.*, 2000.
123. Lennon, Cooper, *et al.*, 2007.
124. Campbell, Sutcliffe, *et al.*, 2006.
125. Sousa, Clark, *et al.*, 2008.
126. Vourc'h, Martin, *et al.*, 2003.
127. Yang, Lung, *et al.*, 2008.
128. Krone, Riepe, *et al.*, 2005.
129. Ruta, Ingudomnukul, *et al.*, 2011.
130. Stiles, 2009.
131. Fraser, Bayazitov, *et al.*, 2008.
132. Balciuniene, Feng, *et al.*, 2007.
133. van der Velden, Vreeburg, *et al.*, 2008.
134. Szatmari, Paterson, *et al.*, 2007.
135. Liu, Paterson, *et al.*, 2008.
136. Duvall, Lu, *et al.*, 2007.
137. Schellenberg, Dawson, *et al.*, 2006.
138. Arking, Cutler, *et al.*, 2008.
139. Hsiung, Kaplan, *et al.*, 2004.
140. Licht and Lynch, 2002.
141. Ma, Cuccaro, *et al.*, 2007.
142. Croen, Goines, *et al.*, 2008.
143. Smith, Woodroffe, *et al.*, 2002.
144. Steele, Al Adeimi, *et al.*, 2001.
145. Abelson, Kwan, *et al.*, 2005.
146. Castermans, Thienpoint, *et al.*, 2008.
147. Battaglia, 2005.
148. Miller, Shen, *et al.*, 2009.
149. Veltman, Thompson, *et al.*, 2004.
150. Soni, Whittington, *et al.*, 2008.
151. Webb, Maina, *et al.* 2008.
152. Ben-Shachar, Lanpher, *et al.*, 2009.
153. Barnby, Abbott, *et al.*, 2005.
154. Philippi, Roschmann, *et al.*, 2005.
155. Weiss, Shen, *et al.*, 2008.
156. Fernandez, Roberts, *et al.*, 2009.
157. Bijlsma, Gijsbers, *et al.*, 2009.
158. Hannes, Sharp, *et al.*, 2009.
159. Asherson, Zhou, *et al.*, 2008.
160. Zhou, Dempfle, *et al.*, 2008.
161. Ullmann, Turner, *et al.*, 2007.
162. Bönisch and Bruss, 2006.
163. Nakamine, Ouchanov, *et al.*, 2008.
164. Havlovicova, Novotna, *et al.*, 2007.
165. Strom, Stone, *et al.*, 2009.
166. Escamilla, Hare, *et al.*, 2009.
167. Amin, Aulchenko, *et al.*, 2009.
168. Allen-Brady, Miller, *et al.*, 2009.
169. Kent, Evans, *et al.*, 1999.
170. Hepburn, Philofsky, *et al.*, 2008.
171. Kobrynski and Sullivan, 2007.
172. Ou, Berg, *et al.*, 2008.
173. Shprintzen, 2008.
174. Durand, Betancur, *et al.*, 2007.

175. Tartaglia, Davis, *et al.*, 2008.
176. McKenzie, Ponte, *et al.*, 2007.
177. Wallerstein, Sugalski, *et al.*, 2008.
178. Wada, 2009.
179. Moser, Raymond, *et al.*, 2005.
180. de Winter, van Dijk, *et al.*, 2009.
181. Burusnukul, de Los Reyes, *et al.*, 2008.
182. Noor, Gainakopoulos, *et al.*, 2009.
183. Artigas-Pallares, Gabau-Vila, *et al.*, 2005.
184. See www.genome.gov.
185. See www.ncbi.nlm.nih.gov/omim.
186. See http://rarediseases.info.nih.gov/GARD.
187. See www.ncbi.nlm.nih.gov/bookshelf/
     br.fcgi?book=gene.
188. Williams, Mars, *et al.*, 2007.
189. Gardener, Spiegelman, *et al.*, 2009.
190. Rice, Harold, *et al.*, 2010.
191. Geva, Eshel, *et al.*, 2008.
192. Leonard, Nassar, *et al.*, 2008.
193. Strang-Karlsson, Raikkonen, *et al.*, 2008.
194. Roza, Steegers, *et al.*, 2008.
195. Juul-Dam, Townsend, *et al.*, 2001.
196. Talarovicova, Krskova, *et al.*, 2007.
197. Insel, 2010.
198. Meyer-Lindenberg, 2008.
199. Andari, Duhamel, *et al.*, 2010.
200. Evans, Shergill, *et al.*, 2010.
201. Johnson and Breedlove, 2010.
202. Kimura, Tanizawa, *et al.*, 1992.
203. Evardone and Alexander, 2009.
204. Breedlove, 2010.
205. Voracek, Pietschnig, *et al.*, 2011.
206. Mouridsen, Rich, *et al.*, 2010.
207. Knickmeyer, Wheelwright, *et al.*, 2008.
208. Geier and Geier, 2007.
209. Auyeung, Baron-Cohen, *et al.*, 2009.
210. Martel, 2009.
211. Falter, Plaisted, *et al.*, 2008.
212. Barbeau, Mendrek, *et al.*, 2009.
213. Manson, 2008.
214. Coleman, 1989.
215. Yamazaki, Chess, *et al.*, 1977.
216. Pinillos-Pison, Llorente-Cereza, *et al.*, 2009.
217. Guerri, Bazinet, *et al.*, 2009.
218. Murthy, Kudlur, *et al.*, 2009.
219. Rodriguez, Olsen, *et al.*, 2009.
220. Bishop, Gahagan, *et al.*, 2007.
221. Bromley, Baker, *et al.*, 2009.
222. Miller, Strömland, *et al.*, 2005.
223. Ornoy, 2009.
224. Kuwagata, Ogawa, *et al.*, 2009.
225. Snow, Hartle, *et al.*, 2008.
226. Ornoy, 2003.
227. Bass, Corwin, *et al.*, 2004.
228. Badawi, Dixon, *et al.*, 2006.
229. Lindstrom, Lagerroos, *et al.*, 2006.
230. Kolevzon, Gross, *et al.*, 2007.
231. Bolton, Murphy, *et al.*, 1997.
232. Bilder, Pinborough-Zimmerman, *et al.*, 2009.
233. Wagner, Schmidt, *et al.*, 2009.
234. Dammann, Naples, *et al.*, 2009.
235. Jangaard, Fell, *et al.*, 2008.
236. Croen, Yoshinda, *et al.*, 2005.
237. Newman, 2003.
238. Royal College of Obstetricians and Gynaecologists, 2010.
239. Rennie, Burman-Roy, *et al.*, 2010.
240. Hulbert-Williams and Hastings, 2008.
241. Curatolo, Paloscia, *et al.*, 2009.
242. Rutter, Kreppner, *et al.*, 2007.
243. Hoksbergen, Laak, *et al.*, 2005.
244. Rutter, Andersen-Wood, *et al.*, 1999.
245. Moulson, Fox, *et al.*, 2009.
246. Beverly, McGuinness, *et al.*, 2008.
247. Colvert, Rutter, *et al.*, 2008b.
248. Colvert, Rutter, *et al.*, 2008a.
249. Camfield and Camfield, 2002.
250. Danielsson, Viggedal, *et al.*, 2008.
251. See www.epilepsy.org.uk
252. Schubert, 2005.
253. Spence and Schneider, 2009.
254. Muñoz-Yunta, Ortiz, *et al.*, 2008.
255. Hara, 2007.
256. Tuchman and Rapin, 2002.
257. Deonna and Roulet, 2006.
258. Tuchman, Moshe, *et al.*, 2009.
259. Malhotra and Gupta, 2002.
260. Murphy, Wheless, *et al.*, 2000.
261. Perez-Jimenez, Villarejo, *et al.*, 2003.
262. Di Nardo, Kramvis, *et al.*, 2009.
263. Bourgeron, 2009.
264. Howlin, 2002.
265. See http://dermatlas.med.jhmi.edu/derm.
266. Muzykewicz, Newberry, *et al.*, 2007.
267. Gillberg, Gillberg, *et al.*, 1994.
268. Gutierrez, Smalley, *et al.*, 1998.
269. Hunt and Shepherd, 1993.
270. Osborne and O'Callaghan, 2003.
271. Bolton, Park, *et al.*, 2002.
272. Lammert, Friedman, *et al.*, 2005.
273. Duong, Bastuji-Garin, *et al.*, 2011.
274. Shilyansky, Karlsgodt, *et al.*, 2010.
275. Martins, Monteiro, *et al.*, 2007.
276. Marui, Hashimoto, *et al.*, 2004.
277. Sacco, Militerni, *et al.*, 2007.
278. van Daalen, Swinkels, *et al.*, 2007.
279. Williams, Dagli, *et al.*, 2008.
280. Kilian, Brown, *et al.*, 2008.
281. Varga, Pastore, *et al.*, 2009.
282. Giunco, Moretti-Ferreira, *et al.*, 2008.
283. Bertrand, Mars, *et al.*, 2001.
284. Gillberg and de Souza, 2002.
285. Deutsch and Joseph, 2003.
286. Tirosh and Canby, 1993.
287. White, O'Reilly, *et al.*, 2009.
288. Tate, Bigler, *et al.*, 2007.
289. Burmeister, Hannay, *et al.*, 2005.
290. Graham, Rosner, *et al.*, 2005.
291. Mostofsky, Bunoski, *et al.*, 2004.
292. Mukaddes, Kilincaslan, *et al.*, 2007.
293. Kumar, Sarvananthan, *et al.*, 2009.
294. Kielinen, Rantala, *et al.*, 2004.
295. Roper, Arnold, *et al.*, 2003.
296. Ekstrom, Hakenas-Plate, *et al.*, 2008.
297. Douniol, Jacquette, *et al.*, 2009.
298. Darke, Bushby, *et al.*, 2006.

299. Hendriksen and Vles, 2008.
300. Young, Barton, *et al.*, 2008.
301. Weidenheim, Goodman, *et al.*, 2001.
302. Pancrudo, Shanske, *et al.*, 2007.
303. Berlit, 2007.
304. Evans, 2009.
305. Tantam, Evered, *et al.*, 1990.
306. Purcell, Jeon, *et al.*, 2001.
307. Lee, Martin-Ruiz, *et al.*, 2002.
308. Perry, Lee, *et al.*, 2001.
309. Hussman, 2001.
310. Aldred, Moore, *et al.*, 2003.
311. Kelley, 2000.
312. Alberti, Pirrone, *et al.*, 1999.
313. Page, 2000.
314. Page and Moseley, 2002.
315. Zafeiriou, Ververi, *et al.*, 2008.
316. Bindu, Shehanaz, *et al.*, 2007.
317. Roper, Arnold, *et al.*, 2003.
318. Millward, Ferriter, *et al.*, 2008.
319. Roman, 2007.
320. Madsen, Hviid, *et al.*, 2002a.
321. Gerber and Offit, 2009.
322. Whiteley, Rodgers, *et al.*, 1999.
323. Kuddo and Nelson, 2003.
324. White, 2003.

325. Nikolov, Bearss, *et al.*, 2009.
326. Campbell, Buie, *et al.*, 2009.
327. Cass, Gringras, *et al.*, 2008.
328. Genuis and Bouchard, 2009.
329. Millward, Ferriter, *et al.*, 2008.
330. Geier, Kern, *et al.*, 2009.
331. Palmer, Blanchard, *et al.*, 2009.
332. Austin and Shandley, 2008.
333. Ha, Kwon, *et al.*, 2009.
334. Lee, Jacobs, *et al.*, 2007.
335. Grandjean and Landrigan, 2006.
336. Rauh, Garfinkel, *et al.*, 2006.
337. Kleinman, Brown, *et al.*, 2011.
338. Bouchard, Bellinger, *et al.*, 2010.
339. Atladottir, Pedersen, *et al.*, 2009.
340. Mouridsen, Rich, *et al.*, 2007.
341. Croen, Grether, *et al.*, 2005.
342. Castellani, Conti, *et al.*, 2009.
343. Cabanlit, Wills, *et al.*, 2007.
344. Saresella, Marventano, *et al.*, 2009.
345. Hughes, 2008.
346. Fazlioglu and Baran, 2008.
347. Gordon, 2009.
348. Church and Dale, 2002.
349. Hirschtritt, Hammond, *et al.*, 2009.
350. Elia, Dell, *et al.*, 2005.

CHAPTER 12 PRESENTATION IN INFANCY AND EARLY CHILDHOOD (THE PRE-SCHOOL YEARS)

1. Chawarska, Paul, *et al.*, 2007.
2. Clifford and Dissanayake, 2008.
3. Clifford, Young, *et al.*, 2007.
4. See, for example, a list produced by the Koegel Autism Center of the University of Santa Barbara at http://education.ucsb.edu/autism/Red-Flags.html.
5. Cox, Klein, *et al.*, 1999.
6. Moore and Goodson, 2003.
7. Schopler, Reichler, *et al.*, 1980.
8. Stone, Coonrod, *et al.*, 2000.
9. Baron-Cohen, Cox, *et al.*, 1996.
10. Howlin and Asgharian, 1999.
11. Soltis, 2004.
12. Hartley and Sikora, 2009a.
13. Hartley and Sikora, 2009b.
14. Rutgers, Bakermans-Kranenberg, *et al.*, 2004.
15. Rutgers, van IJzendoorn, *et al.*, 2007.
16. Oppenheim, Koren-Karie, *et al.*, 2009.
17. Mildenberger, Noterdaeme, *et al.*, 2001.
18. Snyder, Miller, *et al.*, 2008.
19. Martos-Perez and Ayuda-Pascual, 2003.
20. Newman, Macomber, *et al.*, 2007.
21. Barnett, 1997.
22. Creak, 1972.
23. Favazza, 1977.
24. Rutter, Kreppner, *et al.*, 2007.
25. Kanner, 1943.
26. Bettelheim, 1967.
27. Beverly, McGuinness. *et al.*, 2008.
28. Rommelse, Altink, *et al.*, 2008.
29. Rommelse, Altink, *et al.*, 2009.

30. Marcu, Oppenheim, *et al.*, 2009.
31. David, Nina, *et al.*, 2009.
32. Hartley, Sikora, *et al.*, 2008.
33. Hoevenaars-van den Boom, Antonissen, *et al.*, 2009.
34. Nishiyama, Taniai, *et al.*, 2009.
35. Bruining, de Sonneville, *et al.*, 2010.
36. Tantam, 2009.
37. Zhang, Lu, *et al.*, 2011.
38. Kenny, Lees, *et al.*, 2011.
39. Giuffre and De Sanctis, 2010.
40. Tatton-Brown, Cole, *et al.*, 1993–2011.
41. Morrow, Whitman, *et al.*, 1990.
42. Tantam, Evered, *et al.*, 1990.
43. Ball, Sullivan, *et al.*, 2005.
44. de Boer, Röder, *et al.*, 2006.
45. Naqvi, Cole, *et al.*, 2000.
46. Van der Aa, Rooms, *et al.*, 2009.
47. Edelmann, Prosnitz, *et al.*, 2007.
48. Lincoln, Searcy, *et al.*, 2007.
49. Frigerio, Burt, *et al.*, 2006.
50. Young, Lipina, *et al.*, 2008.
51. Santos, Meyer-Lindenberg, *et al.*, 2010.
52. Riby and Hancock, 2009a.
53. Holland, Whittington, *et al.*, 2003.
54. Bellone, Busti, *et al.*, 2011.
55. Soni, Whittington, *et al.*, 2008.
56. Veltman, Craig, *et al.*, 2005.
57. Mukaddes and Herguner, 2007.
58. Campbell, Daly, *et al.*, 2006.
59. Vorstman, Morcus, *et al.*, 2006.
60. Antshel, Aneja, *et al.*, 2007.

61. Durand, Betancur, *et al.*, 2007.
62. Sikora, Pettit-Kekel, *et al.*, 2006.
63. Shelley and Robertson, 2005.
64. Gropman, Duncan, *et al.*, 2006.
65. Lott and Dierssen, 2010.
66. Lowenthal, Paula, *et al.*, 2007.
67. Stancheva, Collins, *et al.*, 2003.
68. Shultz, Glaze, *et al.*, 1993.
69. Johnston, Jeon, *et al.*, 2001.
70. Renieri, Mari, *et al.*, 2009.
71. Subramaniam, Naidu, *et al.*, 1997.
72. Kishi and Macklis, 2005.
73. Young, Bebbington, *et al.*, 2008.
74. Mount, Charman, *et al.*, 2003.
75. Zinn, Roeltgen, *et al.*, 2007.
76. Good, Lawrence, *et al.*, 2003.
77. Geuze, Vermetten, *et al.*, 2005.
78. Russell, Wallis, *et al.*, 2006.
79. Donnelly, Wolpert, *et al.*, 2000.
80. Elgar and Campbell, 2001.
81. Bruining, Swaab, *et al.*, 2009.
82. Boada, Janusz, *et al.*, 2009.
83. van Rijn, Swaab, *et al.*, 2008.
84. Bechara, Didiot, *et al.*, 2009.
85. Zhang, Shen, *et al.*, 2009.
86. Li, Nguyen, *et al.*, 2004.
87. McCoy, Shao, *et al.*, 2002.
88. Wassink, Piven, *et al.*, 2001.
89. Kaufmann, Cortell, *et al.*, 2004.
90. Hall, Lightbody, *et al.*, 2008.
91. Clifford, Dissanayake, *et al.*, 2007.
92. Kent, Emerton, *et al.*, 2008.
93. Macarov, Zeigler, *et al.*, 2007.
94. Tamagaki, Murata, *et al.*, 2000.
95. Quigg, Rust, *et al.*, 2006.
96. Uzumcu, Karaman, *et al.*, 2009.
97. Wessels, Bohnhorst, *et al.*, 2010.
98. Callier, Faivre, *et al.*, 2008.
99. Tantam, Evered, *et al.*, 1990.
100. Jambaque, Chiron, *et al.*, 2000.
101. Klein, Tuchman, *et al.*, 2000.
102. Kolvin, 1971.
103. Heller, 1908.
104. De Sanctis, 1908.
105. For a detailed discussion of the history, see Dhossche, Wing, *et al.*, 2006.
106. Palomo, Thompson, *et al.*, 2008.
107. Fombonne, 2002.
108. Kurita, Koyama, *et al.* 2005b.
109. Kurita, Osada, *et al.*, 2004.
110. Mordekar, Prendergast, *et al.*, 2009.
111. Mouridsen, Rich, *et al.*, 1998.
112. Dover and Le Couteur, 2007.
113. Miles, Takahashi, *et al.*, 2005.
114. Battaglia and Carey, 2006.
115. Reichow and Wolery 2009.
116. Howlin, Magiati, *et al.*, 2009.
117. Wimpory, Hobson, *et al.*, 2007.
118. Girolametto, Sussman, *et al.*, 2007.
119. Wakako, Hiroshi, *et al.*, 2009.
120. Shields, 2001.
121. Parr, 2008.
122. Vismara, Colombi, *et al.*, 2009.
123. Williams, 2006.
124. Greenspan, 2009.
125. Kasari, Paparella, *et al.*, 2008.
126. Carter, Martínez-Pedraza, *et al.*, 2009.
127. Halpin and Nugent, 2007.
128. Goin-Kochel, Mackintosh, *et al.*, 2009.
129. Meilleur and Fombonne, 2009.
130. Hansen, Ozonoff, *et al.*, 2008.
131. De Sanctis, 1908.
132. Gregory, McKenna, *et al.*, 1998.
133. Velakoulis, Walterfang, *et al.*, 2009.
134. Tuchman, 1997.
135. Tuchman, 2009.
136. Stefanatos, 2008.
137. Tsao, 2009.
138. Wheless, Clarke, *et al.*, 2007.
139. Shields, 2006.
140. Caplan, Siddarth, *et al.*, 2002.
141. Tuchman, 2004.
142. Amiet, Gourfinkel-An, *et al.*, 2008.
143. Gillberg, Billstedt, *et al.*, 2009.

CHAPTER 13 PRESENTATION OF ASPERGER SYNDROME IN MIDDLE CHILDHOOD

1. Havighurst, 1971.
2. Pellegrini, Dupuis, *et al.*, 2007, p.261.
3. Nicolopoulou, 2010.
4. Naber, 2008.
5. Naber, Swinkels, *et al.*, 2007.
6. Malti, Gummerum, *et al.*, 2009.
7. Sandberg and Meyer-Bahlburg, 1994.
8. Hobson, Lee, *et al.*, 2009.
9. Legoff and Sherman, 2006.
10. Philip, 2004.
11. Prendeville, Prelock, *et al.*, 2006.
12. Thornton and Cox, 2005.
13. Nikopoulos and Keenan, 2004.
14. Nikopoulos and Keenan, 2007.
15. Jahr, Eldevik, *et al.*, 2000.
16. Spearman, 1904.
17. Detterman and Daniel, 1989.
18. Liss, 2001.
19. López and Scott, 2000, p.3.
20. Baron-Cohen, 2009.
21. Allison, Williams, *et al.*, 2007.
22. Emond, Emmett, *et al.*, 2010.
23. Zucker and Losh, 2008.
24. Ingersoll, 2008.
25. Munson, Faja, *et al.*, 2008.
26. Panayiotou, 2008.
27. Daoust, Lusignan, *et al.*, 2008.
28. Tantam, Kalucy, *et al.*, 1982.
29. Arnold, Bennetto, *et al.*, 2009.
30. Hutman, Siller, *et al.*, 2009.

31. Goldman, 2008.
32. Loth, Gomez, *et al.*, 2008.
33. Larsson, Bergman, *et al.*, 2004.
34. Gadow, Roohi, *et al.*, 2009.
35. Hallett, Ronald, *et al.*, 2009.
36. White, Oswald, *et al.*, 2009.
37. Keeton, Kolos, *et al.*, 2009.
38. White and Roberson-May, 2009.
39. Mancebo, Garcia, *et al.*, 2008.
40. Hartley and Sikora, 2009b.
41. Ivarsson and Melin, 2008.
42. King, Hollander, *et al.*, 2009.
43. Posey, Aman, *et al.*, 2007.
44. Heiser, Turner, *et al.*, 2009.
45. Rutgers, Bakermans-Kranenburg, *et al.*, 2004.
46. Brunet, Heisz, *et al.*, 2009.
47. Yiyuan and Farver, 2009.
48. Titov, Andrews, *et al.*, 2009.
49. Stein and Stein, 2008.
50. Kosson, Blackburn, *et al.*, 2008.
51. Rosen, Miller, *et al.*, 2006.
52. Wolff, 1998.
53. Rapoport, Chavez, *et al.*, 2009. a) p.12.
54. Rapoport and Gogtay, 2011.
55. King and Lord, 2011.
56. Leyfer, Folstein, *et al.*, 2006.
57. Reiersen, Constantino, *et al.*, 2007.
58. Jansiewicz, Goldberg, *et al.*, 2006.
59. Dowell, Mahone, *et al.*, 2009.
60. Rinehart, Tonge, *et al.*, 2006a.
61. Rinehart, Bellgrove, *et al.*, 2006.
62. Rochelle and Talcott, 2006.
63. Gowen and Miall, 2005.
64. Tantam, 1986.
65. Rommelse, Altink, *et al.*, 2009.
66. Stein, 2003.
67. Caron, Mottron, *et al.*, 2004.
68. Treffert, 2009.
69. Kristensen, 2000.

70. Bittner, Egger, *et al.*, 2007.
71. Costa, Pini, *et al.*, 2009.
72. Cartwright-Hatton, McNicol, *et al.*, 2006.
73. Bhardwaj, Agarwall, *et al.*, 2005.
74. Viana, Beidel, *et al.*, 2009.
75. Cunningham, McHolm, *et al.*, 2006.
76. See www.asha.org/public/speech/disorders/ SelectiveMutism.htm
77. Nikolov, Bearss, *et al.*, 2009.
78. Farmer and Oliver, 2005.
79. Hepburn, DiGuiseppi, *et al.*, 2008.
80. Constantino, Lavesser, *et al.*, 2007.
81. Tanguay, 2002.
82. Chalfant, Rapee, *et al.*, 2007.
83. Mastrangelo, 2009.
84. Agyapong, Migone, *et al.*, 2009.
85. Callahan, Henson, *et al.*, 2008.
86. Connor, 1999.
87. Dalrymple and Ruble, 1996.
88. See www.aspergersyndrome.org/Articles/Behaviors-That-May-Be-Personal-Challenges-For-A-St.aspx
89. Cotugno, 2009. a) p.1277.
90. Laird, 2008.
91. Silani, Bird, *et al.*, 2008.
92. Tani, Lindberg, *et al.*, 2004.
93. Swerts and Krahmer, 2008.
94. Krause, Steimer, *et al.*, 1989.
95. Sofronoff, Attwood, *et al.*, 2007.
96. Merlo, Lehmkuhl, *et al.*, 2009.
97. Segal, Rogers, *et al.*, 2007.
98. Hirano, Hirano, *et al.*, 2010.
99. Jones, Happé, *et al.*, 2009.
100. Ashwin, Ashwin, *et al.*, 2009.
101. Elfert and Mirenda, 2006.
102. Flannery, 2005.
103. Sinha, Silove, *et al.*, 2006.
104. Devlin, Leader, *et al.*, 2009.
105. Lau, Chan, *et al.*, 2010.

CHAPTER 14 PRESENTATION OF KANNER SYNDROME IN MIDDLE CHILDHOOD

1. Baron-Cohen, Cox, *et al.*, 1996.
2. Matson, Wilkins, *et al.*, 2008.
3. Groen, Zwiers, *et al.*, 2008.
4. Joffe and Varlokosta, 2007.
5. Stribling, Rae, *et al.*, 2007.
6. Agaliotis and Kalyva, 2008.
7. Hogg, Reeves, *et al.*, 2001.
8. Hoevenaars-van den Boom, Antonissen, *et al.*, 2009.
9. Wilkins and Matson, 2009.
10. Zaja and Rojahn, 2008.
11. Gabriels, Cuccaro, *et al.*, 2005.
12. Gadow, Roohi, *et al.*, 2008.
13. Bakermans-Kranenburg and van IJzendoorn, 2011.
14. Cassidy, Woodhouse, *et al.*, 2011.
15. Ellis, Boyce, *et al.*, 2011.
16. Ellis, Shirtcliff, *et al.*, 2011.

17. Essex, Armstrong, *et al.*, 2011.
18. Knafo, Israel, *et al.*, 2011.
19. Obradovi, Bush, *et al.*, 2011.
20. Pluess and Belsky, 2011.
21. Fasano, Barra, *et al.*, 2008.
22. Evans, Strafella, *et al.*, 2009.
23. O'Sullivan, Evans, *et al.*, 2009.
24. Chartoff, Marck, *et al.*, 2001.
25. Riba, Krämer, *et al.*, 2008.
26. Thakkar, Polli, *et al.*, 2008.
27. Schweimer and Hauber, 2006.
28. Reeves, Mehta, *et al.*, 2007.
29. Sesack and Grace, 2010.
30. Morgan, Grant, *et al.*, 2002.
31. de Krom, Staal, *et al.*, 2009.
32. Gadow, Roohi, *et al.*, 2008.

33. Martínez-Levy, Díaz-Galvis, *et al.*, 2009.
34. Volkow, Wang, *et al.*, 2009.
35. Barnard, Muldoon, *et al.*, 2008.
36. Doig, McLennan, *et al.*, 2009.
37. Forsyth, Colver, *et al.*, 2007.
38. Bondy and Frost, 2001.
39. Angermeier, Schlosser, *et al.*, 2007.
40. Lund and Troha, 2008.
41. Howlin, Gordon, *et al.*, 2007.
42. Ospina, Krebs, *et al.*, 2008.
43. Lambrechts, Kuppens, *et al.*, 2009.
44. Matson and Rivet, 2008.
45. Lee, Amos, *et al.*, 2009.
46. Fisher, 2009.
47. Jones, Cooper, *et al.*, 2008.

48. Wodehouse and McGill, 2009.
49. Harvey, Boer, *et al.*, 2009.
50. Braam, Didden, *et al.*, 2009.
51. Oliver-Africano, Murphy, *et al.*, 2009.
52. Romeo, Knapp, *et al.*, 2009.
53. Matson and Dempsey, 2008.
54. Gal, Dyck, *et al.*, 2009.
55. El-Hattab, Smolarek, *et al.*, 2009.
56. Parikh, Kolevzon, *et al.*, 2008.
57. Renty and Roeyers, 2006.
58. Panerai, Zingale, *et al.*, 2009.
59. Goin-Kochel, Mackintosh, *et al.*, 2009.
60. Mandell, Walrath, *et al.*, 2005.
61. Ammerman, Hersen, *et al.*, 1994.

CHAPTER 15 PRESENTATION OF ASPERGER SYNDROME IN LATER CHILDHOOD AND ADOLESCENCE

1. Dubas, Miller, *et al.*, 2003.
2. Havighurst, 1971.
3. Macmillan, 2006.
4. Aarts, Custers, *et al.*, 2009.
5. Bandura, 1977.
6. Aarts, Custers, *et al.*, 2008.
7. Wei, Russell, *et al.*, 2005.
8. Forstmann, Wolfensteller, *et al.*, 2008.
9. Gudjonsson, Sigurdsson, *et al.*, 2008.
10. Panzer and Viljoen, 2005.
11. Vygotsky, 1966.
12. Bruck, London, *et al.*, 2007.
13. Bright-Paul, Jarrold, *et al.*, 2008.
14. Bubier and Drabick, 2008.
15. Norwalk, Norvilitis, *et al.*, 2009.
16. Makris, Buka, *et al.*, 2008.
17. Parfit, 1971.
18. Haslam, Jetten, *et al.*, 2009.
19. Pasupathi and Hoyt, 2009.
20. Slaughter, Peterson, *et al.*, 2007.
21. Carrington and Graham, 2001.
22. Begeer, Banerjee, *et al.*, 2008.
23. Wischniewski, Windmann, *et al.*, 2009.
24. Kiyonari and Barclay, 2008.
25. Victoroff, 2007.
26. Abelson, 1981.
27. Landen and Rasmussen, 1997.
28. Mukaddes, 2002.
29. Kanbayashi, 1997.
30. Mason, Williams, *et al.*, 2008.
31. Howlin and Ashgarian, 1999.
32. Arnulf, Zeitzer, *et al.*, 2005.
33. Berthier, Santamaria, *et al.*, 1992.
34. Wainscot, Naylor, *et al.*, 2008.
35. Davey, Allen, *et al.*, 2009.
36. Davey, Yucel, *et al.*, 2008.
37. Thomas Scheff, personal communication.
38. Tantam, 1998.
39. Mills, 2005.
40. Humphrey and Lewis, 2008.

41. Van Doorn, Branje, *et al.*, 2008.
42. Smith, Greenberg, *et al.*, 2008.
43. Eisenberg, Hofer, *et al.*, 2008.
44. Kolvin, 1971.
45. Mäki, Miettunen, *et al.*, 2008.
46. Isohanni, Jones, *et al.*, 2001.
47. Phillips and Seidman, 2008.
48. Hurst, Nelson-Gray, *et al.*, 2007.
49. Rumsey, Andreasen, *et al.*, 1986.
50. Whitehouse, Watt, *et al.*, 2009.
51. Hartley and Sikora, 2009b.
52. Simonoff, Pickles, *et al.*, 2008.
53. Mukaddes and Fateh, 2010.
54. Hutton, Goode, *et al.*, 2008.
55. Hammond, Forster-Gibson, *et al.*, 2008.
56. Tantam, 1988c.
57. Balfe and Tantam, 2010.
58. Hofvander, Delorme, *et al.*, 2009.
59. Goffman, 1969.
60. Hill, Berthoz, *et al.*, 2004.
61. Szatmari, Georgiades, *et al.*, 2008.
62. Ryan and Räisänen, 2008.
63. Malhotra, 2007.
64. Castagnini and Berrios, 2009.
65. Kleist, 1974.
66. Srihari, Lee, *et al.*, 2006.
67. Soni, Whittington, *et al.*, 2008.
68. Falip, Carreño, *et al.*, 2009.
69. Dhossche, Reti, *et al.*, 2010.
70. Dhossche, Reti, *et al.*, 2009.
71. Cavanna, Robertson, *et al.*, 2008.
72. Quigley, Lommel, *et al.*, 2009.
73. Dhossche, 2004.
74. Hare and Malone, 2004.
75. Krasnoperova, 2004.
76. Wing and Shah, 2000.
77. Wachtel, Griffin, *et al.*, 2010.
78. Cavanna, Robertson, *et al.*, 2008.
79. Wing and Shah, 2000.
80. Babington and Spiegel, 2007.

81. Menzies, Achard, *et al.*, 2007.
82. Anholt, Cath, *et al.*, 2009.
83. Ivarsson and Melin, 2008.
84. Liu, Paterson, *et al.*, 2008.
85. Cullen, Samuels, *et al.*, 2008.
86. Cath, Ran, *et al.*, 2008.
87. Ruta, Mugno, *et al.*, 2010.
88. Cromer, Schmidt, *et al.*, 2007.
89. For supporting citations, see Menzies, Achard, *et al.*, 2007.
90. Cath, van Grootheest, *et al.*, 2008.
91. Moulding, Kyrios, *et al.*, 2007.
92. Samuels, Bienvenu, *et al.*, 2008.
93. Pertusa, Fullana, *et al.*, 2008.
94. Lechman and Bloch, 2008.
95. Abbott and Rapee, 2004.
96. Simos and Dimitriou, 1994.
97. Munesue, Ono, *et al.*, 2008.
98. DeLong, 1994.
99. Carlson, Potegal, *et al.*, 2009.
100. Nandagopal, DelBello, *et al.*, 2009.
101. Scott, Colom, *et al.*, 2007.
102. Caraballo, Cersósimo, *et al.*, 2004.
103. Turk, Bax, *et al.*, 2009.
104. Hurtado, Koepp, *et al.*, 2006.
105. Galli-Carminati, Deriaz, *et al.*, 2009.
106. Hoebert, van der Heijden, *et al.*, 2009.
107. Russell, Schmidt, *et al.*, 2009.
108. Ulrike Schmidt, personal communication.
109. Bölte, Özkara, *et al.*, 2002.
110. Stichter, Randolph, *et al.*, 2009.
111. Grynszpan, Martin, *et al.*, 2008.
112. Golan and Baron-Cohen, 2006.
113. Muller, Schuler, *et al.*, 2008.
114. Laugeson, Frankel, *et al.*, 2009.

CHAPTER 16 PRESENTATION OF ATYPICAL ASPERGER SYNDROME, OFTEN WITH ADHD, IN LATE CHILDHOOD AND ADOLESCENCE (SECONDARY SCHOOL AND COLLEGE)

1. Harty, Miller, *et al.*, 2009.
2. Carlson, Potegal, *et al.*, 2009.
3. Solanto, Pope-Boyd, *et al.*, 2009.
4. Hare, Camerer, *et al.*, 2009.
5. Adriani, Boyer, *et al.*, 2009.
6. Bauminger, 2007.
7. Anckarsäter, Stahlberg, *et al.*, 2006.
8. Voeller, 1994.
9. Lessing, 1989.
10. Lessing, 2000.
11. Schimmelmann, Friedel, *et al.*, 2009.
12. Rommelse, Altink, *et al.*, 2009.
13. Kessler, Lane, *et al.*, 2007.
14. Reddy, Newman, *et al.*, 2010.
15. Rabiner, Murray, *et al.*, 2010.
16. Steiner, Sheldrick, *et al.*, 2011.
17. Wehmeier, Schacht, *et al.*, 2010.
18. Carpenter, Loo, *et al.*, 2009.
19. Herba, de Bruin, *et al.*, 2008.
20. Sinzig, Mursch, *et al.*, 2008.
21. de Boer, Caramaschi, *et al.*, 2009.
22. Caramaschi, de Boer, *et al.*, 2008.
23. Wegner, 2009.
24. Eisenberg, Michalik, *et al.*, 2007.
25. Russell, Jarrold, *et al.*, 1999.
26. Hill, 2003.
27. Cleckley, 1941.
28. Fairchild, van Goozen, *et al.*, 2009.
29. Leist and Dadds, 2009.
30. Fairchild, van Goozen, *et al.*, 2008.
31. Marsh and Blair, 2008.
32. Gauthier, Furr, *et al.*, 2009.
33. DiLallo, Jones, *et al.*, 2009.
34. Green, Gilchrist, *et al.*, 2000.
35. Brooks, Fos, *et al.*, 1999.
36. Nobili, 2007.
37. Lyketsos, Rosenblatt, *et al.*, 2004.
38. Seitz, Nickel, *et al.*, 2006.
39. Weiss and Murray, 2003.
40. Gadow, DeVincent, *et al.*, 2009.
41. Holtmann, Bölte, *et al.*, 2007.
42. Freeman, Zinner, *et al.*, 2009.
43. Kurlan, 2003.
44. Thomaes, Bushman, *et al.*, 2009.
45. McGrath, Hutaff-Lee, *et al.*, 2008.
46. Re, Pedron, *et al.*, 2007.
47. Brieber, Neufang, *et al.*, 2007.
48. Tantam, 2009.
49. Krueger, Barbey, *et al.*, 2009.
50. Mulligan, Anney, *et al.*, 2009.
51. Nijmeijer, Hoekstra, *et al.*, 2009.
52. See www.macbrain.org/resources.htm
53. Tottenham, Tanaka, *et al.*, 2009.
54. Demurie, De Corel, *et al.*, 2011.
55. Duchaine and Weidenfeld, 2003.
56. Biederman, Milberger, *et al.*, 1995.
57. Pliszka, 2007.
58. NICE, 2008.
59. AACAP, 2007.
60. Heal, Cheetham, *et al.*, 2009.
61. Biederman, Melmed, *et al.*, 2008.
62. Gadow, Sverd, *et al.*, 2007.
63. Keane, 2007.
64. Silva, Muniz, *et al.*, 2008.
65. Abikoff, 2009.
66. Faraone, Spencer, *et al.*, 2004.
67. Golubchik, Sever, *et al.*, 2008.
68. Goksoyr and Nottestad, 2008.
69. Kay, Michaels, *et al.*, 2009.
70. Matza, Paramore, *et al.*, 2005.

71. For a review, see Jahromi, Kasari, *et al.*, 2009.
72. Jahromi, Kasari, *et al.*, 2009.
73. Anckarsäter, Nilsson, *et al.*, 2007.
74. Scragg and Shah, 1994.
75. Newman and Ghaziuddin, 2008.
76. Mordre, Groholt, *et al.*, 2011.
77. DeLoache, Simcock, *et al.*, 2007.
78. Heden and Kristiansson, 2003.
79. Whyte, Petch, *et al.*, 2008.
80. Stokes, Newton, *et al.*, 2007.
81. Lhermitte, Pillon, *et al.*, 1986.

82. Archibald, Mateer, *et al.*, 2001.
83. Silva, Leong, *et al.*, 2004.
84. Wolfe, 2008.
85. Daderman, Lindgren, *et al.*, 2004.
86. Cooper, Mohamed, *et al.*, 1993.
87. Jairam and van Marle 2008.
88. Jones and Okere 2008.
89. Realmuto and Ruble, 1999.
90. Hellemans, Colson, *et al.*, 2007.
91. Balfe, Chen, *et al.*, 2005.
92. Palermo, 2003.

CHAPTER 17 THE PRESENTATION AND CONSEQUENCES OF ASPERGER SYNDROME IN ADULTHOOD

1. Janoff-Bulman, 1992.
2. Arnett, 1998.
3. Massey, Gebhardt, *et al.*, 2008.
4. Office for Disability Issues, 2008.
5. Ambery, Russell, *et al.*, 2006.
6. Cimera and Cowan, 2009.
7. Kessler, Lane, *et al.*, 2008.
8. Reimer, D'Ambrosio, *et al.*, 2007.
9. Sobanski, Sabljic, *et al.*, 2008.
10. Verster, Bekker, *et al.*, 2008.
11. Cox, Moore, *et al.*, 2008.
12. Freud, 1930, p.101.
13. Jones, Zahl, *et al.*, 2001.
14. Causton-Theoharis, Ashby, *et al.*, 2009.
15. Ryan and Räisänen, 2008.
16. Ballas and Dorling, 2007.
17. Gottman and Levenson, 2000.
18. Bauer, McAdams, *et al.*, 2005.
19. Gruehn, Rebucal, *et al.*, 2008.
20. McNulty, O'Mara, *et al.*, 2008.
21. See www.gottman.com/research/gaylesbian/12yearstudy.
22. Punshon, Skirrow, *et al.*, 2009.
23. Huws and Jones, 2008.
24. Frith and Happé, 1999.
25. Balfe, Chen, *et al.*, 2005.
26. Addis, Wong, *et al.*, 2008.
27. Durkheim, 1970.
28. Haugen, Welsh, *et al.*, 2008.
29. Neff and Karney, 2005.
30. Goldin, McRae, *et al.*, 2008.
31. Laursen, Finkelstein, *et al.*, 2001.
32. Whitehouse, Durkin, *et al.*, 2009.
33. Coker, Elliott, *et al.*, 2009.
34. Edwards, Barkley, *et al.*, 2001.
35. Russell, Cutrona, *et al.*, 1984.
36. Gest, Sesma, *et al.*, 2006.
37. Tantam, 1986.

38. Newson, 1982.
39. Howlin and Goode, 1998.
40. Engström, Ekström, *et al.*, 2003.
41. Prichard, 1835.
42. Lough, Kipps, *et al.*, 2006.
43. Koenigs, Young, *et al.*, 2007.
44. Yunjo, Bradley, *et al.*, 2010.
45. Russell, 2006.
46. Wolff, 2000.
47. Bleuler, 1911.
48. Kretschmer, 1925.
49. Tantam, 1988c.
50. Tantam, 1991b.
51. For a counter-example, see Grandin and Scariano, 1986.
52. Fairbairn, 1944.
53. Torgersen, Lygren, *et al.*, 2000.
54. Lysaker, Wickett, *et al.*, 2004.
55. Homer, Solomon, *et al.*, 2008.
56. Blackshaw, Kinderman, *et al.*, 2001.
57. Pinkham, Hopfinger, *et al.*, 2008.
58. Yardley, McDermott, *et al.*, 2008.
59. Alt and Gutmann, 2009.
60. Spain, Lavender, *et al.*, 2009.
61. Munesue, Ono, *et al.*, 2008.
62. Dziobek, Gold, *et al.*, 2007.
63. Levy, Fleming, *et al.*, 2009.
64. Tantam, 1986.
65. Able, Johnston, *et al.*, 2007.
66. Barnard, Harvard, *et al.*, 2001.
67. Clark, Scharaschkin, *et al.*, 2009.
68. Howlin, Alcock, *et al.*, 2005.
69. Argyle and Henderson, 1984.
70. Hellemans, Roeyers, *et al.*, 2010.
71. Solanto, Marks, *et al.*, 2008.
72. Shamay-Tsoory, 2008.
73. Sartre, 2004.

APPENDIX ETHICS AND ASD

1. Allen, Evans, *et al.*, 2008.
2. Mayes and Koegel, 2003.

REFERENCES

Aarts, H., R. Custers, *et al.* (2008). Preparing and motivating behavior outside of awareness. *Science* **319**(5870): 1639.

Aarts, H., R. Custers, *et al.* (2009). Priming and authorship ascription: When nonconscious goals turn into conscious experiences of self-agency. *Journal of Personality and Social Psychology* **96**(5): 967–979.

Abbott, M. J., R. M. Rapee (2004). Post-event rumination and negative self-appraisal in social phobia before and after treatment. *Journal of Abnormal Psychology* **113**(1): 136–144.

Abell, F., M. Krams, *et al.* (1999). The neuroanatomy of autism: A voxel-based whole brain analysis of structural scans. *Neuroreport: For Rapid Communication of Neuroscience Research* **10**(8): 1647–1651.

Abelson, A. G. (1981). The development of gender identity in the autistic child. *Child: Care, Health and Development* **7**(6): 347–356.

Abelson, J. F., K. Y. Kwan, *et al.* (2005). Sequence variants in SLITRK1 are associated with Tourette's syndrome. *Science* **310**(5746): 317–320.

Abikoff, H. (2009). ADHD psychosocial treatments: Generalization reconsidered. *Journal of Attention Disorders* **13**(3):207–210.

Able, S. L., J. A. Johnston, *et al.* (2007). Functional and psychosocial impairment in adults with undiagnosed ADHD. *Psychological Medicine* **37**(1): 97–107.

Abraham, A. and D. Y. von Cramon (2009). Reality = Relevance? Insights from spontaneous modulations of the brain's default network when telling apart reality from fiction. *PLoS ONE* **4**(3): e4741.

Academy of Medical Royal Colleges (2001). *Implementing and Ensuring Safe Sedation Practice for Healthcare Procedures in Adults.* London: Royal College of Anaesthetists.

Acosta, M. T. and P. L. Pearl (2003). The neurobiology of autism: New pieces of the puzzle. *Current Neurology and Neuroscience Reports* **3**(2): 149–156.

Adams, A. M. and S. E. Gathercole (2000). Limitations in working memory: Implications for language development. *International Journal of Language and Communication Disorders* **35**(1): 95–116.

Addington, A. M., J. Gauthier, *et al.* (2011). A novel frameshift mutation in UPF3B identified in brothers affected with childhood onset schizophrenia and autism spectrum disorders. *Molecullar Psychiatry* **16**(3): 238–239.

Addis, D. R., A. T. Wong, *et al.* (2008). Age-related changes in the episodic simulation of future events. *Psychological Science* **19**(1): 33–41.

Adib, N., K. Davies, *et al.* (2005). Joint hypermobility syndrome in childhood: A not so benign multisystem disorder? *Rheumatology* **44**(6): 744–750.

Adler, L. A., T. Spencer, *et al.* (2006). Validity of pilot Adult ADHD Self-Report Scale (ASRS) to rate adult ADHD symptoms. *Annals of Clinical Psychiatry* **18**(3): 145–148.

Adolphs, R. (2001). The neurobiology of social cognition. *Current Opinion in Neurobiology* **11**(2): 231–239.

Adolphs, R. (2006). How do we know the minds of others? Domain-specificity, simulation, and enactive social cognition. *Brain Research* **1079**(1): 25–35.

Adolphs, R. (2009). The social brain: Neural basis of social knowledge. *Annual Review of Psychology* **60**: 693–716.

Adolphs, R., D. Tranel, *et al.* (1994). An impaired recognition of emotion in facial expressions following bilateral damage to the human amygdala. *Nature* **372**(6507): 669–672.

Adolphs, R., M. L. Spezio, *et al.* (2008). Distinct face-processing strategies in parents of autistic children. *Current Biology* **18**(14): 1090–1093.

Adriani, W., F. Boyer, *et al.* (2009). Increased impulsive behavior and risk proneness following lentivirus-mediated dopamine transporter over-expression in rats' nucleus accumbens. *Neuroscience* **159**(1): 47–58.

Agaliotis, I. and E. Kalyva (2008). Nonverbal social interaction skills of children with learning disabilities. *Research in Developmental Disabilities* **29**(1): 1–10.

Agyapong, V., M. Migone, *et al.* (2009). P02–194 Perception of primary school teachers about Asperger's syndrome. *European Psychiatry* **24**: S884.

Ainsworth, M., M. Blehar, *et al.* (1978). *Patterns of Attachment: A Psychological Study of the Strange Situation.* Hillsdale, NJ: Erlbaum.

Aitken, K. J. (2008). Intersubjectivity, affective neuroscience, and the neurobiology of autistic spectrum disorders: A systematic review. *Keio Journal of Medicine* **57**(1): 15–36.

Akbarian, S., R. Z. Chen, *et al.* (2001). Expression pattern of the Rett syndrome gene MeCP2 in primate prefrontal cortex. *Neurobiology of Disease* **8**(5): 784–791.

Akshoomoff, N., C. Lord, *et al.* (2004). Outcome classification of preschool children with autism spectrum disorders using MRI brain measures. *Journal of the American Academy of Child and Adolescent Psychiatry* **43**(3): 349–357.

Alberti, A., P. Pirrone, *et al.* (1999). Sulphation deficit in low-functioning autistic children: A pilot study. *Biological Psychiatry* **46**(3): 420–424.

Albrecht, B., D. Brandeis, *et al.* (2008). Action monitoring in boys with attention-deficit/hyperactivity disorder, their nonaffected siblings, and normal control subjects: Evidence for an endophenotype. *Biological Psychiatry* **64**(7):615–625.

Aldred, S., K. Moore, *et al.* (2003). Plasma amino acid levels in children with autism and their families. *Journal of Autism and Developmental Disorders* **33**(1): 93–97.

Alexander, A. L., J. E. Lee, *et al.* (2007). Diffusion tensor imaging of the corpus callosum in autism. *NeuroImage* **34**(1): 61–73.

Alia-Klein, N., R. Z. Goldstein, *et al.* (2007). What is in a word? No versus Yes differentially engage the lateral orbitofrontal cortex. *Emotion* **7**(4): 649–659.

Allen, D., C. Evans, *et al.* (2008). Offending behaviour in adults with Asperger syndrome. *Journal of Autism and Developmental Disorders* **38**(4): 748–758.

Allen, G. and E. Courchesne (1998). The cerebellum and non-motor function: Clinical implications. *Molecular Psychiatry* **3**(3): 207–210.

Allen-Brady, K., J. Miller, *et al.* (2009). A high-density SNP genome-wide linkage scan in a large autism extended pedigree. *Molecular Psychiatry* **14**(6): 590–600.

Allik, H, J. O. Larsson, *et al.* (2008). Sleep patterns in school-age children with Asperger syndrome or high-functioning autism: A follow-up study. *Journal of Autism and Developmental Disorders* **38**(9): 1625–1633.

Allik, H., J. O. Larsson, *et al.* (2006a). Health-related quality of life in parents of school-age children with Asperger syndrome or high-functioning autism. Health and Quality of Life Outcomes **4**: 1.

Allik, H., J. O. Larsson, *et al.* (2006b). Sleep patterns of school-age children with Asperger syndrome or high-functioning autism. *Journal of Autism and Developmental Disorders* **36**(5): 585–595.

Allison, B. H., D. Auciello, *et al.* (2008). Comparing the convergent validity and clinical utility of the Behavior Assessment System for Children-Parent Rating Scales and Child Behavior Checklist in children with epilepsy. *Epilepsy and Behavior* **13**(1): 237–242.

Allison, C., J. Williams, *et al.* (2007). The Childhood Asperger Syndrome Test (CAST): Test-retest reliability in a high scoring sample. *Autism* **11**(2): 173–185.

Alsaadi, T., J. R. Binder, *et al.* (2000). Pure topographic disorientation: A distinctive syndrome with varied localization. *Neurology* **54**(9): 1864–1866.

Alt, M. and M. L. Gutmann (2009). Fast mapping semantic features: Performance of adults with normal language, history of disorders of spoken and written language, and attention deficit hyperactivity disorder on a word-learning task. *Journal of Communication Disorders* **42**(5):347–364.

Altemeier, W. A. and L. E. Altemeier (2009). How can early, intensive training help a genetic disorder? *Pediatric Annals* **38**(3): 167–170, 172.

Aman, M. G. (2005). Treatment planning for patients with autism spectrum disorders. *Journal of Clinical Psychiatry* **66**(Suppl 10): 38–45.

Amaral, D. G., M. D. Bauman, *et al.* (2003). The amygdala and autism: Implications from non-human primate studies. *Genes, Brain and Behavior* **2**(5): 295–302.

Ambery, F. Z., A. J. Russell, *et al.* (2006). Neuropsychological functioning in adults with Asperger syndrome. *Autism* **10**(6): 551–564.

American Academy of Child and Adolescent Psychiatry (AACAP) (2007). Practice parameters for the assessment and treatment of children and adolescents with attention-deficit/hyperactivity disorder. *Journal of the American Academy of Child and Adolescent Psychiatry* **46**(7): 894–921.

American Psychiatric Association (APA) (1987). *Diagnostic and Statistical Manual of Mental Disorders, Third Edition, Revised* (DSM-III-R). Washington, DC: APA.

American Psychiatric Association (APA) (2001). *Diagnostic and Statistical Manual of Mental Disorders, Fourth Edition, Text Revision* (DSM-IV-TR). Washington, DC: APA.

Ames, C. and C. Jarrold (2007). The problem with using eye-gaze to infer desire: A deficit of cue inference in children with autism spectrum disorder? *Journal of Autism and Developmental Disorders* **37**(9): 1761–1775.

Ames, C. and S. Fletcher-Watson (2010). A review of methods in the study of attention in autism. *Developmental Review* **30**(1): 52–73.

Amiet, C., I. Gourfinkel-An, *et al.* (2008). Epilepsy in autism is associated with intellectual disability and gender: Evidence from a meta-analysis. *Biological Psychiatry* **64**(7): 547–640.

Amin, N., Y. S. Aulchenko, *et al.* (2009). Suggestive linkage of ADHD to chromosome 18q22 in a young genetically isolated Dutch population. *European Journal of Human Genetics* **17**(7): 958–966.

Ammerman, R. T. P., M. P. Hersen, *et al.* (1994). Maltreatment in psychiatrically hospitalized children and adolescents with developmental disabilities: Prevalence and correlates. *Journal of the American Academy of Child and Adolescent Psychiatry* **33**(4): 567–576.

Anatskaya, O. and A. Vinogradov (2010). Somatic polyploidy promotes cell function under stress and energy depletion: Evidence from tissue-specific mammal transcriptome. *Functional and Integrative Genomics* **10**(4): 433–446.

Anckarsäter, H., O. Stahlberg, *et al.* (2006). The impact of ADHD and autism spectrum disorders on temperament, character, and personality development. *American Journal of Psychiatry* **163**(7): 1239–1244.

Anckarsäter, H., T. Nilsson, *et al.* (2007). Prevalences and configurations of mental disorders among institutionalized adolescents. *Developmental Rehabilitation Journal* **10**(1): 57–65.

Andari, E., J-R. Duhamel, *et al.* (2010). Promoting social behavior with oxytocin in high-functioning autism spectrum disorders. *Proceedings of the National Academy of Sciences of the United States of America* **107**(9): 4389–4394.

Anderson, G. M. (2002). Genetics of childhood disorders: XLV. Autism, part 4: Serotonin in autism. *Journal of the American Academy of Child and Adolescent Psychiatry* **41**(12): 1513–1516.

Anderson, M. (2001). Annotation: Conceptions of intelligence. *Journal of Child Psychology and Psychiatry and Allied Disciplines* **42**(3): 287–298.

Anderson, M. L. (2007). Evolution of cognitive function via redeployment of brain areas. *Neuroscientist* **13**(1): 13–21.

Angermeier, K., R. W. Schlosser, *et al.* (2007). Effects of iconicity on requesting with the Picture Exchange Communication System in children with autism spectrum disorder. *Research in Autism Spectrum Disorders* **2**(3): 430–446.

Anholt, G., D. Cath *et al.* (2010). P03-30 Do ADHD and autism symptoms predict specific OC symptom dimensions or OC symptom severity in OCD? *European Psychiatry* **24**(Suppl 1): S1029.

Anisman, H. and D. C. McIntyre (2002). Conceptual, spatial, and cue learning in the Morris water maze in fast or slow kindling rats: Attention deficit comorbidity. *Journal of Neuroscience* **22**(17): 7809–7817.

Annaz, D., A. Karmiloff-Smith, *et al.* (2009). A cross-syndrome study of the development of holistic face recognition in children with autism, Down syndrome, and Williams syndrome. *Journal of Experimental Child Psychology* **102**(4): 456–486.

Annoni, G. M., A. Pegna, *et al.* (1998). Motor perseverations: A function of the side and the site of a cerebral lesion. *European Neurology* **40**(2): 84–90.

Antshel, K. M., A. Aneja, *et al.* (2007). Autistic spectrum disorders in velo-cardio facial syndrome (22q11.2 deletion). *Journal of Autism and Developmental Disorders* **37**(9): 1776–1786.

Araque, A. and M. Navarrete (2010). Glial cells in neuronal network function. *Philosophical Transactions of the Royal Society B: Biological Sciences* **365**(1551): 2375–2381.

Archibald, S. J., C. A. Mateer, *et al.* (2001). Utilization behavior: Clinical manifestations and neurological mechanisms. *Neuropsychology Review* **11**(3): 117–130.

Arcos-Burgos, M. and M. T. Acosta (2007). Tuning major gene variants conditioning human behavior: The anachronism of ADHD. *Current Opinion in Genetics and Development* **17**(3): 234–238.

Argyle, M. and M. Henderson (1984). The rules of friendship. *Journal of Social and Personal Relationships* **1**(2): 211–237.

Arking, D. E., D. J. Cutler, *et al.* (2008). A common genetic variant in the neurexin superfamily member CNTNAP2 increases familial risk of autism. *American Journal of Human Genetics* **82**(1): 160–164.

Arnett, J. J. (1998). Learning to stand alone: The contemporary American transition to adulthood in cultural and historical context. *Human Development* **41**(5–6): 295–315.

Arnold, A. P. (2009). Mouse models for evaluating sex chromosome effects that cause sex differences in non-gonadal tissues. *Journal of Neuroendocrinology* **21**(4): 377–386.

Arnold, J. E., L. Bennetto, *et al.* (2009). Reference production in young speakers with and without autism: Effects of discourse status and processing constraints. *Cognition* **110**(2): 131–146.

Arnsten, A. F. (2006). Fundamentals of attention-deficit/hyperactivity disorder: circuits and pathways. *Journal of Clinical Psychiatry* **67**(Suppl 8): 7–12.

Arnulf, I., J. M. Zeitzer, *et al.* (2005). Kleine-Levin syndrome: A systematic review of 186 cases in the literature. *Brain* **128**(12): 2763–2776.

Artigas-Pallares, J., E. Gabau-Vila, *et al.* (2005). [Syndromic autism: II. Genetic syndromes associated with autism]. *Revista de Neurologia* **40**(Suppl 1): S151–S162.

Asherson, P., K. Zhou, *et al.* (2008). A high-density SNP linkage scan with 142 combined subtype ADHD sib pairs identifies linkage regions on chromosomes 9 and 16. *Molecular Psychiatry* **13**(5): 514–521.

Ashtari, M., S. Kumra, *et al.* (2005). Attention-deficit/hyperactivity disorder: A preliminary diffusion tensor imaging study. *Biological Psychiatry* **57**(5): 448–455.

Ashwin, C., S. Baron-Cohen, *et al.* (2007). Differential activation of the amygdala and the 'social brain' during fearful face-processing in Asperger syndrome. *Neuropsychologia* **45**(1): 2–14.

Ashwin, E., C. Ashwin, *et al.* (2009). Eagle-eyed visual acuity: An experimental investigation of enhanced perception in autism. *Biological Psychiatry* **65**(1): 17–21.

Asperger, H. (1944). Die 'Autistichen Psychopathen' in Kindersalter. *Archiv fur Psychiatrie und Nervenkrankenheiten* **117**: 76–136.

Asperger, H. (1979). Problems of infantile autism. *Communication* **13**(3): 45–52.

Assumpcao, F., R. C. Santos, *et al.* (1999). Brief report: Autism and Aarskog syndrome. *Journal of Autism and Developmental Disorders* **29**(2): 179–181.

Atladottir, H. O., M. G. Pedersen, *et al.* (2009). Association of family history of autoimmune diseases and autism spectrum disorders. *Pediatrics* **124**(2): 687–694.

Austin, D. W. and K. Shandley (2008). An investigation of porphyrinuria in Australian children with autism. *Journal of Toxicology and Environmental Health A* **71**(20): 1349–1351.

Autism and Developmental Disabilities Monitoring Network Surveillance Year 2000 Principal Investigators; Centers for Disease Control and Prevention (2007). Prevalence of autism spectrum disorders – autism and developmental disabilities monitoring network, six sites, United States, 2000. *MMWR Surveillance Summaries* **56**(1): 1–11.

Auyeung, B., S. Baron-Cohen, *et al.* (2009). Fetal testosterone and autistic traits. *British Journal of Psychology* **100**(1): 1–22.

Auyeung, B., S. Wheelwright, *et al.* (2009). The children's empathy quotient and systemizing quotient: Sex differences in typical development and in autism spectrum conditions. *Journal of Autism and Developmental Disorders* **39**(11): 1509–1521.

Aylward, E. H., N. J. Minshew, *et al.* (2002). Effects of age on brain volume and head circumference in autism. *Neurology* **59**(2): 175–183.

Babington, P. W. and D. R. Spiegel (2007). Treatment of catatonia with olanzapine and amantadine. *Psychosomatics* **48**(6): 534–536.

Bach, M. and S. C. Dakin (2009). Regarding 'Eagle-eyed visual acuity: An experimental investigation of enhanced perception in autism'. *Biological Psychiatry* **66**(10): e19–e20.

Bachevalier, J., L. Malkova, *et al.* (2002). Effects of selective neonatal temporal lobe lesions on socioemotional behavior in infant rhesus monkeys (Macaca mulatta). *Behavioral Neuroscience* **115**(3): 545–559.

Badaruddin, D. H., G. L. Andrews, *et al.* (2007). Social and behavioral problems of children with agenesis of the corpus callosum. *Child Psychiatry and Human Development* **38**(4): 287–302.

Badawi, N., G. Dixon, *et al.* (2006). Autism following a history of newborn encephalopathy: More than a coincidence? *Developmental Medicine and Child Neurology* **48**(2): 85–89.

Baddeley, A. and B. Wilson (1988). Frontal amnesia and the dysexecutive syndrome. *Brain and Cognition* **7**(2): 212–230.

Baddeley, A. and G. J. Hitch (1974). Working memory. In G. Bower (ed.) *The Psychology of Learning and Motivation*. New York, NY: Academic Press.

Baieli, S., L. Pavone, *et al.* (2003). Autism and phenylketonuria. *Journal of Autism and Developmental Disorders* **33**(2): 201–204.

Bailey, A. J., S. Braeutigam, *et al.* (2005). Abnormal activation of face processing systems at early and intermediate latency in individuals with autism spectrum disorder: A magnetoencephalographic study. *European Journal of Neuroscience* **21**(9): 2575–2585.

Baillieux, H,. H. J. De Smet, *et al.* (2006). Neurobehavioral alterations in an adolescent following posterior fossa tumor resection. *Cerebellum* **5**(4): 289–295.

Bakare, M. O. and N. N. Ikegwuonu (2008). Childhood autism in a 13 year old boy with oculocutaneous albinism: A case report. Journal of Medical Case Reports **2**: 56.

Bakare, M. O., A. O. Agomoh, *et al.* (2009). Etiological explanation, treatability and preventability of childhood autism: A survey of Nigerian healthcare workers' opinion. *Annals of General Psychiatry* **8**: 6.

Bakermans-Kranenburg, M. J. and M. H. van IJzendoorn (2011). Differential susceptibility to rearing environment depending on dopamine-related genes: New evidence and a meta-analysis. *Development and Psychopathology* **23**(1): 39–52.

Balciuniene, J., N. Feng, *et al.* (2007). Recurrent 10q22-q23 deletions: A genomic disorder on 10q associated with cognitive and behavioral abnormalities. *American Journal of Human Genetics* **80**(5): 938–947.

Balfe, M. and D. Tantam (2010). A descriptive social and health profile of a community sample of adults and adolescents with Asperger syndrome. *BMC Research Notes* **3**(1): 300.

Balfe, M., D. Tantam, *et al.* (2011). Possible evidence for a fall in the prevalence of high-functioning pervasive developmental disorder with age? *Autism Research and Treatment*. doi:10.1155/2011/325495.

Balfe, M., T. Chen, *et al.* (2005). *Sheffield Survey of Health and Social Care Needs of Adolescents and Adults with Asperger Syndro*me. 13. ScHARR Report. Sheffield: School of Health and Related Research.

Balint, S., P. Czobor, *et al.* (2009). Attention deficit hyperactivity disorder (ADHD): Gender- and age-related differences in neurocognition. *Psychological Medicine* **39**(8): 1337–1345.

Ball, L. J., M. D. Sullivan, *et al.* (2005). Speech-language characteristics of children with Sotos syndrome. *American Journal of Medical Genetics A* **136A**(4): 363–367.

Ballas, D. and D. Dorling (2007). Measuring the impact of major life events upon happiness. *International Journal of Epidemiology* **36**(6): 1244–1252.

Ballerini, M., N. Cabibbo, *et al.* (2008). From the cover: Interaction ruling animal collective behavior depends on topological rather than metric distance: Evidence from a field study. *Proceedings of the National Academy of Sciences of the United States of America* **105**(4): 1232–1237.

Banaclocha, M. A. M. (2007). Neuromagnetic dialogue between neuronal minicolumns and astroglial network: A new approach for memory and cerebral computation. *Brain Research Bulletin* **73**(1–3): 21–27.

Bandura, A. (1977). Self-efficacy: Toward a unifying theory of behavioral change. *Psychological Review* **84**(2): 191–215.

Bar, M. and M. Neta (2007). Visual elements of subjective preference modulate amygdala activation. *Neuropsychologia* **45**(10): 2191–2200.

Barbaro, J. and C. Dissanayake (2009). Autism spectrum disorders in infancy and toddlerhood: A review of the evidence on early signs, early identification tools, and early diagnosis. *Journal of Developmental and Behavioral Pediatrics* **30**(5): 447–459.

Barbeau, E. B., A. Mendrek, *et al.* (2009). Are autistic traits autistic? *British Journal of Psychology* **100**(1): 23–28.

Barnard, J., V. Harvard, *et al.* (2001). *Ignored or Ineligible?* London: National Autistic Society.

Barnard, L., K. Muldoon, *et al.* (2008). Profiling executive dysfunction in adults with autism and comorbid learning disability. *Autism* **12**(12): 125–141.

Barnby, G., A. Abbott, *et al.* (2005). Candidate-gene screening and association analysis at the autism-susceptibility locus on chromosome 16p: Evidence of association at GRIN2A and ABAT. *American Journal of Human Genetics* **76**(6): 950–966.

Barnea-Goraly, N., H. Kwon, *et al.* (2004). White matter structure in autism: Preliminary evidence from diffusion tensor imaging. *Biological Psychiatry* **55**(3): 323–326.

Barnett, A. L., L. Kooistra, *et al.* (1998). Clumsiness as syndrome and symptom. *Human Movement Science* **17**(4–5): 435–447.

Barnett, S. A. (1997). Review of "Feral children and clever animals: Reflections on human nature" by D. K. Candland. *Interdisciplinary Science Reviews* **22**(2): 172.

Baron-Cohen, S, M. V. Lombardo, *et al.* (2011). Why are autism spectrum conditions more prevalent in males? *PLoS Biology* **9**(6): e1001081.

Baron-Cohen, S. (2000). Is Asperger syndrome/high-functioning autism necessarily a disability? *Development and Psychopathology* **12**(3): 489–500.

Baron-Cohen, S. (2003). *The Essential Difference: Male and Female Brains and the Truth about Autism.* New York, NY: Basic Books.

Baron-Cohen, S. (2009). Autism: The empathizing-systemizing (E-S) theory. *Annals of the New York Academy of Sciences* **1156**(March): 68–80.

Baron-Cohen, S. and J. Hammer (1997). Is autism an extreme form of the 'male brain'? *Advances in Infancy Research* **11**: 193–317.

Baron-Cohen, S. and M. K. Belmonte (2005). Autism: A window onto the development of the social and the analytic brain. *Annual Review of Neuroscience* **28**: 109–126.

Baron-Cohen, S. and S. Wheelwright (2004). The empathy quotient: An investigation of adults with Asperger syndrome or high functioning autism, and normal sex differences. *Journal of Autism and Developmental Disorders* **34**(2): 163–175.

Baron-Cohen, S., A. Cox, *et al.* (1996). Psychological markers in the detection of autism in infancy in a large population. *British Journal of Psychiatry* **168**(2): 158–163.

Baron-Cohen, S., A. Leslie, *et al.* (1985). Does the autistic child have a 'theory of mind'? *Cognition* **21**(1): 37–46.

Baron-Cohen, S., H. Ring, *et al.* (2000). The amygdala theory of autism. *Neuroscience and Biobehavioral Reviews* **24**(3): 355–364.

Baron-Cohen, S., H. Ring, *et al.* (2006). fMRI of parents of children with Asperger syndrome: A pilot study. *Brain and Cognition* **61**(1): 122–130.

Baron-Cohen, S., J. Allen, *et al.* (1992). Can autism be detected at 18 months? The needle, the haystack and the CHAT. *British Journal of Psychiatry* **161**(December): 839–843.

Baron-Cohen, S., J. Richler, *et al.* (2003). The systemizing quotient: An investigation of adults with Asperger syndrome or high-functioning autism, and normal sex differences. *Philosophical Transactions of the Royal Society B: Biological Sciences* **358**(1430): 361–374.

Baron-Cohen, S., R. Campbell, *et al.* (1995). Are children with autism blind to the mentalistic significance of the eyes. *British Journal of Developmental Psychology* **13**(4): 379–398.

Baron-Cohen, S., S. W. Wright, *et al.* (1998). Engineering and autism: Exploring the link further: Reply to Wolff, Braunsberg and Islam. *Autism* **2**(1): 98–104.

Barr, M. (1898). Some notes on echolalia with the report of an extraordinary case. *Journal of Nervous and Mental Disease* **25**: 20–30.

Barr, W. B. (2003). Delineating the functions of the nondominant hemisphere. *Epilepsy and Behavior* **4**(6): 797–798.

Barry, R. J., A. R. Clarke, *et al.* (2003). A review of electrophysiology in attention-deficit/hyperactivity disorder: I. Qualitative and quantitative electroencephalography. *Clinical Neurophysiology* **114**(2): 171–183.

Bartlett, C. W., N. Gharani, *et al.* (2005). Three autism candidate genes: A synthesis of human genetic analysis with other disciplines. *International Journal of Developmental Neuroscience* **23**: 221–234.

Barton, J. J. S., D. Z. M. Press, *et al.* (2002). Lesions of the fusiform face area impair perception of facial configuration in prosopagnosia. *Neurology* **58**: 71–78.

Bartram, J. L., A. S. Rigby, *et al.* (2005). The Lasso-o tape: stretchability and observer variability in head circumference measurement. *Archives of Disease in Childhood* **90**: 820–821.

Bass, J. L., M. Corwin, *et al.* (2004). The effect of chronic or intermittent hypoxia on cognition in childhood: A review of the evidence. *Pediatrics* **114**(3): 805–816.

Bateson, G., D. Jackson, *et al.* (1956). Toward a theory of schizophrenia. *Behavioral Science* **1**(4): 251–264.

Battaglia, A. (2005). The inv dup(15) or idic(15) syndrome: A clinically recognisable neurogenetic disorder. *Brain and Development* **27**(5): 365–369.

Battaglia, A. and J. C. Carey (2006). Etiologic yield of autistic spectrum disorders: A prospective study. *American Journal of Medical Genetics C: Seminars in Medical Genetics* **142C**(1): 3–7.

Bauer, J. J., D. P. McAdams, *et al.* (2005). Interpreting the good life: Growth memories in the lives of mature, happy people. *Journal of Personality and Social Psychology* **88**(1): 203–217.

Bauman, M. L. and T. L. Kemper (2003). The neuropathology of the autism spectrum disorders: What have we learned? *Novartis Foundation Symposium* **251**: 112–122.

Bauman, M. L. and T. L. Kemper (2005). Neuroanatomic observations of the brain in autism: A review and future directions. *International Journal of Developmental Neuroscience* **23**: 183–187.

Bauminger, N. (2007a). Brief report: Group social-multimodal intervention for HFASD. *Journal of Autism and Developmental Disorders* 37(8): 1605–1615.

Bauminger, N. (2007b). Brief report: Individual social-multimodal intervention for HFASD. *Journal of Autism and Developmental Disorders* 37(8): 1593–1604.

Bauminger, N., M. Solomon, *et al.* (2008). Friendship in high-functioning children with autism spectrum disorder: Mixed and non-mixed dyads. *Journal of Autism and Developmental Disorders* 38(7): 1211–1229.

Beattie, G. W. (1983). *Talk: An Analysis of Speech and Non-Verbal Behaviour in Conversation.* Milton Keynes: Open University Press.

Bebbington, A. and J. Beecham (2007). Social services support and expenditure for children with autism. *Autism* 11(1): 43–61.

Beblo, T., M. Driessen, *et al.* (2006). Functional MRI correlates of the recall of unresolved life events in borderline personality disorder. *Psychological Medicine* 36: 845–856.

Becchio, C., A. Pierno, *et al.* (2007). Motor contagion from gaze: The case of autism. *Brain* 130(9): 2401–2411.

Bechara, E. G., M. C. Didiot, *et al.* (2009). A novel function for fragile X mental retardation protein in translational activation. *PLoS Biology* 7(1): e1000016.

Bedny, M., A. Pascual-Leone, *et al.* (2009). Growing up blind does not change the neural bases of Theory of Mind. *Proceedings of the National Academy of Sciences of the United States of America* 106(27): 11,312–11,317.

Beebe, D. W. (2006). Neurobehavioral morbidity associated with disordered breathing during sleep in children: A comprehensive review. *Sleep* 29(9): 1115–1134.

Begeer, S., R. Banerjee, *et al.* (2008). Self-presentation of children with autism spectrum disorders. *Journal of Autism and Developmental Disorders* 38(6): 1187–1191.

Begeer, S., S. E. Bouk, *et al.* (2009). Underdiagnosis and referral bias of autism in ethnic minorities. *Journal of Autism and Developmental Disorders* 39(1): 142–148.

Beglinger, L. and T. Smith (2005). Concurrent validity of social subtype and IQ after early intensive behavioral intervention in children with autism: A preliminary investigation. *Journal of Autism and Developmental Disorders* 35(3): 295–303.

Bejerot, S. and E. Mortberg (2009). Do autistic traits play a role in the bullying of obsessive-compulsive disorder and social phobia sufferers? *Psychopathology* 42(3): 170–176.

Bellgrove, M. A., Z. Hawi, *et al.* (2005). Association between Dopamine Transporter (DAT1): Genotype, Left-Sided Inattention, and an Enhanced Response to Methylphenidate in Attention-Deficit Hyperactivity Disorder. *Neuropsychopharmacology* 30(12): 2290–2297.

Bellini, S. and J. Peters (2008). Social skills training for youth with autism spectrum disorders. *Child and Adolescent Psychiatric Clinics of North America* 17(4): 857–873.

Bellini, S., J. Peters, *et al.* (2007). Meta-analysis of school-based social skills interventions for children with autism spectrum disorders. *Journal of Remedial and Special Education* 28(3): 153–162.

Bello, K. D., N. Goharpey, *et al.* (2008). A puzzle form of a non-verbal intelligence test gives significantly higher performance measures in children with severe intellectual disability. *BMC Pediatrics* 8: 30.

Bellone, S., A. Busti, *et al.* (2011). Children obesity, glucose tolerance, ghrelin, and Prader-Willi syndrome. In B. Debasis (ed.) *Global Perspectives on Childhood Obesity.* San Diego, CA: Academic Press.

Belmonte, M. K. and R. A. Carper (2006). Monozygotic twins with Asperger syndrome: Differences in behaviour reflect variations in brain structure and function. *Brain and Cognition* 61(1): 110–121.

Ben, B. D., V. Kronfeld-Duenias, *et al.* (2007). Accelerated maturation of white matter in young children with autism: a high b value DWI study. *NeuroImage* 37(1): 40–47.

Ben-David, E., E. Granot-Hershkovitz, *et al.* (2011). Identification of a functional rare variant in autism using genome-wide screen for monoallelic expression. *Human Molecular Genetics* 20(18): 3632–3641.

Bennett, D. S., M. Pitale, *et al.* (2004). Reactive vs. proactive antisocial behavior: Differential correlates of child ADHD symptoms? *Journal of Attention Disorders* 7: 197–204.

Bennett, T., P. Szatmari, *et al.* (2008). Differentiating autism and Asperger syndrome on the basis of language delay or impairment. *Journal of Autism and Developmental Disorders* 38(4): 616–625.

Ben-Sasson, A., S. A. Cermak, *et al.* (2008). Sensory clusters of toddlers with autism spectrum disorders: Differences in affective symptoms. *Journal of Child Psychology and Psychiatry* 49(8): 817–825.

Ben-Shachar, S., B. Lanpher, *et al.* (2009). Microdeletion 15q13.3: A locus with incomplete penetrance for autism, mental retardation, and psychiatric disorders. *Journal of Medical Genetics* 46(6): 382–388.

Benson, P. R. and K. L. Karlof (2009). Anger, stress proliferation, and depressed mood among parents of children with ASD: A longitudinal replication. *Journal of Autism and Developmental Disorders* 39(2): 350–362.

Berger, A., O. Kofman, *et al.* (2007). Multidisciplinary perspectives on attention and the development of self-regulation. *Progress in Neurobiology* 82(5): 256–286.

Berger, H. J. C., F. H. T. M. Aerts, *et al.* (2002). Cognitive styles in adolescents with autism spectrum disorders. *Tijdschrift voor Psychiatrie* 44: 83–94.

Berger, T. and T. Kellner (1964). The construction of reality an exercise in the microsociology of knowledge. *Diogenes* 46: 1–23.

Berlit, P. (2007). Neuropsychiatric disease in collagen vascular diseases and vasculitis. *Journal of Neurology* 254(Suppl 2): II87–II89.

Bernfort, L., S. Nordfeldt, *et al.* (2008). ADHD from a socio-economic perspective. *Acta Paediatrica* 97(2): 239–245.

Berthier, M. L., J. Santamaria, *et al.* (1992). Recurrent hypersomnia in two adolescent males with Asperger's syndrome. *Journal of the American Academy of Child and Adolescent Psychiatry* 31(4): 735–738.

Bertrand, J., A. Mars, *et al.* (2001). Prevalence of autism in a United States population: The Brick Township, New Jersey, investigation. *Pediatrics* 108(5): 1155–1161.

Bettelheim, B. (1967). *The Empty Fortress: Infantile Autism and the Birth of the Self.* New York, NY: Free Press.

Bettelheim, B. (1973). Some thoughts on childhood psychosis: Self and object. *Psychoanalytic Study of the Child* 28: 131–145.

Beverly, B. L., T. M. McGuinness, *et al.* (2008). Communication and academic challenges in early adolescence for children who have been adopted from the former Soviet Union. *Language Speech and Hearing Services in Schools* 39(3): 303–313.

Beversdorf, D. Q., A. Narayanan, *et al.* (2007). Network model of decreased context utilization in autism spectrum disorder. *Journal of Autism and Developmental Disorders* 37(6): 1040–1048.

Beversdorf, D. Q., B. W. Smith, et al. (2000). Increased discrimination of false memories in autism spectrum disorder. *Proceedings of the National Academy of Sciences of the United States of America* **97**: 8734–8737.

Beversdorf, D. Q., J. M. Anderson, et al. (1998). The effect of semantic and emotional context on written recall for verbal language in high functioning adults with autism spectrum disorder. *Journal of Neurology, Neurosurgery and Psychiatry* **65**: 685–692.

Bhardwaj, A., V. Agarwal, et al. (2005). Letter to the Editor. *Journal of Autism and Developmental Disorders* **35**(1): 135–136.

Bickart, K. C., C. I. Wright, et al. (2011). Amygdala volume and social network size in humans. *Nature Neuroscience* **14**(2): 163–164.

Biederman, J., C. R. Petty, et al. (2008). Educational and occupational underattainment in adults with attention-deficit/hyperactivity disorder: A controlled study. *Journal of Clinical Psychiatry* **69**(8): 1217–1222.

Biederman, J., L. J. Seidman, et al. (2008). Effects of stimulant medication on neuropsychological functioning in young adults with attention-deficit/hyperactivity disorder. *Journal of Clinical Psychiatry* **69**(7): 1150–1156.

Biederman, J., R. D. Melmed, et al. (2008). For the SPD a randomized, double-blind, placebo-controlled study of guanfacine extended release in children and adolescents with attention-deficit/hyperactivity disorder. *Pediatrics* **121**(1): e73–e84.

Biederman, J., S. Milberger, et al. (1995). Family-environment risk factors for attention-deficit hyperactivity disorder. A test of Rutter's indicators of adversity. *Archives of General Psychiatry* **52**(6): 464–470.

Bijlsma, E. K., A. C. Gijsbers, et al. (2009). Extending the phenotype of recurrent rearrangements of 16p11.2: Deletions in mentally retarded patients without autism and in normal individuals. *European Journal of Medical Genetics* **52**(2–3): 77–87.

Bilder, D., J. Pinborough-Zimmerman, et al. (2009). Prenatal, perinatal, and neonatal factors associated with autism spectrum disorders. *Pediatrics* **123**(5): 1293–1300.

Bilder, R., F. W. Sabb, et al. (2009). Phenomics: The systematic study of phenotypes on a genome-wide scale. *Neuroscience* **164**(1): 30–42.

Billstedt, E., I. C. Gillberg, et al. (2005). Autism after adolescence: Population-based 13- to 22-year follow-up study of 120 individuals with autism diagnosed in childhood. *Journal of Autism and Developmental Disorders* **35**(3): 351–360.

Billstedt, E., I. C. Gillberg, et al. (2007). Autism in adults: Symptom patterns and early childhood predictors. Use of the DISCO in a community sample followed from childhood. *Journal of Child Psychology and Psychiatry* **48**(11): 1102–1110.

Binder, J. R., R. H. Desai, et al. (2009). Where is the semantic system? A critical review and meta-analysis of 120 functional neuroimaging studies. *Cerebral Cortex* **19**(12): 2767–2796.

Bindu, P. S., K. E. Shehanaz, et al. (2007). Intermediate maple syrup urine disease: Neuroimaging observations in 3 patients from South India. *Journal of Child Neurology* **22**(7): 911–913.

Birmingham, E. and A. Kingstone (2009). A human social attention. *Annals of the New York Academy of Sciences* **1156**: 118–140.

Birnbaum, H. G., R. C. Kessler, et al. (2005). Costs of attention deficit-hyperactivity disorder (ADHD) in the US: Excess costs of persons with ADHD and their family members in 2000. *Current Medical Research and Opinion* **21** (2): 195–206.

Bishop, D. V. (2007). Curing dyslexia and attention-deficit hyperactivity disorder by training motor co-ordination: Miracle or myth? *Journal of Paediatrics and Child Health* **43**(10): 653–655.

Bishop, D. V. and C. F. Norbury (2005). Executive functions in children with communication impairments, in relation to autistic symptomatology. 2: Response inhibition. *Autism* **9**(1): 29–43.

Bishop, S., S. Gahagan, et al. (2007). Re-examining the core features of autism: A comparison of autism spectrum disorder and fetal alcohol spectrum disorder. *Journal of Child Psychology and Psychiatry* **48**(11): 1111–1121.

Bittner, A., H. L. Egger, et al. (2007). What do childhood anxiety disorders predict? *Journal of Child Psychology and Psychiatry* **48**(12): 1174–1183.

Blackshaw, A. J., P. Kinderman, et al. (2001). Theory of mind, causal attribution and paranoia in Asperger syndrome. *Autism* **5**(2): 147–163.

Blair, R. J. (1995). A cognitive developmental approach to mortality: Investigating the psychopath. *Cognition* **57**(1): 1–29.

Blais, C., R. E. Jack, et al. (2008). Culture shapes how we look at faces. *PLoS ONE* **3**(8): e3022.

Blanchard, L. T., M. J. Gurka, et al. (2006). Emotional, developmetal, and behavioral health of American children and their families: A report from the 2003 National Survey of Children's Health. *Pediatrics* **117**: e1202–e1212.

Blanchon, Y. C., C. Gay, et al. (2002). A case of N-acetyl galactosaminidase deficiency (Schindler disease) associated with autism. *Journal of Autism and Developmental Disorders* **32**(2): 145–146.

Blass, E. M. and C. A. Camp (2001). The ontogeny of face recognition: Eye contact and sweet taste induce face preference in 9- and 12-week-old human infants. *Developmental Psychology* **37**(6): 762–774.

Bleuler, E. (1911). *Dementia Praecox oder Gruppen der Schizophrenien*. Leipzig und Wein: Franz Deuticke.

Block-Lerner, J., C. Adair, et al. (2007). The case for mindfulness-based approaches in the cultivation of empathy: Does nonjudgemental, present-moment awareness increase capacity for perspective-taking and empathic concern? *Journal of Marital and Family Therapy* **33**(4): 501–516.

Bloss, C. S. M. and E. P. Courchesne (2007). MRI neuroanatomy in young girls with autism: A preliminary study. *Journal of the American Academy of Child and Adolescent Psychiatry* **46**(4): 515–523.

Bluhm, R. L., E. A. Osuch, et al. (2008). Default mode network connectivity: Effects of age, sex, and analytic approach. *Neuroreport* **19**(8): 887–891.

Blumstein, S. E. and K. Kurowski. (2006). The foreign accent syndrome: A perspective. *Journal of Neurolinguistics* **19**(5): 346–355.

Boada, R., J. Janusz, et al. (2009). The cognitive phenotype in Klinefelter syndrome: A review of the literature including genetic and hormonal factors. *Developmental Disabilities Research Reviews* **15**(4): 284–294.

Boardman, J., B. Grove, et al. (2003). Work and employment for people with psychiatric disabilities. *British Journal of Psychiatry* **182**: 467–468.

Bobee, S., E. Mariette, et al. (2000). Effects of early midline cerebellar lesion on cognitive and emotional functions in the rat. *Behavioural Brain Research* **112**(1–2): 107–117.

Boddaert, N., M. Zilbovicius, et al. (2009). MRI findings in 77 children with non-syndromic autistic disorder. *PLoS ONE* **4**(2): e4415.

Boddaert, N., N. Chabane, *et al.* (2004). Superior temporal sulcus anatomical abnormalities in childhood autism: A voxel-based morphometry MRI study. *NeuroImage* **23**(1): 364–369.

Bodfish, J. W., F. J. Symons, *et al.* (2000). Varieties of repetitive behavior in autism: Comparisons to mental retardation. *Journal of Autism and Developmental Disorders* **30**(3): 237–243.

Boelte, S., N. Uhlig, *et al.* (2002). Abnormal asymmetry in language association cortex in autism. *Annals of Neurology* **52**(5): 588–596.

Boes, A. D., A. Bechara, *et al.* (2009). Right ventromedial prefrontal cortex: A neuroanatomical correlate of impulse control in boys. *Social Cognitive and Affective Neuroscience* **4**(1): 1–9.

Boggio, P., S. Zaghi, *et al.* (2009). Modulation of emotions associated with images of human pain using anodal transcranial direct current stimulation (tDCS). *Neuropsychologia* **47**(1): 212–217.

Bogte, H., B. Flamma, *et al.* (2009). Divided attention capacity in adults with autism spectrum disorders and without intellectual disability. *Autism* **13**(3): 229–243.

Bolduc, M-E. B. O. and C. P. O. Limperopoulos (2009). Neurodevelopmental outcomes in children with cerebellar malformations: A systematic review. *Developmental Medicine and Child Neurology* **51**(4): 256–267.

Bölte, S., I. Dziobek, *et al.* (2009). Brief report: The level and nature of autistic intelligence revisited. *Journal of Autism and Developmental Disorders* **39**(4): 678–682.

Bölte, S., N. Özkara, *et al.* (2002). Autism spectrum disorders and low body weight: Is there really a systematic association? *International Journal of Eating Disorders* **31**(3): 343–351.

Bölte, S., S. Feineis-Matthews, *et al.* (2008). Brief report: Emotional processing in high-functioning autism-physiological reactivity and affective report. *Journal of Autism and Developmental Disorders* **38**(4): 776–781.

Bolton, P. F., M. Murphy, *et al.* (1997). Obstetric complications in autism: consequences or causes of the condition? *Journal of the American Academy of Child and Adolescent Psychiatry* **36**(2): 272–281.

Bolton, P. F., R. J. Park, *et al.* (2002). Neuro-epileptic determinants of autism spectrum disorders in tuberous sclerosis complex. *Brain* **125**(6): 1247–1255.

Bonato, M., K. Priftis, *et al.* (2009). Normal and impaired reflexive orienting of attention after central nonpredictive cues. *Journal of Cognitive Neuroscience* **21**(4): 745–759.

Bondy, A. and L. Frost (2001). The picture exchange communication system. *Behaviour Modification* **25**(5): 725–744.

Bonilha, L., F. Cendes, *et al.* (2008). Gray and white matter imbalance: Typical structural abnormality underlying classic autism? *Brain and Development* **30**(6): 396–401.

Bönisch, H. and M. Bruss (2006). The norepinephrine transporter in physiology and disease. *Handbook of Experimental Pharmacology* **175**: 485–524.

Boomsma, A., N. D. van Lang, *et al.* (2008). A new symptom model for autism cross-validated in an independent sample. *Journal of Child Psychology and Psychiatry* **49**(8): 809–816.

Bora, E., M. Yucel, *et al.* (2009) Neurobiology of human affiliative behaviour: implications for psychiatric disorders. *Current Opinion in Psychiatry* **22**(3): 320–325.

Boraston, Z. L., B. Corden, *et al.* (2008). Brief report: Perception of genuine and posed smiles by individuals with autism. *Journal of Autism and Developmental Disorders* **38**(3): 574–580.

Bos, P. A., J. Panksepp, *et al.* (2011) Acute effects of steroid hormones and neuropeptides on human social-emotional behavior: A review of single administration studies. *Frontiers in Neuroendocrinology.* doi:10.1016/j.yfrne.2011.01.002.

Bosch, S. (2002). Isolation or involvement? The social networks of children with autism included in regular classes. *Dissertation Abstracts International Section A: Humanities and Social Sciences* **62**: 8–A.

Bouchard, M. F., D. C. Bellinger, *et al.* (2010). Attention-deficit/hyperactivity disorder and urinary metabolites of organophosphate pesticides. *Pediatrics* **125**(6): e1270–e1277.

Bourgeron, T. (2009). A synaptic trek to autism. *Current Opinion in Neurobiology* **19**(2): 231–234.

Boyd, B. A., G. T. Baranek, *et al.* (2010). Sensory features and repetitive behaviors in children with autism and developmental delays. *Autism Research* **3**(2): 78–87.

Braam, W., R. Didden, *et al.* (2009). Melatonin decreases daytime challenging behaviour in persons with intellectual disability and chronic insomnia. *Journal of Intellectual Disability Research* **54**(1): 52–59.

Bradshaw, J. L. and D. M. Sheppard (2000). The neurodevelopmental frontostriatal disorders: Evolutionary adaptiveness and anomalous lateralization. *Brain and Language* **73**(2): 297–320.

Bramham, J., F. Ambery, *et al.* (2009). Executive functioning differences between adults with attention deficit hyperactivity disorder and autistic spectrum disorder in initiation, planning and strategy formation. *Autism* **13**(3): 245–264.

Braun, C. M., C. Denault, *et al.* (1994). Discrimination of facial identity and facial affect by temporal and frontal lobectomy patients. *Brain and Cognition* **24**(2): 198–212.

Breedlove, S. M. (2010). Minireview: Organizational hypothesis: instances of the fingerpost. *Endocrinology* **151**(9): 4116–4122.

Bremner, J. D., R. B. Innis, *et al.* (2000). Decreased benzodiazepine receptor binding in prefrontal cortex in combat-related posttraumatic stress disorder. *American Journal of Psychiatry* **157**(7): 1120–1126.

Brentano, F. (1973) (1874) *Psychology from an Empirical Standpoint* (originally published *Psychologie vom Empirischen Standpunkt*). London: Routledge.

Breslau, N., R. C. Kessler, *et al.* (1998). Trauma and posttraumatic stress disorder in the community: The 1996 Detroit Area Survey of Trauma. *Archives of General Psychiatry* **55**(7): 626–632.

Brewer, J. B. and A. Moghekar (2002). Imaging the medial temporal lobe: Exploring new dimensions. *Trends in Cognitive Sciences* **6**(5): 217–223.

Brewster, P. W., C. R. Mullin, *et al.* (2011). Sex differences in face processing are mediated by handedness and sexual orientation. *Laterality* **16**(2): 188–200.

Brieber, S., S. Neufang, *et al.* (2007). Structural brain abnormalities in adolescents with autism spectrum disorder and patients with attention deficit/hyperactivity disorder. *Journal of Child Psychology and Psychiatry* **48**(12): 1251–1258.

Briegel, W., M. Schimek, *et al.* (2009). Autism spectrum disorders in children and adolescents with Moebius sequence. *European Child and Adolescent Psychiatry* **18**(8): 515–519.

Bright-Paul, A., C. Jarrold, *et al.* (2008). Theory-of-mind development influences suggestibility and source monitoring. *Developmental Psychology* **44**(4): 1055–1068.

Broadbent, D. (1958). *Perception and Communication.* London: Pergamon Press.

Brodmann, K. (1909). *Vergleichende Lokalisationslehre der Grosshirnrinde.* Leipzig: Barth-Verlag.

Bromley, R. L., G. A. Baker, *et al.* (2009). Cognitive abilities and behaviour of children exposed to antiepileptic drugs in utero. *Current Opinion in Neurology* 22(2): 162–166.

Brook, U. and M. Boaz (2006). Adolescents with attention deficit and hyperactivity disorder/learning disability and their proneness to accidents. *Indian Journal of Pediatrics* 73(4): 299–303.

Brooks, J., L. A. Fos, *et al.* (1999). Assessment of executive function in patients with mild traumatic brain injury. *Journal of Trauma* 46(1): 159–163.

Brothers, L. (1990). The social brain: A project for integrating primate behaviour and neurophysiology in a new domain. *Concepts in Neuroscience* 15: 27–51.

Brown, R. T., W. S. Freeman, *et al.* (2001). Prevalence and assessment of attention-deficit/hyperactivity disorder in primary care settings. *Pediatrics* 107(3): E43.

Broyd, S. J., C. Demanuele, *et al.* (2009). Default-mode brain dysfunction in mental disorders: A systematic review. *Neuroscience and Biobehavioral Reviews* 33(3): 279–296.

Bruck, M., K. London, *et al.* (2007). Autobiographical memory and suggestibility in children with autism spectrum disorder. *Development and Psychopathology* 19(1): 73–95.

Bruining, H., H. Swaab, *et al.* (2009). Psychiatric characteristics in a self-selected sample of boys with Klinefelter syndrome. *Pediatrics* 123(5): e865–e870.

Bruining, H., L. de Sonneville, *et al.* (2010). Dissecting the clinical heterogeneity of autism spectrum disorders through defined genotypes. *PLoS ONE* 5(5): e10887.

Brun, C. C., R. Nicolson, *et al.* (2009). Mapping brain abnormalities in boys with autism. *Human Brain Mapping* 30(12): 3887–3900.

Brune, M., M. Abdel-Hamid, *et al.* (2007). Mental state attribution, neurocognitive functioning, and psychopathology: What predicts poor social competence in schizophrenia best? *Schizophrenia Research* 92(1–3): 151–159.

Brune, M., M. Abdel-Hamid, *et al.* (2009). Linking social cognition with social interaction: Non-verbal expressivity, social competence and mentalising in patients with schizophrenia spectrum disorders. *Behavioral and Brain Functions* 5: 6.

Brunet, P. M., J. J. Heisz, *et al.* (2009). Shyness and face scanning in children. *Journal of Anxiety Disorders* 23: 909–914.

Bryson, S. A., S. K. Corrigan, *et al.* (2008). Characteristics of children with autism spectrum disorders who received services through community mental health centers. *Autism* 12(1): 65–82.

Bryson, S. E., E. A. Bradley, *et al.* (2008). Prevalence of autism among adolescents with intellectual disabilities. *Canadian Journal of Psychiatry* 53(7): 449–459.

Bryson, S. E., L. Zwaigenbaum, *et al.* (2007). A prospective case series of high-risk infants who developed autism. *Journal of Autism and Developmental Disorders* 37(1): 12–24.

Bryson, S. E., L. Zwaigenbaum, *et al.* (2008). The Autism Observation Scale for Infants: Scale development and reliability data. *Journal of Autism and Developmental Disorders* 38(4): 731–738.

Bubier, J. L. and D. A. Drabick (2008). Affective decision-making and externalizing behaviors: The role of autonomic activity. *Journal of Abnormal Child Psychology* 36: 941–953.

Buccino, G. and M. Amore (2008). Mirror neurons and the understanding of behavioural symptoms in psychiatric disorders. *Current Opinion in Psychiatry* 21(3): 281–285.

Buck, R. and B. Ginsburg, B. (1997). Communicative genes and the evolution of empathy. In W. J. Ickes (ed.) *Emphathetic Accuracy.* New York, NY: Guilford Press.

Buckley, M. J., F. A. Mansouri, *et al.* (2009). Dissociable components of rule-guided behavior depend on distinct medial and prefrontal regions. *Science* 325(5936): 52–58.

Buckner, R. L., J. R. Andrews-Hanna, *et al.* (2008). The brain's default network: Anatomy, function, and relevance to disease. *Annals of the New York Academy of Sciences* 1124: 1–38.

Burgel, U., K. Amunts, *et al.* (2006). White matter fiber tracts of the human brain: Three-dimensional mapping at microscopic resolution, topography and intersubject variability. *NeuroImage* 29(4): 1092–1105.

Burgess, P. W., I. Dumontheil, *et al.* (2007). The gateway hypothesis of rostral prefrontal cortex (area 10) function. *Trends in Cognitive Sciences* 11(7): 290–298.

Burmeister, M., M. G. McInnis, *et al.* (2008). Psychiatric genetics: Progress amid controversy. *Nature Reviews Genetics* 9(7): 527–540.

Burmeister, R., H. J. Hannay, *et al.* (2005). Attention problems and executive functions in children with spina bifida and hydrocephalus. *Child Neuropsychology* 11(3): 265–283.

Burns, T., J. Catty, *et al.* (2009). The impact of supported employment and working on clinical and social functioning: Results of an international study of individual placement and support. *Schizophrenia Bulletin* 35(5): 949–958.

Burusnukul, P., E. C. de Los Reyes, *et al.* (2008). Danon disease: An unusual presentation of autism. *Pediatric Neurology* 39(1): 52–54.

Buschgens, C. J., M. A. van Aken, *et al.* (2008). Differential family and peer environmental factors are related to severity and comorbidity in children with ADHD. *Journal of Neural Transmission* 115(2): 177–186.

Buschmann, A., B. Jooss, *et al.* (2008). Children with developmental language delay at 24 months of age: Results of a diagnostic work-up. *Developmental Medicine and Child Neurology* 50(3): 223–229.

Bush, C. A., R. L. Mullis, *et al.* (2000). Differences in empathy between offender and nonoffender youth. *Journal of Youth and Adolescence* 29(4): 467–478.

Butler, M. G., G. A. Allen, *et al.* (1988). Preliminary communication: Photoanthropometric analysis of individuals with the fragile X syndrome. *American Journal of Medical Genetics* 30(1–2): 165–168.

Buttenschøn, H. N., M. B. Lauritsen, *et al.* (2009). A population-based association study of glutamate decarboxylase 1 as a candidate gene for autism. *Journal of Neural Transmission* 116(3): 381–388.

Buxhoeveden, D. P. and M. F. Casanova (2002). The minicolumn hypothesis in neuroscience. *Brain* 125(5): 935–951.

Cabanlit, M., S. Wills, *et al.* (2007). Brain-specific autoantibodies in the plasma of subjects with autistic spectrum disorder. *Annals of the New York Academy of Sciences* 1107: 92–103.

Cacioppo, J. T., C. J. Norris, *et al.* (2009). In the eye of the beholder: Individual differences in perceived social isolation predict regional brain activation to social stimuli. *Journal of Cognitive Neuroscience* 21(1): 83–92.

Cadesky, E. B., V. L. Mota, *et al.* (2000). Beyond words: How do children with ADHD and/or conduct problems process nonverbal information about affect? *Journal of the American Academy of Child and Adolescent Psychiatry* 39(9): 1160–1167.

Cahn, B. R. and J. Polich (2006). Meditation states and traits: EEG, ERP, and neuroimaging studies. *Psychological Bulletin* 132(2): 180–211.

Calder, A. J., J. D. Beaver, *et al.* (2007). Separate coding of different gaze directions in the superior temporal sulcus and inferior parietal lobule. *Current Biology* 17(1): 20–25.

Callahan, K., R. K. Henson, *et al.* (2008). Social validation of evidence-based practices in autism by parents, teachers, and administrators. *Journal of Autism and Developmental Disorders* **38**(4): 678–692.

Callier, P., L. Faivre, *et al.* (2008). Array-CGH in a series of 30 patients with mental retardation, dysmorphic features, and congenital malformations detected an interstitial 1p22.2-p31.1 deletion in a patient with features overlapping the Goldenhar syndrome. *American Journal of Medical Genetics Part A* **146A**(16): 2109–2115.

Calvo-Merino, B., J. Grèzes, *et al.* (2006). Seeing or doing? Influence of visual and motor familiarity in action observation. *Current Biology* **16**(19): 1905–1910.

Camfield, P. and C. Camfield (2002). C Epileptic syndromes in childhood: Clinical features, outcomes, and treatment. *Epilepsia* **43**(Suppl 3):27–32.

Campbell D.B., D. Datta, *et al.* (2011). Association of oxytocin receptor (OXTR) gene variants with multiple phenotype domains of autism spectrum disorder. *Journal of Neurodevelopmental Disorders* **3**(2): 101–112.

Campbell, D. B., J. S. Sutcliffe, *et al.* (2006). A genetic variant that disrupts MET transcription is associated with autism. *Proceedings of the National Academy of Sciences of the United States of America* **103**(45): 16,834–16,839.

Campbell, D. B., T. M. Buie, *et al.* (2009). Distinct genetic risk based on association of MET in families with co-occurring autism and gastrointestinal conditions. *Pediatrics* **123**(3): 1018–1024.

Campbell, L. E., E. Daly, *et al.* (2006). Brain and behaviour in children with 22q11.2 deletion syndrome: A volumetric and voxel-based morphometry MRI study. *Brain* **129**(5): 1218–1228.

Campbell, R., C. A. Heywood, *et al.* (1990). Sensitivity to eye gaze in prosopagnosic patients and monkeys with superior temporal sulcus ablation. *Neuropsychologia* **28**(11): 1123–1142.

Canino, G. and M. Alegria (2008). Psychiatric diagnosis – is it universal or relative to culture? *Journal of Child Psychology and Psychiatry* **49**(3): 237–250.

Canli, T., M. Qiu, *et al.* (2006). Neural correlates of epigenesis: Proceedings of the National Academy of Sciences **103**(43): 16,033–16,038.

Canu, E., M. Boccardi, *et al.* (2009). HOXA1 A218G polymorphism is associated with smaller cerebellar volume in healthy humans. *Journal of Neuroimaging* **19**(4): 353–358.

Capano, L., D. Minden, *et al.* (2008). Mathematical learning disorder in school-age children with attention-deficit hyperactivity disorder. *Canadian Journal of Psychiatry* **53**(6): 392–399.

Caplan, R., P. Siddarth, *et al.* (2002). Developmental outcome with and without successful intervention. *International Review of Neurobiology* **49**: 269–284.

Caraballo, R., R. Cersósimo, *et al.* (2004). Benign focal seizures of adolescence: A prospective study. *Epilepsia* **45**(12): 1600–1603.

Caramaschi, D., S. F. de Boer, *et al.* (2008). Development of violence in mice through repeated victory along with changes in prefrontal cortex neurochemistry. *Behavioural Brain Research* **189**(2): 263–272.

Caria, A., R. Veit, *et al.* (2007). Regulation of anterior insular cortex activity using real-time fMRI. *NeuroImage* **35**(3): 1238–1246.

Carlson, G. A., M. Potegal, *et al.* (2009). Rages – what are they and who has them? *Journal of Child and Adolescent Psychopharmacology* **19**(3): 281–288.

Carlson, H. B. and M. B. W. Buckwald (1993). Vocational Communication Group treatment in an outpatient head injury facility. *Brain Injury* **7**(2): 183–187.

Carlson, J. M., T. Greenberg, *et al.* (2010). Blind rage? Heightened anger is associated with altered amygdala responses to masked and unmasked fearful faces. *Psychiatry Research: Neuroimaging* **182**(3): 281–283.

Caron, M. J., L. Mottron, *et al.* (2004). Do high functioning persons with autism present superior spatial abilities? *Neuropsychologia* **42**(4): 467–481.

Carothers, D. E. and R. L. Taylor (2004). Understanding orbitofrontal contributions to theory-of-mind reasoning: Implications for autism. *Brain and Cognition* **55**(1): 209–219.

Carpenter, R. E., S. K. Loo, *et al.* (2009). Social functioning difficulties in ADHD: Association with PDD risk. *Clinical Child Psychology and Psychiatry* **14**(3): 329–344.

Carrington, S. and L. Graham (2001). Perceptions of school by two teenage boys with Asperger syndrome and their mothers: A qualitative study. *Autism* **5**(1): 37–48.

Carroll, J. (1993). *Human Cognitive Abilities.* Cambridge, Cambridge University Press.

Carter, A. S., F. de L. Martínez-Pedraza, *et al.* (2009). Stability and individual change in depressive symptoms among mothers raising young children with ASD: Maternal and child correlates. *Journal of Clinical Psychology* **65**(12): 1270–1280.

Cartwright-Hatton, S., K. McNicol, *et al.* (2006). Anxiety in a neglected population: Prevalence of anxiety disorders in pre-adolescent children. *Clinical Psychology Review* **26**(7): 817–833.

Carver, C. S., S. L. Johnson, *et al.* (2008). Serotonergic function, two-mode models of self-regulation, and vulnerability to depression: What depression has in common with impulsive aggression. *Psychological Bulletin* **134**(6): 912–943.

Casanova, M. F. (2006). *Abnormalities of Cortical Circuitry in the Brains of Autistic Individuals.* Presented at the All Wales Autism Resource (AWARES) International Conference, Cardiff.

Casanova, M. F. (2008). The minicolumnopathy of autism: A link between migraine and gastrointestinal symptoms. *Medical Hypotheses* **70**(1): 73–80.

Casanova, M. F. and J. Trippe (2009). Radial cytoarchitecture and patterns of cortical connectivity in autism. *Philosophical Transactions of the Royal Society B: Biological Sciences* **364**(1522): 1433–1436.

Casanova, M. F., A. El-Baz, *et al.* (2009). A reduced gyral window and corpus callosum size in autism: Possible macroscopic correlates of a minicolumnopathy. *Journal of Autism and Developmental Disorders* **39**(5): 751–764.

Casanova, M. F., D. P. Buxhoeveden, *et al.* (2002). Affective expressions during joint attention interactions with an adult: The case of autism. *Psychology: The Journal of the Hellenic Psychological Society* **9**(1): 1–21.

Casanova, M. F., D. P. Buxhoeveden, *et al.* (2003). Disruption in the inhibitory architecture of the cell minicolumn: Implications for autism. *Neuroscientist* **9**(6): 496–507.

Casasanto, D. and K. Jasmin (2010). Good and bad in the hands of politicians: Spontaneous gestures during positive and negative speech. *PLoS ONE* **5**(7): e11805.

Cascio, C., F. McGlone, *et al.* (2008). Tactile perception in adults with autism: A multidimensional psychophysical study. *Journal of Autism and Developmental Disorders* **38**(1): 127–137.

Case-Smith, J. and M. Arbesman (2008). Evidence-based review of interventions for autism used in or of relevance to occupational therapy. *American Journal of Occupational Therapy* **62**(4): 416–429.

Casey, B. J. (2005). Frontostriatal and frontocerebellar circuitry underlying cognitive control. In U. Mayr and S. Keele (eds) *Developing Individuality in the Human Brain: A Tribute to Michael I. Posner*. Washington, DC: American Psychological Association.

Cass, H., P. Gringras, *et al.* (2008). Absence of urinary opioid peptides in children with autism. *Archives of Disease in Childhood* **93**(9): 745–750.

Cassidy, J., S.S. Woodhouse, *et al.* (2011). Enhancing infant attachment security: An examination of treatment efficacy and differential susceptibility. *Development and Psychopathology* **23**(1): 131–148.

Castagnini, A. and G. Berrios (2009). Acute and transient psychotic disorders (ICD-10 F23): A review from a European perspective. *European Archives of Psychiatry and Clinical Neuroscience* **259**(8): 433–443.

Castellani, M. L., C. M. Conti, *et al.* (2009). Autism and immunity: Revisited study. *International Journal of Immunopathology and Pharmacology* **22**(1): 15–19.

Castellanos, F. X., P. P. Lee, *et al.* (2002). Developmental trajectories of brain volume abnormalities in children and adolescents with attention-deficit/hyperactivity disorder. *Journal of the American Medical Association* **288**(14): 1740–1748.

Castelli, F., C. Frith, *et al.* (2002). Autism, Asperger syndrome and brain mechanisms for the attribution of mental states to animated shapes. *Brain* **125**(8): 1839–1849.

Castermans, D., B. Thienpont, *et al.* (2008). Position effect leading to haploinsufficiency in a mosaic ring chromosome 14 in a boy with autism. *European Journal of Human Genetics* **16**(10): 1187–1192.

Catani, M. and D. H. ffytche (2005). The rises and falls of disconnection syndromes. *Brain* **128**(10): 2224–2239.

Catani, M., D. K. Jones, *et al.* (2008). Altered cerebellar feedback projections in Asperger syndrome. *NeuroImage* **41**(4): 1184–1191.

Cath, D. C., N. Ran, *et al.* (2008). Symptom overlap between autism spectrum disorder, generalized social anxiety disorder and obsessive-compulsive disorder in adults: A preliminary case-controlled study. *Psychopathology* **41**(2): 101–110.

Cath, D., D. van Grootheest, *et al.* (2008). Environmental factors in obsessive-compulsive behavior: Evidence from discordant and concordant monozygotic twins. *Behavior Genetics* **38**(2): 108–120.

Cattell, R. B. (1971). *Abilities: Their Structure, Growth, and Action.* Boston, MA: Houghton Mifflin.

Causton-Theoharis, J., C. Ashby, *et al.* (2009). Islands of loneliness: Exploring social interaction through the autobiographies of individuals with autism. *Journal of Intellectual and Developmental Disability* **47**(2): 84–96.

Cavanna, A. E. M., M. M. M. Robertson, *et al.* (2008). Catatonic signs in Gilles De La Tourette syndrome. *Cognitive and Behavioral Neurology* **21**(1): 34–37.

Cecil, K. M., M. P. DelBello, *et al.* (2003). Proton magnetic resonance spectroscopy of the frontal lobe and cerebellar vermis in children with a mood disorder and a familial risk for bipolar disorders. *Journal of Child and Adolescent Psychopharmacology* **13**(4): 545–555.

Cederlund, M. and C. Gillberg (2004). One hundred males with Asperger syndrome: A clinical study of background and associated factors. *Developmental Medicine and Child Neurology* **46**(10): 652–660.

Cederlund, M., B. Hagberg, *et al.* (2008). Asperger syndrome and autism: A comparative longitudinal follow-up study more than 5 years after original diagnosis. *Journal of Autism and Developmental Disorders* **38**(1): 72–85.

Chakrabarti, B., F. Dudbridge, *et al.* (2009). Genes related to sex steroids, neural growth, and social-emotional behavior are associated with autistic traits, empathy, and Asperger syndrome. *Autism Research* **2**(3): 157–177.

Chalfant, A. M., R. Rapee, *et al.* (2007). Treating anxiety disorders in children with high functioning autism spectrum disorders: A controlled trial. *Journal of Autism and Developmental Disorders* **37**(10): 1842–1857.

Challman, T. D., W.J. Barberesi, *et al.* (2003). The yield of the medical evaluation of children with pervasive developmental disorders. *Journal of Autism and Developmental Disorders* **33**(2): 18–7192.

Chamberlain, S. R., Sahakian, B. J. (2007). The neuropsychiatry of impulsivity. *Current Opinion in Psychiatry* **20**(3): 255–261.

Chaminade, T., A. N. Meltzoff, *et al.* (2002). Does the end justify the means? A PET exploration of the mechanisms involved in human imitation. *NeuroImage* **15**(2): 318–328.

Chan, A. S., Y. M. Y. Han, *et al.* (2011). Abnormalities in the anterior cingulate cortex associated with attentional and inhibitory control deficits: A neurophysiological study on children with autism spectrum disorders. *Research in Autism Spectrum Disorders* **5**(1): 254–266.

Chan, E., J. B. Mattingley, *et al.* (2009). Abnormal spatial asymmetry of selective attention in ADHD. *Journal of Child Psychology and Psychiatry* **50**(9): 1064–1072.

Chan, J. M. and M. F. A. O'Reilly (2008). Social stories intervention package for students with autism in inclusive classroom settings. *Journal of Applied Behavior Analysis* **41**(3): 405–409.

Charbonneau, S., B. P. Scherzer, *et al.* (2003). Perception and production of facial and prosodic emotions by chronic CVA patients. *Neuropsychologia* **41**(5): 605–613.

Charman, T. (2003). Why is joint attention a pivotal skill in autism? *Philosophical Transactions of the Royal Society B: Biological Sciences* **358**(1430): 315–324.

Charman, T. (2011). Commentary: Glass half full or half empty? Testing social communication interventions for young children with autism – reflections on Landa, Holman, O'Neill, and Stuart (2011). *Journal of Child Psychology and Psychiatry* **52**(1): 22–23.

Charman, T., E. Taylor, *et al.* (2005). Outcome at 7 years of children diagnosed with autism at age 2: Predictive validity of assessments conducted at 2 and 3 years of age and pattern of symptom change over time. *Journal of Child Psychology and Psychiatry* **46**(5): 500–513.

Charman, T., P. Howlin, *et al.* (2004). Psychoeducational treatment of children with autism and reactive attachment disorder. *Autism* **8**(1): 101–109.

Chartoff, E. H., B. T. Marck, *et al.* (2001). Induction of stereotypy in dopamine-deficient mice requires striatal D1 receptor activation. *Proceedings of the National Academy of Sciences of the United States of America* **98**(18): 10,451–10,456.

Chaudhry, A. M., J. A. Parkinson, *et al.* (2009). Preference judgements involve a network of structures within frontal, cingulate and insula cortices. *European Journal of Neuroscience* **29**(5): 1047–1055.

Chauhan, B, C. J Mathias, *et al.* (2008). Autonomic contributions to empathy: Evidence from patients with primary autonomic failure. *Autonomic Neuroscience* **140**(1–2): 96–100.

Chawarska, K., R. Paul, *et al.* (2007). Parental recognition of developmental problems in toddlers with autism spectrum disorders. *Journal of Autism and Developmental Disorders* **37**(1): 62–72.

Chein, J. M., S. M. Ravizza, *et al.* (2007). Using neuroimaging to evaluate models of working memory and their implications for language processing. *Journal of Neurolinguistics* **16**(4–5): 315–339.

Chen, C. Y., C. Y. Liu, *et al.* (2007). Factors associated with the diagnosis of neurodevelopmental disorders: A population-based longitudinal study. *Pediatrics* **119**(2): e435–e443.

Chen, C. Y., K. H. Chen, *et al.* (2009). Increased risks of congenital, neurologic, and endocrine disorders associated with autism in preschool children: Cognitive ability differences. *Journal of Pediatrics* **154**(3): 345–350e1.

Chen, F. (2009). Inverse correlation between the conceptual and perceptual processing in children with autism may be due to processing bias differences in information recall. *Autism* **13**(2): 193–194.

Chen, G. K., N. Kono, *et al.* (2006). Quantitative trait locus analysis of nonverbal communication in autism spectrum disorder. *Molecular Psychiatry* **11**(2): 214–220.

Chen, M., C. M. Seipp, *et al.* (2008). Mothers' and fathers' attributions and beliefs in families of girls and boys with attention-deficit/hyperactivity disorder. *Child Psychiatry and Human Development* **39**(1): 85–99.

Chen, W., K. Zhou, *et al.* (2008). DSM-IV combined type ADHD shows familial association with sibling trait scores: A sampling strategy for QTL linkage. *American Journal of Medical Genetics B: Neuropsychiatric Genetics* **147**(8): 1450–1460.

Chen, Y. H., J. Rodgers, *et al.* (2009). Restricted and repetitive behaviours, sensory processing and cognitive style in children with autism spectrum disorders. *Journal of Autism and Developmental Disorders* **39**(4): 635–642.

Cheng, Y., P. L. Lee, *et al.* (2008). Gender differences in the mu rhythm of the human mirror-neuron system. *PLoS ONE* **3**(5): e2113.

Chiang, C. H., W. T. Soong, *et al.* (2008). Nonverbal communication skills in young children with autism. *Journal of Autism and Developmental Disorders* **38**(10): 1898–1906.

Chiang, M. C., M. Barysheva, *et al.* (2009). Genetics of brain fiber architecture and intellectual performance. *Journal of Neuroscience* **29**(7): 2212–2224.

Chiao, J. Y., T. Harada, *et al.* (2009). Neural representations of social status hierarchy in human inferior parietal cortex. *Neuropsychologia* **47**(2): 354–363.

Chick, J., L. Waterhouse, *et al.* (1979). Psychological construing in schizoid children grown up. *British Journal of Psychiatry* **135**: 425–430.

Chiu, P. H., M. A. Kayali, *et al.* (2008). Self responses along cingulate cortex reveal quantitative neural phenotype for high-functioning autism. *Neuron* **57**(3): 463–473.

Chomsky, N. (1957). *Syntactic Structures*. The Hague: Mouton.

Chorney, D. B. M., M. F. P. Detweiler, *et al.* (2008). The interplay of sleep disturbance, anxiety, and depression in children. *Journal of Pediatric Psychology Special Issue (continued): Sleep in Pediatric Medical Populations* **33**: 339–348.

Christensen, D. and R. Rosenthal (1982). Gender and nonverbal decoding skill as determinants of interpersonal expectancy effects. *Journal of Personality and Social Psychology* **42**(1): 1–87.

Christensen, H., G. Boysen, *et al.* (2005). Insular lesions, ECG abnormalities, and outcome in acute stroke. *Journal of Neurology, Neurosurgery and Psychiatry* **76**(2): 269–271.

Christoff, K. and J. Gabrieli (2000). The frontopolar cortex and human cognition: Evidence for a rostrocaudal hierarchical organization within the human prefrontal cortex. *Psychobiology* **28**(2): 168–186.

Chudasama, Y., J. D. Kralik, *et al.* (2007). Rhesus monkeys with orbital prefrontal cortex lesions can learn to inhibit prepotent responses in the reversed reward contingency task. *Cerebral Cortex* **17**(5): 1154–1159.

Chugani, H. T., E. Da Silva, *et al.* (1996). Infantile spasms: III. Prognostic implications of bitemporal hypometabolism on positron emission tomography. *Annals of Neurology* **39**: 643–649.

Church, A. J. and R. C. Dale (2002). Antistreptolysin-O titers: Implications for adult PANDAS. Pediatric autoimmune neuropsychiatric disorders associated with streptococcal infections. *American Journal of Psychiatry* **159**(2): 320–327.

Chuthapisith, J., B. diMambro, *et al.* (2009). Effectiveness of a computer assisted learning (CAL) package to raise awareness of autism. *BMC Medical Education* **9**(1): 12.

Ciccarelli, O., M. Catani, *et al.* (2008). Diffusion-based tractography in neurological disorders: concepts, applications, and future developments. *The Lancet Neurology* **7**(8): 715–727.

Cimera, R. E. and R. J. Cowan (2009). The costs of services and employment outcomes achieved by adults with autism in the US. *Autism* **13**(3): 285–302.

Clark, F., A. Scharaschkin, *et al.* (2009). *Supporting People with Autism through Adulthood: Technical Report*. London: National Audit Office.

Clark, T. F., P. Winkielman, *et al.* (2008). Autism and the extraction of emotion from briefly presented facial expressions: Stumbling at the first step of empathy. *Emotion* **8**(6): 803–809.

Cleckley, H. (1941). *The Mask of Sanity*. St Louis, MO: C V Mosby.

Clifford, S. M. and C. Dissanayake (2008). The early development of joint attention in infants with autistic disorder using home video observations and parental interview. *Journal of Autism and Developmental Disorders* **38**(5): 791–805.

Clifford, S., C. Dissanayake, *et al.* (2007). Autism spectrum phenotype in males and females with fragile X full mutation and premutation. *Journal of Autism and Developmental Disorders* **37**(4): 738–747.

Clifford, S., R. Young, *et al.* (2007). Assessing the early characteristics of autistic disorder using video analysis. *Journal of Autism and Developmental Disorders* **37**(2): 301–313.

Cohen, H. (1955). The evolution of the concept of disease; president's address. *Proceedings of the Royal Society of Medicine* **48**(3):155–160.

Cohen, H., Z. Kaplan, *et al.* (2004). Repetitive transcranial magnetic stimulation of the right dorsolateral prefrontal cortex in posttraumatic stress disorder: a double-blind, placebo-controlled study. *American Journal of Psychiatry* **161**(3): 515–524.

Cohen, L., S. Dehaene, *et al.* (2000). Language and calculation within the parietal lobe: A combined cognitive, anatomical and fMRI study. *Neuropsychologia* **38**(10): 1426–1440.

Cohen, M. X., N. David, *et al.* (2009). Gamma-band activity in the human superior temporal sulcus during mentalizing from nonverbal social cues. *Psychophysiology* **46**(1): 43–51.

Coker, T. R., M. N. Elliott, *et al.* (2009). Racial/Ethnic disparities in the mental health care utilization of fifth grade children. *Academic Pediatrics* **9**(2): 89–96.

Coleman, J. and J. Gurd (2006). Introduction to the theme issue on foreign accent syndrome. *Journal of Neurolinguistics* **19**(5): 341–345.

Coleman, M. M. (1989). Young children with autism or autistic-like behavior. *Infants and Young Children* **1**(4): 22–31.

Colle, L., S. Baron-Cohen, *et al.* (2008). Narrative discourse in adults with high-functioning autism or Asperger syndrome. *Journal of Autism and Developmental Disorders* **38**(1): 28–40.

Colom, R., P. C. Shih, *et al.* (2006). The real relationship between short-term memory and working memory. *Memory* **14**(7): 804–813.

Colom, R., R. J. Haier, *et al.* (2003). Gray matter correlates of fluid, crystallized, and spatial intelligence: Testing the P-FIT model. *Intelligence* **37**(2): 124–135.

Colombi, C., K. Liebal, *et al.* (2009). Examining correlates of cooperation in autism: Imitation, joint attention, and understanding intentions. *Autism* **13**(2): 143–163.

Colvert, E., M. Rutter, *et al.* (2008a). Do theory of mind and executive function deficits underlie the adverse outcomes associated with profound early deprivation? Findings from the English and Romanian Adoptees Study. *Journal of Abnormal Child Psychology* **36**(7): 1057–1068.

Colvert, E., M. Rutter, *et al.* (2008b). Emotional difficulties in early adolescence following severe early deprivation: Findings from the English and Romanian adoptees study. *Development and Psychopathology* **20**(2): 547–567.

Commission on Chronic Illness (1957). *Prevention of Chronic Illness.* Cambridge, MA: HUP.

Conciatori, M., C. J. Stodgell, *et al.* (2004). Association between the HOXA1 A218G polymorphism and increased head circumference in patients with autism. *Biological Psychiatry* **55**(4): 413–419.

Connor, K. M., J. R. Davidson, *et al.* (2000). Psychometric properties of the Social Phobia Inventory (SPIN). New self-rating scale. *British Journal of Psychiatry* **176**: 379–386.

Connor, M. (1999). Children on the autistic spectrum: Guidelines for mainstream practice. *Support for Learning* **14**(2): 80–886. Available at www.mugsy.org/connor2.htm, accessed on 27 July 2011.

Constantino, J. N. and R. D. P. Todd (2003). Distribution of Social Responsiveness Scale (SRS) scored as a function of sex (n = 1576): Autistic traits in the general population: a twin study. *Archives of General Psychiatry* **60**(5): 524–530.

Constantino, J. N., A. M. Abbacchi, *et al.* (2009). Developmental course of autistic social impairment in males. *Development and Psychopathology* **21**(1): 127–138.

Constantino, J. N., C. P. Gruber, *et al.* (2004). The factor structure of autistic traits. *Journal of Child Psychology and Psychiatry* **45**(4): 719–726.

Constantino, J. N., J. J. Hudziak, *et al.* (2003). Prevalance of pervasive developmental disorders in the British nationalwide survey of child mental heath. *International Review of Psychiatry* **15**(1–2): 158–165.

Constantino, J. N., P. D. P. Lavesser, *et al.* (2007). Rapid quantitative assessment of autistic social impairment by classroom teachers. *Journal of the American Academy of Child and Adolescent Psychiatry* **46**(12): 1668–1676.

Constantino, J. N., S. A. Davis, *et al.* (2003). Validation of a brief quantitative measure of autistic traits: comparison of the social responsiveness scale with the autism diagnostic interview-revised. *Journal of Autism and Developmental Disorders* **33**(4): 427–433.

Conturo, T. E., D. L. Williams, *et al.* (2008). Neuronal fiber pathway abnormalities in autism: An initial MRI diffusion tensor tracking study of hippocampo-fusiform and amygdalo-fusiform pathways. *Journal of the International Neuropsychological Society* **14**(6): 933–946.

Conty, L., K. N'Diaye, *et al.* (2007). When eye creates the contact! ERP evidence for early dissociation between direct and averted gaze motion processing. *Neuropsychologia* **45**(13): 3024–3037.

Conway, A. R. A., N. Cowan, *et al.* (2002). A latent variable analysis of working memory capacity, short-term memory capacity, processing speed, and general fluid intelligence. *Intelligence* **30**(2): 163–183.

Coo, H., H. Ouellette-Kuntz, *et al.* (2008). Trends in autism prevalence: Diagnostic substitution revisited. *Journal of Autism and Developmental Disorders* **38**(6): 1036–1046.

Coolican, J., I. M. Smith, *et al.* (2010). Brief parent training in pivotal response treatment for preschoolers with autism. *Journal of Child Psychology and Psychiatry* **51**(12): 1321–1330.

Coolidge, F. L., D. L. Segal, *et al.* (2009). Working memory deficits in personality disorder traits: A preliminary investigation in a nonclinical sample. *Journal of Research in Personality* **43**(3): 355–361.

Cooper, S. A., W. N. Mohamed, *et al.* (1993). Possible Asperger's syndrome in a mentally handicapped transvestite offender. *Journal of Intellectual Disability Research* **37**(2): 189–194.

Corbett, B. A., L. J. Constantine, *et al.* (2009). Examining executive functioning in children with autism spectrum disorder, attention deficit hyperactivity disorder and typical development. *Psychiatry Research* **166**(2–3): 210–222.

Corkum, P. P., R. M. Panton, *et al.* (2008). Acute impact of immediate release methylphenidate administered three times a day on sleep in children with attention-deficit/hyperactivity disorder. *Journal of Pediatric Psychology Special Issue (continued): Sleep in Pediatric Medical Populations* **33**: 368–379.

Coskun, M. A., L. Varghese, *et al.* (2009). How somatic cortical maps differ in autistic and typical brains. *Neuroreport* **20**(2): 175–179.

Costa, B., S. Pini, *et al.* (2009). Mutation analysis of oxytocin gene in individuals with adult separation anxiety. *Psychiatry Research* **168**(2): 87–93.

Costantini, M., G. Galati, *et al.* (2008). Empathic neural reactivity to noxious stimuli delivered to body parts and non-corporeal objects. *European Journal of Neuroscience* **28**(6): 1222–1230.

Cotugno, A. J. (2009). Social competence and social skills training and intervention for children with Autism Spectrum Disorders. *Journal of Autism and Developmental Disorders* **39**(9): 1268–1277.

Council on Children with Disabilities, Section on Developmental Behavioral Pediatrics, Bright Futures Steering Committee *et al.* (2006). Medical home initiatives for children with special needs project advisory committee identifying infants and young children with developmental disorders in the medical home: An algorithm for developmental surveillance and screening. *Pediatrics* **118**(1): 405–420.

Courchesne, E., R. Yeung-Courchesne, *et al.* (1988). Hypoplasia of Cerebellar Vermal Lobules VI and VII in Autism. *New England Journal Of Medicine* **318**(21): 1349–1354.

Cox, A., K. Klein, *et al.* (1999). Autism spectrum disorders at 20 and 42 months of age: stability of clinical and ADI-R diagnosis. *Journal of Child Psychology and Psychiatry* **40**(5): 719–732.

Cox, D. J., M. Moore, *et al.* (2008). Rebound effects with long-acting amphetamine or methylphenidate stimulant medication preparations among adolescent male drivers with attention-deficit/hyperactivity disorder. *Journal of Child and Adolescent Psychopharmacology* **18**(1): 1–10.

Craddock, N., M. C. O'Donovan, *et al.* (2009). Psychosis genetics: Modeling the relationship between schizophrenia, bipolar disorder, and mixed (or schizoaffective) psychoses. *Schizophrenia Bulletin* **35**(3): 482–490.

Craig, A. D. (2002). How do you feel? Interoception: The sense of the physiological condition of the body. *Nature Reviews Neuroscience* **3**(8): 655–666.

Craig, A. D. (2009). How do you feel – now? The anterior insula and human awareness. *Nature Reviews Neuroscience* **10**(1): 59–70.

Crane, L., L. Goddard, *et al.* (2009). Sensory processing in adults with autism spectrum disorders. *Autism* **13**(3): 215–228.

Creak, M. (1972). The first observations on the wild-boy of Lacaune (called Victor or the wild-boy of Aveyron): New documents. *Annales Medico Psychologiques* **2**: 465–490.

Crespi, B. (2008). Genomic imprinting in the development and evolution of psychotic spectrum conditions. *Biological Reviews of the Cambridge Philosophical Society* **83**(4): 441–493.

Croen, L. A., C. K. Yoshida, *et al.* (2005). Neonatal hyperbilirubinemia and risk of autism spectrum disorders. *Pediatrics* **115**(2): e135–e138.

Croen, L. A., J. K. Grether, *et al.* (2002). The changing prevalence of autism in California. *Journal of Autism and Developmental Disorders* **32**(3): 207–215.

Croen, L. A., J. K. Grether, *et al.* (2005). Maternal autoimmune diseases, asthma and allergies, and childhood autism spectrum disorders: A case-control study. *Archives of Pediatrics and Adolescent Medicine* **159**(2): 151–157.

Croen, L. A., P. Goines, *et al.* (2008). Brain-derived neurotrophic factor and autism: Maternal and infant peripheral blood levels in the Early Markers for Autism (EMA) Study. *Autism Research* **1**(2): 130–137.

Cromer, K. R., N. B. Schmidt, *et al.* (2007). An investigation of traumatic life events and obsessive-compulsive disorder. *Behaviour Research and Therapy* **45**(7): 1683–1691.

Crozier, S. and M. Tincani (2007). Effects of social stories on prosocial behavior of preschool children with autism spectrum disorders. *Journal of Autism and Developmental Disorders* **37**(9): 1803–1814.

Cullen, B., J. Samuels, *et al.* (2008). Social and communication difficulties and obsessive-compulsive disorder. *Psychopathology* **41**(3): 194–200.

Cunningham, C. E., A. E. McHolm, *et al.* (2006). Social phobia, anxiety, oppositional behavior, social skills, and self-concept in children with specific selective mutism, generalized selective mutism, and community controls. *European Child and Adolescent Psychiatry* **15**(5): 245–255.

Cunningham, J. L. and P. H. Papero (1997). Prototypical nonverbal learning disability (NLD) in a girl with velo-cardio-facial syndrome: A case report. *Archives of Clinical Neuropsychology* **12**(4): 305–306.

Curatolo, P., C. Paloscia, *et al.* (2009). The neurobiology of attention deficit/hyperactivity disorder. *European Journal of Paediatric Neurology* **13**(4): 299–304.

D'Argembeau, A., P. Ruby, *et al.* (2007). Distinct regions of the medial prefrontal cortex are associated with self-referential processing and perspective taking. *Journal of Cognitive Neuroscience* **19**(6): 935–944.

Dadds, M. R., D. J. Hawes, *et al.* (2009). Learning to 'talk the talk': The relationship of psychopathic traits to deficits in empathy across childhood. *Journal of Child Psychology and Psychiatry* **50**(5): 599–606.

Dadds, M. R., K. Hunter, *et al.* (2008). A measure of cognitive and affective empathy in children using parent ratings. *Child Psychiatry and Human Development* **39**(2): 111–122.

Dadds, M., Y. El Masry, *et al.* (2008). A reduced eye gaze explains fear blindness in childhood psychopathic traits. *Journal of the American Academy of Child and Adolescent Psychiatry* **47**(4): 455–463.

Daderman, A. M., M. Lindgren, *et al.* (2004). The prevalence of dyslexia and AD/HD in a sample of forensic psychiatric rapists. *Nordic Journal of Psychiatry* **58**(5): 371–381.

Daley, T. C. (2004). From symptom recognition to diagnosis: Children with autism in urban India. *Social Science and Medicine* **58**(7): 1323–1335.

Dalrymple, N. J. and L. A. Ruble (1996). *Technical Assistance Manual on Autism for Kentucky Schools*. Franfort, KY: Kentucky Department of Education. Available in modified form at www.aspergersyndrome.org/Articles/Behaviors-That-May-Be-Personal-Challenges-For-A-St.aspx, accessed on 27 July 2011.

Dalton, K. M., B. M. Nacewicz, *et al.* (2007). Gaze-fixation, brain activation, and amygdala volume in unaffected siblings of individuals with autism. *Biological Psychiatry* **61**(4): 512–520.

Damasio, A. R. (1996). The somatic marker hypothesis and the possible functions of the prefrontal cortex. *Philosophical Transactions of the Royal Society B: Biological Sciences* **351**(1346): 1413–1420.

Damasio, A. R. and R. G. Maurer (1978). A neurological model for childhood autism. *Archives of Neurology* **35**(12): 777–786.

Damasio, A. R., T. J. Grabowski, *et al.* (2000). Subcortical and cortical brain activity during the feeling of self-generated emotions. *Nature Neuroscience* **3**(10): 1049–1056.

Damasio, H., T. Grabowski, *et al.* (1994). The return of Phineas Gage: Clues about the brain from the skull of a famous patient [published erratum appears in *Science* **265**(5176):1159]. *Science* **264**(5162): 1102–1105.

Dammann, O., M. Naples, *et al.* (2009). SNAP-II and SNAPPE-II and the risk of structural and functional brain disorders in extremely low gestational age newborns: The ELGAN study. *Neonatology* **97**(2): 71–82.

Daniels, J. L., U. Forssen, *et al.* (2008). Parental psychiatric disorders associated with autism spectrum disorders in the offspring. *Pediatrics* **121**(5): e1357–e1362.

Danielsson, S., G. Viggedal, *et al.* (2008). Lack of effects of vagus nerve stimulation on drug-resistant epilepsy in eight pediatric patients with autism spectrum disorders: A prospective 2-year follow-up study. *Epilepsy and Behavior* **12**(2): 298–304.

Daoust, A. M., F. A. Lusignan, *et al.* (2008). Dream content analysis in persons with an autism spectrum disorder. *Journal of Autism and Developmental Disorders* **38**(4): 634–643.

Darke, J., K. Bushby, *et al.* (2006). Survey of behaviour problems in children with neuromuscular diseases. *European Journal of Paediatric Neurology* **10**(3): 129–34.

Davey, C. G., M. Yucel, *et al.* (2008). The emergence of depression in adolescence: Development of the prefrontal cortex and the representation of reward. *Neuroscience and Biobehavioural Reviews* **32**(1): 1–19.

Davey, C. G., N. B. Allen, *et al.* (2010). Being liked activates primary reward and midline self-related brain regions. *Human Brain Mapping* **31**(4): 660–668.

David, A. S., A. Wacharasindhu, *et al.* (1993). Severe psychiatric disturbance and abnormalities of the corpus callosum: Review and case series. *Journal of Neurology, Neurosurgery and Psychiatry* **56**(1): 85–93.

David, O., K. Nina, *et al.* (2009). Maternal insightfulness and resolution of the diagnosis are associated with secure attachment in preschoolers with autism spectrum disorders. *Child Development* **80**(2): 519–527.

Davies, M. (2007). Neural correlates of viewing emotional faces with direct or averted gaze in children with autism spectrum disorders. *International Meeting for Autism Research*. Seattle, WA.

Davis, M. H. and L. A. Kraus (1997). Personality and empathic accuracy. In W. J. Ickes (ed.) *Empathic Accuracy*. New York, NY: Guilford Press.

Dawson, G. (2007). Despite major challenges, autism research continues to offer hope. *Archives of Pediatric and Adolescent Medicine* **161**(4): 411–412.

Dawson, M. (2009). The autism crisis: Science and ethics in the era of autism advocacy. Available at http://autismcrisis. blogspot.com/2009/07/anomaly-in-autism-intervention-research.html, accessed 27 July 2011.

Dawson, M., L. Soulières, *et al.* (2007). The level and nature of autistic intelligence. *Psychological Science* **18**(8): 657–662.

De Bellis, M. D., B. J. Casey, *et al.* (2000). A pilot study of amygdala volumes in pediatric generalized anxiety disorder. *Biological Psychiatry* **48**(1): 51–57.

De Bellis, M. D., M. S. Keshavan, *et al.* (2002). Superior temporal gyrus volumes in pediatric generalized anxiety disorder. *Biological Psychiatry* **51**(7): 553–562.

De Boer, L., I. Röder, *et al.* (2006). Psychosocial, cognitive, and motor functioning in patients with suspected Sotos syndrome: A comparison between patients with and without NSD1 gene alterations. *Developmental Medicine and Child Neurology* **48**(7): 582–588.

De Boer, S. F., D. Caramaschi, *et al.* (2009). The vicious cycle towards violence: focus on the negative feedback mechanisms of brain serotonin neurotransmission. *Frontiers in Behavioral Neuroscience* **3**: 52.

De Bruin, E. I., R. F. Ferdinand, *et al.* (2007). High rates of psychiatric co-morbidity in PDD-NOS. *Journal of Autism and Developmental Disorders* **37**(5): 877–886.

De Giacomo, A., C. Portoghese, *et al.* (2009). Imitation and communication skills development in children with pervasive developmental disorders. *Journal of Neuropsychiatric Disease and Treatment* **5**(3): 355–362.

De Graaf, R., R. C. Kessler, *et al.* (2008). The prevalence and effects of Adult Attention-Deficit/Hyperactivity Disorder (ADHD) on the performance of workers: Results from the WHO World Mental Health Survey Initiative. *Occupational and Environmental Medicine* **65**(12): 835–842.

De Krom M., W. G. Staal, *et al.* (2009). A common variant in DRD3 receptor is associated with autism spectrum disorder. *Biological Psychiatry* **65**(7): 625–630.

De Pisapia, N. and T. S. Braver (2006). A model of dual control mechanisms through anterior cingulate and prefrontal cortex interactions. *Neurocomputing* **69**(10–12): 1322–1326.

De Pisapia, N., J. A. Slomski, *et al.* (2007). Functional specializations in lateral prefrontal cortex associated with the integration and segregation of information in working memory. *Cerebral Cortex* **17**(5): 993–1006.

De Ridder, A. and D. De Graeve (2006). Healthcare use, social burden and costs of children with and without ADHD in Flanders, Belgium. *Clinical Drug Investigation* **26**(2): 75–90.

De Sanctis, S. (1908). Dementia pracocissima catatonica oder Katatonie des frueheren Kindesalters? *Folia Neuro-Biologica (Leipzig)* **2**: 9–12.

De Saussure, F. (1959). *Course in General Linguistics* (trans. by W. Baskin). New York, NY: Philosophical Library.

De Veer, M. W., J. Gallup, *et al.* (2003). An 8-year longitudinal study of mirror self-recognition in chimpanzees (Pan troglodytes). *Neuropsychologia* **41**(2): 229–234.

De Vries, A., I. Noens, *et al.* (2010). Autism spectrum disorders in gender dysphoric children and adolescents. *Journal of Autism and Developmental Disorders* **40**(8): 930–936.

De Waal, F. B. M. (2008). Putting the altruism back into altruism: The evolution of empathy. *Annual Review of Psychology* **59**: 279–300.

De Winter, C. F., F. van Dijk, *et al.* (2009). RCM Behavioural phenotype in Borjeson-Forssman-Lehmann syndrome. *Journal of Intellectual Disability Research* **53**(4): 319–328.

Deak, G. O., T. A. Walden, *et al.* (2008). Driven from distraction: How infants respond to parents' attempts to elicit and re-direct their attention. *Infant Behavior and Development* **31**(1): 34–50.

Decety, J. and C. Lamm (2007). The role of the right temporoparietal junction in social interaction: How low-level computational processes contribute to meta-cognition. *Neuroscientist* **13**(6): 580–593.

Decety, J. and M. Meyer (2008). From emotion resonance to empathic understanding: A social developmental neuroscience account. *Development and Psychopathology* **20**(4): 1053–1080.

Decety, J. and T. Chaminade (2003). Neural correlates of feeling sympathy. *Neuropsychologia* **41**(2): 127–138.

Decety, J. and Y. Moriguchi (2007). The empathic brain and its dysfunction in psychiatric populations: Implications for intervention across different clinical conditions. *Biopsychosocial Medicine* **1**: 22.

Decety, J., K. J. Michalska, *et al.* (2008). Who caused the pain? An fMRI investigation of empathy and intentionality in children. *Neuropsychologia* **46**(11): 2607–2614.

Deitz, J. C., D. Kartin, *et al.* (2007). Review of the Bruininks-Oseretsky test of motor proficiency, Second edition (BOT-2). *Physical and Occupational Therapy in Pediatrics* **27**(4): 87–102.

DeLoache, J. S., G. Simcock, *et al.* (2007). Planes, trains, automobiles – and tea sets: Extremely intense interests in very young children. *Developmental Psychology* **43**(6): 1579–1586.

DeLong, R. (1994). Children with autistic spectrum disorder and a family history of affective disorder *Developmental Medicine and Child Neurology* **36**(8): 674–687.

Demurie, E., M. De Corel, *et al.* (2011). Empathic accuracy in adolescents with autism spectrum disorders and adolescents with attention-deficit/hyperactivity disorder. *Research in Autism Spectrum Disorders* **5**(1): 126–134.

Deonna, T. and E. Roulet (2006). Autistic spectrum disorder: Evaluating a possible contributing or causal role of epilepsy. *Epilepsia* **47**(Suppl 2): 79–82.

DeQuinzio, J. A., D. B. Townsend, *et al.* (2007). Generalized imitation of facial models by children with autism. *Journal of Applied Behavior Analysis* **40**(4): 755–759.

Derks, E. M., J. J. Hudziak, *et al.* (2008). Genetic and environmental influences on the relation between attention problems and attention deficit hyperactivity disorder. *Behaviour Genetics* **38**(1): 11–23.

Derrida, J. (1978). *Writing and Difference*. London and New York: Routledge.

Deruelle, C., C. Rondan, *et al.* (2008). Attention to low- and high-spatial frequencies in categorizing facial identities, emotions and gender in children with autism. *Brain and Cognition* **66**(2): 115–123.

Detterman, D. K. (1999). The psychology of mental retardation. *International Review of Psychiatry* **11**(1): 26–33.

Detterman, D. K. and M. Daniel (1989). Correlations of mental tests with each other and with cognitive variables are highest in low IQ groups. *Intelligence* **13**: 349–360.

Deutsch, C. K. and R. M. Joseph (2003). Brief report: Cognitive correlates of enlarged head circumference in children with autism. *Journal of Autism and Developmental Disorders* **33**(2): 209–215.

DeVito, T. J., D. J. Drost, *et al.* (2007). Evidence for cortical dysfunction in autism: A proton magnetic resonance spectroscopic imaging study. *Biological Psychiatry* **61**(4): 465–473.

Devlin, S., G. Leader, et al. (2009). Comparison of behavioral intervention and sensory-integration therapy in the treatment of self-injurious behavior. *Research in Autism Spectrum Disorders* **3**(1): 223–231.

DeWall, C. N., R. F. Baumeister, et al. (2008). Evidence that logical reasoning depends on conscious processing. *Consciousness and Cognition* **17**(3): 628–645.

Dewey, D., M. Cantell, et al. (2007). Motor and gestural performance in children with autism spectrum disorders, developmental coordination disorder, and/or attention deficit hyperactivity disorder. *Journal of the International Neuropsychological Society* **13**(2): 246–256.

Dhossche, D. M. (2004). Autism as early expression of catatonia. *Medical Science Monitor: International Medical Journal of Experimental and Clinical Research* **10**(3): RA31–RA39.

Dhossche, D. M., I. M. Reti, et al. (2009). Catatonia and autism: A historical review, with implications for electroconvulsive therapy. *Journal of ECT* **25**(1): 19–22.

Dhossche, D. M., I. M. Reti, et al. (2010). Tics as signs of catatonia: Electroconvulsive therapy response in two men. *Journal of ECT* **26**(4): 266–269.

Dhossche, D., L. Wing, et al. (eds) (2006) *Catatonia in Autism Spectrum Disorders.* New York, NY: Academic Press.

Di Martino, A. and F. X. Castellanos (2003). Functional neuroimaging of social cognition in pervasive developmental disorders: A brief review. *Annals of the New York Academy of Sciences* **1008**: 256–260.

Di Martino, A., K. Ross, et al. (2009). Functional brain correlates of social and nonsocial processes in autism spectrum disorders: An activation likelihood estimation meta-analysis. *Biological Psychiatry* **65**(1): 63–74.

Di Martino, A., Z. Shehzad, et al. (2009). Relationship between cingulo-insular functional connectivity and autistic traits in neurotypical adults. *American Journal of Psychiatry* **166**(8): 891–899.

Di Nardo A., I. Kramvis, et al. (2009). Tuberous sclerosis complex activity is required to control neuronal stress responses in an mTOR-dependent manner. *Journal of Neuroscience* **29**(18): 5926–5937.

Diamond, A. (2005). Attention-deficit disorder (attention-deficit/hyperactivity disorder without hyperactivity): a neurobiologically and behaviorally distinct disorder from attention-deficit/hyperactivity disorder (with hyperactivity). *Development and Psychopathology* **17**(3), 807–825.

Dias, E. C., J. J. Foxe, et al. (2003). Changing plans: A high density electrical mapping study of cortical control. *Cerebral Cortex* **13**(7): 701–715.

Dichter, G. S. and A. Belger (2007). A Social stimuli interfere with cognitive control in autism. *NeuroImage* **35**(3): 1219–1230.

Dichter, G. S. and A. Belger (2008). Atypical modulation of cognitive control by arousal in autism. *Psychiatry Research; Neuroimaging* **164**(3): 185–197.

Dichter, G. S., J. N. Felder, et al. (2009). Autism is characterized by dorsal anterior cingulate hyperactivation during social target detection. *Social Cognitive and Affective Neuroscience* **4**(3): 215–226.

Diehl, J. J., L. Bennetto, et al. (2008). Resolving ambiguity: A psycholinguistic approach to understanding prosody processing in high-functioning autism. *Brain and Language* **106**(2): 144–152.

Dietz, C., S. H. Swinkels, et al. (2007). Stability and change of IQ scores in preschool children diagnosed with autistic spectrum disorder. *European Child and Adolescent Psychiatry* **16**(6): 405–410.

Diewald, M. and K. U. Mayer (2003). The sociology of the life course and life span psychology: Integrated paradigm or complementing pathways? *Advances in Life Course Research* **14**(1–2): 5–14.

DiLallo, J. J., M. Jones, et al. (2009). Personality subtypes in disruptive adolescent males. *Journal of Nervous and Mental Disease* **197**(1): 15–23.

DiLavore, P. C., C. Lord, et al. (1995). The pre-linguistic autism diagnostic observation schedule. *Journal of Autism and Developmental Disorders* **25**(4): 355–379.

Dinstein, I., C. Thomas, et al. (2008). A mirror up to nature. *Current Biology* **18**(1): R13–R18.

Dishion, T. J., J. McCord, et al. (1999). When interventions harm: Peer groups and problem behavior. *American Psychologist* **54**(9): 755–764.

Dobbinson, S, M. Perkins, et al. (2003). The interactional significance of formulas in autistic language. *Clinical Linguistics and Phonetics* **17**(4–5): 299–307.

Dockrell, J. E. (2001). Assessing language skills in preschool children. *Child Psychology and Psychiatry Review* **6**(2): 74–85.

Doi, H., K. Ueda, et al. (2009). Neural correlates of the stare-in-the-crowd effect. *Neuropsychologia* **47**(4): 1053–1060.

Doig, J. L., J. D. McLennan, et al. (2009). 'Jumping through hoops': Parents' experiences with seeking respite care for children with special needs. *Child: Care, Health and Development* **35**(2): 234–242.

Dominick, K. C., N. O. Davis, et al. (2007). Atypical behaviors in children with autism and children with a history of language impairment. *Research in Developmental Disabilities* **28**(1): 145–162.

Donaldson, Z. R. and L. J. Young (2008). Oxytocin, vasopressin, and the neurogenetics of sociality. *Science Genetics of Behavior* **322**(5903): 900–904.

Donnelly, S. L., C. M. Wolpert, et al. (2000). Female with autistic disorder and monosomy X (Turner syndrome): Parent-of-origin effect of the X chromosome. *American Journal of Medical Genetics* **96**(3): 312–316.

Doron, K. W. and M. S. Gazzaniga (2008). Neuroimaging techniques offer new perspectives on callosal transfer and interhemispheric communication. *Cortex* **44**(8): 1023–1029.

Dosenbach, N. U. F., B. Nardos, et al. (2010). Prediction of individual brain maturity using fMRI. *Science* **329**(5997): 1358–1361.

dosReis, S., A. Butz, et al. (2006). Attitudes about stimulant medication for attention-deficit/hyperactivity disorder among African American families in an inner city community. *Journal of Behavioral Health Services and Research* **33**(4): 423–430.

Douniol, M., A. Jacquette, et al. (2009). Psychiatric and cognitive phenotype in children and adolescents with myotonic dystrophy. *European Child and Adolescent Psychiatry* **18**(12): 705–715.

Dover, C. J. and A. Le Couteur (2007). How to diagnose autism. *Archives of Disease in Childhood* **92**(6): 540–545.

Dowell, L. R., M. E. Mahone, et al. (2009). Associations of postural knowledge and basic motor skill with dyspraxia in autism: Implication for abnormalities in distributed connectivity and motor learning. *Neuropsychology* **23**(5): 563–570.

Dubas, J. S., K. Miller, et al. (2003). The study of adolescence during the 20th century. *The History of the Family* **8**(3): 375–397.

Duchaine, B. C. and A. Weidenfeld (2003). An evaluation of two commonly used tests of unfamiliar face recognition. *Neuropsychologia* **41**(6): 713–720.

Duffy, A., M. Alda, et al. (2007). The early manifestations of bipolar disorder: A longitudinal prospective study of the offspring of bipolar parents. Bipolar Disorders 9(8): 828–838.

Dumontheil, I., P. W. Burgess, et al. (2008). Development of rostral prefrontal cortex and cognitive and behavioural disorders. Developmental Medicine and Child Neurology 50(3): 168–181.

Dunbar, R. I. M. (2004). Gossip in evolutionary perspective. Review of General Psychology 8(2): 100–110.

Dunn, B. D., T. Dalgleish, at al. (2006). The somatic marker hypothesis: A critical evaluation. Neuroscience and Biobehavioral Reviews 30(2): 239–271.

Dunn, W., B. S. Myles, et al. (2002). Sensory processing issues associated with Asperger syndrome: A preliminary investigation. American Journal of Occupational Therapy 56(1): 97–102.

Duong, T. A., S. Bastuji-Garin, et al. (2011). Evolving pattern with age of cutaneous signs in neurofibromatosis type 1: a cross-sectional study of 728 patients. Dermatology 222(3): 269–273.

Duquette, A., F. Michaud, et al. (2008). Exploring the use of a mobile robot as an imitation agent with children with low-functioning autism. Autonomous Robots 24(2): 147–157.

Durand, C. M., C. Betancur, et al. (2007). Mutations in the gene encoding the synaptic scaffolding protein SHANK3 are associated with autism spectrum disorders. Nature Genetics 39(1): 25–27.

Durkheim, E. (1970). Suicide: A Study in Sociology. London: Routledge & Kegan Paul.

Durston, S., H. E. Hulshoff, et al. (2004). Magnetic resonance imaging of boys with attention-deficit/hyperactivity disorder and their unaffected siblings. Journal of the American Academy of Child and Adolescent Psychiatry 43(3): 332–340.

Durston, S., J. van Belle, et al. (2011). Differentiating frontostriatal and fronto-cerebellar circuits in attention-deficit/hyperactivity disorder: Prefrontal cortical circuits regulating attention, behavior and emotion. Biological Psychiatry 69(12): 1178–1184.

Durston, S., N. T. Tottenham, et al. (2003). Differential patterns of striatal activation in young children with and without ADHD. Biological Psychiatry 53(10): 871–878.

Duvall, J. A., A. Lu, et al. (2007). A quantitative trait locus analysis of social responsiveness in multiplex autism families. American Journal of Psychiatry 164(4): 656–662.

Dziobek, I., K. Rogers, et al. (2008). Dissociation of cognitive and emotional empathy in adults with Asperger syndrome using the Multifaceted Empathy Test (MET). Journal of Autism and Developmental Disorders 38(3): 464–473.

Dziobek, I., S. M. Gold, et al. (2007). Hypercholesterolemia in Asperger syndrome: Independence from lifestyle, obsessive-compulsive behavior, and social anxiety. Psychiatry Research 149(1–3): 321–324.

Dziuk, M. A., J. C. G. Larson, et al. (2007). Dyspraxia in autism: Association with motor, social, and communicative deficits. Developmental Medicine and Child Neurology 49(10): 734–739.

Eaves, L. C., H. H. Ho, et al. (1994). Subtypes of autism by cluster analysis. Journal of Autism and Developmental Disorders 24(1): 3–22.

Eaves, L., H. D. P. Wingert, et al. (2006). Screening for autism spectrum disorders with the social communication questionnaire. Journal of Developmental and Behavioral Pediatrics 27(2): S95–S103.

Edelmann, L., A. Prosnitz, et al. (2007). An atypical deletion of the Williams-Beuren syndrome interval implicates genes associated with defective visuospatial processing and autism. Journal of Medical Genetics 44(2): 136–143.

Edwards, G., R. A. Barkley, et al. (2001). Parent-adolescent conflict in teenagers with ADHD and ODD. Journal of Abnormal Child Psychology 29(6): 557–572.

Effron, D. A., P. M. Niedenthal, et al. (2006). Embodied temporal perception of emotion. Emotion 6(1): 1–9.

Eigsti, I. M. and L. Bennetto (2009). Grammaticality judgments in autism: Deviance or delay. Journal of Child Language 36(5): 999–1021.

Eigsti, I. M., L. Bennetto, et al. (2007). Beyond pragmatics: Morphosyntactic development in autism. Journal of Autism and Developmental Disorders 37(6): 1007–1023.

Eippert, F., R. Veit, et al. (2007). Regulation of emotional responses elicited by threat-related stimuli. Human Brain Mapping 28(5): 409–423.

Eisenberg, L. (2007). Commentary with a historical perspective by a child psychiatrist: When ADHD was the brain-damaged child. Journal of Child and Adolescent Psychopharmacology 17(3): 279–283.

Eisenberg, L. and Kanner, L. (1956). Early infantile autism, 1943–1955. American Journal of Orthopsychiatry 26(3): 556–566.

Eisenberg, N., C. Hofer, et al. (2008). Understanding mother-adolescent conflict discussions: Concurrent and across-time prediction from youths' dispositions and parenting. Monographs of the Society for Research in Child Development 73(2): vii–viii, 1–160.

Eisenberg, N., N. Michalik, et al. (2007). The relations of effortful control and impulsivity to children's sympathy: A longitudinal study. Cognitive Development 22(4): 544–567.

Eisenberg, N., R. A. Fabes, et al. (1996). The relations of children's dispositional empathy-related responding to their emotionality, regulation, and social functioning. Developmental Psychology 32(2): 195–209.

Eisenberg, N., R. Fabes, et al. (2006). Prosocial development. In W. Damon and R. Lerner (eds) Handbook of Child Psychology. Sixth edition. Chichester: Wiley.

Ekman, P. (1994). Strong evidence for universals in facial expressions: A reply to Russell's mistaken critique. Psychological Bulletin 115(2): 268–287.

Ekman, P. and W. Friesen (1969a). Nonverbal leakage and cues to deception. Psychiatry 32(1): 88–106.

Ekman, P. and W. Friesen (1969b). The repertoire of nonverbal behavior: Categories, origins, usage, and coding. Semiotica 1(1): 49–98.

Ekstrom, A. B., L. Hakenas-Plate, et al. (2008). Autism spectrum conditions in myotonic dystrophy type 1: A study on 57 individuals with congenital and childhood forms. American Journal of Medical Genetics B: Neuropsychiatric Genetics 147B(6): 918–926.

El Abd, S., M. A. Patton, et al. (1999). Social, communicational, and behavioral deficits associated with ring X Turner syndrome. American Journal of Medical Genetics 88(5): 510–516.

Elfert, M. and P. Mirenda (2006). The experiences of behavior interventionists who work with children with autism in families' homes. Autism 10(6): 577–591.

Elfgren, C., D. van Westen, et al. (2006). fMRI activity in the medial temporal lobe during famous face processing. NeuroImage 30(2): 609–616.

Elgar, K. and R. Campbell (2001). Annotation: The cognitive neuroscience of face recognition: implications for developmental disorders. Journal of Child Psychology and Psychiatry and Allied Disciplines 42(6): 705–717.

El-Hattab, A. W., T. A. Smolarek, *et al.* (2009). Redefined genomic architecture in 15q24 directed by patient deletion/duplication breakpoint mapping. *Human Genetics* **126**(4): 589–602.

Elia, J. and M. Devoto (2007). ADHD genetics: 2007 update. *Current Psychiatry Reports* **9**(5): 434–439.

Elia, J., M. L. Dell, *et al.* (2005). PANDAS with catatonia: A case report. Therapeutic response to lorazepam and plasmapheresis. *Journal of the American Academy of Child and Adolescent Psychiatry* **44**(11): 1145–1150.

Elliott, E. J., J. Payne, *et al.* (2008). Fetal alcohol syndrome: A prospective national surveillance study. *Archives of Disease in Childhood* **93**(9): 732–737.

Ellis, B.J., W.T. Boyce, *et al.* (2011). Differential susceptibility to the environment: An evolutionary–neurodevelopmental theory. *Development and Psychopathology* **23**(1): 7–28.

Ellis, B.J., E.A. Shirtcliff, *et al.* (2011). Quality of early family relationships and the timing and tempo of puberty: Effects depend on biological sensitivity to context. *Development and Psychopathology* **23**(1): 85–99.

Elsabbagh, M., A. Volein, *et al.* (2009a). Neural correlates of eye gaze processing in the infant broader autism phenotype. *Biological Psychiatry* **65**(1): 31–38.

Elsabbagh, M., A. Volein, *et al.* (2009b). Visual orienting in the early broader autism phenotype: Disengagement and facilitation. *Journal of Child Psychology and Psychiatry* **50**(5): 637–642.

Eluvathingal, T. J., M. E. Behen, *et al.* (2006). Cerebellar lesions in tuberous sclerosis complex: Neurobehavioral and neuroimaging correlates. *Journal of Child Neurology* **21**(10): 846–851.

Emerson, E. and C. Hatton (2007). Mental health of children and adolescents with intellectual disabilities in Britain. *British Journal of Psychiatry* **191**: 493–499.

Emery, N. J. (2000). The eyes have it: The neuroethology, function and evolution of social gaze. *Neuroscience and Biobehavioral Reviews* **24**(6): 581–604.

Emond, A., P. Emmett, *et al.* (2010). Feeding symptoms, dietary patterns, and growth in young children with autism spectrum disorders. *Pediatrics* **126**(2): e337–e342.

Ene, M. (1999). High-functioning autism or Asperger Syndrome? A comparison of emotion perception abilities and neurocognitive functioning. *Dissertation Abstracts International: Section B: The Sciences and Engineering* **60**: 1849.

Engell, A. D. and J. V. Haxby (2007). Facial expression and gaze-direction in human superior temporal sulcus. *Neuropsychologia* **45**(14): 3234–3241.

English, A. and J. Essex (2001). *Report on Autistic Spectrum Disorders: A Comprehensive Report into Identification, Training and Provision Focusing on the Needs of Children and Young People with Autistic Spectrum Disorder and their Families within the West Midlands Region.* Warwick, Warwickshire County Council for the West Midlands Autistic Society.

Engström, I., L. Ekström, *et al.* (2003). Psychosocial functioning in a group of Swedish adults with Asperger syndrome or high-functioning autism. *Autism* **7**(1): 99–110.

Erikson, E. (1963). *Childhood and Society.* New York, NY: W. W. Norton.

Ernst, M., A. S. Kimes, *et al.* (2003). Neural substrates of decision making in adults with attention deficit hyperactivity disorder. *American Journal of Psychiatry* **160**(6): 1061–1070.

Escamilla, M. M. D., E. P. Hare, *et al.* (2009). Schizophrenia gene locus on chromosome 17q21 in a new set of families of Mexican and Central American ancestry: Evidence from the NIMH genetics of schizophrenia in Latino populations study. *American Journal of Psychiatry* **166**(4): 442–449.

Escobar, R., A. Hervas, *et al.* (2008). Attention deficit/hyperactivity disorder: Burden of the disease according to subtypes in recently diagnosed children. *Actas Espanolas de Psiquiatria* **36**(5): 285–294.

Eshel, N., E. E. Nelson, *et al.* (2007). Neural substrates of choice selection in adults and adolescents: Development of the ventrolateral prefrontal and anterior cingulate cortices. *Neuropsychologia* **45**(6): 1270–1279.

Eslinger, P. J. and K. R. Biddle (2000). Adolescent neuropsychological development after early right prefrontal cortex damage. *Developmental Neuropsychology* **18**(3): 297–329.

Eslinger, P. J., C. V. Flaherty-Craig, *et al.* (2004). Developmental outcomes after early prefrontal cortex damage. *Brain and Cognition* **55**(1): 84–103.

Esposito, G. and P. Venuti (2008). Analysis of toddlers' gait after six months of independent walking to identify autism: A preliminary study. *Perceptual and Motor Skills* **106**(1): 259–269.

Esposito, G., P. Venuti, *et al.* (2009). An exploration of symmetry in early autism spectrum disorders: Analysis of lying. *Brain and Development* **31**: 131–138.

Essex, M.J., J.M. Armstrong, *et al.* (2011). Biological sensitivity to context moderates the effects of the early teacher–child relationship on the development of mental health by adolescence. *Development and Psychopathology* **23**(1): 149–161.

Estecio, M. R-H., A. C. Fett-Conte, *et al.* (2002). Molecular and Cytogenetic Analyses on Brazilian Youths with Pervasive Developmental Disorders Autism. *Journal of Autism and Developmental Disorders* **32**(1): 35–41.

Esterberg, M. L., H. D. Trotman, *et al.* (2008). Childhood and current autistic features in adolescents with schizotypal personality disorder. *Schizophrenia Research* **104**(1–3): 265–273.

Evans, A. H., A. P. Strafella, *et al.* (2009). Impulsive and compulsive behaviors in Parkinson's disease. *Movement Disorders* **24**(11): 1561–1570.

Evans, D. G. (2009). Neurofibromatosis type 2 (NF2): A clinical and molecular review. *Orphanet Journal of Rare Diseases* **4**: 16.

Evans, S., S. S. Shergill, *et al.* (2010). Oxytocin decreases aversion to angry faces in an associative learning task. *Neuropsychopharmacology* **35**: 2502–2509.

Evardone, M. and G. M. Alexander (2009). Anxiety, sex-linked behaviors, and digit ratios (2D:4D). *Archives of Sexual Behavior* **38**(3): 442–455.

Fagerlund, A., S. Heikkinen, *et al.* (2006). Brain metabolic alterations in adolescents and young adults with fetal alcohol spectrum disorders. *Alcoholism: Clinical and Experimental Research* **30**(12): 2097–2104.

Fair, D. A., A. L. Cohen, *et al.* (2009). Functional brain networks develop from a local to distributed organization. *PLoS Computational Biology* **5**(5): e1000381.

Fairbairn, W. (1944). Endopsychic structure considered in terms of object relationships. *International Review of Psycho-Analysis* **25**: 70–92.

Fairchild, G., S. H. van Goozen, *et al.* (2008). Cortisol diurnal rhythm and stress reactivity in male adolescents with early-onset or adolescence-onset conduct disorder. *Biological Psychiatry* **64**(7): 599–606.

Fairchild, G., S. H. van Goozen, *et al.* (2009). Deficits in facial expression recognition in male adolescents with early-onset or adolescence-onset conduct disorder. *Journal of Child Psychology and Psychiatry* **50**(5): 627–636.

Fairhall, S. L. and A. Ishai (2007). Effective connectivity within the distributed cortical network for face perception. *Cerebral Cortex* **17**(10): 2400–2406.

Fajardo, C., M. I. Escobar, et al. (2008). Economo neurons are present in the dorsolateral (dysgranular) prefrontal cortex of humans. *Neuroscience Letters* **435**(3): 215–218.

Falcaro, M., A. Pickles, et al. (2008). The SLI Consortium Genetic and phenotypic effects of phonological short-term memory and grammatical morphology in specific language impairment. *Genes, Brain, and Behavior* **7**(4): 393–402.

Falip, M., M. Carreño, et al. (2009). Postictal psychosis: A retrospective study in patients with refractory temporal lobe epilepsy. *Seizure* **18**(2): 145–149.

Falk, D. (2009). New information about Albert Einstein's brain. *Frontiers in Evolutionary Neuroscience* **1**: 3.

Falter, C. M., K. C. Plaisted, et al. (2008). Visuo-spatial processing in autism: Testing the predictions of extreme male brain theory. *Journal of Autism and Developmental Disorders* **38**(3): 507–515.

Fan, Y-T., J. Decety, et al. (2010). Unbroken mirror neurons in autism spectrum disorders. *Journal of Child Psychology and Psychiatry* **51**(9): 981–988.

Faraone, S. V. and J. Biederman (1997). Do attention deficit hyperactivity disorder and major depression share familial risk factors? *Journal of Nervous and Mental Disease* **185**(9): 533–541.

Faraone, S. V., J. Biederman, et al. (1997). Attention deficit disorder and conduct disorder: Longitudinal evidence for a familial subtype. *Psychological Medicine*. **27**(2): 291–300.

Faraone, S. V., T. Spencer, et al. (2004). Meta-analysis of the efficacy of methylphenidate for treating adult attention-deficit/hyperactivity disorder. *Journal of Clinical Psychopharmacology* **24**(1): 24–29.

Farley, M. A., W. M. McMahon, et al. (2009). Twenty-year outcome for individuals with autism and average or near-average cognitive abilities. *Autism Research* **2**(2): 109–118.

Farmer, M. and A. Oliver (2005). Assessment of pragmatic difficulties and socio-emotional adjustment in practice. *International Journal of Language and Communication Disorders* **40**(4): 403–429.

Farrow, T. F. D., Y. Zheng, et al. (2001). Investigating the functional anatomy of empathy and forgiveness. *Neuroreport: For Rapid Communication of Neuroscience Research* **12**(11): 2433–2438.

Farrugia, D. (2009). Exploring stigma: Medical knowledge and the stigmatisation of parents of children diagnosed with autism spectrum disorder. *Sociology of Health and Illness* **31**(7): 1011–1027.

Fasano, A., A. Barra, et al. (2008). Cocaine addiction: From habits to stereotypical-repetitive behaviors and punding. *Drug and Alcohol Dependence* **96**(1–2): 178–182.

Fatemi, S. H., A. R. Halt, et al. (2002). Purkinje cell size is reduced in cerebellum of patients with autism. *Cellular and Molecular Neurobiology* **22**(2): 2–175.

Favazza, A. R. (1977). Feral and isolated children. *British Journal of Medical Psychology* **50**(1): 105–111.

Fayyad, J., R. de Graaf, et al. (2007). Cross-national prevalence and correlates of adult attention-deficit hyperactivity disorder. *British Journal of Psychiatry* **190**: 402–409.

Fazlioglu, Y. and G. Baran (2008). A sensory integration therapy program on sensory problems for children with autism. *Perceptual and Motor Skills* **106**(2): 415–422.

Fecteau, S., L. Mottron, et al. (2003). Developmental changes of autistic symptoms. *Autism* **7**(3): 255–268.

Feinberg, A. P. M. (2008). Epigenetics at the epicenter of modern medicine. *Journal of the American Medical Association* **299**(11): 1345–1350.

Fernandez, B. A., W. Roberts, et al. (2010). Phenotypic spectrum associated with de novo and inherited deletions and duplications at 16p11.2 in individuals ascertained for diagnosis of autism spectrum disorder. *Journal of Medical Genetics* **47**(3): 195–203.

Fernandez-Miranda, J. C., A. L. Rhoton, et al. (2008). The claustrum and its projection system in the human brain: A microsurgical and tractographic anatomical study. *Journal of Neurosurgery* **108**(4): 764–774.

Fernell, E., C. Gillberg, et al. (1991). Autistic symptoms in children with infantile hydrocephalus. *Acta Paediatrica Scandinavia* **80**(4): 451–457.

Fernell, E., F. Norrelgen, et al. (2002). Developmental profiles and auditory perception in 25 children attending special preschools for language-impaired children. *Acta Paediatrica* **91**(10): 1108–1115.

Ferrari, P. F., E. Kohler, et al. (2000). The ability to follow eye gaze and its emergence during development in macaque monkeys. *Proceedings of the National Academy of Sciences of the United States of America* **97**(25): 13,997–14,002.

Ferrari, P. F., E. Visalberghi, et al. (2006). Neonatal imitation in rhesus macaques. *PLoS Biology* **4**(9): e302.

Ferreira, P. E., A. Palmini, et al. (2009). Differentiating attention-deficit/hyperactivity disorder inattentive and combined types: A (1)H-magnetic resonance spectroscopy study of fronto-striato-thalamic regions. *Journal of Neural Transmission* **116**(5): 623–629.

Fiehler, K., M. Burke, et al. (2009). The human dorsal action control system develops in the absence of vision. *Cerebral Cortex* **19**(1): 1–12.

Field, T., T. Field, et al. (2001). Children with autism display more social behaviors after repeated imitation sessions. *Autism* **5**(3): 317–323.

Filipek, P. A. (1999). Neuroimaging in the developmental disorders: The state of the science. *Journal of Child Psychology and Psychiatry and Allied Disciplines* **40**(1): 113–128.

Filipek, P. A., P. J. Accardo, et al. (1999). The screening and diagnosis of autistic spectrum disorders. *Journal of Autism and Developmental Disorders* **29**(6): 439–484.

Fine, C. (2010). *Delusions of Gender*. London: Icon Books.

Fisher, M. H. (2009). Literature analysis to determine the inclusion of children with disabilities in abuse interventions. *Child Abuse and Neglect* **33**(6): 326–327.

Fisher, S. E., C. Francks, et al. (2002). A genomewide scan for loci involved in attention-deficit/hyperactivity disorder. *American Journal of Human Genetics* **70**(5):1183–1196.

Fitzgerald, M. (2000). Einstein: Brain and behavior. *Journal of Autism and Developmental Disorders* **30**(6): 620–621.

Fitzgerald, M. (2005). *The Genesis of Artistic Creativity*. London: Jessica Kingsley Publishers.

Flannery, R. (2005). Precipitants to psychiatric patient assaults on staff: Review of empirical findings, 1990–2003, and risk management implications. *Psychiatric Quarterly* **76**(4): 317–326.

Fletcher, P. C., F. Happé, et al. (1995). Other minds in the brain: A functional imaging study of theory of mind in story comprehension. *Cognition* **57**(2): 109–128.

Fletcher-Watson, S., S. R. Leekam, et al. (2009). Eye-movements reveal attention to social information in autism spectrum disorder. *Neuropsychologia* **47**(1): 248–257.

Floel, A., D. Poeppel, et al. (2004). Prefrontal cortex asymmetry for memory encoding of words and abstract shapes. *Cerebral Cortex* **14**(4): 404–409.

Flosnik, D. L., B. M. Cortese, et al. (2009). Cataplexy in anxious patients: Is subclinical narcolepsy underrecognized in anxiety disorders? *Journal of Clinical Psychiatry* **70**(6): 810–816.

Folstein, S. and M. Rutter (1977). Infantile autism: A genetic study of 21 twin pairs. *Journal of Child Psychology and Psychiatry* **18**(4): 297–321.

Fombonne, E. (2002). Prevalence of childhood disintegrative disorder. *Autism* **6**(2): 149–157.

Fombonne, E. (2003). Modern views of autism. *Canadian Journal of Psychiatry* **48**(8): 503–505.

Fombonne, E., C. Du Mazaubrun, *et al.* (1997). Autism and associated medical disorders in a French epidemiological survey. *Journal of The American Academy of Child and Adolescent Psychiatry.* **36**(11): 1561–1569.

Fombonne, E., H. Simmons, *et al.* (2003). Editorial. *Journal of Child Psychology and Psychiatry and Allied Disciplines* **44**(4): 475–476.

Fombonne, E., R. Zakarian, *et al.* (2006). Pervasive developmental disorders in Montreal, Quebec, Canada: Prevalence and links with immunizations. *Pediatrics* **118**(1): e139–e150.

Fonteneau, E. and H. K. van der Lely (2008). Electrical brain responses in language-impaired children reveal grammar-specific deficits. *PLoS ONE* **3**(3): e1832.

Forstmann, B. U., U. Wolfensteller, *et al.* (2008). When the choice is ours: Context and agency modulate the neural bases of decision-making. *PLoS ONE* **3**(4): e1899.

Forsyth, R., A. Colver, *et al.* (2007). Participation of young severely disabled children is influenced by their intrinsic impairments and environment. *Developmental Medicine and Child Neurology* **49**(5): 345–349.

Franc, N., M. Maury, *et al.* (2009). [ADHD and attachment processes: Are they related?]. *Encephale* **35**(3): 256–261.

Fransson, P., B. Skiöld, *et al.* (2007). Resting-state networks in the infant brain. *Proceedings of the National Academy of Sciences of the United States of America* **104**(39): 15,531–15,536.

Fraser, M. M., I. T. Bayazitov, *et al.* (2008). Phosphatase and tensin homolog, deleted on chromosome 10 deficiency in brain causes defects in synaptic structure, transmission and plasticity, and myelination abnormalities. *Neuroscience* **151**(2): 476–488.

Frazier, T. W. and A. Y. Hardan (2009). A meta-analysis of the corpus callosum in autism. *Biological Psychiatry* **66**(10): 935–941.

Freeman, J. L., G. H. Perry, *et al.* (2006). Copy number variation: New insights in genome diversity. *Genome Research* **16**(8): 949–961.

Freeman, R. D. M., S. H. M. Zinner, *et al.* (2009). Coprophenomena in Tourette syndrome. *Developmental Medicine and Child Neurology* **51**(3): 218–227.

Freeth, M., D. Ropar, *et al.* (2010). The eye gaze direction of an observed person can bias perception, memory, and attention in adolescents with and without autism spectrum disorder. *Journal of Experimental Child Psychology* **105**(1–2): 20–37.

Freitag, C. M., C. Kleser, *et al.* (2007). Quantitative assessment of neuromotor function in adolescents with high functioning autism and Asperger syndrome. *Journal of Autism and Developmental Disorders* **37**(5): 948–959.

Freitag, C. M., C. Konrad, *et al.* (2008). Perception of biological motion in autism spectrum disorders. *Neuropsychologia* **46**(5): 1480–1494.

Freitag, C. M., K. Agelopoulos, *et al.* (2009). Adenosine A(2A) receptor gene (ADORA2A) variants may increase autistic symptoms and anxiety in autism spectrum disorder. *European Child and Adolescent Psychiatry* **19**(1): 67–74.

Freitas, C., and F. Fregni, *et al.* (2009). A meta-analysis of the effects of repetitive transcranial magnetic stimulation (rTMS) on negative and positive symptoms in schizophrenia. *Schizophrenia Research* **108**(1–3): 11–24.

Freud, S. (1930). *Civilization and its Discontents.* London: Hogarth.

Freud, S. (1932). Libidinal types. *Psychoanalytic Quarterly* **1**(1): 3–6.

Friedman, N. P., A. Miyake, *et al.* (2008). Individual differences in executive functions are almost entirely genetic in origin. *Journal of Experimental Psychology: General* **137**(2): 201–225.

Friedman, S. D. P., D. W. W. M. Shaw, *et al.* (2006). Gray and white matter brain chemistry in young children with autism. *Archives of General Psychiatry* **63**(7): 786–794.

Friedman-Weieneth, J. L., E. A. Harvey, *et al.* (2007). The relation between 3-year-old children's skills and their hyperactivity, inattention, and aggression. *Journal of Educational Psychology* **99**(3): 671–681.

Frigerio, E., D. M. Burt, *et al.* (2006). Is everybody always my friend? Perception of approachability in Williams syndrome. *Neuropsychologia* **44**(2): 254–259.

Frith, C. (1999). When conscious recollection disrupts memory. *Archives of General Psychiatry* **56**(7): 645–646.

Frith, C. D. and U. Frith (2008). The self and its reputation in autism. *Neuron* **57**(3): 331–332.

Frith, U. (2003). *Explaining the Enigma* (Second edition). Oxford: Blackwell.

Frith, U. and C. D. Frith (1974). Labeling: A study of an autistic child. *Journal of Family Counseling* **2**: 71–80.

Frith, U. and C. D. Frith (2003). Development and neurophysiology of mentalizing. *Philosophical Transactions of the Royal Society B: Biological Sciences* **358**(1431): 459–473.

Frith, U. and F. Happé (1996). Mary has more: Sex differences, autism, coherence, and theory of mind. *Behavioural and Brain Sciences* **19**: 253–254.

Frith, U. and F. Happé (1999). Theory of mind and self-consciousness: What is it like to be autistic? *Mind and Language* **14**(1): 1–22.

Fujiwara, J., P. N. Tobler, *et al.* (2009). Segregated and integrated coding of reward and punishment in the cingulate cortex. *Journal of Neurophysiology* **101**(6): 3284–3293.

Funnell, E. and N. J. Pitchford (2010). Reading disorders and weak verbal IQ following left hemisphere stroke in children: No evidence of compensation. *Cortex* **46**(10): 1248–1249.

Gabig, C. S. (2008). Verbal working memory and story retelling in school-age children with autism. *Language, Speech and Hearing Services in Schools* **39**(4): 498–511.

Gabrieli, J. D. E. (2009). Dyslexia: A new synergy between education and cognitive neuroscience. *Science* **325**(5938): 280–283.

Gabriels, R. L., M. L. Cuccaro, *et al.* (2005). Repetitive behaviors in autism: Relationships with associated clinical features. *Research in Developmental Disabilities* **26**(2): 169–181.

Gadow, K. D., C. J. DeVincent, *et al.* (2009). Comparative study of children with ADHD only, autism spectrum disorder + ADHD, and chronic multiple tic disorder + ADHD. *Journal of Attention Disorders* **12**(5): 474–485.

Gadow, K. D., J. Roohi, *et al.* (2008). Association of ADHD, tics, and anxiety with dopamine transporter (DAT1) genotype in autism spectrum disorder. *Journal of Child Psychology and Psychiatry* **49**(12): 1331–1338.

Gadow, K. D., J. Roohi, *et al.* (2009). Association of COMT (Val158Met) and BDNF (Val66Met) gene polymorphisms with anxiety, ADHD and tics in children with autism spectrum disorder. *Journal of Autism and Developmental Disorders* **39**(11): 1542–1551.

Gadow, K. D., J. Sverd, *et al.* (2007). Immediate-release methylphenidate for ADHD in children with comorbid chronic multiple tic disorder. *Journal of the American Academy of Child and Adolescent Psychiatry* **46**(7): 840–848.

Gal, E., M. J. Dyck, *et al.* (2009). The relationship between stereotyped movements and self-injurious behavior in children with developmental or sensory disabilities. *Research in Developmental Disabilities* **30**(2): 342–352.

Gallagher, H. L., F. Happé, *et al.* (2000). Reading the mind in cartoons and stories: An fMRI study of 'theory of mind' in verbal and nonverbal tasks. *Neuropsychologia* **38**(1): 11–21.

Gallese, V. (2003). The roots of empathy: The shared manifold hypothesis and the neural basis of intersubjectivity. *Psychopathology* **36**(4): 171–180.

Gallese, V. and T. Metzinger (2003). Motor ontology: The representational reality of goals, actions, and selves. *Philosophical Psychology* **13**(3): 365–388.

Gallese, V., M. Rochat, *et al.* (2009). Motor cognition and its role in the phylogeny and ontogeny of action understanding. *Developmental Psychology* **45**(1): 103–113.

Galli-Carminati, G., N. Deriaz, *et al.* (2009). Melatonin in treatment of chronic sleep disorders in adults with autism: A retrospective study. *Swiss Medical Weekly* **139**(19–20): 293–296.

Gallup, G. G., Jr. (1970). Chimpanzees: Self-recognition. *Science* **167**(914): 86–87.

Gannett, L. (2010). The Human Genome Project. In E. Zalta (eds) *Stanford Encyclopedia of Philosophy.* Available at http://plato.stanford.edu/archives/fall2010/entries/human-genome/%3E, accessed on 16 September 2011.

Ganz. M. L. (2007). The lifetime distribution of the incremental societal costs of autism. *Archives of Pediatric and Adolescent Medicine* **161**(4): 343–349.

Gao, W., H. Zhu, *et al.* (2009). Evidence on the emergence of the brain's default network from 2-week-old to 2-year-old healthy pediatric subjects. *Proceedings of the National Academy of Sciences of the United States of America* **106**(16): 6790–6795.

Garcia-Perez, R. M., R. P. Hobson, *et al.* (2008). Narrative role-taking in autism. *Journal of Autism and Developmental Disorders* **38**(1): 156–168.

Garcia-Villamisar, D. and C. Hughes (2007). Supported employment improves cognitive performance in adults with autism. *Journal of Intellectual Disability Research* **51**(2): 142–150.

Gardener, H., D. Spiegelman, *et al.* (2009). Prenatal risk factors for autism: Comprehensive meta-analysis. *British Journal of Psychiatry* **195**(1): 7–14.

Garner, J. P., C. L. Meehan, *et al.* (2003). Stereotypies in caged parrots, schizophrenia and autism: Evidence for a common mechanism. *Behavioural Brain Research* **145**(1–2): 125–134.

Garon, N., S. E. Bryson, *et al.* (2008). Executive function in preschoolers: A review using an integrative framework. *Psychological Bulletin* **134**(1): 31–60.

Garrard, P., N. H. Martin, *et al.* (2008). Cognitive and social cognitive functioning in spinocerebellar ataxia: A preliminary characterization. *Journal of Neurology* **255**(3): 398–405.

Gasic, G. P., J. W. Smoller, *et al.* (2009). BDNF, relative preference, and reward circuitry responses to emotional communication. *American Journal of Medical Genetics Part B: Neuropsychiatric Genetics* **150B**(6): 762–781.

Gater, R., D. Goldberg, *et al.* (1997). The care of patients with chronic schizophrenia: A comparison between two services. *Psychological Medicine* **27**(6): 1325–1336.

Gau, S. S. and H. L. Chiang (2009). Sleep problems and disorders among adolescents with persistent and subthreshold attention-deficit/hyperactivity disorders. *Sleep* **32**(5): 671–679.

Gauthier, I., C. Klaiman, *et al.* (2009). Face composite effects reveal abnormal face processing in Autism spectrum disorders. *Vision Research* **49**(4): 470–478.

Gauthier, K. J., R. M. Furr, *et al.* (2009). Differentiating impulsive and premeditated aggression: Self and informant perspectives among adolescents with personality pathology. *Journal of Personality Disorders* **23**(1): 76–84.

Gaymard, B., C. François, *et al.* (2003). A direct prefrontotectal tract against distractibility in the human brain. *Annals of Neurology* **53**(4): 542–545.

Gaytan-Tocaven, L. and M. E. Olvera-Cortes (2004). Bilateral lesion of the cerebellar-dentate nucleus impairs egocentric sequential learning but not egocentric navigation in the rat. *Neurobiology of Learning and Memory* **82**(2): 120–127.

Gazzaniga, M. S. (2000). Cerebral specialization and interhemispheric communication: Does the corpus callosum enable the human condition? *Brain* **123**(7): 1293–1326.

Gazzaniga, M. S. (2005). Forty-five years of split-brain research and still going strong. *Nature Reviews Neuroscience* **6**(8): 653–659.

Geier, D. A. and M. R. Geier (2007). A prospective assessment of androgen levels in patients with autistic spectrum disorders: Biochemical underpinnings and suggested therapies. *Neuro Endocrinology Letters* **28**(5): 565–573.

Geier, D. A., J. K. Kern, *et al.* (2009). Biomarkers of environmental toxicity and susceptibility in autism. *Journal of the Neurological Sciences* **280**(1–2): 101–108.

Gendry, M. I., M. Zilbovicius, *et al.* (2005). Autism severity and temporal lobe functional abnormalities. *Annals of Neurology* **58**(3): 466–469.

Genuis, S. J. and T. P. Bouchard (2009). Celiac disease presenting as autism. *Journal of Child Neurology* **25**(1): 114–119.

George, C., Kaplan, N. *et al.* (1985). *The Berkeley Adult Attachment Interview.* Oakland, CA: Berkeley.

Georgiades, S., P. Szatmari, *et al.* (2007). Structure of the autism symptom phenotype: A proposed multidimensional model. *Journal of the American Academy of Child and Adolescent Psychiatry* **46**(2): 188–196.

Gepner, B. and F. Feron (2009). Autism: A world changing too fast for a mis-wired brain? *Neuroscience and Biobehavoral Reviews* **33**(8): 1227–1242.

Gerber, J. S. and P. A. Offit (2009). Vaccines and autism: A tale of shifting hypotheses. *Clinical Infectious Disseases* **48**(4): 456–461.

Gernsbacher, M. A., E. A. Sauer, *et al.* (2008). Infant and toddler oral- and manual-motor skills predict later speech fluency in autism. *Journal of Child Psychology and Psychiatry* **49**(1): 43–50.

Geschwind, D. H. (2008). Autism: Family connections. *Nature* **454**(7206): 838–839.

Geschwind, D. H. (2009). Advances in autism. *Annual Review of Medicne* **60**: 367–380.

Geschwind, D. H. and S. J. Spence (2008). Genetics of autism. *CONTINUUM: Lifelong Learning in Neurology* **14**(2): 49–64.

Geschwind, N. (1970). The organization of language and the brain. *Science* **170**(961): 940–944.

Geschwind. N. and A. M. Galaburda (1985). Cerebral lateralization: Biological mechanisms, associations, and pathology: I. Ahypothesis and a program for research. *Archives of Neurology* **42**(5): 428–459.

Gest, S., A. Sesma, *et al.* (2006). Childhood peer reputation as a predictor of competence and symptoms 10 years later. *Journal of Abnormal Child Psychology* **34**(4): 507–524.

Geurts, H. M. and M. Embrechts (2008). Language Profiles in ASD, SLI, and ADHD. *Journal of Autism and Developmental Disorders* **38**(10): 1931–1943.

Geurts, H. M., B. Corbett, *et al.* (2009). The paradox of cognitive flexibility in autism. *Trends in Cognitive Sciences* **13**(2): 74–82.

Geuze, E., E. Vermetten, *et al.* (2005). MR-based in vivo hippocampal volumetrics: 2. Findings in neuropsychiatric disorders. *Molecular Psychiatry* **10**: 160–184.

Geva, R., R. Eshel, *et al.* (2008). Verbal short-term memory span in children: Long-term modality dependent effects of intrauterine growth restriction. *Journal of Child Psychology and Psychiatry* **49**(12): 1321–1330.

Gewirtz, J. C. and M. Davis (1997). Second-order fear conditioning prevented by blocking NMDA receptors in amygdala. *Nature* **388**(6641): 471–474.

Ghaziuddin, M. (2008). Defining the behavioral phenotype of Asperger syndrome. *Journal of Autism and Developmental Disorders* **38**(1): 138–142.

Ghika, J. (2008). Paleoneurology: Neurodegenerative diseases are age-related diseases of specific brain regions recently developed by homo sapiens. *Medical Hypotheses* **71**(5): 788–801.

Giannotti, F., F. Cortesi, *et al.* (2008). An investigation of sleep characteristics, EEG abnormalities and epilepsy in developmentally regressed and non-regressed children with autism. *Journal of Autism and Developmental Disorders* **38**(10): 1888–1897.

Gibson, J. J. (1979). *The Ecological Approach to Visual Perception.* Boston: MA, Houghton Mifflin.

Giger, M. L., H.-P. Chan, *et al.* (2008). Anniversary Paper: History and status of CAD and quantitative image analysis: The role of Medical Physics and AAPM. *Medical Physics* **35**(12): 5799–5820.

Gilbert, P. (1992). *Depression: The Evolution of Powerlessness.* New York, NY: Guilford Press.

Gilbert, S. J., G. Bird, *et al.* (2008). Atypical recruitment of medial prefrontal cortex in autism spectrum disorders: An fMRI study of two executive function tasks. *Neuropsychologia* **46**(9): 2281–2291.

Gillberg, C. and L. de Souza (2002). Head circumference in autism, Asperger syndrome, and ADHD: A comparative study. *Developmental Medicine and Child Neurology* **44**(5): 296–300.

Gillberg, C. L. (1992). The Emanuel Miller Memorial Lecture 1991. Autism and autistic-like conditions: Subclasses among disorders of empathy. *Journal of Child Psychology and Psychiatry* **33**(5): 813–842.

Gillberg, C., E. Billstedt, *et al.* (2009). Mortality in autism: A prospective longitudinal community-based study. *Journal of Autism and Developmental Disorders* **40**(3): 352–357.

Gillberg, I. C., C. Gillberg, *et al.* (1994). Autistic behaviour and attention deficits in tuberous sclerosis: A population-based study. *Developmental Medicine and Child Neurology* **36**(1): 50–56.

Gillott, A. and Standen, P. J. (2007). Levels of anxiety and sources of stress in adults with autism. *Journal of Intellectual Disabilities* **11**(4): 359–370.

Girgis, R. R., N. J. Minshew, *et al.* (2007). Volumetric alterations of the orbitofrontal cortex in autism. *Progress in Neuropsychopharmacology and Biological Psychiatry* **31**(1): 41–45.

Girolametto, L., F. Sussman, *et al.* (2007). Using case study methods to investigate the effects of interactive intervention for children with autism spectrum disorders. *Journal of Communication Disorders* **40**(6): 470–492.

Giuffre, M. and L. De Sanctis (2010). Genetic syndrome suspicion: Examples of clinical approach in the neonatal unit. *Minerva Pediatrica* **62**(3 Suppl 1): 199–201.

Giunco, C. T., D. Moretti-Ferreira, *et al.* (2008). MOMO syndrome associated with autism: A case report. *Genetics and Molecular Research* **7**(4): 1223–1225.

Gläscher, J. and R. Adolphs (2003). Processing of the arousal of subliminal and supraliminal emotional stimuli by the human amygdala. *Journal of Neuroscience* **23**(32): 10,274–10,282.

Gläscher, J., D. Rudrauf, *et al.* (2010). Distributed neural system for general intelligence revealed by lesion mapping. *Proceedings of the National Academy of Sciences of the United States of America* **107**(10): 4705–4709.

Glaser, D. (2000). Child abuse and neglect and the brain: A review. *Journal of Child Psychology and Psychiatry* **41**(1): 97–116.

Gobbini, M. I. and J. V. Haxby (2006). Neural response to the visual familiarity of faces. *Brain Research Bulletin* **71**(1–3): 76–82.

Gobbini, M. I., A. C. Koralek, *et al.* (2007). Two takes on the social brain: A comparison of theory of mind tasks. *Journal of Cognitive Neuroscience* **19**(11): 1803–1814.

Goez, H. and N. Zelnik (2008). Handedness in patients with developmental coordination disorder. *Journal of Child Neurology* **23**(2): 151–154.

Goffin, A., L. H. Hoefsloot, *et al.* (2001). PTEN mutation in a family with Cowden syndrome and autism. *American Journal of Medical Genetics* **105**(6): 521–524.

Goffman, E. (1969). On face work. In E. Goffman (ed.) *Where the Action is.* London: Allen Lane.

Goffman, E. (2001). The presentation of self in everyday life. In C. Lemert and A. Branaman (eds) *The Goffman Reader.* Oxford: Blackwell.

Goin-Kochel, R. P., V. H. Mackintosh, *et al.* (2007). Parental reports on the efficacy of treatments and therapies for their children with autism spectrum disorders. *Research in Autism Spectrum Disorders* **3**: 528–537.

Goksoyr, P. K. and J. A. Nottestad (2008). The burden of untreated ADHD among adults: The role of stimulant medication. *Addictive Behavior* **33**(2): 342–346.

Goin-Kochel, R.P., V.H. Mackintosh, *et al.* (2004). Parental reports on the efficacy of treatments and therapies for their children with autism spectrum disorders. *Research in Autism Spectrum Disorders* **3**(2): 528–537.

Golan, O. and S. Baron-Cohen (2006). Systemizing empathy: Teaching adults with Asperger syndrome or high-functioning autism to recognize complex emotions using interactive multimedia. *Development and Psychopathology* **18**(2): 591–617.

Golarai, G., K. Grill-Spector, *et al.* (2006). Autism and the development of face processing. *Clinical Neuroscience Research* **6**(3–4): 145–160.

Goldie, P. (2003). *The Emotions.* Oxford: Oxford University Press.

Goldin, P. R., K. McRae, *et al.* (2008). The neural bases of emotion regulation: Reappraisal and suppression of negative emotion. *Biological Psychiatry* **63**(6): 577–586.

Goldman, S. (2008). Brief report: Narratives of personal events in children with autism and developmental language disorders: Unshared memories. *Journal of Autism and Developmental Disorders* **38**(10): 1982–1988.

Goldstein, G., D. N. Allen, *et al.* (2008). The structure of intelligence in children and adults with high functioning autism. *Neuropsychology* **22**(3): 301–312.

Golubchik, P., J. Sever, *et al.* (2008). Methylphenidate in the treatment of female adolescents with cooccurrence of attention deficit/hyperactivity disorder and borderline personality disorder: A preliminary open-label trial. *International Clinical Psychopharmacology* **23**(4): 228–231.

Gomez, J. C. (2009). Embodying meaning: Insights from primates, autism, and Brentano. *Neural Networks* **22**(2): 190–196.

Gonigle-Chalmers, M., K. Bodner, *et al.* (2008). Size sequencing as a window on executive control in children with autism and Asperger's syndrome. *Journal of Autism and Developmental Disorders* **38**(7):1382–1390.

Good, C. D., K. Lawrence, *et al.* (2003). Dosage-sensitive X-linked locus influences the development of amygdala and orbitofrontal cortex, and fear recognition in humans. *Brain* **126**(11): 2431–2446.

Goodlin-Jones, B., K. Tang, *et al.* (2009). Sleep problems, sleepiness and daytime behavior in preschool-age children. *Journal of Child Psychology and Psychiatry* **50**(12): 1532–1540.

Goodlin-Jones, B., S. Waters, *et al.* (2009). Objective sleep measurement in typically and atypically developing preschool children with ADHD-like profiles. *Child Psychiatry and Human Development* **40**(2): 257–268.

Goraya, J. S., M. Cruz, *et al.* (2009). Sleep study abnormalities in children with attention deficit hyperactivity disorder. *Pediatric Neurology* **40**(1): 42–46.

Gordon, N. (2009). Sydenham's chorea, and its complications affecting the nervous system. *Brain and Development* **31**(1): 11–14.

Gotham, K., S. Risi, *et al.* (2008). A replication of the Autism Diagnostic Observation Schedule (ADOS) revised algorithms. *Journal of the American Academy of Child and Adolescent Psychiatry* **47**(6): 642–651.

Gottman, J. and R. Levenson (2000). The timing of divorce: Predicting when a couple will divorce over a 14-year period. *Journal of Marriage and Family* **62**(3): 737–745.

Goursaud, A. P. and J. Bachevalier (2007). Social attachment in juvenile monkeys with neonatal lesion of the hippocampus, amygdala and orbital frontal cortex. *Behavioural Brain Research* **176**(1): 75–93.

Gove, W. R. (1970). Societal reaction as an explanation of mental illness: An evaluation. *American Sociological Review* **35**(5): 873–884.

Gowen, E. and R. C. Miall (2005). Behavioural aspects of cerebellar function in adults with Asperger syndrome. *Cerebellum* **4**(4): 279–289.

Graham, J. M., Jr., B. Rosner, *et al.* (2005). Behavioral features of CHARGE syndrome (Hall-Hittner syndrome): Comparison with Down syndrome, Prader-Willi syndrome, and Williams syndrome. *American Journal of Medical Genetics A* **133A**(3): 240–247.

Grandin, T. and M. Scariano (1986). *Emergence: Labelled Autistic.* Novato, CA: Arena Press.

Grandjean, P. and P. J. Landrigan (2006). Developmental neurotoxicity of industrial chemicals. *The Lancet* **368**(9553): 2167–2178.

Gray, C. (2000). *The New Social Story Book: Revisions by Carol Gray.* Arlington, TX: Gray Center.

Gray, J. and M. McNaughton (2000). *The Neuropsychology of Anxiety.* Oxford: Oxford University Press.

Gray, K. M., B. J. Tonge, *et al.* (2008). Using the Autism Diagnostic Interview-Revised and the Autism Diagnostic Observation Schedule with young children with developmental delay: Evaluating diagnostic validity. *Journal of Autism and Developmental Disorders* **38**(4): 657–667.

Green, J., A. Gilchrist, *et al.* (2000). Social and psychiatric functioning in adolescents with Asperger syndrome compared with conduct disorder. *Journal of Autism and Developmental Disorders* **30**(4): 279–293.

Greenspan, S. and S. Wieder (2009). *Engaging Autism: Using the Floortime Approach to Help Children Relate, Communicate, and Think (A Merloyd Lawrence Book).* Cambridge, MA: Da Capo.

Gregory, C. A., P. J. McKenna, *et al.* (1998). Dementia of frontal type and simple schizophrenia: Two sides of the same coin? – Review. *Neurocase: The Neural Basis of Cognition* **4**: 1–6.

Gregory, S., J. Connelly, *et al.* (2009). Genomic and epigenetic evidence for oxytocin receptor deficiency in autism. BMC Medicine **7**(1): 62.

Greven, C. U., F. V. Rijsdijk, *et al.* (2011). A twin study of ADHD symptoms in early adolescence: hyperactivity-impulsivity and inattentiveness show substantial genetic overlap but also genetic specificity. *Journal of Abnormal Child Psychology* **39**(2), 265–275.

Grèzes, J., C. D. Frith, *et al.* (2004). Inferring false beliefs from the actions of oneself and others: An fMRI study. *NeuroImage* **21**(2): 744–750.

Grindle, C. F., H. Kovshoff, *et al.* (2009). Parents' experiences of home-based applied behavior analysis programs for young children with autism. *Journal of Autism and Developmental Disorders* **39**(1): 42–56.

Gringras, P. (2000). Practical paediatric psychopharmacological prescribing in autism: The potential and the pitfalls. *Autism* **4**(3): 229–247.

Groen, W. B., M. P. Zwiers, *et al.* (2008). The phenotype and neural correlates of language in autism: An integrative review. *Neuroscience and Biobehavioral Reviews* **32**(8): 1416–1425.

Groman, S. M., A. S. James, *et al.* (2009). Poor response inhibition: At the nexus between substance abuse and attention deficit/hyperactivity disorder. *Neuroscience and Biobehavioral Reviews* **33**(5): 690–698.

Gropman, A. L., W. C. Duncan, *et al.* (2006). Neurologic and developmental features of the Smith-Magenis syndrome (del 17p11.2). *Pediatric Neurology* **34**(5): 337–350.

Grossmann, T., M. H. Johnson, *et al.* (2007). Social perception in the infant brain: Gamma oscillatory activity in response to eye gaze. *Social Cognitive and Affective Neuroscience* **2**(4): 284–291.

Gruber, R., T. Xi, *et al.* (2009). Sleep disturbances in prepubertal children with attention deficit hyperactivity disorder: A home polysomnography study. *Sleep* **32**(3): 343–350.

Gruehn, D., K. Rebucal, *et al.* (2008). Empathy across the adult lifespan: Longitudinal and experience-sampling findings. *Emotion* **8**(6): 753–765.

Grynszpan, O., J. C. Martin, *et al.* (2008). Multimedia interfaces for users with high functioning autism: An empirical investigation. *International Journal of Human-Computer Studies* **66**(8): 628–639.

Guan, J. S., S. J. Haggarty, *et al.* (2009). HDAC2 negatively regulates memory formation and synaptic plasticity. *Nature* **459**(7243): 55–60.

Guastella, A. J., S. L. Einfeld, *et al.* (2010). Intranasal oxytocin improves emotion recognition for youth with autism spectrum disorders. *Biological Psychiatry* **67**(7): 692–694.

Gudjonsson, G. H., J. F. Sigurdsson, *et al.* (2008). Interrogative suggestibility, compliance and false confessions among prisoners and their relationship with attention deficit hyperactivity disorder (ADHD) symptoms. *Psychological Medicine* **38**(7): 1037–1044.

Guerri, C., A. Bazinet, *et al.* (2009). Foetal alcohol spectrum disorders and alterations in brain and behaviour. *Alcohol and Alcoholism* **44**(2): 108–114.

Guevara, J., P. Lozano, *et al.* (2001). Utilization and cost of health care services for children with attention-deficit/hyperactivity disorder. *Pediatrics* **108**(1): 71–78.

Guilmatre, A., C. Dubourg, *et al.* (2009). Recurrent rearrangements in synaptic and neurodevelopmental genes and shared biologic pathways in schizophrenia, autism, and mental retardation. *Archives of General Psychiatry* **66**(9): 947–956.

Gunji, A., M. Inagaki, *et al.* (2009). Event-related potentials of self-face recognition in children with pervasive developmental disorders. *Brain and Development* **31**(2): 139–147.

Guo, G., Y. Tong, *et al.* (2007). Dopamine transporter, gender, and number of sexual partners among young adults. *European Journal of Human Genetics* **15**(3): 279–287.

Guo, Y., J. Xu, *et al.* (2007). Verifying the hypothesis of disconnection syndrome in patients with conduction aphasia using diffusion tensor imaging. *Neural Regeneration Research* **2**: 217–220.

Gutierrez, G. C., S. L. Smalley, *et al.* (1998). Autism in tuberous sclerosis complex. *Journal of Autism and Developmental Disorders* **28**(2): 97–103.

Ha, M., H. J. Kwon, *et al.* (2009). Low blood levels of lead and mercury and symptoms of attention deficit hyperactivity in children: A report of the Children's Health and Environment Research (CHEER). *Neurotoxicology* **30**(1): 31–36.

Habel, U., C. Windischberger, *et al.* (2007). Amygdala activation and facial expressions: Explicit emotion discrimination versus implicit emotion processing. *Neuropsychologia* **45**(10): 2369–2377.

Hadjikhani, N., R. M. Joseph, *et al.* (2009). Body expressions of emotion do not trigger fear contagion in autism spectrum disorder. *Social Cognitive and Affective Neuroscience* **4**(1): 70–78.

Hagan, C. C. B., F. M. D. Hoeft, *et al.* (2008). Aberrant neural function during emotion attribution in female subjects with fragile X syndrome. *Journal of the American Academy of Child and Adolescent Psychiatry* **47**(12): 1443–1454.

Hagmann, P., L. Cammoun, *et al.* (2008). Mapping the structural core of human cerebral cortex. *PLoS Biology* **6**(7): e159.

Haier, R. J., R. Colom, R, *et al.* (2003). Gray matter and intelligence factors: Is there a neuro-g? *Intelligence* **37**(2): 136–144.

Hall, J. (2007). *Handbook of Physical Measurements.* Oxford: Oxford University Press.

Hall, S. S., A. A. Lightbody, *et al.* (2008). Compulsive, self-injurious, and autistic behavior in children and adolescents with fragile X syndrome. *American Journal on Mental Retardation* **113**(1): 44–53.

Hallahan, B., E. M. Daly, *et al.* (2009). Brain morphometry volume in autistic spectrum disorder: A magnetic resonance imaging study of adults. *Psychological Medicine* **39**(2): 337–346.

Hallett, M. (2001). Neurophysiology of tics. *Advances in Neurology* **85**: 237–244.

Hallett, V., A. Ronald, *et al.* (2009). Investigating the association between autistic-like and internalizing traits in a community-based twin sample. *Journal of the American Academy of Child and Adolescent Psychiatry* **48**(6): 618–627.

Hallmayer, J., S. Cleveland, *et al.* (2011). Genetic heritability and shared environmental factors among twin pairs with autism. *Archives Of General Psychiatry.* doi:10.1001/archgenpsychiatry.2011.76.

Halperin, J. M. and K. P. Schulz (2006). Revisiting the role of the prefrontal cortex in the pathophysiology of attention-deficit/hyperactivity disorder. *Psychological Bulletin* **132**(4): 560–581.

Halpin, J. and B. Nugent (2007). Health visitors' perceptions of their role in autism spectrum disorder. *Community Practitioner* **80**(1): 18–22.

Ham, H. S., M. Corley, *et al.* (2008). Imitation of meaningless gestures in individuals with Asperger syndrome and high-functioning autism. *Journal of Autism and Developmental Disorders* **38**(3): 569–573.

Hamann, S. (2001). Cognitive and neural mechanisms of emotional memory. *Trends in Cognitive Sciences* **5**(9): 394–400.

Hamilton, A. F. (2008). Emulation and mimicry for social interaction: a theoretical approach to imitation in autism. *Quarterly Journal of Experimental Psychology (Colchester)* **61**(1): 101–115.

Hammond, P., C. Forster-Gibson, *et al.* (2008). Face-brain asymmetry in autism spectrum disorders. *Molecular Psychiatry* **13**(6): 614–623.

Hannes, F. D., A. J. Sharp, *et al.* (2009). Recurrent reciprocal deletions and duplications of 16p13.11: The deletion is a risk factor for MR/MCA while the duplication may be a rare benign variant. *Journal of Medical Genetics* **46**(4): 223–232.

Hans, N. (2003). The digital origin of human language: A synthesis. *BioEssays* **25**(5): 489–500.

Hänsel, A. and R. von Känel (2008). The ventro-medial prefrontal cortex: A major link between the autonomic nervous system, regulation of emotion, and stress reactivity? *BioPsychoSocial Medicine* **2**(1): 21.

Hansen, R. L., S. Ozonoff, *et al.* (2008). Regression in autism: prevalence and associated factors in the CHARGE Study. *Ambulatory Pediatrics* **8**(1): 25–31.

Happé, F. (1994). An advanced test of theory of mind: Understanding of story characters' thoughts and feelings by able autistic, mentally handicapped and normal children and adults. *Journal of Autism and Developmental Disorders* **24**(2): 129–154.

Happé, F. (2003). Theory of mind and the self. *Annals of the New York Academy of Sciences* **1001**: 134–144.

Happé, F. and A. Ronald (2008). The 'fractionable autism triad': A review of evidence from behavioural, genetic, cognitive and neural research. *Neuropsychology Review* **18**(4): 287–304.

Happé, F. and P. Vital (2009). What aspects of autism predispose to talent? *Philosophical Transactions of the Royal Society B: Biological Sciences* **364**(1522): 1369–1375.

Happé, F. and U. Frith (2009). The beautiful otherness of the autistic mind. *Philosophical Transactions of the Royal Society B: Biological Sciences* **364**(1522): 1346–1350.

Happé, F., H. Brownell, *et al.* (1999). Acquired theory of mind impairments following stroke. *Cognition* **70**(3): 211–240.

Happé, F., J. Briskman, *et al.* (2001). Exploring the cognitive phenotype of autism: Weak 'central coherence' in parents and siblings of children with autism: I. Experimental tests. *Journal of Child Psychology and Psychiatry* **42**(3): 299–307.

Hara, H. (2007). Autism and epilepsy: A retrospective follow-up study. *Brain and Development* **29**(8): 486–490.

Hare, D. J. (2006). Autistic catatonia: Continuity or comorbidity? *Journal of Applied Research in Intellectual Disabilities* **19**(3): 271.

Hare, D. J. and C. Malone, C. (2004). Catatonia and autistic spectrum disorders. *Autism* **8**(2): 183–195.

Hare, D. J., S. Jones, *et al.* (2006). Objective investigation of the sleep-wake cycle in adults with intellectual disabilities and autistic spectrum disorders. *Journal of Intellectual Disability Research* **50**(10): 701–710.

Hare, T. A., C. F. Camerer, *et al.* (2009). Self-control in decision-making involves modulation of the vmPFC valuation system. *Science* **324**(5927): 646–648.

Harley, E. M., W. B. Pope, *et al.* (2009). Engagement of fusiform cortex and disengagement of lateral occipital cortex in the acquisition of radiological expertise. *Cerebral Cortex* **19**(11): 2746–2754.

Harrington, J. W. (2008). Are we overmedicating our children? *Pediatrics* **122**(1): 211–212.

Harris, K. M., E. M. Mahone, *et al.* (2008). Nonautistic motor stereotypies: Clinical features and longitudinal follow-up. *Pediatric Neurology* **38**(4): 267–272.

Harris, N. S., E. Courchesne, *et al.* (1999). Neuroanatomic contributions to slowed orienting of attention in children with autism. *Cognitive Brain Research* **8**(1): 61–71.

Harrison, A. G., M. J. Edwards, *et al.* (2007). Identifying students faking ADHD: Preliminary findings and strategies for detection. *Archives of Clinical Neuropsychology* **22**(5): 577–588.

Harrison, N. A., L. Brydon, *et al.* (2009). Neural origins of human sickness in interoceptive responses to inflammation. *Biological Psychiatry* **66**(5): 415–422.

Hartley, S. L. and D. M. Sikora (2009a). Sex differences in autism spectrum disorder: An examination of developmental functioning, autistic symptoms, and coexisting behavior problems in toddlers. *Journal of Autism and Developmental Disorders* **39**:1715–1722.

Hartley, S. L. and D. M. Sikora (2009b). Which DSM-IV-TR criteria best differentiate high-functioning autism spectrum disorder from ADHD and anxiety disorders in older children? *Autism* **13**(5): 485–509.

Hartley, S. L., D. M. Sikora, *et al.* (2008). Prevalence and risk factors of maladaptive behaviour in young children with autistic disorder. *Journal of Intellectual Disability Research* **52**(10): 819–829.

Hartshorne, T. S., T. L. Grialou, *et al.* (2005). Autistic-like behavior in CHARGE syndrome. *American Journal of Medical Genetics A* **133A**(3): 257–261.

Harty, S. C., C. J. Miller, *et al.* (2009). Adolescents with childhood ADHD and comorbid disruptive behavior disorders: Aggression, anger, and hostility. *Child Psychiatry and Human Development* **40**(1): 85–97.

Harvey, S. T., D. Boer, *et al.* (2009). Updating a meta-analysis of intervention research with challenging behaviour: Treatment validity and standards of practice. *Journal of Intellectual and Developmental Disabilities* **34**: 67–80.

Haslam, S. A., J. Jetten, *et al.* (2009). Social identity, health and well-being: An emerging agenda for applied psychology. *Applied Psychology* **58**(1): 1–23.

Haswell, C. C., J. Izawa, *et al.* (2009). Representation of internal models of action in the autistic brain. *Nature Neuroscience* **12**(8): 970–972.

Hatfield, E., J. Cacioppo, *et al.* (1994). *Emotional Contagion.* Cambridge: Cambridge University Press.

Hauber, W. and S. Sommer (2009). Prefrontostriatal circuitry regulates effort-related decision making. *Cerebral Cortex* **19**(10): 2240–2247.

Haugen, P. T., D. P. Welsh, *et al.* (2008). Empathic accuracy and adolescent romantic relationships. *Journal of Adolescence* **31**(6): 709–727.

Havas, D., A. Glenberg, *et al.* (2010). Cosmetic use of botulinum toxin-A affects processing of emotional language. *Psychological Science* **21**(7): 895–900.

Havighurst, R. (1971). *Developmental Tasks and Education.* New York: Longman.

Havlovicova, M., D. Novotna, *et al.* (2007). A girl with neurofibromatosis type 1, atypical autism and mosaic ring chromosome 17. *American Journal of Medical Genetics A* **143A**(1): 76–81.

Hayakawa, Y., T. Nakajima, *et al.* (2002). Human cerebellar activation in relation to saccadic eye movements: A functional magnetic resonance imaging study. *Ophthalmologica* **216**: 399–405.

Hazlett, H. C., M. Poe, *et al.* (2005). Magnetic resonance imaging and head circumference study of brain size in autism: Birth through age 2 years. *Archives of General Psychiatry* **62**(12): 1366–1376.

Hazlett, H. C., M. Poe, *et al.* (2006). Cortical gray and white brain tissue volume in adolescents and adults with autism. *Biological Psychiatry* **59**(1): 1–6.

Haznedar, M. M., M. S. Buchsbaum, *et al.* (2000). Limbic circuitry in patients with autism spectrum disorders studied with positron emission tomography and magnetic resonance imaging. *American Journal of Psychiatry* **157**(12): 1994–2001.

Heal, D. J., S. C. Cheetham, *et al.* (2009). The neuropharmacology of ADHD drugs in vivo: Insights on efficacy and safety. *Neuropharmacology* **57**(7–8): 608–618.

Hedden, T., S. Ketay, *et al.* (2008). Cultural influences on neural substrates of attentional control. *Psychological Science* **19**(1): 12–17.

Hedden. T. and J. D. E. Gabrieli (2010). Shared and selective neural correlates of inhibition, facilitation, and shifting processes during executive control. *NeuroImage* **51**(1): 421–431.

Heden, F. and M. Kristiansson (2003). [Three cases illustrate that there are several possible explanations of erotomania, not only psychosis. In some of the cases autism is the basic problem]. *Lakartidningen* **100**(48): 3962–3964, 3967.

Hedley, D. and R. Young (2006). Social comparison processes and depressive symptoms in children and adolescents with Asperger syndrome. *Autism* **10**(2): 137–151.

Heidegger, M. (1927). *Being and Time.* New York, NY: Harper & Row.

Hein, G. and T. Singer (2008). I feel how you feel but not always: The empathic brain and its modulation. *Current Opinion in Neurobiology* **18**(2): 153–158.

Heinrich, H., H. Gevensleben, *et al.* (2007). Annotation: Neurofeedback – train your brain to train behaviour. *Journal of Child Psychology and Psychiatry* **48**: 3–16.

Heinrichs, M. and G. Domes (2008). Neuropeptides and social behaviour: Effects of oxytocin and vasopressin in humans. *Progress in Brain Research* **170**: 337–350.

Heiser, N. A., S. M. Turner, *et al.* (2009). Differentiating social phobia from shyness. *Journal of Anxiety Disorders* **23**(4): 469–476.

Hellemans, H., H. Roeyers, *et al.* (2010). Sexual behavior in male adolescents and young adults with autism spectrum disorder and borderline/mild mental retardation. *Sexuality and Disability* **28**(2): 93–104.

Hellemans, H., K. Colson, *et al.* (2007). Sexual behavior in high-functioning male adolescents and young adults with autism spectrum disorder. *Journal of Autism and Developmental Disorders* **37**(2): 260–269.

Heller, T. (1908). Ueber Dementia infantilis. *Zeitschrift fuer die Erforschung und Behandlung des Jugendlichen Schwachsinns* **2**: 17–28.

Helps, S., C. James, *et al.* (2008). Very low frequency EEG oscillations and the resting brain in young adults: A preliminary study of localisation, stability and association with symptoms of inattention. *Journal of Neural Transmission* **115**: 279–285.

Helt, M., E. Kelley, *et al.* (2008). Can children with autism recover? If so, how? *Neuropsychology Review* **18**(4): 339–366.

Hemmerdinger, J. M., S. D. Stoddart, *et al.* (2007). A systematic review of tests of empathy in medicine. *BMC Medical Education* **7**: 24.

Hempel, A., F. L. Giesel, *et al.* (2004). Plasticity of cortical activation related to working memory during training. *American Journal of Psychiatry* **161**(4): 745–747.

Henderson, H. A., N. E. Zahka, *et al.* (2009). Self-referenced memory, social cognition, and symptom presentation in autism. *Journal of Child Psychology and Psychiatry* **50**(7): 853–861.

Henderson, L. M., P. J. Yoder, *et al.* (2002). Getting the point: Electrophysiological correlates of protodeclarative pointing. *International Journal of Developmental Neuroscience* **20**(3–5): 449–458.

Henderson, S. and D. Sugden (1992). *The Movement Assessment Battery for Children*. New York, NY: Psychological Corporation.

Hendren, R. L., I. De Backer, *et al.* (2000). Review of neuroimaging studies of child and adolescent psychiatric disorders from the past 10 years. *Journal of the American Academy of Child and Adolescent Psychiatry* **39**(7): 815–828.

Hendriksen, J. G. and J. S. Vles (2008). Neuropsychiatric disorders in males with duchenne muscular dystrophy: Frequency rate of attention-deficit hyperactivity disorder (ADHD), autism spectrum disorder, and obsessive-compulsive disorder. *Journal of Child Neurology* **23**(5): 477–481.

Henseler, I., S. Krüger, *et al.* (2011). A gateway system in rostral PFC? Evidence from biasing attention to perceptual information and internal representations. NeuroImage **56**(3): 1666–1676.

Hepburn, S. L., A. Philofsky, *et al.* (2008). Autism symptoms in toddlers with Down syndrome: A descriptive study. *Journal of Applied Research in Intellectual Disabilities* **21**(1): 48–57.

Hepburn, S. L., C. DiGuiseppi, *et al.* (2008). Use of a teacher nomination strategy to screen for autism spectrum disorders in general education classrooms: A pilot study. *Journal of Autism and Developmental Disorders* **38**(2): 373–382.

Herba, C. M., E. de Bruin, *et al.* (2008). Face and emotion recognition in MCDD versus PDD-NOS. *Journal of Autism and Developmental Disorders* **38**(4): 706–718.

Hermans, E. J., G. van Wingen, *et al.* (2009). Reduced spontaneous facial mimicry in women with autistic traits. *Biological Psychology* **80**(3): 348–353.

Hernandez, N., A. Metzger, *et al.* (2009). Exploration of core features of a human face by healthy and autistic adults analyzed by visual scanning. *Neuropsychologia* **47**(4): 1004–1012.

Herrington, J. D., A. Mohanty, *et al.* (2005). Emotion-modulated performance and activity in left dorsolateral prefrontal cortex. *Emotion* **5**: 200–207.

Hess, K. L., M. J. Morrier, *et al.* (2008). Autism treatment survey: Services received by children with autism spectrum disorders in public school classrooms. *Journal of Autism and Developmental Disorders* **38**(5): 961–971.

Hesslinger, B., T. Thiel, *et al.* (2001). Attention-deficit disorder in adults with or without hyperactivity: Where is the difference? A study in humans using short echo (1) H-magnetic resonance spectroscopy. *Neuroscience Letters* **304**: 117–119.

Hickok, G. and M. Hauser (2010). (Mis)understanding mirror neurons. *Current Biology* **20**(14): R593–R594.

Hietanen, J. K., L. Nummenmaa, *et al.* (2006). Automatic attention orienting by social and symbolic cues activates different neural networks: An fMRI study. *NeuroImage* **33**(1): 406–413.

Hikosaka, O., M. Isoda (2010). Switching from automatic to controlled behavior: Cortico-basal ganglia mechanisms. *Trends in Cognitive Sciences* **14**(4):154–161.

Hill, A. L., D. G. Rand, *et al.* (2010). Emotions as infectious diseases in a large social network: The SISa model. *Proceedings of the Royal Society B: Biological Sciences* **277**(1701): 3827–3835.

Hill, E., S. Berthoz, *et al.* (2004). Brief report: Cognitive processing of own emotions in individuals with autistic spectrum disorder and in their relatives. *Journal of Autism and Developmental Disorders* **34**(2): 229–235.

Hill, J. (2003). Early identification of individuals at risk for antisocial personality disorder. *British Journal of Psychiatry* **182**(144): s11–s14.

Hill, J., T. Inder, *et al.* (2010). Similar patterns of cortical expansion during human development and evolution. *Proceedings of the National Academy of Sciences* **107**(29): 13135–13140.

Hilton, C., L. Wente, *et al.* (2007). Relationship between motor skill impairment and severity in children with Asperger syndrome. *Research in Autism Spectrum Disorders* **1**(4): 339–349.

Hines, M. (2010). Sex-related variation in human behavior and the brain. *Trends in Cognitive Sciences* **14**(10): 448–456.

Hirano, Y., S. Hirano, *et al*, (2010). Auditory gating deficit to human voices in schizophrenia: A MEG study. *Schizophrenia Research* **117**(1): 61–67.

Hirao, K., J. Miyata, *et al.* (2008). Theory of mind and frontal lobe pathology in schizophrenia: A voxel-based morphometry study. *Schizophrenia Research* **105**(1–3): 165–174.

Hirschtritt, M. E., C. J. Hammond, *et al.* (2009). Executive and attention functioning among children in the PANDAS subgroup. *Child Neuropsychology* **15**(2): 179–194.

Hobbes, T. (1660). *Leviathan.* Available from Project Gutenberg at www.gutenberg.org/ebooks/3207, accessed 7 July 2011.

Hobbs, K., A. Kennedy, *et al.* (2007). Retrospective fetal ultrasound study of brain size in autism. *Biological Psychiatry* **62**(9):1048–1055.

Hobson, R. P. (1995). *Autism and the Development of Mind.* New York, NY: Psychology Press.

Hobson, R. P. (2007). Communicative depth: Soundings from developmental psychopathology. *Infant Behavior Development* **30**(2): 267–277.

Hobson, R. P., A. Lee, *et al.* (2009). Qualities of symbolic play among children with autism: A social-developmental perspective. *Journal of Autism and Developmental Disorders* **39**(1):12–22.

Hodzic, A., A. Kaas, *et al.* (2009). Distinct cortical networks for the detection and identification of human body. *NeuroImage* **45**(4): 1264–1271.

Hoebert, M., K. B. van der Heijden, *et al.* (2009). Long-term follow-up of melatonin treatment in children with ADHD and chronic sleep onset insomnia. *Journal of Pineal Research* **47**(1): 1–7.

Hoekstra, R. A., M. Bartels, *et al.* (2007). Heritability of autistic traits in the general population. *Archives of Pediatrics and Adolescent Medicine* **161**(4): 372–377.

Hoevenaars-van den Boom, M. A. A., A. C. F. M. Antonissen, *et al.* (2009). Differentiating characteristics of deafblindness and autism in people with congenital deafblindness and profound intellectual disability. *Journal of Intellectual Disability Research* **53**(6): 548–558.

Hofvander, B., R. Delorme, *et al.* (2009). Psychiatric and psychosocial problems in adults with normal-intelligence autism spectrum disorders. *BMC Psychiatry* **9**: 35.

Hogg, J., D. Reeves, *et al.* (2001). Mudford consistency, Context and confidence in judgements of affective communication in adults with profound intellectual and multiple disabilities. *Journal of Intellectual Disability Research* **45**(1): 18–29.

Hoksbergen, R., J. T. Laak, *et al.* (2005). Post-Institutional Autistic Syndrome in Romanian Adoptees. *Journal of Autism and Developmental Disorders* **35**(5): 615–623.

Holland, A., J. Whittington, *et al.* (2003). The paradox of Prader-Willi syndrome: A genetic model of starvation. *The Lancet* **362**(9388): 989–991.

Holtmann, M., S. Bölte, *et al.* (2007). Attention deficit hyperactivity disorder symptoms in pervasive developmental disorders: Association with autistic behavior domains and coexisting psychopathology. *Psychopathology* **40**(3): 172–177.

Home Office. (2006) *British Crime Survey, 2004–2005.* London: Home Office.

Homer, B. D., T. M. Solomon, *et al.* (2008). Methamphetamine abuse and impairment of social functioning: A review of the underlying neurophysiological causes and behavioral implications. *Psychological Bulletin* **134**(2): 301–310.

Hong, H. and E. Hong (2000). *The Essential Kirkegaard.* Princeton, NJ: Princeton University Press.

Hooker, C. I., K. A. Paller, *et al.* (2003). Brain networks for analyzing eye gaze. *Cognitive Brain Research* **17**(2): 406–418.

Hopkins, M. J., J. Dywan, *et al.* (2002). Altered electrodermal response to facial expression after closed head injury. *Brain Injury* **16**(3): 245–257.

Hornak, J., J. Bramham, *et al.* (2003). Changes in emotion after circumscribed surgical lesions of the orbitofrontal and cingulate cortices. *Brain* **126**(7): 1691–1712.

Houghton, S., G. Douglas, *et al.* (1999). Differential patterns of executive function in children with attention-deficit hyperactivity disorder according to gender and subtype. *Journal of Child Neurology* **14**(12): 801–805.

Howard, M. A., P. E. Cowell, *et al.* (2000). Convergent neuroanatomical and behavioural evidence of an amygdala hypothesis of autism. *Neuroreport* **11**(13): 2931–2935.

Howlin, P. (2001). Autistic features in Cohen syndrome: A preliminary report. *Developmental Medicine and Child Neurology* **43**(10): 692–696.

Howlin, P. (2002). Tuberous sclerosis.

Howlin, P. and A. Asgharian (1999). The diagnosis of autism and Asperger syndrome: Findings from a survey of 770 families. *Developmental Medicine and Child Neurology* **41**(12): 834–839.

Howlin, P. and A. Moore (1997). Diagnosis in autism. *Autism* **1**(2): 135–162.

Howlin, P. and S. Goode (1998). Outcome in adult life for people with autism and Asperger's syndrome. In Volkmar, F.R. (ed.) *Autism and Persuasive Developmental Disorders, Cambridge Monographs in Child and Adolescent Psychiatry.* Cambridge: Cambridge University Press.

Howlin, P., I. Magiati, *et al.* (2009). Systematic review of early intensive behavioral interventions for children with autism. *American Journal of Intellectual and Developmental Disabilities* **114**(1): 23–41.

Howlin, P., J. Alcock, *et al.* (2005). An 8 year follow-up of a specialist supported employment service for high-ability adults with autism or Asperger syndrome. *Autism* **9**(5): 533–549.

Howlin, P., R. K. Gordon, *et al.* (2007). The effectiveness of Picture Exchange Communication System (PECS) training for teachers of children with autism: A pragmatic, group randomised controlled trial. *Journal of Child Psychology and Psychiatry* **48**(5): 473–481.

Howlin, P., S. Baron-Cohen, *et al.* (1999). *Teaching Children with Autism to Mind-read: A Practical Guide for Teachers and Parents.* Chichester: Wiley.

Hoza, B., S. Mrug, *et al.* (2005). What aspects of peer relationships are impaired in children with attention-deficit/hyperactivity disorder? *Journal of Consulting and Clinical Psychology* **73**(3): 411–423.

Hsiung, G. Y., B. J. Kaplan, *et al.* (2004). A dyslexia susceptibility locus (DYX7) linked to dopamine D4 receptor (DRD4) region on chromosome 11p15.5. *American Journal of Medical Genetics B Neuropsychiatric Genetics* **125B**(1): 112–119.

Hu, V. W., T. Sarachana, *et al.* (2009). Gene expression profiling differentiates autism case-controls and phenotypic variants of autism spectrum disorders: evidence for circadian rhythm dysfunction in severe autism. *Autism Research* **2**(2): 78–97.

Hubbard, K. and D. A. Trauner (2007). Intonation and emotion in autistic spectrum disorders. *J Psycholinguist Res* **36**(2): 159–173.

Hubert, B. E., B. Wicker, *et al.* (2009). Electrodermal reactivity to emotion processing in adults with autistic spectrum disorders. *Autism* **13**(1): 9–19.

Hughes, B. (2005). What can a Foucauldian analysis contribute to disability theory? In S. Tremain (ed.) *Foucault and the Government of Disability.* Ann Arbor, MI: University of Michigan Press.

Hughes, J. R. (2008). A review of recent reports on autism: 1000 studies published in 2007. *Epilepsy and Behavior* **13**(3): 425–437.

Hulbert-Williams, L. and R. P. Hastings (2008). Life events as a risk factor for psychological problems in individuals with intellectual disabilities: A critical review. *Journal of Intellectual Disability Research* **52**(11): 883–895.

Hume, K., R. Loftin, *et al.* (2009). Increasing independence in autism spectrum disorders: A review of three focused interventions. *Journal of Autism and Developmental Disorders* **39**(9): 1329–1338.

Humphrey, N. and S. Lewis (2008). 'Make me normal': The views and experiences of pupils on the autistic spectrum in mainstream secondary schools. *Autism* **12**(1): 23–46.

Hunt, A. and C. Shepherd (1993). A prevalence study of autism in tuberous sclerosis. *Journal of Autism and Developmental Disorders* **23**(2): 323–339.

Hurst, R. M., R. O. Nelson-Gray, *et al.* (2007). The relationship of Asperger's characteristics and schizotypal personality traits in a non-clinical adult sample. *Journal of Autism and Developmental Disorders* **37**(9): 1711–1720.

Hurt, E. A., B. Hoza, *et al.* (2007). Parenting, family loneliness, and peer functioning in boys with attention-deficit/hyperactivity disorder. *Journal of Abnormal Child Psychology* **35**(4): 543–555.

Hurtado, B., M. J. Koepp, *et al.* (2006). The impact of levetiracetam on challenging behavior. *Epilepsy and Behavior* **8**(3): 588–592.

Hurtig, T., H. Ebeling, *et al.* (2007). ADHD symptoms and subtypes: Relationship between childhood and adolescent symptoms. *Journal of the American Academy of Child and Adolescent Psychiatry* **46**(12): 1605–1613.

Hussman, J. P. (2001). Suppressed GABAergic inhibition as a common factor in suspected etiologies of autism. *Journal of Autism and Developmental Disorders* **31**(2): 247–248.

Hutchinson, A. D., J. L. Mathias, *et al.* (2008). Corpus callosum morphology in children and adolescents with attention deficit hyperactivity disorder: A meta-analytic review. *Neuropsychology* **22**(3): 341–349.

Hutman, T., M. Siller, *et al.* (2009). Mothers' narratives regarding their child with autism predict maternal synchronous behavior during play. *Journal of Child Psychology and Psychiatry* **50**(10): 1255–1263.

Hutton, J., S. Goode, *et al.* (2008). New-onset psychiatric disorders in individuals with autism. *Autism* **12**(4): 373–390.

Huws, J. C. and R. S. Jones (2008). Diagnosis, disclosure, and having autism: An interpretative phenomenological analysis of the perceptions of young people with autism. *Journal of Intellectual and Developmental Disabilities* **33**(2): 99–107.

Iacoboni, M. (2009). Imitation, Empathy, and Mirror Neurons. *Annual Review of Psychology* **60**: 653–670.

Iacoboni, M. and J. C. Mazziotta (2007). Mirror neuron system: Basic findings and clinical applications. *Annals of Neurology* **62**(3): 213–218.

Iaria, G., N. Bogod, *et al.* (2009). Developmental topographical disorientation: Case one. *Neuropsychologia* **47**(1): 30–40.

Iarocci, G., J. Yager, *et al.* (2007). What gene-environment interactions can tell us about social competence in typical and atypical populations. *Brain and Cognition* **65**(1): 112–127.

Ickes, W. (1993). Empathic accuracy. *Journal of Personality* **61**(4): 587–610.

Ijichi, S., N. Ijichi, *et al.* (2008). For others: Epistasis and the evolutionary survival of an extreme tail of the quantitative distribution of autistic assets. *Medical Hypotheses* **70**(3): 515–521.

Ingersoll, B. P. (2008). The social role of imitation in autism: Implications for the treatment of imitation deficits. *Infants and Young Children* **21**(2): 107–119.

Insel, T. (2010). The challenge of translation in social neuroscience: A review of oxytocin, vasopressin, and affiliative behavior. *Neuron* **65**(6): 768–779.

Isaki, E., T. J. Spaulding, *et al.* (2008). Contributions of language and memory demands to verbal memory performance in language-learning disabilities. *Journal of Communication Disorders* **41**(6): 512–530.

Ishijima, M. and H. Kurita (2007). Brief report: Identical male twins concordant for Asperger's disorder. *Journal of Autism and Developmental Disorders* **37**(2): 386–389.

Isles, A. R. and L. S. Wilkinson (2008). Epigenetics: What is it and why is it important to mental disease? *British Medical Bulletin* **85**: 35–45.

Isohanni, M., P. B. Jones, *et al.* (2001). Early developmental milestones in adult schizophrenia and other psychoses. A 31-year follow-up of the Northern Finland 1966 Birth Cohort. *Schizophrenia Research* **52**(1–2): 1–19.

Itier, R. J. and M. Batty (2009). Neural bases of eye and gaze processing: The core of social cognition. *Neuroscience and Biobehavioral Reviews* **33**(6): 843–863.

Ito, H., K. Mori, *et al.* (2005). Findings of brain 99mTc-ECD SPECT in high-functioning autism: 3-dimensional stereotactic ROI template analysis of brain SPECT. *The Journal of Medical Investigation* **52**(1–2): 49–56.

Ivarsson, T. and K. Melin (2008). Autism spectrum traits in children and adolescents with obsessive-compulsive disorder (OCD). *Journal of Anxiety Disorders* **22**(6): 969–978.

Jabbi, M., J. Bastiaansen, *et al.* (2008). A common anterior insula representation of disgust observation, experience and imagination shows divergent functional connectivity pathways. *PLoS ONE* **3**(8): e2939.

Jabbi, M., M. Swart, *et al.* (2007). Empathy for positive and negative emotions in the gustatory cortex. *NeuroImage* **34**(4): 1744–1753.

Jabourian, A, J. C. Turpin, *et al.* (2002). Autisme de l'enfant lie a une mucopolysaccharidose: Autistic like disorders and Sanfilippo syndrome. *Annales Medico-Psychologiques, Revue Psychiatrique* **160**(5–6): 421–426.

Jahr, E., S. Eldevik, *et al.* (2000). Teaching children with autism to initiate and sustain cooperative play. *Research in Developmental Disabilities* **21**(2): 151–169.

Jahromi, L. B., C. L. Kasari, *et al.* (2009). Positive effects of methylphenidate on social communication and self-regulation in children with pervasive developmental disorders and hyperactivity. *Journal of Autism and Developmental Disorders* **39**(3): 395–404.

Jairam, J. and H. J. van Marle (2008). [The treatment of hypersexuality in a male with obsessive compulsive disorder as psychiatric co-morbidity]. *Tijdschrift voor Psychiatrie* **50**(2): 113–117.

Jambaque, I., C. Chiron, *et al.* (2000). Mental and behavioural outcome of infantile epilepsy treated by vigabatrin in tuberous sclerosis patients. *Epilepsy Research* **38**(2–3): 151–160.

Jangaard, K. A., D. B. Fell, *et al.* (2008). Outcomes in a population of healthy term and near-term infants with serum bilirubin levels of >or=325 micromol/L (>or=19 mg/dL) who were born in Nova Scotia, Canada, between 1994 and 2000. *Pediatrics* **122**(1): 119–124.

Janoff-Bulman, R. (1992). *Shattered Assumptions: Towards a New Psychology of Trauma.* New York, NY: The Free Press.

Jansiewicz, E. M., M. C. Goldberg, *et al.* (2006). Motor signs distinguish children with high functioning autism and Asperger's syndrome from controls. *Journal of Autism and Developmental Disorders* **36**(5): 613–621.

Janson, U. (1993). Normal and deviant behavior in blind children with ROP. *Acta Ophthalmologica* **210**: 20–26.

Jarbrink, K. (2007). The economic consequences of autistic spectrum disorder among children in a Swedish municipality. *Autism* **11**(5): 453–463.

Jarbrink, K. and M. Knapp (2001). The economic impact of autism in Britain. *Autism* **5**(1): 7–22.

Jarbrink, K., P. McCrone, *et al.* (2007). Cost-impact of young adults with high-functioning autistic spectrum disorder. *Research in Developmental Disabilities* **28**(1): 94–104.

Jarvinen-Pasley, A., J. Pasley, *et al.* (2008). Is the linguistic content of speech less salient than its perceptual features in autism? *Journal of Autism and Developmental Disorders* **38**(2): 239–248.

Jarvinen-Pasley, A., S. Peppe, *et al.* (2008). The relationship between form and prosodic abilities in autism. *Journal of Autism and Developmental Disorders* **38**(7): 1328–1340.

Javorsky, J. (1996). An examination of youth with attention-deficit/hyperactivity disorder and language learning disabilities: A clinical study. *Journal of Learning Disabilities* **29**(3): 247–258.

Jennes-Coussens, M., J. Magill-Evans, *et al.* (2006). The quality of life of young men with Asperger syndrome: A brief report. *Autism* **10**(4): 403–414.

Joffe, V. and S. Varlokosta (2007). Patterns of syntactic development in children with Williams syndrome and Down's syndrome: Evidence from passives and wh-questions. *Clinical Linguistics and Phonetics* **21**(9): 705–727.

Johansen, E. B., P. R. Killeen, *et al.* (2009). Origins of altered reinforcement effects in ADHD. *Behavioural and Brain Functions* **5**: 7.

Johansson, M., E. Billstedt, *et al.* (2007). Autism spectrum disorder and underlying brain mechanism in the oculoauriculovertebral spectrum. *Developmental Medicine and Child Neurology* **49**(4): 280–288.

Johnson, A. K., A. Barnacz, *et al.* (2005). Me, myself, and lie: The role of self-awareness in deception. *Personality and Individual Differences* **38**(8): 1847–1853.

Johnson, C. P., S. M. Myers, *et al.* (2007). Identification and evaluation of children with autism spectrum disorders. *Pediatrics* **120**(5): 1183–1215.

Johnson, K. A., I. H. Robertson, *et al.* (2007). Dissociation in performance of children with ADHD and high-functioning autism on a task of sustained attention. *Neuropsychologia* **45**(10): 2234–2245.

Johnson, R. T. and S. M. Breedlove (2010). Human trust: Testosterone raises suspicion. *Proceedings of the National Academy of Sciences of the United States of America* **107**(25): 11,149–11,150.

Johnston, C. and J. L. Ohan (2005). The importance of parental attributions in families of children with attention-deficit/hyperactivity and disruptive behavior disorders. *Clinical Child and Family Psychology Review* **8**(3): 167–182.

Johnston, M. V., O. H. Jeon, *et al.* (2001). Neurobiology of Rett syndrome: A genetic disorder of synapse development. *Brain and Development* **23**(Suppl 1): S206–S213.

Jolliffe, D. and D. P. Farrington (2004). Empathy and offending: A systematic review and meta-analysis. *Aggression and Violent Behavior* **9**(5): 441–476.

Jones, A. (2001). Pretending to be normal: Living with Asperger's syndrome. *British Journal of Learning Disabilities* **29**(1): 37–38.

Jones, A. (2002). Pretending to be normal: Living with Asperger's syndrome. *British Journal of Learning Disabilities* **30**(2): 82–83.

Jones, C. R. G., F. Happé, *et al.* (2009). Auditory discrimination and auditory sensory behaviours in autism spectrum disorders. *Neuropsychologia* **47**(13): 2850–2858.

Jones, M. C. and K. Okere (2008). Treatment of hypersexual behavior with oral estrogen in an autistic male. *Southern Medical Journal* **101**(9): 959–960.

Jones, R. S. P., A. Zahl, *et al.* (2001). First-hand accounts of emotional experiences in autism: A qualitative analysis. *Disability and Society* **16**(3): 393–401.

Jones, S., S. A. Cooper, *et al.* (2008). Prevalence of, and factors associated with, problem behaviors in adults with intellectual disabilities. *Journal of Nervous and Mental Disease* **196**(9): 678–686.

Jones, W., K. Carr, *et al.* (2008). Absence of preferential looking to the eyes of approaching adults predicts level of social disability in 2-year-old toddlers with autism spectrum disorder. *Archives of Geneal Psychiatry* **65**(8): 946–954.

Jones, W., J. Hesselink, *et al.* (2002). Cerebellar abnormalities in infants and toddlers with Williams syndrome. *Developmental Medicine and Child Neurology* **44**(10): 688–694.

Joosten, A. V., A. C. Bundy, *et al.* (2009). Intrinsic and extrinsic motivation for stereotypic and repetitive behavior. *Journal of Autism and Developmental Disorders* **39**(3): 521–531.

Just, M. A., V. L. Cherkassky, *et al.* (2004). Cortical activation and synchronization during sentence comprehension in high-functioning autism: evidence of underconnectivity. *Brain* **127**(8): 1811–1821.

Just, M. A., V. L. Cherkassky, *et al.* (2007). Functional and anatomical cortical underconnectivity in autism: Evidence from an fMRI study of an executive function task and corpus callosum morphometry. *Cerebral Cortex* **17**(4): 951–961.

Justus, T., S. M. Ravizza, *et al.* (2005). Reduced phonological similarity effects in patients with damage to the cerebellum. *Brain and Language* **95**(2): 304–318.

Juul-Dam, N., J. Townsend, *et al.* (2001). Prenatal, perinatal, and neonatal factors in autism, pervasive developmental disorder-not otherwise specified, and the general population. *Pediatrics* **107**(4): E63.

Kaiser, M. D., C. M. Hudac, *et al.* (2010). Neural signatures of autism. *Proceedings of the National Academy of Sciences of the United States of America* **107**(49): 21,223–21,228.

Kaiser, M. D., L. Delmolino, *et al.* (2010). Comparison of visual sensitivity to human and object motion in autism spectrum disorder. *Autism Research* **3**(4): 1–5.

Kaland, N., A. Moller-Nielsen, *et al.* (2002). A new 'advanced' test of theory of mind: Evidence from children and adolescents with Asperger syndrome. *Journal of Child Psychology and Psychiatry* **43**(4): 517–528.

Kaland, N., K. Callesen, *et al.* (2008). Performance of children and adolescents with Asperger syndrome or high-functioning autism on advanced theory of mind tasks. *Journal of Autism and Developmental Disorders* **38**(6): 1112–1123.

Kalin, N. H., S. E. Shelton, *et al.* (2001). The primate amygdala mediates acute fear but not the behavioral and physiological components of anxious temperament. *Journal of Neuroscience* **21**(6): 2067–2074.

Kamp-Becker, I., M. Ghahreman, *et al.* (2009). Dimensional structure of the autism phenotype: Relations between early development and current presentation. *Journal of Autism and Developmental Disorders* **39**(4): 557–571.

Kan, C. C., J. K. Buitelaar, *et al.* (2008). [Autism spectrum disorders in adults]. *Nederlands Tijdschrift voor Geneeskunde* **152**(24): 1365–1369.

Kana, R. K., T. A. Keller, *et al.* (2007). Inhibitory control in high-functioning autism: Decreased activation and underconnectivity in inhibition networks. *Biological Psychiatry* **62**(3): 198–206.

Kana, R. K., T. A. Keller, *et al.* (2009). Atypical frontal-posterior synchronization of Theory of Mind regions in autism during mental state attribution. *Social Neuroscience* **4**(2): 135–152.

Kanbayashi, Y. (1997). Gender identity disorder of a boy with autistic disorder. *Journal of Mental Health* **43**: 41–46.

Kanne, S. M., A. M. Abbacchi, *et al.* (2009). Multi-informant ratings of psychiatric symptom severity in children with autism spectrum disorders: The importance of environmental context. *Journal of Autism and Developmental Disorders* **39**(6): 856–864.

Kanne, S., S. Christ, *et al.* (2009). Psychiatric symptoms and psychosocial difficulties in young adults with autistic traits. *Journal of Autism and Developmental Disorders* **39**(6): 827–833.

Kanner, L. (1943). Autistic disturbances of affective contact. *Nervous Child* **2**: 217–250.

Kanner, L. (1972). How far can autistic children go in matters of social adaptation? *Journal of Autism and Childhood Schizophrenia* **2**(1): 9–33.

Kanner, L. and L. Eisenberg (1957). Early infantile autism, 1943–1955. *Psychiatric Research Reports* **7**: 55–65.

Kanner, L., A. Rodriguez, *et al.* (1972). How far can autistic children go in matters of social adaptation? *Journal of Autism and Childhood Schizophrenia* **2**(1): 9–33.

Karama, S., Y. Ad-Dab'bagh, *et al.* (2003). Positive association between cognitive ability and cortical thickness in a representative US sample of healthy 6 to 18 year-olds. *Intelligence* **37**(2): 145–155.

Karande, S., N. Satam, *et al.* (2007). Clinical and psychoeducational profile of children with specific learning disability and co-occurring attention-deficit hyperactivity disorder. *Indian J Med Sci* **61**(12): 639–647.

Kasari, C., T. Paparella, *et al.* (2008). Language outcome in autism: Randomized comparison of joint attention and play interventions. *Journal of Consulting and Clinical Psychology* **76**(1):125–137.

Kaufmann, W. E., K. L. Cooper, *et al.* (2003). Specificity of Cerebellar Vermian Abnormalities in Autism: A Quantitative Magnetic Resonance Imaging Study. *Journal of Child Neurology* **18**(7): 463–470.

Kaufmann, W. E., R. Cortell, *et al.* (2004). Autism spectrum disorder in fragile X syndrome: Communication, social interaction, and specific behaviors. *American Journal of Medical Genetics* **129A**(3): 225–234.

Kay, G. G., M. A. Michaels, *et al.* (2009). Simulated driving changes in young adults with ADHD receiving mixed amphetamine salts extended release and atomoxetine. *Journal of Attention Disorders* **12**(4): 316–329.

Kaya, M., S. Karasalihoglu, *et al.* (2002). The relationship between 99mTc-HMPAO brain SPECT and the scores of real life rating scale in autistic children. *Brain and Development* **24**(2):77–81.

Kayaalp, L., A. Dervent, *et al.* (2007). EEG abnormalities in West syndrome: Correlation with the emergence of autistic features. *Brain and Development* **29**(6): 336–345.

Ke, X., S. Hong, *et al.* (2008). Voxel-based morphometry study on brain structure in children with high-functioning autism. *Neuroreport* **19**(9): 921–925.

Ke, X., T. Tang, *et al.* (2009). White matter impairments in autism, evidence from voxel-based morphometry and diffusion tensor imaging. *Brain Research* **1265**: 171–177.

Keane, H. (2007). Pleasure and discipline in the uses of Ritalin. *The International Journal on Drug Policy* **19**(5):401–409.

Keary, C., N. Minshew, *et al.* (2009). Corpus callosum volume and neurocognition in autism. *Journal of Autism and Developmental Disorders* **39**(6): 834–841.

Kedia, G., S. Berthoz, *et al.* (2008). An agent harms a victim: A functional magnetic resonance imaging study on specific moral emotions. *Journal of Cognitive Neuroscience* **20**(10): 1788–1798.

Keehn, B., L. Brenner, *et al.* (2009). Brief report: Eye-movement patterns during an embedded figures test in children with ASD. *Journal of Autism and Developmental Disorders* **39**(2): 383–387.

Keen, D. V., F. D. Reid, *et al.* (2010). Autism, ethnicity and maternal immigration. *British Journal of Psychiatry* **196**(4): 274–281.

Keeton, C, A. C. Kolos, *et al.* (2009). Pediatric generalized anxiety disorder: Epidemiology, diagnosis, and management. *Pediatric Drugs* **11**(3): 171–183.

Kegel, C. A. T., A. G. Bus, *et al.* (2011). Differential susceptibility in early literacy instruction through computer games: The role of the Dopamine D4 Receptor Gene (DRD4). *Mind, Brain, and Education* **5**(2): 71–78.

Keller, F. and A. M. Persico (2003). The neurobiological context of autism. *Molecular Neurobiology* **28**(1): 1–22.

Keller, T. A., R. K. Kana, *et al.* (2007). A developmental study of the structural integrity of white matter in autism. *Neuroreport* **18**(1): 23–27.

Kelley, R. I. (2000). Inborn errors of cholesterol biosynthesis. *Advances in Pediatrics* **47**: 1–53.

Kelly, A. B., M. S. Garnett, *et al.* (2008). Autism spectrum symptomatology in children: The impact of family and peer relationships. *Journal of Abnormal Child Psychology* **36**(7): 1069–1081.

Kennard, C. and F. C. Rose (1988). *Physiological Aspects of Clinical Neuro-ophthalmology.* London: Chapman & Hall.

Kennedy, D. P. and E. Courchesne (2008a). Functional abnormalities of the default network during self- and other-reflection in autism. *Social Cognitive and Affective Neuroscience* **3**(2): 177–190.

Kennedy, D. P. and E. Courchesne (2008b). The intrinsic functional organization of the brain is altered in autism. *NeuroImage* **39**(4): 1877–1885.

Kennedy, D. P., K. Semendeferi, *et al.* (2007). No reduction of spindle neuron number in frontoinsular cortex in autism. *Brain and Cognition* **64**(2): 124–129.

Kennerley, S. W. and J. D. Wallis (2009). Reward-dependent modulation of working memory in lateral prefrontal cortex. *Journal of Neuroscience* **29**(10): 3259–3270.

Kenny, J., M. M. Lees, *et al.* (2011). Sotos syndrome, infantile hypercalcemia, and nephrocalcinosis: A contiguous gene syndrome. *Pediatric Nephrology* **26**(8): 1331–1334.

Kent, L., J. Emerton, *et al.* (2008). X linked ichthyosis (steroid sulphatase deficiency) is associated with increased risk of attention deficit hyperactivity disorder, autism and social communication deficits. *Journal of Medical Genetics* **45**(8): 519–524.

Kent, L., J. Evans, *et al.* (1999). Comorbidity of autistic spectrum disorders in children with Down syndrome. *Developmental Medicine and Child Neurology* **41**(3): 153–158.

Kenworthy, L., D. O. Black, *et al.* (2009). Are executive control functions related to autism symptoms in high-functioning children? *Child Neuropsychology* **15**(5): 1–16.

Kertèsz, A. (2010). From 'scientific revolution' to 'unscientific revolution': An analysis of approaches to the history of generative linguistics. *Language Sciences* **32**(5): 507–527.

Kesler, S. R. P., A. L. M. Reiss, *et al.* (2008). Brain volume reductions within multiple cognitive systems in male preterm children at age twelve. *Journal of Pediatrics* **152**(4): 513–520e1.

Kessler, R. C., M. Lane, *et al.* (2008). The prevalence and workplace costs of adult attention deficit hyperactivity disorder in a large manufacturing firm. *Psychological Medicine* **39**(1): 1–11.

Kielinen, M., H. Rantala, *et al.* (2004). Associated medical disorders and disabilities in children with autistic disorder: A population-based study. *Autism* **8**(1): 49–60.

Kilian, S., W. S. Brown, *et al.* (2008). Regional callosal morphology in autism and macrocephaly. *Developmental Neuropsychology* **33**(1): 74–99.

Kilincaslan, A. and N. M. Mukaddes (2009). Pervasive developmental disorders in individuals with cerebral palsy. *Developmental Medicine and Child Neurology* **51**(4): 289–294.

Kimura, T., O. Tanizawa, *et al.* (1992). Structure and expression of a human oxytocin receptor. *Nature* **356**(6369): 526–529.

King, B. H. and C. Lord (2011). Is schizophrenia on the autism spectrum? *Brain Research* **22**(1380): 34–41.

King, B. H., E. Hollander, *et al.* (2009). Lack of efficacy of citalopram in children with autism spectrum disorders and high levels of repetitive behavior: Citalopram ineffective in children with autism. *Archives of General Psychiatry* **66**(6): 583–590.

Kingstone, A., C. K. Friesen, *et al.* (2000). Reflexive joint attention depends on lateralized cortical connections. *Psychological Science* **11**(2): 159–166.

Kircher, T., B. Straube, *et al.* (2009). Neural interaction of speech and gesture: Differential activations of metaphoric co-verbal gestures. *Neuropsychologia* **47**(1): 169–179.

Kirwan, C. B. and C. E. Stark (2004). Medial temporal lobe activation during encoding and retrieval of novel face-name pairs. *Hippocampus* **14**(7): 919–930.

Kishi, N. and J. D. Macklis (2005). Dissecting MECP2 function in the central nervous system. *Journal of Child Neurology* **20**(9): 753–759.

Kiyonari, T. and P. Barclay (2008). Cooperation in social dilemmas: Free riding may be thwarted by second-order reward rather than by punishment. *Journal of Personality and Social Psychology* **95**(4): 826–842.

Klein, S. K., R. F. Tuchman, *et al.* (2000). The influence of premorbid language skills and behavior on language recovery in children with verbal auditory agnosia. *Journal of Child Neurology* **15**(1): 36–43.

Kleinhans, N. M., T. Richards, *et al.* (2008). Abnormal functional connectivity in autism spectrum disorders during face processing. *Brain* **131**(4): 1000–1012.

Kleinman, J. M., P. E. Ventola, *et al.* (2008). Diagnostic stability in very young children with autism spectrum disorders. *Journal of Autism and Developmental Disorders* **38**(4): 606–615.

Kleinman, R. E., R. T. Brown, *et al.* (2011). A research model for investigating the effects of artificial food colorings on children with ADHD. *Pediatrics* **127**(6): e1575–e1584.

Kleist, K. (1974). Cycloid, paranoid and epileptoid psychoses and the problem of degenerative psychoses. In S. Hirsch and M. Shepherd (eds) *Themes and Variations in European Psychiatry*. Bristol: John Wright.

Klin, A. (2000). Attributing social meaning to ambiguous visual stimuli in higher-functioning autism and Asperger syndrome: The Social Attribution Task. *Journal of Child Psychology and Psychiatry* **41**(7): 831–846.

Klin, A., C. A. Saulnier, *et al.* (2007). Social and communication abilities and disabilities in higher functioning individuals with autism spectrum disorders: The Vineland and the ADOS. *Journal of Autism and Developmental Disorders* **37**(4): 748–759.

Klin, A., D. J. Lin, *et al.* (2009). Two-year-olds with autism orient to non-social contingencies rather than biological motion. *Nature* **459**(7244): 257–261.

Klin, A., F. R. Volkmar, *et al.* (1995). Validity and neuropsychological characterization of Asperger syndrome: Convergence with nonverbal learning disabilities syndrome. *Journal of Child Psychology and Psychiatry and Allied Disciplines* **36**(7): 1127–1140.

Klin, A., L. C. Mayes, *et al.* (1995). Multiplex developmental disorder. *Journal of Developmental and Behavioral.Pediatrics* **16**(3, Suppl): S7–S11.

Knafo, A., S. Israel, *et al.* (2011). Heritability of children's prosocial behavior and differential susceptibility to parenting by variation in the dopamine receptor D4 gene. *Development and Psychopathology* **23**(1): 53–67.

Knafo, A., C. Zahn-Waxler, *et al.* (2009). Empathy in early childhood. *Annals of the New York Academy of Sciences* **1167**: 103–114.

Knapp, M. (1997). Costs of schizophrenia. *British Journal of Psychiatry* **171**: 509–518.

Knauft, B. M. (1991). Violence and sociality in human-evolution. *Current Anthropology* **32**(4): 391–428.

Knickmeyer, R. C., S. Wheelwright, *et al.* (2008). Sex-typical play: Masculinization/defeminization in girls with an autism spectrum condition. *Journal of Autism and Developmental Disorders* **38**(6): 1028–1035.

Knight, T. A. and A. F. Fuchs (2007). Contribution of the frontal eye field to gaze shifts in the head-unrestrained monkey: effects of microstimulation. *Journal of Neurophysiology* **97**(1): 618–634.

Knoch, D., A. Pascual-Leone, *et al.* (2006). Diminishing reciprocal fairness by disrupting the right prefrontal cortex. *Science* **314**(5800): 829–832.

Knoch, D., L. R. R. Gianotti, *et al.* (2006). Disruption of right prefrontal cortex by low-frequency repetitive transcranial magnetic stimulation induces risk-taking behavior. *The Journal of Neuroscience* **26**(24): 6469–6472.

Knoester, M., F. M. Helmerhorst, *et al.* (2007). Matched follow-up study of 5 8-year-old ICSI singletons: Child behaviour, parenting stress and child (health-related) quality of life. *Human Reproduction* **22**(12): 3098–3107.

Kobrynski, L. J. and K. E. Sullivan (2007). Velocardiofacial syndrome, DiGeorge syndrome: The chromosome 22q11.2 deletion syndromes. *The Lancet* **370**(9596): 1443–1452.

Kodak, T. and C. C. Piazza (2008). Assessment and behavioral treatment of feeding and sleeping disorders in children with autism spectrum disorders. *Child and Adolescent Psychiatric Clinics of North America* **17**(4): 887–905.

Koegel, R. L., L. Schreibman, *et al.* (1983). The personality and family-interaction characteristics of parents of autistic children. *Journal of Consulting and Clinical Psychology* **51**(5): 683–692.

Koenigs, M., L. Young, *et al.* (2007). Damage to the prefrontal cortex increases utilitarian moral judgements. *Nature* **446**(7138): 908–911.

Kogan, M. D., S. J. Blumberg, *et al.* (2009). Prevalence of parent-reported diagnosis of autism spectrum disorder among children in the US, 2007. *Pediatrics* **124**(5): 1395–1403.

Kolevzon, A. M., R. M. Gross, *et al.* (2007). Prenatal and perinatal risk factors for autism: A review and integration of findings. *Archives of Pediatrics and Adolescent Medicine* **161**(4): 326–333.

Kolvin, I. (1971). Studies in the childhood psychoses: Diagnostic criteria and classification. *British Journal of Psychiatry* **118**(545): 381–384.

Koren-Karie, N., D. Oppenheim, *et al.* (2009). Mothers of securely attached children with autism spectrum disorder are more sensitive than mothers of insecurely attached children. *Journal of Child Psychology and Psychiatry* **50**(5): 643–650.

Koshino, H., R. K. Kana, *et al.* (2008). fMRI investigation of working memory for faces in autism: Visual coding and underconnectivity with frontal areas. *Cerebral Cortex* **18**(2): 289–300.

Kosson, D. S., R. Blackburn, *et al.* (2008). Assessing interpersonal aspects of schizoid personality disorder: Preliminary validation studies. *Journal of Personality Assessment* **90**(2): 185–196.

Kraepelin, E. (1904). Psychiatrisches aus Java. *Zentralblatt fur Nervenheilkunde und Psychiatrie* **27**: 468–489.

Krain, A. L. and F. X. Castellanos (2006). Brain development and ADHD. *ClinicalPsychology Review* **26**(4): 433–444.

Krasnoperova, M. G. (2004). [Clinical aspects of childhood autism with endogenous manifesting psychosis and mental retardation]. *Zh Nevrol Psikhiatr Im S S Korsakova* **104**(2): 5–10.

Krause, R., E. Steimer, *et al.* (1989). Facial expression of schizophrenic patients and their interaction partners. *Psychiatry* **52**(1): 1–12.

Kravchenko, A. V. (2007). Essential properties of language, or, why language is not a code. *Language Sciences* **29**(5): 650–671.

Kretschmer, E. (1925). *Physique and Character* (trans. by W. J. H. Sprott). London: Kegan Paul, Trench, Trubner.

Kringelbach, M. L., I. E. T. de Araujo, *et al.* (2008). Taste-related activity in the human dorsolateral prefrontal cortex. *NeuroImage* **21**(2): 781–788.

Kristensen, H. (2000). Selective mutism and comorbidity with developmental disorder/delay, anxiety disorder, and elimination disorder. *Journal of the American Academy of Child and Adolescent Psychiatry* **39**(2): 249–256.

Kristensen, H. and B. Oerbeck (2006). Is selective mutism associated with deficits in memory span and visual memory? An exploratory case-control study. *Depression and Anxiety* **23**(2): 71–76.

Kroenke, K., R. L. Spitzer, *et al.* (2001). The PHQ-9: Validity of a Brief Depression Severity Measure. *Journal of General Internal Medicine* **16**(9): 606–613.

Krone, N., F. G. Riepe, *et al.* (2005). Congenital adrenal hyperplasia due to 11-hydroxylase deficiency: Functional characterization of two novel point mutations and a three-base pair deletion in the CYP11B1 gene. *The Journal of Clinical Endocrinology and Metabolism* **90**(6): 3724–3730.

Krueger, F., A. K. Barbey, *et al.* (2009). The medial prefrontal cortex mediates social event knowledge. *Trends in Cognitive Sciences* **13**(3): 103–109.

Krysko, K. M. and M. D. Rutherford (2009). A threat-detection advantage in those with autism spectrum disorders. *Brain and Cognition* **69**(3): 472–480.

Kubler, A., V. Dixon, *et al.* (2006). Automaticity and reestablishment of executive control: An fMRI study. *Journal of Cognitive Neuroscience* **18**(8): 1331–1342.

Kuddo, T. M. D. and K. B. M. Nelson (2003). How common are gastrointestinal disorders in children with autism? (Editorial). *Current Opinion in Pediatrics* **15**(3): 339–343.

Kuemerle, B., F. Gulden, *et al.* (2007). The mouse Engrailed genes: A window into autism. *Behavioural Brain Research* **176**(1): 121–132.

Kumandas, S., M. Akcakus, *et al.* (2004). Joubert syndrome: review and report of seven new cases. *European Journal of Neurology* **11**(8): 505–510.

Kumar, A., N. Sarvananthan, *et al.* (2009). Asperger syndrome associated with idiopathic infantile nystagmus: A report of 2 cases. *Strabismus* **17**(2): 63–65.

Kurita, H. (1997). A comparative study of Asperger syndrome with high-functioning atypical autism. *Psychiatry and Clinical Neurosciences* **51**(2): 67–70.

Kurita, H., H. Osada, *et al.* (2004). External validity of childhood disintegrative disorder in comparison with autistic disorder. *Journal of Autism and Developmental Disorders* **34**(3): 355–362.

Kurita, H., T. Koyama, *et al.* (2005a). Autism-Spectrum Quotient-Japanese version and its short forms for screening normally intelligent persons with pervasive developmental disorders. *Psychiatry and Clinical Neurosciences* **59**(4): 490–496.

Kurita, H., T. Koyama, *et al.* (2005b). Comparison of childhood disintegrative disorder and disintegrative psychosis not diagnosed as childhood disintegrative disorder. *Psychiatry and Clinical Neurosciences* **59**(2): 200–205.

Kurlan, R. (2003). Tourette's syndrome: Are stimulants safe? *Current Neurology and Neuroscience Reports* **3**(4): 285–288.

Kurscheidt, J. C., P. Peiler, *et al.* (2008). Acute effects of methylphenidate on neuropsychological parameters in adults with ADHD: Possible relevance for therapy. *Journal of Neural Transmission* **115**(2): 357–362.

Kurtz, M. M. and K. T. Mueser (2008). A meta-analysis of controlled research on social skills training for schizophrenia. *Journal of Consulting and Clinical Psychology* **76**(3): 491–504.

Kuwagata, M., T. Ogawa, *et al.* (2009). Observation of fetal brain in a rat valproate-induced autism model: A developmental neurotoxicity study. *International Journal of Developmental Neuroscience* **27**(4): 399–405.

Labelle, C. A. (2003). Examining the feedback hypothesis of the executive function deficit in autism. *Dissertation Abstracts International: Section B: The Sciences and Engineering* **63**: 7-B.

Ladavas, E. (2002). Functional and dynamic properties of visual peripersonal space. *Trends in Cognitive Sciences* **6**(1): 17–22.

LaGraize, S. C., C. J. Labuda, *et al.* (2004). Differential effect of anterior cingulate cortex lesion on mechanical hypersensitivity and escape/avoidance behavior in an animal model of neuropathic pain. *Experimental Neurology* **188**(1): 139–148.

Laird, J. (2008). *Feelings: The Perception of Self.* Oxford: Oxford University Press.

Lambrechts, G., S. Kuppens, *et al.* (2009). Staff variables associated with the challenging behaviour of clients with severe or profound intellectual disabilities. *Journal of Intellectual Disability Research* **53**(7): 620–632.

Lamm, C., E. C. Porges, *et al.* (2008). Perspective taking is associated with specific facial responses during empathy for pain. *Brain Research* **1227**: 153–161.

Lamm, C., H. C. Nusbaum, *et al.* (2007). What are you feeling? Using functional magnetic resonance imaging to assess the modulation of sensory and affective responses during empathy for pain. *PLoS ONE* **2**(12): e1292.

Lammert, M., J. M. Friedman, *et al.* (2005). Prevalence of neurofibromatosis 1 in German children at elementary school enrollment. *Archives of Dermatology* **141**(1): 71–74.

Lancaster, K., D. M. Dietz, *et al.* (2007). Abnormal social behaviors in young and adult rats neonatally infected with Borna disease virus. *Behavioural Brain Research* **176**(1): 141–148.

Lancker Sidtis, D. V. (2007). Does functional neuroimaging solve the questions of neurolinguistics? *Brain and Language* **102**(2): 200–214.

Landa, R. J. (2008). Diagnosis of autism spectrum disorders in the first 3 years of life. *Nature Clinical Practice Neurology* **4**(3): 138–147.

Landen, M. and P. Rasmussen (1997). Gender identity disorder in a girl with autism: A case report. *European Child and Adolescent Psychiatry* **6**(3): 170–173.

Landgren, M., C. Gillberg, *et al.* (1992). Goldenhar syndrome and autistic behaviour. *Developmental Medicine and Child Neurology* **34**(11): 999–1005.

Lanius, R. A., P. C. Williamson, *et al.* (2004). The nature of traumatic memories: A 4-T FMRI functional connectivity analysis. *American Journal of Psychiatry* **161**(1): 36–44.

Larsson, J. O., L. R. Bergman, *et al.* (2004). Behavioral profiles in 4–5 year-old children: Normal and pathological variants. *Child Psychiatry and Human Development* **35**(2): 143–162.

Lassus-Sangosse, D., M. A. N'guyen-Morel, *et al.* (2008). Sequential or simultaneous visual processing deficit in developmental dyslexia? *Vision Research* **48**(8): 979–988.

Lau, W-y., C. K-y. Chan, *et al.* (2010). Effectiveness of group cognitive-behavioral treatment for childhood anxiety in community clinics. *Behaviour Research and Therapy* **48**(11): 1067–1077.

Laugeson, E. A., F. Frankel, *et al.* (2009). Parent-assisted social skills training to improve friendships in teens with autism spectrum disorders. *Journal of Autism and Developmental Disorders* **39**(4): 596–606.

Laursen, B., B. Finkelstein, *et al.* (2001). A developmental meta-analysis of peer conflict resolution. *Developmental Review* **21**(4): 423–449.

Lawer, L., E. Brusilovskiy, *et al.* (2009). Use of vocational rehabilitative services among adults with autism. *Journal of Autism and Developmental Disorders* **39**(3): 487–494.

Lawrence, E. J., P. Shaw, *et al.* (2004). Measuring empathy: Reliability and validity of the Empathy Quotient. *Psychological Medicine* **34**(5): 911–919.

Le Couteur, A., G. Haden, *et al.* (2008). Diagnosing autism spectrum disorders in pre-school children using two standardised assessment instruments: The ADI-R and the ADOS. *Journal of Autism and Developmental Disorders* **38**(2): 362–372.

Le Couteur, A., M. Rutter, et al. (1989). Autism Diagnostic Interview: A standardized investigator-based instrument. *Journal of Autism and Developmental Disorders* **19**(3): 363–387.

Le Doux, J. (1999). *The Emotional Brain.* London: Weidenfeld & Nicolson.

Leckman, J. F. and M. H. Bloch (2008). A Developmental and Evolutionary Perspective on Obsessive-Compulsive Disorder: Whence and Whither Compulsive Hoarding? *American Journal of Psychiatry* **165**(10): 1229–1233.

Lee, D. H., D. R. Jacobs, et al. (2007). Association of serum concentrations of persistent organic pollutants with the prevalence of learning disability and attention deficit disorder. *Journal of Epidemiology and Community Health* **61**(7): 591–596.

Lee, D. O. and O. Y. Ousley (2006). Attention-deficit hyperactivity disorder symptoms in a clinic sample of children and adolescents with pervasive developmental disorders. *Journal of Child and Adolescent Psychopharmacology* **16**(6): 737–746.

Lee, L. C., R. A. Harrington, et al. (2008). Children with autism: Quality of life and parental concerns. *Journal of Autism and Developmental Disorders* **38**(6): 1147–1160.

Lee, M., C. Martin-Ruiz, et al. (2002). Nicotinic receptor abnormalities in the cerebellar cortex in autism. *Brain* **125**(7): 1483–1495.

Lee, P. J., A. Amos, et al. (2009). Adults with late diagnosed PKU and severe challenging behaviour: A randomised placebo-controlled trial of a phenylalanine-restricted diet. *Journal of Neurology, Neurosurgery and Psychiatry* **80**(6): 631–635.

Lee, P. S., J. Foss-Feig, et al. (2007). Atypical neural substrates of Embedded Figures Task performance in children with Autism Spectrum Disorder. *NeuroImage* **38**(1): 184–193.

Lee, T. W., O. Josephs, et al. (2006). Imitating expressions: Emotion-specific neural substrates in facial mimicry. *Social Cognitive and Affective Neuroscience* **1**(2): 122–135.

Lee, T. W., R. J. Dolan, et al. (2008). Controlling emotional expression: Behavioral and neural correlates of nonimitative emotional responses. *Cerebral Cortex* **18**(1): 104–113.

Leff, A. P., P. Iverson, et al. (2009). Vowel-specific mismatch responses in the anterior superior temporal gyrus: An fMRI study. *Cortex* **45**(4): 517–526.

Leff, J. and C. Vaughn. (1985). *Expressed Emotion in Families.* New York, NY: Guilford Press.

Legoff, D. B. and M. Sherman (2006). Long-term outcome of social skills intervention based on interactive LEGO play. *Autism* **10**(4): 317–329.

Leist, T. and M. R. Dadds (2009). Adolescents' ability to read different emotional faces relates to their history of maltreatment and type of psychopathology. *Clinical Child Psychology and Psychiatry* **14**(2): 237–250.

Leiter, V. (2007). Nobody's just normal, you know: The social creation of developmental disability. *Social Science and Medicine* **65**(8): 1630–1641.

Lemon, R. N. and S. A. Edgley (2010). Life without a cerebellum. *Brain* **133**(3): 652–654.

Lennon, P. A., M. L. Cooper, et al. (2007). Deletion of 7q31.1 supports involvement of FOXP2 in language impairment: clinical report and review. *American Journal of Medical Genetics A* **143A**(8): 791–798.

Leonard, H., N. Nassar, et al. (2008). Relation between intrauterine growth and subsequent intellectual disability in a ten-year population cohort of children in Western Australia. *American Journal of Epidemiology* **167**(1): 103–111.

Lepagnol-Bestel, A. M., G. Maussion, et al. (2008). SLC25A12 expression is associated with neurite outgrowth and is upregulated in the prefrontal cortex of autistic subjects. *Molecular Psychiatry* **13**(4): 385–397.

Leslie, D. L. and A. Martin (2007). Health care expenditures associated with autism spectrum disorders. *Archives of Pediatrics and Adolescent Medicine* **161**(4): 350–355.

Leslie, K. R., S. H. Johnson-Frey, et al. (2004). Functional imaging of face and hand imitation: Towards a motor theory of empathy. *NeuroImage* **21**(2): 601–607.

Lessing, D. (1989). *The Fifth Child.* London: Paladin.

Lessing, D. (2000). *Ben, in the World.* London: Flamingo.

Levin, H. S., J. Scheller, et al. (1996). Dyscalculia and dyslexia after right hemisphere injury in infancy. *Archives of Neurology* **53**(1): 88–96.

Levy, D., M. Ronemus, et al. (2011). Rare de novo and transmitted copy-number variation in autistic spectrum disorders. *Neuron* **70**(5): 886–897.

Levy, F., D. A. Hay, et al. (1997). Attention-deficit hyperactivity disorder: a category or a continuum? Genetic analysis of a large-scale twin study. *Journal of the American Academy of Child and Adolescent Psychiatry* **36**(6): 737–744.

Levy, L. D., J. P. Fleming, et al. (2009). Treatment of refractory obesity in severely obese adults following management of newly diagnosed attention deficit hyperactivity disorder. *International Journal of Obesity* **33**(3): 326–334.

Levy, S. E., E. Giarelli, et al. (2010) Autism spectrum disorder and co-occurring developmental, psychiatric, and medical conditions among children in multiple populations of the United States. *Journal of Developmental and Behavioural Pediatrics* **31**(4): 267–275.

Leyfer, O., S. Folstein, et al. (2006). Comorbid psychiatric disorders in children with autism: Interview development and rates of disorders. *Journal of Autism and Developmental Disorders* **36**(7): 849–861.

Lhermitte, F. (1983). 'Utilization behaviour' and its relation to lesions of the frontal lobes. *Brain* **106**(2): 237–255.

Lhermitte, F., B. Pillon, et al. (1986). Human autonomy and the frontal lobes. Part I: Imitation and utilization behavior: A neuropsychological study of 75 patients. *Annals of Neurology* **19**(4): 326–334.

Li, J., L. Nguyen, et al. (2004). Lack of evidence for an association between WNT2 and RELN polymorphisms and autism. *American Journal of Medical Genetics B: Neuropsychiatric Genetics* **126B**(1): 51–57.

Li, J., M. R. Delgado, et al. (2011). How instructed knowledge modulates the neural systems of reward learning. *Proceedings of the National Academy of Sciences* **108**(1): 55–60.

Licht, D. J. and D. R. Lynch (2002). Juvenile dentatorubral-pallidoluysian atrophy: New clinical features. *Pediatric Neurology* **26**(1): 51–54.

Lim, M. M., I. F. Bielsky et al. (2005). Neuropeptides and the social brain: Potential rodent models of autism. *International Journal of Developmental Neuroscience* **23**(2–3): 235–243.

Limperopoulos, C., H. Bassan, et al. (2008). Positive screening for autism in ex-preterm infants: Prevalence and risk factors. *Pediatrics* **121**(4): 758–765.

Lincoln, A. J., D. Taylor, et al. (2010). Impaired behavior regulation under conditions of concurrent variable schedules of reinforcement in children with ADHD. *Journal of Attention Disorders* **13**(4): 358–368.

Lincoln, A. J., Y. M. Searcy, et al. (2007). Social interaction behaviors discriminate young children with autism and Williams syndrome. *Journal of the American Academy of Child and Adolescent Psychiatry* **46**(3): 323–331.

Lind, S. E. and D. M. Bowler (2009). Delayed self-recognition in children with autism spectrum disorder. *Journal of Autism and Developmental Disorders* **39**(4): 643–650.

Lindstrom, K., P. Lagerroos, *et al.* (2006). Teenage outcome after being born at term with moderate neonatal encephalopathy. *Pediatric Neurology* **35**(4): 268–274.

Liptak, G. S., L. B. Benzoni, *et al.* (2008). Disparities in diagnosis and access to health services for children with autism: Data from the national survey of children's health. *Journal of Developmental and Behavioral Pediatrics* **29**(3): 152–160.

Liss, M. N. (2001). Rhythmic behaviors in typically developing infants, and infants with later diagnosed autism or developmental delay. *Dissertation Abstracts International: Section B: The Sciences and Engineering* **62**: 5-B.

Liszkowski, U., M. Carpenter, *et al.* (2007). Reference and attitude in infant pointing. *Journal of Child Language* **34**(1): 1–20.

Little, L. (2001). Peer victimization of children with Asperger spectrum disorders. *Journal of the American Academy of Child and Adolescent Psychiatry* **40**(9): 995–996.

Litvack-Miller, W. (1993). The structure and development of dispositional empathy during middle childhood and its relationship to prosocial behavior. *Dissertation Abstracts International* **54**: 427.

Litvack-Miller, W., D. McDougall, *et al.* (1997). The structure of empathy during middle childhood and its relationship to prosocial behavior. *Genetic, Social, and General Psychology Monographs* **123**(3): 303–324.

Liu, X. Q., A. D. Paterson, *et al.* (2008). Genome-wide linkage analyses of quantitative and categorical autism subphenotypes. *Biological Psychiatry* **64**(7): 561–570.

Liu, X., N. Novosedlik, *et al.* (2009). The DLX1 and DLX2 genes and susceptibility to autism spectrum disorders. *European Journal of Human Genetics* **17**(2): 228–235.

Lobo, I. (2008). Epistasis: Gene interaction and the phenotypic expression of complex diseases like Alzheimer's. *Nature Education* **1**(1) (serial on the internet).

Lopes, F. L., T. M. Azevedo, *et al.* (2009). Freezing reaction in panic disorder patients associated with anticipatory anxiety. *Depression and Anxiety* **26**(10): 917–921.

López, J. and J. Scott (2000). *Social Structure*. Buckingham: Open University Press.

LoPresti, M. L., K. Schon, *et al.* (2008). Working memory for social cues recruits orbitofrontal cortex and amygdala: A functional magnetic resonance imaging study of delayed matching to sample for emotional expressions. *Journal of Neuroscience* **28**(14): 3718–3728.

Lord, C., M. Rutter, *et al.* (1989). Autism Diagnostic Observation Schedule: A standardized observation of communicative and social behaviour. *Journal of Autism and Developmental Disorders* **19**(2): 185–212.

Lord, C., M. Rutter, *et al.* (1994). Autism Diagnostic Interview Revised: A revised version of a diagnostic interview for caregivers of individuals with possible pervasive developmental disorders. *Journal of Autism and Developmental Disorders* **24**(5): 659–686.

Lord, C., S. Risi, *et al.* (2000). The Autism Diagnostic Observation Schedule – Generic: A standard measure of social and communication deficits associated with the spectrum of autism. *Journal of Autism and Developmental Disorders* **30**(3): 205–223.

Lorena, R. R. G. (2009). Tonic activity level in the right prefrontal cortex predicts individuals' risk taking. *Psychological Science* **20**(1): 33–38.

Losh, M., R. Adolphs, *et al.* (2009). Neuropsychological profile of autism and the broad autism phenotype. *Archives of General Psychiatry* **66**(5): 518–526.

Loth, E., J. C. Gomez, *et al.* (2008). Event schemas in autism spectrum disorders: The role of theory of mind and weak central coherence. *Journal of Autism and Developmental Disorders* **38**(3): 449–463.

Lott, I. T. and M. Dierssen (2010). Cognitive deficits and associated neurological complications in individuals with Down's syndrome. *The Lancet Neurology* **9**(6): 623–633.

Lotter, V. (1966). Epidemiology of autistic conditions in young children. I. Prevalence. *Social Psychiatry* **1**(3): 124–137.

Loucas, T., T. Charman, *et al.* (2008). Autistic symptomatology and language ability in autism spectrum disorder and specific language impairment. *Journal of Child Psychology and Psychiatry* **49**(11): 1184–1192.

Lough, S., and J. R. Hodges (2002). Measuring and modifying abnormal social cognition in frontal variant frontotemporal dementia. *Journal of Psychosomatic Research* **53**(2): 639–646.

Lough, S., C. M. Kipps, *et al.* (2006). Social reasoning, emotion and empathy in frontotemporal dementia. *Neuropsychologia* **44**(6): 950–958.

Loveland, K. A., J. Bachevalier, *et al.* (2008). Fronto-limbic functioning in children and adolescents with and without autism. *Neuropsychologia* **46**(1): 49–62.

Lowenthal, R., C. Paula, *et al.* (2007). Prevalence of pervasive developmental disorder in Down's syndrome. *Journal of Autism and Developmental Disorders* **37**(7): 1394–1395.

Lucarelli, C. (2008). *Via delle Oche*. New York, NY: Europa Editions.

Lucht, M. J., S. Barnow, *et al.* (2009). Associations between the oxytocin receptor gene (OXTR) and affect, loneliness and intelligence in normal subjects. *Progress in Neuropsychopharmacology and Biological Psychiatry* **33**(5): 860–866.

Luckenbaugh, D. A., R. L. Findling, *et al.* (2009). Earliest symptoms discriminating juvenile-onset bipolar illness from ADHD. *Bipolar Disorders* **11**(4): 441–451.

Luders, E., K. L. Narr, *et al.* (2009). Decreased callosal thickness in attention-deficit/hyperactivity disorder. *Biological Psychiatry* **65**(1): 84–88.

Luna, B., N. J. Minshew, *et al.* (2002). Neocortical system abnormalities in autism: An fMRI study of spatial working memory. *Neurology* **59**(6): 834–840.

Luna, B., S. K. Doll, *et al.* (2007). Maturation of executive function in autism. *Biological Psychiatry* **61**(4): 474–481.

Lund, S. and J. Troha (2008). Teaching young people who are blind and have autism to make requests using a variation on the picture exchange communication system with tactile symbols: A preliminary investigation. *Journal of Autism and Developmental Disorders* **38**(4): 719–730.

Lundgren, K., H. Brownell, *et al.* (2010). Training theory of mind following right hemisphere damage: A pilot study. *Brain and Language* **103**(8): 209–210.

Luo, Q., D. Peng, *et al.* (2004). Emotional valence of words modulates the subliminal repetition priming effect in the left fusiform gyrus: An event-related fMRI study. *NeuroImage* **21**(1): 414–421.

Luyster, R., M. Kadlec, *et al.* (2008). Language assessment and development in toddlers with autism spectrum disorders. *Journal of Autism and Developmental Disorders* **38**(8): 1426–1438.

Lyketsos, C. G., A. Rosenblatt, *et al.* (2004). Forgotten frontal lobe syndrome or executive dysfunction syndrome. *Psychosomatics* **45**(3): 247–255.

Lysaker, P. H., A. M. Wickett, *et al.* (2004). Neurocognitive deficits and history of childhood abuse in schizophrenia spectrum disorders: Associations with Cluster B personality traits. *Schizophrenia Research* **68**(1): 87–94.

Ma, D. Q., M. L. Cuccaro, et al. (2007). Dissecting the locus heterogeneity of autism: Significant linkage to chromosome 12q14. *Molecular Psychiatry* **12**: 376–384.

Macarov, M., M. Zeigler, et al. (2007). Deletions of VCX-A and NLGN4: A variable phenotype including normal intellect. *Journal of Intellectual Disability Research* **51**(5): 329–333.

MacDonald, K. B. (2008). Effortful control, explicit processing, and the regulation of human evolved predispositions. *Psychological Review* **115**(4): 1012–1031.

Mackie, S., P. Shaw, et al. (2007). Cerebellar development and clinical outcome in attention deficit hyperactivity disorder. *American Journal of Psychiatry* **164**(4): 647–655.

MacLean, P. D. (1990). *The Triune Brain in Evolution: Role in Paleocerebral Functions.* New York, NY: Plenum Press.

Macmillan, R. (2006). 'Constructing adulthood': Agency and subjectivity in the transition to adulthood. *Advances in Life Course Research* **11**: 3–29.

MacNeil, B. M., V. A. Lopes, et al. (2009). Anxiety in children and adolescents with Autism Spectrum Disorders. *Research in Autism Spectrum Disorders* **3**(1): 1–21.

MacSweeney, M., R. Campbell, et al. (2004). Dissociating linguistic and nonlinguistic gestural communication in the brain. *NeuroImage* **22**(4): 1605–1618.

Madsen, K. M., A. Hviid, et al. (2002a). Population-based study of measles, mumps, and rubella vaccination and autism. *New England Journal of Medicine* **347**(19): 1477–1482.

Madsen, K. M., A. Hviid, et al. (2002b). Impaired recognition of social emotions following amygdala damage. *Journal of Cognitive Neuroscience* **14**(8): 1264–1274.

Maestrini, E., A. T. Pagnamenta, et al. (2009). High-density SNP association study and copy number variation analysis of the AUTS1 and AUTS5 loci implicate the IMMP2L-DOCK4 gene region in autism susceptibility. *Molecular Psychiatry* **15**: 954–968.

Maestro, S., F. Muratori, et al. (2005). Course of autism signs in the first year of life. *Psychopathology* **38**(1): 26–31.

Mah, L., M. C. Arnold, et al. (2004). Impairment of social perception associated with lesions of the prefrontal cortex. *American Journal of Psychiatry* **161**: 1247–1255.

Main, M. (1996). Introduction to the special section on attachment and psychopathology: 2. Overview of the field of attachment. *Journal of Consulting and Clinical Psychology* **64**(2): 237–243.

Mäki, P., J. Miettunen, et al. (2008). Negative features of psychosis precede onset of psychosis in a prospective general population sample of adolescents. *Schizophrenia Research* **98**: 10.

Makris, N., J. Biederman, et al. (2007). Cortical thinning of the attention and executive function networks in adults with attention-deficit/hyperactivity disorder. *Cerebral Cortex* **17**(6): 1364–1375.

Makris, N., S. L. Buka, et al. (2008). Attention and executive systems abnormalities in adults with childhood ADHD: A DT-MRI study of connections. *Cerebral Cortex* **18**(5): 1210–1220.

Malhotra, S. (2007). Acute and transient psychosis: A paradigmatic approach. *Indian Journal of Psychiatry* **49**(4): 233–243.

Malhotra, S. and N. Gupta (2002). Autistic symptoms following herpes encephalitis. *European Child and Adolescent Psychiatry* **11**(3): 3–146.

Mallinowski, B. (1934). *Magic, Science, and Religion.* Garden City, NY: Doubleday.

Malloy-Diniz, L., D. Fuentes, et al. (2007). Impulsive behavior in adults with attention deficit/ hyperactivity disorder: Characterization of attentional, motor and cognitive impulsiveness. *Journal of the International Neuropsychological Society* **13**(4): 693–698.

Malti, T., M. Gummerum, et al. (2009). Children's moral motivation, sympathy, and prosocial behavior. *Child Development* **80**(2): 442–460.

Mancebo, M., A. M. Garcia, et al. (2008). Juvenile-onset OCD: Clinical features in children, adolescents and adults. *Acta Psychiatrica Scandinavica* **118**(2): 149–159.

Mandell, D. S., C. M. Walrath, et al. (2005). The prevalence and correlates of abuse among children with autism served in comprehensive community-based mental health settings. *Child Abuse and Neglect* **29**: 1359–1372.

Mandell, D. S., K. H. Morales, et al. (2008). Psychotropic medication use among Medicaid-enrolled children with autism spectrum disorders. *Pediatrics* **121**(3): e441–e448.

Mandell, D. S., L. D. Wiggins, et al. (2009). Racial/ethnic disparities in the identification of children with autism spectrum disorders. *American Journal of Public Health* **99**(3): 493–498.

Mandell, D. S., W. W. Thompson, et al. (2005). Trends in diagnosis rates for autism and ADHD at hospital discharge in the context of other psychiatric diagnoses. *Psychiatric Services* **56**: 56–62.

Mano, Y., T. Harada, et al. (2009). Perspective-taking as part of narrative comprehension: A functional MRI study. *Neuropsychologia* **47**(3): 813–824.

Manoach, D. S., N. S. White, et al. (2004). Hemispheric specialization of the lateral prefrontal cortex for strategic processing during spatial and shape working memory. *NeuroImage* **21**(3): 894–903.

Manson, J. E. (2008). Prenatal exposure to sex steroid hormones and behavioral/cognitive outcomes. *Metabolism* **57**(Suppl 2): S16–S21.

Mantini, D., M. G. Perrucci, et al. (2007). Electrophysiological signatures of resting state networks in the human brain. *Proceedings of the National Academy of Sciences of the United States of America* **104**(32): 13,170–13,175.

Mar, R. A. (2004). The neuropsychology of narrative: Story comprehension, story production and their interrelation. *Neuropsychologia* **42**(10): 1414–1434.

Marazziti, D. and D. M. Catena (2008). The role of oxytocin in neuropsychiatric disorders. *Current Medicinal Chemistry* **15**(7): 698–704.

Marchetta, N. D. J., P. P. M. Hurks, et al. (2008). Interference control, working memory, concept shifting, and verbal fluency in adults with attention-deficit/hyperactivity disorder (ADHD). *Neuropsychology* **22**(1): 74–84.

Marco, R., A. Miranda, et al. (2009). Delay and reward choice in ADHD: An experimental test of the role of delay aversion. *Neuropsychology* **23**(3): 367–380.

Marco-Pallares, J., D. Cucurell, et al. (2009). Genetic variability in the dopamine system (dopamine receptor D4, catechol-O-methyltransferase) modulates neurophysiological responses to gains and losses. *Biological Psychiatry* **66**(2): 154–161.

Marcu, I., D. Oppenheim, at al. (2009). Attachment and symbolic play in preschoolers with autism spectrum disorders. *Journal of Autism and Developmental Disorders* **39**(9): 1321–1328.

Mariën, P., H. Baillieux, et al. (2009). Cognitive, linguistic and affective disturbances following a right superior cerebellar artery infarction: A case study. *Cortex* **45**(4): 527–536.

Marino, L., C. Butti, et al. (2008). A claim in search of evidence: Reply to Manger's thermogenesis hypothesis of cetacean brain structure. *Biological Reviews of the Cambridge Philosophical Society* **83**(4): 417–440.

Marsden, G., N. Kalter, et al. (1974). Response productivity: A methodological problem in content analysis studies in psychotherapy. *Journal of Consulting and Clinical Psychology* **42**(2): 224–230.

Marsh, A. A. and R. J. R. Blair (2008). Deficits in facial affect recognition among antisocial populations: A meta-analysis. *Neuroscience and Biobehavioral Reviews* **32**(3): 454–465.

Martel, M. M. (2009). Conscientiousness as a mediator of the association between masculinized finger-length ratios and attention-deficit/hyperactivity disorder (ADHD). *Journal of Child Psychology and Psychiatry* **50**(7): 790–798.

Martel, M. M., J. T. Nigg, *et al.* (2009). How do trait dimensions map onto ADHD symptom domains? *Journal of Abnormal Child Psychology* **37**(3): 337–348.

Martineau, J., S. Cochin, *et al.* (2008). Impaired cortical activation in autistic children: Is the mirror neuron system involved? *International Journal of Psychophysiology* **68**(1): 35–40.

Martínez-Levy, G., J. Díaz-Galvis, *et al.* (2009). Genetic interaction analysis for DRD4 and DAT1 genes in a group of Mexican ADHD patients. *Neuroscience Letters* **451**(3): 257–260.

Martins, C. L., J. P. Monteiro, *et al.* (2007). [Managing children with neurofibromatosis type 1: What should we look for?]. *Acta Medica Portuguesa* **20**(5): 393–400.

Marton, I., J. Wiener, *et al.* (2009). Empathy and social perspective taking in children with attention-deficit/hyperactivity disorder. *Journal of Abnormal Child Psychology* **37**(1): 107–118.

Martos-Perez, J. and R. Ayuda-Pascual (2003). [Autism and hyperlexia]. *Revue Neurologique* **36**(Suppl 1): S57–S60.

Marui, T., O. Hashimoto, *et al.* (2004). Association between the neurofibromatosis-1 (NF1) locus and autism in the Japanese population. *American Journal of Medical Genetics* **131B**(1): 43–47.

Mason, R. A., D. L. Williams, *et al.* (2008). Theory of Mind disruption and recruitment of the right hemisphere during narrative comprehension in autism. *Neuropsychologia* **46**(1): 269–280.

Massey, E. K., W. A. Gebhardt, *et al.* (2008). Adolescent goal content and pursuit: A review of the literature from the past 16 years. *Developmental Review* **28**: 421–460.

Mastrangelo, S. (2009). Play and the child with autism spectrum disorder: From possibilities to practice. *International Journal of Play Therapy* **18**(1): 13–30.

Matano, S. and E. Hirasaki (1997). Volumetric comparisons in the cerebellar complex of anthropoids, with special reference to locomotor types. *American Journal of Physical Anthropology* **103**(2): 173–183.

Materna, S., P. W. Dicke, *et al.* (2008). The posterior superior temporal sulcus is involved in social communication not specific for the eyes. *Neuropsychologia* **46**: 2759–2765.

Matson, J. L. and J. A. Boisjoli (2008). The token economy for children with intellectual disability and/or autism: A review. *Research in Developmental Disabilities* **30**(2): 240–248.

Matson, J. L. and T. Dempsey (2009). The nature and treatment of compulsions, obsessions, and rituals in people with developmental disabilities. *Research in Developmental Disabilities* **30**(3): 603–611.

Matson, J. L. and T. T. Rivet (2008). Characteristics of challenging behaviours in adults with autistic disorder, PDD-NOS, and intellectual disability. *Journal of Intellectual and Developmental Disabilities* **33**(4): 323–329.

Matson, J. L., J. Wilkins, *et al.* (2001). Early identification and diagnosis in autism spectrum disorders in young children and infants: How early is too early? *Research in Autism Spectrum Disorders* **2**(1): 75–84.

Matson, J. L., J. Wilkins, *et al.* (2008). Autism in adults with severe intellectual disability: An empirical study of symptom presentation. *Journal of Intellectual and Developmental Disabilities* **33**(1): 36–42.

Matsumoto, D. and B. Willingham (2009). Spontaneous facial expressions of emotion of congenitally and noncongenitally blind individuals. *Journal of Personality and Social Psychology* **96**(1): 1–10.

Matthew, C. K. (2008). The evolutionary persistence of genes that increase mental disorders risk. *Current Directions in Psychological Science* **17**(6): 395–399.

Matthew, D. A., S. H. Valerie, *et al.* (2010). COMT Val158Met genotype as a risk factor for problem behaviors in youth. *Journal of the American Academy of Child and Adolescent Psychiatry* **49**(8): 841–849.

Mattila, M. L., M. P. Kielinen, *et al.* (2007). An epidemiological and diagnostic study of Asperger syndrome according to four sets of diagnostic criteria. *Journal of the American Academy of Child and Adolescent Psychiatry* **46**(5): 636–646.

Matza, L. S., C. Paramore, *et al.* (2005). A review of the economic burden of ADHD. *Cost Effectiveness and Resource Allocation* **3**: 5.

Maussion, G., J. Carayol, *et al.* (2008). Convergent evidence identifying MAP/microtubule affinity-regulating kinase 1 (MARK1) as a susceptibility gene for autism. *Human Molecular Genetics* **17**(6): 2541–2551.

Mayes, S. D. and S. L. Calhoun (2006). WISC-IV and WISC-III profiles in children with ADHD. *Journal of Attention Disorders* **9**(3): 486–493.

Mayes, S. D. and S. L. Calhoun (2007). WISC-IV and WIAT-II Profiles in children with high-functioning autism. *Journal of Autism and Developmental Disorders* **38**(3): 428–439.

Mayes, S. D., S. L. Calhoun, *et al.* (2001). Does DSM-IV Asperger's disorder exist? *Journal of Abnormal Child Psychology* **29**(3): 263–271.

Mayes, S. D., S. L. Calhoun, *et al.* (2009). ADHD subtypes and comorbid anxiety, depression, and oppositional-defiant disorder: Differences in sleep problems. *Journal of Pediatr Psychology* **34**(3): 328–337.

Mayes, T. A. and R. L. Koegel (2003). Persons with autism and criminal justice. *Journal of Positive Behavior Interventions* **5**(2): 92–100.

Mazza, M., A. De Risio, *et al.* (2001). Selective impairments of theory of mind in people with schizophrenia. *Schizophrenia Research* **47**(2–3): 299–308.

Mbarek, O., S. Marouillat, *et al.* (1999). Association study of the NF1 gene and autistic disorder. *American Journal of Medical Genetics* **88**(6): 729–732.

McAlonan, G. M., J. Suckling, *et al.* (2008). Distinct patterns of grey matter abnormality in high-functioning autism and Asperger's syndrome. *Journal of Child Psychology and Psychiatry* **49**(12): 1287–1295.

McAlonan, G. M., V. Cheung, *et al.* (2005). Mapping the brain in autism: A voxel-based MRI study of volumetric differences and intercorrelations in autism. *Brain* **128**(2): 268–276.

McAlonan, G. M., V. Cheung, *et al.* (2007). Mapping brain structure in attention deficit-hyperactivity disorder: A voxel-based MRI study of regional grey and white matter volume. *Psychiatry Research* **154**(2): 171–180.

McCann, J., S. Peppe, *et al.* (2007). Prosody and its relationship to language in school-aged children with high-functioning autism. *International Journal of Language and Communication Disorders* **42**: 682–702.

McCoy, P. A., Y. Shao, *et al.* (2002). No association between the WNT2 gene and autistic disorder. *American Journal of Medical Genetics* **114**(1):106–109.

McGovern, C. W. and M. Sigman (2005). Continuity and change from early childhood to adolescence in autism. *Journal of Child Psychology and Psychiatry* **46**(4): 401–408.

McGrath, L. M., C. Hutaff-Lee, *et al.* (2008). Children with comorbid speech sound disorder and specific language impairment are at increased risk for attention-deficit/ hyperactivity disorder. *Journal of Abnormal Child Psychology* **36**: 151–163.

McGurk, S. R., K. T. Mueser, *et al.* (2009). Work, recovery, and comorbidity in schizophrenia: A randomized controlled trial of cognitive remediation. *Schizophrenia Bulletin* **35**: 319–335.

McIntosh, D., A. Reichmann-Decker, *et al.* (2006). When the social mirror breaks: Deficits in automatic, but not voluntary, mimicry of emotional facial expressions in autism. *Developmental Science* **9**(3): 295–302.

McKenzie, O., I. Ponte, *et al.* (2007). Aristaless-related homeobox gene, the gene responsible for West syndrome and related disorders, is a Groucho/transducin-like enhancer of split dependent transcriptional repressor. *Neuroscience* **146**(1): 236–247.

McLoughlin, G., A. Ronald, *et al.* (2007). Genetic support for the dual nature of attention deficit hyperactivity disorder: Substantial genetic overlap between the inattentive and hyperactive-impulsive components. *Journal of Abnormal Child Psychology* **35**(6): 999–1008.

McLuhan, M. (1962). *The Gutenberg Galaxy: The Making of Typographic Man.* Toronto: University of Toronto Press.

McNeil, M. C., E. A. Polloway, *et al.* (1984). Feral and isolated children – Historical review and analysis. *Education and Training in Mental Retardation and Developmental Disabilities* **19**: 70–79.

McNulty, J. K., E. M. O'Mara, *et al.* (2008). Benevolent cognitions as a strategy of relationship maintenance: Don't sweat the small stuff…but it is not all small stuff. *Journal of Personality and Social Psychology* **94**(4): 631–646.

Mechanic, D. (1982). The concept of illness behaviour. *Journal of Chronic Disease* **15**: 189–194.

Meilleur, A. A. and E. Fombonne (2009). Regression of language and non-language skills in pervasive developmental disorders. *Journal of Intellectual Disability Research* **53**(2): 115–124.

Meinhardt-Injac, B., M. Persike, *et al.* (2010). The time course of face matching by internal and external features: Effects of context and inversion. *Vision Research* **50**(16): 1598–1611.

Melke, J., B. H. Goubran, *et al.* (2008). Abnormal melatonin synthesis in autism spectrum disorders. *Molecular Psychiatry* **13**(1): 90–98.

Meltzoff, A. and M. Moore (1977). Imitation of facial and manual gestures by human neonates. *Science* **198**(4312): 75–78.

Menzies, L., S. Achard, *et al.* (2007). Neurocognitive endophenotypes of obsessive-compulsive disorder. *Brain* **130**: 3223–3236.

Merin, N., G. S. Young, *et al.* (2007). Visual fixation patterns during reciprocal social interaction distinguish a subgroup of 6-month-old infants at-risk for autism from comparison infants. *Journal of Autism and Developmental Disorders* **37**: 108–121.

Merlo, L. J., H. D. Lehmkuhl, *et al.* (2009). Decreased family accommodation associated with improved therapy outcome in pediatric obsessive-compulsive disorder. *Journal of Consulting and Clinical Psychology* **77**(2): 355–360.

Merritt, M. (2008). Nativism and neurobiology: Representations, representing, and the continuum of cognition. *Review of General Psychology* **12**(2): 181–191.

Merton, R. (1948). The self-fulfilling prophecy. *Antioch Review* **8**: 190–194.

Mervis, C. B., B. F. Robinson, *et al.* (2000). The Williams syndrome cognitive profile. *Brain and Cognition* **44**(3): 604–628.

Meunier, D., S. Achard, *et al.* (2009). Age-related changes in modular organization of human brain functional networks. *NeuroImage* **44**(3): 715–723.

Meyer-Lindenberg, A. (2008). Impact of prosocial neuropeptides on human brain function. *Progress in Brain Research* **170**: 463–470.

Micali, N., S. Chakrabarti, *et al.* (2004). The broad autism phenotype: Findings from an epidemiological survey. *Autism* **8**(1): 21–37.

Miklowitz, D. J., D. A. Axelson, *et al.* (2008). Family-focused treatment for adolescents with bipolar disorder: Results of a 2-year randomized trial. *Archives of General Psychiatry* **65**(9): 1053–1061.

Miklowitz, D. J., D. A. Axelson, *et al.* (2009). Expressed emotion moderates the effects of family-focused treatment for bipolar adolescents. *Journal of the American Academy of Child and Adolescent Psychiatry* **48**(6): 643–651.

Mildenberger, K., M. Noterdaeme, *et al.* (2001). [Behavioral problems in children with specific and pervasive developmental disorders, evaluated with the psychopathology assessment scale (AMDP)]. [German]. *Praxis der Kinderpsychologie und Kinderpsychiatrie* **50**(8): 649–663.

Miles, J. H. and R. E. Hillman (2000). Value of a clinical morphology examination in autism. *American Journal of Medical Genetics* **91**(4): 245–253.

Miles, J. H., L. L. Hadden, *et al.* (2000). Head circumference is an independent clinical finding associated with autism. *American Journal of Medical Genetics* **95**(4): 339–350.

Miles, J. H., T. N. Takahashi, *et al.* (2005). Essential versus complex autism: Definition of fundamental prognostic subtypes. *American Journal of Medical Genetics A* **135**(2): 171–180.

Miller, D. T., Y. Shen, *et al.* (2009). Microdeletion/duplication at 15q13.2q13.3 among individuals with features of autism and other neuropsychiatric disorders. *Journal of Medical Genetics* **46**(4): 242–248.

Miller, G. (1951). *Language and Communication.* New York, NY: McGraw-Hill.

Miller, G. A. (2003). The cognitive revolution: A historical perspective. *Trends in Cognitive Sciences* **7**(3): 141–144.

Miller, M. T., K. Strömland, *et al.* (2005). Autism associated with conditions characterized by developmental errors in early embryogenesis: A mini review. *International Journal of Developmental Neuroscience* **23**(2–3): 201–219.

Miller, P. A. and M. Jansen-op-de-Haar (1997). Emotional, cognitive, behavioral, and temperament characteristics of high-empathy children. *Motivation and Emotion* **21**(1): 109–125.

Miller, T. W., J. T. Nigg, *et al.* (2009). Attention deficit hyperactivity disorder in African American children: What can be concluded from the past ten years? *Clinical Psychology Review* **29**(1): 77–86.

Mills, R. S. L. (2005). Taking stock of the developmental literature on shame. *Developmental Review* **25**(1): 26–63.

Millward, C., M. Ferriter, *et al.* (2008). Gluten- and casein-free diets for autistic spectrum disorder. *Cochrane Database of Systematic Reviews* **16**(2): CD003498.

Milne, E., H. Griffiths, *et al.* (2009). Vision in children and adolescents with autistic spectrum disorder: evidence for reduced convergence. *Journal of Autism and Developmental Disorders* **39**(7): 965–975.

Minio-Paluello, I., S. Baron-Cohen, *et al.* (2009). Absence of embodied empathy during pain observation in Asperger syndrome. *Biological Psychiatry* **65**(1): 55–62.

Miniscalco, C., B. Hagberg, *et al.* (2007). Narrative skills, cognitive profiles and neuropsychiatric disorders in 7–8-year-old children with late developing language. *International Journal of Language and Communication Disorders* **42**(6): 665–681.

Minshawi, N. F. (2008). Behavioral assessment and treatment of self-injurious behavior in autism. *Child and Adolescent Psychiatric Clinics of North America* **17**(4): 875–886, x.

Mitchell, J. P., C. N. Macrae, *et al.* (2006). Dissociable medial prefrontal contributions to judgments of similar and dissimilar others. *Neuron* **50**(4): 655–663.

Miyashita, T., N. Ichinohe, *et al.* (2007). Differential modes of termination of amygdalothalamic and amygdalocortical projections in the monkey. *The Journal of Comparative Neurology* **502**(2): 309–324.

Mizuhiki, T., B. J. Richmond, *et al.* (2007). Differences between single neuronal responses in anterior and posterior insula during multi-trial reward schedules. *Neuroscience Research* **58**(Suppl 1): S170–S170.

Molina, J. D., J. M. Ruata, *et al.* (1986). Letter: Is there a right-hemisphere dysfunction in Asperger's syndrome. *British Journal of Psychiatry* **148**: 745–746.

Moll, G. H., H. Heinrich, *et al.* (2003). Methylphenidate and intracortical excitability: Opposite effects in healthy subjects and attention-deficit hyperactivity disorder. *Acta Psychiatrica Scandinavica* **107**(1): 69–72.

Montag, C., F. Schubert, *et al.* (2008). Prefrontal cortex glutamate correlates with mental perspective-taking. *PLoS ONE* **3**(12): e3890.

Montag, C., J. Gallinat, *et al.* (2008). Theodor Lipps and the concept of empathy: 1851–1914. *American Journal of Psychiatry* **165**(10): 1261.

Montes, G. and J. S. Halterman (2008). Association of childhood autism spectrum disorders and loss of family income. *Pediatrics* **121**(4): e821–e826.

Montgomery, K. J. and J. V. Haxby (2008). Mirror neuron system differentially activated by facial expressions and social hand gestures: A functional magnetic resonance imaging study. *Journal of Cognitive Neuroscience* **20**(10): 1866–1877.

Moody, E. J., D. N. McIntosh, *et al.* (2007). More than mere mimicry? The influence of emotion on rapid facial reactions to faces. *Emotion* **7**: 447–457.

Mooney, E. L., K. M. Gray, *et al.* (2009). Factor analytic study of repetitive behaviours in young children with Pervasive Developmental Disorders. *Journal of Autism and Developmental Disorders* **39**(5): 765–774.

Moore, V. and S. Goodson (2003). How well does early diagnosis of autism stand the test of time? Follow-up study of children assessed for autism at age 2 and development of an early diagnostic service. *Autism* **7**(1): 47–63.

Mooshagian, E., M. Iacoboni, *et al.* (2009). Spatial attention and interhemispheric visuomotor integration in the absence of the corpus callosum. *Neuropsychologia* **47**(3): 933–937.

Moran, J. M., G. S. Wig, *et al.* (2004). Neural correlates of humor detection and appreciation. *NeuroImage* **21**(3): 1055–1060.

Mordekar, S. R., M. Prendergast, *et al.* (2009). Corticosteroid treatment of behaviour, language and motor regression in childhood disintegrative disorder. *European Journal of Paediatric Neurology* **13**(4): 367–369.

Mordre, M., B. Groholt, *et al.* (2011). The impact of ADHD and conduct disorder in childhood on adult delinquency: A 30 years follow-up study using official crime records. *BMC Psychiatry* **11**(1): 57.

Moretti, P., S. U. Peters, *et al.* (2008). Autistic symptoms, developmental regression, mental retardation, epilepsy, and dyskinesias in CNS folate deficiency. *Journal of Autism and Developmental Disorders* **38**(6): 1170–1177.

Morgan, C., M. Charalambides, *et al.* (2010). Migration, ethnicity, and psychosis: Toward a sociodevelopmental model. *Schizophrenia Bulletin* **36**(4): 655–664.

Morgan, D., K. A. Grant, *et al.* (2002). Social dominance in monkeys: Dopamine D2 receptors and cocaine self-administration. *Nature Neuroscience* **5**(2): 169–174.

Mori, K., T. Hashimoto, *et al.* (2001). [Proton magnetic resonance spectroscopy of the autistic brain]. [Japanese]. *No to Hattatsu [Brain and Development]* **33**(4): 329–335.

Moriguchi, Y., T. Ohnishi, *et al.* (2009). The human mirror neuron system in a population with deficient self-awareness: An fMRI study in alexithymia. *Hum Brain Mapping* **30**(7): 2063–2076.

Morin, A. and J. Michaud (2007). Self-awareness and the left inferior frontal gyrus: Inner speech use during self-related processing. *Brain Research Bulletin* **74**(6): 387–396.

Morita, T., S. Itakura, *et al.* (2008). The role of the right prefrontal cortex in self-evaluation of the face: A functional magnetic resonance imaging study. *Journal of Cognitive Neuroscience* **20**(2): 342–355.

Morrow, J. D., B. Y. Whitman, *et al.* (1990). Autistic disorder in Sotos syndrome: A case report. *European Journal of Pediatrics* **149**(8): 567–569.

Mosconi, M. W., H. Cody-Hazlett, *et al.* (2009). Longitudinal study of amygdala volume and joint attention in 2- to 4-year-old children with autism. *Archives of General Psychiatry* **66**(5): 509–516.

Mosconi, M. W., M. Kay, *et al.* (2010). Neurobehavioral abnormalities in first-degree relatives of individuals with autism. *Archives of General Psychiatry* **67**(8): 830–840.

Mosconi, M. W., P. B. Mack, *et al.* (2005). Taking an intentional stance on eye-gaze shifts: A functional neuroimaging study of social perception in children. *NeuroImage* **27**(1): 247–252.

Mosconi, M. W., R. J. Steven, *et al.* (2009). The Social Orienting Continuum and Response Scale (SOC-RS): A dimensional measure for preschool-aged children. *Journal of Autism and Developmental Disorders* **39**(2): 242–250.

Moser, H. W., G. V. Raymond, *et al.* (2005). Adrenoleukodystrophy: New approaches to a neurodegenerative disease. *Journal of the American Medical Association* **294**(24): 3131–3134.

Moss, J., I. Magiati, *et al.* (2008). Stability of the autism diagnostic interview-revised from pre-school to elementary school age in children with autism spectrum disorders. *Autism and Developmental Disorders* **38**(6): 1081–1091.

Moss, S. B., R. Nair, *et al.* (2007). Attention deficit/hyperactivity disorder in adults. *Diagnostic and Statistical Manual of Mental Disorders* **34**(3): 445–473.

Mostofsky, S. H., A. L. Reiss, *et al.* (1998). Evaluation of cerebellar size in attention-deficit hyperactivity disorder. *Journal of Child Neurology* **13**(9): 434–439.

Mostofsky, S. H., M. P. Burgess, *et al.* (2007). Increased motor cortex white matter volume predicts motor impairment in autism. *Brain* **130**(8): 2117–2122.

Mostofsky, S. H., R. Bunoski, *et al.* (2004). Challenging behavior in CHARGE syndrome. *Mental Health Aspects of Developmental Disabilities* **7**: 41–52.

Mostofsky, S. H., S. K. Powell, *et al.* (2009). Decreased connectivity and cerebellar activity in autism during motor task performance. *Brain* **132**(9): 2413–2425.

Moulding, R., M. Kyrios, *et al.* (2007). Autogenous and reactive obsessions: Further evidence for a two-factor model of obsessions. *Journal of Anxiety Disorders* **21**(5): 677–690.

Moulson, M. C., N. A. Fox, *et al.* (2009). Early adverse experiences and the neurobiology of facial emotion processing. *Developmental Psychology* **45**(1): 17–30.

Mount, R. H., R. P. Hastings, *et al.* (2001). Behavioural and emotional features in Rett syndrome. *Disability and Rehabilitation: An International Multidisciplinary Journal* **23**(3–4): 129–138.

Mount, R. H., T. Charman, *et al.* (2003). Features of autism in Rett syndrome and severe mental retardation. *Journal of Autism and Developmental Disorders* **33**(4): 435–442.

Mouridsen, S. E., B. Rich, *et al.* (1998). Validity of childhood disintegrative psychosis: General findings of a long-term follow-up study. *British Journal of Psychiatry* **172**: 263–267.

Mouridsen, S. E., B. Rich, *et al.* (2007a). Autoimmune diseases in parents of children with infantile autism: A case-control study. *Developmental Medicine and Child Neurology* **49**(6): 429–432.

Mouridsen, S. E., B. Rich, *et al.* (2008). Psychiatric disorders in the parents of individuals with infantile autism: A case-control study. *Psychopathology* **14**(1): 5–12.

Mouridsen, S. E., B. Rich, *et al.* (2010). Sibling sex ratio of individuals diagnosed with autism spectrum disorder as children. *Developmental Medicine and Child Neurology* **52**(3):289–292.

Mouridsen, S. E., H. Bronnum-Hansen, *et al.* (2008). Mortality and causes of death in autism spectrum disorders: An update. *Autism* **12**(4): 403–414.

Mraz, K. D., J. Green, *et al.* (2007). Correlates of head circumference growth in infants later diagnosed with autism spectrum disorders. *Journal of Child Neurology* **22**(6): 700–713.

Mugno, D., L. Ruta, *et al.* (2007). Impairment of quality of life in parents of children and adolescents with pervasive developmental disorder. *Health and Quality of Life Outcomes* **5**: 22.

Muhle, R., S. V. Trentacoste, *et al.* (2004). The genetics of autism. *Pediatrics* **113**(5): e472–e486.

Mukaddes, N. M. (2002). Gender identity problems in autistic children. *Child Care, Health and Development* **28**(6): 529–532.

Mukaddes, N. M. and S. Herguner (2007). Autistic disorder and 22q11.2 duplication. *The World Journal of Biological Psychiatry* **8**(2): 127–130.

Mukaddes, N. M. and R. Fateh (2010). High rates of psychiatric co-morbidity in individuals with Asperger's disorder. *World Journal of Biological Psychiatry* **11**(2): 486–492.

Mukaddes, N. M., A. Kilincaslan, *et al.* (2007). Autism in visually impaired individuals. *Psychiatry and Clinical Neurosciences* **61**(1): 39–44.

Mukaetova-Ladinska, E. B., H. Arnold, *et al.* (2004). Depletion of MAP2 expression and laminar cytoarchitectonic changes in dorsolateral prefrontal cortex in adult autistic individuals. *Neuropathology and Applied Neurobiology* **30**(6): 615–623.

Muldoon, O. T., K. Schmid, *et al.* (2009). Political violence and psychological well-being: The role of social identity. *Applied Psychology: An International Review* **58**: 129–145.

Muller, E., A. Schuler, *et al.* (2008). Social challenges and supports from the perspective of individuals with Asperger syndrome and other autism spectrum disabilities. *Autism* **12**(2): 173–190.

Mulligan, A., R. J. Anney, *et al.* (2009). Autism symptoms in Attention-Deficit/Hyperactivity Disorder: A familial trait which correlates with conduct, oppositional defiant, language and motor disorders. *Journal of Autism and Developmental Disorders* **39**(2): 197–209.

Muncer, S. J. and J. Ling (2006). Psychometric analysis of the empathy quotient (EQ) scale. *Personality and Individual Differences* **40**(6): 1111–1119.

Mundy, P. (2003). Annotation: The neural basis of social impairments in autism: The role of the dorsalmedial-frontal cortex and anterior cingulate system. *Journal of Child Psychology and Psychiatry* **44**(6): 793–789.

Mundy, P., L. Sullivan, *et al.* (2009). A parallel and distributed-processing model of joint attention, social cognition and autism. *Autism Research* **2**(1): 2–21.

Munesue, T., Y. Ono, *et al.* (2008). High prevalence of bipolar disorder comorbidity in adolescents and young adults with high-functioning autism spectrum disorder: A preliminary study of 44 outpatients. *Journal of Affective Disorders* **111**(2–3): 170–175.

Muñoz-Yunta, J. A., T. Ortiz, *et al.* (2008). Magnetoencephalographic pattern of epileptiform activity in children with early-onset autism spectrum disorders. *Clinical Neurophysiology* **119**(3): 626–634.

Munson, J., S. Faja, *et al.* (2008). Neurocognitive predictors of social and communicative developmental trajectories in preschoolers with autism spectrum disorders. *Journal of the International Neuropsychological Society* **14**(6): 956–966.

Murphy, D. G. M., J. Beecham, *et al.* (2011). Autism in adults. New biologicial findings and their translational implications to the cost of clinical services. *Brain Research* **1380**: 22–33.

Murphy, D. G., E. Daly, *et al.* (2006). Cortical serotonin 5-HT2A receptor binding and social communication in adults with Asperger's syndrome: An in vivo SPECT study. *American Journal of Psychiatry* **163**(5): 934–936.

Murphy, D. G., H. D. Critchley, *et al.* (2002). Asperger syndrome: A proton magnetic resonance spectroscopy study of brain. *Archives of General Psychiatry* **59**(10): 885–891.

Murphy, J. V., J. W. Wheless, *et al.* (2000). Left vagal nerve stimulation in six patients with hypothalamic hamartomas. *Pediatric Neurology* **23**(2): 167–168.

Murphy, M., P. F. Bolton, *et al.* (2000). Personality traits of the relatives of autistic probands. *Psychological Medicine* **30**(6): 1411–1424.

Murphy, P., N. Brady, *et al.* (2009). No evidence for impaired perception of biological motion in adults with autistic spectrum disorders. *Neuropsychologia* **47**(14): 3225–3235.

Murray, E. A. and B. J. Richmond (2001). Role of perirhinal cortex in object perception, memory, and associations. *Current Opinion in Neurobiology* **11**(2): 188–193.

Murthy, P. M., S. M. Kudlur, *et al.* (2009). A clinical overview of fetal alcohol syndrome. *Addictive Disorders and Their Treatment* **8**: 1–12.

Muscarella, L. A., V. Guarnieri, *et al.* (2007). HOXA1 gene variants influence head growth rates in humans. *American Journal of Medical Genetics B: Neuropsychiatric Genetics* **144B**(3): 388–390.

Muzykewicz, D. A., P. Newberry, *et al.* (2007). Psychiatric comorbid conditions in a clinic population of 241 patients with tuberous sclerosis complex. *Epilepsy and Behavior* **11**(4): 506–513.

Myers, B. J., V. H. Mackintosh, *et al.* (2009). My greatest joy and my greatest heart ache: Parents' own words on how having a child in the autism spectrum has affected their lives and their families' lives. *Research in Autism Spectrum Disorders* **3**(3): 670–684.

Naber, F. B. A., S. H. N. Swinkels, *et al.* (2007). Attachment in toddlers with autism and other developmental disorders. *Journal of Autism and Developmental Disorders* **37**(6): 1123–1138.

Naber, F., M. J. Bakermans-Kranenburg, *et al.* (2008a). Joint attention development in toddlers with autism. *European Child and Adolescent Psychiatry* **17**(3): 143–152.

Naber, F., M. J. Bakermans-Kranenburg, *et al.* (2008b). Play behavior and attachment in toddlers with autism. *Journal of Autism and Developmental Disorders* **38**(5): 857–866.

Nagel, T. (1979). *Mortal Questions.* Cambridge: Cambridge University Press.

Nagy, E. (2008). Innate intersubjectivity: Newborns' sensitivity to communication disturbance. *Developmental Psychology* **44**(6): 1779–1784.

Najib, A., J. P. Lorberbaum, *et al.* (2004). Regional brain activity in women grieving a romantic relationship breakup. *American Journal of Psychiatry* **161**(12): 2245–2256.

Nakamine, A., L. Ouchanov, *et al.* (2008). Duplication of 17(p11.2p11.2) in a male child with autism and severe language delay. *American Journal of Medical Genetics A* **146A**(5): 636–643.

Nan, Y., A. D. Friederici, *et al.* (2008). Dissociable pitch processing mechanisms in lexical and melodic contexts revealed by ERPs. *Brain Research* **1263**: 104–113.

Nandagopal, J. J., M. P. DelBello, *et al.* (2009). Pharmacologic treatment of pediatric bipolar disorder. *Child and Adolescent Psychiatric Clinics of North America* **18**(2): 455–469, x.

Naqvi, N. H. and A. Bechara (2009). The hidden island of addiction: The insula. *Trends in Neurosciences* **32**(1): 56–67.

Naqvi, S., T. Cole, *et al.* (2000). Cole-Hughes macrocephaly syndrome and associated autistic manifestations. *American Journal of Medical Genetics* **94**(2): 149–152.

Nardi, A. E., F. L. Lopes, *et al.* (2009). Panic disorder and social anxiety disorder subtypes in a caffeine challenge test. *Psychiatry Research* **169**(2): 149–153.

Narendran, R., W. G. Frankle, *et al.* (2005). Altered prefrontal dopaminergic function in chronic recreational ketamine users. *American Journal of Psychiatry* **162**: 2352–2359.

Nation, K. and S. Penny (2008). Sensitivity to eye gaze in autism: Is it normal? Is it automatic? Is it social? *Development and Psychopathology* **20**(1): 79–97.

National Autistic Society (2007). *Advocacy and Autism.* London: National Autistic Society.

National Autistic Society (2011). Asperger syndrome: the triad of impairments. Available at www.autism.org.uk/working-with/education/educational-professionals-in-schools/breaking-down-barriers-to-learning/asperger-syndrome-the-triad-of-impairments.aspx, accessed on 5 October 2011.

National Initiative for Autism: Screening and Assessment (2003). *National Autism Plan for Children.* London: National Autistic Society.

National Institute for Health and Clinical Excellence (NICE) (2008). *Attention Deficit Hyperactivity Disorder: Diagnosis and Management of ADHD in Children, Young People and Adults.* London: NICE.

National Skin Centre (1995). Approach to Congenital Pigmentary Disorders. Available at www.nsc.gov.sg/showpage.asp?id=229, accessed on 28 July 2011.

Naylor, P., J. Dawson, *et al.* (in press) Bullying of pupils with and without SEN. *Journal of Adolescence.*

Nazarali, N., C. M. Glazebrook, *et al.* (2009). Movement planning and reprogramming in individuals with autism. *Journal of Autism and Developmental Disorders* **39**(10): 1401–1411.

Neff, L. A. and B. R. Karney (2005). To know you is to love you: The implications of global adoration and specific accuracy for marital relationships. *Journal of Personality and Social Psychology* **88**: 480–497.

Nemeth, D. J., K., V. I. Balogh, *et al.* (2010). Learning in autism: Implicitly superb. *PLoS ONE* **5**(7): e11731.

Nente, F., R. Carrillo-Mezo, *et al.* (2007). Pathological hyperfamiliarity for others from a left anterior cingulate lesion. *Journal of Neuropsychiatry and Clinical Neurosciences* **19**: 345–346.

Neubauer, A. C. and A. Fink (2003). Intelligence and neural efficiency: Measures of brain activation versus measures of functional connectivity in the brain. *Intelligence* **37**(2): 223–229.

Neuman, R. J., R. D. Todd, *et al.* (1999). Evaluation of ADHD typology in three contrasting samples: A latent class approach. *Journal of the American Academy of Child and Adolescent Psychiatry* **38**(1): 25–33.

New York State Department of Health (1999). Clinical Practice Guideline, Report of the Recommendations, Autism/Pervasive Developmental Disorders, Assessment and Intervention for Young Children (Age 0–3 Years). Available at www.health.ny.gov/community/infants_children/early_intervention/disorders/autism/ch4_pt1.htm, accessed on 16 September 2011.

Newman, S. S. and M. Ghaziuddin (2008). Violent crime in Asperger syndrome: The role of psychiatric comorbidity. *Journal of Autism and Developmental Disorders* **38**(10): 1848–1852.

Newman, T. B. (2003). The power of stories over statistics. *British Medical Journal* **327**(7429): 1424–1427.

Newman, T., D. Macomber, *et al.* (2007). Hyperlexia in children with autism spectrum disorders. *Journal of Autism and Developmental Disorders* **37**(4): 760–774.

Newmeyer, A., T. Degrauw, *et al.* (2007). Screening of male patients with autism spectrum disorder for creatine transporter deficiency. *Neuropediatrics* **38**(6): 310–312.

Newson, E., M. Dawson, *et al.* (1982). *The Natural History of Able Autistic People: Their Management and Functioning in Social Context.* Nottingham: University of Nottingham Child Development Unit.

Nicolopoulou, A. (2010). Play and narrative in the process of development: Commonalities, differences, and interrelations. *Cognitive Development* **20**(4): 495–502.

Nietzsche, F. (1888). The twilight of the idols. In W. Kaufman (ed.) (1968). *The Portable Nietzsche.* Princeton, NJ: Princeton University Press.

Nijmeijer, J. S., P. J. Hoekstra, *et al.* (2009). PDD symptoms in ADHD: An independent familial trait? *Journal of Abnormal Child Psychology* **37**(3): 443–453.

Nikolov, R. N., K. E. Bearss, *et al.* (2009). Gastrointestinal symptoms in a sample of children with pervasive developmental disorders. *Journal of Autism and Developmental Disorders* **39**(3): 405–413.

Nikopoulos, C. K. and M. Keenan (2004). Effects of video modeling on social initiations by children with autism. *Journal of Applied Behavior Analysis* **37**(1): 93–96.

Nikopoulos, C. K. and M. Keenan (2007). Using video modeling to teach complex social sequences to children with autism. *Journal of Autism and Developmental Disorders* **37**(4): 678–693.

Nishiyama, T., H. Taniai, *et al.* (2009). Genetic correlation between autistic traits and IQ in a population-based sample of twins with autism spectrum disorders (ASDs). *Journal of Human Genetics* **54**(1): 56–61.

Nitschke, J. B., E. E. Nelson, *et al.* (2008). Orbitofrontal cortex tracks positive mood in mothers viewing pictures of their newborn infants. *NeuroImage* **21**(2): 583–592.

Nixon, G. M., J. M. Thompson, *et al.* (2008). Short sleep duration in middle childhood: Risk factors and consequences. *Sleep* **31**(1): 71–78.

Nobili, L. (2007). Nocturnal frontal lobe epilepsy and non-rapid eye movement sleep parasomnias: Differences and similarities. *Sleep Medicine Reviews* **11**(4): 251–254.

Noonan, S. K., F. Haist, et al. (2009). Aberrant functional connectivity in autism: Evidence from low-frequency BOLD signal fluctuations. Brain Research 1262: 48–63.

Noor, A., P. J. Gianakopoulos, et al. (2009). Copy number variation analysis and sequencing of the X-linked mental retardation gene TSPAN7/TM4SF2 in patients with autism spectrum disorder. Psychiatric Genetics 19(3): 154–155.

Nordahl, C. W., D. Dierker, et al. (2007). Cortical folding abnormalities in autism revealed by surface-based morphometry. Journal of Neuroscience 27(43): 11,725–11,735.

Nordin, V. and C. Gillberg (1996). Autism spectrum disorders in children with physical or mental disability or both. I: Clinical and epidemiological aspects. Developmental Medicine and Child Neurology 38(4): 297–313.

Norwalk, K., J. M. Norvilitis, et al. (2009). Symptomatology and its relationship to factors associated with college adjustment. Journal of Attention Disorders 13(3): 251–258.

Numis, A. L., P. Major, et al. (2011). Identification of risk factors for autism spectrum disorders in tuberous sclerosis complex. Neurology 76(11): 981–987.

Nummenmaa, L., J. Hirvonen, et al. (2008). Is emotional contagion special? An fMRI study on neural systems for affective and cognitive empathy. NeuroImage 43(3): 571–580.

Nunez, J. M., B. J. Casey, et al. (2005). Intentional false responding shares neural substrates with response conflict and cognitive control. NeuroImage 25(1): 267–277.

Nyden, A., K. J. Myren, et al. (2007). Long-term psychosocial and health economy consequences of ADHD, autism, and reading-writing disorder: A prospective service evaluation project. Journal of Attention Disorders 12(2): 141–148.

O'Connell, R. G., M. A. Bellgrove, et al. (2009). The neural correlates of deficient error awareness in attention-deficit hyperactivity disorder (ADHD). Neuropsychologia 47(4): 1149–1159.

O'Donovan, M. C., N. J. Craddock, et al. (2009). Genetics of psychosis: Insights from views across the genome. Human Genetics 126(1): 3–12.

O'Sullivan, S. S., A. H. Evans, et al. (2009). Dopamine dysregulation syndrome: An overview of its epidemiology, mechanisms and management. CNS Drugs 23(2): 157–170.

Oberman, L. M. and V. S. Ramachandran (2007). The simulating social mind: The role of the mirror neuron system and simulation in the social and communicative deficits of autism spectrum disorders. Psychological Bulletin 133(2): 310–327.

Oberman, L. M. and V. S. Ramachandran (2008). Preliminary evidence for deficits in multisensory integration in autism spectrum disorders: The mirror neuron hypothesis. Social Neuroscience 3(3–4): 348–355.

Obradovi, J., N.R. Bush, et al. (2011). The interactive effect of marital conflict and stress reactivity on externalizing and internalizing symptoms: The role of laboratory stressors. Pluess 101–114.

Office for Disability Issues (2008). Independent Living: A Cross-Government Strategy about Independent Living for Disabled People. London: Office for Disability Issues.

Ogdie, M. N., S. E. Fisher, et al. (2004). Attention deficit hyperactivity disorder: fine mapping supports linkage to 5p13, 6q12, 16p13, and 17p11. American Journal of Human Genetics 75(4): 661–668.

Okamoto-Barth, S., J. Call, et al. (2007). Great apes' understanding of other individuals' line of sight. Psychological Science 18: 462–468.

Olaniyan, O., S. dosReis, et al. (2007). Community perspectives of childhood behavioral problems and ADHD among African American parents. Ambulatory Pediatrics 7(3): 226–231.

Olesen, P. J., H. Westerberg, et al. (2004). Increased prefrontal and parietal activity after training of working memory. Nature Neuroscience 7(1): 75–79.

Oliver-Africano, P., D. Murphy, et al. (2009). Aggressive behaviour in adults with intellectual disability: Defining the role of drug treatment. CNS Drugs 23(11): 903–913.

Oller, D., P. Niyogic, et al. (2010). Automated vocal analysis of naturalistic recordings from children with autism, language delay, and typical development. Proceedings of the National Academy of Sciences of the United States of America 107(30): 13,354–13,359.

Oner, O., H. Devrimci-Ozguven, et al. (2007). MR spectroscopy: higher right anterior cingulate N-acetylaspartate/choline ratio in Asperger syndrome compared with healthy controls. American Journal of Neuroradiology 28(8): 1494–1498.

Oosterling, I. J., S. H. Swinkels, et al. (2009). Comparative analysis of three screening instruments for autism spectrum disorder in toddlers at high risk. Journal of Autism and Developmental Disorders 39: 879–909.

Oppenheim, D., N. Koren-Karie, et al. (2009). Maternal insightfulness and resolution of the diagnosis are associated with secure attachment in preschoolers with autism spectrum disorders. Child Development 80: 519–527.

Oram Cardy, J. E., E. J. Flagg, et al. (2008). Auditory evoked fields predict language ability and impairment in children. International Journal of Psychophysiology 68(2): 170–175.

Ornoy, A. (2003). The impact of intrauterine exposure versus postnatal environment in neurodevelopmental toxicity: Long-term neurobehavioral studies in children at risk for developmental disorders. Toxicology Letters 140–141: 171–181.

Ornoy, A. (2009). Valproic acid in pregnancy: How much are we endangering the embryo and fetus? Reproductive Toxicology 28(1): 1–10.

Orphanet (2008). Autism – Facial port-wine stain. Available at www.orpha.net/consor/cgi-bin/Disease_Search.php?lng=EN&data_id=16743&Disease_Disease_Search_diseaseGroup=autism&Disease_Disease_Search_diseaseType=Pat&Disease(s)%20concerned=Autism---facial-port-wine-stain&title=Autism---facial-port-wine-stain&search=Disease_Search_Simple, accessed on 28 July 2011.

Orr, J. M. and D. H. Weissman (2009). DH anterior cingulate cortex makes 2 contributions to minimizing distraction. Cerebral Cortex 19(3): 703–711.

Orsmond, G. I., H. Y. Kuo, et al. (2009). Siblings of individuals with an autism spectrum disorder: Sibling relationships and wellbeing in adolescence and adulthood. Autism 13(1): 59–80.

Osaka, N., Y. Otsuka, et al. (2007). Transcranial magnetic stimulation (TMS) applied to left dorsolateral prefrontal cortex disrupts verbal working memory performance in humans. Neuroscience Letters 418(3): 232–235.

Osborne, J. P. and F. J. K. O'Callaghan (2003). The management of tuberous sclerosis. Current Paediatrics 13(5): 365–370.

Ospina, M. B., S. J. Krebs, et al. (2008). Behavioural and developmental interventions for autism spectrum disorder: A clinical systematic review. PLoS ONE 3(11): e3755.

Otsuka, H., M. Harada, et al. (1999). Brain metabolites in the hippocampus-amygdala region and cerebellum in autism: An 1H-MR spectroscopy study. Neuroradiology 41: 517–519.

Ou, Z. M., J. S. M. P. Berg, et al. (2008). Microduplications of 22q11.2 are frequently inherited and are associated with variable phenotypes. Genetics in Medicine 10(4): 267–277.

Ouellette-Kuntz, H., H. Coo, et al. (2007). Trends in special education code assignment for autism: Implications for prevalence estimates. Journal of Autism and Developmental Disorders 37(10): 1941–1948.

Owens, J. A., R. Maxim, et al. (2000). Parental and self-report of sleep in children with attention-deficit/hyperactivity disorder. Archives of Pediatrics and Adolescent Medicine 154(6): 549–555.

Owens, J., R. B. Sangal, et al. (2009). Subjective and objective measures of sleep in children with attention-deficit/hyperactivity disorder. Sleep Medicine 10(4): 446–456.

Ozdemir, S. (2008). The effectiveness of social stories on decreasing disruptive behaviors of children with autism: Three case studies. Journal of Autism and Developmental Disorders 38(9): 1689–1696.

Ozgen, H. M., J. W. Hop, et al. (2008). Minor physical anomalies in autism: A meta-analysis. Molecular Psychiatry 15(3): 300–307.

Ozonoff, S. and J. N. Miller (1996). An exploration of right-hemisphere contributions to the pragmatic impairments of autism. Brain and Language 52(3): 411–434.

Ozonoff, S., M. South, et al. (2000). DSM-IV-defined Asperger syndrome: Cognitive, behavioral and early history differentiation from high-functioning autism. Autism 4(1): 29–46.

Page, T. (2000). Metabolic approaches to the treatment of autism spectrum disorders. Journal of Autism and Developmental Disorders 30(5): 463–469.

Page, T. and C. Moseley (2002). Metabolic treatment of hyperuricosuric autism. Progress in Neuro-Psychopharmacology and Biological Psychiatry 26(2): 397–400.

Palermo, M.T. (2003). Preventing filicide in families with autistic children. International Journal of Offender Therapy and Comparative Criminology 47(1): 1–57.

Palmer, R. F., S. Blanchard, et al. (2009). Proximity to point sources of environmental mercury release as a predictor of autism prevalence. Health Place 15(1): 18–24.

Palminteri, S., T. Boraud, et al. (2009). Brain hemispheres selectively track the expected value of contralateral options. Journal of Neuroscience 29(43): 13,465–13,472.

Palomo, R., M. Thompson, et al. (2008). A case study of childhood disintegrative disorder using systematic analysis of family home movies. Journal of Autism and Developmental Disorders 38: 1853–1858.

Panayiotou, G. (2008). Emotional dimensions reflected in ratings of affective scripts. Personality and Individual Differences 44(8): 1795–1806.

Pancrudo, J., S. Shanske, et al. (2007). Mitochondrial myopathy associated with a novel mutation in mtDNA. Neuromuscular Disorders 17(8): 651–654.

Pandi-Perumal, S. R., V. Srinivasan, et al. (2007). Role of the melatonin system in the control of sleep: therapeutic implications. CNS Drugs 21(12): 995–1018.

Panerai, S., M. Zingale, et al. (2009). Special education versus inclusive education: The role of the TEACCH program. Journal of Autism and Developmental Disorders 39(6): 874–882.

Panos, P. T., S. S. Porter, et al. (2001). An evaluation of a case of agenesis of the corpus callosum with Rourke's nonverbal learning disorder model. Archives of Clinical Neuropsychology 16(5): 507–521.

Panzer, A. and M. Viljoen (2005). Supportive neurodevelopmental evidence for ADHD as a developmental disorder. Medical Hypotheses 64(4): 755–758.

Papez, J. (1937). A proposed mechanism of emotion. Archives of Neurology and Psychiatry 79: 217–224.

Parfit, D. (1971). Personal identity. The Philosophical Review 80(1): 3–27.

Parikh, M. S., A. Kolevzon, et al. (2008). Psychopharmacology of aggression in children and adolescents with autism: A critical review of efficacy and tolerability. Journal of Child and Adolescent Psychopharmacology 18(2): 157–178.

Parise, C. V. and C. Spence (2009). When birds of a feather flock together: Synesthetic correspondences modulate audiovisual integration in non-synesthetes. PLoS ONE 4(5): e5664.

Parmeggiani, A., A. Posar, et al. (2007). Epilepsy in patients with pervasive developmental disorder not otherwise specified. Journal of Child Neurology 22(10): 1198–1203.

Parr, J. (2008). Autism. Clinical Evidence [Online]. pii: 0322.

Parr, L. A., B. M. Waller, et al. (2005). Emotional communication in primates: Implications for neurobiology. Current Opinion in Neurobiology 15(6): 716–720.

Pascual, R., E. Verdu, et al. (1999). Early social isolation decreases the expression of calbindin D-28k in rat cerebellar Purkinje cells. Neuroscience Letters 272(3): 171–174.

Pascual, R., M. C. Hervias, et al. (1998). Purkinje cell impairment induced by early movement restriction. Biology of the Neonate 73(1): 47–51.

Pascual-Castroviejo, I., C. Roche, et al. (1998). Hypomelanosis of ITO. A study of 76 infantile cases. Brain and Development 20(1): 36–43.

Pasupathi, M. and T. Hoyt (2009). The development of narrative identity in late adolescence and emergent adulthood: The continued importance of listeners. Developmental Psychology 45(2): 558–574.

Paul, L. K., D. Lancker-Sidtis, et al. (2003). Communicative deficits in agenesis of the corpus callosum: Nonliteral language and affective prosody. Brain and Language 85(2): 313–324.

Paulus, M. P., J. S. Feinstein, et al. (2004). Trend detection via temporal difference model predicts inferior prefrontal cortex activation during acquisition of advantageous action selection. NeuroImage 21(2): 733–743.

Peay, H. L., P. M. Veach, et al. (2008). Psychiatric disorders in clinical genetics I: Addressing family histories of psychiatric illness. Journal of Genetic Counseling 17(1): 6–17.

Peirce, C. (1958). Selected Writings. New York, NY: Dover.

Pellegrini, A. D. (2008). The roles of aggressive and affiliative behaviors in resource control: A behavioral ecological perspective. Developmental Review 28(4): 461–487.

Pellegrini, A. D., D. Dupuis, et al. (2007). Play in evolution and development. Developmental Review 27: 261–276.

Pelphrey, K. A. and E. J. Carter (2008). Brain mechanisms for social perception: Lessons from autism and typical development. Annals of the New York Academy of Sciences Learning, Skill Acquisition, Reading, and Dyslexia 1145: 283–299.

Pelphrey, K. A., J. P. Morris, et al. (2007). Perception of dynamic changes in facial affect and identity in autism. Social Cognitive and Affective Neuroscience 2(2): 140–149.

Perez-Jimenez, A., F. J. Villarejo, et al. (2003). Continuous giggling and autistic disorder associated with hypothalamic hamartoma. Epileptic Disorders 5(1): 31–37.

Perlbarg, V. and G. Marrelec (2008). Contribution of exploratory methods to the investigation of extended large-scale brain networks in functional MRI: Methodologies, results, and challenges. International Journal of Biomedical Imaging. doi:10.1155/2008/218519.

Perlov, E., P. Alexandra, *et al.* (2008). Spectroscopic findings in attention-deficit/hyperactivity disorder: Review and meta-analysis. *World Journal of Biological Psychiatry* **10**(2): 355–365.

Perry, E. K., M. L. Lee, *et al.* (2001). Cholinergic activity in autism: Abnormalities in the cerebral cortex and basal forebrain. *American Journal of Psychiatry* **158**: 1058–1066.

Pertusa, A., M. A. Fullana, *et al.* (2008). Compulsive hoarding: OCD symptom, distinct clinical syndrome, or both? *American Journal of Psychiatry* **165**: 1289–1298.

Peru, A., A. Beltramello, *et al.* (2003). Temporary and permanent signs of interhemispheric disconnection after traumatic brain injury. *Neuropsychologia* **41**(5): 634–643.

Pescucci, C., I. Meloni, *et al.* (2003). Chromosome 2 deletion encompassing the MAP2 gene in a patient with autism and Rett-like features. *Clincal Genetics* **64**(6): 497–501.

Peterson, C. C., H. M. Wellman, *et al.* (2005). Steps in theory-of-mind development for children with deafness or autism. *Child Development* **76**: 502–517.

Peters-Scheffer, N., R. Didden, *et al.* (2008). The behavior flexibility rating scale-revised (BFRS-R): Factor analysis, internal consistency, inter-rater and intra-rater reliability, and convergent validity. *Research in Developmental Disabilities* **29**(5): 398–407.

Pham, A. V., J. S. Carlson, *et al.* (2010). Ethnic differences in parental beliefs of attention-deficit/hyperactivity disorder and treatment. *Journal of Attention Disorders* **13**(6): 584–591.

Phan, K. L., C. S. Sripada, *et al.* (2010). Reputation for reciprocity engages the brain reward center. *Proceedings of the National Academy of Sciences* **107**(29): 13,099–13,104.

Phan, K. L., D. A. Fitzgerald, *et al.* (2005). Neural substrates for voluntary suppression of negative affect: a functional magnetic resonance imaging study. *Biological Psychiatry* **57**: 210–219.

Phan, K. L., D. A. Fitzgerald, *et al.* (2006). Association between amygdala hyperactivity to harsh faces and severity of social anxiety in generalized social phobia. *Biological Psychiatry* **59**(5): 424–429.

Philip, W. (2004). Fostering communication and shared play between mainstream peers and children with autism: Approaches, outcomes and experiences. *British Journal of Special Education* **31**(4): 215–222.

Philippi, A., E. Roschmann, *et al.* (2005). Haplotypes in the gene encoding protein kinase c-beta (PRKCB1) on chromosome 16 are associated with autism. *Molecular Psychiatry* **10**(10): 950–960.

Phillips, L. K. and L. J. Seidman (2008). Emotion processing in persons at risk for schizophrenia. *Schizophrenia Bulletin* **34**(5): 888–903.

Pierce, K. and E. Courchesne (2000). Exploring the neurofunctional organization of face processing in autism. *Archives of General Psychiatry* **57**(4): 344–346.

Pierce, K. and E. Redcay (2008). Fusiform function in children with an autism spectrum disorder is a matter of 'who'. *Biological Psychiatry* **64**(7): 552–560.

Pierce, K., C. Carter, *et al.* (2011). Detecting, Studying, and Treating Autism Early: The One-Year Well-Baby Check-Up Approach. *The Journal of Pediatrics* **159**(3): 458–465.

Pierce, K., D. Conant, *et al.* (2011). Preference for geometric patterns early in life as a risk factor for autism. *Archives of General Psychiatry* **68**(1): 101–109.

Pierce, K., R. A. Muller, *et al.* (2001). Face processing occurs outside the fusiform 'face area' in autism: evidence from functional MRI. *Brain* **124**(10): 10–73.

Pietz, J., F. Ebinger, *et al.* (2003). Prosopagnosia in a preschool child with Asperger syndrome. *Developmental Medicine and Child Neurology* **45**: 55–57.

Piggot, J., D. Shirinyan, *et al.* (2009). Neural systems approaches to the neurogenetics of autism spectrum disorders. *Neuroscience* **164**(1): 247–256.

Pika, S. and K. Zuberbuhler (2007). Social games between bonobos and humans: Evidence for shared intentionality? *American Journal of Primatology* **70**(3): 207–210.

Pinillos-Pison, R., M. T. Llorente-Cereza, *et al.* (2009). Congenital infection by cytomegalovirus: A review of our 18 years' experience of diagnoses. *Revista Neurologica* **48**(7): 349–353.

Pinkham, A. E., J. B. Hopfinger, *et al.* (2008). Neural bases for impaired social cognition in schizophrenia and autism spectrum disorders. *Schizophrenia Research* **99**(1–3): 164–175.

Pinto, D., A. T. Pagnamenta, *et al.* (2010). Functional impact of global rare copy number variation in autism spectrum disorders. *Nature* **466**(7304): 368–372.

Plantin, L. and K. Daneback (2009). Parenthood, information and support on the internet: A literature review of research on parents and professionals online. *BMC Family Practice* **10**: 34.

Plessen, K. J. M., R. P. Bansal, *et al.* (2006). Hippocampus and amygdala morphology in attention-deficit/hyperactivity disorder. *Archives of General Psychiatry* **63**(7): 795–807.

Plioplys, S., D. W. Dunn, *et al.* (2007). 10-year research update review: Psychiatric problems in children with epilepsy. *Journal of the American Academy of Child and Adolescent Psychiatry* **46**(11): 1389–1402.

Pliszka, S. (2007). Practice parameter for the assessment and treatment of children and adolescents with attention-deficit/hyperactivity disorder. *Journal of the American Academy of Child and Adolescent Psychiatry* **46**: 894–921.

Plotnik, J. M., F. B. M. de Waal, *et al.* (2006). Self-recognition in an Asian elephant. *Proceedings of the National Academy of Sciences of the United States of America* **103**(45): 17,053–17,057.

Pluess, M. and Belsky, J. (2011). Prenatal programming of postnatal plasticity? *Development and Psychopathology* **23**(1): 29–38.

Polanczyk, G., M. S. de Lima, *et al.* (2007). The worldwide prevalence of ADHD: A systematic review and metaregression analysis. *American Journal of Psychiatry* **164**: 942–948.

Poldrack, R. A. (2008). The role of fMRI in cognitive neuroscience: Where do we stand? *Current Opinion in Neurobiology* **18**(2): 223–227.

Polezzi, D., I. Daum, *et al.* (2008). Mentalizing in economic decision-making. *Behavioural Brain Research* **190**(2): 218–223.

Pollard, K. S., S. R. Salama, *et al.* (2006). An RNA gene expressed during cortical development evolved rapidly in humans. *Nature* **443**(7108): 167–172.

Porter, M. A., M. Coltheart, *et al.* (2008). Theory of mind in Williams syndrome assessed using a nonverbal task. *Journal of Autism and Developmental Disorders* **38**(5): 806–814.

Posey, D. J., M. G. Aman, *et al.* (2007). Positive effects of methylphenidate on inattention and hyperactivity in pervasive developmental disorders: An analysis of secondary measures. *Biological Psychiatry* **61**(4): 538–544.

Posner, K., G. A. Melvin, *et al.* (2007). Clinical presentation of attention-deficit/hyperactivity disorder in preschool children: The Preschoolers with Attention-Deficit/Hyperactivity Disorder Treatment Study (PATS). *Journal of Child and Adolescent Psychopharmacology* **17**(5): 547–562.

Posner, M. I. and M. K. Rothbart (2007). Research on attention networks as a model for the integration of psychological science. *Annual Review of Psychology* **58**: 1–23.

Posner, M. I. and S. E. Petersen (1990). The attention system of the human brain. *Annual Review of Neuroscience* **13**: 25–42.

Posserud, B., A. J. Lundervold, *et al.* (2008). Factor analysis of the Autism Spectrum Screening Questionnaire. *Autism* **12**(1): 99–112.

Posserud, M. B., A. J. Lundervold, *et al.* (2006). Autistic features in a total population of 7–9-year-old children assessed by the ASSQ (Autism Spectrum Screening Questionnaire). *Journal of Child Psychology and Psychiatry* **47**(2): 167–175.

Pottie, C. G., J. Cohen, *et al.* (2009). Parenting a child with autism: Contextual factors associated with enhanced daily parental mood. *Journal of Pediatric Psychology* **34**(4): 419–429.

Prather, M. D., P. Lavenex, *et al.* (2001). Increased social fear and decreased fear of objects in monkeys with neonatal amygdala lesions. *Neuroscience* **106**(4): 653–658.

Prehn-Kristensen, A., C. Wiesner, *et al.* (2009). Induction of empathy by the smell of anxiety. *PLoS ONE* **4**(6): e5987.

Premack, D. and G. Woodruff (1978). Does the chimpanzee have a theory of mind? *Behavioral and Brain Science* **1**(4): 515–526.

Prendergast, M. A., W. J. Jackson, *et al.* (1998). Age-related differences in distractibility and response to methylphenidate in monkeys. *Cerebral Cortex* **8**(2): 164–172.

Prendeville, J. A., P. A. Prelock, *et al.* (2006). Peer play interventions to support the social competence of children with autism spectrum disorders. *Seminars in Speech and Language* **27**(1): 32–46.

Preston, S. D. and F. B. M. de Waal (2002). Empathy: Its ultimate and proximate bases. *Behavioral and Brain Science* **25**(1): 1–71.

Price, L. S. (2001). Finding the man in the soldier-rapist: Some reflections on comprehension and accountability. *Women's Studies International Forum* **24**(2): 211–227.

Prichard, J. C. (1835). *Moral Insanity*. London: Sherwood, Gilbert & Piper.

Prior, H., A. Schwarz, *et al.* (2008). Mirror-induced behavior in the magpie: Evidence of self-recognition. *PLoS Biology* **6**(8): e202.

Prior, M., R. Eisenmajer, *et al.* (1998). Are there subgroups within the autistic spectrum? A cluster analysis of a group of children with autistic spectrum disorders. *Journal of Child Psychology and Psychiatry* **39**: 893–902.

Punshon, C., P. Skirrow, *et al.* (2009). The not guilty verdict: Psychological reactions to a diagnosis of Asperger syndrome in adulthood. *Autism* **13**(3): 265–283.

Purcell, A. E., O. H. Jeon, *et al.* (2001). Postmortem brain abnormalities of the glutamate neurotransmitter system in autism. *Neurology* **57**(9):1618–1628.

Pyers, J. and A. Senghas (2009). Language promotes false-belief understanding: Evidence from learners of a new sign language. *Psychological Science* **20**(7): 805–812.

Qin, S., E. J. Hermans, *et al.* (2009). Acute psychological stress reduces working memory-related activity in the dorsolateral prefrontal cortex. *Biological Psychiatry* **66**(1): 25–32.

Quigg, M. M., R. S. M. Rust, *et al.* (2006). Clinical findings of the phakomatoses: Hypomelanosis of Ito. *Neurology* **66**(12): E45.

Quigley, J., K. M. Lommel, *et al.* (2009). Catatonia in an adolescent with Asperger's disorder. *Journal of Child and Adolescent Psychopharmacology* **19**(1): 93–96.

Quirmbach, L. M., A. J. Lincoln, *et al.* (2009). Social stories: Mechanisms of effectiveness in increasing game play skills in children diagnosed with autism spectrum disorder using a pretest posttest repeated measures randomized control group design. *Journal of Autism and Developmental Disorders* **39**(2): 299–321.

Rabiner, D. L., D. W. Murray, *et al.* (2010). A randomized trial of two promising computer-based interventions for students with attention difficulties. *Journal of Abnormal Child Psychology* **38**(1): 131–142.

Ragland, J. D., R. C. Gur, *et al.* (2004). Event-related fMRI of frontotemporal activity during word encoding and recognition in schizophrenia. *American Journal of Psychiatry* **161**: 1004–1015.

Ramnani, N. and A. M. Owen (2004). Anterior prefrontal cortex: insights into function from anatomy and neuroimaging. *Nature Reviews Neuroscience* **5**(3): 184–194.

Ranta, M. E., D. Crocetti, *et al.* (2009). Manual MRI parcellation of the frontal lobe. *Psychiatry Research: Neuroimaging* **172**(2): 147–154.

Rapin, I. (1996). Practitioner review: Developmental language disorders: A clinical update. *Journal of Child Psychology and Psychiatry* **37**(6): 643–655.

Rapin, I. and M. Dunn (2003). Update on the language disorders of individuals on the autistic spectrum. *Brain and Development* **25**(3): 166–172.

Rapin, I. and R. F. Tuchman (2008). What is new in autism? *Current Opinion in Neurology* **21**(2): 143–149.

Rapin, I., M. Dunn, *et al.* (2009). Subtypes of language disorders in school-age children with autism. *Developmental Neuropsychology* **34**(1): 66–84.

Rapoport, J. L. and N. Gogtay (2011). Childhood onset schizophrenia: Support for a progressive neurodevelopmental disorder. *International Journal of Developmental Neuroscience* **29**(3): 251–258.

Rapoport, J., A. Chavez, *et al.* (2009). Autism spectrum disorders and childhood-onset schizophrenia: Clinical and biological contributions to a relation revisited. *Journal of the American Academy of Child and Adolescent Psychiatry* **48**(1): 10–18.

Raposo, A., S. Han, *et al.* (2009). Ventrolateral prefrontal cortex and self-initiated semantic elaboration during memory retrieval. *Neuropsychologia* **47**(11): 2261–2271.

Rauh, V. A., R. Garfinkel, *et al.* (2006). Impact of prenatal chlorpyrifos exposure on neurodevelopment in the first 3 years of life among inner-city children. *Pediatrics* **118**(6): e1845–e1859.

Ravaja, N., T. Kauppinen, *et al.* (2000). Relationships between hostility and physiological coronary heart disease risk factors in young adults: The moderating influence of depressive tendencies. *Psychological Medicine* **30**(2): 381–393.

Re, A. M., M. Pedron, *et al.* (2007). Expressive writing difficulties in children described as exhibiting ADHD symptoms. *Journal of Learning Disabilities* **40**(3): 244–255.

Realmuto, G. M. and L. A. Ruble (1999). Sexual behaviors in autism: Problems of definition and management. *Journal of Autism and Developmental Disorders* **29**(2): 121–127.

Reaven, J. A., S. L. Hepburn, *et al.* (2008). Use of the ADOS and ADI-R in children with psychosis: importance of clinical judgment. *Clinical Child Psycholology and Psychiatry* **13**(1): 81–94.

Redcay, E. (2008). The superior temporal sulcus performs a common function for social and speech perception: Implications for the emergence of autism. *Neuroscience and Biobehavioral Reviews* **32**(1): 123–142.

Reddy, L. A., E. Newman, *et al.* (2010). Concurrent validity of the pediatric attention disorders diagnostic screener for children with ADHD. *Child Neuropsychology* **16**(5): 478–493.

Reed, C. L., P. M. Beall, *et al.* (2007). Brief report: Perception of body posture – what individuals with autism spectrum disorder might be missing. *Journal of Autism and Developmental Disorders* **37**(8): 1576–1584.

Reeves, S. J., M. A. Mehta, *et al.* (2007). Striatal dopamine (D2) receptor availability predicts socially desirable responding. *NeuroImage* **34**(4): 1782–1789.

Reichenberg, A. P., R. M. Gross, *et al.* (2006). Advancing paternal age and autism. *Archives of General Psychiatry* **63**(9): 1026–1032.

Reichow, B. and M. Wolery (2009). Comprehensive synthesis of early intensive behavioral interventions for young children with autism based on the UCLA young autism project model. *Journal of Autism and Developmental Disorders* **39**(1): 23–41.

Reiersen, A. M., J. N. Constantino, *et al.* (2007). Autistic traits in a population-based ADHD twin sample. *Journal of Child Psychology and Psychiatry* **48**(5): 464–472.

Reiersen, A. M., J. N. Constantino, *et al.* (2008). Evidence for shared genetic influences on self-reported ADHD and autistic symptoms in young adult Australian twins. *Twin Research and Human Genetics* **11**(6): 579–585.

Reilly, J. S., J. Stiles, *et al.* (1995). Affective facial expression in infants with focal brain damage. *Neuropsychologia* **33**(1): 83–99.

Reimer, B., L. A. D'Ambrosio, *et al.* (2007). Task-induced fatigue and collisions in adult drivers with attention deficit hyperactivity disorder. *Traffic Injury Prevention* **8**(3): 290–299.

Reiss, A. L. (2009). Childhood developmental disorders: An academic and clinical convergence point for psychiatry, neurology, psychology and pediatrics. *Journal of Child Psychology and Psychiatry* **50**(1–2): 87–98.

Reiss, D. and L. Marino (2001). Mirror self-recognition in the bottlenose dolphin: A case of cognitive convergence. *Proceedings of the National Academy of Sciences of the United States of America* **98**(10): 5937–5942.

Renieri, A., F. Mari, *et al.* (2009). Diagnostic criteria for the Zappella variant of Rett syndrome (the preserved speech variant). *Brain and Development* **31**(3): 208–216.

Rennie, J., S. Burman-Roy, *et al.* (2010). Neonatal jaundice: summary of NICE guidance. *British Medical Journal* **340**: c2409.

Renty, J. and H. Roeyers (2006). Satisfaction with formal support and education for children with autism spectrum disorder: The voices of the parents. *Child Care, Health and Development* **32**(3): 371–385.

Research Autism (2011). Treatments and Therapies for Autism Spectrum Disorders Currently Under Scientific Evaluation by Research Autism. Available at www.researchautism.net/interventionlist.ikml, accessed on 28 July 2011.

Reverberi, C., A. Toraldo, *et al.* (2005). Better without (lateral) frontal cortex? Insight problems solved by frontal patients. *Brain* **128**(12): 2882–2890.

Reynolds, S. and S. J. Lane (2008). Diagnostic validity of sensory over-responsivity: A review of the literature and case reports. *Journal of Autism and Developmental Disorders* **38**(3): 516–529.

Rhoades, R., A. Scarpa, *et al.* (2007). The importance of physician knowledge of autism spectrum disorder: Results of a parent survey. *BMC Pediatrics* **7**: 37.

Riba, J., U. Krämer, *et al.* (2008). Dopamine agonist increases risk taking but blunts reward-related brain activity. *PLoS ONE* **3**(6): e2479.

Riby, D. M. and M. J. Doherty (2009). Tracking eye movements proves informative for the study of gaze direction detection in autism. *Research in Autism Spectrum Disorders* **3**(3): 723–733.

Riby, D. M. and P. J. Hancock (2009a). Do faces capture the attention of individuals with Williams syndrome or autism? Evidence from tracking eye movements. *Journal of Autism and Developmental Disorders* **39**(3): 421–431.

Riby, D. M. and P. J. Hancock (2009b). Looking at movies and cartoons: Eye-tracking evidence from Williams syndrome and autism. *Journal of Intellectual Disability Research* **53**(2): 169–181.

Rice, F., G. T. Harold, *et al.* (2010). The links between prenatal stress and offspring development and psychopathology: Disentangling environmental and inherited influences. *Psychological Medicine* **40**(2): 1–11.

Riches, N. G., T. Loucas, *et al.* (2010). Sentence repetition in adolescents with specific language impairments and autism: An investigation of complex syntax. *International Journal of Language and Communication Disorders* **45**(1): 1–22.

Richler, J., S. L. Bishop, *et al.* (2007). Restricted and repetitive behaviors in young children with autism spectrum disorders. *Journal of Autism and Developmental Disorders* **37**(1): 73–85.

Ridley, R. M. (1994). The psychology of perserverative and stereotyped behaviour. *Progress in Neurobiology* **44**(2): 221–231.

Riem, M. M. E., M. J. Bakermans-Kranenburg, *et al.* (2011). Oxytocin modulates amygdala, insula, and inferior frontal gyrus responses to infant crying: A randomized controlled trial. *Biological Psychiatry* **70**(3): 291–297.

Riikonen, R., I. Salonen, *et al.* (1999). Brain perfusion SPECT and MRI in foetal alcohol syndrome. *Developmental Medicine and Child Neurology* **41**(10): 652–659.

Riley, C., G. J. DuPaul, *et al.* (2008). Combined type versus ADHD predominantly hyperactive-impulsive type: Is there a difference in functional impairment? *Journal of Developmental and Behavioral Pediatrics* **29**(4): 270–275.

Rimland, B. (1964). *Infantile Autism*. New York, NY: Appleton Century Crofts.

Rinehart, N. J., B. J. Tonge, *et al.* (2006a). Gait function in children with high functioning autism and Asperger's: Evidence for basal-ganglia and cerebellar involvement. *European Journal of Child and Adolescent Psychiatry* **15**(5), 256–264.

Rinehart, N. J., B. J. Tonge, *et al.* (2006b). Gait function in newly diagnosed children with autism: Cerebellar and basal ganglia related motor disorder. *Developmental Medicine and Child Neurology* **48**(10): 819–824.

Rinehart, N. J., J. L. Bradshaw, *et al.* (2000). Atypical interference of local detail on global processing in high-functioning autism and Asperger's disorder. *Journal of Child Psychology and Psychiatry* **41**(6): 769–778.

Rinehart, N. J., M. A. Bellgrove, *et al.* (2006). An examination of movement kinematics in young people with high-functioning autism and Asperger's disorder: Further evidence for a motor planning deficit. *Journal of Autism and Developmental Disorders* **36**(6): 757–767.

Ring, H., M. Woodbury-Smith, *et al.* (2008). Clinical heterogeneity among people with high functioning autism spectrum conditions: Evidence favouring a continuous severity gradient. *Behavioral and Brain Functions* **4**: 11.

Ritvo, E. R., B. J. Freeman, *et al.* (1989). The UCLA-University of Utah epidemiologic survey of autism: prevalence. *American Journal of Psychiatry* **146**(2): 194–199.

Riva, D. (2000). Cerebellar contribution to behaviour and cognition in children. *Journal of Neurolinguistics* **13**(2–3): 215–225.

Rizzolatti, G., M. Fabbri-Destro, *et al.* (2009). Mirror neurons and their clinical relevance. *Nature Clinical Practice Neurology* **5**(1): 24–34.

Rizzolatti, G., P. F. Ferrari, *et al.* (2006). The inferior parietal lobule: Where action becomes perception. *Novartis Foundation Symposium* **270**: 129–140.

Roberts, J. and M. Prior (2006). *A Review of the Research to Identify the Most Effective Models of Practice in Early Intervention of Children with Autism Spectrum Disorders.* Canberra: Australian Government Department of Health and Ageing.

Roberts, R. E., C. R. Roberts, *et al.* (2009). One-year incidence of psychiatric disorders and associated risk factors among adolescents in the community. *Journal of Child Psychology and Psychiatry* **50**(4): 405–415.

Robins, D. L., D. Fein, *et al.* (2001a). Reply to Charman *et al.*'s commentary on the Modified Checklist for Autism in Toddlers. *Journal of Autism and Developmental Disorders* **31**(2): 149–151.

Robins, D. L., D. Fein, *et al.* (2001b). The Modified Checklist for Autism in Toddlers: An initial study investigating the early detection of autism and pervasive developmental disorders. *Journal of Autism and Developmental Disorders* **31**(2): 131–144.

Rochelle, K. S. and J. B. Talcott (2006). Impaired balance in developmental dyslexia? A meta-analysis of the contending evidence. *Journal of Child Psychology and Psychiatry* **47**: 1159–1166.

Rockwell, T. (2008). Dynamic empathy: A new formulation for the simulation theory of mind reading. *Cognitive Systems Research* **9**(1–2): 52–63.

Rodriguez, A., J. Olsen, *et al.* (2009). Is prenatal alcohol exposure related to inattention and hyperactivity symptoms in children? Disentangling the effects of social adversity. *Journal of Child Psychology and Psychiatry* **50**(9): 1073–1083.

Rogers, K., I. Dziobek, *et al.* (2007). Who cares? Revisiting empathy in Asperger syndrome. *Journal of Autism and Developmental Disorders* **37**(4): 709–715.

Rogers, S. J. and S. Newhart-Larson (1989). Characteristics of infantile autism in five children with Leber's congenital amaurosis. *Developmental Medicine and Child Neurology* **31**(5): 598–608.

Rojas, D. C., E. Peterson, *et al.* (2006). Regional gray matter volumetric changes in autism associated with social and repetitive behavior symptoms. *BMC Psychiatry* **6**: 56.

Rolls, E. T. (2000). The orbitofrontal cortex and reward. *Cerebral Cortex* **10**(3): 284–294.

Roman, G. C. (2007). Autism: Transient in utero hypothyroxinemia related to maternal flavonoid ingestion during pregnancy and to other environmental antithyroid agents. *Journal of the Neurological Sciences* **262**(1–2): 15–26.

Romanski, L. M. (2007). Representation and integration of auditory and visual stimuli in the primate ventral lateral prefrontal cortex. *Cerebral Cortex* **17**(Suppl 1): i61–i69.

Romeo, R., M. Knapp, *et al.* (2009). The treatment of challenging behaviour in intellectual disabilities: Cost-effectiveness analysis. *Journal of Intellectual Disability Research* **53**(7): 633–643.

Rommelse, N. N., M. E. Altink, *et al.* (2008). Relationship between endophenotype and phenotype in ADHD. *Behavioural and Brain Functions* **4**: 4.

Rommelse, N. N., M. E. Altink, *et al.* (2009). Comorbid problems in ADHD: Degree of association, shared endophenotypes, and formation of distinct subtypes. Implications for a future DSM. *Journal of Abnormal Child Psychology* **37**(6): 793–804.

Roper, L., P. Arnold, *et al.* (2003). Co-occurrence of autism and deafness: Diagnostic considerations. *Autism* **7**(3): 245–253.

Rorty, A. (ed.) (1980). *Explaining Emotions.* Berkeley, CA: University of California Press.

Rosen, J. L., T. J. Miller, *et al.* (2006). Comorbid diagnoses in patients meeting criteria for the schizophrenia prodrome. *Schizophrenia Research* **85**(1–3): 124–131.

Rosenberg, R. E., D. S. Mandell, *et al.* (2010). Psychotropic medication use among children with autism spectrum disorders enrolled in a national registry, 2007–2008. *Journal of Autism and Developmental Disorders* **40**(3): 342–351.

Rosenberg, R. E., J. K. Law, *et al.* (2009). Characteristics and concordance of autism spectrum disorders among 277 twin pairs. *Archives of Pediatrics and Adolescent Medicine* **163**(10): 907–914.

Ross, A. O. (1967). The effects of short-term social and sensory isolation upon behavior, EEG and averaged evoked potentials in PPPIES. *Physiology and Behavior* **2**(2): 145–151.

Rourke, B. P. and K. D. Tsatsanis (2000). Syndrome of nonverbal learning difficulties and Asperger syndrome. In A. Klin, F. Volkmar, *et al.* (eds) *Asperger Syndrome.* New York, NY: Guilford Press.

Rourke, B. P., J. E. Del Dotto, *et al.* (1990). Nonverbal learning disabilities: The syndrome and a case study. *Journal of School Psychology* **28**: 361–385.

Roux, S., N. Bruneau, *et al.* (1997). Bioclinical profiles of autism and other developmental disorders using a multivariate statistical approach. *Biological Psychiatry* **42**(12): 1148–1156.

Roy, M., A. Lebuis A, *et al.* (2011). The modulation of pain by attention and emotion: A dissociation of perceptual and spinal nociceptive processes. *European Journal of Pain* **15**(6): 641.e1–641.e10.

Royal College of Obstetricians and Gynaecologists (2010). *Neonatal Jaundice.* London: National Institute for Health and Clinical Excellence.

Royet, J. P., O. Koenig, *et al.* (1999). Functional anatomy of perceptual and semantic processing of odors. *Journal of Cognitive Neuroscience* **11**(1): 94–109.

Roza, S. J., E. A. P. Steegers, *et al.* (2008). What is spared by fetal brain-sparing? Fetal circulatory redistribution and behavioral problems in the general population. *American Journal of Epidemiology* **68**(10): 1145–1152.

Rubinsten, O. and A. Henik (2009). Developmental dyscalculia: Heterogeneity might not mean different mechanisms. *Trends in Cognitive Sciences* **13**(2): 92–99.

Ruesch, J. and G. Bateson (1951). *Communication: The Social Matrix of Psychiatry.* New York, NY: W. W. Norton.

Rumsey, J. M., N. Andreasen, *et al.* (1986). Thought, language, communication and affective flattening in autistic adults. *Archives of General Psychiatry* **43**(8): 771–777.

Ruppert, V. and B. Maisch (2003). Genetics of human hypertension. *Herz* **28**(8): 655–662.

Russell, D., C. E. Cutrona, *et al.* (1984). Social and emotional loneliness: An examination of Weiss's typology of loneliness. *Journal of Personality and Social Psychology* **46**(6): 1313–1321.

Russell, H. F., D. Wallis, *et al.* (2006). Increased prevalence of ADHD in Turner syndrome with no evidence of imprinting effects. *Journal of Pediatric Psychology* **31**(9): 945–955.

Russell, J., C. Jarrold, *et al.* (1999). Two intact executive capacities in children with autism: Implications for the core executive dysfunctions in the disorder. *Journal of Autism and Developmental Disorders* **29**(2): 103–112.

Russell, M. (2006). *Husserl: A Guide for the Perplexed.* London: Continuum.

Russell, T. A., U. Schmidt, *et al.* (2009). Aspects of social cognition in anorexia nervosa: Affective and cognitive theory of mind. *Psychiatry Research* **168**(3): 181–185.

Russo, G. S., D. A. Backus, *et al.* (2002). Neural activity in monkey dorsal and ventral cingulate motor areas: comparison with the supplementary motor area. *Journal of Neurophysiology* **88**(5): 2612–2629.

Russo, N., T. Flanagan, *et al.* (2007). Deconstructing executive deficits among persons with autism: Implications for cognitive neuroscience. *Brain and Cognition* **65**(1): 77–86.

Ruta, D., D. Mugno, *et al.* (2010). Obsessive-compulsive traits in children and adolescents with Asperger syndrome. *European Child and Adolescent Psychiatry* **19**(1): 17–24.

Ruta, L., E. Ingudomnukul, *et al.* (2011). Increased serum androstenedione in adults with autism spectrum conditions. *Psychoneuroendocrinology* **36**(8): 1154–1163.

Rutgers, A. H., M. H. van IJzendoorn, *et al.* (2007). Autism and attachment: The Attachment Q-Sort. *Autism* **11**(2): 187–200.

Rutgers, A. H., M. J. Bakermans-Kranenburg, *et al.* (2004). Autism and attachment: A meta-analytic review. *Journal of Child Psychology and Psychiatry* **45**(6): 1123–1134.

Rutherford, M. D. and A. M. Towns (2008). Scan path differences and similarities during emotion perception in those with and without autism spectrum disorders. *Journal of Autism and Developmental Disorders* **38**(7): 1371–1381.

Rutherford, M. D. and K. M. Krysko (2008). Eye direction, not movement direction, predicts attention shifts in those with autism spectrum disorders. *Journal of Autism and Developmental Disorders* **38**(10): 1958–1965.

Rutherford, M. D., E. D. Richards, *et al.* (2007). Evidence of a divided-attention advantage in autism. *Cognitive Neuropsychology* **24**(5): 505–515.

Rutter, M., J. Kreppner, *et al.* (2007). Early adolescent outcomes of institutionally deprived and non-deprived adoptees. III. Quasi-autism. *Journal of Child Psychology and Psychiatry* **48**(12): 1200–1207.

Rutter, M., J. Kreppner, *et al.* (2009). Lecture: attachment insecurity, disinhibited attachment, and attachment disorders: Where do research findings leave the concepts? *Journal of Child Psychology and Psychiatry* **50**(5): 529–543.

Rutter, M., L. Andersen-Wood, *et al.* (1999). Quasi-autistic patterns following severe early global privation. English and Romanian Adoptees (ERA) Study Team. *Journal of Child Psychology and Psychiatry and Allied Disciplines* **40**(4): 537–549.

Ryan, S. and U. Räisänen (2008). 'It's like you are just a spectator in this thing': Experiencing social life the 'aspie' way. *Emotion, Space and Society* **1**(2): 135–143.

Ryburn, B., V. Anderson, *et al.* (2009). Asperger syndrome: How does it relate to non-verbal learning disability? *Journal of Neuropsychology* **3**(1): 107–123.

Rypma, B. and V. Prabhakaran (2003). When less is more and when more is more: The mediating roles of capacity and speed in brain-behavior efficiency. *Intelligence* **37**(2): 207–222.

Sabbagh, M. A. (2004). Understanding orbitofrontal contributions to theory-of-mind reasoning: Implications for autism. *Brain and Cognition* **55**(1): 209–219.

Sabbagh, M. A., M. C. Moulson, *et al.* (2004). Neural correlates of mental state decoding in human adults: An event-related potential study. *Journal of Cognitive Neuroscience* **16**(3): 415–426.

Sacco, R., R. Militerni, *et al.* (2007). Clinical, morphological, and biochemical correlates of head circumference in autism. *Biological Psychiatry* **62**(9): 1038–1047.

Sacco, T. and B. Sacchetti (2010). Role of secondary sensory cortices in emotional memory storage and retrieval in rats. *Science* **329**(5992): 649–656.

Sacnacchal, C., J. Forget, *et al.* (2003). Vigabatrin and newer interventions in succinic semialdehyde dehydrogenase deficiency. *Annals of Neurology* **54**(Suppl 6): S66–S72.

Sahiner, B., H.-P. Chan, *et al.* (2008). Classifier performance prediction for computer-aided diagnosis using a limited dataset. *Medical Physics* **35**(4): 1559–1570.

Sahyoun, C., I. Soulières, *et al.* (2009). Cognitive differences in pictorial reasoning between high-functioning autism and Aspergers syndrome. *Journal of Autism and Developmental Disorders* **39**(7): 1014–1023.

Sakai, Y., C. A. Shaw *et al.* (2011). Protein interactome reveals converging molecular pathways among autism disorders. *Science Translational Medicine* **3**(86): 86ra49.

Saldana, D., R. M. Alvarez, *et al.* (2009). Objective and subjective quality of life in adults with autism spectrum disorders in southern Spain. *Autism* **13**(3): 303–316.

Sallee, F. R., A. Lyne, *et al.* (2009). Long-term safety and efficacy of guanfacine extended release in children and adolescents with attention-deficit/hyperactivity disorder. *Journal of Child and Adolescent Psychopharmacology* **19**(5): 215–226.

Salmond, C. H., F. Vargha-Khadem, *et al.* (2007). Heterogeneity in the patterns of neural abnormality in autistic spectrum disorders: Evidence from ERP and MRI. *Cortex* **43**(6): 686–699.

Salter, G., A. Seigal, *et al.* (2008). Can autistic children read the mind of an animated triangle? *Autism* **12**(4): 349–371.

Samson, D., I. A. Apperly, *et al.* (2004). Left temporoparietal junction is necessary for representing someone else's belief. *Nature Neuroscience* **7**(5): 499–500.

Samson, D., I. A. Apperly, *et al.* (2005). Seeing it my way: A case of a selective deficit in inhibiting self-perspective. *Brain* **128**(5): 1102–1111.

Samuels, J. F., O. J. Bienvenu, *et al.* (2008). Prevalence and correlates of hoarding behavior in a community-based sample. *Behaviour Research and Therapy* **46**(7): 836–844.

Sanchez-Valle, E., M. Posada, *et al.* (2008). Estimating the burden of disease for autism spectrum disorders in Spain in 2003. *Journal of Autism and Developmental Disorders* **38**(2): 288–296.

Sandberg, D. E. and H. F. Meyer-Bahlburg (1994). Variability in middle childhood play behavior: Effects of gender, age, and family background. *Archives of Sexual Behavior* **23**(6): 645–663.

Sanders, L. D., V. Ameral, *et al.* (2009). Event-related potentials index segmentation of nonsense sounds. *Neuropsychologia* **47**(4): 1183–1186.

Sanders, S. J., A. G. Ercan-Sencicek, *et al.* (2011). Multiple recurrent de novo CNVs, including duplications of the 7q11.23 Williams syndrome region, are strongly associated with autism. *Neuron* **70**(5): 863–885.

Santos, A., A. Meyer-Lindenberg, *et al.* (2010). Absence of racial, but not gender, stereotyping in Williams syndrome children. *Current Biology* **20**(7): R307–R308.

Saresella, M., I. Marventano, *et al.* (2009). An autistic endophenotype results in complex immune dysfunction in healthy siblings of autistic children. *Biological Psychiatry* **66**(10): 978–984.

Sartre, J. P. (1969). *Being and Nothingness.* London: Routledge.

Sartre, J. P. (2004). *Critique of Dialectical Reason.* London: Verso.

Sasson, N., N. Tsuchiya, *et al.* (2007). Orienting to social stimuli differentiates social cognitive impairment in autism and schizophrenia. *Neuropsychologia* **45**(11): 2580–2588.

Satpute, A. B. and M. D. Lieberman (2006). Integrating automatic and controlled processes into neurocognitive models of social cognition. *Brain Research* **1079**(1): 86–97.

Savazzi, S., M. Fabri, *et al.* (2007). Interhemispheric transfer following callosotomy in humans: Role of the superior colliculus. *Neuropsychologia* **45**(11): 2417–2427.

Savic, I. and B. Gulyas (2000). PET shows that odors are processed both ipsilaterally and contralaterally to the stimulated nostril. *Neuroreport* **11**(13): 2861–2866.

Scalais, E., C. Nuttin, *et al.* (2005). Developmental dyspraxia. *Current Management in Child Neurology*.

Scambler, D. J., S. Hepburn, *et al.* (2007). Emotional responsivity in children with autism, children with other developmental disabilities, and children with typical development. *Journal of Autism and Developmental Disorders* **37**(3): 553–563.

Schachter, H. (2002). How efficacious and safe is short-term methylphenidate for the treatment of attention-deficit disorder in children and adolescents? A meta-analysis. *Canadian Medical Association Journal* **165**(11): 1475–1488.

Schachter, H., A. Girardi, *et al.* (2008). Effects of school-based interventions on mental health stigmatization: A systematic review. *Child and Adolescent Psychiatry and Mental Health* **2**(1): 18.

Schaefer, S. M., D. C. Jackson, *et al.* (2008). Modulation of amygdalar activity by the conscious regulation of negative emotion. *Journal of Cognitive Neuroscience* **14**(6): 913–921.

Scheeren, A. M. and J. E. A. Stauder (2008). Broader autism phenotype in parents of autistic children: Reality or myth? *Journal of Autism and Developmental Disorders* **38**(2): 276–287.

Schell-Apacik, C. C., K. Wagner, *et al.* (2008). Agenesis and dysgenesis of the corpus callosum: Clinical, genetic and neuroimaging findings in a series of 41 patients. *American Journal of Medical Genetics A* **146A**(19): 2501–2511.

Schellenberg, G. D., G. Dawson, *et al.* (2006). Evidence for multiple loci from a genome scan of autism kindreds. *Molecular Psychiatry* **11**(11): 1049–1060.

Schienle, A., R. Stark, *et al.* (2002). The insula is not specifically involved in disgust processing: An fMRI study. *Neuroreport* **13**(16): 2023–2026.

Schiller, D., J. B. Freeman, *et al.* (2009). A neural mechanism of first impressions. *Nature Neuroscience* **12**(4): 508–514.

Schimmelmann, B. G., S. Friedel, *et al.* (2009). Exploring the genetic link between RLS and ADHD. *Journal of Psychiatric Research* **43**(10): 941–945.

Schippers, M. B., A. Roebroeck, *et al.* (2010). Mapping the information flow from one brain to another during gestural communication. *Proceedings of the National Academy of Sciences of the United States of America* **107**(20): 9388–9393.

Schmahmann, J. D. (2004). Disorders of the cerebellum: Ataxia, dysmetria of thought, and the cerebellar cognitive affective syndrome. *Journal of Neuropsychiatry and Clinical Neurosciences* **16**(3): 367–378.

Schmithorst, V. J. (2003). Developmental sex differences in the relation of neuroanatomical connectivity to intelligence. *Intelligence* **37**(2): 164–173.

Schmitz, C., J. Martineau, *et al.* (2003). Motor control and children with autism: Deficit of anticipatory function? *Neuroscience Letters* **348**(1): 17–20.

Schneider, M. F., C. M. Krick, *et al.* (2010). Impairment of fronto-striatal and parietal cerebral networks correlates with attention deficit hyperactivity disorder (ADHD) psychopathology in adults: A functional magnetic resonance imaging (fMRI) study. *Psychiatry Research: Neuroimaging* **183**(1): 75–84.

Schopler, E. (1996). Are autism and Asperger syndrome (AS) different labels or different disabilities? *Journal of Autism and Developmental Disorders* **26**(1): 109–110.

Schopler, E., G. B. Mesibov, *et al.* (1998). Preface. In E. Schopler, G. B. Mesibov, *et al.* (eds) *Asperger Syndrome or High-functioning Autism?* New York, NY: Plenum Press.

Schopler, E., R. J. Reichler, *et al.* (1980). Toward objective classification of childhood autism: Childhood Autism Rating Scale (CARS). *Journal of Autism and Developmental Disorders* **10**(1): 91–103.

Schubert, R. (2005). Attention deficit disorder and epilepsy. *Pediatric Neurology* **32**(1): 1–10.

Schultz, R. J., D. G. Glaze, *et al.* (1993). The pattern of growth failure in Rett syndrome. *American Journal of Diseases of Children* **147**(6): 633–637.

Schultz, R. T., I. Gauthier, *et al.* (2000). Abnormal ventral temporal cortical activity during face discrimination among individuals with autism and Asperger syndrome. *Archives of General Psychiatry* **57**(4): 331–340.

Schumann, C. M., C. C. Barnes, *et al.* (2009). Amygdala enlargement in toddlers with autism related to severity of social and communication impairments. *Biological Psychiatry* **66**(10): 942–949.

Schwartz, C. B., H. A. Henderson, *et al.* (2009). Temperament as a predictor of symptomotology and adaptive functioning in adolescents with high-functioning autism. *Journal of Autism and Developmental Disorders* **39**(6): 842–855.

Schweimer, J. and W. Hauber (2006). Dopamine D1 receptors in the anterior cingulate cortex regulate effort-based decision making. *Learning and Memory* **13**(6): 777–782.

Scott, J., F. Colom, *et al.* (2007). A meta-analysis of relapse rates with adjunctive psychological therapies compared to usual psychiatric treatment for bipolar disorders. *International Journal of Neuropsychopharmacology* **10**(1): 123–129.

Scragg, P. and A. Shah (1994). Prevalence of Asperger's syndrome in a secure hospital. *British Journal of Psychiatry* **165**(5): 679–682.

Sebastian, C., S. J. Blakemore, *et al.* (2009). Reactions to ostracism in adolescents with autism spectrum conditions. *Journal of Autism and Developmental Disorders* **39**(8):1122–1130.

Seedat, S. P., K. M. P. Scott, *et al.* (2009). Cross-national associations between gender and mental disorders in the World Health Organization world mental health surveys. *Archives of General Psychiatry* **66**(7): 785–795.

Segal, M. M., G. F. Rogers, *et al.* (2007). Hypokalemic sensory overstimulation. *Journal of Child Neurology* **22**(12): 1408–1410.

Segenreich, D., D. Fortes, *et al.* (2009). Anxiety and depression in parents of a Brazilian non-clinical sample of attention-deficit/hyperactivity disorder (ADHD) students. *Brazilian Journal of Medical and Biological Research* **42**(5): 465–469.

Seida, J. K., M. B. Ospina, *et al.* (2009). Systematic reviews of psychosocial interventions for autism: an umbrella review. *Developmental Medicine and Child Neurology* **51**(2): 95–104.

Seitz, R. J., J. Nickel, *et al.* (2006). Functional modularity of the medial prefrontal cortex: Involvement in human empathy. *Neuropsychology* **20**(6): 743–751.

Seltzer, M. M., M. W. Krauss, *et al.* (2003). The symptoms of autism spectrum disorders in adolescence and adulthood. *Journal of Autism and Developmental Disorders* **33**(6): 565–581.

Senju, A., K. Yaguchi, *et al.* (2003). Eye contact does not facilitate detection in children with autism. *Cognition* **89**(1): B43–B51.

Senju, A., M. Maeda, *et al.* (2007). Absence of contagious yawning in children with autism spectrum disorder. *Biology Letters* **3**(6): 706–708.

Senju, A., V. Southgate, *et al.* (2009). Mindblind eyes: An absence of spontaneous theory of mind in Asperger syndrome. *Science* **325**(5942): 883–885.

Senju, A., Y. Kikuchi, *et al.* (2009). Brief report: Does eye contact induce contagious yawning in children with autism spectrum disorder? *Journal of Autism and Developmental Disorders* **39**(11): 1598–1602.

Senju, A., Y. Tojo, *et al.* (2004). Reflexive orienting in response to eye gaze and an arrow in children with and without autism. *Journal of Child Psychology and Psychiatry* **45**(3): 445–458.

Sesack, S. R. and A. A. Grace (2010). Cortico-basal ganglia reward network: Microcircuitry. *Neuropsychopharmacology* **35**(1):27–47.

Shackman, A. J., B. W. McMenamin, *et al.* (2009). Right dorsolateral prefrontal cortical activity and behavioral inhibition. *Psychological Science* **20**(12): 1500–1506.

Shafritz, K. M., K. E. Marchione, *et al.* (2004). The effects of methylphenidate on neural systems of attention in attention deficit hyperactivity disorder. *American Journal of Psychiatry* **161**(11): 1990–1997.

Shah, A. and U. Frith (1983). An islet of ability in autistic children: A research note. *Journal of Child Psychology and Psychiatry* **24**(4): 613–620.

Shallice, T. (1982). Specific impairments of planning. *Philosophical Transactions of the Royal Society B: Biological Sciences* **298**(1089): 199–209.

Shamay-Tsoory, S. G. (2008). Recognition of 'fortune of others' emotions in Asperger syndrome and high functioning autism. *Journal of Autism and Developmental Disorders* **38**(8): 1451–1461.

Shamay-Tsoory, S. G., J. Aharon-Peretz, *et al.* (2009). Two systems for empathy: A double dissociation between emotional and cognitive empathy in inferior frontal gyrus versus ventromedial prefrontal lesions. *Brain* **132**(3): 617–627.

Shamay-Tsoory, S. G., M. Fischer, *et al.* (2009). Intranasal administration of oxytocin increases envy and schadenfreude (gloating). *Biological Psychiatry* **66**(9): 864–870.

Shamay-Tsoory, S. G., R. Tomer, *et al.* (2003). Characterization of empathy deficits following prefrontal brain damage: The role of the right ventromedial prefrontal cortex. *Journal of Cognitive Neuroscience* **15**(3): 324–337.

Shamay-Tsoory, S. G., Y. Tibi-Elhanany, *et al.* (2007). The green-eyed monster and malicious joy: The neuroanatomical bases of envy and gloating (schadenfreude). *Brain* **130**(6): 1663–1678.

Shannon, C. (1948). A mathematical theory of communication. *The Bell System Technical Journal* **27**: 379–423.

Shattuck, P. T., M. Durkin, *et al.* (2009). Timing of identification among children with an autism spectrum disorder: Findings from a population-based surveillance study. *Journal of the American Academy of Child and Adolescent Psychiatry* **48**(5): 474–483.

Shattuck, P. T., M. M. Seltzer, *et al.* (2007). Change in autism symptoms and maladaptive behaviors in adolescents and adults with an autism spectrum disorder. *Journal of Autism and Developmental Disorders* **37**(9): 1735–1747.

Shaw, P., E. J. Lawrence, *et al.* (2004). The impact of early and late damage to the human amygdala on 'theory of mind' reasoning. *Brain* **127**(7): 1535–1548.

Shaw, P., N. J. Kabani, *et al.* (2008). Neurodevelopmental trajectories of the human cerebral cortex. *Journal of Neuroscience* **28**(14): 3586–3594.

Shelley, B. P. and M. M. Robertson (2005). The neuropsychiatry and multisystem features of the Smith-Magenis syndrome: A review. *The Journal of Neuropsychiatry and Clinical Neurosciences* **17**(1): 91–97.

Shelton, J. F., D. J. Tancredi, *et al.* (2010). Independent and dependent contributions of advanced maternal and paternal ages to autism risk. *Autism Research* **3**(1): 30–39.

Shepherd, S. V., J. T. Klein, *et al.* (2009). Mirroring of attention by neurons in macaque parietal cortex. *Proceedings of the National Academy of Sciences of the United States of America* **106**(23): 9489–9494.

Shi, L., S. E. Smith, *et al.* (2009). Activation of the maternal immune system alters cerebellar development in the offspring. *Brain, Behavior, and Immunity* **23**(1): 116–123.

Shields, J. (2001). The NAS earlybird programme: Partnership with parents in early intervention. *Autism* **5**(1): 49–56.

Shields, W. D. (2006). Infantile spasms: Little seizures, BIG consequences. *Epilepsy Currents* **6**(3): 63–69.

Shilyansky, C., K. H. Karlsgodt, *et al.* (2010). Neurofibromin regulates corticostriatal inhibitory networks during working memory performance. *Proceedings of the National Academy of Sciences of the United States of America* **107**(29): 13141–13146.

Shimabukuro, T. T., S. D. Grosse, *et al.* (2008). Medical expenditures for children with an autism spectrum disorder in a privately insured population. *Journal of Autism and Developmental Disorders* **38**(3): 546–552.

Shimoji, T. and N. Tomiyama (2004). Mild trigonocephaly and intracranial pressure: Report of 56 patients. *Child's Nervous System* **20**(10):749–756.

Shimoji, T., S. Shimabukuro, *et al.* (2002). Mild trigonocephaly with clinical symptons: Analysis of surgical results in 65 patients. *Child's Nervous System* **18**(5): 5–224.

Shprintzen, R. J. (2008). Velo-cardio-facial syndrome: 30 years of study. *Developmental Disabilities Research Reviews* **14**(1): 3–10.

Shu, B. C. (2009). Quality of life of family caregivers of children with autism: The mother's perspective. *Autism* **13**(1): 81–91.

Siebert, M., H. J. Markowitsch, *et al.* (2003). Amygdala, affect and cognition: Evidence from 10 patients with Urbach-Wiethe disease. *Brain* **126**(12): 2627–2637.

Sigman, M., P. Mundy, *et al.* (1986). Social interactions of autistic, mentally retarded and normal children and their caregivers. *Journal of Child Psychology and Psychiatry* **27**(5): 647–656.

Sikora, D. M., K. Pettit-Kekel, *et al.* (2006). The near universal presence of autism spectrum disorders in children with Smith–Lemli–Opitz syndrome. *American Journal of Medical Genetics Part A* **140A**(14): 1511–1518.

Silani, G., G. Bird *et al.* (2008). Levels of emotional awareness and autism: An fMRI study. *Social Neuroscience* **3**(2): 97–112.

Siller, M. and M. Sigman (2008). Modeling longitudinal change in the language abilities of children with autism: Parent behaviors and child characteristics as predictors of change. *Developmental Psychology* **44**(6): 1691–1704.

Silva, J. A., G. B. Leong, *et al.* (2004). A neuropsychiatric developmental model of serial homicidal behavior. *Behavioral Sciences and the Law* **22**(6): 787–799.

Silva, R., R. Muniz, *et al.* (2008). Treatment of children with attention-deficit/hyperactivity disorder: Results of a randomized, multicenter, double-blind, crossover study of extended-release Dexmethylphenidate and d,l-Methylphenidate and placebo in a laboratory classroom setting. *Psychopharmacol Bulletin* **41**(1): 19–33.

Silverman, J. L., S. M. Turner, *et al.* (2011). Sociability and motor functions in Shank1 mutant mice. *Brain Research* **22**(1380): 120–137.

Silvestri, R., A. Gagliano, *et al.* (2009). Sleep disorders in children with Attention-Deficit/Hyperactivity Disorder (ADHD) recorded overnight by video-polysomnography. *Sleep Medicine* **10**(10): 1132–1338.

Simmonds, H. A., J. A. Duley, *et al.* (1997). When to investigate for purine and pyrimidine disorders: Introduction and review of clinical and laboratory indications. *Journal of Inherited Metabolic Diseases* **20**(2): 214–226.

Simon, J. R., M. Stollstorff, *et al.* (2011). Dopamine transporter genotype predicts implicit sequence learning. *Behavioural Brain Research* **216**(1): 452–457.

Simonoff, E. M. D., A. P. Pickles, *et al.* (2008). Psychiatric disorders in children with autism spectrum disorders: Prevalence, comorbidity, and associated factors in a population-derived sample. *Journal of the American Academy of Child and Adolescent Psychiatry* **47**(8): 921–929.

Simos, G. and E. Dimitriou (1994). Cognitive-behavioural treatment of culturally bound obsessional ruminations: A case report. *Behavioural and Cognitive Psychotherapy* **22**(4): 325–330.

Singer, T., B. Seymour, *et al.* (2004). Empathy for pain involves the affective but not sensory components of pain. *Science* **303**(5661): 1157–1162.

Singleton, J. L. and M. D. Tittle (2000). Deaf parents and their hearing children. *Journal of Deaf Studies and Deaf Education* **5**(3): 221–236.

Sinha, Y., N. Silove, *et al.* (2006). Auditory integration training and other sound therapies for autism spectrum disorders: A systematic review. *Archives of Disease in Childhood* **91**(12): 1018–1022.

Sinzig, J., D. Morsch, *et al.* (2008). Inhibition, flexibility, working memory and planning in autism spectrum disorders with and without comorbid ADHD-symptoms. *Child and Adolescent Psychiatry and Mental Health* **2**(1): 4.

Sinzig, J., N. Bruning, *et al.* (2008). Attention profiles in autistic children with and without comorbid hyperactivity and attention problems. *Acta Neuropsychiatrica* **20**(4): 207–215.

Slaughter, V., C. C. Peterson, *et al.* (2007). Mind what mother says: Narrative input and theory of mind in typical children and those on the autism spectrum. *Child Development* **78**(3): 839–858.

Slifer, K. J., T. Diver, *et al.* (2003). Assessment of facial emotion encoding and decoding skills in children with and without oral clefts. *Journal of Cranio-Maxillofacial Surgery* **31**(5): 304–315.

Smith, A. B., E. Taylor, *et al.* (2006). Task-specific hypoactivation in prefrontal and temporoparietal brain regions during motor inhibition and task switching in medication-naive children and adolescents with attention deficit hyperactivity disorder. *American Journal of Psychiatry* **163**: 1044–1051.

Smith, C. J., C. M. Lang, *et al.* (2009). Familial associations of intense preoccupations, an empirical factor of the restricted, repetitive behaviors and interests domain of autism. *Journal of Child Psychology and Psychiatry* **50**(8): 982–990.

Smith, C., D. Felce, *et al.* (2002). Individualized education for children with learning disorders. *Chinese Mental Health Journal* **16**: 751–767.

Smith, H. and E. Milne (2009). Reduced change blindness suggests enhanced attention to detail in individuals with autism. *Journal of Child Psychology and Psychiatry* **50**(3): 300–306.

Smith, I. M. and S. E. Bryson (2007). Gesture imitation in autism. II. Symbolic gestures and pantomimed object use. *Cognitve Neuropsychology* **24**(7): 679–700.

Smith, L. E., J. S. Greenberg, *et al.* (2008). Symptoms and behavior problems of adolescents and adults with autism: Effects of mother-child relationship quality, warmth, and praise. *American Journal on Mental Retardation* **113**(5): 387–402.

Smith, L. E., M. M. Seltzer, *et al.* (2008). A comparative analysis of well-being and coping among mothers of toddlers and mothers of adolescents with ASD. *Journal of Autism and Developmental Disorders* **38**(5): 876–889.

Smith, M., A. Woodroffe, *et al.* (2002). Molecular genetic delineation of a deletion of chromosome 13q12-q13 in a patient with autism and auditory processing deficits. *Cytogenet Genome Research* **98**(4): 233–239.

Smith, M., J. R. Escamilla, *et al.* (2001). Molecular genetic delineation of 2q37.3 deletion in autism and osteodystrophy: Report of a case and of new markers for deletion screening by PCR. *Cytogenetics and Cell Genetics* **94**(1–2): 15–22.

Smith, S. D. (2007). Genes, language development, and language disorders. *Mental Retardation and Developmental Disabilities Research Reviews* **13**(1): 96–105.

Snow, A., L. Lecavalier, *et al.* (2009). The structure of the Autism Diagnostic Interview-Revised: diagnostic and phenotypic implications. *Journal of Child Psychology and Psychiatry* **50**(6): 734–742.

Snow, W. M., K. Hartle, *et al.* (2008). Altered morphology of motor cortex neurons in the VPA rat model of autism. *Developmental Psychobiology* **50**(7): 633–639.

Snowling, M. J. P. and M. E. P. Hayiou-Thomas (2006). The dyslexia spectrum: Continuities between reading, speech, and language impairments. *Topics in Language Disorders Dyslexia in the Current Context* **26**(2): 110–126.

Snyder, A. (2009). Explaining and inducing savant skills: Privileged access to lower level, less-processed information. *Philosophical Transactions of the Royal Society B: Biological Sciences* **364**(1522): 1399–1405.

Snyder, D. M. M., K. M. Miller, *et al.* (2008). It looks like autism: Caution in diagnosis. *Journal of Developmental and Behavioral Pediatrics* **29**(1): 47–50.

Sobanski, E., D. Sabljic, *et al.* (2008). Driving-related risks and impact of methylphenidate treatment on driving in adults with attention-deficit/hyperactivity disorder (ADHD). *Journal of Neural Transmission* **115**(2): 347–356.

Sodian, B. and C. Thoermer (2008). Precursors to a theory of mind in infancy: Perspectives for research on autism. *Quarterly Journal of Experimental Psychology (Colchester)* **61**(1): 27–39.

Sofronoff, K., T. Attwood, *et al.* (2007). A randomized controlled trial of a cognitive behavioural intervention for anger management in children diagnosed with Asperger syndrome. *Journal of Autism and Developmental Disorders* **37**(7): 1203–1214.

Sokhadze, E., J. Baruth, *et al.* (2009). Event-related potential study of novelty processing abnormalities in autism. *Applied Psychophysiology and Biofeedback* **34**(1): 37–51.

Solanto, M. V., D. J. Marks, *et al.* (2008). Development of a new psychosocial treatment for adult ADHD. *Journal of Attention Disorders* **11**(6): 728–736.

Solanto, M. V., S. A. Pope-Boyd, *et al.* (2009). Social functioning in predominantly inattentive and combined subtypes of children with ADHD. *Journal of Attention Disorders* **13**(1): 27–35.

Soltis, J. (2004). The signal functions of early infant crying. *Behavioral and Brain Sciences* **27**(4): 443–458.

Soni, S., J. Whittington, *et al.* (2008). The phenomenology and diagnosis of psychiatric illness in people with Prader-Willi syndrome. *Psychological Medicine* **38**(10): 1505–1514.

Sonnby-Borgstroem, M. (2002a). Automatic mimicry reactions as related to differences in emotional empathy. *Scandinavian Journal of Psychology* **43**(5): 433–443.

Sonnby-Borgstrom, M. (2002b). [The facial expression says more than words. Is emotional contagion via facial expression the first step toward empathy?]. *Lakartidningen* **99**(13): 1438–1442.

Sonuga-Barke, E. J., J. Lasky-Su, *et al.* (2008). Does parental expressed emotion moderate genetic effects in ADHD? An exploration using a genome wide association scan. *American Journal of Medical Genetics Part B: Neuropsychiatric Genetics* **147B**(8): 1359–1368.

Sonuga-Barke, E. J., R. D. Oades, *et al.* (2009). Dopamine and serotonin transporter genotypes moderate sensitivity to maternal expressed emotion: The case of conduct and emotional problems in attention deficit/hyperactivity disorder. *Journal of Child Psychology and Psychiatry* **50**(9): 1052–1063.

Sourander, A. M., P. M. Jensen, *et al.* (2007). Childhood bullies and victims and their risk of criminality in late adolescence: The Finnish 'from a boy to a man' study. *Archives of Pediatrics and Adolescent Medicine* **161**(6): 546–552.

Sousa, I., T. G. Clark, *et al.* (2008). MET and autism susceptibility: Family and case-control studies. *European Journal of Human Genetics* **17**(6): 749–758.

Sowell, E. R., P. M. Thompson, *et al.* (2003). Cortical abnormalities in children and adolescents with attention-deficit hyperactivity disorder. *The Lancet* **362**(9397): 1699–1707.

Spain, D., T. Lavender, *et al.* (2009). Comorbidities in adult attendees of a specialist autism clinic. International Meeting for Autism Research, Chicago, IL, 7–9 May.

Spalletta, G., A. Pasini, *et al.* (2001). Prefrontal blood flow dysregulation in drug naive ADHD children without structural abnormalities. *Journal of Neural Transmission* **108**(10): 1203–1216.

Spearman, C. (1904). General intelligence, objectively determined and measured. *American Journal of Psychology* **15**(2): 201–293.

Spek, A. A., E. M. Scholte, *et al.* (2008). Brief report: The use of WAIS-III in adults with HFA and Asperger syndrome. *Journal of Autism and Developmental Disorders* **38**(4): 782–787.

Spence, S. J. and M. T. Schneider (2009). The role of epilepsy and epileptiform EEGs in autism spectrum disorders. *Pediatric Research* **65**(6): 599–606.

Spinella, M. (2002). A relationship between smell identification and empathy. *International Journal of Neuroscience* **112**(6): 605–612.

Spitzer, R. L., K. Kroenke, *et al.* (2006). A Brief Measure for Assessing Generalized Anxiety Disorder: The GAD-7. *Archives of Internal Medicine* **166**: 1092–1097.

Srihari, V. H., T. S. W. Lee, *et al.* (2006). Revisiting cycloid psychosis: A case of an acute, transient and recurring psychotic disorder. *Schizophrenia Research* **82**(2–3): 261–264.

Stancheva, I., A. L. Collins, *et al.* (2003). A mutant form of MeCP2 protein associated with human Rett syndrome cannot be displaced from methylated DNA by notch in Xenopus embryos. *Molecular Cell* **12**(2): 425–435.

State, M. W. (2010). The genetics of child psychiatric disorders: Focus on autism and Tourette syndrome. *Neuron* **68**(2): 254–269.

Stavro, G. M., M. L. Ettenhofer, *et al.* (2007). Executive functions and adaptive functioning in young adult attention-deficit/hyperactivity disorder. *Journal of the International Neuropsychological Society* **13**(2): 324–334.

Steele, M. M., M. Al Adeimi, *et al.* (2001). Brief report: A case of autism with interstitial deletion of chromosome 13. *Journal of Autism and Developmental Disorders* **31**(2): 231–234.

Stefanatos, G. A. (2008). Regression in autistic spectrum disorders. *Neuropsychology Review* **18**(4): 305–319.

Stein, J. (2003). Visual motion sensitivity and reading. *Neuropsychologia* **41**(13): 1785–1793.

Stein, M. B. and D. J. Stein (2008). Social anxiety disorder. *The Lancet* **371**(9618): 1115–1125.

Steiner, N. J., R. C. Sheldrick, *et al.* (2011). Computer-based attention training in the schools for children with attention deficit/hyperactivity disorder: A preliminary trial. *Clinical Pediatrics* **50**(7): 615–622.

Steinlin, M., M. Styger, *et al.* (1999). Cognitive impairments in patients with congenital nonprogressive cerebellar ataxia. *Neurology* **53**(5): 966–973.

Stephens, G. J., L. J. Silbert, *et al.* (2010). Speaker-listener neural coupling underlies successful communication. *Proceedings of the National Academy of Sciences of the United States of America* **107**(32): 14425–14430.

Stern, C. E., A. M. Owen, *et al.* (2000). Activity in ventrolateral and mid-dorsolateral prefrontal cortex during nonspatial visual working memory processing: Evidence from functional magnetic resonance imaging. *NeuroImage* **11**(5): 392–399.

Stevens, M. C., D. A. Fein, *et al.* (2000). Subgroups of children with autism by cluster analysis: A longitudinal examination. *Journal of the American Academy of Child and Adolescent Psychiatry* **39**(3): 346–352.

Stevens, S. E., E. J. Sonuga-Barke, *et al.* (2008). Inattention/overactivity following early severe institutional deprivation: presentation and associations in early adolescence. *Journal of Abnormal Child Psychology* **36**(3): 385–398.

Stewart, J. L., R. Levin-Silton, *et al.* (2008). Anger style, psychopathology, and regional brain activity. *Emotion* **8**(5): 701–713.

Stichter, J. P., J. K. Randolph, *et al.* (2009). The use of structural analysis to develop antecedent-based interventions for students with autism. *Journal of Autism and Developmental Disorders* **39**(6): 883–896.

Stiles, B. L. (2009). Phosphatase and tensin homologue deleted on chromosome 10: Extending its PTENtacles. *International Journal of Biochemistry and Cell Biology* **41**(4): 757–761.

Stinear, C. M., J. P. Coxon, *et al.* (2009). Pimary motor cortex and movement prevention: Where Stop meets Go. *Neuroscience and Biobehavioral Review* **33**: 662–673.

Stokes, M., N. Newton, *et al.* (2007). Stalking, and social and romantic functioning among adolescents and adults with autism spectrum disorder. *Journal of Autism and Developmental Disorders* **37**(10): 1969–1986.

Stone, J. (2008). What does this study test, and why? *Archives of Disease in Childhood* **93**(10): 905–907.

Stone, W. L., C. R. McMahon, *et al.* (2008). Use of the Screening Tool for Autism in Two-Year-Olds (STAT) for children under 24 months: An exploratory study. *Autism* **12**(5): 557–573.

Stone, W. L., E. E. Coonrod, *et al.* (2000). Brief report: Screening tool for autism in two-year-olds (STAT): Development and preliminary data. *Journal of Autism and Developmental Disorders* **30**(6): 607–612.

Strang-Karlsson, S., K. Raikkonen, *et al.* (2008). Very low birth weight and behavioral symptoms of attention deficit hyperactivity disorder in young adulthood: The Helsinki study of very-low-birth-weight adults. *American Journal of Psychiatry* **165**(10): 1345–1353.

Stribling, P., J. Rae, *et al.* (2007). Two forms of spoken repetition in a girl with autism. *International Journal of Language and Communication Disorders* **42**(4): 427–444.

Strom, S. P., J. L. Stone, et al. (2009). High-density SNP association study of the 17q21 chromosomal region linked to autism identifies CACNA1G as a novel candidate gene. *Molecular Psychiatry* **15**(10): 996–1005.

Strömland, K., L. Sjögreen, et al. (2002). Möbius sequence: A Swedish multidiscipline study. *European Journal of Paediatric Neurology* **6**(1): 1–45.

Stroop, R. (1935). Studies of interference in serial verbal reactions. *Journal of Experimental Psychology* **18**(6): 643–662.

Sturm, H., E. Fernell, et al. (2004). Autism spectrum disorders in children with normal intellectual levels: associated impairments and subgroups. *Developmental Medicine and Child Neurology* **46**(7): 444–447.

Sturm, V. E., H. J. Rosen, et al. (2006). Self-conscious emotion deficits in frontotemporal lobar degeneration. *Brain* **129**(9): 2508–2516.

Subramaniam, B., S. Naidu, S, et al. (1997). Neuroanatomy in Rett syndrome: Cerebral cortex and posterior fossa. *Neurology* **48**(2): 399–407.

Sugie, Y., H. Sugie, et al. (2009). Study of HOXD genes in autism particularly regarding the ratio of second to fourth digit length. *Brain and Development* **32**(5): 356–361.

Sullivan, E. V., A. J. Harding, et al. (2003). Disruption of frontocerebellar circuitry and function in alcoholism. *Alcoholism: Clinical and Experimental Research* **27**: 301–309.

Suomi, S. J., F. C. van der Horst, et al. (2008). Rigorous experiments on monkey love: An account of Harry F. Harlow's role in the history of attachment theory. *Integrative Psychological and Behavioral Science* **42**(4): 354–369.

Sutera, S., J. Pandey, et al. (2007). Predictors of optimal outcome in toddlers diagnosed with autism spectrum disorders. *Journal of Autism and Developmental Disorders* **37**(1): 98–107.

Suzuki, K., A. Yamadori, et al. (2000). [Hyperlexia in an adult patient with lesions in the left medial frontal lobe]. *Rinsho Shinkeigaku* **40**: 393–397.

Swain, J. E., J. P. Lorberbaum, et al. (2007). Brain basis of early parent-infant interactions: psychology, physiology, and in vivo functional neuroimaging studies. *Journal of Child Psychology and Psychiatry* **48**(3–4): 262–287.

Sweeten, T. L., D. J. Posey, et al. (2002). The amygdala and related structures in the pathophysiology of autism. *Pharmacology Biochemistry and Behavior* **71**(3): 449–455.

Swerts, M. and E. Krahmer (2008). Facial expression and prosodic prominence: Effects of modality and facial area. *Journal of Phonetics* **36**(2): 219–238.

Szatmari, P., A. D. Paterson, et al. (2007). Mapping autism risk loci using genetic linkage and chromosomal rearrangements. *Nature Genetics* **39**(3): 319–328.

Szatmari, P., S. Georgiades, et al. (2008). Alexithymia in parents of children with autism spectrum disorder. *Journal of Autism and Developmental Disorders* **38**(10): 1859–1865.

Tabelow, K., V. Piëch, et al. (2009). High-resolution fMRI: Overcoming the signal-to-noise problem. *Journal of Neuroscience Methods* **178**(2): 357–365.

Tager-Flusberg, H. and K. Sullivan (1994). A second look at second-order belief attribution in autism. *Journal of Autism and Developmental Disorders* **24**(5): 577–586.

Tager-Flusberg, H., S. Rogers, et al. (2009). Defining spoken language benchmarks and selecting measures of expressive language development for young children with autism spectrum disorders. *Journal of Speech, Language, and Hearing Research* **52**: 643–652.

Takagi, M., P. Trillenberg, et al. (2001). Adaptive control of pursuit, vergence and eye torsion in humans: Basic and clinical implications. *Vision Research* **41**: 3331–3344.

Takagi, M., R. Tamargo, et al. (2003). Effects of lesions of the cerebellar oculomotor vermis on eye movements in primate: Binocular control. *Progress in Brain Research* **142**: 19–33.

Takahashi, T. N., J. E. Farmer, et al. (2005). Joubert syndrome is not a cause of classical autism. *American Journal of Medical Genetics A* **132**(4): 347–351.

Takarae, Y., N. J. Minshew, et al. (2007). Atypical involvement of frontostriatal systems during sensorimotor control in autism. *Psychiatry Research* **156**(2): 117–127.

Talarovicova, A., L. Krskova, et al. (2007). Some assessments of the amygdala role in suprahypothalamic neuroendocrine regulation: A minireview. *Endocrine Regulations* **41**(4): 155–162.

Tamagaki, C., A. Murata, et al. (2000). [Two siblings with adult-type metachromatic leukodystrophy: correlation between clinical symptoms and neuroimaging]. *Seishin Shinkeigaku Zasshi* **102**(4): 399–409.

Tan, A., M. Salgado, et al. (1997). The characterization and outcome of stereotypical movements in nonautistic children. *Movement Disorders* **12**(1): 47–52.

Tanguay, P. E. (2002). Screening young people for autism with the Development Behavior Checklist. *Journal of the American Academy of Child and Adolescent Psychiatry* **41**(11): 1369–1375.

Tani, P., N. Lindberg, et al. (2004). Asperger syndrome, alexithymia and perception of sleep. *Neuropsychobiology* **49**(2): 64–70.

Taniai, H., T. Nishiyama, et al. (2008). Genetic influences on the broad spectrum of autism: Study of proband-ascertained twins. *American Journal of Medical Genetics B: Neuropsychiatric Genetics* **147B**(6): 844–849.

Tantam, D. (1986). Eccentricity and autism: A clinical and experimental study of 60 adult psychiatric patients, including 46 able autistic adults, with a social disability attributable to personality or developmental disorder. 1–418. Thesis, University of London.

Tantam, D. (1988a). *A Mind of Their Own*. London: National Autistic Society.

Tantam, D. (1988b). Asperger's syndrome. *Journal of Child Psychology and Psychiatry* **29**(3): 245–255.

Tantam, D. (1988c). Lifelong eccentricity and social isolation. I. Psychiatric, social, and forensic aspects. *British Journal of Psychiatry* **153**(6): 777–782.

Tantam, D. (1988d). Lifelong eccentricity and social isolation. II: Asperger's syndrome or schizoid personality disorder? *British Journal of Psychiatry* **153**(6): 783–791.

Tantam, D. (1991a). Asperger's syndrome in adulthood. In U. Frith (ed.) *Autism and Asperger's Syndrome*. Cambridge: Cambridge University Press.

Tantam, D. (1991b). Shame and groups. *Group Analysis* **23**(1): 31–44.

Tantam, D. (1992). Characterizing the fundamental social handicap in autism. *Acta Paedopsychiatrica* **55**(2): 83–91.

Tantam, D. (1995). Empathy, persistent aggression, and antisocial personality disorder. *Journal of Forensic Psychiatry* **6**(1): 10–18.

Tantam, D. (1996a). Fairbairn. In G. Berrios and H. Freeman (eds) *150 Years of British Psychiatry*. London: Athlone Press.

Tantam, D. (1996b). Psychotherapy and traditional healing. In D. Tantam, A. Duncan, et al. (eds) *Psychiatry for the Developing World*. London, Gaskell.

Tantam, D. (1998). Shame and the presentation of emotional disorders. In P. Gilbert and B. Andrews (eds) *Shame: Interpersonal Behaviour, Psychopathology and Culture*. Oxford: Oxford University Press.

Tantam, D. (2000). Adolescence and adulthood of individuals with Asperger syndrome. In A. Klin, F. Volkmar, *et al.* (eds) *Asperger Syndrome.* New York, NY: Guilford Press.

Tantam, D. (2002a). *Psychotherapy and Counselling in Practice.* Cambridge: Cambridge University Press.

Tantam, D. (2002b). Reasons and psychological explanation. *International Journal of Psychotherapy* **7**(2): 165–173.

Tantam, D. (2003). The flavour of emotions. *Psychology and Psychotherapy: Theory, Research and Practice* **76**(1): 23–45.

Tantam, D. (2009). *Can the World Afford Autistic Spectrum Disorder? Nonverbal Communication, Asperger Syndrome and the Interbrain.* London: Jessica Kingsley Publishers.

Tantam, D. (2012). Psychoanalytic approaches. In F. Volkmar (ed.) *Encyclopedia of Autism Spectrum Disorders.* Stuttgart: Springer.

Tantam, D. and G. McGrath (1989a). Prolonged use of neuroleptics in schizophrenia: A review for the practitioner. *International Clinical Psychopharmacology* **4**(3): 167–194.

Tantam, D. and G. McGrath (1989b). Psychiatric day hospitals – another route to institutionalization? *Social Psychiatry and Psychiatric Epidemiology* **24**(2): 96–101.

Tantam, D., C. Evered, *et al.* (1990). Asperger's syndrome and ligamentous laxity. *Journal of the American Academy of Child and Adolescent Psychiatry* **29**(6): 892–896.

Tantam, D., L. Monaghan, *et al.* (1989). Autistic children's ability to interpret faces: A research note. *Journal of Child Psychology and Psychiatry* **30**(4): 623–630.

Tantam, D., R. Kalucy *et al.* (1982). Sleep, scratching and dreams in eczema: A new approach to alexithymia. *Psychotherapy and Psychosomatics* **37**(1): 26–85.

Tardif, C., F. Laine, *et al.* (2007). Slowing down presentation of facial movements and vocal sounds enhances facial expression recognition and induces facial-vocal imitation in children with autism. *Journal of Autism and Developmental Disorders* **37**(8): 1469–1484.

Tartaglia, N., S. Davis, *et al.* (2008). A new look at XXYY syndrome: Medical and psychological features. *American Journal of Medical Genetics A* **146A**(12): 1509–1522.

Tate, D. F., E. D. Bigler, *et al.* (2007). The relative contributions of brain, cerebrospinal fluid-filled structures and non-neural tissue volumes to occipital-frontal head circumference in subjects with autism. *Neuropediatrics* **38**(1): 18–24.

Tateno, M. M., Y. M. Tateno, *et al.* (2008). Comorbid childhood gender identity disorder in a boy with Asperger syndrome. *Psychiatry and Clinical Neurosciences* **62**(2): 238.

Tatton-Brown, K., T. Cole, *et al.* (1993–2011). Sotos syndrome. In R. A. Pagon, T. D. Bird, *et al.* (eds) *GeneReviews* (online). Seattle, WA: University of Washington.

Taylor, D. C., B. G. Neville, *et al.* (1999). Autistic spectrum disorders in childhood epilepsy surgery candidates. *European Child and Adolescent Psychiatry* **8**(3): 189–192.

Taylor, E. L., M. Target, *et al.* (2008). Attachment in adults with high-functioning autism. *Attachment and Human Development* **10**(2): 143–163.

Taylor, S. F., R. C. Welsh, *et al.* (2004). A functional neuroimaging study of motivation and executive function. *NeuroImage* **21**(3): 1045–1054.

Teasdale, J. D., R. J. Howard, *et al.* (1999). Functional MRI study of the cognitive generation of affect. *American Journal of Psychiatry* **156**(2): 209–215.

Tebruegge, M., V. Nandini, *et al.* (2004). Does routine child health surveillance contribute to the early detection of children with pervasive developmental disorders? An epidemiological study in Kent, UK. *BMC Pediatrics* **4**: 4.

Tehee, E, R. Honan, *et al.* (2009). Factors contributing to stress in parents of individuals with autistic spectrum disorders. *Journal of Applied Research in Intellectual Disabilities* **22**(1): 34–42.

Teherani, A., K. E. Hauer, *et al.* (2008). Can simulations measure empathy? Considerations on how to assess behavioral empathy via simulations. *Patient Education and Counseling* **71**(2): 148–152.

Teman, P. T., M. Tippmann-Peikert, *et al.* (2009). Idiopathic rapid-eye-movement sleep disorder: Associations with antidepressants, psychiatric diagnoses, and other factors, in relation to age of onset. *Sleep Medicine* **10**(1): 60–65.

Tendolkar, I. (2008). How semantic and episodic memory contribute to autobiographical memory: Commentary on Burt. *Language Learning* **58**: 143–147.

Tepest, R., E. Jacobi, *et al.* (2010). Corpus callosum size in adults with high-functioning autism and the relevance of gender. *Psychiatry Research: Neuroimaging* **183**(1): 38–43.

Thakkar, K. N., F. E. Polli, *et al.* (2008). Response monitoring, repetitive behaviour and anterior cingulate abnormalities in autism spectrum disorders (ASD). *Brain* **131**(9): 2464–2478.

Thomaes, S., B. J. Bushman, *et al.* (2009). Reducing narcissistic aggression by buttressing self-esteem: An experimental field study. *Psychological Science* **20**(12): 1536–1542.

Thomas, A., L. Bonanni, *et al.* (2007). Symptomatic REM sleep behaviour disorder. *Journal of the Neurological Sciences* **28**(Suppl 1): S21–S36.

Thome, J. (2008). An estimated 3.4% of adults have adult attention-deficit hyperactivity disorder. *Evidence-Based Mental Health* **11**(11): 31.

Thompson, C. C. and G. B. Potter (2000). Thyroid hormone action in neural development. *Cerebral Cortex* **10**(10): 939–945.

Thompson, L. A., D. M. Malloy, *et al.* (2009). Lateralization of visuospatial attention across face regions varies with emotional prosody. *Brain and Cognition* **69**: 108–115.

Thornton, K. and F. Cox (2005). Play and the reduction of challenging behaviour in children with ASD and learning disabilities. *Autism* **6**: 32–46.

Thurm, A., C. Lord, *et al.* (2007). Predictors of language acquisition in preschool children with autism spectrum disorders. *Journal of Autism and Developmental Disorders* **37**(9): 1721–1734.

Tirosh, E. and J. Canby (1993). Autism with hyperlexia: A distinct syndrome? *American Journal on Mental Retardation* **98**(1): 84–92.

Tischfield, M. A., T. M. Bosley, *et al.* (2005). Homozygous HOXA1 mutations disrupt human brainstem, inner ear, cardiovascular and cognitive development. *Nature Genetics* **37**(10): 1035–1037.

Titov, N., G. Andrews, *et al.* (2009). Shyness programme: Longer term benefits, cost-effectiveness, and acceptability. *Australian and New Zealand Journal of Psychiatry* **43**: 36–44.

Topcu, M., I. Saatci, *et al.* (2002). D-glyceric aciduria in a six-month-old boy presenting with West syndrome and autistic behaviour. *Neuropediatrics* **33**(1):47–50.

Torgersen, S., S. Lygren, *et al.* (2000). A twin study of personality disorders. *Comprehensive Psychiatry* **41**(6): 416–425.

Torriero, S., M. Oliveri, *et al.* (2007). Cortical networks of procedural learning: Evidence from cerebellar damage. *Neuropsychologia* **45**(6): 1208–1214.

Tottenham, N., J. W. Tanaka, *et al.* (2009). The NimStim set of facial expressions: Judgments from untrained research participants. *Psychiatry Research* **168**(3): 242–249.

Townsend, J., M. Westerfield, *et al.* (2001). Event-related brain response abnormalities in autism: evidence for impaired cerebello-frontal spatial attention networks. *Cognitive Brain Research* **11**(1): 127–145.

Treffert, D. A. (2009). The savant syndrome: An extraordinary condition. A synopsis: past, present, future. *Philosophical Transactions of the Royal Society B: Biological Sciences* **364**(1522): 1351–1357.

Troiani, V., S. Ash, *et al.* (2006). The neural correlates of narrative discourse: An investigation using arterial spin-labeling. *Brain and Language* **99**(1–2): 191–192.

Truss, L. (2003). *Eats, Shoots & Leaves.* London: Profile Books.

Tsao, C. Y. (2009). Current trends in the treatment of infantile spasms. *Neuropsychiatric Disease and Treatment* **5**: 289–299.

Tsao, C. Y. and J. R. Mendell (2007). Autistic disorder in 2 children with mitochondrial disorders. *Journal of Child Neurology* **22**(9): 1121–1123.

Tuchman, R. (2004). AEDs and psychotropic drugs in children with autism and epilepsy. *Mental Retardation and Developmental Disability Research Reviews* **10**(2): 135–138.

Tuchman, R. (2009). CSWS-related autistic regression versus autistic regression without CSWS. *Epilepsia* **50**(Suppl 1): 18–20.

Tuchman, R. and I. Rapin (2002). Epilepsy in autism. *The Lancet Neurology* **1**(6): 352–358.

Tuchman, R. F. (1997). Acquired epileptiform aphasia. *Seminars in Pediatric Neurology* **4**(2): 93–101.

Tuchman, R., S. L. Moshe, *et al.* (2009). Convulsing toward the pathophysiology of autism. *Brain and Development* **31**(2): 95–103.

Turk, J., M. Bax, *et al.* (2009). Autism spectrum disorder in children with and without epilepsy: impact on social functioning and communication. *Acta Paediatrica* **98**(4): 675–681.

Turner, B. M., S. Paradiso, *et al.* (2007). The cerebellum and emotional experience. *Neuropsychologia* **45**(6): 1331–1341.

Tustin, F. (1972). *Autism and Childhood Psychosis.* London: Hogarth Press.

Twemlow, S. W. M. and P. P. Fonagy (2005). The prevalence of teachers who bully students in schools with differing levels of behavioral problems. *American Journal of Psychiatry* **162**(12): 2387–2389.

Twenge, J. M., R. F. Baumeister, *et al.* (2007). Social exclusion decreases prosocial behavior. *Journal of Personality and Social Psychology* **92**(1): 56–66.

Uddin, L. Q., A. M. Kelly, *et al.* (2008). Network homogeneity reveals decreased integrity of default-mode network in ADHD. *Journal of Neuroscience Methods* **169**(1): 249–254.

Ullman, M. T. (2001). A neurocognitive perspective on language: The declarative/procedural model. *Nature Reviews Neuroscience* **2**(10): 717–726.

Ullmann, R., G. Turner, *et al.* (2007). Array CGH identifies reciprocal 16p13.1 duplications and deletions that predispose to autism and/or mental retardation. *Human Mutation* **28**(7): 674–682.

Uzumcu, A., B. Karaman, *et al.* (2009). Molecular genetic screening of MBS1 locus on chromosome 13 for microdeletions and exclusion of FGF9, GSH1 and CDX2 as causative genes in patients with Moebius syndrome. *European Journal of Medical Genetics* **52**(5): 315–320.

Vaish, A., M. Carpenter, *et al.* (2009). Sympathy through affective perspective taking and its relation to prosocial behavior in toddlers. *Developmental Psychology* **45**(2): 534–543.

Valera, E. M., S. V. Faraone, *et al.* (2006). Meta-analysis of structural imaging findings in attention-deficit/hyperactivity disorder. *Biological Psychiatry* **61**(12): 1361–1369.

Valla, J. M. and S. J. Ceci. (2011). Can sex differences in science be tied to the long reach of prenatal hormones? *Perspectives on Psychological Science* **6**(2): 134–146.

Van Daalen, E., S. H. Swinkels, *et al.* (2007). Body length and head growth in the first year of life in autism. *Pediatric Neurology* **37**(5): 324–330.

Van de Lagemaat, L. N. and S. G. N. Grant (2010). Genome variation and complexity in the autism spectrum. *Neuron* **67**(1): 8–10.

Van den Heuvel, M. P. and H. E. Hulshoff Pol (2010). Exploring the brain network: A review on resting-state fMRI functional connectivity. *European Neuropsychopharmacology* **20**(8): 519–534.

Van der Aa, N., L. Rooms, *et al.* (2009). Fourteen new cases contribute to the characterization of the 7q11.23 microduplication syndrome. *European Journal of Medical Genetics* **52**(2–3): 94–100.

Van der Velden, J. J. A. J., M. M. Vreeburg, *et al.* (2008). Skin abnormalities in individuals with macrocephaly: Cowden disease from a dermatologist's point of view. *International Journal of Dermatology Innovative in Care, Teaching and Research – Evening Seminar Series 2008 of the Department of Dermatology, Maastricht* **47**(Suppl 1): 45–48.

Van Doorn, M. D., S. J. T. Branje, *et al.* (2008). Conflict resolution in parent-adolescent relationships and adolescent delinquency. *Journal of Early Adolescence* **28**(4): 503–527.

Van Essen, D. C. (2005). A Population-Average, Landmark- and Surface-based (PALS) atlas of human cerebral cortex. *NeuroImage* **28**(3): 635–662.

Van Eylen. L., B. Boets, *et al.* (2011). Cognitive flexibility in autism spectrum disorder: Explaining the inconsistencies? *Research in Autism Spectrum Disorders* **5**(4): 1390–1401.

Van Kooten, I. A. J., S. J. M. C. Palmen, *et al.* (2008). Neurons in the fusiform gyrus are fewer and smaller in autism. *Brain* **131**(4): 987–999.

Van Meel, C. S., J. Oosterlaan, *et al.* (2005). Motivational effects on motor timing in attention-deficit/hyperactivity disorder. *Journal of the American Academy of Child and Adolescent Psychiatry* **44**(5): 451–460.

Van Rijn, S., H. Swaab, *et al.* (2008). Social behavior and autism traits in a sex chromosomal disorder: Klinefelter (47XXY) syndrome. *Journal of Autism and Developmental Disorders* **38**(9): 1634–1641.

Van Santen, J. P. H., E. T. Prud'hommeaux, *et al.* (2009). Automated assessment of prosody production. *Speech Communication* **51**(11): 1082–1097.

Van Wieren, T. A., C. A. Reid, *et al.* (2008). Workplace discrimination and autism spectrum disorders: The National EEOC Americans with Disabilities Act Research project. *Work* **31**(3): 299–308.

Vance, A., T. J. Silk, *et al.* (2007). Right parietal dysfunction in children with attention deficit hyperactivity disorder, combined type: A functional MRI study. *Molecular Psychiatry* **12**(9): 793, 826–832.

Varga, E. A., M. Pastore, *et al.* (2009). The prevalence of PTEN mutations in a clinical pediatric cohort with autism spectrum disorders, developmental delay, and macrocephaly. *Genetics in Medcine* **11**(2): 111–117.

Vasanta, D. (2005). Language cannot be reduced to biology: Perspectives from neuro-developmental disorders affecting language learning. *Journal of Biosciences* **30**(5): 129–137.

Vaurio, L., E. P. Riley, *et al.* (2008). Differences in executive functioning in children with heavy prenatal alcohol exposure or attention-deficit/hyperactivity disorder. *Journal of the International Neuropsychological Society* **14**(1): 119–129.

Velakoulis, D., M. Walterfang, *et al.* (2009). Frontotemporal dementia presenting as schizophrenia-like psychosis in young people: Clinicopathological series and review of cases. *British Journal of Psychiatry* **194**(4): 298–305.

Veltman, M. W. M., E. E. Craig, *et al.* (2005). Autism spectrum disorders in Prader-Willi and Angelman syndromes: A systematic review. *Psychiatric Genetics* **15**(4): 243–254.

Veltman, M. W., R. J. Thompson, *et al.* (2004). Prader-Willi syndrome: A study comparing deletion and uniparental disomy cases with reference to autism spectrum disorders. *European Child and Adolescent Psychiatry* **13**(1): 42–50.

Verkerk, A. J., C. A. Mathews, *et al.* (2003). CNTNAP2 is disrupted in a family with Gilles de la Tourette syndrome and obsessive compulsive disorder. *Genomics* **82**(1): 1–9.

Verster, J. C., E. M. Bekker, *et al.* (2008). Methylphenidate significantly improves driving performance of adults with attention-deficit hyperactivity disorder: A randomized crossover trial. *Journal of Psychopharmacology* **22**(3): 230–237.

Verte, S., H. Roeyers, *et al.* (2003). Developing a scale of self-efficacy in personal relationships for adolescents. *Psychological Reports* **92**(1): 1–184.

Viana, A. G., D. C. Beidel, *et al.* (2009). Selective mutism: A review and integration of the last 15 years. *Clinical Psychology Review* **29**(1): 57–67.

Viaud-Delmon, I., O. Warusfel, *et al.* (2006). High sensitivity to multisensory conflicts in agoraphobia exhibited by virtual reality. *European Psychiatry* **21**(7): 501–508.

Victoroff, J. (2007). Aggression, science, and law: The origins framework. *International Journal of Law and Psychiatry* **32**(4): 189–197.

Vidal, C. N., R. Nicolson, *et al.* (2006). Mapping corpus callosum deficits in autism: An index of aberrant cortical connectivity. *Biological Psychiatry* **60**(3): 218–225.

Vigilant, L. (2007). Bonobos. *Current Biology* **17**(3): R74–R75.

Viskontas, I. V., K. L. Possin, *et al.* (2007). Symptoms of frontotemporal dementia provide insights into orbitofrontal cortex function and social behavior. *Annals of the New York Academy of Sciences* **1121**: 528–545.

Vismara, L. A., C. Colombi, *et al.* (2009). Can one hour per week of therapy lead to lasting changes in young children with autism? *Autism* **13**(1): 93–115.

Vivanti, G., A. Nadig, *et al.* (2008). What do children with autism attend to during imitation tasks? *Journal of Experimental Child Psychology* **101**(3): 186–205.

Voeller, K. K. (1994). Techniques for measuring social competence in children. In G. R. Lyon (ed.) *Frames of Reference for the Assessment of Learning Disabilities: New Views on Measurement Issues*. Baltimore, MD: Brookes.

Voineagu, I., X. Wang *et al.* (2011) Transcriptomic analysis of autistic brain reveals convergent molecular pathology. *Nature* **474**(7351): 251–412.

Volden, J., J. Coolican, *et al.* (2009). Brief report: pragmatic language in autism spectrum disorder: Relationships to measures of ability and disability. *Journal of Autism and Developmental Disorders* **39**(2): 388–393.

Volkow, N. D., G. J. Wang, *et al.* (2009). Evaluating dopamine reward pathway in ADHD: Clinical implications. *Journal of the American Medical Association* **302**(10): 1084–1091.

Vollm, B. A., A. N. Taylor, *et al.* (2006). Neuronal correlates of theory of mind and empathy: A functional magnetic resonance imaging study in a nonverbal task. *NeuroImage* **29**(1): 90–98.

Voracek, M., J. Pietschnig, *et al.* (2011). Digit ratio (2D:4D) and sex-role orientation: Further evidence and meta-analysis. *Personality and Individual Differences* **51**(4):417–422.

Vorstman, J. A. S., M. E. J. Morcus, *et al.* (2006). The 22q11.2 Deletion in Children: High Rate of Autistic Disorders and Early Onset of Psychotic Symptoms. *Journal of the American Academy of Child and Adolescent Psychiatry* **45**(9): 1104–1113.

Vourc'h, P., I. Martin, *et al.* (2003). Mutation screening and association study of the UBE2H gene on chromosome 7q32 in autistic disorder. *Psychiatric Genetics* **13**(4): 221–225.

Vuilleumier, P. (2002). Facial expression and selective attention. *Current Opinion in Psychiatry* **15**(3): 291–300.

Vygotsky, L. (1966). *Thought and Language*. Cambridge, MA: Harvard University Press.

Waal, F. D. (1989). *Peacemaking Among Primates*. London: Penguin.

Wachtel, L. E., M. Griffin, *et al.* (2010). Brief report: Electroconvulsive therapy for malignant catatonia in an autistic adolescent. *Autism* **14**(4): 349–358.

Wada, T. (2009). [X-linked alpha-thalassemia/mental retardation syndrome]. *Rinsho Byori* **57**(4): 382–390.

Wagner, A. I., N. L. Schmidt, *et al.* (2009). The limited effects of obstetrical and neonatal complications on conduct and attention-deficit hyperactivity disorder symptoms in middle childhood. *Journal of Developmental and Behavioral Pediatrics* **30**(3): 217–225.

Wainscot, J., P. Naylor, *et al.* (2008). Relationships with peers and use of the school environment of mainstream secondary school pupils with Asperger syndrome (high-functioning autism): A case-control study. *International Journal of Psychology and Psychological Therapy* **8**(1): 25–38.

Waiter, G. D., J. H. Williams, *et al.* (2004). A voxel-based investigation of brain structure in male adolescents with autistic spectrum disorder. *NeuroImage* **22**(2): 619–625.

Wakako, S., Y. Hiroshi, *et al.* (2009). Shared minds: Effects of a mother's imitation of her child on the mother-child interaction. *Infant Mental Health Journal* **30**: 145–157.

Walker, C. (1995). Karl Jaspers and Edmund Husserl IV: Phenomenology and empathic understanding. *Philosophy, Psychiatry, and Psychology* **2**(3): 247–266.

Wallace, G. L., J. A. Silvers, *et al.* (2009). Brief report: Further evidence for inner speech deficits in autism spectrum disorders. *Journal of Autism and Developmental Disorders* [Epub].

Wallerstein, R., R. Sugalski, *et al.* (2008). Expansion of the ARX spectrum. *Clinical Neurology Neurosurgery* **110**(6): 631–634.

Wang, A. T., S. S. Lee, *et al.* (2007). Reading affect in the face and voice: Neural correlates of interpreting communicative intent in children and adolescents with autism spectrum disorders. *Archives of General Psychiatry* **64**(6): 698–708.

Wang, J., T. Jiang, *et al.* (2007). Characterizing anatomic differences in boys with attention-deficit/hyperactivity disorder with the use of deformation-based morphometry. *American Journal of Neuroradiology* **28**(3): 543–547.

Wang, M., B. P. Ramos, *et al.* (2007). ARNSTEN, AFT [alpha]2A-adrenoceptors strengthen working memory networks by inhibiting cAMP-HCN channel signaling in prefrontal cortex. *Cell* **129**(2): 397–410.

Warden, D. and S. Mackinnon (2003). Prosocial children, bullies and victims: An investigation of their sociometric status, empathy and social problem-solving strategies. *British Journal of Developmental Psychology* **21**(3): 367–385.

Warren, M. P. (1994). The missing link: The role of empathy in communicative psychoanalysis. *International Journal of Communicative Psychoanalysis and Psychotherapy* **9**(2): 35–39.

Warreyn, P., H. Roeyers, *et al.* (2005). Early social communicative behaviours of preschoolers with autism spectrum disorder during interaction with their mothers. *Autism* **9**(4): 342–361.

Warreyn, P., H. Roeyers, *et al.* (2007). Temporal coordination of joint attention behavior in preschoolers with autism spectrum disorder. *Journal of Autism and Developmental Disorders* **37**(3): 501–512.

Wassink, T. H. and J. Piven (2000). The molecular genetics of autism. *Current Psychiatry Reports* **2**(2): 170–175.

Wassink, T. H., J. Piven, *et al.* (2001). Evidence supporting WNT2 as an autism susceptibility gene. *American Journal of Medical Genetics* **105**(5): 406–413.

Wassmer, E., P. Davies, *et al.* (2003). Clinical spectrum associated with cerebellar hypoplasia. *Pediatric Neurology* **28**(5): 347–351.

Watson, L. R., G. T. Baranek, *et al.* (2007). The first year inventory: Retrospective parent responses to a questionnaire designed to identify one-year-olds at risk for autism. *Journal of Autism and Developmental Disorders* **37**(1): 49–61.

Wazana, A., M. Bresnahan, *et al.* (2007). The autism epidemic: Fact or artifact? *Journal of the American Academy of Child and Adolescent Psychiatry* **46**(6): 721–730.

Webb, S. J. P. and E. J. H. P. Jones (2009). Early identification of autism: Early characteristics, onset of symptoms, and diagnostic stability. *Infants and Young Children* **22**(2): 100–118.

Webb, T., E. Maina, *et al.* (2008). In search of the psychosis gene in people with Prader-Willi syndrome. *American Journal of Medical Genetics* **146A**(7): 843–853.

Weber, A. M. and D. N. Franz (1997). Nonverbal learning disability pattern observed in a case of adult-onset metachromatic leukodystrophy. *Archives of Clinical Neuropsychology* **12**(4): 424–425.

Weber, A. M., J. C. Egelhoff, *et al.* (2000). Autism and cerebellum: Evidence from tuberous sclerosis. *Journal of Autism and Developmental Disorders* **30**(6): 511–518.

Webster, S. D. and A. R. Beech (2000). The nature of sexual offenders' affective empathy: A grounded theory analysis. *Sexual Abuse: A Journal of Research and Treatment* **12**(4): 249–261.

Wechsler, D. (2003). *Wechsler Intelligence Scale for Children—Fourth Edition (WISC–IV)*. San Antonio, TX: Pearson Education.

Wechsler, D. (2008). *Wechsler Adult Intelligence Scale—Fourth Edition (WAIS–IV)*. San Antonio, TX: Pearson Education.

Wegner, D. M. (2009). How to think, say, or do precisely the worst thing for any occasion. *Science* **325**(5936): 48–50.

Wehmeier, P. M., A. Schacht, *et al.* (2010). PW01-66: Does atomoxetine improve executive function and inhibitory control as measured by an objective computer-based test? A randomized, placebo-controlled study. *European Psychiatry* **25**(Suppl 1): 1482.

Wei, M., D. W. Russell, *et al.* (2005). Adult attachment, social self-efficacy, self-disclosure, loneliness, and subsequent depression for freshman college students: A longitudinal study. *Journal of Counseling Psychology* **52**(4): 602–614.

Weidenheim, K. M., L. Goodman, *et al.* (2001). Etiology and pathophysiology of autistic behavior: Clues from two cases with an unusual variant of neuroaxonal dystrophy. *Journal of Child Neurology* **16**(11): 809–819.

Weimer, A. K., A. M. Schatz, *et al.* (2001). Motor impairment in Asperger syndrome: Evidence for a deficit in proprioception. *Journal of Developmental and Behavioral Pediatrics* **22**(2): 92–101.

Weinstein, C. S., R. J. Apfel, *et al.* (1998). Description of mothers with ADHD with children with ADHD. *Psychiatry* **61**(1): 12–19.

Weiser, M., A. Reichenberg, *et al.* (2008). Advanced parental age at birth is associated with poorer social functioning in adolescent males: Shedding light on a core symptom of schizophrenia and autism. *Schizophrenia Bulletin* **34**(6): 1042–1046.

Weiss, L. A., Y. Shen, *et al.* (2008). The autism consortium association between microdeletion and microduplication at 16p11.2 and autism. *The New England Journal of Medicine* **358**(7): 667–675.

Weiss, M. and C. Murray (2003). Assessment and management of attention-deficit hyperactivity disorder in adults. *Canadian Medical Association Journal* **168**(6): 715–722.

Weiss, R. (1973). *The Experience of Emotional and Social Isolation*. Cambridge, MA: MIT Press.

Weissenbock, H., M. Hornig, *et al.* (2000). Microglial activation and neuronal apoptosis in Bornavirus infected neonatal Lewis rats. *Brain Pathology* **10**(2): 260–272.

Wellman, H. M., S. Baron-Cohen, *et al.* (2002). Thought-bubbles help children with autism acquire an alternative to a theory of mind. *Autism* **6**(4): 4–363.

Welsh, T. N., M. C. Ray, *et al.* (2009). Does Joe influence Fred's action? Not if Fred has autism spectrum disorder. *Brain Research* **1248**: 141–148.

Wessels, K., B. Bohnhorst, *et al.* (2010). Novel CHD7 mutations contributing to the mutation spectrum in patients with CHARGE syndrome. *European Journal of Medical Genetics* **53**(5): 280–285.

Westen, D., O. Nakash *et al.* (2006). Clinical assessment of attachment patterns and personality disorder in adolescents and adults. *Journal of Consulting and Clinical Psychology* **74**(6): 1065–1085.

Whalen, P. J., S. L. Rauch, *et al.* (1998). Masked presentations of emotional facial expressions modulate amygdala activity without explicit knowledge. *Journal of Neuroscience* **18**(1): 411–418.

Whatmough, C., H. Chertkow, *et al.* (2002). Dissociable brain regions process object meaning and object structure during picture naming. *Neuropsychologia* **40**(2): 174–186.

Wheless, J. W., D. F. Clarke, *et al.* (2007). Treatment of pediatric epilepsy: European expert opinion, 2007. *Epileptic Disorders* **9**(4): 353–412.

Whitaker, D. S. (1985). *Using Groups to Help People*. London: Routledge & Kegan Paul.

White, J. F. (2003). Intestinal pathophysiology in autism. *Experimental Bioligy and Medicine (Maywood)* **228**(6): 639–649.

White, S. W. and R. Roberson-Nay (2009). Anxiety, social deficits, and loneliness in youth with autism spectrum disorders. *Journal of Autism and Developmental Disorders* **39**(7): 1006–1013.

White, S. W., D. Oswald, *et al.* (2009). Anxiety in children and adolescents with autism spectrum disorders. *Clinical Psychology Review* **29**(3): 216–229.

White, S., H. O'Reilly, *et al.* (2009). Big heads, small details and autism. *Neuropsychologia* **47**(5): 1274–1281.

Whitehouse, A. J., H. J. Watt, *et al.* (2009). Adult psychosocial outcomes of children with specific language impairment, pragmatic language impairment and autism. *International Journal of Language and Communication Disorders* **44**(4): 511–528.

Whitehouse, A. J., J. G. Barry, *et al.* (2008). Further defining the language impairment of autism: Is there a specific language impairment subtype? *Journal of Communication Disorders* **41**(4): 319–336.

Whitehouse, A. J., K. Durkin, *et al.* (2009). Friendship, loneliness and depression in adolescents with Asperger's Syndrome. *Journal of Adolescent Health* **32**(2): 309–322.

Whiteley, P., J. Rodgers, *et al.* (1999). A gluten-free diet as an intervention for autism and associated spectrum disorders: Preliminary findings. *Autism* **3**(1): 45–65.

Whorf, B. (1972). *Language, Thought, and Reality*. Cambridge, MA: MIT Press.

Whyte, S., E. Petch, *et al.* (2008). Who stalks? A description of patients at a high security hospital with a history of stalking behaviour. *Criminal Behaviour and Mental Health* **18**(1): 27–38.

Wicks, R. (2003). Schopenhauer. Available from http://plato. stanford.edu/entries/schopenhauer/#4, accessed on 29 July 2011.

Wicks-Nelson, R. and A. C. Israel (2003). Acquired theory of mind impairments in individuals with bilateral amygdala lesions. *Neuropsychologia* **41**(2): 2–220.

Wiener, N. (1948). *Cybernetics; or, Control and Communication in the Animal and the Machine.* Cambridge, MA: MIT Press.

Wild, B., M. Erb, *et al.* (2003). Why are smiles contagious? An fMRI study of the interaction between perception of facial affect and facial movements. *Psychiatry Research: Neuroimaging* **123**(1): 17–36.

Wilkins, J. and J. L. Matson (2009). A comparison of social skills profiles in intellectually disabled adults with and without ASD. *Behavior Modification* **33**(2): 143–155.

Williams, C. A., A. Dagli, *et al.* (2008). Genetic disorders associated with macrocephaly. *American Journal of Medical Genetics A* **146A**(15): 2023–2037.

Williams, D. (2006). *The Jumbled Jigsaw.* London: Jessica Kingsley Publishers.

Williams, D. and F. Happé (2009). Pre-conceptual aspects of self-awareness in autism spectrum disorder: The case of action-monitoring. *Journal of Autism and Developmental Disorders* **39**(2): 251–259.

Williams, D., N. Botting, *et al.* (2008). Language in autism and specific language impairment: Where are the links? *Psychological Bulletin* **134**(6): 944–963.

Williams, J. and E. Taylor (2006). The evolution of hyperactivity, impulsivity and cognitive diversity. *Journal of the Royal Society Interface* **3**(8): 399–413.

Williams, J. G., J. P. Higgins, *et al.* (2006). Systematic review of prevalence studies of autism spectrum disorders. *Archives of Disease in Childhood* **91**(1): 8–15.

Williams, J. H. G., A. Whiten, *et al.* (2001). Imitation, mirror neurons and autism. *Neuroscience and Biobehavioral Reviews* **25**(4): 287–295.

Williams, J. H., G. D. Waiter, *et al.* (2005). An fMRI study of joint attention experience. *NeuroImage* **25**(1): 133–140.

Williams, K. R. (2006). The Son-Rise Program intervention for autism: Prerequisites for evaluation. *Autism* **10**(1): 86–102.

Williams, K., M. Chambers, *et al.* (1996). Association of common health symptoms with bullying in primary school children. *British Medical Journal* **313**(7048): 17–19.

Williams, K., M. Tuck, *et al.* (2008). The Autism Spectrum Disorder Steering Group Diagnostic labelling of autism spectrum disorders in NSW. *Journal of Paediatrics and Child Health* **44**(3): 108–113.

Williams, T. A. P., A. E. M. Mars, *et al.* (2007). Risk of autistic disorder in affected offspring of mothers with a glutathione S-Transferase P1 haplotype. *Archives of Pediatrics and Adolescent Medicine* **161**(4): 356–361.

Wills, S., M. Cabanlit, *et al.* (2009). Detection of autoantibodies to neural cells of the cerebellum in the plasma of subjects with autism spectrum disorders. *Brain, Behavior, and Immunity* **23**(1): 64–74.

Wilmer, J. B., L. Germine, *et al.* (2010). Human face recognition ability is specific and highly heritable. *Proceedings of the National Academy of Sciences of the United States of America* **107**(11): 5238–5241.

Wilson, J. and G. Jungner (1968). *Principles and Practice of Screening for Disease.* Geneva: World Health Organization.

Wiltermuth, S. and C. Heath (2009). Synchrony and cooperation. *Psychological Science* **20**(1): 1–5.

Wimmer, H. and J. Perner (1983). Beliefs about beliefs: Representation and constraining function of wrong beliefs in young children's understanding of deception. *Cognition* **13**(1): 103–128.

Wimpory, D. C., R. P. Hobson, *et al.* (2007). What facilitates social engagement in preschool children with autism? *Journal of Autism and Developmental Disorders* **37**(3): 564–573.

Wing, L. (1981). Asperger's syndrome: A clinical account. *Psychological Medicine* **11**(1): 115–129.

Wing, L. (1996a). Autistic spectrum disorders: No evidence for or against an increase in prevalence. *British Medical Journal* **312**(7027): 327–328.

Wing, L. (1996b). *The Autistic Spectrum.* London: Constable.

Wing, L. and A. Shah (2000). Catatonia in autistic spectrum disorders. *British Journal of Psychiatry* **176**: 357–362.

Wing, L. and J. Gould (1978). Systematic recording of behaviors and skills of retarded and psychotic children. *Journal of Autism and Childhood Schizophrenia* **8**(1): 79–97.

Wing, L. and J. Gould (1979). Severe impairments of social interaction and associated abnormalities in children: epidemiology and classification. *Journal of Autism and Developmental Disorders* **9**(1): 11–29.

Winston, J. S., J. O'Doherty (2003). Common and distinct neural responses during direct and incidental processing of multiple facial emotions. *NeuroImage* **20**(1): 84–97.

Wischniewski, J., S. Windmann, *et al.* (2009). Rules of social exchange: Game theory, individual differences and psychopathology. *Neuroscience and Biobehavioral Reviews* **33**(3): 305–313.

Wittfoth, M., C. Schroder, *et al.* (2010). On emotional conflict: Interference resolution of happy and angry prosody reveals valence-specific effects. *Cerebral Cortex* **20**(2): 383–392.

Wittgenstein, L. (1958). *Philosophical Investigations.* Oxford: Basil Blackwell.

Witwer, A. N. and L. Lecavalier (2008). Examining the validity of autism spectrum disorder subtypes. *Journal of Autism and Developmental Disorders* **38**(9): 1611–1624.

Wobber, V., R. Wrangham, *et al.* (2010). Bonobos exhibit delayed development of social behavior and cognition relative to chimpanzees. *Current Biology* **20**(3): 226–230.

Wodehouse, G. and P. McGill (2009). Support for family carers of children and young people with developmental disabilities and challenging behaviour: What stops it being helpful? *Journal of Intellectual Disability Research* **53**(7): 644–653.

Wolanczyk, T., A. Banaszkiewicz, *et al.* (2000). Nadpobudliwosc psychoruchowa i zaburzenia behawioralne w przebiegu choroby Sanfilippo A (mukopolisacharydozy typu IIIA): Opis przypadku i przeglad pismiennictwa. [Hyperactivity and behavioral disorders in Sanfilippo A (mucopolysaccharidosis type IIIA): Case report and review of the literature]. *Psychiatry Polska* **34**(5): 831–837.

Wolfe T. (2008). *Bonfire of the Vanities.* New York, NY: Picador.

Wolff, S. (1991). 'Schizoid' personality in childhood and adult life. I: The vagaries of diagnostic labelling. *British Journal of Psychiatry* **159**(5): 615–620.

Wolff, S. (1998). Schizoid personality in childhood: The links with Asperger syndrome, schizophrenia spectrum disorders, and elective mutism. In E. Schopler, G. B. Mesibov, *et al.* (eds) *Asperger Syndrome or High-functioning Autism?* New York, NY: Plenum Press.

Wolff, S. (2000). Schizoid personality in childhood and Asperger syndrome. In A. Klin, F. Volkmar, *et al.* (eds) *Asperger Syndrome.* New York, NY: Guilford Press.

Wolosin, S. M., M. E. Richardson, *et al.* (2007). Abnormal cerebral cortex structure in children with ADHD. *Human Brain Mapping* **30**(1): 175–184.

Wolsko, C., C. Lardon, *et al.* (2007). Stress, coping, and well-being among the Yup'ik of the Yukon-Kuskokwim Delta: The role of enculturation and acculturation. *International Journal of Circumpolar Health* **66**(1): 51–61.

Wong, D., M. Maybery, *et al.* (2006). Profiles of executive function in parents and siblings of individuals with autism spectrum disorders. *Genes, Brain, and Behavior* **5**(8): 561–576.

Wong, T. K., P. C. Fung, *et al.* (2009). Spatiotemporal dipole source localization of face processing ERPs in adolescents: A preliminary study. *Behavioral and Brain Functions* **5**: 16.

Wong, V. C. (2009). Use of complementary and alternative medicine (CAM) in autism spectrum disorder (ASD): Comparison of Chinese and Western culture (Part A). *Journal of Autism and Developmental Disorders* **39**(3): 454–463.

Wood, J. and J. Grafman (2003). Human prefrontal cortex: Processing and representational perspectives. *Nature Reviews Neuroscience* **4**(2): 130–147.

Wood, J. J., A. Drahota, *et al.* (2009). Cognitive behavioral therapy for anxiety in children with autism spectrum disorders: A randomized, controlled trial. *Journal of Child Psychology and Psychiatry* **50**(3): 224–234.

Woodrow, S. L. and N. P. Burrows (2003). Pachydermodactyly in association with Asperger syndrome. *Clinical and Experimental Dermatology* **28**(6): 674–675.

Woollett, K., H. J. Spiers, *et al.* (2009). Talent in the taxi: A model system for exploring expertise. *Philosophical Transactions of the Royal Society B: Biological Sciences* **364**(1522): 1407–1416.

World Health Organization (WHO) (1977). *The International Statistical Classification of Diseases and Related Health Problems, Ninth Revision* (ICD-9). Geneva: WHO.

World Health Organization (WHO) (1992). *The International Statistical Classification of Diseases and Related Health Problems, Tenth Revision* (ICD-10). Geneva: WHO.

Worthen, M. F. (2000). The role of empathy in adolescent friendship. *Dissertation Abstracts International: Section B: The Sciences and Engineering* **61**: 1116.

Worthington, E., C. Witvliet, *et al.* (2007). Forgiveness, health, and well-being: A review of evidence for emotional versus decisional forgiveness, dispositional forgivingness, and reduced unforgiveness. *Journal of Behavioral Medicine* **30**(4): 291–302.

Xiao, X., J. Qiu, *et al.* (2009). The dissociation of neural circuits in a Stroop task. *Neuroreport* **20**(8): 674–678.

Xu, X, X. Zuo, *et al.* (2009). Do you feel my pain? Racial group membership modulates empathic neural responses. *Journal of Neuroscience* **29**(26): 8525–8529.

Xue, M., M. Brimacombe, *et al.* (2008). Autism spectrum disorders: Concurrent clinical disorders. *Journal of Child Neurology* **23**(1): 6–13.

Yamada, M., K. Hirao, *et al.* (2007). Social cognition and frontal lobe pathology in schizophrenia: A voxel-based morphometric study. *NeuroImage* **35**(1): 292–298.

Yamamoto, T., Y. Oomura, *et al.* (1984). Monkey orbitofrontal neuron activity during emotional and feeding behaviors. *Brain Research Bulletin* **12**(4): 441–443.

Yamashita, Y., C. Fujimoto, *et al.* (2003). Possible association between congenital cytomegalovirus infection and autistic disorder. *Journal of Autism and Developmental Disorders* **33**(4): 455–459.

Yamasue, H., H. Kuwabara, *et al.* (2009). Oxytocin, sexually dimorphic features of the social brain, and autism. *Psychiatry and Clinical Neurosciences* **63**(2): 129–140.

Yamazaki, K., S. Chess, *et al.* (1977). Follow-up report on autism in congenital rubella. *Journal of Autism and Childhood Schizophrenia* **7**(1): 69–81.

Yang, P., F. W. Lung, *et al.* (2008). Association of the homeobox transcription factor gene ENGRAILED 2 with autistic disorder in Chinese children. *Neuropsychobiology* **57**(1): 3–8.

Yardley, L., L. McDermott, *et al.* (2008). Psychosocial consequences of developmental prosopagnosia: A problem of recognition. *Journal of Psychosomatic Research* **65**(5): 445–451.

Yeargin-Allsopp, M., C. Rice, *et al.* (2003). Prevalence of autism in a US metropolitan area. *Journal of the American Medical Association* **289**(1): 49–55.

Yeo, R. A., D. E. Hill, *et al.* (2003). Proton magnetic resonance spectroscopy investigation of the right frontal lobe in children with attention-deficit/hyperactivity disorder. *Journal of the American Academy of Child and Adolescent Psychiatry* **42**(3): 303–310.

Yianni-Coudurier, C., C. Darrou, *et al.* (2008). What clinical characteristics of children with autism influence their inclusion in regular classrooms? *Journal of Intellectual Disability Research* **52**(10): 855–863.

Yip, J., J. J. Soghomonian, *et al.* (2007). Decreased GAD67 mRNA levels in cerebellar Purkinje cells in autism: Pathophysiological implications. *Acta Neuropathologica* **113**(5): 559–568.

Yip, J., J. J. Soghomonian, *et al.* (2008). Increased GAD67 mRNA expression in cerebellar interneurons in autism: Implications for Purkinje cell dysfunction. *Journal of Neuroscience Research* **86**(3): 525–530.

Yip, J., J. J. Soghomonian, *et al.* (2009). Decreased GAD65 mRNA levels in select subpopulations of neurons in the cerebellar dentate nuclei in autism: An in situ hybridization study. *Autism Research* **2**(1): 50–59.

Yiyuan, X. and J. A. Farver (2009). What makes you shy? Understanding situational elicitors of shyness in Chinese children. *International Journal of Behavioral Development* **33**: 97–104.

Yoshimura, I., A. Sasaki, *et al.* (1989). A case of congenital myotonic dystrophy with infantile autism. *No To Hattatsu* **21**(4): 379–384.

Young, D. J., A. Bebbington, *et al.* (2008). The diagnosis of autism in a female: Could it be Rett syndrome? *European Journal of Pediatrics* **167**(6): 661–669.

Young, E. C., J. J. Diehl, *et al.* (2005). The use of two language tests to identify pragmatic language problems in children with autism spectrum disorders. *Language, Speech, and Hearing Services in Schools* **36**(1): 62–72.

Young, E. J., T. Lipina, *et al.* (2008). Reduced fear and aggression and altered serotonin metabolism in Gtf2ird1-targeted mice. *Genes, Brain, and Behavior* **7**(2): 224–234.

Young, H. K., B. A. Barton, *et al.* (2008). Cognitive and psychological profile of males with Becker muscular dystrophy. *Journal of Child Neurology* **23**(2): 155–162.

Yu, C., F. Lin, *et al.* (2003). Occult white matter damage contributes to intellectual disability in tuberous sclerosis complex. *Intelligence* **37**: 174–180.

Yuan, T. F. (2009). Einstein's brain: Gliogenesis in autism? *Medical Hypotheses* **72**(6): 753.

Yunjo, L., D. Bradley, *et al.* (2010). Three cases of developmental prosopagnosia from one family: Detailed neuropsychological and psychophysical investigation of face processing. *Cortex: A Journal Devoted to the Study of the Nervous System and Behavior* **46**(8): 949–964.

Zafeiriou, D. I., A. Ververi, *et al.* (2008). L-2-Hydroxyglutaric aciduria presenting with severe autistic features. *Brain and Development* **30**(4): 305–307.

Zaffanello, M., G. Zamboni, *et al.* (2003). A case of partial biotinidase deficiency associated with autism. *Neuropsychology, Development and Cognition, Section C: Child Neuropsychology* **9**(3): 184–188.

Zahn, R., J. Moll, *et al.* (2007). Social concepts are represented in the superior anterior temporal cortex. *The Proceedings of the National Academy of Sciences USA* **104**(15): 6430–6435.

Zahn, R., R. de Oliveira-Souza, *et al.* (2009). Subgenual cingulate activity reflects individual differences in empathic concern. *Neuroscience Letters* **457**(2): 107–110.

Zaja, R. H. and J. Rojahn (2008). Facial emotion recognition in intellectual disabilities. *Current Opinion in Psychiatry* **21**(5):441–444.

Zaki, J. and K. Ochsner (2009). The need for a cognitive neuroscience of naturalistic social cognition. *Annals of the New York Academy of Sciences* **1167**(1): 16–30.

Zaki, J., K. Hennigan, *et al.* (2010). Social cognitive conflict resolution: Contributions of domain-general and domain-specific neural systems. *Journal of Neuroscience* **30**(25): 8481–8488.

Zald, D. H. (2003). The human amygdala and the emotional evaluation of sensory stimuli. *Brain Research Reviews* **41**(1): 88–123.

Zalla, T., A. M. Sav, *et al.* (2009). Faux pas detection and intentional action in Asperger syndrome: A replication on a French sample. *Journal of Autism and Developmental Disorders* **39**(2): 373–382.

Zang, Y. F., Z. Jin, *et al.* (2005). Functional MRI in attention-deficit hyperactivity disorder: Evidence for hypofrontality. *Brain and Development* **27**(8): 544–550.

Zatorre, R. J. and J. T. Gandour (2008). Neural specializations for speech and pitch: Moving beyond the dichotomies. *Philosophical Transactions of the Royal Society B: Biological Sciences* **363**(1493): 1087–1104.

Zeidner, M., R. D. Roberts, *et al.* (2008). The science of emotional intelligence: Current consensus and controversies. *European Psychologist* **13**(1): 64–78.

Zentall, T. and C. Akins (2001). Imitation in animals: Evidence, function and mechanisms. In R. G. Cook (ed.) *Avian Visual Cognition*. Available at www.pigeon.psy.tufts.edu/avc/zentall, accessed on 6 October 2011.

Zhang, A, C. H. Shen, *et al.* (2009). Altered expression of autism-associated genes in the brain of Fragile X mouse model. *Biochemical and Biophysical Research Communications* **379**(4): 920–923.

Zhang, H., X. Lu, *et al.* (2011). Reversed clinical phenotype due to a microduplication of Sotos syndrome region detected by array CGH: Microcephaly, developmental delay and delayed bone age. *American Journal of Medical Genetics A* **155**(6): 1374–1378.

Zhang, K., J. Gao, *et al.* (2007). An association study between cathechol-O-methyltransferase gene and mental retardation in the Chinese Han population. *Neuroscience Letters* **419**(1): 83–87.

Zhao, X., A. Leotta, *et al.* (2007). A unified genetic theory for sporadic and inherited autism. *Proceedings of the National Academy of Sciences USA* **104**(31): 12831–12836.

Zhou, K., A. Dempfle, *et al.* (2008). Meta-analysis of genome-wide linkage scans of attention deficit hyperactivity disorder. *American Journal of Medical Genetics B: Neuropsychiatric Genetics* **147B**(8): 1392–1398.

Zhou, Q., C. Valiente, *et al.* (2003). Empathy and its measurement. In S. J. Lopez (ed.) *Positive Psychological Assessment: A Handbook of Models and Measures.* Washington, DC: American Psychological Association.

Ziatas, K., K. Durkin, *et al.* (2003). Differences in assertive speech acts produced by children with autism, Asperger syndrome, specific language impairment, and normal development. *Development and Psychopathology* **15**(1): 73–94.

Zillmer, E. A., J. D. Ball, *et al.* (1991). Wechsler Verbal-Performance IQ discrepancies among psychiatric inpatients: Implications for subtle neuropsychological dysfunctioning. *Archives of Clinical Neuropsychology* **6**(1–2): 61–71.

Zinn, A. R., D. Roeltgen, *et al.* (2007). A Turner syndrome neurocognitive phenotype maps to Xp22.3. *Behavioral and Brain Functions* **3**(1): 24.

Zola, I. K. (1993). Disability statistics, what we count and what it tells us: A personal and political analysis. *Journal of Disability Policy Studies* **4**(2): 9–39.

Zucker, N. L. and M. Losh (2008). Repetitive behaviours in anorexia nervosa, autism, and obsessive-compulsive personality disorder. *Psychiatry* **7**(4): 183–187.

Zwaigenbaum, L., S. Bryson, *et al.* (2009). Clinical assessment and management of toddlers with suspected autism spectrum disorder: Insights from studies of high-risk infants. *Pediatrics* **123**(5): 1383–1391.

INDEX